STAGES OF LITERACY DEVELOPMENT	CHARACTERISTICS	TYPES OF INSTRUCTIONAL EMPHASES
Ages: 6–10 **Grades:** 1 to mid-4th (continued)	*Word Study: Within Word Pattern* • Spells most single-syllable, short-vowel words correctly; developing understanding of spelling long-vowel patterns, less frequent spelling patterns, and *r*-influenced vowel patterns	*Word Study* Spelling: • Sort words according to long-vowel patterns, complex consonant units, less common vowel patterns, and homophones and homographs. Vocabulary: • Examine compound words and simple morphological (word formation) processes (root words plus affixes).
Ages: 8–14 **Grades:** 3–8	*Reading* • Reads with good fluency and expression; prefers silent reading as it is now faster than reading aloud; students self-select reading materials and can independently prepare for literature discussions • Beginning to develop a critical stance and is able to independently back up opinions with evidence to support them • Acquires new vocabulary and domain-specific knowledge from reading and researching *Writing* • Written responses are more sophisticated and critical • Beginning to compose longer pieces of writing in a variety of genres • Revision and editing come to play bigger roles • Beginning to write for a wider variety of purposes, including note taking and outlining *Word Study: Syllables and Affixes* • Spells correctly most single-syllable words; errors are at the juncture of multisyllabic words and in unaccented syllables • Beginning to use a variety of print and digital resources to deepen their word knowledge and interest in words and language	*Reading* • Continue to read aloud to students and develop critical thinking skills. • Guide silent reading and reading discussions of literature and informational text. • Include self-selected and assigned silent reading of novels of different genres and of informational texts. • Help students develop study skills, including textbook reading, note taking, adjusting reading rates based on purpose, and test-taking skills. *Writing* • Use mentor texts to introduce students to more sophisticated writing and author's craft moves. • Help with report writing, reference work, and exploration of primary sources. • Teach how to write for a variety of audiences and purposes. *Word Study* Spelling: • Teach plural and inflectional endings, compound words, syllable juncture patterns, unaccented syllables. Vocabulary: • Include word-formation processes—Latin and Greek roots and affixes—as they occur in *general-academic* and *domain-specific* vocabulary. • Begin to explore the *etymology* of words to support word consciousness.
Ages: 12 and above **Grades:** 6 and above	*Reading* • Reads fluently and with good expression • Fully explores the genres within literature and informational texts with more sophisticated responses • Reads and analyzes primary source material in depth *Writing* • Capable of more sophisticated and critical compositions • Experiments with a wider range of genres and craft moves • Uses the writing process to intentionally develop and improve compositions *Word Study: Derivational Relations* • Capable of understanding more advanced spelling/ morphological processes: assimilated prefixes, spelling–meaning alternations, easily confused suffixes	*Reading* • Refine study skills, note taking, adjusting reading rates for different purposes, and test-taking strategies. • Refine competencies in *disciplinary literacy*. • Support the exploration and reading of primary source material and digital and print references. *Writing* • Refine the structure and language of narratives and informational texts. • Develop more intensively the *argument* form of writing. *Word Study* • For both spelling and vocabulary, examine less common Greek and Latin roots, prefixes, and suffixes. • Refine *general academic* and *domain-specific* vocabulary in the context of different disciplines. • Develop *etymology* as a rich source of vocabulary knowledge.

INTERMEDIATE

SKILLFUL

Teaching Reading and Writing

The Developmental Approach

Shane Templeton
University of Nevada, Reno

Kristin M. Gehsmann
St. Michael's College
Colchester, Vermont

PEARSON

Boston Columbus Indianapolis New York San Francisco Upper Saddle River
Amsterdam Cape Town Dubai London Madrid Milan Munich Paris Montreal Toronto
Delhi Mexico City São Paulo Sydney Hong Kong Seoul Singapore Taipei Tokyo

Vice President/Editorial Director: Jeffery Johnston
Editor in Chief/Vice President: Aurora Martínez Ramos
Acquisitions Editor: Kathryn Boice
Editorial Assistant: Michelle Hochberg
Executive Marketing Manager: Krista Clark
Project Manager: Karen Mason
Manufacturing Buyer: Linda Sager
Manager, Visual Research: Jorgensen Fernandez
Manager, Rights and Permissions: Johanna Burke

Permissions: Tania Zamora
Cover: Diane Lorenzo
Cover Photos: (1) Kirill Polovnoy/Fotolia, (2 and 3) Hope Madden Wolfington, (4) Monkey Business/Fotolia, (5) ZouZou/Shutterstock
Full-Service Project Management: Cenveo® Publisher Services
Composition: Cenveo® Publisher Services
Printer/Binder: LSCCommunications

Photo and text credits begin on page 478, which constitutes a continuation of the copyright page.

Library of Congress Cataloging-in-Publication Data

Templeton, Shane.
   Teaching reading and writing: the developmental approach/Shane Templeton, University
      of Nevada, Reno, Nevada, Kristin M. Gehsmann, St. Michael's College, Colchester, Vermont. pages ; cm
   Includes bibliographical references and index.
   ISBN-13: 978-0-205-45632-1
   ISBN-10: 0-205-45632-4
   1. Language arts (Elementary)--United States. 2. Language arts
      (Middle school)--United States. 3. Developmental reading. I. Title.
   LB1576.T459 2013
   372.6'044--dc23
                                                                                    2013012699

10 2019

ISBN 10: 0-205-45632-4
ISBN 13: 978-0-205-45632-1

*To Ayden, Ansel, Ashley, and Abigail,
and their teachers—past, present, and future*

About the Authors

Shane Templeton is Foundation Professor Emeritus of Literacy Studies, University of Nevada, Reno. A former classroom teacher at the primary and secondary levels, he has focused his research on the development of orthographic and vocabulary knowledge. He has written several books on the teaching and learning of reading and language arts and is a member of the Usage Panel of the *American Heritage Dictionary*.

Kristin M. Gehsmann is Associate Professor of Education and Coordinator of the Master's in Reading Concentration at Saint Michael's College in Colchester, Vermont. A former elementary school teacher and PreK–12 literacy consultant, she conducts research on narrowing the achievement gap in high-poverty communities, and bringing research-based practices to scale through ongoing professional development.

Brief Contents

CHAPTER 1: **The Foundations of Literacy Instruction**   1

CHAPTER 2: **Language, Thought, and Literacy Development**   32

CHAPTER 3: **Effective Literacy Instruction: Principles and Practices**   71

CHAPTER 4: **Prioritizing Student-Centered Assessment and Instruction**   112

CHAPTER 5: **Foundations of Language and Literacy Instruction for English Learners**   153

CHAPTER 6: **Emergent Literacy: Engaging the World of Print, Developing Oral Language, and Vocabulary**   173

CHAPTER 7: **Beginning Conventional Reading and Writing**   219

CHAPTER 8: **Transitional Reading and Writing**   270

CHAPTER 9: **Intermediate Reading and Writing**   315

CHAPTER 10: **Skillful Literacy: Developing Critical Engagements with Texts, Language, and Vocabulary**   364

CHAPTER 11: **Response to Instruction: Intervention and Acceleration for Readers Who Struggle**   414

Contents

Preface xvii

CHAPTER 1:
The Foundations of Literacy Instruction 1

What *Is* "Literacy"? 3

The Importance of Print and Digital Literacy 4

■ Strategies for the Classroom: Is There One "Best Method" for Teaching Reading? 5

The Many Faces of Literacy 5

The Literacy Essentials 6

The Literacy Essentials: The "What" of Effective Instruction 7

■ The Language of Your Instruction: Schema Theory and Comprehension 8

■ Children's Literature Connection: Historical Fiction – *Al Capone Does My Shirts* 12

■ The Language of Your Instruction: Standards and Their Influence 18

The Literacy Essentials from a Developmental Perspective 18

Stages of Literacy Development 19

The Sociocultural Contexts of Literacy Learning 24

Learning Cultural Practices 24

Developing a Culture of the Classroom 25

■ The Language of Your Instruction: Talking *With*, not Just *To*, Your Students 26

Levels of Support and the Gradual Release of Responsibility Model 26

Gradual Release of Responsibility Model 27

Differentiating Instruction 27

Chapter Summary 28

Suggested Extension Activities 28

Recommended Professional Resources 29

Online Resources 29

How to Use This Book 30

CHAPTER 2:
Language, Thought, and Literacy Development 32

Characteristics of Oral Language 34

Phonological Knowledge 34

Semantic Knowledge 35

Syntactic Knowledge 37

Pragmatic Knowledge 37

Characteristics of Thought 38

Characteristics of Written Language: Word Level 40

Correspondences at the Level of Sound: Alphabet and Pattern 41

Correspondences at the Level of Meaning: Morphology 43

Characteristics of Written Language: Text Level 44

What Makes Texts Complex? 46

■ The Language of Your Instruction: Why the Emphasis on Text Complexity? 47

■ Children's and Young Adults' Literature Connection: Reading for Boys and Young Adult Males 49

The Developmental Model of Literacy 49

Understanding the Developmental Continuum 49

Emergent Reading and Writing (Preschool to Early First Grade) 55

■ Strategies for the Classroom: Scaffolding Young Children's Speech Discrimination 57

Beginning Conventional Reading and Writing (Kindergarten to Early Grade 2) 58

Transitional Reading and Writing (Late Grade 1 to Mid-Grade 4) 60

Intermediate Reading and Writing (Grade 3 through Grade 8) 62

Skillful Reading and Writing (Grade 6 and Above) 65

Chapter Summary 68

Suggested Extension Activities 69

Recommended Professional Resources 69

Online Resources 70

CHAPTER 3:
Effective Literacy Instruction: Principles and Practices 71

Characteristics of Highly Effective Teachers 73

■ **The Language of Your Instruction: Building a Community of Thoughtful Communicators and Deep Thinkers 74**

Your Classroom Environment and Students' Motivation to Learn 74

Organizing Your Classroom Environment 75

A Print-Rich Environment 75

Classroom Management and Student Engagement 77

Conclusion: Your Classroom Environment 77

■ **Reading and Writing in Digital Contexts: Using Multiple Literacies in Your Classroom 78**

Your Classroom Library 78

Quantity of Books 79

Quality and Variety of Books 79

■ **Strategies for the Classroom: To Level or Not to Level, That Is the Question 80**

Your Daily Literacy Block 81

■ **Working and Collaborating: The Role of Paraprofessionals in Your Literacy Block 81**

Reading Workshop: An Overview 82

Managing Your Time in Reading Workshop 82

Shared Reading 82

Interactive Read-Aloud 83

■ **Children's Literature Connection: Books to Start the School Year 84**

Mini-Lessons: Explicit, Whole Class, Standards-Based Instruction 84

Small Group Reading Instruction 87

■ **Accommodating English Learners: Creating an Environment that Supports Risk Taking and Collaboration 90**

Independent Reading Time: Time Spent Reading 90

Managing Small Group Instruction and Independent Reading across the Week 92

Wrapping Up the Workshop: Share Time 93

Writing Workshop: An Overview 93

Mentor Texts 94

Mini-Lessons 94

Independent Writing Practice 95

Small Group Writing Instruction and Conferring 95

Share 97

Word Study Instruction: An Overview 97

Sorting 98

Student Talk and Reflection 99

Different Types of Sorts 99

Sorting Throughout the Week 102

Extension Activities 103

Managing Word Study Instruction Across the Week 107

Your Word Study Lesson Plan Sequence 107

Word Study Assessment 108

Individual Learning Contracts 108

Comprehensive Core Reading Programs 108

Chapter Summary 110

Suggested Extension Activities 110

Recommended Professional Resources 111

Online Resources 111

CHAPTER 4:
Prioritizing Student-Centered Assessment and Instruction 112

A Brief and Recent History of Assessment and School Reform 115

"A Nation at Risk" 115

The "Reading Wars" 116

No Child Left Behind and High-Stakes
Testing 117

■ **The Language of Your Instruction: Helping
Students Succeed with High-Stakes
Assessment 117**

The Misuses and Unintended Consequences
of High-Stakes Assessment 118

A New Era of Reform: Common Core State
Standards 118

■ **Working and Collaborating: Talking with
Parents and Families about High-Stakes
Assessment 120**

Types and Purposes of Assessment 121

Norm-Referenced Assessment 121

Criterion-Referenced Assessment 122

Summative Assessment 123

Formative Assessment 123

■ **Strategies for the Classroom: Planning
Assessment *Before* Your Instruction 125**

The Qualities of a "Good" Assessment 125

Reliability 125

Validity 126

Instructional Transparency 126

■ **Accommodating English Learners: Equitable
Literacy Assessment for English Learners 127**

A Comprehensive Literacy Assessment
Program 127

Assessing the "Literacy Essentials" 129

Word Structure: Pinpointing Development with Qualitative Spelling Inventories 129

Assessing Foundational Skills: Phonological Awareness
Literacy Screening (PALS) 132

Assessing Reading Comprehension 133

■ **Reading and Writing in Digital Contexts:
The Role of Electronic Data Management
Systems 133**

Informal Reading Inventories 136

■ **Children's Literature Connection: Doing Your
Best: Books about Perseverance and Overcoming
Obstacles 136**

Assessing Fluency 139

Assessing Vocabulary and Morphological
Knowledge 141

Interest Inventories and Motivation Surveys 143

Special Considerations for Emergent and Beginning
Readers 143

Using Ongoing Formative Assessment
in Your Classroom 144

Conferring 144

Records of Oral Reading 145

Rubrics 145

Student Self-Assessment and Ongoing Feedback 146

Portfolios 150

Chapter Summary 150

Suggested Extension Activities 151

Recommended Professional Resources 151

Online Resources 152

CHAPTER 5:
**Foundations of Language and Literacy
Instruction for English Learners 153**

The Foundations of Teaching English Learners 155

Examining Our Dispositions 156

Characteristics of English Learners 158

■ **Working and Collaborating: Tips for
Effective Home-School Communication 159**

Culturally Responsive and Culturally
Inclusive Teaching 159

Effective Instructional Practices 160

Examining Students' Home Languages and Their
Literacy Experiences 161

■ **Accommodating English Learners: Speakers
of Variant/Vernacular Dialects 162**

Determining Levels of English Learners'
Proficiency in English 164

Literacy Instruction with Your English
Learners 165

■ **Children's Literature Connection: Evaluating
Language, Racial, Ethnic, and Culturally Diverse
Aspects of Literature 167**

Reading to Your English Learners: Supporting
Language and Literacy Development 168

Wide Reading and Purposeful Writing 168

Vocabulary Instruction 169

■ **The Language of Your Instruction: Moving Beyond the Literal: Idiomatic Expressions 170**

Spelling Instruction 170

■ **Strategies for the Classroom: "Modeling" Academic Language 171**

Chapter Summary 171

Suggested Extension Activities 172

Recommended Professional Resources 172

Online Resources 172

CHAPTER 6:
Emergent Literacy: Engaging the World of Print, Developing Oral Language, and Vocabulary 173

An Introduction to the Emergent Stage of Development 175

Oral Language Development: The Foundation of Literacy 176

Enriching the Language Environment in Your Classroom 176

Density of Talk 177

Quality of Talk 177

The Role of Syntax 178

Authentic and Sustained Conversation 178

■ **Strategies for the Classroom: Building a Tower of Talk 179**

Language and Literacy Development in Meaningful Contexts 180

■ **Strategies for the Classroom: Literacy-Rich Centers 181**

Engaging the World of Print: The Role of Exposure to Written Texts 182

Storybook Reading 182

Reading Informational Text 184

■ **Children's Literature Connection: Guidelines for Choosing High-Quality Informational Text 186**

Other Texts for Emergent Readers 188

Poetry, Fingerplays, Nursery Rhymes, and Songs 188

Environmental and Functional Print 188

■ **Children's Literature Connection: Favorite Books and Resources for Poetry, Nursery Rhymes, Fingerplays, and Songs 189**

Concept Books 189

■ **The Language of Your Instruction: Talking with Children about Print in Their Environment 190**

Predictable Pattern Books 190

Wordless Picture Books 190

Big Books 191

Reading to Children: Developing Listening Comprehension and Vocabulary 191

Dialogic Read-Alouds 191

■ **Children's Literature Connection: Resources for Selecting a Good Read-Aloud 192**

Text Talk 193

Deciding Which Words to Teach 195

Anchored Vocabulary Instruction 196

Developing Conceptual Knowledge 196

■ **Strategies for the Classroom: Anchored Vocabulary Instruction 197**

Developing Concepts about Print: Its Forms and Functions 198

Shared Reading 198

Independent Reading Practice 200

■ **Working and Collaborating: Reading with Your Child at Home 201**

Learning the Alphabet and the Role of Letters 202

■ **Reading and Writing in Digital Contexts: Resources for Evaluating Learning Applications 203**

Alphabet Books 204

Beginning Consonant Sounds and Letters 204

Beginning Sound Sorts 205

Extensions 206

Learning about Units of Print and Units of Language 206

■ **Accommodating English Learners: Predictable Consonant Confusions for English Learners 207**

Phonological Sensitivity and Awareness of Words 207

Awareness of Syllables 208

Rhyming 208

Awareness of Onset-Rime 208

■ **Strategies for the Classroom: Shared Reading, Print Referencing, and Rhyme 209**

Awareness of Phonemes 209

Phonics 211

Phonological Awareness and Language: A Strong Foundation 211

Concept of Word 212

Writing in the Emergent Stage 213

Putting All the Pieces Together: The Reading-Writing-Language Connection 214

Chapter Summary 216

Suggested Extension Activities 217

Recommended Professional Resources 217

Online Resources 218

CHAPTER 7:
Beginning Conventional Reading and Writing 219

Overview of Beginning Readers, Writers, and Letter Name-Alphabetic Spellers 221

Word Knowledge: The Linchpin of Literacy Development 222

Alphabet Knowledge 222

Phonological and Phonemic Awareness 224

Concept of Word in Text 224

■ **Strategies for the Classroom: Hearing and Representing Sounds 225**

Sight Word Vocabulary 228

■ **Accommodating English Learners: Building Sight Vocabulary 230**

Word Study: Phonics, Spelling, and Vocabulary 232

Phonics 232

Letter Name–Alphabetic Spellers 233

Vocabulary Development 237

■ **Strategies for the Classroom: Word Study in Practice: A Sample Five-Day Lesson Plan 238**

Small Group Reading Instruction for Beginning Readers 241

Guided Reading 242

■ **The Language of Your Instruction: Prompting Readers to Be Strategic 246**

What Beginning Readers Can Read Themselves 247

■ **Working and Collaborating: Paired Reading 247**

Beginning Fluency: From Automaticity to Expressive Reading 252

Fluency Instruction for Beginning Readers 252

■ **Reading and Writing in Digital Contexts: Technology Assisted Repeated Readings 253**

Reading *To* and *With* Children: Guiding Comprehension Development 254

Before Reading: Activating Prior Knowledge, Previewing, Predicting, and Setting a Purpose 254

During Reading: Monitoring and Questioning 255

After Reading: Retelling 257

■ **Children's Literature Connection: Texts That Stimulate Children to Ask Questions 257**

The Beginning of Conventional Writing 260

Getting Started with Writing Workshop 261

Getting Started with Narrative Writing 262

Writing to Inform: Procedural "How-To" Writing, "All-About" Texts, and Persuasive "Argument" Writing 263

The Writing Process 264

Chapter Summary 266

Suggested Extension Activities 268

Recommended Professional Resources 268

Online Resources 269

CHAPTER 8:
Transitional Reading and Writing 270

Overview of Transitional Readers, Writers, and Within Word Pattern Spellers 272

■ **Within Word Pattern Spellers: Moving from Sound to Pattern** 273

Characteristics of Early, Middle, and Late Within Word Pattern Spellers 274

Studying Vowels in Single-Syllable Words 276

Studying Consonants in Single-Syllable Words 279

■ **Accommodating English Learners: Teaching the Vowel Sounds of English** 280

■ **Working and Collaborating: Talking with Families about Word Study Instruction** 281

Vocabulary Development: Spelling Instruction and Beyond 282

Homophones, Homographs, and Other Features of the Late Within Word Pattern Stage 282

Shades of Meaning: Synonym and Antonym Lines 283

Generative Vocabulary Instruction: Early Morphological Awareness 284

■ **Strategies for the Classroom: Teaching the Prefix "un–" to Transitional Readers** 284

Interactive Read-Alouds: Developing Engaged Listeners and Deep Thinkers 286

Reader Response Theory in Action: Supporting Comprehension Development 287

Talking Well, Thinking Well: The Power of Talk in the Development of Comprehension 289

Supporting Children's Conversations about Books 289

■ **Children's Literature Connection: Interactive Read-Alouds for Developing Critical Thinking in the Transitional Stage of Development** 290

Collaborative Reasoning and Argument Schema 291

■ **The Language of Your Instruction: Collaborative Reasoning in Action** 291

From Talking Well to Writing Well: Written Response to Text 293

Quick Writes 293

■ **Reading and Writing in Digital Contexts: Blogging in Response to Text** 294

From Quick Writes to Response Essays 294

Books for Transitional Readers: Independent and Small Group Reading Practice 297

Early Transitional Readers 298

Middle Transitional Readers 298

■ **The Language of Your Instruction: Teaching Children to Infer** 299

Late Transitional Readers 300

■ **Children's Literature Connection: Other Books for Transitional Readers** 302

Developing Transitional Readers' Fluency and Comprehension: Research-Based "Best" Practices 303

Wide Reading 303

Repeated Reading 303

Comprehension Routines: Reciprocal Teaching in Action 304

■ **The Language of Your Instruction: Conferring with Transitional Readers and Writers** 305

Reading and Writing Connections: Helping Transitional Writers Write Well 306

Narrative 307

Research and Reports 309

Persuasive Pieces: The Seeds of Argument 309

Chapter Summary 312

Suggested Extension Activities 313

Recommended Professional Resources 314

Online Resources 314

CHAPTER 9:
Intermediate Reading and Writing 315

Overview of Intermediate Readers, Writers, and Syllables and Affixes Spellers 317

Developing Comprehension and Understanding of Texts 318

Strategies for Approaching Texts: Predicting, Questioning, Clarifying, Summarizing, Extending 318

Types of Texts and Approaches to Reading 318

■ **Strategies for the Classroom: "Reading with a Pencil"** 319

Reading Informational Texts 320

■ **Strategies for the Classroom: Accountable Talk** 322

Reading Literature: Narrative Fiction 324

Reading Literature: Poetry 325

- ■ **Strategies for the Classroom: Book Clubs 327**
- ■ **Young Adult Literature Connection: For Middle School Students at the Intermediate Stage 330**

Developmental Word Knowledge 330

Spelling: Exploring Syllable Patterns and Morphology 330

- ■ **The Language of Your Instruction: Spelling Features at the Intermediate Stage 331**

Vocabulary Development 336

- ■ **Strategies for the Classroom: Teaching Morphology at the Intermediate Level with Root Words and Affixes 339**

Applying What They Are Learning: Decoding and Learning Longer Words in Reading 341

- ■ **Strategies for the Classroom: Teaching Morphology at the Intermediate Level with Greek and Latin Roots 342**

Systematic Instruction in *General Academic* and *Domain-Specific* Vocabulary 346

Fluency: The Bridge to Comprehension 349

- ■ **Accommodating English Learners: Awareness and Understanding of Cognates 351**

Modeling Fluent Reading 352

Bridging from Read-Alouds to Students' Reading of Anchor Texts 352

Writing 352

The Writing Process in the Intermediate Stage 354

- ■ **The Language of Your Instruction: Writing Traits 356**

The Traits of Writing 356

Getting Under Way with Informational Writing: RAFT Papers 358

- ■ **Strategies for the Classroom: Author's Craft Lessons 360**
- ■ **Reading and Writing in Digital Contexts: Connecting Content Learning and Technological Literacy 360**

Chapter Summary 362

Suggested Extension Activities 363

Recommended Professional Resources 363

Online Resources 363

CHAPTER 10:
Skillful Literacy: Developing Critical Engagements with Texts, Language, and Vocabulary 364

Overview of Skillful Readers, Writers, and Derivational Relations Spellers 367

Characteristics of Texts for Skillful Readers 367

- ■ **Young Adult Literature Connection: The Uses of Mythology 369**

Developing Comprehension and Understanding: In-Depth Critical Engagements with More Complex Texts 371

Literature 371

- ■ **The Language of Instruction: Provoking a Persuasive Stance 372**

Independent Reading: Motivating and Engaging Readers with Self-Selected Reading 378

- ■ **Young Adult Literature Connection: Literature for LGBTQI Students 379**

Informational Texts and Academic Language 381

Developmental Spelling Knowledge: Derivational Relationships 384

- ■ **Reading and Writing in Digital Contexts: Critical Literacy in Action on the Web 388**

Vocabulary Development 394

- ■ **Strategies for the Classroom: Skillful Readers with "Spelling Issues" 395**

Advanced Generative Vocabulary Instruction 395

The Role of Etymological Knowledge in Growing and Deepening Vocabulary Knowledge 398

Systematic Instruction in General Academic and Domain-Specific Vocabulary 400

- ■ **Strategies for the Classroom: Reading Workshop Mini-Lesson: Author's Craft 404**

Writing in the Skillful Stage 405

Analyzing Narrative 405

Analyzing and Constructing an Argument 407

Chapter Summary 412

Suggested Extension Activities 412

Recommended Professional Resources 412

Online Resources 413

CHAPTER 11:

Response to Instruction: Intervention and Acceleration for Readers Who Struggle 414

What Is Response to Instruction? 416

■ **The Language of Your Instruction: Student-First Language 419**

Tiered Instruction 419

The Role of Assessment in Response to Instruction 420

■ **Accommodating English Learners: Determining the Presence of a Learning Disability in an English Learner 420**

Profiles of Students Experiencing Difficulty in Learning to Read 421

Automatic Word Callers: Readers with Strong Word Recognition, Weak Vocabulary and Comprehension 422

Word Stumblers: Readers with Strong Vocabulary and Comprehension, Weaker Word Recognition and Fluency 423

Struggling Word Callers: Readers Experiencing Difficulty with Word Recognition and Comprehension 423

Slow and Steady Comprehenders: Readers with Strong Comprehension and Word Recognition and Weaker Fluency 424

Slow Word Callers: Readers with Strong Word Recognition and Weak Fluency and Comprehension 424

Students with Specific Learning Disabilities in Reading 424

■ **Reading and Writing in Digital Contexts: Assistive Technology in the Literacy Classroom 425**

Accommodating Students Experiencing Difficulty with Literacy 425

Supporting the Development of *All* Students: Research-Based Best Practices 426

■ **Working and Collaborating: Helping Students with Learning Disabilities Be Successful with Homework 427**

Word Sorts: Varying the Complexity 428

■ **Children's Literature Connection: Great Books about Children and Adolescents with Learning Difficulties 428**

Building Background Knowledge and Using Graphic Organizers 429

Increase "High-Success" Reading Practice 431

■ **Strategies for the Classroom: Tips for Teaching Comprehension Strategies 431**

Morphological Analysis: Helping Students "Unlock" the Meaning of Words 432

Attend to Motivation and Engagement 433

Chapter Summary 434

Suggested Extension Activities 434

Recommended Professional Resources 435

Online Resources 435

Glossary 436

References 442

References for Children's and Young Adult Literature 461

Index 466

Photo and Text Credits 478

Preface

Today's teachers face many challenges, including teaching all students, teaching them well, and teaching them in the context of rising expectations and high-stakes assessment. Today's students come from increasingly diverse socioeconomic, cultural, linguistic, racial, and ethnic backgrounds. Because of your dedication to these children, you embrace the challenges and opportunities of teaching in today's dynamic and diverse classroom environments. In this book we provide the foundation for meeting the challenges of teaching literacy in these contexts, providing you with the knowledge and tools necessary to teach literacy in a developmentally responsive and integrated way.

Purpose

Understanding developmentally responsive instruction allows you to teach in students' instructional zones, accelerating their literacy learning and development. We have written *Teaching Reading and Writing: The Developmental Approach* (PreK to Grade 8) to provide you with the knowledge and strategies for this type of teaching, including up-to-date research on literacy development, instruction, assessment, and intervention. In this book, we address three goals:

1. Provide foundational knowledge in the nature and progression of literacy development, identifying what learners are able to understand about the essential elements of literacy at different developmental stages, and when and how are they able to apply those understandings with your help as well as independently.

2. Provide an understanding of the essential elements of literacy and how related instructional strategies support deep and meaningful engagements with texts.

3. Provide an understanding of the foundations and nature of culturally responsive literacy instruction.

Using This Book

Intended for preservice and experienced teachers alike, this book provides a wealth of content and does so in a conversational, approachable style that connects theory to practice by including:

- Vignettes and sample lessons from real classrooms
- Authentic student work samples
- Ways to use and integrate print-based and digital texts across the curriculum
- Tools for organizing and managing a comprehensive, developmentally responsive literacy program

Whether you're preparing to teach or have a classroom of your own, *Teaching Reading and Writing: The Developmental Approach* promises to provide you with the tools and knowledge necessary to confidently and competently meet the diverse needs of students in today's class-rooms. It is designed to help you teach in a student-centered, research-based way. Beginning with assessment, you'll learn to identify students' stages of development as a means for determining not only *what* to teach, but *how* to teach it. Most methods texts dedicate separate chapters to the essential elements of literacy—word analysis skills, fluency, vocabulary, comprehension, writing, and motivation—but our chapters reflect an integrated model of literacy instruction that is based on the understanding that reading and writing are developmental processes. As such, you will see these components of literacy addressed in *every* chapter.

- Each chapter begins with real-life scenarios that illustrate the theory in practice. This will help you immediately see the relevance and application of theory.

- Student work samples are included in each chapter to help you actually see the kind of work students at each stage of development create so you will know what to expect from learners across the developmental continuum. We also help you learn how to analyze student work to identify your student's stages of development and instructional needs.

- Sample lessons not only make the text engaging and accessible but they also make the text come to life. These samples help you put the theory and research into practice with real students in real classrooms. Each lesson is aligned with the *Common Core State Standards for English Language Arts*.

- Literature for children and young adults is integrated throughout the text. In each instructional chapter you'll find a list of titles appropriate for that stage of development; in other chapters you will find titles appropriate for the various topics that are addressed. With the Common Core's emphasis on text complexity, these lists are timely and extremely helpful for teachers who are planning Common Core-aligned lessons each day.

- An illustrative companion text, Newbury Honor Award-winning *Al Capone Does My Shirts* by Gennifer Choldenko (2004), is available.

- Each chapter ends with a comprehensive chapter summary, suggested extension activities, recommended professional resources, and additional online resources.

The first two foundational chapters of *Teaching Reading and Writing: The Developmental Approach* address the nature of development and interaction of thought, language, and literacy. They introduce you to the developmental model, the literacy essentials, historical trends in the field, as well as the current policy environment in which the Common Core State Standards and Response to Intervention (RTI) figure prominently. By giving you an overview of these topics early on, we're able to build on this knowledge in each of the subsequent chapters.

The third foundational chapter addresses the principles and practices of effective, developmentally responsive literacy instruction, and the fourth grounds your understanding of development and instruction in effective assessment.

Chapters 6 through 10 are dedicated, respectively, to each stage of literacy development: *emergent, beginning, transitional, intermediate*, and *skillful*. Within each chapter, you'll learn how to differentiate instruction for students within each stage, meet the expectations of the new Common Core State Standards for English Language Arts, accommodate English learners, collaborate with other professionals, integrate print and digital literacies, and build home–school connections. The literacy essentials are addressed in each of these chapters with a special focus on the unique needs of learners at each specific stage of development. You will learn *what* to teach, *when* to teach it, and *how* to teach it.

In addition to a special feature titled "Accommodating English Learners" in each chapter, the fifth chapter of this book is dedicated to the special needs of English learners. The chapter addresses specific accommodations English learners may need in the literacy classroom, as well as the importance of culturally relevant pedagogy. A specific chapter on teaching readers who struggle provides an overview of Response to Intervention as well as profiles of readers who struggle. For each profile, you will learn about research-based methods proven to accelerate the achievement of these readers. General suggestions for accelerating the achievement of all learners are included at the end of the chapter.

At the end of Chapter 1 you will find the section "How to Use This Book," which provides much more specific information and advice on the purpose and application of the organization of the book and the features of each chapter. These features include *Strategies for the Classroom, The Language of Your Instruction, Accommodating English Learners, Reading and Writing in Digital Contexts, Children's Literature Connection*, and *Working and Collaborating*.

We hope you'll find *Teaching Reading and Writing: The Developmental Approach* to be the foundation and guide for your literacy instruction that we have intended it to be. It will support your dedication, excitement, and commitment to the very best of literacy instruction—a guide to helping your students move toward reading and comprehending literary and informational texts independently and proficiently, and toward writing for a range of tasks, purposes, and audiences.

Supplements

The following supplements comprise an outstanding array of resources that facilitate learning about literacy instruction. For more information, ask your local Pearson representative. For technology support, please contact technical support directly at 1-800-677-6337 or online at **www.247.pearsoned.com.**

Instructor's Resource Manual and Test Bank

For each chapter, the instructor's resource manual features activities and resources for instructors to use in the classroom. Answers to the Self-Check questions for each chapter from the text are also included. In addition, the TestBank includes multiple-choice, essential terms, and short-answer items. Page references to the main text, suggested answers, and skill types have been added to each question to help instructors create and evaluate student tests. (Available for download from the Instructor Resource Center at **www.pearsonhighered.com/irc.**)

PowerPoint™ Slides

Ideal for lecture presentations or student handouts, the PowerPoint™ presentation provides dozens of ready-to-use graphic and text images.

Acknowledgments

A project as intensive and extensive as this book could not have been undertaken, much less completed, without support and ideas from so many dear friends and professional colleagues. Space does not allow the inclusion of all of their names here, but we wish to acknowledge those who have impacted this project most specifically.

Aurora Martínez, who realized, sustained, and supported the vision; Erin Grelak, who was there in the beginning and throughout most of the journey, and who believed and invested in so many ways; Kathryn Boice, who took over the reigns and skillfully and considerately guided us to a successful conclusion; Beth Jacobson, extraordinary developmental editor, who attended this project, nurtured, and provided feedback as if it were the only book on which she was working, but we of course knew better; Karen Mason, project manager and mastermind of permissions, production, and so much more; Tania Zamora, who negotiated the intricacies and challenges of permissions with expediency and good humor; Michelle Hochberg, logistics planner extraordinaire; Libby Bonesteel, who graciously and with all due dispatch took on the Herculean project of writing the Instructor's Resource Manual and Test Bank, and of preparing the chapter PowerPoint™ slides. We could easily write a page of gratitude for each of the following individuals: Donald Bear, Marcia Invernizzi, Francine Johnston, Kevin Flanigan, Tisha Hayes, Darrell Morris, Tamara Baren, Carol Caserta-Henry, Sandy Madura, Kara Moloney, Shari Dunn, Brenda Sabey, Dianna Townsend, Diane Barone, Cindy Brock, Julie Pennington, Pete and Stephanie Cobin, David and Regina Smith, Karen Carpenter, Janet Bellavance, Matthew Hajdun, Lynda Siegel, Suzy Tenenbaum, David Mendenhall, Karen Jeffrey, Nicole Doner, Alexis Scott, Jessica Pepin, and Allison Drake.

We also gratefully acknowledge the reviewers, whose time, commitment, and feedback during the development of this book were extraordinary and invaluable. Because of their efforts, we believe this book is a much stronger resource: Bruce F. Brodney, St. Petersburg College; Melissa Caraway, University of Dallas; Ann Crutchfield, Pfeiffer University; Annette M. Dobrasz, Niagara University, D'Youville College, Niagara Community College; Meadow Sherrill Graham, West Virginia University; Ellen Jampole, Coastal Carolina University; Robert Timothy Rush, University of Wyoming; and Kim S. Truesdell, Buffalo State College.

Thank you, too, to those elementary and middle school students who generously shared their work with us and with you, and to the undergraduate and graduate students of Saint Michael's College who read and responded to early drafts of the manuscript. We are most grateful for their suggestions and encouragement. And finally, we are especially grateful to our families, who have been more than supportive and understanding of the countless hours we've invested in this project.

The Foundations of Literacy Instruction

Chapter Outline

» What *Is* Literacy?

» The Importance of Print and Digital Literacy

» The Many Faces of Literacy

» The Literacy Essentials

» The Literacy Essentials from a Developmental Perspective

» The Sociocultural Contexts of Literacy Learning

» Levels of Support and the Gradual Release of Responsibility Model

1. How are "print literacy" and "digital literacy" alike? How are they different?
2. Why is each of the following *essential* to the development of proficient reading and writing: *Comprehension, Writing, Vocabulary, Word Structure, Fluency, Motivation*?
3. What is the importance of understanding the developmental nature of literacy across the five stages: *Emergent, Beginning, Transitional, Intermediate, Skillful*?
4. Describe the sociocultural contexts of literacy learning and how they may impact your teaching of literacy.
5. Why is the "Gradual Release of Responsibility" model for instruction such a powerful framework for teaching literacy?

I t is shortly after 9:00 a.m. on a Tuesday morning in September. Ms. Arlene Robinson, principal of Compello Elementary School, has invited you to accompany her as she visits each classroom during literacy block. The primary grades have a two-hour block; intermediate grades meet for an hour and a half. Arlene visits the classrooms every day; her previous school, she mentions, was simply too large to be able to do that—so she worked out a rotation. And she doesn't always visit the classrooms at Compello Elementary in the mornings; quite often, she does her "walkabout," as she calls it, in the afternoons. Like most effective elementary principals, Arlene makes it a point to know the names of every student well before the holiday break in December.

As you're walking down the kindergarten/first-grade wing, you can't help but notice the lively voices pouring out into the hallway from every classroom; all doors are propped open. Arlene chuckles. "You know," she says, "when I began teaching, my principal told all of the new teachers that when he walked down our hallway he wanted our kids to be so quiet that he'd be able to hear a pin drop! Needless to say, I crossed some swords with that gentleman!" Arlene went on to share how every teacher at Compello understood that learning is a social phenomenon, and that students have to be able to talk with one another in order to learn. "*Most* of the time," she winks, "they're using their indoor voices!"

When we enter Karleen Echevarria's first-grade classroom, several of the children move quickly across the room to give Arlene a hug, which she receives with smiles, hugs them in return, but then gently eases them back toward what they had been engaged in doing. These particular children had been working at their desks on their science unit, sorting pictures into different categories: creatures that live on land, in water, or both on land and in water. The children resumed a spirited debate about whether one particular creature could be placed in the "both land and water" category, then agreed to put it in an "oddball" category—they'd check on it later with Ms. Echevarria. Karleen was in the reading corner, meeting with another group of seven children. They were earnestly discussing why the animals who Henny Penny told "the sky is falling" all went along with her without asking her how she knew this! Karleen followed up by asking them if there'd ever been a time when *they* had followed along with a group without asking why.

A bit later, as you and Principal Robinson turn into the fourth/fifth-grade wing, Arlene shares that the district adopted a new reading program the previous year. The state had mandated that schools adopt a program. "Now, I know I've got several experienced teachers at Compello who are excellent teachers of reading and writing. I'm pretty certain they don't need a program to teach well. Most of the teachers here, though, are within their first three or four years of teaching, and I like having that program as a resource for them that they can draw from and lean on for support when they need to. Our veteran teachers—we've got a very supportive school culture—help them sort out and focus on what is of most help in the program for their kids, and what they don't really need to bother with. Otherwise, those programs can be overwhelming to teachers early in their careers! Together with the support they receive from the veterans, I think our newer teachers are doing a pretty good job of becoming effective literacy teachers!"

You ask if there is a literacy coach or specialist at Compello Elementary. Arlene shares that the district has budgeted for a literacy coach for every three "bubble" schools—those not quite qualifying for free and reduced lunch—and that the coach does her best, "but it sure is difficult if that person isn't living every day in your school!" The district does a pretty good job of providing professional development during the year, Arlene adds, but more and more the focus has been placed on building and trying to support effective professional learning communities *within* each school. "They're trying to get us to have more within- and between-grade

discussions," she comments, "focusing on 'data-driven' instruction—how do we know how well our students are doing in reading and what adjustments can we then make in our instruction? This had been part of our RTI [Response to Intervention] framework the last few years, and we've been working not only to use the assessments we are mandated to use, but [and here Arlene winks again] adding a couple of assessments that we feel give us perhaps better 'classroom-based' information about individual students.

"You know, another big push we began a couple of years ago was how to adjust our reading instruction to fit the new Common Core State Standards that our state is mandated to use. Teachers throughout the district have expressed some concern that the new grade-level expectations may be too advanced for many of our students. Our mission as administrators throughout the district is to support the teachers' efforts to achieve the higher expectations for reading and writing but to do so in ways that reflect good instruction. Fortunately, most administrators understand a *developmental model* of learning—almost all of us are former classroom teachers—so we are better able to set the appropriate tone for our teachers." ■

This vignette captures several important themes that we will address in this text: the social nature of literacy learning; the differentiation of instruction, which involves meeting with small groups of students while other students are working independently or at literacy work stations; the importance of getting to know your students well; and a vocabulary activity and a literature discussion in which the children are *actively* involved. Arlene also touches on some of the practical situations that every teacher experiences and must learn how to negotiate—using a mandated curriculum, following district-mandated procedures while appropriately exercising the experienced teachers' and principal's professional judgment in customizing instruction and assessment.

What *Is* "Literacy"?

Simply put, literacy is the ability to read and write. Reading is thinking guided by print (Calkins, 2000), and writing is using print to guide the thinking of others. Do you remember how you learned to read? To write? Were those experiences joyful ones—or challenging? Do you enjoy reading today? Writing? What do you use reading and writing to *do*?

These are important questions. You will be reflecting on them as you read and apply teaching strategies and activities we will be sharing in this book. This is because teaching reading and writing will probably be the most important responsibility you will have as a teacher. Your own experience in learning to read and write will influence how you approach this responsibility. How you were taught determines:

- What you think about reading and writing
- How you use reading and writing
- How you will be learning to teach reading and writing to others

If you have pleasant memories—or at least had a few teachers who inspired you—you are fortunate in being able to build on your personal experiences as you prepare to teach your students. You may recognize those teachers in this book. If you did *not* have enjoyable experiences—if in fact you do not like to read all that much today—we hope you will learn, as we move through this text together, how you can change your own experiences and in turn support children's joyful and purposeful learning.

In a best-selling book published many years ago titled *Why Johnny Can't Read*, a journalist wrote that all we have to do is teach a child the sounds that the letters make, and that child will learn to read (Flesch, 1956). If it were that simple, of course, we probably wouldn't need teachers. There is no question that it is necessary to learn how letters represent sounds, but becoming literate involves so much more than that. You'll not only be teaching your students *about* reading, but you'll also be helping them learn how this tool will empower them to learn and to think more critically. Many students, unfortunately, experience difficulty in developing literacy right from the beginning. Many other students learn easily, but run into difficulty later on. This is because literacy—reading and writing—is also complex. Becoming literate and using the tool of literacy develop over many years, and how well this tool is acquired and used depends in large part on the teachers students will have—on you.

The Importance of Print and Digital Literacy

A generation ago, being able to read at the eighth-grade level would suffice in many occupations (Wagner, 2010). In the twenty-first century, however, that is not enough. The levels at which students must be able to read are considerably higher because requirements for getting a job are more stringent in an increasingly globalized economy. Globalization and information technology have merged. Because of this reality, literacy must develop and support students' abilities to think critically, problem solve, communicate effectively, and collaborate. As Principal Arlene Robinson pointed out, at the present time in the United States this awareness is reflected in new standards for literacy in general and for literacy in the specific content areas or domains (*Common Core State Standards Initiative*, 2010).

We all know that the digital world is changing in profound ways how young people, as well as those who teach them, are looking at and thinking about their worlds (Gee, 2007; Carr, 2010). Changes in society and technology have led a number of educators and scholars to think about literacy in broader terms: They point out that there are many ways to "read" and "write" the world. Some are beginning to ask if there will still be a role for "print" literacy—for abilities based on paper, pen, turning pages, books on shelves in libraries—in this digital revolution. As the content of this book will show, there definitely will be: Much of the ability to understand and navigate digital environments, as well as to use social media responsibly and effectively, is grounded in skills that come right out of print literacy. Texts and the thinking that goes into understanding them *(reading)* and creating them *(writing)* provide frameworks for thinking about what's going on in the real world and the digital world. It has been estimated that textbooks—one of the traditional means of delivering content in schools for centuries—will be totally digital by 2017, accessible for all students on low-cost e-tablets (State Educational Technology Directors Association [SETDA], 2012).

This is why we will emphasize your teaching of literacy in *print*-based contexts, which we define as information and stories presented in printed texts as well as on screens that can be

The Many Faces of Literacy

Strategies for the Classroom

Is There One "Best Method" for Teaching Reading?

No. Education in general, and literacy in particular, are shaped by social, political, economic, and technological influences (Graff, 2010; Smith, 1965). At different times throughout history, different methods have held sway. They usually have to do with how to teach beginning reading, but the different positions educators take also have implications for upper grade levels as well.

You may be aware of the debates about how "best" to teach reading (Carnine, Silbert, Kame'enui, & Tarver, 2009; Goodman, 1986; 1993; Lehmann, 1997). Over the years, the loudest debaters—and those who often have influenced national policy regarding how reading should be taught—have usually fallen into either of two positions:

- Those who say we should begin with the parts—sounds and letters—and build up from there to the whole
- Those who say we should begin with the whole—a text—and work down to the parts

Throughout your teaching career you will see different shifts and emphases. It is important to bear in mind, though, that these changes will not overturn everything you know about how to teach literacy. Understanding the developmental model—how literacy knowledge and skills evolve over time, one after the other—will be your constant instructional compass and companion. The technologies certainly will change, affecting how you arrange and provide instruction, but the underlying mechanisms of students' learning will remain reassuringly constant.

Frank Smith (2004) addressed the reality that teachers "on the ground" must deal with:

> The primary role of reading teachers is to ensure that children have adequate demonstrations of written language being used for meaningful purposes and to help children to fulfill such purposes themselves. Where children see little relevance in reading, then teachers must show that reading is worthwhile. Where children find little interest in reading, then teachers must create interesting situations. No one ever taught reading to a child who wasn't interested in reading, and interest can't be demanded. (p. 212)

Teaching letters and sounds, therefore, without providing a model of what reading *is* will not make sense, and eventually interest will fall away. Attempting to teach using whole texts without providing systematic instruction in the ways letters and sounds correspond will not make sense either, because children are not being provided the tools for fulfilling their own purposes for reading. The truth of the matter, of which you are also probably aware, is that the recipe for "How Best to Teach Reading" includes several essential components or ingredients, and how much of each ingredient is provided for each child at different points in time depends on where that child is along the continuum of literacy development.

So, although there is no "best method" (the word "method" itself suggests a narrower, more exclusive focus), there *is* one "trusted approach": The *developmental* approach best supports your teaching of reading—and *writing* as well—in a way that will make sense to your students. You teach your students what they are ready to learn; they are more likely to be interested, and they will attend more closely to what you are demonstrating and helping them learn how to do. Teaching students the "basics" as well as the *application* of this basic knowledge continues throughout the school years. Effective instruction in reading *and* writing will enable and empower your students as they access, understand, and evaluate their informational and narrative worlds.

scrolled and hyperlinked. In these contexts you will teach not only *basics* such as letters and sounds but *critical* literacy as well (Frey, Fisher, & Berkin, 2009; *Common Core State Standards Initiative*, 2010). Although students may be "digital natives," they will still need you to reveal and guide them through the nature and implications of print—of reading and of writing.

The Many Faces of Literacy

A number of scholars and educators describe *literacy* in terms of a set of flexible "practices for communicating purposefully in multiple social and cultural contexts" (Mills, 2010, p. 247). Increasingly, of course, these contexts include *digitized* experiences, because we are now living in a "hypermediated" environment—television, movies, digital books, video games, and social media with almost instant connectivity. Students' experiences with fictional characters occur across several formats in what scholars term "branded fiction" and "genre mixing" (Lefstein & Snell, 2011; Sekeres, 2009). Just think of Harry Potter (books, movies, websites, clothing, theme park), Selena Gomez (music, television, movies, website), and the *American Girl* series (books, clothing, dolls, movies). There is an exciting new literacy frontier stretching out through these new interconnections and technologies. There are also unparalleled seductions: How are reading and writing affected, and what will they mean in this New World?

We can begin to answer this question by turning to the Old World. The essence, insight, and meaning of critical thinking have not changed at least since Socrates' time over 2,000 years ago. And dating from Socrates' day, we have had at least four "technological" revolutions that have affected reading and writing directly and significantly:

- An alphabet that can represent all the sounds in a language
- The development of the book
- The invention of the printing press
- The development of the Internet

What we are seeing now in the digital and social media environments—e-tablets, incredibly sophisticated Internet-enabled smartphones, the ability to store and do work in the "cloud"—are but way stations along the development of the Internet's vast highway system. In the future, your students will see and use far more fascinating and capable devices and platforms to access and live in the Internet's digital worlds.

There is no question that, with each new technology, how people "do" literacy is significantly affected. Indeed, each technological revolution has also accelerated the arts, humanities, and sciences as well as social, economic, and political developments (Olson & Cole, 2006). Throughout each of these revolutions, however, the true meaning and potential of reading and writing has remained and will continue to remain remarkably constant: *thinking* critically and very often *feeling* deeply so that we may communicate with ourselves, with others, and with our world. That's what reading and writing have meant, and what they will continue to mean.

The Literacy Essentials

Reading and writing are *reciprocal* processes. As students learn to read and write, each ability supports the other. As they read and think in different genres—for example, mystery, biography, poetry—students learn, with teacher guidance, how writers *use* the language and structure of those genres to affect readers: how readers think, how they learn, how they feel, how they are entertained, and how they behave. Our students then use these models to guide their own writing. Understanding this reciprocal process, your approach to teaching reading and writing will be based on your knowledge of:

- *What* needs to be taught and understanding effective ways to teach it
- The *development* of language, thought, and literacy in children and older students

First, we will address the *what*; second, we will lay the cornerstones for the *developmental* foundation.

The Literacy Essentials: The "What" of Effective Instruction

We've mentioned that reading and writing involve the use of print to guide thinking. Texts are like "blueprints" for constructing meaning (Spiro, 1980). Reading involves purposefully engaging a text—following the blueprint—in ways that ensure we are constructing as best we can the meaning that the author intended. When we *write*, we use our understanding of those same "blueprints" to help our readers construct the meaning we are trying to convey. So that we may teach students how best to build meanings as they interact with texts, it's necessary that we understand the essential components involved in this process of meaning construction. Attention to these essentials is necessary to enable all the other literacies:

- Comprehension
- Writing
- Vocabulary
- Word structure
- Fluency
- Motivation

Comprehension

To comprehend is to understand. Comprehending or understanding what we read may occur at different levels—deeply, or more superficially—depending on our purpose for reading. And that is the key: Comprehension is *active*, not passive. "Meaning" is not literally on the page to be passively lifted off. Understanding what we read is not somehow a by-product of identifying the words on the page. Driven by our purpose, meaning must be constructed from the blueprint that the information on the page suggests, together with the background knowledge we bring to the page. Because every reader brings a unique set of background experiences and understandings to every reading, whenever a reader reads a text, a new meaning is constructed that did not exist before.

In general, comprehension of any text is a process that proceeds in the following manner (Perfetti, 1985, 2007):

- The meaning of the words is determined.
- The order of and relationships among the words within each sentence are processed.
- The sentences are related to each other.
- Larger chunks of text are related to each other.
- An overall "model" of the text is created in the reader's mind.

From the author's blueprint to the reader's construction of the model—that's what comprehension is about. Importantly, readers' models of texts seldom contain the *exact* wording of the text (that would seriously overload their memories) but rather construct a more general understanding or sense of what the text is about.

For many years, reading comprehension has been described in terms of three levels: *literal*, *inferential*, and *critical* (Irwin, 2006; Israel & Duffy, 2008). Generations of teachers have tried to help students understand these levels by using the phrases *reading the lines* (literal), *reading between the lines* (inferential), and *reading beyond the lines* (critical). These phrases made sense if students already understood the levels of comprehension, but were of little help if they didn't. Over the last several years, educators have developed more effective ways to discuss and support students' understanding of how they can actively engage texts to best achieve their purposes for reading (McLaughlin, 2009; Raphael, Highfield, & Au, 2006).

Common Core Connection

Reading Standards for Literature and Informational Text: Key Ideas and Details; Integration of Knowledge and Ideas

Common Core Connection

Speaking and Listening: Comprehension and Collaboration

The Language of Your Instruction

Schema Theory and Comprehension

An important part of our background knowledge—its content and how it is organized—relies on specific experiences we have had. For example, if we are reading about a particular soccer match, our ability to understand the information about fielders, goals, penalty kicks, and so forth relies on the experiences we have had with soccer matches. If we haven't had much experience, then we're not going to be able to comprehend very much of the article. Schema theory explains this phenomenon (Anderson, Spiro, & Montague, 1977; Freebody & Anderson, 1983; McVee, Dunsmore, & Gavelek, 2005). **Schema theory** provides an important perspective for much of our understanding about comprehension in reading. If you read and understand fairly easily the article on the soccer match, for instance, it is because you have a robust mental *schema* for soccer matches. Your soccer schema has been constructed over time as you have learned more and more about soccer, and perhaps even played it. The *schemas* (or *schemata*) for different types of experiences apply to all social and *cognitive*, or thinking, activity. For example, someone whose "restaurant schema" has been constructed based only on experiences in more expensive establishments might enter a MacDonald's or Burger King and stand around waiting to be seated by the *maitre d'*—admittedly a silly example, but one we hope illustrates the nature of schema theory.

Our schemas organize our concepts and vocabulary and apply them to specific situations. Our concept of "net," for example, is applied to our soccer schema and has to do with where goals are scored, although the net looks different from the net in basketball. Similarly, our concept of "net" is used differently in our "fishing schema" and in our "Internet schema"—the result of our experiences in fishing with our uncle and using the Web. The implications for learning in general and reading comprehension in particular are profoundly important.

Our purposes for reading a particular text—what information or experience we are looking for, and why—determine how we approach any reading we do. This is because our purposes will guide what we look for and the degree to which we need to rely on our own background knowledge as we read.

And our *purposes* for reading a text vary, of course: We may simply want to escape and enjoy a narrative world, fictional or real; we may need information right now to solve a problem we are having with our printer; or we may—as is so often the case with students—be reading because a teacher has required us to and given us questions to answer. Regardless, readers must be able to apply strategies that will help them in accessing the *sources of information* they will need in order to achieve their purposes:

- Some information sources will be "right there," explicitly stated in the text;
- Other information sources may be inferred from the text by "thinking and searching";
- Still other information sources may be accessed by combining information that is explicit or implied in the text with the reader's background knowledge or "in the head" information (Raphael, Highfield, & Au, 2006).

As teachers, we teach our students strategies for accessing these information sources. We want them to grow from applying these strategies consciously and deliberately to applying them almost effortlessly, without even thinking about it (Afflerbach, Pearson, & Paris, 2008; Frey, Fisher, & Berkin, 2009).

The strategies we teach assist students in learning what to do *before*, *during*, and *after* reading. The chapters in this book are structured to reflect these strategies, priming your thinking before you get into the substance of the chapter and supporting your active engagement before, during, and after your reading. These tactics help define your purposes and what you pay attention to during your reading of the chapter. The chapter summary for each chapter pulls together the important information keyed by the initial focus questions. Although we include snippets of narratives throughout the text, because this is primarily an *informational* text, the chapters are *structured* in such a way that purposes and information will be developed, sustained, and hopefully learned.

We've just noted the types of texts your students will listen to and read: *narrative* and *informational*. An important part of the background knowledge about reading that you will help your students learn is the structure of these types of texts.

The notion of *narrative*, or "story," runs deep in every culture in the world. Many have said that we organize and make sense of our lives through the structure of a story or narrative. The power of stories in the lives of children, first heard and later read, cannot be overstated. "As they are told and retold, stories have the function of wrestling with the ultimately inexplicable chaos of reality around us. They give it form, and in shaping and reshaping the form, they help us gain control over it" (Jabbour, cited in Templeton, 1996). Stories or narratives offer a structure that helps younger children and older students take on problems and, over time, resolve those problems. Narratives may take on different forms in different cultures—Latino and Hispanic, for example, and Native American/Indigenous and African—but they serve the same function in all cultures: teaching and reassuring us as we grapple with life's challenges, large and small. For example, Sandra Madura, a teacher at Compello Elementary School, selects *Al Capone Does My Shirts* (Choldenko, 2004) for her fifth-grade class. The main characters are children of parents who are working in the maximum-security prison on the island of Alcatraz in San Francisco Bay. Sandra wants her students to read and explore this text because, as a work of historical fiction, it connects to her instruction in U.S. History and its narrative reflects the timeless struggles and worries of young people on the verge of puberty.

While a sense of narratives may be "wired in" to our collective psychology and experience, *informational* texts are not (Havelock, 1988; Ong, 2002). They structure information to accomplish different purposes: inform, describe, argue, or persuade. Our ability to reason logically, however, may develop based on our experience with the structure and the language of informational texts (Olson, 1996). Informational, or as it's often referred to, *expository* text, does not "tell stories" in the narrative sense. It's structured to convey and represent information in supportive and accessible ways—or at least it *should* be. When it isn't, students should be led to inquire "Why not?" Such inquiry is an important part of critical thinking and reading. For example, middle school students might come to question a history text that states the primary cause of the Spanish-American war was the explosion of the battleship *Maine*.

Informational texts also are usually characterized by the use of **Academic Language** (Brock, Lapp, Salas, & Townsend, 2009; Schleppergrell, 2004; WIDA, 2011; Zwiers, 2008). Academic Language includes challenging *vocabulary*—new and abstract nouns and verbs, for example—and more complex *sentences* (Nagy & Townsend, 2012). These sentences are more complex because they're longer, often contain a number of clauses, and include connective words and phrases such as *therefore*, *subsequently*, and *as a consequence*.

Comprehension Strategies   What are the comprehension strategies for narrative and informational texts that you will be teaching your students? You will see different labels, but most educators (e.g., Block & Pressley, 2007) agree that they involve:

- Predicting
- Questioning
- Drawing inferences
- Identifying important information
- Summarizing
- Monitoring

Each of these strategies will be taught in the context of specific narrative and informational texts. They will also overlap in places. You will teach them directly, individually, but will also demonstrate how they may be used in combination. Learning them, and learning how and when to use them, is a *developmental* process. We'll describe each briefly here, and then unpack them in later chapters.

- **Predicting.** Decades ago, Russell Stauffer (1969) revolutionized the way many educators thought about reading instruction by encouraging teachers to ask students "What do you think will happen next?" before and during the reading of a story. For many years, reading had been taught as if students were passive recipients of information, but this simple question emphasized that students could and should read actively—and that if they did, their understanding, recall, and retention would improve. Getting students to predict what they will learn or find out, and then revise or confirm their predictions as they read, is powerful. Prediction involves bringing background knowledge to bear, often *visualizing* what might occur. For example, after reading the blurb on the back cover of *Al Capone Does My Shirts* (Choldenko, 2004), Sandra Madura asks her students, "What do you think might be the kinds of trouble Moose Flanagan [the novel's main character] could get into on Alcatraz?" The resulting discussion not only primes the students for their reading but it also gives Sandra helpful information about her students' background knowledge.

- **Questioning.** Like predicting, asking questions before and during reading makes it much more likely that readers will understand and recall the information. Of course, these questions are often posed by teachers, but we will support our students' learning about how to pose questions themselves. One question that inevitably springs from Sandra Madura's fifth graders before reading the first chapter of *Al Capone Does My Shirts* is "Why is this kid living on Alcatraz, anyway?" The answer, found on the first page of Chapter 1, "Devil's Island," is "My mother said I had to." Of course, this answer only begs more questions—the kinds of questions students would naturally ask of their world, because their minds are set up this way. Teachers simply remind them to do this when they read or listen to texts, and teachers model how to do it when the going gets tough.

- **Drawing inferences.** This is one of the most complex processes in the act of reading and one of the most important to teach students how to do. Inferring relies on the reader's background knowledge. For example, consider the two sentences "Shelley is eleven years old. Her sister, Julie, is fourteen." Now answer the question "Who is older, Shelley or Julie?" This may seem fairly simple, but you can read those two sentences all day long and not find the answer to the question unless you also use your background knowledge about numbers. Similarly, your ability to infer the relationship between the following two sentences relies on your background knowledge: "The citizens demonstrated loudly in the streets. The government cut benefits significantly." Answering the question "Why did the citizens demonstrate?" relies on your drawing an inference based on your background knowledge: The *order* of the sentences might suggest the government cut benefits *because* the citizens demonstrated, but your knowledge of current events, relationships between governments and their citizens, and so forth, led you to infer that the citizens demonstrated *because* of the government's actions.

These examples are meant to illustrate not only the nature and subtlety of inferring but also the importance of being sensitive to students' reading levels and background knowledge. What may appear to us or some of our students to be "right there" on the page is often *not* obvious to other students. This highlights the significance of demonstrating and walking students through the strategy of *how* to draw inferences.

- **Identifying important information.** Depending on the reader's purpose, in both narratives and informational texts, it is necessary to determine what is essential and what is not, and to understand the relationships among this information. Students often assume that *all* information in a book is important—otherwise, wouldn't the author have left it out? That is why it is important to emphasize the *purpose* for reading. For example, the chapter on Andrew Jackson, "Old Hickory," in Joy Hakim's (1993) *The New Nation* includes boxes with interesting if not fascinating information about Jackson and his era. In one of these boxes we learn that Jackson bought 20 spittoons for the East Room of the White House at a fairly steep price. Although that type of information may catch our eye as we are previewing the chapter before reading more carefully—and we might remember it because of its interest—it may not be the most important information to focus on when we go back and read the chapter thoroughly. As the teacher, you will walk students through the chapter, showing them how the topic sentences in each paragraph help "label" the essential information and point to supporting details. In this case, most paragraphs describe the chronology of Jackson's life and how his experiences shaped his perspective when he was later elected President of the United States.

- **Summarizing.** A summary answers the question "What is this text *really* about?" It is a shorter version of the text, capturing the main point or points. Crafting a summary is the most challenging strategy, as it relies on and pulls together all of the other strategies. Some educators make a helpful distinction between "summarizing" and "writing a summary" (e.g., Frey, Fisher, & Berkin, 2009). Summarizing during reading is one way of ensuring that readers are making sense of the reading and getting the big picture. In this sense, summarizing is a way of *monitoring* one's reading, which we explore in the next section. But summarizing *after* reading either by sharing orally or writing a couple of sentences, or by writing a more developed composition, draws on the same types of information and strategies.

When you first address summarizing, begin with narratives. Younger children can learn the basics of summarizing, even though they may not be writing summaries for a while. What are the most important things or events that happened in the story? What did they all add up to? For informational text, students learn that the headings, subheadings, and boldfaced text represent the most important ideas. As we'll see in later chapters, putting this information into one's own words is important, and we will support our students in doing so.

- **Monitoring.** During reading, we should be aware of how it's going—are we cruising along with most things making sense, or are we encountering some problems in making sense of some sentences? Being aware of (1) the degree to which we're making sense as we read and (2) what to do about it when we aren't, involves monitoring. If we are encountering difficulty, self-monitoring helps determine where the difficulty lies and how to fix it, which involves plugging in another strategy.

Strategies versus Skills   The strategies we've listed here are often referred to as *skills*. So is there a difference between strategies and skills? Yes, and this difference has to do with the degree to which readers are aware of them. A *strategy* is what we teach and students consciously learn to apply over time. When our students reach the point where they are applying a strategy without thinking about it, it has become a skill (Afflerbach, Pearson, & Paris, 2008). Strategies are conscious and deliberate; skills are automatic. Our objective, of course, is for these strategies to become automatically applied by our students. When they are self-monitoring and encounter difficulty when they read, it is our hope that they will remember a strategy and apply it, as needed.

One last, very important, point: You will encounter many labels for strategies, types of questions, and types of support. These labels and strategies appear in your curriculum guides, standards, and articles you may read. Despite all the labels and terminology, just remember the basics of good comprehension instruction: Through your support and guidance

- You are helping your students grow and develop their background knowledge, which includes their own world knowledge and what they are learning about the structure of the particular type of texts they are reading.

Children's Literature Connection

Historical Fiction – *Al Capone Does My Shirts*

At different places throughout this book you will see a Penguin icon. It indicates those places we refer to Gennifer Choldenko's *Al Capone Does My Shirts* (2004)—a Newbery Honor Book award recipient, published by Penguin Press, and an excellent work of historical fiction. We will be sharing examples of how the various components of literacy may be illustrated and taught with this literature connection. We share examples of many other types of literature as well, but by referring often to Choldenko's text we will be able to experience with you—and you with your students, present or future—the types of "close, attentive reading that is at the heart of understanding and enjoying . . . literature" as well as the "deep, and thoughtful engagement . . . [that] builds knowledge, enlarges experience, and broadens worldviews" (*Common Core State Standards*, 2010, p. 3).

Al Capone Does My Shirts effectively illustrates the elements of literature and literary devices that writers use. Because of that, Choldenko provides us many opportunities to guide students' thinking and exploration of language; of perspective; of history (the setting for the novel is Alcatraz and San Francisco in the mid-1930s during the Great Depression); of diversity, including the main character's sister Natalie, who is autistic; and of moral decisions and the challenges they often present to young people.

An excellent companion volume for *Al Capone* is *Children of Alcatraz: Growing up on the Rock* by Claire Rudolf

Murphy (2006). An informational picture book, *Children of Alcatraz* addresses the historical sweep of the island. Throughout most of that history—before, during, and after the federal prison was maintained on Alcatraz—children lived there.

- You are showing your students how to activate and use their background/prior knowledge to deepen their understanding of text before, during, and after reading.
- Your students are learning to do this based on their purpose/goal/intention for reading.

Writing

Common Core Connection

Writing Standards: Text Types and Purposes

Our expanded definition of *literacy* includes a wide range of purposes and types of writing. As we've noted, the texts our students read are blueprints for constructing meaning. Importantly, these texts will also be the blueprints for constructing the meaning that our students, through their writing, want their readers to construct.

Traditionally, the readers of our students' writing have been teachers, but teachers should not be the *sole* readers of everything students write. We should be facilitators of our students' developing ability to communicate with, and influence, their immediate contexts and the broader world beyond. As students learn through your reading instruction how authors structure arguments, provide information and explanation, and create narrative worlds, they will apply this knowledge in composing their own texts. They will think carefully about their audience and how their writing may best be structured to affect that audience. For example:

- A second-grader writes about why the *Henry and Mudge* (Cynthia Rylant) books are her favorites, offering her opinion, supported by two or three reasons, using linking words such as *because*, and providing a conclusion.

- A seventh-grader writes a persuasive essay in support of teachers allowing writing in an online fanzine to count for class credit in English. The fanzine in this case is dedicated to the "vampire and werewolves" fantasy genre. In her paper, she addresses the teachers in the English/Language Arts department in her middle school. She begins her persuasive piece by introducing her point. She then organizes and supports her point with appropriate reasons and evidence, chooses words and phrases that explicitly establish the relationship between her topic and the support she offers, and adopts the appropriate tone or style for this type of argument.

For our students' informational writing, there is at present an increased focus in the Common Core State Standards on **argument**. We're not referring here to the heated in-your-face type of exchange, but rather the more objective, logical presentation of a point of view. Well-constructed arguments are invaluable in both education and the workplace. The argument form is used to change points of view, move others to act in a certain way, or convince others of the reasonableness of your position. Unlike *persuasive* writing, however, its power is in its structure. Whereas *persuasive* writing is usually *selective* in presenting a point of view and appealing to the reader's emotions, arguments rest on the power of the structure and reasoning in the writing. *Informative* and *explanatory* writing are used both to examine and to convey information and ideas with clarity and accuracy. This type of writing supports our students' learning as well as their communication with others.

Like the reading of narratives, *narrative writing* supports students' developing understanding of themselves and their world, and provides a form through which they can try out these developing understandings with others. It also helps them develop further insight into the narratives they read and the ideas and themes that narratives explore.

You will support your students' understanding of the *process* of writing. The work of published authors does not spring, magically, from their pens or keyboards in perfect final-draft form. Many students, however, have this naïve belief. In reality, however, just about every composition is developed over time through planning, revising, and editing. Think back to our questions at the beginning of this chapter: Do *you* enjoy writing? Many teachers may not enjoy or choose to do a lot of writing outside of the profession, and yet they must encourage and support their students in doing so. Some very wise writing teachers have encouraged us that by writing with our students, sharing and modeling our writing, we not only help the students' development but also come to enjoy writing ourselves (Calkins, 1994; Fletcher, 1996; Graves, 1983; Routman, 2005). Over the years, the *National Writing Project* (*www.nwp.org*) has supported thousands of teachers in becoming writers and in supporting their teaching of writing, and we encourage you to become involved yourself with this excellent project.

> **Common Core Connection**
>
> Writing Standards: Production and Distribution of Writing

Vocabulary

Students' understanding of words and the concepts the words represent is one of the best predictors of their success in school (Anglin, 1993; Schleppegrell, 2004; Stahl & Nagy, 2006). Vocabulary "sets the ceiling" on students' comprehension (Biemiller, 2005). Regardless of the grade or grades you teach, you will be teaching your students specific words as well as teaching them *about* words—the processes of word formation that apply to most of those hundreds of thousands of words in English (Nagy, 2007; Templeton, 2012). Your instruction will be what educators call *generative*: Knowing how words "work" will help students *generate*, from one word, an understanding of several other related words. Your instruction will also be engaging and motivating, helping students develop an interest in and wish to explore words (Baumann, Ware, & Edwards, 2007; Bear, Invernizzi, Templeton, & Johnston, 2012; Scott, Skobel, & Wells, 2008).

> **Common Core Connection**
>
> Language Standards: Vocabulary Acquisition and Use

Three Layers of Vocabulary Instruction We will frame vocabulary instruction throughout this book within three layers that we've adapted from Stahl and Nagy (2006):

1. Immerse the learner in rich oral language and in wide reading and purposeful writing. Learners of all ages must be surrounded by rich oral language and should be reading widely. For many students, this is going to occur only in their classrooms. The words, phrases, and nuances of meaning students encounter in their reading should also be tried out and exercised in their writing—further extending students' understandings of the underlying concepts. You will support your students' wide reading, and for children who are emergent and beginning readers, and therefore not able to read widely, you read to the children books that reflect a range of words in contexts that are compelling and engaging.

Although wide reading is absolutely necessary for growing a large vocabulary, it is not sufficient. The next two layers provide the additional sufficient support.

2. Explicitly teach and talk about word structure. The structure of words gives important clues to their meaning. So many of the words students will encounter in their reading, and should use in their writing, are created by combining the meaningful elements of **prefixes**, **suffixes**, and **roots**. Younger students, for example, are walked through the simple relationships involved in taking the word *help* and adding prefixes and suffixes:

> help
> help*ing*
> help*ful*
> *un*help*ful*

Older students explore how a word such as *courage* is affected by the addition of different prefixes and suffixes:

> courage
> courage*ous*
> courage*ously*
> *en*courage
> *dis*courage
> *dis*courag*ingly*
> *dis*courage*able*
> *undis*courag*ed*
> *en*courage*ment*
> *en*courag*ingly*

3. Engage in deep, intense study of specific words. The words that represent the most important concepts in a text or unit of study deserve focused instruction. Looking at how they are used in context and examining their structure supports the learning of these words. They should also, however, be explored through activities that involve learners in comparing and contrasting the words and their concepts in ways that construct deep and lasting understandings. For example, fourth-graders learning about classical Greek civilization will learn or expand understanding of concepts such as *democracy, city-states, myth,* and *legend. Democracy* may be contrasted with *autocracy:* How are they alike (a form of government) and different (rights and freedoms enjoyed by citizens)? How might an understanding of the meaningful parts that make up *democracy* and *autocracy* support learning and remembering the concepts they represent (*cracy* means "rule or govern," *demo* refers to "people," and *auto* refers to "self"—rule by the *people* versus rule by an *individual*).

Three Major Types of Vocabulary There are three major types of vocabulary: (1) everyday conversational vocabulary; (2) more "academic" vocabulary that occurs in all content areas and subjects, referred to as *general* academic vocabulary; and (3) academic vocabulary that primarily occurs within each specific *content area* or subject, more recently referred to as *domain-specific* vocabulary. You will also see the labels "Tier 1, Tier 2, and Tier 3" to refer to these three types (Beck, McKeown, & Kucan, 2002), Tier 1 being the equivalent of conversational vocabulary, Tier 2 general academic, and Tier 3 content-specific.

- **Conversational vocabulary** refers to the basic, most frequently used words in the language. The words often label common things or actions and they seldom require direct instruction because they are used so frequently—for example, *chair, fun, happy,* and *ran.* As we'll explore in later chapters, however, many of our new English learners may need instruction in some of these words.

- **General academic vocabulary** refers to words that students encounter often in their reading and should be able to use in their writing. These words are also likely to occur in formal oral language contexts such as lectures. They occur across all content areas—examples are *coincidence, energetic, fortunate,* and *paradox.* Often, students have the underlying concepts for the words but just need to learn the new labels.

- **Content-** or **domain-specific academic vocabulary** refers to words that occur in specific content areas such as mathematics *(numerator, rectilinear),* science *(enzyme, magnetic field),* the arts *(bass clef, impressionism),* and history and social science *(antebellum, preamble).* The domain-specific vocabulary in English/Language Arts is often referred to as *literary vocabulary*—for example, *foreshadowing* and *rhyme scheme* (Hiebert & Lubliner, 2008). In contrast to general academic vocabulary, much domain-specific academic vocabulary represents new concepts, or familiar concepts with new applications.

Selecting Specific Words for In-Depth Study   How do you know which specific words to select for deep and intense study? We will address specific guidelines later in the developmental chapters, but in general, for the primary grades, we ensure that children, especially English learners, acquire the most frequently occurring words they may not be picking up in conversation. We also emphasize appropriate general academic vocabulary, and begin to explore the domain-specific vocabulary that will represent important concepts in content-area units of study. For the intermediate grades, both general academic and domain-specific vocabulary will receive significant emphasis. In the middle grades, domain-specific vocabulary receives primary emphasis.

For example, although several unfamiliar terms appear in the first few chapters of *Al Capone Does My Shirts,* teacher Sandra Madura chose those that she believed were critical to her students' understanding of the developing narrative and were important for them to learn by the intermediate grades. Some of the words she selected were *convict, criminal, electrician, innocent, affliction,* and *Eleanor Roosevelt.* Sandra knew that most of her students have at least heard most if not all of these words, and some have some knowledge about them. She also knew that most of the words are important general academic vocabulary terms—thus requiring a deeper understanding—and those that are domain-specific are important in the context of the narrative. She skipped those that were *not* critical to understanding the chapter or the larger themes—words such as *embezzler* and *conniver,* the meaning of which she could simply mention along the way.

A final word about vocabulary. Knowing a word is not an all-or-nothing, "either you know it or you don't" situation. There are *degrees* of knowing a word. Before beginning a unit on "Oceans," for example, Kim Leslie has her fifth-grade students self-assess their knowledge of the important vocabulary words that will be addressed in the unit: For the word *plankton,* for instance, each student indicates if she or he:

- Has never heard of the word
- Has heard it but does not know what it means
- Has some ideas about what it means
- Knows it well

Not only does this preassessment provide Kim with important information about her students' prior knowledge about oceans, it also pulls her students into the topic and gives them a sense of ownership of their developing understanding. Over the course of the unit, they will see how their knowledge grows for the words and the concepts they represent.

Word Structure

Common Core Connection

Language Standards:
Conventions of
Standard English

Does the spelling of English words make sense? Most folks would answer "Of course not!" But there is far more logic in the way words are spelled than most people realize, and we will be exploring how we can support our students' understanding of this logic throughout this book. Yes, there are famous examples of the *illogic* of spelling (for example, *though, tough, through, bough*), but when taken together with most words in the language, these examples are fairly few in number. Learning to read and spell words in English involves learning about the logic at the level of *sound* and the logic at the level of *meaning*. We'll briefly examine the logic at the level of *meaning* here, and address this more deeply as well as the logic at the level of *sound* in Chapter 2. Subsequent chapters will provide support in how we *teach* about these levels to students at different developmental levels.

Recall from the previous section how the structure of words gives important clues to their meaning. Among words that are related in meaning there is a strong *visual* connection, captured in the *spelling* of the related words. This relationship is referred to as the **spelling–meaning connection**: "Words that are related in meaning are often related in spelling as well, despite changes in sound" (Templeton, 1983, 2012). It also explains most of the "odd" spellings in the English language. For example, why are there silent consonants in the following words?

bomb   *sign*   *muscle*

They are there because they maintain the visual relationship with words to which they are related in meaning:

bomb   *sign*   *muscle*
bombard   *signature*   *muscular*

Why do vowel letters have different sounds, as with the letter *i* in the following words?

define

definition

definitive

Although it stands for three different sounds, the letter *i* is there because it helps to maintain the *visual* relationship among these words, which of course are related in *meaning*.

Why do many consonant letters stand for different sounds? The spelling–meaning connection explains most of these: When reading *Al Capone Does My Shirts*, for example, Sandra Madura and her students discussed the profession of Moose Flanagan's dad: *electrician*. Sandra wrote the word *electric* on the white board and then the word *electrician* underneath it. She underlined the final *c* in both words and reminded the students how words related in meaning are often related in their spelling. Even though the sound that the *c* represents changes when *-ian* is added to *electric*, the spelling does *not* change because of the meaning relationship that these two words share.

As we will explore later, when students develop an awareness and understanding of these connections between spelling and meaning, their vocabularies may also grow in breadth and in depth. This is the "second layer" of vocabulary instruction, discussed above on page 14.

Students will develop insight into the logic of sound and meaning only if we are aware and understand this logic ourselves. If you are just coming to this awareness, know that we will explore these relationships in some depth in several other chapters. As Hughes and Searle (1997) point out, "Many teachers themselves see spelling as more arbitrary than systematic; at least, they give that impression to their students . . . . If we teachers do not believe that spelling has logical, negotiable patterns, how can we hope to help [students] develop that insight?"

Fluency

Fluency refers to the ability to identify words quickly and accurately and to read orally with expression (Rasinski, Reutzel, Chard, & Linan-Thompson, 2011). Becoming a reader who is able to read an unfamiliar text with expression, sounding natural, is a developmental phenomenon. It fundamentally depends on the ability to identify all or almost all words automatically, without having to stop to **decode** or figure them out. For this reason, fluency has been described as the bridge between word decoding and comprehension (Pikulski & Chard, 2005). It is impossible to read aloud naturally without being able to decode almost all the words in a text automatically and accurately. This means that instruction should emphasize attention to the structure of printed words as well as plenty of opportunities to read texts at appropriate levels, encountering the most frequent words and word patterns in the language over and over. Rasinski (2011) has pointed out that readers who are able to read orally with good expression are also better able to comprehend material when reading silently. If oral reading is awkward and "disfluent," comprehension during silent reading will suffer.

Although fluency depends on word knowledge and the rapid and automatic recognition of words in text, fluency also depends on the related ability to recognize and read in phrases or "phrasal units" (Benjamin & Schwanenflugel, 2010; Rasinski, 2011). This ability, too, is a developmental phenomenon. It depends on experience with text, advancing word knowledge, and overall language development. Occasionally, students who seem to be fine in all these areas still struggle with reading fluently at the more rapid rate than their abilities would suggest. We will address this challenge in Chapter 11.

Motivation

Motivation is key to success in learning. Students are motivated to read if they're interested. Again, as Smith (2004) observed, "No one ever taught reading to a child who wasn't interested in reading, and interest can't be demanded" (p. 212). If students are not motivated to read, then they will not be able to bring their attention to bear on a text, much less apply the strategies you have been teaching. The motivation and love of reading come from being "hooked" by a particular book, author, or topic and then going from there. When a student experiences success with reading because she or he is interested and motivated, the teacher may then build on that to develop a willingness to read material in which the child is *not* naturally interested. We set that stage by developing background knowledge; for example, before reading a chapter about the parts of a cell.

When students are motivated and engaged readers, they can overcome what otherwise are often challenging obstacles to the rate and extent of their literacy development, including parental education and income (Guthrie, 2004). A number of researchers have confirmed that the following practices will help establish the environment for nurturing students' motivation to read and expansion of interests (Duke & Pearson, 2002; Guthrie & Humenick, 2004; Langer 2001):

- Allow opportunities for students to choose what to read. When you get to know your students and what motivates them in their own lives, you will know what topics and books to make available. Listen to and value their opinions.
- Provide students with easy access to interesting texts.
- Read real texts for genuine reasons and purposes.
- Provide students opportunities to discuss readings.
- Provide a range of genres.

Common Core Connection

Reading Standards: Foundational Skills – Fluency

The Language of Your Instruction

Standards and Their Influence

The topic of *standards* is part of your instructional language because the terminology used in literacy standards inevitably becomes a significant part of the terminology you use in the classroom. Over the last decade, elementary teachers and students in the United States have faced a considerable increase in grade-specific standards and testing. Some have argued that this trend has resulted in a narrowing of the curriculum, a decrease in morale among educators, and an increase in "one-size-fits-all" teaching practices (Allington, 2002; Gehsmann & Templeton, 2011/2012; Nichols & Berliner, 2007). In June 2010, the National Governor's Association and the Council of Chief State School Officers unveiled a new set of standards, the *Common Core State Standards (CCSS)* (www.corestandards.org). Throughout this and the other chapters, you'll notice a margin icon that signals important connections to this new set of standards. In contrast to a number of standards documents in the past, we are encouraged because this new set of standards acknowledges the realities of elementary teachers and the diverse learners they teach. The *CCSS* affirm that "instruction should be *differentiated*.... The point is to teach students what they need to learn . . . to discern when particular children or activities warrant more or less attention" (p. 15, emphasis added). These acknowledgments in such an influential standards document are important and very appropriate.

A word about standards may be helpful here: To a greater or lesser degree, there have always been grade-level expectations or their equivalent in education. They determine what is taught and tested. Unavoidably, they often clash with classroom realities that reflect the range of abilities among students. Although not disagreeing with the intent of standards, educators who understand learning in a developmental perspective have often criticized *what* and *how much* is expected by the end of each grade level. Over the course of a generation, the expectations for children's reading and writing have increased, and occur earlier in the standards. What used to be the first-grade curriculum is now addressed in kindergarten,

for example, and this shift ripples on through the grades: Middle school expectations of a decade ago now appear in grades 4 and 5.

The *CCSS* are the current version of this phenomenon and will define the instructional landscape in almost all states for the next several years (a handful of states have not adopted these standards; they elected to retain their existing state standards). The broad-based literacy expectations of the *CCSS* are admirable, as we will note. When we drill down into some of the specifics—expectations for which you will likely be held accountable—there may be some challenges. Throughout this text, we will demonstrate how a developmental model of literacy grounds effective literacy instruction and will support you as you negotiate the ever-present tension between (1) providing literacy instruction that is in children's "construction zones" (González, Moll, & Amanti, 2005; Newman, Griffin, & Cole, 1989) and (2) addressing grade-level standards for which you may be accountable.

The *Common Core State Standards* reflect what your students will be expected to learn, but another important set of standards reflects what teachers are expected to learn and be able to apply in their teaching and in their interactions with the broader community: the International Reading Association's (IRA) *Standards for Reading Professionals* (2010; listed in the *Online Resources* at the end of this chapter). This document informs much of the information and support we provide you in this text. The IRA *Standards* provide six overarching standards that include foundations for literacy instruction, what and how to teach, the effective assessment of literacy learning and development, understanding diversity and teaching from a culturally responsive perspective, establishing a supportive literacy environment, and a commitment to lifelong learning and collaboration with other educators and the broader community through professional learning and leadership. In addition, specific standards for different instructional roles are provided. Those for pre-K through elementary and middle/high school classroom reading teachers are reflected in this book.

The Literacy Essentials from a Developmental Perspective

As discussed earlier, reading and writing are *reciprocal* processes. The mutually supportive relationship between these two abilities begins in the preschool years and will continue to be the foundation for students' literacy development. We take a *developmental* approach to the teaching of literacy because this supports our teaching to where students *are* rather than where they are *not*.

Determining where your students fall along the continuum of literacy development ensures that you will be teaching them in their instructional zone or level, so your instruction will make sense (Morris, 2008). You will know how far you can "stretch" your students without winding up in their frustration zone. When you meet your students in their appropriate instructional zones, you are able to build on what they already know and what they are trying to do.

If this sounds quite obvious to you and you're thinking "Of course!" that's a very good sign. Unfortunately, as we will address throughout this text, you often may feel pressured to teach content or concepts that are beyond particular students' learning zones. But if your literacy instruction is grounded in the developmental perspective, you will be able to move your students farther along toward that content and those concepts by teaching *in*, rather than *beyond*, their instructional zones.

Certainly the development of literacy takes time, but it is the examination of *how* literacy development proceeds, and what it looks like, that informs our teaching during this time span. A classic study of first-, second-, and third-graders who were learning to read found that children "displayed much greater uniformity in what they knew about reading and print than in how they brought their knowledge to bear on text . . . . Many differences . . . turned out to be more a matter of how [the children] *used* knowledge than of knowledge acquisition or knowing per se" (Bussis, Chittenden, Amarel, & Klausner, 1985, p. 65, emphasis added). The developmental model, then, helps us determine what our students are likely to know at any point along the developmental continuum, and therefore how better to support their *use* of that knowledge.

Stages of Literacy Development

Whereas all students at some level are trying to make meaning when they read, the ease with which they are able to do so *during* reading, and how well they adjust when the reading becomes challenging, depend on their stage of reading development. The degree to which students are able to write—to encode their thinking at the word and sentence level while keeping in mind the purpose of their writing—depends on their stage of literacy development. Chapter 2 will explore the characteristics of development at each of these stages in some depth, and Chapters 6 through 10 will address *instruction* at each of these developmental stages. To set the stage, however, here we offer a brief introduction to these stages of literacy development.

Emergent Stage

The **emergent stage** ranges from the preschool years through kindergarten, and it is not unusual to find some first-graders who are in the emergent stage. This stage is an important foundational time during which children develop **concepts about print**:

- Print represents spoken language.
- Print carries meaning and performs different functions (for example, labels things, tells stories).
- Print has directionality—in English, top-to-bottom, left-to-right, with a return sweep at the end of each line.
- Print represents words and sounds.
- The smallest units of writing are *letters*, and there is a limited number of letters that occur over and over again.

Emergent learners develop concepts of "story" and often of "nursery rhyme." With little effort, over time they memorize favorite texts and "read" them back, turning the pages at exactly the right places. This is not true reading, of course, but an extremely important foundational understanding for reading to develop. Their written productions evolve from random scribbles to letterlike forms. See Figure 1.1.

FIGURE 1.1 Child's Writing: "Dinosaur"

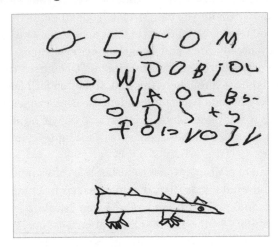

Beginning Stage

The **beginning stage** is when learners attend much more closely to print. The children are coming to understand that units on the printed page or screen correspond to speech, and they develop an increasingly sensitive awareness of how this correspondence works. Over time, while teachers are continuing to model how print "works," children are also learning about letters, letter names, and some of the sounds the letters stand for. This immersion in actual texts and learning about the smallest elements of these texts (letters) gradually helps children learn to "read the spaces" (Clay, 1991, 2001), and develop a **concept of word in text** (Flanigan, 2007; Morris, Bloodgood, Lomax, & Perney, 2003).

After they have a functional understanding of words in text—that words have beginnings and endings, indicated by spaces—children's awareness of all the sounds that a word contains develops rapidly. They become fully aware of **phonemes**, the smallest units of speech, and come to understand the **alphabetic principle** that letters represent sounds and are matched in a left-to-right sequence within the printed word. These understandings in turn lay the foundation for developing a **sight vocabulary**—words that the learner recognizes immediately both in text and in isolation. Like emergent learners, they continue to benefit from repeated readings of predictable texts. They also benefit from reading some **decodable texts** that are written to contain several examples of the phonic/spelling patterns the children are learning in their word study instruction. When beginning readers encounter a new text, their reading rate is quite slow and choppy, often described as "word by word." Reading fluency obviously has yet to develop, because beginning readers are spending so much of their "thinking space" focused on identifying the words on the page.

Because of the read-alouds you will be conducting with your children at this stage, they will be developing a more elaborate concept of story as well as developing a beginning understanding of informational texts and how they work. The students are able to learn that each type of text usually has different purposes. Interestingly, young boys often respond with more interest to informational texts than to narratives (Zambo & Brozo, 2009), a point we will explore further in Chapter 2.

Learners at the beginning stage are able to exercise their developing knowledge about print through their *writing*. Just as with their reading, their writing is slow going, definitely not fluent.

FIGURE 1.2 Child's Writing: "I Like Sitting Under My Favorite Tree"

They expend so much thinking space and energy matching up letters with the sounds they want to represent, while still trying to hold onto the topic of their writing (not to mention the pencil!). It is important not to set too many expectations on them during these initial attempts with respect to quality and correctness of writing. If they wish to, or are required to, revise a piece of writing, then care should be taken on how much is addressed during the revision process. Simple conventions—capitalization at the beginning of a sentence and a period at the end—and any wording changes they might wish should be about the maximum expectation. First-grader Elisa's writing (Figure 1.2) took a few minutes to complete.

Some children move into the beginning reading stage in kindergarten, while most move through this stage in first grade; some children are still in this stage in second grade.

Transitional Stage

The **transitional stage** is a time when learners move toward fluency in their reading—that is, increasing rate and expression. This development is grounded in their increasing word knowledge—understanding how printed words work—and their growing familiarity with narrative and informational texts. The children's store of sight words increases dramatically. During this stage, they will become silent readers, which is something beginning readers simply cannot do. All of this knowledge about words and print allows them to recognize words more rapidly and automatically, which in turn frees up more thinking space *as* they read. Because there is more space on their brain's "desktop" while they read, they are better able to analyze, summarize, and generalize based on their *own* reading rather than just on the texts that are read *to* them by the teacher (Applebee, 1978; Barone, 1989; Madura, 1998).

Because of their growing familiarity with and understanding of the nature and functions of print and texts, transitional learners are also becoming more fluent in their *writing*. Their processes of encoding words and ideas become more rapid, and they are able to hold information and ideas in their heads better as they are encoding that information. They are also better able to keep in mind the purpose and audience for their writing. For transitional learners, *revision* of their writing is a realistic expectation. Figure 1.3 represents two entries from second-grader Kirstin's journal.

FIGURE 1.3 Transitional Writer's Journal Entries

> Sharons frind brocke her arm yesterday by jumping off a swing.
>
> I cant whate till tomarow.

Many children move into the transitional stage in first grade; most will move through this period in second or third grade, though a few are still at this stage in fourth grade.

The Intermediate Stage

Many students move into the **intermediate stage** in third grade; for most, however, movement into this stage corresponds to the intermediate grades—grades four and five. A number of middle-grade students are still in this stage as well. The children's developing understanding of texts allows for reading more extensive texts, and sustaining their reading over longer periods of time. Fluency develops further, allowing quite natural-sounding oral reading of on-level texts. Their reading interests may expand considerably, and they may immerse themselves for weeks on end in particular series books or particular genres. Students in the intermediate stage develop the ability to step back and think in more depth about the structure and content of what they read—a noted foundation for the more sophisticated **cognition** that will come in just a few years. Importantly, this is the stage during which students' acquisition of vocabulary from wide reading begins to increase dramatically.

Intermediate writers incorporate the more complex patterns and features of both narrative and informational texts. They are better able to "orchestrate" the many cognitive demands of writing—more fluently encoding at the word and sentence levels, while sustaining focus and intent. Writing also becomes a vehicle for *learning* (Scardamalia, 1981), not only in response to the reading that the students are doing but also through their original compositions. It is a powerful medium through which they discover who they are, work toward establishing their identities, and learn that who they are and what they do really *matters*.

Figure 1.4 shows an entry from fifth-grader Richard's learning log; he has been reading different informational texts that address the topic of extinct animals. His misspellings ("exstinked," "indangerd," and the different attempts at *species*–"speceys"/"speaces") are revealing examples of his underlying word knowledge, although he is clearly able to read these words in text. As we'll explore in Chapter 2, when students move into the transitional stage, and then continuing throughout their development, there will usually be a gap between words that they are able to read and their ability to spell those words correctly.

FIGURE 1.4 Intermediate Writer's Journal Entry

> I thought it was fun to learn about birds that are exstinked and indangerd speceys and about the dodo bird I didn't know there was. I thought that it was a joke about the dodo bird. It's cool to learn about other indangered speaces and I loved talking about the dodo bird. Whats' inchrasting is that they eat a plant called the dodo plant!

Skillful Literacy Stage

The **skillful literacy stage** represents a level that many students do not attain. But they certainly are capable of developing the language and thinking skills to grow into this level. Some students at the upper elementary level and many more in the middle grades are capable of this level of development. At the skillful literacy stage, the ability to read deeply, thoughtfully, and critically may be applied to a wide range of genres, although there will always be room for fine-tuning the strategies with which particular genres or the literature in particular disciplines may be read. Reading can become much more flexible and strategic. Students become increasingly able to analyze themes and character motivations, as well as relate contemporary literary characters and themes to earlier works. Word knowledge may grow into an appreciation not only of the frequently occurring Greek and Latin word elements but also the histories of words. This insight affords more nuanced understanding and appreciation of words and their use, across disciplines and literary texts.

Students' writing at this stage often displays complex analysis and interpretation, reflecting a more sophisticated, discipline-specific vocabulary. The degree to which students develop this insight in their writing will depend on the support and guidance they receive from their teachers. Twelve-year-old Catherine's personal narrative in Figure 1.5 shows her understanding of how the form of this genre, including the first person as narrator, may be used to develop suspense. Also apparent is Catherine's more sophisticated use of the conventions of writing such as semicolons and ellipses, and her correct spelling of more complex words such as *competition* and *visualized*. Her vocabulary knowledge is suggested through her appropriate and effective use of the word *conceded* in this context, and she has effectively used and punctuated dialogue.

FIGURE 1.5 Catherine's Personal Narrative – *A Nerve-Wracking First Time*

It was early competition season: November, maybe even December, and it was our first time tumbling on tumble track in awhile; we'd been so busy working on perfecting our routines. Once we took two, maybe three turns each, I did my back layout. As I got out of the dusty pit full of foam blocks that cushioned my landing, my coach shouted, "Wow! That was so high! Double next time."

"What?!" I nervously asked. "I have never done a double back before . . ."

"It's okay," she answered. "Just set your arms up, circle them back, grab your legs and pull your flip around twice, until you hit the pit."

"Alright," I conceded. I was not totally convinced. When I got back in line, I was asking all of my friends who had done a double before, "Is it hard? Is it scary?" They all told me it was a piece of cake and that I'd be fine.

It was almost my turn. I visualized all of the double backs I had seen before and tried to picture myself doing the same motions. The line moved up, I was next. Panic rushed through my body.

"Okay," I told myself. "Just set, circle and keep pulling, I will be fine." Around me, my team chanted and cheered my name, encouraging me to go for it. But I was in my own world. With my body shaking, I closed my eyes, took a deep breath and prepared . . .

The Sociocultural Contexts of Literacy Learning

Common Core Connection

Speaking and
Listening:
Comprehension and
Collaboration

We talked earlier about the new digital age and its implications for literacy instruction. That is a very important context, but social and cultural contexts are equally if not more important in terms of how they impact your teaching and your students' learning of literacy. When your students walk through the door in the morning, they bring their language, family, and a community heritage with them. If you are to be effective, your instruction must be responsive to the cultures that language, family, and community represent (Au, 2005; Moll, 2005). How our students see themselves, who and what they value, how they behave, and how they learn—all are a function of the embedded contexts in which they live. Figure 1.6 represents the embedded nature of these sociocultural contexts.

Learning Cultural Practices

For many of our students, it's not just content and a new language that they are trying to learn—it's a whole set of cultural practices as well. These practices are reflected in school and in the larger societal mainstream. Most middle-class English-speaking children have grown up in these practices, hardly noticing them. For learners outside the mainstream, however, these norms will need to be made explicit (Delpit, 1995). Because of the range of diversity in so many of the nation's schools, as these cultural norms are learned, there are also many opportunities to learn about nonmainstream students' lives and experiences. If we as teachers are open, we will never cease to be impressed with the integrity of their lives and experiences, and open to ways

FIGURE 1.6 Embedded Contexts for Schooling

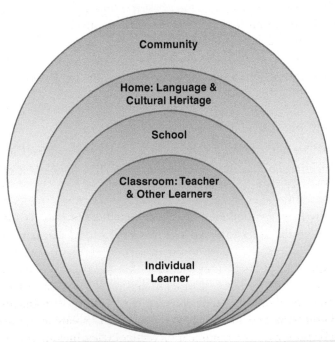

Community

Home: Language &
Cultural Heritage

School

Classroom: Teacher
& Other Learners

Individual
Learner

in which those lives can inform and enrich our own. Not the least of these ways is the possibility of English-only students beginning to learn the new language spoken by some classmates, as the new classmates learn English. Surely, in more ways than one, language learning is a two-way street (Suárez-Orozco, Suárez-Orozco, & Todorova, 2008; Templeton, 2010).

As you are also well aware, there are communities in which the out-of-school challenges are significant and daunting—such as extreme poverty, not enough to eat, and instability and insecurity at home and in the community—and they inevitably affect the classroom. Many teachers who choose to teach in these contexts, however, discover that their rewards may be greater in the long run, in terms of personal satisfaction and helping to change lives for the better.

Broadly speaking, a **culture** reflects the language, beliefs, values, literature, art, and institutions of a group. A culture is a framework for making meaning (Templeton, 1997), and the students in our classrooms see themselves in terms of the culture from which they come. They have learned how to interact with children and adults, and bring this understanding into the classroom. The classroom offers the most promising context in which different cultural and language communities may interface, communicate, and learn from one another.

We've already talked about the critically important role that *you* will play in orchestrating this interaction and communication. You're a part of your students' sociocultural context, right down to how you feel on a particular day and how that affects your interaction with your students. We spoke earlier of the importance of your making literacy interesting and purposeful to your students. You will be successful with this to the extent that you understand and value your students' different backgrounds, expectations, and voices. If you keep this in mind and respond to these differences, at the same time supporting your students' developing understanding of societal norms and mainstream culture, you will be an effective teacher of literacy. Susan Florio-Ruane (2001) best summed this up when she observed that when we as teachers understand that "language, identity, education, and culture are inextricably entwined, we may approach the teaching of literacy with greater sensitivity, insight, and imagination."

Developing a Culture of the Classroom

As we explore briefly below and later in Chapter 3, you will work to develop a culture of the classroom that establishes norms for how your students use space, time, and resources, and how they behave and interact. This culture of the classroom will support the social engagements that underlie true learning, because we know that "any function . . . in development appears twice: First, on the social level, and later, on the individual level" (Vygotsky, 1978). Vygotsky went on to note that "all the higher functions originate as actual relations between human individuals" (p. 57). This is true for our students' out-of-school learning as well as for their learning in our classroom.

The expectations you hold for the types of literacy you wish your students to develop are first addressed through social collaboration, in whole class and small groups. We, as teachers, are supporting our students in their growth toward "the close, attentive reading that is at the heart of understanding and enjoying complex works of literature" (*CCSS*, 2010) and in the reasoning processes with which they analyze and evaluate both literary and informational texts. This ability will grow through our support of students' developing *critical literacy* skills. These involve students learning how to evaluate information that is presented within a single text and in texts across multiple subject areas. They will learn that the creators of messages will be using and crafting information in certain ways in order to influence what they believe and how they think. This will ground their understanding of how different forms of media are linked, often in a Web-based environment, and how these forms are used to create information and narratives. These new information and communication technologies, including social media, will be

The Language of Your Instruction

Talking *With*, not Just *To*, Your Students

As novice teachers, and often as experienced teachers as well, we must step outside our own view of how "school" works and our own role in schooling. We've begun that process of reflection by discussing our awareness and understanding of the different backgrounds our students bring with them into the classroom. This process continues with thinking about how we use *language* to structure our interactions with our students.

Your language conveys the following messages:

- What is important and therefore what learners should pay attention to
- Who your students *are* as individuals in the culture of the classroom and in the wider world
- How students may use language to think about themselves and one another
- Who *you* are—a facilitator and guide or a judge and the source of "truth"?

Although we may never say it explicitly, *how* we address and talk with our students may send a message that they are not as bright or valued as much, or have the potential to learn very much, if they:

- Speak a nonstandard dialect of English
- Struggle to learn English as a new language
- Make errors in their reading and writing
- Answer a question with a response that may be thoughtful but not what the curriculum guide suggests is correct or acceptable

In his important and instructive book, *Choice Words: How Our Language Affects Children's Learning* (2004), Peter Johnston demonstrates how the teacher's language "actually creates realities and invites identities" (p. 9) and underscores the ways in which "each conversational exchange . . . provides building material for children's understanding of a wide range of literate concepts, practices, and possibilities, and helps shape their identities" (p. 10). Our language is powerful, Johnston reminds us. It's not just the way we try to teach children how to read and write—it's also the way we help *or hinder* our students' construction of their own identities and sense of self-worth.

explored for their potential to link individuals globally as well as here at home. The worldview and understanding you are helping your students construct through their literacy engagements may literally be informed by fellow students in other countries from different cultural and language contexts.

Levels of Support and the Gradual Release of Responsibility Model

As with the teachers in Compello Elementary School, because you are teaching literacy developmentally, you will balance whole-class instruction with small-group instruction. To teach the essential components of literacy in a developmentally responsive way, the daily "literacy diet" you provide your students includes reading, writing, word study, and *your* reading to the students (Flanigan et al., 2010; Willows, 2002). The proportion of time you allocate to these ingredients will vary depending on the developmental level of your students, but you will work to ensure that the ingredients will be addressed—whole class, small group, and independent work.

Chapter 3 addresses classroom organization, management, and grouping

It's a significant undertaking to orchestrate these different class and group configurations to support your classroom culture. You will experience more success (and far fewer headaches!) if you walk your students through these configurations and involve them in evaluating how successfully they can negotiate movement and responsibility. This will take time at first, but gradually, students will build behaviors and expectations that can be maintained over the course of the

FIGURE 1.7 Gradual Release of Responsibility

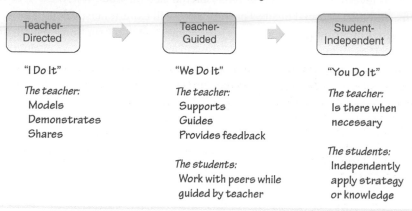

year (Boushey & Moser, 2006). Your goal is for both younger and older students to be trusted to handle most of their interactions and tasks on their own.

Gradual Release of Responsibility Model

In teaching tasks and expectations, but most definitely in teaching literacy strategies and content, most educators agree that we should follow the **Gradual Release of Responsibility** model (Pearson & Gallagher, 1983). See Figure 1.7.

For generations, an "I Do It" (or "I Say It") and then "You Do It" model prevailed in most classrooms. Ironically, this model left out perhaps the most essential aspect of teaching: the *social* aspect in which the teacher supports students' application of what she has modeled, demonstrated, or shared. The teacher-guided step is the critical bridge linking Vygotsky's (1978) "first on the social level, later on the individual level" insight. This model will be applied, in the developmental context, throughout this text.

Differentiating Instruction

You will be able to demonstrate, share, and model a great deal in a whole-class format, and because you will have learners at different points along the developmental continuum, you will also meet your students in small groups. It is critical that instruction be *differentiated* in this manner, to provide more appropriate instruction—both in what is taught and in "face time" with your students.

For example, after reading a chapter in Katherine Paterson's (2004) *Bridge to Terabithia* to her fourth-grade class, Kellie Hiatt had her students respond to the following statement: *Most boys of Jesse's age wouldn't become involved in either the real or make-believe world of Terabithia.* Most of her students were able to discuss, argue, and evaluate their responses at a fairly critical level. When Kellie meets her *transitional*-level readers in small groups, however, they read and discuss a transitional-level text with the theme of friendship. Had they been required to read and respond to *Bridge to Terabithia* on their own, they most likely would have become frustrated and disengaged. The effort required to identify the words in the text would have prevented the transitional-level students from constructing and thinking about the meaning in the text.

At the present time, you will very often hear **differentiated instruction** discussed in the context of **tiered instruction** (Walpole, McKenna, & Philippakos, 2011). Often addressed in the *Response to Intervention (RTI)* model (Lipson & Wixson, 2010), reading instruction is conceptualized in three tiers: Tier 1 is the "core" grade-level instruction that should be provided every student. This level of instruction is differentiated based on students' stages of development, strengths, and instructional needs. For those who still experience difficulty, however, instruction is further differentiated. First, they will receive Tier 2 instruction—usually small-group, more focused, with more support. Students who are still struggling are evaluated for Tier 3 instruction—generally intensive, one-to-one, and usually sustained over a period of time. We'll discuss in Chapter 11 the particulars of this model, and our extension of it, as we apply the model to students who are struggling in their literacy learning.

Chapter Summary

Literacy is the ability to read and write. *Print literacy* refers specifically to the skills necessary to understand information and stories that appear in both printed texts and on digital screens. Reading and writing are *reciprocal* processes, each ability supporting the other. Proficient reading and writing depend on the following literacy essentials:

- **Comprehension**—*An active and not a passive process*, comprehension is constructed as we read a text, drawing on our background knowledge and the information "blueprint" that the text provides.
- **Writing**—*Constructing a "blueprint" for readers who in turn construct the meaning we intend.* What and how we write depends on our understanding of literature and of informational texts—how we create a narrative world or present information.
- **Vocabulary**—*Understanding the concepts that words represent and the relationships among those concepts.* Learning vocabulary involves learning specific words and learning *about* words, such as how prefixes, suffixes, and roots combine to form words.

- **Word structure**—*The ways in which words are written or spelled and the information that the spelling represents.* This information is at the levels of *sound* and *meaning*.
- **Fluency**—*The ability to identify printed words quickly and accurately and to read orally with expression.*

Becoming literate is a *developmental* process that occurs across five developmental stages: emergent, beginning, transitional, intermediate, and skillful. Determining where each of your students is along this continuum gives you more precise insight into what you will teach.

Literacy instruction occurs in embedded sociocultural contexts. Students' ability to learn is influenced by the classroom, school, language, and cultural heritage of the home and the larger community.

The Gradual Release of Responsibility model for instruction makes explicit what and why something is to be learned. This model provides teachers a vehicle for ensuring that students will be successful in applying and using what they have learned.

Suggested Extension Activities

Observe: Make arrangements to observe in a primary (K–2), intermediate (3–5), or middle school (6–8) classroom during the reading/literature or writing block. Your observation may be of either a small-group or whole-class lesson. Based on the perspective presented in this chapter on the reading and writing processes and how teachers may facilitate their learning and development, pay particular attention to the following:

- Which literacy essentials is the teacher addressing in her or his lesson?
- How does the teacher interact with the students? How does she or he present a lesson and follow the Gradual Release of Responsibility model?
- Every few minutes during the lesson, focus on a different student and observe the degree to which he is engaged in the activity. If the student is not that engaged, why not? If the student is

engaged, why? How does the teacher facilitate engagement?

- If possible, make notes of your observations during the lesson. If this is not feasible, jot down your observations as soon after observing as possible. In either case, jot down your impressions afterward. What leapt out at you, impressed you, puzzled you?

It may not be possible for you to observe in an actual classroom because of the time of year or because you are a classroom teacher and it isn't convenient at this time to make arrangements to observe in a colleague's classroom. In that case, go to MyEducationLab and select a literacy instructional video from one of these three levels to watch and respond to.

Reflect: What are three big ideas or "takeaways" from this chapter that have given you the most insight into teaching and/or learning literacy? Write these down. Then, briefly explain why each has really caught your attention. Meet in a small group with fellow students or teachers to share and discuss. If face-to-face discussion is not possible, share in the online threaded discussion forum your instructor has provided for the course.

Engage: If you plan to read *Al Capone Does My Shirts* as the companion exemplar text for this book, please do the following before you being reading:

1) Take no more than 5 minutes and write down what first comes to mind when you think about each of these topics: *The Great Depression, Alcatraz, Al Capone, Autism.* Get your thoughts down in whatever manner is most comfortable for you—a list, short sentences or phrases, a cluster—the form doesn't matter.

2) Meet in a small group or online to share these initial thoughts. If you're not clear about what someone has shared, ask him or her. Your colleagues, of course, may ask you as well.

3) After you've shared, add to your initial jottings: What additional information did you learn? How were these topics elaborated and/or clarified for you? What new information did you learn? Were there any surprises? What questions do you have?

Recommended Professional Resources

Bear, D. R., & Templeton, S. (1998). Explorations in developmental spelling: Foundations for learning and teaching phonics, spelling, and vocabulary. *The Reading Teacher, 52,* 222–242.

Johnston, P. (2004). *Choice words: How our language affects children's learning.* Portland, ME: Stenhouse.

Morrow, L., Shanahan, T., & Wixson, K. K. (Eds.). (2013). *Teaching with the Common Core State Standards for English Language Arts, PreK–2.* New York: Guilford.

Morrow, L., Shanahan, T., & Wixson, K. K. (Eds.). (2013). *Teaching with the Common Core State Standards for English Language Arts, 3–5.* New York: Guilford.

Online Resources

To familiarize yourself with some of the online resources for literacy instruction, explore the following websites of some of the most important and supportive professional organizations in literacy education:

International Reading Association

www.reading.org

National Council of Teachers of English

www.ncte.org

National Writing Project

www.nwp.org

To further your understanding of policy initiatives affecting literacy, explore one of the following websites. We will be revisiting them throughout this text.

International Reading Association's Standards for Reading Professionals

www.reading.org/General/CurrentResearch/ Standards/ProfessionalStandards2010.aspx

Common Core State Standards for English/ Language Arts

www.corestandards.org/

How to Use This Book

To the extent that it is possible in a book or online format, we have tried in this text to develop an ongoing conversation with you. While this conversation is obviously one-sided, we still have tried to present content and ask questions just as we would if we were sitting across from you. With this goal in mind, we have organized this text so as to provide (1) effective and, we hope, efficient delivery of content; (2) opportunities to engage your critical thinking about the teaching of literacy; and (3) realistic opportunities to apply ideas, strategies, and activities.

In each chapter you will find:

- Focus questions that target the major topics.
- Opening vignettes that provide a real-world context for the level and types of instruction that are addressed in each chapter. These vignettes are based on and reflect the instruction of exemplary teachers and administrators who we know and have worked with extensively.
- Feature boxes throughout each chapter that address significant topics and themes in literacy instruction.
- Chapter-ending features and resources.

You will have students who are at different developmental levels of literacy in your classroom, and so throughout this text we offer support for accommodating these different levels. As you read each developmental chapter (Chapters 6 through 10), you may find it helpful to refer from time to time to Table 2.1 (pages 50–54), a comprehensive chart that summarizes the developmental continuum, to remind you of the characteristics of students at each particular developmental level.

The feature boxes in the chapters are organized around the following themes:

- **Strategies for the Classroom**—This feature succinctly presents practical activities and strategies for teaching the content addressed in each chapter.
- **The Language of Your Instruction**—This feature will provide models of language and questioning that you can use to initiate, engage, and facilitate students' thinking about and discussion of texts and words.
- **Accommodating English Learners**—In each developmental chapter, aspects of accommodating literacy instruction for English learners are presented.

- **Reading and Writing in Digital Contexts**—In each developmental chapter, examples of reading and writing instruction and application are provided.
- **Children's Literature Connection**—Chapters 3 through 11 include recommended titles across genres and cultures. In Chapter 10, this feature is labeled *Young Adult Literature Connection.*
- **Working and Collaborating**—Chapters 6 through 10 include suggestions for how you may collaborate and partner with your students' homes and the community—fellow educators, parents, and volunteers—with examples for supporting literacy instruction and intervention for learners specific to each developmental stage.

As we've done in this chapter, throughout this text we will be making connections with the *Common Core State Standards*, specifically those that address reading, writing, and language. As a literacy teacher, in most states you will be expected to address these standards, and your students' progress toward meeting these standards will be assessed. What we have learned about effective instruction is reflected in these standards. Our connections will be of two types: (1) *discussing* aspects and applications of the *CCSS* and (2) *calling out* instruction that supports the *CCSS* through a marginal icon.

The resources at the end of each chapter include those you've just seen here in Chapter 1:

- **Chapter Summary**—The summary is keyed to the focus questions presented at the beginning of each chapter.
- **Suggested Activities with Students**—These provide you the opportunity to apply the chapter information with students—either your own or those in your preservice field-based experiences.
- **Your Ongoing Professional Development— Questions to Explore with Fellow Students/ Colleagues**—These provide you the opportunity to explore collaboratively and problem solve, with your classroom colleagues or fellow teachers, specific situations and case studies. Your instructor may require these questions to be addressed in class or on the website for the course.

- **Recommended Professional Resources**—We have kept two points in mind in selecting and recommending significant authors/books/articles on particular topics: (1) We know your time for reading beyond this assigned text is limited and (2) because of that, we have tried to select wisely. Our recommendations provide further background information and practical application to help you grow and develop your teaching repertoire and knowledgeably apply this information.
- **Online Resources**—You are already familiar with the experience of doing an online search—for example, for "phonics instruction" or "critical reading"—and coming up with thousands of hits. Many of them are likely to be quite good, but how do you know, and how do you decide? We provide criteria for doing so (just as you will help your own students in their online explorations), but we also recommend some very helpful sites—those that provide good instructional ideas and activities that have a solid research base.

We've already begun in this chapter to refer to *Al Capone Does My Shirts*, by Gennifer Choldenko. Though not written for younger students, this work of historical fiction is an excellent book for those in the intermediate and middle grades. We will make reference to it often to illustrate the strategies and activities we discuss in the areas of word study and vocabulary, comprehension and literature response activities, and writing. These examples will include how this and similar books may be used for on-, above-, and below-level students. For younger students, many of the types of texts we have used as examples may be found on *www.wegivebooks.org*.

Language, Thought, and Literacy Development

2

Chapter Outline

» **Characteristics of Oral Language**

» **Characteristics of Thought**

» **Characteristics of Written Language: Word Level**

» **Characteristics of Written Language: Text Level**

» **The Developmental Model of Literacy**

1. How are the development of oral language and the development of thought related?
2. What is *orthographic knowledge?* Why is it such a critical foundation for reading and writing?
3. What affects the complexity of *literature* and *informational* texts?
4. Describe what this observation means: "Oral language is a foundation for literacy, but literacy later becomes the foundation for further development in oral language and in thought."
5. How does your understanding of development affect what you teach?

Mike Wallin, a third-grade teacher at Compello Elementary, is talking with Donita Grolin, literacy coach for Compello and two other elementary schools in the district. Mike is concerned about Rordel, a new student who transferred into his class the previous week. Rordel's stage of literacy development and oral language level is quite a bit behind the rest of the students in class. Mike has managed to pull Rordel aside a few times to talk with him, and shares that Rordel's oral language level might be similarly behind. Although Rordel seems to hang back and not engage much—Mike acknowledges that this is normal for a new student—he tells Donita that he thinks this is more than just shyness. Mike has listened to Rordel read and has examined his spellings on a qualitative spelling inventory; he's concluded that Rordel is at the *beginning* literacy stage. The student reads haltingly, pausing on several words, and has difficulty in recalling what he has read. His spellings confirmed this level: He spelled *bed* and *ship*, for example, as *bad* and *sep*. Mike thinks he knows what type of instruction Rordel needs, but is seeking Donita's advice in how to accommodate Rordel in the regular classroom, as well as making sure the child is able to get intensive one-to-one additional literacy instruction as soon as possible.

Donita confirms with Mike that addressing Rordel's oral language is crucial—building vocabulary and syntactic knowledge, over time, should be front and center. Although Rordel will be reading primarily from materials on his independent and instructional levels, he will be listening to texts that he could not read on his own and afterwards talk about the text with two other children. He will listen to a text several times over the course of a week, looking at and following along with the highlighted words on an e-tablet screen as he listens. This is where he will be exposed to more vocabulary and more complex syntactic structures.

Rordel will also benefit from Mike's read-alouds—the language in the books will provide excellent models of vocabulary and syntax. When Mike pauses to talk with the children about an aspect of the read-aloud, he often has them turn to a buddy to talk; this, too, will support Rordel's language development in a comfortable and nonthreatening way. This focus on oral language will support Rordel's literacy growth as well.

Because she sees so many classrooms and children, Donita is able to reassure Mike that his concentrated developmental focus on Rordel's language and literacy will certainly help Rordel. And, if he should move again, it may be just the right amount of support and encouragement to give Rordel the lift he needs to continue, having experienced success in an instructionally appropriate and socially welcoming environment at Compello Elementary. ■

In Chapter 1 we explored how the processes of reading and writing involve language and thought. In this chapter, we look more closely at the characteristics of language and thought, setting the stage for (1) how they support the development of literacy and (2) how literacy supports and extends the development of language and thought.

Characteristics of Oral Language

At all developmental levels, learners bring their language knowledge to the task of reading and writing. Language users possess four types of knowledge, and they are in play just about every time we speak:

- **Phonological knowledge.** *How* we speak our language—the sounds we make as well as the emphasis we place on words and phrases.
- **Semantic knowledge.** Our understanding of the meaning of words and of word parts (prefixes, suffixes, and roots).
- **Syntactic knowledge.** Our ability to order or arrange words into phrases and sentences.
- **Pragmatic knowledge.** How we *use* our language in different situations and contexts.

These types of knowledge interact in real time as we communicate. Much of the knowledge underlying these four types is subconscious—we just seem to "know" it without thinking about it (Templeton, 1986; Tomasello, 2008). Effective teachers help students bring these types of knowledge to the surface, developing and extending them, and applying them in their learning. Let's look at each of these types of knowledge more closely.

Phonological Knowledge

Common Core Connection

Reading Standards: Foundational Skills – Phonological Awareness

Phonological knowledge refers to the sounds and contours of language. When we hear the words *sit* and *bit*, how do we know they are different? Only by the sounds we hear at the beginning of each word. How about *rip* and *ripe*? We can tell the differences between these two words by the sounds we hear in the middle of each word. These individual sounds are called **phonemes**, and they are the smallest unit of speech that helps us distinguish one word from another (*sit* vs. *bit*). Figure 2.1 presents the common phonemes in Standard American English along with their most common spellings. Our knowledge of the phonemes in our language is part of our *phonological* knowledge. In Standard English, there are 44 distinct phonemes. Phonemes combine into **syllables**. As we'll explain later, *using* knowledge of phonemes in listening and speaking is pretty much subconscious. Becoming consciously aware of phonemes, however, is a more challenging task.

Phonological knowledge also includes **prosody**, the rhythmic flow of speech. This flow varies in terms of loudness, duration, pitch or intonation, and pausing. Speakers use these features to give particular emphasis to what they are saying. Where we place stress or accent, for example, as well as the rising and falling intonation in our language, conveys meaning. For example, think about how the change in emphasis affects the meaning in the sentence "Jeb ate the kumquat":

Jeb ate the *kumquat*? (instead of the cauliflower)
Jeb ate the kumquat? (rather than Suzie)
Jeb *ate* the kumquat? (as opposed to throwing it, which he usually does when he doesn't like a particular food)

FIGURE 2.1 Major Phonemes of Standard American English

Consonants					Vowels	
/b/	bit				ă	bat
/ch/	chick	stretch			ā	cake pay
/d/	dog				â	rare air wear
/f/	fit	stuff	phrase	tough	ä	father
/g/	get	tag			ě	wet
/h/	hot	who			ē	me
/hw/	which	when			ĭ	sit
/j/	jump	gentle			ī	side
/k/	cat	sack	school		î	pierce
/kw/	choir	queen			ŏ	hot
/l/	lap	needle	fall		ô	paw
/m/	slam	comb			ō	smoke
/n/	not	hidden			oi	spoil
/ng/	song	pink			ou	cloud
/p/	pan				ŭ	sum
/r/	roar	rhyme	wrap		û	turn
/s/	sip	moss	scene			
/sh/	shop	fish	issue		o͝o	shook
/t/	top	missed			o͞o	moon
/th/	math	think			/ə/	about mitten
/th/	bathe	that				
/v/	van	wave				
/w/	win					
/y/	yes					

Note: The symbols for the sounds used here are those used in the *American Heritage Children's Dictionary*. They are the most common symbols for these sounds in materials intended for use by elementary and middle grade students.

Semantic Knowledge

Semantic knowledge involves *meaning*. It's the relationship between spoken and written words, word parts (prefixes, suffixes, and roots), and the underlying concepts they label. We organize our experiences and our world in terms of concepts and their interrelationships: For example, the *Civil War* and the *Revolutionary War* are different concepts, but they are related in that they are both important wars that are part of American history. They differ in terms of their historical context and their significant individuals and personalities. They are similar in terms of geography and in terms of slavery being an issue in both. As we'll explore throughout this text, vocabulary learning has to do with the exploration, extension, and differentiation of semantic knowledge—of concepts and of their labels.

Words have *denotations* and *connotations:* The literal or dictionary meaning of a word is what it **denotes**. The **connotative** meaning of a word is the associations that the word takes on— what the word **connotes** or suggests to us, how it makes us feel, and the personal associations we bring to it beyond the word's denotative meaning. For example, one of the denotative meanings of *absent* is "not present." For many students, however, the word *absent* in connection with *parent* takes on a sad or unpleasant connotation—a father or mother, for example, who is on an extended tour of duty overseas.

Common Core Connection

Language Standards: Vocabulary Acquisition and Use

In addition to denotation and connotation, words can be used *figuratively*: for instance, compare a *bouquet* of flowers with a *bouquet* of ideas. **Figurative language** refers to words or phrases that are not used in their literal sense but instead to compare, emphasize, clarify, or open up a new way of looking at and thinking about our world. When we look more closely at figurative language we see that language scholars have broken it down into several categories: for example *simile/metaphor*, *hyperbole*, and *personification*.

In *Al Capone Does My Shirts*, Moose describes Mrs. Kelly as "a short round ball of a woman with hair the color of plumbing pipes" (Choldenko, 2004, p. 126). Mrs. Kelly isn't *literally* a "ball," but this metaphorical use of the word/concept provokes a pretty vivid mental image of her. (Had Moose said she is *like* a ball, we would call that a *simile*. The only difference between a simile and a metaphor is that similes use "like" or "as"; metaphors do not.) Describing Mrs. Kelly's hair as "the color of plumbing pipes" is a bit of *hyperbole*—exaggerating or stretching the truth a bit, in the process giving us a pretty vivid image!

For most of the words we know, the following types of information are a part of our underlying knowledge (adapted from Miller, 1999; Stahl & Nagy, 2006):

* The *range of meanings of the word*, both literal and figurative. *Cloud* literally refers to a body of particles—for example, water or dust—suspended in the atmosphere; it may also figuratively refer to obscuring someone's thinking or judgment.
* The *web of relationships* the word shares with other words and concepts. Using the same example of *cloud,* we might have "billowing," "hazy," "obscuring," and "weather."
* The *situations and contexts to which the word applies*, including informal and formal speech and writing. Speaking or writing about "clouding someone's judgment" is a bit more formal; in casual conversation we're more likely to talk about someone "being confused."
* Knowing *other words that are likely to occur* with the word, such as a *bank* of clouds (not a carton or a bushel of clouds) and *cloudy* weather (not cloudy patios). If someone *does* put words together that normally don't go together—for instance, "bushel of clouds" or "cloudy patios"—they do so to grab our attention or provide a new way of looking at things. They are using these words *metaphorically*.
* Knowing the *probability of meeting the word*. In a chapter on weather patterns, we'll probably run into the word *cloud* a lot; in a chapter in a math textbook, not so much.
* How the *grammatical form of a word* affects its meaning:
    Cloud, a verb, is the *action* of obscuring something.
    Cloudy, an adjective, applies the characteristics of "cloud" to something or someone.
    Cloudiness, a noun, is the condition of being cloudy.

By encountering new words in a variety of contexts, we develop nuanced and flexible understandings for that word that include these types of knowledge (Landauer & Dumais, 1997).

Morphology refers to the correspondence between meaningful word parts and their underlying meaning, and the processes by which those word parts combine to form words. The term **morpheme** refers to the smallest unit of meaning in the language. For example, the word *highest* contains two morphemes: the word *high* and the suffix *–est*. Whenever we hear the word *high* applied to an object we know that it means that object extends upward pretty far. Whenever we hear *–est* at the end of a word we know that it has to do with the ultimate condition of something—the *highest* building means, of course, there is no other building as high as this one. There are two types of morphemes: **free morphemes,** which can occur by themselves *(words)* and **bound morphemes**, which cannot occur by themselves but must be bound or connected to other meaningful parts. Bound morphemes are suffixes such as *–est* and *–ible*, and prefixes such as *un–* and *re–*. Morphological knowledge is an important aspect of our semantic knowledge. In fact, most words in English are created by combining prefixes, suffixes, and roots: *high/er,* *high/est, re/work, work/able, pre/dict/ion.* We will explore morphology in more depth later in this chapter in the section on word-level characteristics of written language, and provide the "what" and "how to's" of morphology instruction in Chapters 8, 9, and 10.

Syntactic Knowledge

When we try to organize our semantic knowledge in order to communicate with someone else, we are using our syntactic knowledge. Syntactic knowledge is what we use in order to arrange words into phrases and simple sentences, and phrases into longer sentences. How we arrange these elements expresses the relationships among concepts in speech and in writing.

Common Core Connection

Language Standards: Conventions of Standard English

We all have an underlying, subconscious knowledge of the syntactic categories or families in our language. For all languages, any sentence uttered may be broken into two parts: a subject and what that subject does. In most languages, including English, this distinction is between a subject and a verb. It may be quite basic and simple: *She/ran.* A subject phrase and a verb phrase may become quite complex: *The lithe, stunning young lady/leapt breathtakingly from one table to another in the crowded lunchroom.*

There are syntactic categories in which we capture distinctions among the roles that words play. The most familiar categories are probably those of parts of speech—the categories of *noun*, *verb*, *adjective*, *adverb*, and *pronoun* represent *content words.* Content words have such a clear meaning that they produce images: things, actions, and characteristics of things and actions. In contrast, the parts of speech known as *conjunctions* (*but, and, so*), *prepositions* (*over, under, on*), and *determiners* (*the, some, this, a*) are difficult to visualize. They do not have a clear meaning on their own but rather serve as *function* words, gluing concrete words together. For example, it is difficult to point to an example of *a* or *the* in the real world, but each word functions to specify a type of word that will follow. In the case of *the*, it signals that the noun that will follow is a specific example of something—a particular person, geometric figure, vegetable. On the other hand, *a* signals that a less specific noun will follow—any old geometric figure, person, or vegetable.

How words are arranged within sentences follow rules that we all discover as we learn to speak our native language. For the most part, we are not aware of these rules—humans seem to be naturally "wired" to develop language (Chomsky, 1959; Lenneberg, 1967). English-speaking children learn that adjectives usually precede nouns *(happy child)*, while Spanish-speaking children learn that adjectives follow nouns *(niño feliz).*

Pragmatic Knowledge

How we *use* our language in different social contexts reflects our pragmatic knowledge—the form our language takes, and why we use a particular form. For example, when talking with friends at lunch, we're usually informal, we use a simpler vocabulary and often speak in sentence fragments. When making a presentation to the local school board, we're more formal, use more "academic" language and vocabulary, and try to speak in grammatically correct and complete sentences. You'll sometimes see the terms **register** and **code switching** used to refer to these distinctions among language use—more relaxed, informal language use versus more formal, academic language use. As children are exposed to different language contexts (for example, the home, the classroom, the playground, friends' homes, and other contexts such as stores, banks, and post offices), they begin to realize that language can be used for a variety of purposes and that it takes a variety of forms as well. One of the fundamental roles of teachers is to help students successfully negotiate the many forms and functions of oral and written language.

Common Core Connection

Language Standards: Knowledge of Language

A number of linguists have described the different ways in which our pragmatic knowledge is used. One of the most widely accepted ways of classifying language use was suggested by Michael

Halliday (1993/2003, 1999/2003). Halliday describes six *functions* of language, developed in early childhood and elaborated throughout the school years and beyond:

Regulatory—Using language to influence others so as to get them to do what you want. Depending on the context, for example, you may issue commands or requests: *"We've got no more time to lose—we have to move on this right now!" "Don't you agree that this way might allow us to bring many more students along with us?"*

Interactional—Using language in social contexts to establish a comfortable mood and to build interpersonal relationships: *"I like how you helped me understand how the others usually do this."*

Personal—Using language to establish one's identity and present oneself in different social contexts—how we attract attention to ourselves: *"That is soooo not like me!" "I am truly honored to have this opportunity to meet you."*

Representational—Using language to share information: *"Here's what I found out about these flagellates."*

Heuristic—Using language in the process of learning—how, when, why we ask questions: *"So, let me see . . . what you are saying is that . . ."* (restating a student's question to show you value it, and also perhaps to clarify their thinking in the process) *"There is no right answer, so what would be your best answer?"* (Zwiers, 2008)

Imaginative—Using language to investigate and explore our imaginations. Such language often comes out of experiences with narratives and the language of narrative: *"I feel like I've become a softwire, inside the inner workings of a Droid." "The way the fog settled on the mountain this morning made me feel like I was riding my bike through Middle Earth."*

This perspective on language *use* highlights another important point: Neither informal nor formal speech is better than the other, nor is standard any better than nonstandard English (see, for example, Lefstein, 2009). Because effective language depends on the context in which it is used, informal speech works better in some circumstances, formal in others; standard in some instances, nonstandard in others.

Characteristics of Thought

It is almost impossible to discuss oral language without reference to thought or thinking—and vice-versa. The development of thought was threaded throughout our description of the characteristics of oral language. Thought, or more precisely, cognition, is involved in the development of language from the very beginning.

Just as with their language, it is difficult for young children to be aware of their thinking—what psychologists refer to as **metacognition** (Metcalfe & Shimamura, 1994). As children grow, however, they begin to develop the ability to step back and think about their own thinking. This awareness helps them realize how to adjust to developing situations rather than respond impulsively. (Admittedly, this ability is not always applied; even adults, of course, often respond impulsively, but most have the ability to monitor themselves so that such responses—we hope— occur infrequently.)

Because of the binding relationship between language and thought, the course and timing of children's cognitive development will depend over time on how they are encouraged to explore their environments and the social situations within them. The nature and development of cognition have been explored by many researchers and applied widely to education in general and literacy in particular. Just a few notable resources over the years are Anderson and Krathwohl (2000), Anderson, Spiro, and Montagu (1977), Bloom (1956), Bruner (1973), Piaget and Inhelder (1969), and Vygotsky (1962).

The terms that you will encounter in your studies and in your teaching reflect the legacy of this research in cognitive development and learning. The most common terms are *remembering, understanding, applying, analyzing, evaluating, synthesizing,* and the many variations and extensions of these. Note some of our parenthetical examples in Figure 2.2. All of these terms address the increasing complexity of cognitive processes required as we move from concrete to more abstract thinking. From experiencing and remembering, through application, then deeper understanding through analysis—ultimately, these prior levels of understanding are employed as students compare and contrast across different examples and situations. Often presented in a pyramid, with concrete understanding at the base and more complex understanding at the tip (Bloom, 1956; Anderson & Krathwohl, 2000), we prefer a slightly adapted version (Figure 2.2) expressed in an inverted pyramid in which each level, broader in scope and deeper in quality, represents more advanced and generalizable cognition.

In a nutshell, these successive levels represent developing levels of *reasoning.* As we'll see in our discussion of literacy development later in this chapter, children's ability to engage in these types of reasoning also develops over time—critically, with the guidance of a teacher. As scholars and philosophers have known for a very long time, however, "thinking" is impossible to observe. So, as teachers, we base our instruction on what is *observable*—our students' oral language and how they engage written language. These will be our signposts for responding to our students as we guide and extend their reasoning abilities.

FIGURE 2.2 Levels of Understanding

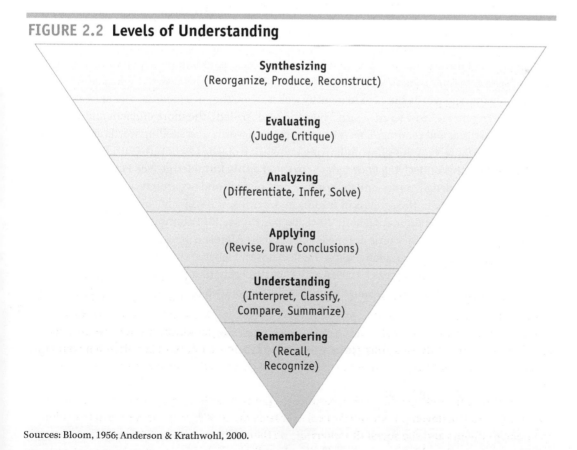

Sources: Bloom, 1956; Anderson & Krathwohl, 2000.

Characteristics of Written Language: Word Level

In Chapter 1, we noted how the comprehension of any text is a process that involves the following:

- The meaning of the words is determined.
- The order of and relationships among the words within each sentence are processed.
- The sentences are related to each other.
- Larger chunks of text are related to each other.
- An overall "model" of the text is created in the reader's mind.

As the first two steps in this process imply, it is no accident that vocabulary knowledge and syntactic knowledge, more than any other reading skill, are the major determinants of understanding: inferring, understanding sequence, summarizing, and so on. And in reading, in order to determine the meaning of the words, they must *first* be correctly identified. In *writing*, in order to encode what one wants to say—what one wants to *mean*—one must first connect with the form of the word and write it down. This is why students' knowledge of word structure is such a critical component, the foundation on which the other literacy abilities build (Templeton & Bear, 1992, 2011).

Common Core Connection

Foundational Skills:
Phonics and Word
Recognition

When it comes to learning about the printed form of words, our minds are not like cameras: We do not learn a printed word by "staring" at it long enough until its image becomes imprinted on our brains like images on film or a computer chip, or by looking at it over and over while repeating it out loud. The images that we have of words are constructed over time and reflect our understanding of (1) the structure of words *in general* (letters, sounds, spelling, and meaning patterns) and (2) *specific* words that we may know. This is why we will emphasize later in this chapter and throughout this text that by looking at how your students *spell* words, you'll be able to determine their *general* knowledge about word structure—that is, the information they use not only to write words but also to identify words when they are reading. The more students understand *in general* "how words work" (how they are spelled), the more efficient and effective will be their writing and reading. This is because reading words and spelling words are not separate processes but rely on the same underlying knowledge of word structure (Ehri, 1997).

The term for this underlying knowledge is **orthographic knowledge** (see Figure 2.3). Orthographic knowledge guides and determines how quickly and accurately we are able to negotiate the very first step in the process of reading and writing, the step on which all else depends (Perfetti, 2007; Perfetti, Landi, & Oakhill, 2005; Rapp & Kipka, 2011; Templeton & Bear, 2011).

But what about the way words are spelled in English? Almost a century ago, a scholar remarked that of all the world's languages, "English has the most antiquated, inconsistent, and illogical spelling" (cited in Venezky, 1999, p. vii). Unfortunately, that perspective still prevails. It is beginning to change, however, because many teachers—yourself included—are learning that the

FIGURE 2.3 The Underlying Role and Importance of Orthographic Knowledge

Decoding:	*Encoding:*
Reading Words	**Writing Words**
↖	↗
Orthographic Knowledge	

FIGURE 2.4 Important Terminology: Phonology, Phonics, and Spelling

Consonants and Vowels	The two major categories of speech sounds in language. The terms are also used to refer to the letters that represent these sounds.
Syllable	A unit of speech that contains a vowel. A consonant or consonants may come before or after the vowel.
Consonant	As you speak, a consonant sound is made by obstructing the flow of air somewhere between your throat and your lips. For example: The /k/ sound at the beginning of *cash* is made by quickly stopping and then releasing the flow of air in your throat. The /t/ sound at the beginning of *top* is made by interrupting the flow of air by placing your tongue on the ridge just behind your upper front teeth. The /sh/ sound at the end of *cash* is made by forcing the flow of air through a very narrow opening.
Vowel	In contrast to consonants, a vowel sound is made by *not* obstructing the flow of air but by changing the shape of your throat and mouth and the position of your tongue. The terms *long* and *short* are used to refer to vowel sounds. We will address these categories in more depth in later chapters. For now, however, the difference between long and short is determined by the simple question "Does the vowel say its name?" Is the sound the same as the name of the letter? If so, we call that a "long" vowel. The vowel sound in *so* is /ō/, which is of course the name of the letter *o*. The vowel sound "says its name," therefore it is long. A *short* vowel sound, as in *cash*, does *not* say its name—there is no letter whose name has that sound.
Diphthong	There are two diphthongs in English: /oi/ as in <u>oi</u>l and /ow/ as in <u>hou</u>se. Diphthongs are vowel sounds within single syllables in which you begin with one vowel sound and glide into another. You can get a sense of this when you slow down your pronunciation of /oi/ and /ow/ and pay attention to where you begin and where you end.
Consonant Digraph	Two consonant letters that represent one sound: <u>ch</u>eck, <u>th</u>is, <u>ph</u>one, <u>sh</u>ape
Consonant Blend	Two or three consonant letters in which each letter keeps the sound it would have if it occurred by itself: <u>bl</u>end, <u>fr</u>og, <u>sn</u>ake, <u>str</u>ike
Vowel Digraph or Vowel Pair	Two vowel letters that represent a single vowel sound: r<u>ai</u>n, s<u>oa</u>p, h<u>ea</u>d
Grapheme	One or more letters that represent a single phoneme. In the word *fan*, *f* is the grapheme that represents /f/; in *phone*, *ph* is the grapheme that represents /f/.
Sight Word	This term is used in two ways: (1) A word that a reader can identify immediately, in text or in isolation, when she sees it. It is not necessary to analyze or sound out the letters in the word in order to identify it. (2) One of the approximately 300 words that occur most frequently in spoken and written English, and which children are expected to learn (usually, the first 150 by the end of first grade, and all 300 by the end of second grade).
Sight Vocabulary	All the words that a student can identify immediately by sight.

way words are spelled usually *does* makes sense. To understand why, we'll explore the two levels that the spelling system represents: *sound* and *meaning*. Figure 2.4 defines the terms that are an important part of this exploration.

Correspondences at the Level of Sound: Alphabet and Pattern

At the level of sound, the **alphabetic layer** of spelling is the most straightforward and obvious: Letters are matched to the sequence of sounds in a word in a left-to-right fashion, as in the words *tip*, *grab*, and *so*. As we'll discuss later, this type of representation corresponds to the way in which

Common Core Connection

Language Standards:
Conventions of
Standard English

young children expect spelling to work. The **pattern layer** represents regular sound/spelling correspondences *within* syllables and *between* syllables. This pattern layer is one step up from the alphabetic level: Within a single syllable, a group or pattern of letters functions as a single unit that corresponds to sound. For example, in the word *slope* the vowel/consonant/silent *e* (VC*e*) spelling pattern represents a long vowel pronunciation; the silent *e* in this spelling pattern distinguishes this "long *o*" pronunciation from the "short *o*" pronunciation in the word *slop*.

Within syllables, the pattern layer also includes the effects of a sound's *position* on its spelling. How a lot of sounds are spelled often depends on where they are within a syllable and their relationship to other sounds within the syllable. For example:

- In one-syllable words with short vowels such as *back, rock,* and *pick,* the final /k/ sound is consistently spelled *ck*. At the beginning of a syllable, however, /k/ will *never* be spelled *ck*. *Where the sound occurs* is an important key to how it is spelled.
- In one-syllable words that end in /k/, as we've just seen, that sound is spelled *ck* after a *short* vowel; after a *long* vowel, however, the /k/ sound is usually spelled *ke*. How a sound is spelled often depends on *other sounds that are next to that sound.*

At this point you may be thinking, "I learned to spell these words and I knew nothing about these patterns!" That may be true, but most of us did not *enjoy* learning to spell. Our efforts to learn correct spelling moved along despite instruction that was probably based on heavy memorization and writing of words several times each. As we'll see in later chapters, your students are much more likely to *enjoy* learning about words while they are learning correct spelling.

And while enjoyment is important, even *more* important is the result of this type of exploration. Exploring words and their patterns pays off in the following ways:

- Students feel more empowered as they exercise their developing knowledge, because they are learning there is a *logic* to spelling that they are coming to control and effectively apply their spelling knowledge.
- Students strengthen connections among sound, spelling, and meaning, and these stronger connections result in more automatic word identification in *reading*, leaving more cognitive space available for thinking. This thinking enables both more elaborate meaning-making as well as enjoyment of what is being read. These connections support more rapid encoding of words in *writing*, providing more thinking space to consider purpose and audience during writing.

Common Core Connection

Language Standards:
Vocabulary Acquisition
and Use

A word about the role of *meaning* at this level: Although it influences spelling most extensively through morphology, meaning also plays a role in determining certain spelling *patterns* within single-syllable words. It explains why there are **homophones** in the language—words such as *sale* and *sail* that sound the same but are spelled differently. There is no "rule" that tells us when the long *a* sound is spelled *a*-consonant-*e* as in *sale* or *ai* as in *sail*. What *does* explain the difference in spelling is the *meaning* of each of the words: Are we writing about a boat or a ship on the water, or about selling something? We don't have to stop and think "Which spelling is it?" because the *meaning* determines the spelling—*always*. Generations have complained about homophones because we've obsessed about spelling *sounds* consistently, but when we switch the focus to *meaning* and always talk about the *meaning* of a word when we are learning the spelling, then homophones make more sense.

Meaning is also a player in words such as *bow* and *dove*, which are pronounced differently depending on their meanings:

When you *bow* to someone out of respect; or play a violin with a *bow*
The *dove*, a type of bird; or yesterday when you *dove* off of the diving board several times

These words are examples of **homographs**, or words that have the same spelling but different meanings, and quite often have different pronunciations as well. When they have the *same* spelling and pronunciation—for example, as in *bear* (animal versus carrying a burden) and *present* (a gift versus giving something to someone)—they are most often referred to as **multiple-meaning words**.

Between syllables, the pattern principle is also at work: It influences the spelling where syllables join. For example, when inflectional endings such as *–ed* and *–ing* are added to one-syllable words, letters at the end of the word are doubled, dropped, or left alone. What determines this is the spelling pattern within the word and the vowel sound it represents. For example, *mop* + *–ing* = *mopping*; *mope* + *–ing* = *moping*. The final consonant in *mop* must be doubled because of the short vowel pattern. This way, we can differentiate *mopping* from *moping*. The knowledge of when to double and when not to double also applies in words like *dinner* and *diner*. Because the vowel in the first syllable of *dinner* is short, the *n* is doubled; because the vowel in the first syllable of *diner* is long, the following consonant is not doubled. This feature is fairly consistent in English: Vowel sounds that are not long are often followed by *doubled* consonants; long vowel sounds are usually followed by a *single* consonant.

Correspondences at the Level of Meaning: Morphology

Morphological knowledge is the foundation for students' *generative* knowledge about words. When students understand basic processes of morphology, they can *generate* knowledge of literally tens of thousands of words.

Most words in English are created by combining morphemes—meaningful word parts. Linguists have identified three components of morphology: compounding, inflectional morphology, and derivational morphology. **Compounding** is the process from which we get compound words such as *seagull* and *strawberry*. It unites two or three words that represent a single concept. **Inflectional morphology** indicates verb tense and number, such as walk*ed*/walk*ing*; cat*s*. Inflectional suffixes are most commonly referred to as inflectional *endings*. And as you will see, **derivational morphology** is the richest of the three components. In English, literally hundreds of thousands of words are *derived* from roots through combination with **affixes**, which are prefixes and suffixes, and other roots. **Derivational suffixes** often change the syntactic role of a root, although the core meaning of the root is usually retained: *respect* (verb), *respect* + *–able* (adjective).

Common Core Connection

Language Standards: Vocabulary Acquisition and Use

Derivational suffixes are really the "workhorses" of morphology. There aren't many of them—some of the most frequent are *–ful*, *–ion*, *–ment*, and *–ity*—but they allow us to *derive* any number of additional words from a single root. By exploring how these suffixes affect the roots to which they are attached, and how they usually change the part of speech of the word, students grow their understanding of English morphology, develop a foundation for learning the Greek and Latin component of English, expand their vocabulary, and increase their syntactic awareness.

Using the word *respect* as an example, let's examine morphology at work:

respect: I *respect* your right to disagree with that point of view. [verb]
respectable: You should know, however, that it is a very *respectable* point of view. [adjective]
respectably: She behaves *respectably* when she disagrees. [adverb]
respectability: The *respectability* of that point of view is hard to challenge. [noun]
respectful: We are *respectful* of the office of the presidency. [adjective]
disrespectful: Seriously, your behavior is totally *disrespectful*—I'm going to ask you to leave! [adjective]

Notice that when you take off prefixes and suffixes in a word, what remains is the *root* of the word. Often the root is a word. For example, when the affixes *un–* and *–able* in *unbreakable* are taken off, the **root word** *break* remains. (In addition to the term *root word*, you'll see the terms **base** or **base word** used—they mean exactly the same thing as *root word*.) Other times, however, the root cannot stand by itself as a word. We say it is a *bound* root, meaning that it occurs only in words in which it is *bound* to other morphemes. For example, *respect* may be broken down further into the prefix *re–* and the bound root, *spect*, which comes from Latin and means "look." Literally, the meaning of *respect* originally had to do with looking *(spect)* again *(re)* at someone. If you respected and admired someone, he or she was worthy of looking at more than once.

Most of the roots in English come from Latin and Greek. Sometimes they pop up by themselves as words: *Graph,* for instance, comes from Greek and means "write." Most of the time, however, these Greek and Latin roots occur as bound roots, such as pre*dict*ion (literally, "saying before" something happens) and in*aud*ible (not capable of being heard).

To say that the English spelling system is logical does not mean that it may be mastered quickly or easily. Children's understanding develops over time. *Your* understanding of the logic that underlies sound and meaning will guide your students' developmentally based understanding, and their learning of word patterns at the levels of sound and meaning will be more efficient, meaningful, and motivating.

Characteristics of Written Language: Text Level

Once again, let's consider how comprehension of a text proceeds—once the meaning of and the relationships among the words are processed:

- The sentences are related to each other.
- Larger chunks of text are related to each other.
- An overall "model" of the text is created in the reader's mind.

How readers read, how they build the overall model of the text, depends on the type of text they're reading—narrative or informational—and on their purpose for reading. Are they reading for pleasure or for information—or both? Are they reading deeply or superficially? Assuming they are doing a careful read, their knowledge of the genre and type of text they will read will determine the overall model of the text they will be constructing.

Readers must be able to process information and relationships within and between sentences, between chunks of sentences—paragraphs—and larger chunks of texts, such as sections and their headings (if an informational text), and between chapters. There are different structural layers in texts, and writers construct them in particular ways. Your students will be learning about that structure and be expected to analyze it in reading and apply it in writing.

Figure 2.5 provides an overview of the types of texts students will be learning about in grades K–8. Broadly speaking, texts fall into either one of two categories: literature or informational.

As students learn to relate sentences to each other, they are constructing *paragraph-level* understanding—usually how a main idea is developed and supported by the sentences in that paragraph. Paragraph-level understanding of course occurs in both narrative and informational texts, but follows a more deliberate, logical structure in informational texts. The main idea of each paragraph is in turn a building block for larger ideas the text is developing, but understanding at the overall text level depends on the understandings built from the paragraph level.

FIGURE 2.5 **Types of Text: Literature and Informational**

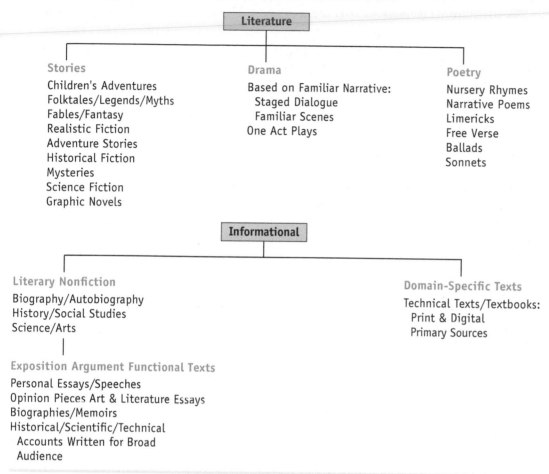

Literature

Stories
Children's Adventures
Folktales/Legends/Myths
Fables/Fantasy
Realistic Fiction
Adventure Stories
Historical Fiction
Mysteries
Science Fiction
Graphic Novels

Drama
Based on Familiar Narrative:
  Staged Dialogue
  Familiar Scenes
One Act Plays

Poetry
Nursery Rhymes
Narrative Poems
Limericks
Free Verse
Ballads
Sonnets

Informational

Literary Nonfiction
Biography/Autobiography
History/Social Studies
Science/Arts

Domain-Specific Texts
Technical Texts/Textbooks:
  Print & Digital
  Primary Sources

Exposition Argument Functional Texts
Personal Essays/Speeches
Opinion Pieces Art & Literature Essays
Biographies/Memoirs
Historical/Scientific/Technical
  Accounts Written for Broad
  Audience

Narrative structure reflects the psychological framework with which we usually make sense of our world: Problems arise, characters take certain steps to resolve these problems, and we hope there will be a satisfactory conclusion. From a young age, children engage narratives this way: There is an initial *problem*, a *plot structure* consisting of a sequence of *episodes* or *events* through which the problem is addressed, working toward a final *resolution*. Resolutions do not always work out as we might wish, of course, but that is an essential value of narratives: While they may help us temporarily escape from our problems, they also help us learn how to deal with them. *Fiction* can shape our reality as much as information and fact.

In *Al Capone Does My Shirts* (Choldenko, 2004), as with any longer narrative, we learn early on that there are a number of problems that Moose Flanagan is going to be dealing with—and many of them are precisely the type of problems *most* 12-year-old boys have to deal with: fitting in with others, becoming aware of how awkward being around certain girls increasingly seems to be. In addition, however, there are some problems that are more unique: living on Alcatraz, communicating with convicted and dangerous criminals, trying to be supportive of a sister with autism at a time when autism was not even recognized as a significant condition. These problems don't roll out all at once, but over time, and are interwoven within the overall plot. As readers move through the book, they are both constructing the text model and carrying it along with them. This is not difficult to do with an interesting and engaging narrative, and effective teachers will make use of this type of reading experience to scaffold students' engagements with more challenging and perhaps not as interesting (at least at first) narratives.

The structure of *informational texts* varies considerably:

- Textbooks in print and in digital format
- The large domain of *literary nonfiction* that includes biographies and autobiographies as well as books that are not in a textbook format but which address contemporary issues, history, social studies, science, and the arts—these texts often include features of narrative structure as well
- Formal letters
- Opinion pieces
- Technical "how-to" directions/manuals
- Graphically displayed information

Common Core Connection

Reading Standards for
Informational Text:
Craft and Structure

Features of traditional textbooks are presented straightforwardly: chapter titles, paragraphs, headings, subheadings, bolded and italicized vocabulary, introductory chapter questions, and end-of-chapter summaries. The table of contents, index, and glossary are important features that help provide appropriate scaffolding and navigational tools. Their online presence is more fluid, often in an array on one side of the screen or in a drop-down menu, which may only be located by learning about and negotiating icons on the screen. Using online navigational tools is often much quicker than with the printed text, but a fluency with typing skills also comes into play. The trade-off between online text navigation and print navigation often is speed of access versus grasp of the overall structure of the topic and text.

Not as obvious in informational texts are underlying structures or patterns such as *compare/contrast, cause/effect, problem/solution, sequence,* and *description.* These structures are found in most academic texts, and several will usually occur within the same text. They are often signaled by particular words and phrases such as *although, as a result, on the other hand,* and *if . . . then.* Here are some examples from the literary nonfiction science text *Guide to Savage Earth* by Trevor Day (2006):

> *Although scientists are getting better at predicting eruptions, they do not know what form an eruption will take* (p. 12).
>
> *Although tremors can occur anywhere, they are more frequent in earthquake zones* (p. 18).
>
> *The Apollo butterfly has adapted to the cool climate of mountains. If global warming makes its habitat too warm, it will have nowhere left to go* (p. 44).

The first two examples, using the signal word *although,* indicate a *comparison/contrast* pattern; the third, including the signal word *if,* indicates a *cause/effect* pattern.

As we move through the grades, Academic Language is a predominant feature of both narrative and informational texts. Academic Language is a more formal register of English and characterizes most informational texts, including literary nonfiction texts. Characterized by increasing vocabulary load and complexity of syntactic structure, each academic domain—science, math, social studies/history—has its own characteristic features in addition to sharing some features with other domains.

What Makes Texts Complex?

Common Core Connection

Reading Standards
for Literature and
Informational Text:
Range of Reading
and Level of Text
Complexity

What determines how "difficult" a text is to understand? Obvious reasons include unfamiliar vocabulary, long sentences, and lack of background knowledge on the part of the reader. When we look further, however, we see a more complex issue, beginning at the sentence level: In written texts, particularly as we move through the grades, sentences often tend to get longer and become more complex, much more so than in speech. Longer sentences do not always mean more difficulty in understanding, as we'll see, but usually they do. This is because longer sentences usually contain embedded clauses. The information these clauses represent, and the relationship of the clauses to the subject and verb, can become complex and challenge both short- and long-term memory. This is especially true for students who are not yet fluent readers and those with limited oral language exposure.

To describe sentence-, paragraph-, and text-level relationships, language scholars use the term **cohesion** (Freebody & Anderson, 1983; Halliday & Hasan, 1976), referring to how explicitly—or implicitly—the author has made connections among the information in the text. What is the relationship between the information in the text and the background knowledge a reader may bring to that text? A text with a high degree of cohesion reflects explicit connections among words and sentences, more concrete language, and repeats and/or summarizes important points along the way. Texts with low cohesion place more demands on readers, requiring them to infer more connections among the information.

Over the years, educators and educational researchers have attempted to assign complexity levels to texts (Fisher, Frey, & Lapp, 2012). Until the last couple of decades, such measures have been primarily

Quantitative, which means looking at words and sentences, and expressing difficulty in terms of *grade level* (see Chall & Dale, 1995; Fry, 1968; Stenner, Smith, Horiban, & Smith, 1987), or *Qualitative,* which involves considering texts in terms of enjoyment/interest, genre, multicultural representation, themes across texts, and quality of illustrations and how they work with the text—with the result of assigning different *levels* to texts (Fountas & Pinnell, 2005).

More recently, however, a more comprehensive approach to determining complexity blends and extends these two traditional approaches; in addition to quantitative information and

The Language of Your Instruction

Why the Emphasis on Text Complexity?

The argument for increasing students' experiences with complex or more challenging texts, and doing so earlier, goes like this: Over the last 50 years, the reading requirements and expectations at the college level have remained pretty much the same. During that same period, however, the difficulty or complexity of the reading material students have been expected to read in grades K–12 has *decreased* (Adams, 2010/2011; Williams, 2005). The result? There is a very large gap between the level of text complexity at which students are reading when they graduate from high school and the levels of text complexity they encounter as college freshmen. Researchers contend that this is one reason why, although more students are entering college than a half-century ago, more are struggling and dropping out than ever before.

A second reason for increasing the complexity of texts students read is the expectation at the college level that students will read many complex texts on their own, with little if any support, and be expected to deal with them critically in writing and discussion. Over the last few decades, along with the decline in text difficulty at the K–12 level, it's argued that there's also been a trend toward more support or scaffolding of students' engagements with texts. In itself, scaffolding is a good thing. However, many argue that this support is rarely withdrawn, and that students are seldom required to critically process and apply the content and ideas presented in texts. Thus, many students who graduate high school and go on to college or technical/trade professions have few experiences reading complex texts on their own.

That's the argument. The belief that the degree of support teachers offer may seldom be withdrawn may be more true at the elementary level, but it is less so at the middle and secondary levels. And the support offered at the elementary level may be due in part to *more* complex texts *actually* being introduced to many children at the primary level than was the case in previous generations (Hiebert, 2005; Hiebert & Sailors, 2008). With respect to *writing* across the grade levels it is indeed probably the case that students are less likely to be required to grapple with complex ideas than in the past.

qualitative information, we now consider the specific text and the reader (Chall, Bissex, Conrad, & Harris-Sharples, 1996). Let's elaborate a bit on each of these.

Quantitative Evaluation—This evaluation uses a readability measure or measures. These measures are based on aspects of the text, including

1) The frequency of the words in a text.—how often they occur in spoken and written English—and the length of sentences. Less-frequent words are usually less familiar, resulting in a greater vocabulary load; longer sentences usually require more cognitive energy to process, resulting in a more complex or "difficult" text.

2) The ways in which words and phrases are interconnected across an entire text—their repetition, reference, and depth of meaning (Graesser, McNamara, & Louwerse, 2011).

There is more to text complexity, of course, than assessments based on counting words and sentences. This is where knowledgeable educators step in. They analyze a text with a number of factors in mind that are not directly reflected in numbers–qualitative information and the specific text and the reader:

Qualitative Evaluation—Four factors need to be considered when evaluating a text from a qualitative perspective, and this perspective is in some ways similar to the traditional qualitative approach we just described, but also different:

1) *Levels of Meaning.* Is the text straightforward with a single level, or is it, for example, an allegory or satire that can operate at both literal and figurative levels?

2) *Structure.* Does the text follow a conventional layout with higher cohesion, or is the organization implicit with lower cohesion? For example: Is a narrative simple, with a linear sequence of events and a single point of view, or more complex, with flashbacks and changing points of view? Does an informational text have clearly labeled sections and graphics, or is it a domain-specific text with complex graphics?

3) *Language Conventionality and Clarity.* Is the language straightforward, contemporary, and conversational, or is it more figurative, formal, and characterized by general- or domain-specific Academic English? Does it reflect a different time period?

4) *Knowledge Demands.* Does the text assume readers may not have (a) many life experiences that are similar to or relate to the content of the text; (b) deep or more extensive cultural and literary experiences to support understanding of the text; or (c) content or domain knowledge? Or does the text assume that this background knowledge *is* present?

If you are a preservice teacher, you will find that many of the texts with which you will be expected to engage your students will have already been selected—they will be a part of the reading curriculum in your school and district. As you become more familiar with them and with these qualitative features, it will become easier over time to think explicitly about a text in terms of these features. Your reflection will be the foundation for thinking about how a particular text will work with a particular student—and what you may need to do to support that student's experience of the text. You will be exercising your own professional judgment in matching a particular text with particular students, and that is the third component for determining complexity:

Evaluation of the Specific Text and the Reader—The teacher must consider a particular student's background knowledge, reading developmental level, and motivation, all in relation to the purpose for reading the text and the tasks the reader will be expected or required to do while engaged with the text.

As we've noted, out of the three components, this third will be the one you'll be attending to most closely and over which you'll have most control. Table 2.1 will help you think about the intersection of your students' developmental stage and the types and levels of text you'll use in their reading instruction.

Children's and Young Adults' Literature Connection

Reading for Boys and Young Adult Males

Pulitzer prize–winning author and university professor Junot Díaz, of Dominican heritage, shared in an interview (2012):

> I loved Encyclopedia Brown as a kid. Donald Sobol passed recently, and that really brought it all back to me, how important his books were to my little self. I didn't learn to read until I was 7, so I missed out on the early stuff, jumped right to chapter books, right to Encyclopedia Brown. What I loved about Boy Detective Leroy Brown was that (1) he was unabashedly smart (smart was not cool when and where I grew up) and (2) his best friend was a girl, tough Sally Kimball, who was both Leroy's bodyguard and his intellectual equal. Sobol did more to flip gender scripts in my head than almost anybody in my early years.

As we think about bringing together specific texts and readers, we should acknowledge that so many young boys and young adult males unfortunately are not engaged by reading. The reasons are complex, and as Díaz implies, even if they are engaged, it may literally be dangerous to admit to it. We need to ensure that all the principles of motivation we presented in Chapter 1 are followed with all students, of course, but the need to intentionally engage young boys from the start, and older young adult males, is critical. The issue of social justice is particularly pressing here: Disproportionate numbers of male students of poverty and of color do not learn to read at necessary functional and academic levels.

So it is important to find and make available texts with which boys connect—even if they may still feel the need to hide the books deep within their backpacks.

Many young boys prefer informational texts over narrative texts, and you never know what author or titles may be the spark. For those who do prefer narratives, make available a range of titles—those reflecting the culture and language of these young readers while also making sure the "tried and true" authors and titles such as Encyclopedia Brown continue to be available, as Junot Díaz reminds us. The book Bright Beginnings for Boys: Engaging Young Boys in Active Literacy (2009) by Deborah Zambo and William Brozo is also an excellent resource.

For young adult males, you will find the work of Alfred Tatum and Jimmy Baca particularly compelling. Tatum's focus is on black male adolescents, and he shows how teachers can tap into a "textual lineage" that grounds and gives a transcendent meaning to their lives. So many of the books he discusses would be appropriate for the middle grades—for example, A Narrative of the Life of Frederick Douglass (1996). Baca's work (2010a, 2010b) addresses at-risk adolescents and relies primarily on his own experiences: From a life that led to five years in a maximum security prison—during which he discovered reading and began to write poetry—to a life of writing and working with at-risk youth.

For young adults, taking narratives inside themselves, living with them as they are read, then holding them close ever afterward will have an effect in ways that might not be measured in the short term. Over time, however, these texts may provide one of the few, but most potent, counterweights to the day-to-day struggles of the street that so many youth have to deal with.

The Developmental Model of Literacy

In Chapter 1, you were introduced to the five stages of literacy development: emergent, beginning, transitional, intermediate, and skillful. Each of these stages is partitioned into three phases: early, middle, and late. Table 2.1 summarizes the different types of knowledge that support literacy growth and development over the course of these stages.

Understanding the Developmental Continuum

Students build fluency and confidence through reading and writing texts at their developmental level, then stretching themselves with appropriately challenging material. They advance through each stage of literacy and advance toward the next stage by (1) exploring words and texts at their present level of understanding, then (2) applying their present knowledge to words and texts

TABLE 2.1 Developmental Stages of Literacy

Grade Range	Literacy Stage	Characteristics of Reading and Writing	Orthographic Knowledge	Text Example: Student Instructional Level	Text Level* Guided Reading	DRA	Lexile
PreK–Early 1st	**Early/Middle Emergent**	"Pretend" reading; pictures "contain" the story. Later, print "tells" the story and children will point to it as they "read" a memorized text.	Squiggles and letterlike forms	*My Dog* We can run.			NA
	Middle/Late Emergent	Messages are conveyed through scribbles, drawings, pretend writing, and random marks, including letter and number forms. Later, spells most obvious consonant sounds.	***ITM*** – "I went home." ***IY2MKNS*** – "I went to my Grandma's."	*Cat on the Mat* The cat sat on the mat.	A	1	
	Late Emergent/Early Beginning				B	2	
K–Early 1st	**Early Beginning**	Reading of new texts is word-by-word, out loud, eventually reading most words with a simple CVC short vowel pattern.	**Early Alphabetic/ Letter Name** bed – ***bd*** ship – ***sp*** float – ***ft*** drive – ***gf***	*Hide and Seek* "Yes, it's me!" said Puppy. "This is fun!" said Bear.	C	3	NA
1st	**Middle Beginning**	Writing is focused on letter–sound correspondence; majority of effort is directed toward spelling. Still uses pictures to communicate message. Labels pictures and writes simple stories to go with pictures.	**Middle Alphabetic/ Letter Name** bed – ***bad*** ship – ***shep*** float – ***fot*** drive – ***jriv***	*The Mitten* The bear was cold. The bear got into the warm mitten. *No Snacks, Jack!* Dad had a sandwich. Len and Kate had popcorn. Jack wanted snacks, too.	D E	4–8	NA

Grade Range	Literacy Stage	Characteristics of Reading and Writing	Orthographic Knowledge	Text Example: Student Instructional Level	Text Level*		
					Guided Reading	DRA	Lexile
1st–Early 2nd	Late Beginning		**Late Alphabetic/ Letter Name** bed – correct ship – correct stick – *stik* float – *flot* drive – *driv*	*Curious George and the Newspapers* George rode his bike down the street. He gave the newspapers to all the people. *A Snowy Day* (Informational) Snow is made from water in the sky. In winter, the water freezes and becomes snow.	F G	10–12	200–400
Late 1st– Early 2nd	Early Transitional	Rate increases, moving toward fluency/expression; oral reading begins to sound more "natural." Beginning to independently monitor reading and employ strategies to self-correct reading.	**Early Within Word Pattern** Spells most single-syllable short vowel words correctly; uses digraphs and two-letter blends at the beginning of words correctly; attempts long vowel markers: when – correct jump – correct float – *flote* train – *trane*	*Bear's Tail* (Folktale) Bear liked to talk. Bear talked about the sky and the snow. He talked about the lake and the trees. But most of all, Bear loved to talk about his long, brown tail. *Tian Tian, a Giant Panda* (Informational) "This is Tian Tian. He is a giant Panda. Most giant pandas have black and white fur like Tian Tian."	H I	14–16	
2nd	Middle Transitional	Students have increased stamina. Writing is longer. Ideas are developed more fully with greater depth in expression and detail.	**Middle Within Word Pattern** float – correct train – correct stick – correct fright – *fright* table – *tabul*	*Charlie Needs a Cloak* Charlie was a shepherd. He had a cozy house, a big hat, a crook, and a flock of fat sheep. *Nate the Great and the Stolen Base* I, Nate the Great, am a detective. Sometimes I'm a baseball player. This morning I was a detective *and* a baseball player.	J K	18–20	300–600

TABLE 2.1 (*Continued*)

Grade Range	Literacy Stage	Characteristics of Reading and Writing	Orthographic Knowledge	Text Example: Student Instructional Level	Text Level* Guided Reading	DRA	Lexile
2nd–mid-4th	**Late Transitional**	By the end of this stage, most reading is done silently. Growth has occurred in different forms of writing. Revision and editing become more integral to the writing process.	**Late Within Word Pattern** bright - correct spoil - *spoyle* chewed - *chood* switch - *swich* smudge - *smuge* color - *coler*	*Come Back, Amelia Bedelia* "Good morning," said Amelia Bedelia. "I will have some cereal with my coffee this morning," said Mrs. Rogers. "All right," said Amelia Bedelia. Mrs. Rogers went into the dining room. *Coyote and Rabbit—A Tale from the Southwest* Coyote was very excited about what he had heard. He had once chased Rabbit up that canyon; but then Rabbit had made a leap sideways, and he had gone through a hole too small for Coyote to get through. Now Coyote could try this again. This time the small hole would be gone.	L M	24–28	
3rd	**Early Intermediate**	Reads with good fluency and expression; prefers silent reading as it is now faster than reading aloud; students self-select reading materials and can independently prepare for literature discussions. Written responses are more sophisticated and critical. Begins to explore longer pieces of writing in a variety of genres. Revision and editing come to play bigger roles. Begins to write for a wider variety of purposes, including note taking and outlining. Uses author's craft techniques such as dialogue, special print, and metaphor.	**Early Syllables & Affixes** Spells most single-syllable words correctly, makes some errors at the juncture of syllables and in unaccented syllables. crawl - *crall* shopping - *shoping* amazing - *amazzing* serving - *surving* bottle - *botel*	*Sidewalk Story* She jumped the last two steps, yanked the front door open, plunked herself down on the wide brownstone steps, and leaned against the heavy-looking black metal railing. She touched her ears. "I'm never going to get real gold earrings. Never!" *Dad's Garden* "What are you laughing about, Dad?" he asked. "David," said his father, "did you know your homework is about some plants that I've been working on recently? It looks like the two of us are finally going to work together." They both got caught up in the lesson. They read and talked about habitats and species.	N O P	30–36	500–800

Grade Range	Literacy Stage	Characteristics of Reading and Writing	Orthographic Knowledge	Text Example: Student Instructional Level	Text Level*		
					Guided Reading	DRA	Lexile
4th	**Middle Intermediate**		**Middle Syllables & Affixes** correspond - *coraspond* damage - *damige* parading - *peraiding* fortunate - *forchinet* opposition - *opacizion* civilization - *civalasation*	*Mysteries from Long Ago* Then about fifty years ago, scientists found dinosaur footprints on an island in the cold Arctic, near the North Pole. This was the first piece of evidence that dinosaurs lived in cold places. Now scientists believed that dinosaurs could have lived all over Earth—not just in warm areas. What they didn't know was how these dinosaurs were able to survive in these cold places.	Q R S	40–44	600–900
5th	**Middle/Late Intermediate to Early Skilled/Proficient**		**Late Syllables & Affixes** dominance - *dominace* opposition - *opisision* criticize - *critisize* civilization - *civilazation*	*The River Kept Rising* A system of levees—huge, sloped walls of packed earth—had been built to keep the river within its banks. However, by April of 1927, the storm-swollen Mississippi threatened to spill over the levees or wash portions away.	T U V	50	
6th	**Late Intermediate to Middle Skilled/Proficient**	Reads accurately and with appropriate rate, tone, and expression; reads faster silently than aloud; reads a variety of genres, including textbooks; reads for a variety of purposes. Writing includes a variety of genres, including report writing in content areas; writing is longer and sophisticated; evidence of craft moves; students write literary analyses.	**Early Derivational Relations** Spells most high-frequency words correctly; makes few spelling errors; may misspell low-frequency multisyllabic words derived from Greek and Latin. confidence - *confedence* emphasize - *emphesize* commotion - *comotion* monarchy - *monarchie* opposition - *oposition*	*Louise Arner Boyd and Glaciers* In 1926, Boyd was finally ready. Her first trip to the Arctic was the culmination of months of training. Boyd hired a boat called the *Hobby* that was specially equipped to navigate the Arctic ice.	W X Y	60	800–1050

(Continued)

TABLE 2.1 *(Continued)*

Grade Range	Literacy Stage	Characteristics of Reading and Writing	Orthographic Knowledge	Text Example: Student Instructional Level	Text Level*		
					Guided Reading	DRA	Lexile
7th – 8th	**Early Skilled/ Proficient to Middle Skilled/Proficient**	Extends potential to read deeply in different disciplines and types of texts. This in turn extends the ability to think critically. Critical thinking is extended in writing. The process of writing becomes one that in turn extends thinking—the full reciprocity of reading different types of texts and writing different types of texts is developed.	**Middle** **Derivational Relations** commotion - correct opposition - correct circumference – *circumfrence* chlorine - *clorine* dominance - *dominence* succession - *succesion*	*Cathedral* In order to construct the vaulted ceiling a wooden scaffold was erected connecting the two walls of the choir one hundred and thirty feet above ground. On the scaffolding wooden centerings like those used for the flying buttresses were installed. They would support the arched stone ribs until the mortar was dry, at which times the ribs could support themselves.	W–Z	70–80	850– 1150

* These are the most common approaches for determining the level of texts. For many years, *Guided Reading Levels* (Fountas & Pinnell, 1996, 2001) and *Developmental Reading Assessment (iDRA)* levels (Beaver & Carter, 2005) have been the standard in most schools. More recently, *Lexile Levels* have been emphasized (Lexile Framework for Reading. 2013). They are the primary leveling criteria used by the Common Core State Standards, so you are much more likely today to see reference to Lexile Levels in the consideration of selecting appropriate texts for students—at both their instructional levels and their "stretch" levels. It is important to note that the Lexile Level ranges in this table more closely approximate developmentally appropriate texts for students. You will be encouraged, however, also to engage your students with texts at their Lexile "stretch" levels (Lexile Framework for Reading, 2013) because of the emphasis on text complexity in the Common Core State Standards (2013).

Representative texts for Lexile Levels are:

300L – Bridwell, N. (1986). *Clifford's Manners*. Scholastic.

400L – Lobel, A. (1972). *Frog and Toad Are Friends*. Harper.

500L – Cole, J. (1992). *The Magic Schoolbus inside the Earth*. Scholastic.

600L – Spinelli, J. (2004) *Stargirl*. Laurel Leaf

700L – Howe, J. (2006). *Bunnicula: A Rabbit Tale of Mystery*. Atheneum.

800L – Collodi, C. (2010). *The Adventures of Pinocchio*. Aeterna.

900L – Appleton, V. (2009). *Tom Swift in the Land of Wonders*. Book Jungle.

1000L – Sewell, A. (2011). *Black Beauty*. CreateSpace Independent Publishing Platform.

1100 – Austen, J. (2013). *Pride and Prejudice*. Collector's Library.

that are characteristic of the next stage of development. This back-and-forth between current understandings and future understandings on the edge of the "zone" is the soul of literacy learning. If instruction is targeted at only the upper point in this dynamic, however, then growth will be delayed, difficult, and most likely frustrated (Cobin, Templeton, & Burner, 2011; Harre, 1984).

Movement through stages is not like rolling down a track, picking up and piling on information. Rather, with each new stage of language and literacy development, information and understandings are rearranged and reorganized (Clay, 1991; Ehri, 1997; Kohlberg, 1987; Templeton & Bear, 1992). For example, understanding flashbacks in narratives builds on—and in the process further develops—prior understandings about characters, point of view, setting, and episode structure. It may be too much to expect many second-graders to infer the moral of a fable they have tried to read on their own, especially when the fable is at a level of complexity that is beyond their instructional or developmental level in reading. Through their teacher's guidance, however, they may be able to deal with these more abstract ideas when the fable is read *to* them and discussed.

Literacy is based on oral language, but it does not simply record and reflect oral language. A theme we have begun to develop and will continue to explore is that oral language and literacy exchange roles as children develop. While oral language is a foundation for literacy, literacy later becomes the foundation for further development in oral language as well as in thought. We'll trace the evolution of this relationship between oral language and literacy in the context of each stage of literacy development.

Emergent Reading and Writing (Preschool to Early First Grade)

During the emergent stage of development, children learn the functions and elements of print. Their oral language is the foundation for this developing knowledge, and toward the end of this stage, their developing knowledge about print will give them new insights into and awareness of oral language.

Oral language develops at a truly impressive rate during the preschool years (Clark, 2003; Karmilov & Karmilov-Smith, 2001; Tomasello, 2008). During her first year, an infant develops the ability to produce many of the significant phonemes in her native language. Over the next two years, her **expressive vocabulary** increases significantly, averaging between 1,000 and 3,000 words. These are the words she uses in her own communication. The child's **receptive vocabulary**—words she at some level understands when she hears them in context—will be much, much larger (Goswami, 2001). By the beginning of kindergarten, the child will have an average of between 4,000 to 6,000 words in her expressive vocabulary.

As with language development in general, the number and range of words children learn depends on both nature (children's biological endowment) and nurture (the number and type of experiences and the accompanying language in the children's home, daycare, and preschool). It's important to emphasize the importance of nurture. In particular, children of poverty face significant challenges. When they begin school, perhaps their most significant educational challenge is the vocabulary gap and what it reflects. This is a gap associated much, much more with their exposure to language in their environments than with nature. A classic series of studies (Hart & Risley, 1995) found that, by the age of 3, children from high-poverty backgrounds have heard fewer than one-third the number of words as children in professional homes, and only one-half the number of words as children in working-class homes. This gap exists regardless of race or ethnicity. Strikingly, in the Hart and Risley studies, the quality of language spoken by 3-year-old children from professional homes was richer than that of *adults* in welfare homes. This underscores a critical aspect of the role of adult caregiver interaction in young children's

Chapter 6 addresses instruction for Emergent Learners

Common Core Connection

Language Standards: Vocabulary Acquisition and Use

language development: It's not just the number of words heard that makes such a difference but also (1) the richer syntax with which those words are expressed, as well as (2) the greater length of the conversational exchanges between child and adult. All of this adds up to a richer network of underlying concepts that such children have developed.

A hallmark of language learning throughout the preschool years and beyond is the tendency to overgeneralize an aspect of language, especially vocabulary and syntax. This is a natural part of almost all learning processes. For example, the word *dog* may be associated with a large furry animal and this word might then be used to refer to *all* furry animals—cats, horses, and bears. Similarly, the word *car* or *truck* might mean *any* sort of moving vehicle. These overgeneralizations persist throughout the early childhood years until the child's vocabulary grows to include more precise labels for concepts. When young children are learning inflectional morphemes in English, they overgeneralize: When his grandma picked him up after his first day at preschool, Ansel excitedly told her, "I *see'd* a lot of kids today!" English has a number of strong ("irregular") verbs like *saw*, and they will be learned later on. In the meantime, though, despite Ansel having heard the verb "saw" used numerous times, the power of pattern and rule won out, so his brain picked up the pattern or rule in which English past-tense verbs are usually created: simply add /ed/.

The more words that young children learn, the more they need to focus on the sounds within the words in order to store and use them effectively. Awareness of speech itself, apart from what it means, is referred to as **phonological awareness**. This awareness is essential in learning to read (Lonigan, Anthony, Burgess, & Phillips, 2000; Neuman & Dickinson, 2011; Wagner, Torgeson, & Rashotte, 1994), and begins with children's sensitivity to syllables and rhymes. Nursery rhymes and rhythmic texts, including songs and jingles, help children become aware of syllables in words. For instance, a preschooler or kindergartner will be able to clap the syllables in words like *yell* and *yellow,* recognizing that the second has more "beats" or syllables than the first, and *yellowing* has even more. These rhymes and rhythms are playful and often nonsensical. Especially when accompanied by music, rhymes and rhythms help children memorize these short texts. This memory for the text supports children's revisiting the text—*telling* the memorized poem or singing the memorized song to the page is the foundation for becoming aware of word units, and later, for matching letters on the page to sounds in speech.

Rhyming words in texts also help children develop sensitivity to sounds smaller than a syllable. They do this in two ways. First, rhyming words stand out because they are part of language structures that are rhythmic and because the words sound similar. Second, in order to tell rhyming words apart, a child has to attend to their only contrasting features: They end the same way, but they *begin* differently. This beginning sound is therefore highlighted, so children gradually begin to attend to it. This is children's first conscious analysis of a spoken word into its component sound parts—the beginning element (usually a consonant) and the rest of the word (the vowel and what follows it). These two elements are the **onset** and the **rime**: An onset is the initial consonant sound or sounds in a single syllable (/*b*/, /*dr*/, /*spl*/) and the rime is the vowel and any consonants that follow it. In the word *bed*, /*b*/ is the onset and /*ĕd*/ is the rime. In the word *drive*, /*dr*/ is the onset and /*īv*/ is the rime.

Learning *about* words—what they are and how their printed form corresponds to their spoken form—will take time. Although young children often delight their parents by pointing to the Target™ sign and squealing "Target!," they are not "reading" the word in a conventional sense. Well before they can read in a conventional way, children become aware of print in their environment and they can recognize many signs, symbols, labels and logos. Parents and caregivers help young children "read" these words by pointing to them and saying their names. Other times, children pick these words up simply by context. Our own children were quick to notice the word *Cheerios* on their morning cereal box and the word *STOP* on the sign at the end of the street.

Common Core Connection

Reading Standards: Foundational Skills – Phonological Awareness

Strategies for the Classroom

Scaffolding Young Children's Speech Discrimination

It is not unusual for children in the preschool years to have difficulty producing all the sounds of English accurately, particularly sounds that are similar such as /v/ and /f/, and those that are articulated in a similar way such as /t/ and /d/ or /k/ and /g/. If you've spent time with young children, you have also noticed that some sounds—like /r/ and /l/, /sh/ and /th/, and /sp/ and /tr/, can be especially difficult for them to articulate. Perhaps you have even heard young children pronounce words *rabbit, three,* and *spaghetti* as *wabbit, free,* and *pasghetti* or even *busghetti.* While these are rather endearing approximations, they are also grand opportunities to fine-tune young children's sensitivity to the English sound system.

You will gently scaffold children's speech discrimination by providing accurate models of pronunciation. This is also a good time to extend their language practice, too. For example:

Child: I want pasghetti.

*Adult: You would like **spaghetti** for lunch? (Wait for a reply.) Now you try, **spa-ghet-ti, spaghetti** (segmenting the word into syllables and emphasizing the /sp/ sound at the beginning and then blending it back together). Let's make **spaghetti** with marinara sauce. What ingredients will we need to get started?*

Sometimes young children omit sounds they cannot produce on their own, as in *gandma* for *grandma* or *tore*

for *store* (Byrnes & Wasik, 2008). Again, it is useful to provide supportive corrections: "It can be tricky to hear and say the 'gr' in **gr**andma. Do you hear it? **Grrr**-andma. Now you try: **gr**andma. Nice." (Or "Good try!") "What will you do with your grandma this weekend?"

While it is important for children to develop correct pronunciations, you will want to be thoughtful in selecting which words and how many you correct, because it is not practical or appropriate to address *every* developmentally based mispronunciation. Selecting words that children use quite frequently in their conversations can be most valuable: names, familiar objects, or common places in the school or home. Further, your corrections should feel natural, positive, and not too disruptive to the conversation. Sometimes they are even as subtle as this:

Child: I got an aminal at the fair.

*Teacher: Great! You got an **animal** at the fair! (Or, What kind of **animal** did you get at the fair?)*

It is helpful to remember that most native English speakers don't master all of these speech production skills until around age 7 or 8, so some variability in pronunciations is to be expected throughout much of the preschool and early elementary school years, and even longer for English learners and some other children.

Young children and preschoolers become aware of print in their environment as early as 2 years old (Ferreiro & Teberosky, 1982; Strickland & Snow, 2002). From these early exposures to print and other symbols in their environment (for example, traffic lights, crosswalk signals, the "golden arches"), they begin to realize that print and symbols represent spoken words and that they convey meaning. Recognizing these signs and symbols gives young children a sense of pride and accomplishment. This recognition, though, is based on the context in which these signs and symbols occur; if we show them a word out of context, they usually are not able to identify it (Hiebert & Raphael, 1998). In time, they may identify a word both in and out of context by remembering its shape. For instance, *turkey* might be recognized because the word dips down at the end. Children's word reading at this early stage has been described as "logographic" (Frith, 1985)—it's much like reading or recognizing a logo, with very little if any analysis of the word or logo itself. Words in children's environment, including their peers' and family members' names, will become some of their first sight words—words they are able to identify automatically when they see them. By the end of the emergent stage of development, most children will have acquired about 20 words they know by sight.

When young children attend to the printed page, they see it quite differently than we do. Where we see a coherent presentation of letters, words, and obvious spaces, emergent children see pretty much a jumble of squiggles. The order that print represents emerges over time—as a child watches a caregiver's moving finger pass over the lines as she or he reads to the child,

> **Common Core Connection**
>
> Reading Standards: Foundational Skills – Print Concepts

moving in harmony with a voice that will say the same thing over and over when that same page is read again and again. The words on the page will gradually emerge, highlighted by the spaces that mark a group of letters that have a beginning and an end. While becoming phonologically aware begins with syllables, rhymes, and beginning consonants, analyzing speech into segments *smaller* than onsets and rimes requires instruction in beginning reading (Henderson, 1981; Ziegler & Goswami, 2005). As we'll explore in Chapter 6, how you talk about and model how print works for young children will support their dawning awareness, over time, of the pieces of spoken language that print represents.

Emergent children's writing development supports their developing understanding of how print represents language. More specifically, their writing will support their awareness of how letters can represent sound and help them learn about printed words. Regardless of culture and language, all young children begin writing with back-and-forth and circular scribbling (Ferreiro & Teberosky, 1982). Over time, their writing takes on the features of the writing system to which they are exposed—its directionality, its characters, its spacing. As these language-specific features develop, children learn that writing serves a symbolic purpose, that it somehow represents language and meaning (Puranik & Lonigan, 2011; Tolchinsky, 2003). Intriguingly, many children go through a phase in which the length of their writing is also associated with the size of the object they are writing about (Ferreiro & Teberosky, 1982). For example, the word *dinosaur* (refer to Figure 1.1) has a lot of "letters," whereas the word *mouse* would have only two or three.

Common Core Connection

Reading Standards: Foundational Skills – Phonological Awareness

As they learn about and write the letters of the alphabet and are engaged in print-related activities and experiences, children will eventually match up some sounds in speech with letters. For example, as part of her "Elephant Story," Lee, a kindergartner, wrote *PPLSMETSK* ("The people saw him eating strawberry cake") (Bear, Invernizzi, Templeton, & Johnston, 2012). Lee has represented the sounds that "popped out" for her, usually at the beginning or ending of syllables, but her writing does not reflect all of the sounds or the boundaries of words. She doesn't yet have a concept of word in text, but she is certainly well on her way. Words will now begin to "stand still" for Lee, so that she can begin to pay attention to more than just a few sounds (Morris, Bloodgood, Lomax, & Perney, 2003; Ouellette & Sénéchal, 2008).

Beginning Conventional Reading and Writing (Kindergarten to Early Grade 2)

As children experience different language contexts—the home, the classroom, the playground, friends' homes, big box stores, and more—they begin to realize that language can be used for a variety of purposes and that it takes a variety of forms as well. As teachers, you will help your students successfully negotiate the many forms and functions of oral and written language, including the "discourse" of schooling. During this time, children's reasoning during and after their reading is primarily of the "remembering" type (see Figure 2.2). They are, however, beginning to develop conscious and deliberate abilities to go beyond this basic level as they respond to stories and informational texts that are read *to* them.

Chapter 7 addresses instruction for Beginning Learners

Not too long after writing her "Elephant Story," Lee wrote: *KNYE ETSNOKNS* ("Can we eat snow cones?"). What's different between this writing and Lee's writing in the "Elephant Story" is that the sounds that are "popping" for Lee are primarily beginning and ending sounds in words. She has what we call a "rudimentary" *concept of word in text,* because she is now aware of and trying to spell the sounds that define the boundaries of a word. Although the representation of vowels is spotty, she is sensitive to most of the consonants. The foundational development in language and print awareness that occurred during the emergent stage supports beginners, such as Lee, in further critical development in language awareness. Such beginners have become *letter name–alphabetic* spellers.

Lee's spelling is another way of telling us that she is "reading the spaces" between words. We can also see this when she is reading a memorized text and gets off track. It takes her a few seconds to get back on track when **fingerpoint reading**, often involving going back to the beginning of the line or sentence she is reading and then reading up to the word that threw her off.

How does beginners' awareness of words as units in print develop further, as well as their understanding of how the letters within the words represent all the sounds in the word? The concept of word in text—the child's ability to point to each word accurately as she reads lines of memorized text—will lead to *full* phonemic awareness: the ability consciously to attend to every consonant and vowel sound within a syllable. As you continue to model reading for children in appropriate texts, you are also involving them in reading and rereading texts that they are able to access themselves (see Table 2.1). Together, with their explorations of letters and sounds as well as their writing, these experiences lead to their awareness of the middle of words—the vowel letters. Their thinking goes something like this:

Young beginning readers know that letters capture sounds and do so in a linear, left-to-right way. They expect this because this is how you've shown them how writing "works": left to right. They have learned about the names and many of the sounds of these letters. As they write and spell words, they pronounce, slowly, what they want to write down. They listen for sounds and think of the letters that represent those sounds.

A child wishing to write the sentence *My bear ate some honey* may sound it out this way:

MY BR AT SIM HINE

Were he to see this sentence in print, however, it may appear to him as follows (the Xs represent the parts of the words that his brain does not have enough orthographic knowledge to process):

MY BXXR ATX SOMX HONEX

When he reads each word, his brain is scanning, left to right, each letter in the word. The brain "notices" the letters that the child's orthographic knowledge allows him to understand. While his reading is quite slow, he is able to decode the words correctly because *context* (the story and accompanying illustrations) provide additional support for the letters he correctly decodes.

Over time, however, decoding becomes a bit easier because children are seeing lots of words in print and in their reading. And, because you have chosen texts appropriately, they are seeing words with simple spelling patterns that fit their expectations of how letters and sounds match up. You're helping them read and learn about words that have a simple consonant-vowel-consonant structure; these are important because they make sense in terms of their own ideas about how the system works: *c – a – t*. You're also, however, helping them learn to read words that do *not* match up with their theory: words such as *bike*, which they've likely been spelling *bik* since it fits with their left-to-right letter–sound match-up theory.

For example, in Table 2.1 the sample text that would be appropriate for a child in the middle of the beginning stage of development contains two two-syllable words—*sandwich* and *popcorn*—that the child may be able to figure out, confirming with picture clues. It also contains the name *Kate*, containing a long-vowel pattern that the child will come to see more often in her reading. She can learn these words as sight words, and over time their spelling patterns will begin to be incorporated into her underlying orthographic knowledge. Toward the end of the beginning stage, children will have built up a sight vocabulary of approximately 150 words (Bear, Templeton, Helman, & Baren, 2003).

Alejanda, whose home language is Spanish, wrote about her sister at the end of her first-grade year. Her writing in Figure 2.6 illustrates her level of orthographic knowledge—she is in the

Common Core Connection

Language Standards: Conventions of Standard English

Common Core Connection

Reading Standards: Foundational Skills – Phonics and Word Recognition

FIGURE 2.6 **Reader/Writer in the Late Beginning Stage**

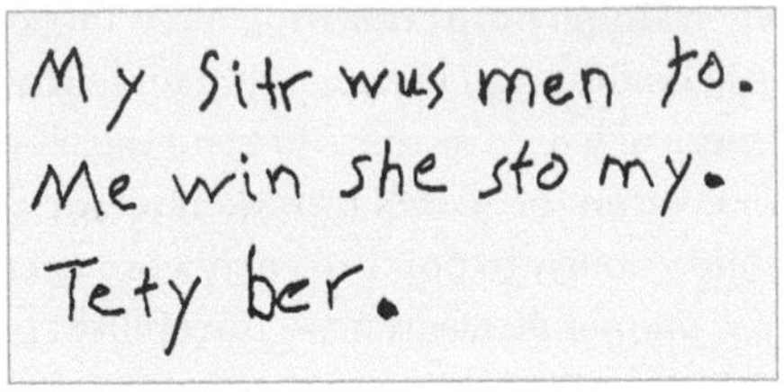

late beginning stage of development. Alejanda is clearly applying her knowledge of short vowel spellings, even when incorrect from the standpoint of conventional spelling *(wus/was, sitr/sister)*. She also has a rule about where periods go—at the end of every line!

> My sister was mean to.
> Me when she stole my.
> Teddy bear.

Transitional Reading and Writing (Late Grade 1 to Mid-Grade 4)

Common Core Connection

Language Standards: Vocabulary Acquisition and Use

As with earlier developmental stages, it is so very important that teachers continue to engage and extend children's oral language throughout the school day. Oral language competence—syntax, vocabulary, and awareness of a wider range of contexts and discourses—will be the necessary and critical foundation for their comprehension during their reading (Duke & Carlisle, 2011; Hulme, Muter, Snowling, & Stevenson, 2004). In both vocabulary growth and syntactic development, children's oral language during the transitional stage grows quite significantly. It's estimated that at this time children begin to acquire, on average, around 3,000 new words a year (Beck & McKeown, 1991), most of which are learned incidentally, without direct instruction. The children's syntactic growth reflects the language of the adults around them and the language they pick up from books, both those read to them and the ones they are reading themselves. The material they are now reading stretches them appropriately, requiring more advanced vocabulary and more developed syntax. In fact, children's syntactic knowledge will come to play an important role in supporting their comprehension of texts during this developmental stage, as well as forever after in their development (Roth, Speech, & Cooper, 2002; Storch & Whitehurst, 2002).

Chapter 8 addresses instruction for Transitional Learners

Transitional readers are moving toward a better balance between word identification and comprehension during their reading, and this may also be reflected in their writing. The process of writing is becoming more fluent, because the children are better able to sustain the idea or topic about which they are writing as they encode that information—through word choice, sentence structure, and conventions such as spelling and punctuation.

Children's reasoning abilities grow as well, reflecting their experiences with oral and written language: they develop competence in summarizing, analyzing, and generalizing beyond what is read. Whereas beginning readers are starting to evidence these abilities, it is primarily in response to books read *to* them and guided discussion by the teacher. Transitional children, on the other hand, are able to apply these reasoning abilities during their own reading as well as afterward (Barone, 1989; Madura, 1995, 1998).

Common Core Connection

Writing Standards: Range of Writing

Figure 2.7 is second-grader Mandy's version of her "Terrible Day," modeled on Judith Viorst's *Alexander and the Terrible, Horrible, No Good, Very Bad Day* (1972), a classic that has delighted

FIGURE 2.7 **Transitional Child's Writing**

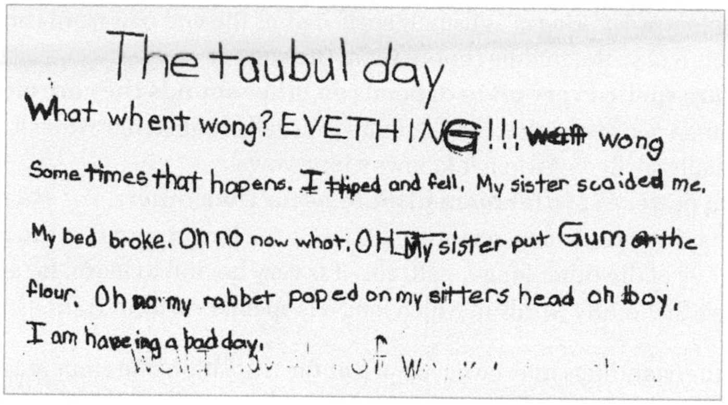

and continues to delight every new generation. Mandy's writing shows us what she is learning about words and texts—it illustrates features of transitional-stage children's word knowledge and developing sensitivity to text and different genres. Mandy has crafted a humorous narrative, using capitalization and punctuation for emphasis.

The Terrible Day

What went wrong? EVERYTHING!!! went wrong
Sometimes that happens. I tripped and fell. My sister scared me.
My bed broke. Oh no now what. OH My sister put Gum on the
Floor. Oh no my rabbit pooped on my sitter's head oh boy.
I am having a bad day.

Common Core Connection

Language Standards: Conventions of Standard English

During this transitional stage, children's orthographic knowledge reflects their developing understanding of *within word patterns.* Their sight vocabularies have grown to include between 250 and 400 words, and many of these words have silent letters—words that end in *e* (*kite, rope*), for example, and those that spell long vowel sounds with other silent letters (*rain, boat*). Children start using these spelling patterns in their writing—they're getting to the point where it makes sense to them that some letters do not make sounds. For example, they may write *snaik* for *snake, coame* for *comb.* Such spellings reveal a very important insight: The students have learned that chunks or *groups* of letters can work together to correspond to sound—they have discovered the pattern layer in English spelling (Ehri, 2005). Words that they had been reading correctly but misspelling, they are now learning to spell. Misspellings often reflect this pattern knowledge. The children are "using but confusing" particular patterns they are learning—for example, Mandy's *flour* for *floor*—but this process is actually critical in the learning process: Through their writing, they are "exercising" their developing word knowledge. In Chapter 8, we will discuss how you may encourage children to apply what they are learning while at the same time respond to these efforts that result in misspellings.

Another challenge awaits children at this transitional stage, however: How will they learn that sometimes a long *a* is spelled like *tail* and sometimes like *tale*? How will they learn about the same sounds being spelled with different letters? Using the type of information discussed earlier in this chapter, their teacher will guide them through the following understandings:

• **Answer the question: "Is the word a homophone?"** These words are spelled differently because they mean different things.

- **How sounds are spelled very often depends on where they are within a word**. Looking at homophones more closely, children will learn how words such as *say* and *rain* reveal that, in single-syllable words, "long *a*" is usually spelled *ay* at the end of a word (but rarely in the middle) and often *ai* in the middle (but never at the end).
- **How sounds are spelled very often depends on other sounds they are close to**. Words such as *ridge* and *cage* reveal that the /j/ sound is usually spelled *dge* when it follows a short vowel, and usually spelled *ge* when it follows a long vowel.
- **Some spelling patterns are far more likely to occur than others**. For example, there are more words that have the *a*-consonant-*e* pattern for the long *a* sound in the middle of a syllable than for any of the other long-*a* patterns. It is very helpful to learn, for example, that there just aren't that many words in which long *a* is spelled *ea*, as in *great*.

All of these understandings may be developed at the transitional literacy stage. Importantly, as teachers support children's learning of spelling patterns in single-syllable words at this stage, they are also showing them how to use that knowledge to decode longer words that they encounter in reading. For instance, learning about *ai* in *paint* and *train* helps children figure out words such as *contain* and *exclaim*.

Common Core Connection

Reading Standards: Foundational Skills – Phonics and Word Recognition

How are children's brains *reading* words at this stage? They scan the beginning of a word or syllable, and the vowel and what follows the brain picks up a spelling *pattern* and processes it as a single unit or chunk: cup = *c-up*, damp = *d-amp*, contain = *c-on / t-ain*.

We help children develop a *flexible* approach as they apply their growing phonics knowledge to unfamiliar words they encounter in their reading. For example, let's say a child runs into the word *heavy* in this sentence: *Kenny didn't know how heavy the bundle was until he grabbed it*. The child notices that *heavy* contains the vowel pair *ea*. He's learned words such as *eat, each*, and *mean*, in which *ea* stands for the long *e* sound. He tries /hēvy/, which doesn't sound like a word he knows and doesn't make sense. But then he tries the short *e* sound, which of course does make sense. This is the flexible strategy we teach children to apply.

Common Core Connection

Reading Standards: Foundational Skills – Fluency

Because they are able to process words in print more economically now, picking up patterns as opposed to individual letters, *fluency* develops significantly. This involves the children's rate, accuracy, and prosody. Recall that prosody is the natural, more rhythmic flow of speech, which is an important aspect of "reading with expression." In fact, as fluency develops in these transitional readers, it may in turn support the comprehension of more challenging texts—primarily through the reading and rereading of such texts with appropriate expression (Schwanenflugel et al., 2006; Stahl, Heubach, & Holcomb, 2005).

Intermediate Reading and Writing (Grade 3 through Grade 8)

Chapter 9 addresses instruction for Intermediate Learners

We sometimes hear in education about a significant spurt of overall brain growth occurring during the intermediate school years, and that this corresponds to a significant advance in cognitive development. The reality is not quite this simplistic (Johnson, Munakata, & Gilmore, 2008). There *is* a significant increase in the growth and complexity of connections within different areas of the brain. Part of this development is due to *nature* (it is "wired in") but so much of it is because of *nurture*. Teachers can help students at this level unleash their potential to exercise some rather striking powers of reasoning. They can help students see the world anew and consciously reflect on it in ways previously unavailable to them. At a very basic level, this type of instruction leads to the establishment of increasing neural connections in the brain. Students become more adept at applying the higher levels of reasoning in Figure 2.2, particularly *evaluating* and *synthesizing*.

Brian's revision of his informational composition in Figure 2.8, which he will edit before publication, reflects both descriptive and compare/contrast patterns. It reveals that he has a good sense of how this type of informational text is structured. Some of Brian's misspellings are those we would expect from transitional learners *(shaps, nead, spead)*, but these can be addressed by targeting these specific vowel patterns in mini-lessons. For the majority of spelling instruction, most of Brian's word study at this level will address patterns in words of more than one syllable (*sistoms, metle, rememberd*). He is a *syllables and affixes* speller. As we will note in our discussion of assessment in Chapter 4 and in later developmental chapters, it is important to point out the value of errors. They provide important insight into what students are learning and how they are making sense of incoming information about words and texts (Bahr, Silliman, & Berninger, 2009; Bear et al., 2012). Using Brian as an example, if he knew he was going to be held accountable for spelling all words correctly in all phases of his writing—or if he received the message that errors were always "wrong"—he would not take risks in his writing or in his reading. We wouldn't see the depth of detail as Brian communicates his "expert" knowledge or the richness of vocabulary as he shares the domain-specific vocabulary about planes, jets, and bombers.

Common Core Connections

Writing Standards: Text Types and Purposes; Production and Distribution of Writing

Common Core Connection

Language Standards: Conventions of Standard English

FIGURE 2.8 Intermediate Reader and Writer

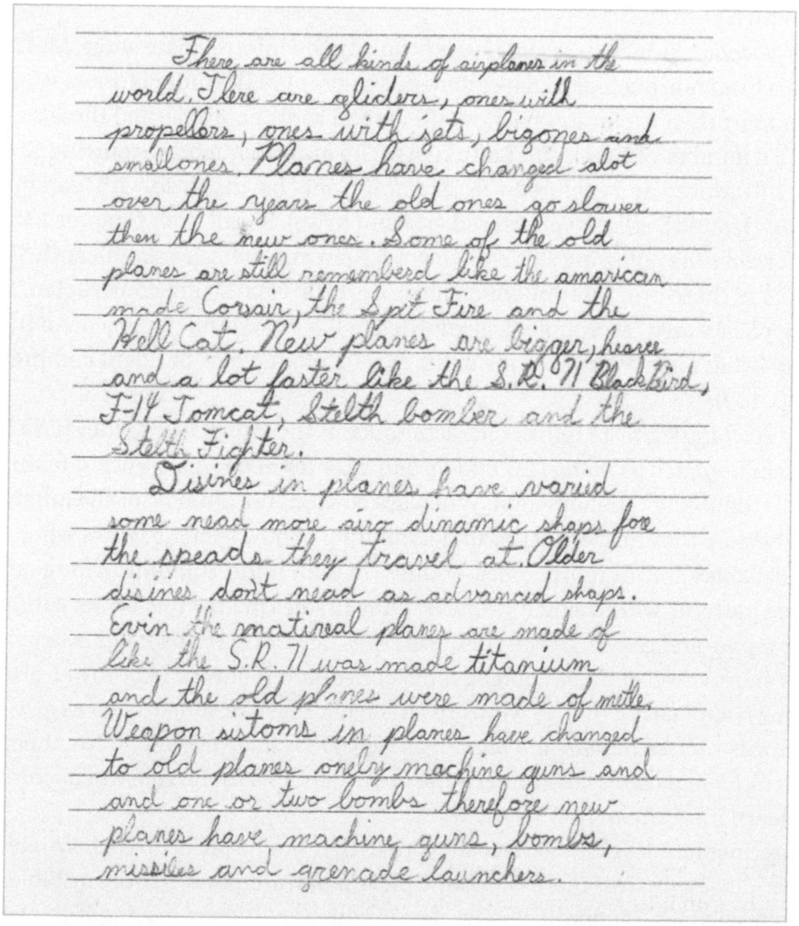
There are all kinds of airplanes in the world. There are gliders, ones with propellors, ones with jets, bigones and smallones. Planes have changed alot over the years the old ones go slower then the new ones. Some of the old planes are still rememberd like the american made Corsair, the Spit Fire and the Hell Cat. New planes are bigger, heaver and a lot faster like the S.R. 71 BlackBird, F-14 Tomcat, Stelth bomber and the Stelth Fighter.

Disines in planes have varied some nead more airo dinamic shaps for the speads they travel at. Older disines don't nead as advanced shaps. Evin the matireal planes are made of like the S.R. 71 was made titanium and the old planes were made of metle. Weapon sistoms in planes have changed to old planes onely machine guns and and one or two bombs therefore new planes have machine guns, bombs, missiles and grenade launchers.

Most students at this level have the resources to build stamina as they engage with longer texts. As we explore in the developmental chapters, this becomes increasingly important in the later grades as students are expected to read, analyze, and respond to more complex texts. Such expectations require "staying power," and while students usually have no problem sticking with whatever they enjoy, they need to develop capacity for sticking with appropriately challenging texts. From the intermediate grades on, they will encounter in these texts more complex syntactic structures and more advanced vocabulary (numbers of words and new concepts).

This in turn can support continuing oral language development (Chall, Jacobs, & Baldwin, 1991; Nippold, 2007). By the way, this is why we share *Al Capone Does My Shirts* with intermediate-level students. The book pulls them in, and they want to keep reading—stamina is not an issue. We use this book to teach a number of narrative features and vocabulary, and possibly to anchor a history unit or unit in character development. Students will be able to apply the insights and understandings gained in this engaging text to other more challenging, and perhaps at first, less interesting narratives.

These more complex texts should influence writing development as well. Students have the potential to compose longer texts, to go through subsequent revisions, and to understand better how to align their writing and its purpose for their intended audience—including the expectations of writing assessments. Writing, of course, requires stamina, and stamina is sustained by purpose and commitment. By bringing students together with representative, exemplary texts as models, teachers then use these different types of texts to scaffold students' organization and ideas in their own writing.

Students' *vocabulary* increases significantly during the intermediate stage. Much of this growth comes from morphological development (Anglin, 1993). Students' increasing cognitive capacities support their exploration of how affixes and roots combine, and these explorations will extend to a number of Greek and Latin roots. The most frequently occurring Greek and Latin roots will be introduced and explored—for example, roots having to do with "communication," such as *–phon–* (sound), *–dict–* (speak), and *–scrib–* (write). Recall from Chapter 1 that this type of learning is *generative*, allowing students to grow their vocabularies significantly through the understanding of these processes by which most words in English are constructed. In addition to expanding vocabulary, "Morphological knowledge is a wonderful dimension of the child's uncovering of 'what's in a word,' and one of the least exploited aids to fluent comprehension" (Wolf, 2007, p. 130).

Students' *spelling* begins to reflect characteristics of the longer words they have been decoding in their reading, such as *middel* for *middle* and *alow* for *allow*. A significant feature of English spelling is this "doubling" phenomenon: When are consonants doubled at the juncture of syllables and when are they not? Students' understanding of how spelling works when word parts are joined—syllables and/or morphemes—builds on their understanding of long- and short-vowel spelling patterns within single syllables. They first learn how this works with words such as *gripped/gripping* and *griped/griping*: In these types of words, a consonant is usually doubled if it follows a short vowel and not doubled if the consonant follows a long vowel. Students learn that this pattern applies not only to words to which endings are added, such as *grip* and *gripe*, but also to words such as *human* and *pattern* as well. Does it always apply? No; there are exceptions such as *habit* and *cabin*. Over time, however, exceptions to the rule will become explained as students learn more about how words work.

When intermediate-level students read words, their brains picks up each syllable as a unit: *dump – ster* and *bat – tle*. This more economic pickup of word parts—entire syllables as opposed to parts within syllables—supports further development in fluency, leaving still more cognitive space available for thinking about what is being read.

Skillful Reading and Writing (Grade 6 and Above)

The middle school years are a particularly critical time for young adolescents' social and moral development, and what teachers guide them to read, write, and discuss has profound consequences for their development. This is because moral, ethical, and psychosocial development usually is grounded in cognitive development. Most students at the middle school level have the cognitive capacity to address the complexity of topics, texts, and experiences that young adulthood may present. Psychosocially, however, they are primarily concerned with establishing their identity. On the one hand, they want to conform to the dictates of their group (band, jocks, emo, goth, gangstah, nerds, skaters, and so forth) and try to define their own identity in terms of that group; on the other hand, they still wish for a supportive, firm hand to define limits (whether they realize it or not!). Morally, they are motivated by acceptance by their group. For a number of reasons, therefore, a great many middle school students are not naturally disposed to valuing academics—such as reading the books that adults are going to be telling them to read, or studying the topics that adults will be telling them to study. Some want to escape from reading, others seek refuge in it, and still others can take it or leave it (Crumpler & Wednick, 2011). For students who *are* engaged in literacy, online social media and "underground" writing sites influence and provide opportunities for them to try out their identity and creativity.

Effective literacy teachers use literacy engagements in part to reach these students where they are. They then use these engagements to scaffold the students' moral as well as cognitive development—helping them grow beyond the narrow yet comfortable world of their particular peer group so they might better deal with the larger issues that will ultimately define them and their relationship to a much larger world. For many students, the texts in which we eventually will be engaging them and stretching them will have ideas or ambiguities that are unsettling, as the cartoon in Figure 2.9 reflects (Telgemeier, 2002). Effective literacy teachers will also be effective guides through this uncertainty, helping students reach greater insight and awareness. They understand how texts can resonate with young adults' lives and enrich those lives in ways they will only gradually become aware of.

Figure 2.10 shows two excerpts from Abbie's writing assignment for her seventh-grade English class. The composition is in response to her social studies text, *The Story of the World: Ancient Times* (Bauer, 2006). The teacher's grading rubric for the assignment included several criteria: *Lead and Gist, Voice, Historical Detail, Ambient Details* (the "flavor" of ancient Rome), *Conclusion,* and *G.U.M.* (grammar, usage, mechanics). Abbie chose the diary format; her first entry is titled "A New Beginning: 72 A.D.," and the second "The Finale: 81 A.D." Abbie's writing demonstrates her ability effectively to integrate historical information within personal narrative, and establish a sense of continuity with Celcus as he moves from slave, to gladiator, to free citizen. She is applying her developing academic vocabulary (for example, *repulsive*) and an easily confused word, *prospective*, rather than the more precise *perspective.*

What about middle school students who are not yet skillful readers? They certainly have the cognitive capacity to engage with the ideas and concepts in the texts they are expected to experience. Middle school teachers will engage them through discussion, read-alouds, modeling, and—if the text is not too far beyond their skills in terms of complexity—reading it themselves after such

Common Core Connection

Reading Standards for Literature: Integration of Knowledge and Ideas; Range of Reading and Level of Text Complexity

Chapter 10 addresses instruction for Learners at the Skillful Literacy Stage

FIGURE 2.9

FIGURE 2.10 Journal Entries: Seventh-Grader's First-Person Historical Fiction

A New Beginning: 72 A.D.

Dear Diary,

I used to be called a worthless man who had nothing but strength; I was repulsive, and despised by most because of my background. I was poor and unattractive; nobody wanted me. Everywhere I worked as a slave I was sold after little time. I had always felt rejected, never quite fitting in, until the year of 72 AD: the year the Colosseum was built; a place where gladiators would fight each other to death for the entertainment of Roman citizens. Many Romans went traveling at this time, looking for gladiators. They knew that when the Colosseum was finished they'd need many strong fighters for the inaugural ceremony. This event would last 100 days-each day full of battles among gladiators and slaves. They began with the least experienced fighters and worked up to the strongest best two fighters.

I was found in a quarry, sweat beads soaking my tunic; immediately I was a stand out for the Romans. I worked hard even though I knew that being a slave was cruel and unethical. This is when I was discovered. They picked me out of the crowd of all the victims: "You." Their tone was strong and demanding. "Come back to Rome with us and you will undergo a major change; you will become a confident and successful gladiator." I followed, obeying their instructions. This was the start to my new life . . .

The Finale: 81 AD

Dear Diary,

Applause fill the arena. My heart races as it always does before these gatherings. More fear rushes through me every step I get closer to my opponent. When I reach him I receive a punishing glare. His cockiness does not weaken me; it only makes me want to find harder.

"Vade!" The referee shouts. And the combat begins . . .

. . . Not only do I live, but I am also set free. I receive a wooden sword which means I no longer have to be a gladiator; I can live life as an honorary Roman. This is a rare achievement for gladiators so I am very satisfied. I am excited to see the world from a new prospective. I will not be a British slave or a Roman gladiator; I will be me, Celcus Atillux, a free and popular man.

~Celcus

scaffolding. Technology is supportive here: Students can access complex texts by reading along as they listen online. They will also need to continue to have access to and read texts that are at their independent and instructional levels.

For students in the middle grades who *do* possess the supportive literacy skills, their cognitive and language potential will allow them to explore and become aware of the ever-increasing depth and complexity of ideas and texts, as Abbie's composition illustrates. They will learn much more about language and its structure, and will appreciate how this knowledge may in turn develop their own knowledge and ways of thinking. Their *generative* vocabulary knowledge may increase significantly. They continue to learn important Greek and Latin roots both in literature and in specific domains, as well as discuss in more depth than in the earlier grades how the meaning of so many roots contributes to the meaning of the words in which they occur. For instance, at first the words *senior*, *senator*, and *senile* may not seem to have much in common, but by thinking about the Latin root *–sen–* and its meaning, "old," students can get into an interesting if not humorous discussion about these words' relationships.

Common Core Connection

Language Standards: Knowledge of Language; Vocabulary Acquisition and Use

Orthographic knowledge at this level potentially grows to include a rich domain of derivational morphological information that will nourish vocabulary and spelling development, as well as supporting even more rapid and effective word identification during reading (Berninger, Abbott, Nagy, & Carlisle, 2009; Nagy, Berninger, & Abbott, 2006). Students at this stage are referred to as *derivational relations* spellers, because they have the foundation for exploring in depth the ways in which many *related* words can be *derived* from a single root. In addition to more in-depth investigation of Greek and Latin roots, spelling–meaning features of word structure may also be examined in greater depth; for example:

- The influence of language origin on spelling, as with /k/ spelled *ch (chlorophyll)* and /s/ spelled *ps (psychology)*. (These examples are from Greek.)
- The widespread phenomenon referred to as **assimilated prefixes**, which seem to be everywhere in texts in the middle grades and beyond. In the word *attract*, *at–* is an absorbed prefix. It started out as *ad–* (meaning "to or toward"), and when combined with the Latin root *–tract–* (meaning "pull"), changed to *at–*. Why? We'll explore this in Chapter 10; understanding this phenomenon develops vocabulary further as well as the spelling of that vocabulary.

We've emphasized students may "potentially" develop more advanced orthographic knowledge: For most students, these insights will not develop unless, as at the intermediate level, teachers introduce and guide the students' exploration. Students' spelling can be a very good guide to their underlying orthographic knowledge at previous stages, but it is not as precise a measure at this level. This is because, although students may in fact be spelling most words correctly, they may not be aware of or know much about the morphology that these spellings represent. Moreover, if they aren't aware of or know the meaning of some of the bound morphemes within those words—affixes and roots—their depth of understanding when reading will not be as rich as that of students who do have this awareness and knowledge.

And finally, at the word level during reading, readers who are at the skillful level use alphabetic, within-syllable, and between-syllable information to read words. They also use morphological information much more effectively, which means that their brains pick up meaning units or *morphemes:* for example, *anthrop – ology*. There is even more cognitive space available for thinking about what they are reading.

Chapter Summary

The development of thought and of language are interrelated throughout a child's development. Figure 2.11 represents the major characteristics of oral language and of thought that we've discussed in this chapter.

Comprehending, learning from, and enjoying any text depends on the quality of the reader's underlying *orthographic knowledge*—knowledge *in general* of how words work and their structure—as well as knowledge of *specific* words. This knowledge supports the decoding of words in reading and the encoding of words in writing. The knowledge develops, over time, from understanding at the level of the sound/alphabetic and pattern layers, to understanding at the meaning layer. Figure 2.12 represents the types of knowledge within each layer, as well as the developmental nature of their overlap.

The nature and structure of written texts depends on the particular genre. The two broad categories, *literature* and *informational*, each include a range of text types. Determining their complexity depends on quantitative, qualitative, and text/reader characteristics.

As students learn about words and texts, their literacy development depends on, and in turn influences, the development of oral language and thought. Learners advance in predictable stages of literacy development. As students advance into each new stage of language and literacy development, their information and understandings are rearranged and reorganized.

FIGURE 2.11 Characteristics of Oral Language and Thought

Characteristics of Oral Language			
Phonological Knowledge: *How* we speak our language	**Semantic Knowledge:** Understanding of the meaning of words and of word parts	**Syntactic Knowledge:** Our ability to order or arrange words into phrases and sentences	**Pragmatic Knowledge:** How we *use* our language in different situations and contexts

Phonemes
Syllables
Prosody
	Denotation
	Connotation
	Figurative
	    Language
	Range of Meanings
	    of Words
	Morphology:
	    Free Morphemes
	    Bound Morphemes:
	        Prefixes & Suffixes
	        Greek/Latin Roots
		Content Words:
		    Nouns
		    Verbs
		    Adjectives
		    Adverbs Pronouns
		"Glue" Words:
		    Conjunctions
		    Prepositions
		    Determiners
			Register:
			    Formal vs. Informal
			Functions of Language:
			    Regulatory
			    Interactional
			    Personal
			    Representational
			    Heuristic
			    Imaginative

Characteristics of Thought			

Remembering → *Understanding* → *Applying* → *Analyzing* → *Evaluating* → *Synthesizing*

FIGURE 2.12 Characteristics of Written Language

Characteristics of Written Language: Word Level			
			MEANING
		PATTERN	
ALPHABET			
Letter Name	Within Word ↓ Vowel Patterns	Between Syllables ↓ Syllable Patterns ↓ Basic Word-Formation Processes: Inflectional Morphology Derivational Morphology Root word + affixes	Advanced Word-Formation Processes: Derivational Morphology Greek/Latin roots + affixes

Characteristics of Written Language: Text Level	
LITERATURE	INFORMATIONAL
Narrative Structure	Literary Nonfiction
Drama	Domain-Specific Texts
Poetry	

Suggested Extension Activities

- Read a picture book to a preschool or kindergarten child. Then ask her to "read" a page or two back to you. Watch what she does: Does she point to the print? If so, in what way? Do you think she is beginning to develop a *concept of word in print?* Why or why not?

- Ask a student in grade 3 or higher to explain the difference between reading "stories" and reading "informational books." What are the purposes of each? Which type do they prefer reading? Why?

- Study several students' writing samples and match their writing to the stages of development described in this chapter. Use Table 2.1 to help determine your instructional priorities for each child.

Recommended Professional Resources

Baca, J. (2010a). *Adolescents on the edge: Stories and lessons to transform learning.* Portsmouth, NH: Heinemann.

Baca, J. (2010b). *Stories from the edge.* Portsmouth, NH: Heinemann.

Bear, D. R., Invernizzi, M., Templeton, S., & Johnston, F. (2012). *Words their way: Word study for phonics, vocabulary, and spelling instruction* (5th ed.). Boston: Pearson/ Allyn & Bacon.

Tatum, A. (2009). *Reading for their life: (Re)Building the textual lineages of African American adolescent males.* Portsmouth, NH: Heinemann.

Zambo, D., & Brozo, W. (2009). *Bright beginnings for boys: Engaging young boys in active literacy.* Newark, DE: International Reading Association.

Online Resources

National Association for the Education of Young Children (NAEYC)

www.naeyc.org

NAEYC is an organization dedicated to developmentally appropriate education, particularly in the early childhood years. Visit its website and review NAEYC's position statements on early reading, family involvement, and cultural and linguistic diversity.

Reading A-Z

www.readinga-z.com/correlation-chart.php

Visit the Reading A-Z text-leveling resource site and explore the text-leveling correlations and criteria. This information may be helpful as you work to level your own classroom library.

The Education Alliance at Brown University

www.alliance.brown.edu/tdl/elemlit/orallanguage.shtml

The Education Alliance at Brown University is a clearinghouse for research on effective best practices. Visit the Education Alliance to learn more about developing your English Learner's oral language competence.

TextProject

www.textproject.org

This site offers resources for teachers to support beginning and struggling readers, including appropriate texts. Research reports are available as well, supporting the strategies and activities available on the site.

Effective Literacy Instruction: Principles and Practices

Chapter Outline

» **Closing the Achievement Gap**

» **Your Classroom Environment and Students' Motivation to Learn**

» **Your Classroom Library**

» **Your Daily Literacy Block**

» **Reading Workshop: An Overview**

» **Writing Workshop: An Overview**

» **Word Study Instruction: An Overview**

» **Managing Word Study Instruction Across the Week**

» **Comprehensive Core Reading Programs**

③ Focus Questions

1. What are the practices of highly effective literacy teachers?
2. What are the characteristics of classroom environments that support high levels of student achievement?
3. What are some ways you'll engage and motivate your students?
4. Describe how you'll organize and manage whole group and small group instruction in reading, writing, and word study.
5. How can you use your knowledge of literacy development and effective instruction to create a program that supports *all* learners?

Deeni Antonucci, the newly hired fifth-grade teacher at Eduardo Elementary School, joins her grade-level colleagues and the literacy coach for a meeting the week before school starts. She has before her a copy of the Common Core State Standards, several teacher resource guides, and a stack of assessment portfolios—one for each student. As she listens to her colleagues talk about the first weeks of school and the reading/English language arts curriculum, she starts to feel overwhelmed. This is not unusual for novice teachers; many experienced teachers feel similarly at the start of a new school year. The school's literacy coach, Janet Lawton, notices Deeni's expression and asks, "What's on your mind? How can we help you?" Deeni looks relieved to be part of such a supportive community, but she isn't quite sure how to reply. After a moment or two she says, "I am familiar with the literacy essentials: word structure, fluency, vocabulary, comprehension, writing, and motivation, and I've looked over my students' assessment profiles. I know I should teach in their 'zones of proximal development' and I need to address the standards, too . . . ." After a brief hesitation, she confides, "I'm just not sure how to pull all of the pieces together."

Janet rests a knowing hand on Deeni's arm and with a genuine smile she assures her that she's not alone in this concern. The other teachers also reassure Deeni as they begin to talk about their different paths to becoming effective literacy teachers. As Deeni listens, she realizes everyone does things a little bit differently in their classrooms, but there are some common themes. She picks up her pen and jots some notes:

Key Principles and Practices

— *Classroom community that supports deep thinking, collaboration, student response, choice, and reflection*

— *Developmentally responsive small group instruction*

— *Time for meaningful and engaged practice*

After several minutes of discussion, Janet sums up the conversation by saying, "There's no shortage of great ideas, approaches, or strategies for teaching literacy; the issue isn't finding more of them but rather selecting those that create predictable routines for children so they can become independent and purposeful readers, writers, and thinkers." This comment reassures Deeni and helps her set her goals and priorities for the coming year. ■

Characteristics of Highly Effective Teachers

Like you, Deeni Antonucci aspires to be a highly effective teacher of literacy. She understands that children's literacy achievement can affect their future success in school and their later career opportunities, too. She also knows that a large number of students—too many in the United States—struggle with literacy. Researchers estimate that approximately eight million students in grades 4 through 12 are not able to read grade-level text proficiently (Biacarosa & Snow, 2006). This is troublesome for many reasons, particularly because we know adolescents' difficulties with reading so often lead to their decision to drop out of school (Biancarosa & Snow, 2006; Kamil, 2003). As you might expect, high school dropouts face limited employment opportunities, and those who do find work earn considerably less (Barton, 2005; Carnevale, 2001). Even students who successfully complete high school have difficulty finding gainful employment; of the high school graduates not enrolled in college between 2006 and 2011, only 27 percent are employed full time (Horn, Zukin, Szeltner, & Stone, 2012). With limited career prospects for high school graduates, and even fewer opportunities for the estimated 7,000 students who drop out of high school each day (Alliance for Excellent Education, 2013), preventing and addressing students' reading challenges *early* and *effectively* are critical priorities for our nation's schoolchildren and the economy.

While your students' levels of literacy can significantly shape their educational outcomes and career opportunities, an equally compelling reason, if not a *more* compelling reason to be concerned about your students' success is the belief that literacy and literate behaviors such as reading, writing, talking, thinking, debating, analyzing, and questioning are necessary for the preservation and advancement of our nation's democracy (Bomer & Bomer, 2001; Hoffman, 2000; Johnston, 2012). Researcher Joe Kretovics explains this position: **Critical literacy** provides students "with the conceptual tools necessary to critique and engage society along with its inequalities and injustices. . . . Critical literacy can stress the need for students to develop a collective vision of what it might be like to live in the best of all societies and how such a vision might be made practical" (Kretovics, 1985, p. 51). In this view, literacy, education, and critical thinking are essential to realize the ideals of liberty, freedom, and social justice.

In recent years, social scientists and cognitive psychologists have affirmed these beliefs with scientific evidence that *reading does indeed change the brain* (Carr, 2011; Paul, 2012). Some studies have found that reading fiction influences peoples' personality traits, emotions, and sense of empathy and concern for others (Djikic, Oatley, Zoeterman, & Peterson, 2009; Kaufman & Libby, 2012; Oatley, 1999). Avid readers of fiction are more likely to understand the perspectives of other people and imagine experiences beyond the limits of their own realities (Djikic et al., 2009; Kaufman & Libby, 2012). Becoming literate is an important and worthy goal because it has the potential to contribute positively to the quality of people's lives and relationships, and it enhances the vitality, health, and inclusiveness of our society. By focusing your attention on becoming a highly effective teacher of literacy, both you and Deeni Antonucci will play an important role in preparing today's children and youth for their future success in school, their careers, and well beyond.

Researchers Snow, Burns, and Griffin affirm that highly effective teachers are the "single best weapon" in the prevention of reading difficulties (1998, p. 343). Another researcher, Linda Darling-Hammond, writes, "The effects of well-prepared teachers on student achievement can be stronger than the influences of student background factors such as poverty, language background, and minority status" (1999, p. 38). So what makes a literacy teacher highly effective? Researchers have sought to answer this question for many years and some important trends are

The Language of Your Instruction

Building a Community of Thoughtful Communicators and Deep Thinkers

The way you talk to and with children contributes to their sense of identity, their relationships with others, and their learning, too (Johnston, 2004). Peter Johnston, noted language and literacy researcher, has studied the discourse patterns of highly effective teachers and their students and has come to this conclusion:

> The social relationships within which they [children] learn are part of their learning. Children, like adults, learn better in a supportive environment in which they can risk trying out new strategies and concepts and stretching themselves intellectually. This is not just because a supportive community enables individuals to extend their minds beyond themselves without risk, but also because the relationship associated with the learning is an inextricable part of what is learned. (p. 65)

Your thoughtful use of language can shape the culture of your classroom community, the relationships children have with each other and you, and your students' learning outcomes, too. Being mindful of your language can make a significant difference not only in the effectiveness of your teaching but also in students' sense of belonging and their care for themselves and others.

beginning to emerge from these studies (Allington & Johnston, 2002; Gehsmann & Woodside-Jiron, 2005; Mosenthal, Lipson, Torncello, Russ, & Mekkelsen, 2004; Pressley, Allington, Wharton-McDonald, Collins Block, & Morrow, 2001; Taylor, Pearson, Clark, & Walpole, 1999). Highly effective literacy teachers:

- Are knowledgeable and articulate about their practice
- Teach phonics *and* comprehension
- Connect word study instruction to meaningful reading and writing activities
- Engage students in authentic and extended reading and writing practice
- Use assessment data and their understanding of literacy development to guide and inform their grouping practices and instructional priorities

The most effective teachers also dedicate a significant amount of time to teaching literacy each day (2 or more hours a day) and most of this time is spent in small group instruction (Taylor et al., 1999). These teachers hold high expectations for student learning, engage students in higher-order thinking and questioning, and communicate regularly and effectively with colleagues and families.

Throughout this chapter and book, you will begin to acquire the knowledge, skills, and understandings necessary for you to become a highly effective teacher of literacy.

Your Classroom Environment and Students' Motivation to Learn

Deeni Antonucci understands the influence a classroom environment can have on children's literacy development, motivation, and achievement. She knows the environment should reflect the things she values most: children's social interactions, their independent and supported reading and writing practice, as well as their exploration of interesting content. She also wants her environment to support her students' *social construction of knowledge* (Bruner, 1996; Vygotsky, 1978). Ongoing conversations, collaborations, and interactions with materials, the environment, and each other allow children to learn from one another and build new understandings and insights together. This **constructivist approach** to teaching makes their learning more meaningful, more motivating, and more memorable (Bruner, 1996; Guthrie, 2002; Vygotsky, 1978). With these goals in mind, organizing your classroom space will be one of your first priorities.

Organizing Your Classroom Environment

The organization of your classroom environment can affect the types of activities children choose to engage in and the benefits of these engagements (Morrow, Reutzel, & Casey, 2006; Morrow & Tracey, 1997; Morrow & Weinstein, 1986). In Italy, educators see the classroom environment as being so important, they refer to it as "an educator" (Edwards, Gandihi, & Forman, 1998).

As you begin to envision your future or current classroom, it's helpful to think about how the arrangement of your classroom furniture and materials can support your teaching as well as your students' learning. To begin, consider creating many smaller learning spaces within your larger classroom environment including:

- Whole group meeting area
- Small group meeting area
- Spaces for independent reading and writing practice
- Classroom library
- Learning centers, particularly in the primary grades

You'll also want to consider the supplies and materials you'll need readily accessible in these areas, including:

- Computer and Smart Board and/or LCD projector and screen
- Easel and chart paper
- Dry erase board (preferably magnetic)
- Pocket charts
- Writing paper and utensils
- Children's book boxes and work folders
- Miscellaneous supplies and materials such as scissors, staplers, colored pencils, pens, markers, paper, Post-it notes, and glue sticks

Whenever possible, store your supplies and materials, and students' work folders and book collections, in clearly marked baskets and containers. Store these materials at a height that's comfortable for your students to access, usually at eye level or lower. In the first weeks of school, demonstrate where to find and how to use these materials so children can access them independently as needed (Denton & Kriete, 2000; Wong & Wong, 2009). Figure 3.1 will help you assess various aspects of your learning environment.

A Print-Rich Environment

Creating an environment that is "print rich" will be another of your many priorities when designing your classroom environment. A **print-rich environment** is just that—a classroom environment that is nearly saturated with print! Of course it won't look this way the first week of school, but over time, you'll add to the environment, leaving "tracks of children's thinking" on charts and

FIGURE 3.1 **Classroom Environment Checklist**

Use this checklist to help you design or assess your own classroom environment.

General Atmosphere

- ❏ As you enter the room, how do you feel? Is it welcoming? Engaging? stimulating?
- ❏ Is the classroom neat, orderly, and attractive?
- ❏ Do students have choice and ownership of at least some of their activities and some of the books they read?
- ❏ Are there opportunities for students to collaborate and interact socially with peers?

Space and Room Arrangement

- ❏ Is there a defined meeting place where the whole class can work together?
- ❏ Can every student see and hear read alouds, charts, and/ or the digital display comfortably?
- ❏ Are there places for students to work independently and in small groups?
- ❏ Is the teacher able to see all children in the classroom at all times?
- ❏ Is the furniture arranged to allow for easy movement and smooth transitions?

Books

- ❏ Is the classroom library well supplied with books—a minimum of 500 to 600 books?
- ❏ Are there a wide variety of genres and types of text (for example, fiction, informational, reference, poetry, graphic novels, magazines, digital texts, biographies)?
- ❏ Are there a variety of levels of text available for students to choose from?
- ❏ Are the books accessible and is the collection inviting (books displayed with covers facing forward, neatly arranged)? Do you want to spend time in the classroom library?
- ❏ Are books displayed in many parts of the room?
- ❏ Are at least some of the books categorized by topic, author, genre, series, and/or theme?
- ❏ Are some of the books (about one-third) leveled so readers can easily find a book at their independent level when they're having difficulty finding a "just-right" text?

Materials and Supplies

- ❏ Are there adequate and varied supplies for writing and artistic response?
- ❏ Are the materials students need readily accessible and clearly labeled?
- ❏ Are there special places for students to store and retrieve their literacy work and materials (crates, baskets, folders, or baggies), including take-home reading materials?
- ❏ Are there computers and other digital media available in the classroom?
- ❏ Are there tools for technology-assisted reading and writing (for example, Kindles, iPods, keyboards, and voice-recognition software)?

Evidence of Routines

- ❏ Is there evidence of instructional routines?
- ❏ Are students able to independently select "just-right" texts?
- ❏ Are classroom rules and expectations displayed and easily understood by students and visitors alike?
- ❏ Does the daily schedule allow for large blocks of uninterrupted time for literacy instruction and practice?
- ❏ Are students able to sustain their reading and writing practice for at least 30 minutes?

Environmental Print

- ❏ Is environmental print neatly prepared, useful, and regularly accessed by students?
- ❏ In the primary grades, is the alphabet displayed at the child's eye level with models for how to appropriately form the letters?
- ❏ Are the teacher's charts free of errors in spelling, grammar, word usage, and mechanics?
- ❏ Is children's work, particularly their writing, displayed?
- ❏ Is there as much informational text displayed throughout the room as other forms of text?
- ❏ Is there a word wall and evidence of word study?

posters (Miller, 2002)—displaying their literacy work, including "work in progress"; labeling objects, bins, and baskets; displaying books and texts; and creating charts that summarize the big ideas of your instruction.

Your charts and displays will combine a mixture of traditional print literacy and aspects of **visual literacy**, too. Your goal for these charts and displays is to make them useful and interactive for your students. Whenever possible, include photos or quotes from your current student on your charts and posters, and be sure to include their names. This increases their sense of community and stimulates the likelihood that they'll reread and access these charts in the days and weeks to come.

Classroom Management and Student Engagement

High levels of student engagement and on-task behavior are the hallmarks of effective teachers (Marzano, Pickering, & Pollock, 2004; Mosenthal et al., 2004; Taylor et al., 1999). Clearly communicating your expectations for student behavior and learning will positively affect your students' engagement with literacy activities and their learning, too (Evertson & Weinstein, 2006; Morrow, Reutzel, & Casey, 2006; Reutzel, Morrow, & Casey, 2009). Like all effective teachers, you will promote on-task, engaged behavior and a positive classroom environment by providing students with:

* Appropriately challenging work (McKenna, 2001; Vygotsky, 1978)
* Relevant and meaningful activities that engage students in authentic reading and writing activities (for example, writing for real audiences, researching topics that interest them, talking about books that move them) (Good & Brophy, 2003; Guthrie, 2002, 2004; Taylor et al., 1999)
* Thoughtful and specific feedback (Wiggins, 1998; Kohn, 1999)
* Opportunities for collaboration and choice (Johnson & Johnson, 1998; Guthrie, 2002, 2004)

You'll also foster a more positive and caring community by being attentive and responsive to children's needs. This is especially important for students who have difficulty with *self-regulation*, because they are less likely to verbalize their needs and wants (Blair, Protzko, & Ursache, 2011). You will build both their social and cognitive competence through your ability and willingness to read their nonverbal communication, anticipate their needs, and help them develop the language skills necessary to form positive social relationships with peers and adults alike (Blair, Protzko, & Ursache, 2011). Your efforts here are crucial to these learners' success: Social competence and self-regulation are strongly correlated with students' achievement in key content areas such as early literacy and numeracy (Blair, Protzko, & Ursache, 2011; Lyons, 2001).

Conclusion: Your Classroom Environment

In sum, your classroom environment is an expression of your values and your priorities. It supports children in their social, emotional, and intellectual development. Some educators have come to see the classroom environment as a "fellow educator." Investing time in planning and thinking about your environment will positively affect how your students will interact with and within this environment. This investment will allow you to focus your attention on other important matters, such as planning and implementing rich and interesting curriculum and forming meaningful relationships with your students.

For more information on the first weeks of school and creating an inspiring and productive classroom environment, consider these professional resources: *The First Six Weeks of School* (Denton & Kriete, 2000), *Space and Places* (Diller, 2008), and *The First Days of School* (Wong & Wong, 2009).

Reading and Writing in Digital Contexts

Using Multiple Literacies in Your Classroom

The students in your classroom are **digital natives** (Prensky, 2001). They've grown up with technology in their environment and it's a natural part of their lives. Perhaps you identify with being a digital native, but there are others who feel more like digital immigrants (Prensky, 2001). **Digital immigrants** have to consciously think about how to integrate technology into their lives and especially their teaching (McKenna, Labbo, Conradi, & Baxter, 2010). Whether you're a digital native or a digital immigrant, today's students are quite familiar with technology and they expect it to be part of their learning. Given this reality, you'll want to think about different ways you can use technology as both a *tool* for learning and a *topic* of study.

Ways Technology Can Be a Tool for Learning

The Common Core State Standards emphasize the importance of students being able to "research to build and present knowledge" (2010, pp. 18, 41). Technology plays an important role in both! To satisfy the goals of the Common Core and other learning intentions, here are some ways you can use technology as a tool for learning:

- Although today's students continue to use traditional formats to show what they know (for example, word-processed documents, pamphlets, PowerPoint presentations, and graphs and figures), their presentations are expanding well beyond these. Increasingly, they are using blogs, wikis, glogsters, prezis, podcasts, personal websites, and specialized presentation techniques such as PechaKucha (www.pechakucha.org) to share their research and knowledge—a critical focus of the Common Core State Standards. When creating their presentations and documents, students often use online document-sharing resources such as Google Docs (www.docs.google.com) to co-construct and share their work with classmates and other audiences.
- Digital storytelling is an especially motivating means for children to retell storybooks, write their own stories, and present their research by combining print,

still images, video, and even sound! Suggestions for digital storytelling can be found at: www.techteachers.com/digitalstorytelling.htm. Be sure to check out the *Toontastic* and *Animation Desk* apps for students who are especially interested in digital storytelling and animation.

Technology as a Topic of Study

In addition to using technology as a teaching and learning tool, **media literacy** is an important topic that you'll teach as well. The Common Core State Standards emphasize this point: "[Students] have to become adept at gathering information, evaluating sources, and citing material accurately" (2010, p. 41). Several organizations and state education agencies have begun to recognize the need for media literacy, too. The state of Minnesota, for example, has included media literacy standards in their new Common Core–aligned language arts standards, which can be found at http://education.state.mn.us/MDE/EdExc/StanCurri/K-12 AcademicStandards/index.htm. The Center for Media Literacy is another helpful resource when developing your curricular goals for media literacy: www.medialit.org/reading-room/educational-standards-and-media-literacy. Among these goals, consider the following suggestions for your own curriculum. Students will be able to:

- Efficiently search digital sources for information, images, and other media
- Effectively evaluate the credibility of information found on websites or from other digital sources
- Skillfully analyze information from digital sources
- Accurately cite digital resources
- Practice and uphold standards for the ethical and safe use of personal and social media

Using technology as both a tool and topic of instruction will motivate and engage your students and deepen their knowledge, while simultaneously broadening their horizons. Whether a digital immigrant or digital native, it's important to intentionally integrate technology into your daily routines and curriculum (McKenna et al., 2010).

Your Classroom Library

One of the most important areas of your learning environment will be your classroom library. You'll want your library space to be large enough to accommodate several students at a time, yet cozy enough that it will encourage students to linger (Morrow & Weinstein, 1986; Neuman & Roskos, 1992). Consider including soft chairs, warm lighting, carpeting, and attractive colors to make the space more appealing.

In the primary grades, include literacy props such as puppets or stuffed animals of favorite storybook characters, flannel boards for retelling stories, poetry charts for rereading, and **big books**. In the intermediate and upper elementary grades, and in middle school, too, include reference books such as the *Merriam-Webster New Book of Word Histories* (1991), *Cryptomania: Teleporting into Greek and Latin with the Cryptokids* (Fine & Doner, 2004), and multimedia to support content-area exploration and word study as well. You'll also teach your students how to access book reviews from credible online resources and by using print references such as *500 Great Books for Teens* (Silvey, 2006). With all age groups, you'll facilitate your students' sharing of book recommendations.

Book recommendations can be informal reflections written on Post-it notes and placed inside book covers, or you can create more elaborate systems such as online blogs for your students to share thoughts about books. You'll also encourage students to give **book talks—** short yet engaging "infomercials" that give listeners just enough information to interest them in reading a book. Book talks often end with a "cliff-hanger" to further entice the listener.

Researchers have found that students often choose to read a particular book because a friend is reading it or a friend recommended it (Pressley et al., 2001; Roskos, Tabors, & Lenhart, 2009). However you structure it, providing students with a vehicle for talking about and recommending books helps build a classroom community that values reading, response, and collaboration.

Common Core Connection

Speaking and Listening: Comprehension and Collaboration

Quantity of Books

Researchers consistently affirm the importance of children's access to books. One study (Neuman, 1999) found children's reading increased by 60 percent simply by adding books to the classroom library. Researchers vary in their estimates of how many books are enough, but some of the most effective schools have upwards of 500 books in their classroom libraries, and many of the most effective teachers have collections closer to 1,500 titles (Allington & Johnston, 2002; Mosenthal et al., 2004)! Children in the primary grades will need an especially large collection of books because their books are shorter and they will read them quickly (Fountas & Pinnell, 1996). If you don't have at least 500 books in your collection, consider borrowing books from your school library or the public library to supplement your collection. Access to **trade books** increases students' motivation to read, and it's been proven to increase their achievement in reading as well (Guthrie, 2002, 2004; Wells & Chang-Wells, 1992).

Quality and Variety of Books

Quantity isn't the only consideration when stocking the shelves of your library; you'll want to be sure the books you include are of high quality, too. These books will span several grade levels and represent many different genres, as noted in Figure 3.2. These books should be attractive, in good condition, and interesting to students in the grade level you teach (Neuman, 1999). They should also represent a wide range of cultures and peoples—intentionally including stories of children and youth with differing abilities and various racial, ethnic, socioeconomic, cultural, and linguistic backgrounds.

It's important that you evaluate the books in your collection for bias. If a book includes language or stereotypes that might be offensive to some, consider the value the book provides. If it still merits inclusion in your library, then take the time to explain to your students the perspectives, discourse patterns, and/or word choices that may challenge them. Situate these issues, as appropriate, within the broader historical or cultural context and talk about them from many different perspectives. As students become more skillful in their reading, they will be able to

Common Core Connection

Reading Standards for Literature and Informational Texts: Range of Reading and Level of Text Complexity

FIGURE 3.2 Sample Genres and Types of Texts for Your Classroom Library

Historical fiction	Concept books
Realistic fiction	ABC books
Science fiction	Wordless picture books
Fantasy	Graphic novels
Adventure	Poetry
Mystery	Autobiography/Biography
Folktales	Informational text
Fables	Functional text
Myths	Humor/Jokes/Riddles
Plays	Magazines
Speeches	Short stories
Fairy tales	Sports stories
Magazines	Newspapers/Newsletters
Reference books	Picture books

critically analyze these texts with greater levels of independence, in part because you and other teachers have provided this important scaffolding and instruction.

While it's possible to purchase many affordable books at yard sales or book sales, be thoughtful about your selections. Choose only the highest-quality literature and informational texts, and books that are current enough for today's students. Whether you agree with it or not, your students will judge books by their covers, and outdated illustrations or tattered pages will affect their interest and engagement with the books in your library (Neuman, 1999). A beautiful and well-stocked library will entice your readers to visit often and read more.

In each of this book's developmental chapters, you'll find resources and recommendations for the types of books appropriate for each stage of development.

Strategies for the Classroom

To Level or Not to Level, That Is the Question

In recent years there's been an increased focus on using leveled text in small group reading instruction and in the classroom in general. This has led many teachers to wonder whether they should label the books in their classroom libraries according to their level of difficulty. Like many good questions, there's not one "right" answer to this question, but we do have some thoughts on the topic.

Having a portion of the texts in your library leveled can be helpful for students who have difficulty finding a "just-right" book. When some of your library is leveled, you can suggest to a student that selecting "green dot" books, for example, might be a "just-right" choice. Over time, however, you'll help these students realize that knowing a book's level isn't quite enough information to make a thoughtful book choice (Bang-Jensen, 2010; Halladay, 2012).

If you decide to use a text-leveling system for some of the books and texts in your classroom library, consider these suggestions:

- Level no more than one-third of your library. This allows children to learn how to select texts that are in line with both their reading ability and interests.
- Integrate leveled texts into the bins and baskets of books you already have in your classroom library.

Organize the books in your collection by topic, author, genre, and theme rather than by level.

- When leveling texts, consider using colored dots that represent a range of levels rather than specific numbers or letters. Place these dots on the back of the book or inside the front cover.

Text levels can provide teachers with a helpful rubric for understanding the complexity of texts. This information can be especially helpful when planning small group guided reading instruction for beginning and transitional readers. Text leveling, however, is not an exact science, nor should a text's level be the only factor you or your students consider when deciding which books to read. Over time you'll feel more comfortable matching children to books and helping them select books to read based on other factors such as their motivation; their background knowledge; their interest in a particular topic, title, author, or genre; and their own assessment of their ability to read and understand texts independently (Bang-Jensen, 2010; Halladay, 2012).

Your Daily Literacy Block

As literacy coach Janet Lawton advised in the opening vignette, there's no shortage of great ideas for teaching literacy; it's the thoughtful selection and organization of these ideas that makes your teaching powerful. As a novice or veteran teacher, you'll find that a predictable instructional routine is critical to your students' learning and your sense of efficacy. While there are several different models of literacy instruction, we've selected one in particular that allows for an important balance of whole class standards-based instruction and modeling, as well as differentiated small group instruction and independent practice. This model, the Reading, Writing, Word Study Workshop, can be adjusted to fit your unique circumstances and available time. In the following sections of this chapter, we will share an overview of this instructional model. Each aspect of the Reading, Writing, Word Study Workshop will be described in greater detail through classroom vignettes and sample lessons in each of the developmental chapters. Occasionally, we'll direct you to these specific examples in these chapters. Our goal in doing so is to make the connection between theory and practice clear and help you see how all the pieces of literacy instruction and development come together to create a cohesive whole or "big picture."

Working and Collaborating

The Role of Paraprofessionals in Your Literacy Block

In many schools across the country, *paraprofessionals*, also called *teachers' aides* and *para-educators*, are hired to help and support students who struggle, particularly readers who experience difficulty. All too often, paraprofessionals become responsible for teaching reading to our most vulnerable learners. Although this is a common practice, it's not a "best practice" (Causton-Theoharis, Giangreco, Doyle, & Vadasy, 2007). Research consistently affirms the need for the most qualified teachers to teach those in the greatest need (Allington, 2009, 2012; Snow, Burns, & Griffin, 1998). Unfortunately, most paraprofessionals do not have the training needed to make a significant difference in students' literacy achievement (Gerber, Finn Achilles, & Boyd-Zaharias, 2001; Gray, McCloy, Dunbar, Mitchell, & Ferguson, 2007; Rowan & Guthrie, 1989). So what's an appropriate role for paraprofessionals in your classroom or school? The following recommendations are adapted from the research of Causton-Theoharis and colleagues (2007):

1. Engage paraprofessionals in *supplementing* the literacy instruction provided by the classroom teacher and/or special educator by reading word bank cards with students, leading a literacy game, supervising computer-based skills practice, talking about texts, or engaging children in reading or writing practice.

2. When paraprofessionals do work with children one-to-one or in small groups, be sure they're using research-based approaches that are designed by highly qualified teachers of reading. Paraprofessionals should never be expected to make instructional decisions or plan instruction. Instead, the materials and teaching plan should be carefully prepared for them to follow. Well-chosen research-based programs such as *Word Study in Action* (Bear, Invernizzi, Templeton, & Johnston, 2012) and *Soar to Success* (Cooper, 2001), or well-designed tutoring approaches such as *Book Buddies* (Johnston, Invernizzi, Juel, & Lewis-Wagner, 2009) can be valuable starting points for engaging paraprofessionals in meaningful and effective supplemental instruction for readers who struggle.

3. It's essential that paraprofessionals receive ongoing training in the materials and methods they're implementing and regular feedback that helps them reflect on and improve their practice. Again, this needs to be a collaborative process that includes the classroom teacher and other professionals such as your special educator, reading specialist, and even your school principal.

Students' progress will also need to be monitored to ensure the lessons and activities continue to be appropriate over time. This is the responsibility of the classroom teacher, special educator, and reading specialist. Modeling "best practice," frequent communication, and thoughtful, well-planned lessons are the keys to engaging paraprofessionals in productive and satisfying ways.

Reading Workshop: An Overview

Reading workshop is a one- to two-hour block of time where your sole focus is reading instruction and practice. Reading workshop has several component parts, including shared reading (preK–2), interactive read-aloud, a mini-lesson, small group and one-to-one reading instruction, independent reading practice, and, finally, a share or wrap-up at the end of the block (Atwell, 1998; Calkins, 2000, Fountas & Pinnell, 2001). Many of these same structures will be part of your writing workshop, too.

Word study instruction can be embedded in either your reading or writing workshop, though many teachers prefer to include it in another part of their day. We'll discuss word study instruction later in the chapter.

Managing Your Time in Reading Workshop

Teachers in the primary grades will likely need close to two hours to meet the needs of their students in reading workshop, especially if they integrate word study into this block. Teachers in the upper elementary and middle grades may be able to manage the pieces of the block in just over an hour's time, especially if they integrate some of the parts of their literacy instruction into their content-area instruction. Regardless of the grade level, the most effective teachers are sure to include more differentiated small group instruction than whole group instruction, and at least 30 minutes of reading practice each day. Figure 3.3 will help you envision the component parts of your reading workshop.

Shared Reading

Shared reading (Holdaway, 1979) is a form of interactive read-aloud typically found in preschool, kindergarten, and first-grade classrooms. Using enlarged texts (charts, poems, songs, and "big books"), you'll show children how print works by pointing to each word as it's read aloud. You'll support children's literacy development and their emerging identities as readers when you read

FIGURE 3.3 Components of Reading Workshop

Shared Reading (PreK–1)

(15–20 minutes)

Configuration: Usually whole class as part of morning meeting

Focus: Concepts of print, phonological awareness, alphabetic principle, concept of word

Interactive Read-Aloud

(20–30 minutes)

Configuration: Whole class usually situated before the mini-lesson, but it can be during another part of the day if your block isn't long enough.

Focus: Vocabulary, comprehension strategies, thinking skills, response

Mini-Lesson

(5–15 minutes)

Configuration: Whole class

Focus: Procedural lessons, strategy lessons, literary analysis

Small-Group Instruction, Conferring, and Independent Reading Practice

(45–60 minutes total)

Configuration: Small group and one-to-one

Focus: At least 30 minutes of independent reading practice and 15 to 20 minutes of small-group instruction 2 to 5 days per week (depending on stage of development and student needs); one-to-one conferring at least once per week for each child

Share/Closure/Wrap-Up

(5–10 minutes)

Configuration: Whole class

Focus: Student reflection and sharing of their reading work and connections to the mini-lesson and/or interactive read-aloud

these texts over and over again until the children memorize them and "read" along with you. This level of familiarity and engagement allows you to use these texts to teach emergent and beginning literacy skills such as phonological awareness, concepts about print, alphabet knowledge, and concept of word. Eventually, you'll use these texts to teach decoding strategies and sight word recognition. Detailed shared reading lesson plans and explanations of how to teach these foundational skills are found in the emergent and beginning literacy chapters.

Interactive Read-Aloud

Interactive read-aloud is a 20- to 30-minute block of time where you'll share a piece of literature, poetry, or informational text with your students. You'll intentionally select this text based on your learning goals. It's common to choose an on-grade-level or above-grade-level text so you can expose students to age-appropriate vocabulary and concepts—something that's especially important for students who are not able to independently read these texts themselves (Alexander

Children's Literature Connection

Books to Start the School Year

Books to Start the Year in the Primary Grades

Cannon, J. (2004). *Pinduli*. New York: Harcourt Children's Books.

Child, L. (2004). *I Am Absolutely Too Small for School*. Somerville, MA: Candlewick.

Choi, Y. (2001). *The Name Jar*. New York: Knopf.

Creech, S. (2001). *A Fine, Fine School*. New York: HarperCollins.

Henkes, K. (1991). *Chrysanthemum*. New York: Greenwillow.

Henkes, K. (2000). *Wemberly Worried*. New York: Greenwillow.

Herrera, J. F. (2000). *The Upside Down Boy / El Niño de Cabeza*. New York: Children's Books Press / Lee & Low Books.

Park, F., & Park, G. (2000). *The Royal Bee*. Honesdale, PA: Boyds Mill.

Books to Start the Year in Grades 4-8

Abbott, T. (2006). *Firegirl*. New York: Little, Brown.

Clements, A. (2007). *No Talking*. New York: Aladdin/Simon & Schuster.

Draper, S. (2010). *Out of My Mind*. New York: Atheneum Books for Young Readers.

Gephart, D. (2010). *How to Survive Middle School*. New York: Yearling/Random House.

Hill, K. (2000). *The Year of Ms. Agnes*. New York: M. K. McElderry.

Lord, C. (2006). *Rules*. New York: Scholastic.

Palacio, R. J. (2012). *Wonder*. New York: Knopf.

Spinelli, J. (2000). *Stargirl*. New York: Knopf Books for Young Readers.

& Jetton, 2000; Sticht & James, 1984). You'll also use interactive read-alouds to model and teach fluent reading and the strategies proficient readers use when reading and responding to text.

As part of your daily interactive read-aloud, invite your students to co-construct the meaning of the text by regularly talking with partners and with you. Sometimes you'll invite your students to try out the strategies you've modeled through the read-aloud while they're listening to you read. More often than not, you'll connect what you've modeled in the read-aloud to your mini-lesson and encourage your readers to apply what they've learned in these two settings to their independent reading practice. This, as you recall from Chapter 1, is a good example of how you'll gradually release responsibility to your learners beginning with modeling, then guided practice, and eventually independent application (Pearson & Gallagher, 1983).

Throughout each of the developmental chapters, you'll learn specific techniques for teaching vocabulary and comprehension strategies, as well as thinking and reasoning skills during your interactive read-aloud time. You'll also learn how to select books to achieve your specific learning goals.

Mini-Lessons: Explicit, Whole Class, Standards-Based Instruction

Mini-lessons are relatively short, whole class lessons that are connected to your interactive read-alouds and the work you expect children to try during independent reading time (Atwell, 1998; Calkins, 2000; Fountas & Pinnell, 2001). In your mini-lessons, you'll explicitly model the habits and strategies of proficient readers and your expectations for the workshop time, too.

The specific topics for your lessons will come from the Common Core State Standards, from your local curriculum, and from formal and informal assessments of student learning. For example, when you notice that a majority of your students need support in a particular strategy, procedure, or understanding, this will become the topic of a future mini-lesson. When only a

FIGURE 3.4 Sample Reading Mini-Lesson Topics

Your mini-lessons will fall into one of the following three categories: procedural lessons, reading strategy lessons, or analysis of text. Here you'll find a list of topics to get you thinking about the different kinds of mini-lessons you'll plan for.

Procedural Lessons	Strategy Lessons	Analysis of Text
• Where and how to sit during mini-lessons and independent reading • How to transition from one activity, center, or location of the room to another • Where to access and how to use materials • Selecting a "just-right" book and returning books to the library • How to give a book talk • What to do when you finish a book • How to talk with a reading partner • How to set reading goals • Protocols for guided reading groups, partner reading, and/or literature circles	• Concepts about print • Concept of word in text • Decoding words • Building stamina—keeping your focus while reading • Making predictions, asking questions, and clarifying • Retelling or summarizing • Making inferences • Determining importance • Monitoring one's understanding and using "fix-up" strategies • How to read (and understand) a book over time • How to read dialogue or punctuation • Using Post-its or response logs to keep track of your thinking	• Comparing and contrasting books, authors, and/or themes • Studying and imitating author's craft • Writing a personal response to text • Using evidence to back up your thinking/opinions • Studying and using literary devices (for example, similes, metaphors, foreshadowing, flashbacks) • Studying genre, text features, and text structure • Examining text through multiple lenses/perspectives • Digging deeper: working with partners to excavate the "big ideas" of texts • Evaluating online sources

few students need support in a particular area, you'll provide this instruction in guided reading, a strategy group lesson, or a one-to-one conference. Figure 3.4 provides some suggestions for mini-lessons topics to get you started.

Your mini-lessons will follow a predictable sequence—one that you now recognize as "the gradual release of responsibility" (Pearson & Gallagher, 1983). They will also be very short, ranging from 5 to 15 minutes. Since these lessons are so short, it's important to plan your instruction carefully so you're not tempted to extend these lessons beyond the 15-minute threshold. Extending the length of mini-lessons very rarely yields better learning outcomes; more often it results in off-task behavior.

If your lesson *must* go longer than 15 minutes, find a way to actively involve your students in guided practice for a period of 2 to 5 minutes before asking them to focus on your direct instruction again. This will improve their engagement and the likelihood of them retaining your intended learning (Jensen, 2005; Sousa, 2011). Planning is really the key to the success with mini-lessons!

The Structure of a Mini-Lesson

Mini-lessons, like other structures within the workshop, follow a predictable sequence as described here (Calkins, 2000).

Connection This first part of the mini-lesson is built on the understanding that new learning is more likely to be retained when it's connected to students' prior knowledge and experiences. As you recall from Chapter 1, this is called *schema theory*. When you connect new learning to prior knowledge, you get the brain's attention and you provide a "hook" or "mental Velcro" to which the new information will adhere. Your connections may sound something like this:

- "Readers, yesterday we talked about . . ."
- "The last couple of days we've been learning . . . [how to make plausible predictions and back them up using evidence from the text]."
- "Remember in today's read-aloud how we . . ."

Teaching Point Although it's difficult to select just one strategy or procedure to teach in your mini-lessons, you'll do so thoughtfully and build on yesterday's lesson today and today's lesson will set the stage for tomorrow's lesson. In this way, your well-sequenced mini-lessons will build on one another to form a unit of study.

Figure 3.4 highlights examples of the three different kinds of reading mini-lessons you'll teach: procedural, strategy, and analysis of text. *Procedural lessons* tend to be more common at the beginning of the year, whereas reading *strategy lessons* can happen at any time. Lessons on *literary or textual analysis* are more common in the middle to late part of the year, except at the later stages of development when students spend most of their time honing their comprehension and critical literacy skills.

From the "connection" phase of the lesson, you might introduce your teaching point with language like this:

- "So today we're going to learn . . ."
- "Today we're going to add to yesterday's strategy . . ."
- "Readers, another way to . . ."

Model/Demonstrate After introducing the topic of the lesson and explaining why it's important, you'll model the procedure or strategy for students by thinking aloud as you demonstrate. If it's a text-based strategy, you'll return to a familiar piece of text or use a short piece of new text. Your demonstration may sound something like this:

- "As I'm reading aloud, I'm going to . . . [stop and think about questions I have, and as I do, listen to the way I start my questions. In a few minutes, we'll talk about different ways to pose questions . . .]."
- "Readers, today I'd like to show you how . . . [to use the parts of words to help you unlock their meaning]."

Active Involvement After modeling the strategy or procedure, you'll want your students to practice it while they're still sitting in the meeting area. This guided practice can be done independently, with reading partners, or with small groups of students before they leave the whole group meeting.

In order to provide immediate feedback, eavesdrop as your students try the strategy or procedure. Also look for confusions that you can address in this or a future mini-lesson. The purpose of active involvement is to provide specific and supportive feedback in a timely manner, and to help students transfer this learning from the whole group setting to their independent reading or writing time.

If you notice a few students having difficulty or excelling with the lesson, you may choose to bring these students together for a strategy group meeting where you'll reteach or extend the lesson. Other times it may be more effective to do this in a one-to-one conference.

Link After reinforcing students' attempts with the strategy or procedure and addressing any lingering confusions, you'll link the lesson to the students' independent reading work and set the expectation that they try the procedure or strategy in their reading practice right away, or in the days to come. You'll also invite students to share what they learned from their practice at the end of the workshop. Your link may sound something like this:

- "Readers, today when you go into independent reading time, I'd like you to . . ."
- "Today during independent reading, I'll be watching to see how you . . ."
- "If you think this is a strategy you can try during independent reading time today, please raise your hand. Great! I'll count on you to share what you learned at the end of the workshop during share time."

Small Group Reading Instruction

When you think back to your elementary school years, can you remember what small group reading instruction looked like and sounded like? If you can, you might remember children sitting around a table reading in sequential order. You probably remember how hard it was to follow along as you simultaneously tried to anticipate the part that you'd have to read when your turn came. Sometimes you would silently read that part over and over again—hoping to get it just right before it was your turn to "perform" it. Perhaps you enjoyed reading your page or paragraph aloud, but most people remember that it was difficult to concentrate on the whole story while waiting for their turn. Other people will remember the anxiety of reading aloud, or how hard it was to listen to some of their classmates who really struggled with reading. As you might guess, this form of small group reading instruction, commonly known as **round robin reading**, is not particularly effective. In fact, round robin reading has the potential to actually harm children's progress by encouraging passive, disengaged reading behaviors. It also limits children's opportunities to actually read text and apply their decoding and problem-solving skills, as well as comprehension strategies (Opitz & Rasinski, 2008).

A variation of this approach is called **popcorn reading**. When using this approach, the teacher calls on children to read at random, presumably thinking this will keep them "engaged." Unfortunately, more often than not, this practice makes students feel anxious and they lose their focus and interest in reading the text (Opitz & Rasinski, 2008). Both popcorn reading and round robin reading are examples of instructional practices that have endured throughout the years despite a lack of sound research to support their use.

While these approaches to small group reading instruction can still be found in some schools, your classroom will be different. Your instructional decisions will be based on current research and best practice. As such, you'll group students according to their stage of development and use small group instructional approaches such as guided reading, strategy lessons, book clubs, and reading conferences.

Guided Reading

Guided reading is an approach to teach reading to small groups of children at the same stage of development. Using *instructional-level texts*, you'll model and teach the strategies your students need to read increasingly complex texts. Guided reading can be used with any age group or developmental stage, but it's most frequently used in kindergarten through grade 3. When students are at the end of the transitional literacy stage, book clubs become the more prevalent form of small group reading instruction, although guided reading can extend well into the middle school years.

> **Common Core Connection**
>
> Reading Standards for Literature: Range of Reading and Level of Text Complexity

There are three important parts to every guided reading lesson and they occur *before, during,* and *after* students read the text (Fountas & Pinnell, 1996; Calkins, 2000):

1) Before reading: Book selection and introduction
- Select a book that is in line with your students' instructional level and interests.
- Preview the text to identify any language, syntactical forms, words, or concepts that may present a challenge for your students. Plan how you will introduce these.

- Plan a simple introduction to orient your students to the gist of the story, provide background knowledge if necessary, and introduce some of the features that you've identified as being potentially challenging. As appropriate, provide students with problem-solving strategies rather than just telling them what they need to know to be successful reading this book.
- Set a purpose for their reading. (For example, read to find out how George and Martha solved their disagreement, or notice how the punctuation affects the meaning of the story and be prepared to share your observations.)

2) During reading: Reading practice, teacher observation and coaching

- Children independently read the text silently or in whisper voices as you move around the group listening to them read and taking notes about their strengths and challenges.
- As necessary, coach students to use their word-solving strategies, or fix-up strategies when meaning breaks down. (See suggested prompts in Chapter 7 on page 246.)
- Study your readers to find trends in their oral reading and their comprehension of the text. Be thinking about what your teaching point may be at the end of the lesson.

3) After reading: Your teaching point and link to independent practice

- After children finish reading the text, have a conversation that connects back to the purpose you set at the beginning of the reading. Also discuss the overall meaning of the text.
- After this discussion, select one teaching point that will help the students not only read this text better but help them read other books better, too. Examples include how to read dialogue in a way that makes meaning clear, how to decode multisyllabic words, or how to repair your comprehension when meaning breaks down. The teaching point should be based on the information you collected while listening to your readers in the "during reading" phase. In this way, your teaching point is timely and student-centered.
- After modeling your teaching point and providing students with the opportunity to try it out while you observe and provide feedback, encourage them to use this strategy during independent reading. Expecting students to try out their new learning builds in accountability and encourages the transference of this learning to other settings—a primary goal of all instruction!

In Chapter 7 you'll find a detailed description of how to plan a guided reading lesson as well as a sample lesson plan.

Strategy Lessons

Using information from your reading or writing conferences, you'll sometimes identify a group of students who are experiencing difficulty with a specific strategy or concept. Other times you'll notice a group that's ready for more advanced work. In either case, you'll bring these students together in a strategy group. Strategy groups are small groups of students who may be at different developmental stages but they have a common need. These groups typically meet only once or twice a week for the purpose of learning or reinforcing a specific reading or writing strategy or procedure such as selecting a "just-right" book. Strategy lessons are just one more example of an effective means for small group student-centered instruction.

Book Clubs and Literature Circles

As students move into the intermediate and skillful stages of literacy, more of their time will be spent in critical discussion of books and texts they've read. You'll still have a role to play in teaching them how to analyze and evaluate books and other texts from multiple perspectives, but your students will become increasingly self-directed and independent at these stages. They'll read for longer periods of time and manage their own reading goals and activities with a partner or small group of peers.

Book clubs are a common structure for organizing these interactions among students (Calkins, 2000). Book clubs are also called *literature circles* (Daniels, 2002) and they grow out of guided reading groups at the earlier stages of development. They are intended to help deepen students' comprehension and enhance their engagement with texts. Book clubs are discussed in greater detail beginning in Chapter 9.

Reading Conferences

Reading conferences are short instructional opportunities that you'll plan for several times per week. Using information you've collected about each reader through the different structures of reading workshop, you'll enter the conference with a "theory of the reader or writer" and some thoughts about what you might teach each student (Calkins, 1994, 2000). Your conferences will have three steps or phases (Calkins, 1994, 2000; Anderson, 2000):

1) **Research: Gathering information.** In the research phase of the conference, invite your students to talk about their reading work and goals, listen to them read a short portion of text aloud, and/or talk about the texts they are currently reading. This phase of the conference is a give-and-take of information and not a "test." Be careful not to quiz your readers. Instead, show genuine interest in what they are thinking and doing as developing readers. As you're listening, think to yourself, "What's the one thing I could teach this reader that would propel his or her reading skills forward?"

2) **Decide: Contemplating your instructional focus.** After a couple of minutes of conversation and/or listening to your student read, you'll need to select one teaching point. This is indeed a difficult choice, especially when working with readers who struggle, because they so often have many things they need to learn. Even in these cases, select only one thing to teach in the reading conference.

3) **Teach: Connect, model, guided practice, and link.** When you've selected a teaching point, begin your instruction with a connection. Share some of your observations with your student—for example, "I noticed that your summaries have improved a great deal since the last time we met. When you said the gist of the story was . . . [insert the gist statement], I thought, 'Wow! She's got it!'" After sharing your observation, elicit the student's reflection on this before moving to your teaching point: "So today I was thinking that we could talk about moving beyond a summary to thinking about the theme of a book." From here you will model and guide how to find themes in a text.

   Conclude your conference by linking this lesson to the student's broader experiences with reading. You might say something like this: "Readers get a lot more enjoyment and information from their reading when they think about themes and big ideas. In the next few days, revisit some of your old favorites and see if you can identify the themes or big ideas of these texts and jot a note about them in your response journal. The next time we confer, I'd like to see what you're thinking about these books. You can also share your thinking during share time."

As you can see, reading conferences are an efficient means of providing student-centered instruction. Importantly, you'll keep records of your conferences so you can follow up with your students and hold them accountable for the learning goals you set in these meetings. A description of how to keep records of your conferences can be found in Chapter 4.

It's an appropriate goal to confer or meet in a strategy group with every student in your class at least one time per week. As you meet with students one-to-one and in guided reading and

Accommodating English Learners

Creating an Environment that Supports Risk Taking and Collaboration

Your English learners will be learning to read and write while simultaneously learning to speak in English. This is indeed challenging, and there are some things you can do to support your English learners' development and well-being. Researchers Helman, Bear, Templeton, Invernizzi, and Johnston (2012, p. 61) recommend the following support strategies:

- **Create a low-stress environment.** Encourage student collaboration and minimize competition. Include multisensory and enjoyable activities such as playing games, singing songs, acting out stories and new vocabulary words, partner reading, and other hands-on and collaborative activities such as word sorting (described later in the chapter).
- **Encourage student-to-student interaction.** Provide ample opportunities for students to talk and work with one another during reading, writing, and word study instruction. Be sure to set the expectation that it's always okay to ask someone for help or clarification. Encourage students to work together by planning purposeful collaborative activities such as partner reading, peer editing, and book club discussions.

- **Have high expectations for all students.** Your expectations are apparent in what you say, what you do, how you say things, and your body language, too. Encourage your students to do their best. Avoid saying things like, "This isn't for you . . . ," "You won't understand . . . ," and "You can't . . . ." Be aware of the tone of your voice, eye contact, and posture. Encourage students with both your verbal and nonverbal communication, recognizing each student's assets, and finding opportunities to build from their strengths rather than focusing on their challenges.
- **Make student–teacher connections.** Teachers who get to know and value their students create communities in which it's okay to make mistakes. Students who feel safe and comfortable in an environment are more likely to take risks to advance their learning, and they're more likely to persist with learning tasks even though they may be challenging. Use your small group time and reading and writing conferences to get to know your students better and provide individualized instruction and ongoing support.

strategy lessons, you'll be looking at your students' strengths, needs, and challenges, as these will inform your selection of future mini-lesson topics, as will the Common Core State Standards and your local curriculum. For more information about reading conferences, see the feature, "The Language of Your Instruction," in Chapter 8.

Independent Reading Time: Time Spent Reading

Like most things in life, your students' reading cannot improve without practice (Allington, 1977; Anderson, Wilson, & Fielding, 1988; Krashen, 2004). Simply stated, students with the best reading performance read more (Anderson, Wilson, & Fielding, 1988; Caldwell & Gaine, 2000; Donahue, Finnegan, Lutkus, Allen, Campbell, 2001; Taylor et al., 1999). In your classroom, you'll intentionally provide students *at least* 30 minutes a day of reading practice, and you'll encourage out-of-school reading each day, too.

Independent Reading and Sustained Silent Reading

Independent reading time is different from other approaches to reading practice such as Sustained Silent Reading (SSR) or Drop Everything and Read (DEAR). Independent reading is a time for more purposeful reading practice. Your students will be reading a lot during independent reading time and they'll be pursuing individualized improvement goals, as well as intentionally practicing the skills, strategies, and habits of proficient readers. This reading practice, like the writing practice in your writing workshop, is a time when students are also held accountable for specific learning goals.

Many teachers also aim to provide their students with more recreational reading practice through structures such as SSR or DEAR throughout the week. These opportunities are scheduled outside of the Reading, Writing, Word Study Workshop. The goal of these silent reading times is pure enjoyment and even relaxation with books. Some researchers believe that this recreational reading helps students access more complex texts (Krashen, 2004), yet others caution its regular use in the classroom because it can take time away from more purposeful practice (NICHD, 2000). If your schedule allows for this added reading practice, we encourage you to include it in your daily or weekly schedule.

Student Book Choice: A Powerful Motivator

Your students will visit your classroom library at least once per week with the intention of browsing for and selecting the independent-level books they'll be reading during independent reading time. They'll keep these in their book boxes or desks and will likely carry them between home and school for extended reading practice. Primary-grade children may have as many as 8 to 10 little books for reading and rereading during the week, whereas older students may have just a few—often a novel, a piece of informational text, and another piece of reading that can be picked up and put down when they have just a few moments to read (short stories, magazines, informational text, poetry). It's critical to students' motivation and achievement that they select books they *want* to read and books they *can* read (Ehri, Dreyer, Flugman, & Gross, 2007; Guthrie, 2002).

Helping Students Choose a "Just-Right" Book

Just-right books are texts your students can read with high levels of comprehension and accuracy (about 95 percent or greater accuracy in the primary grades and 97 percent or greater for older students). Beginning readers will be working to read the words in these books accurately and with increasing automaticity, whereas transitional readers and others will focus on fluent reading. All readers should be reading for meaning, but beginners may need to reread their books a few times to move beyond word-level processing.

When students select books that are clearly too difficult for them, you'll want to do one of three things:

1) Provide instruction that will support their efforts to read the book well.
2) Coach them to make another selection.
3) Give them some time to problem solve on their own.

When talking with students about a book that's a little (or a lot) beyond their current level of achievement or understanding, it's tempting to tell them to make another choice. Unfortunately, this doesn't provide them with the tools or strategies necessary to self-monitor while reading, nor does it provide guidance for how to select a just-right text in the future. It's more helpful to make observations or ask questions to help influence children's reflections and choices. Try these examples:

- I'm wondering if this is a book that's making your feel confident in your reading, or is it mostly confusing? Tell me about it . . . "
- "Wow! This is a real 'stretch book.' This is the kind of book you'll definitely grow into by June. Let's talk about 'just right' books for this time of year."
- "This is a great 'read-along' book. Why don't you take this home and invite [insert name] to read it with you and we'll find a just-right book for you to read in class."

Supporting Appropriate Book Choice for Readers Below Grade Level. Some children will need more support and encouragement to find just-right books. Your readers who are reading below grade level are most likely to need your support, as it can be especially difficult for them to find books they can read and feel good about reading. You can support their selection of appropriate books in a number of ways, including:

- Stocking your library with high-interest, lower-level books and texts
- Providing technology to assist these students when they are really interested in texts that are too challenging for them to read independently
- Offering "controlled choice," which means inviting these students to select from a smaller collection of texts at their independent level and on topics of interest
- Frequently providing book talks about books that are below grade level to make these choices more socially acceptable
- Creating partnerships with younger students so readers who struggle will be encouraged to choose and perfect their reading of below-level texts so they can be shared with their younger reading buddies
- Creating multilevel text sets on popular topics so a range of readers can successfully participate in what Frank Smith (2004) calls "the literacy club"

It's critical that you remember that reading is a social activity and your students want and need to fit in with their peers. By following some of these suggestions, you'll not only help your students find a just-right texts but you'll also build their esteem and identities as readers. In sum, your students need books they're interested in reading and books they can read with high levels of success for at least 30 minutes each day, and, ideally, another 30 minutes outside of school.

Managing Small Group Instruction and Independent Reading across the Week

After your mini-lesson, you will have anywhere from 45 to 60 minutes of instructional time before you conclude the reading block with a share time. Most of your students will be engaged in independent reading practice for at least 30 minutes (and longer for older students). Some of your students will be working with you in small groups or in one-to-one configurations for part of this block, too.

During this time in the workshop, you're doing one of three main things: leading a guided reading group or literature circle, teaching a strategy lesson, or conferring with a student or partnership. So how do you fit it all in? Figure 3.5 illustrates how you can ensure all students receive adequate small group instruction and opportunities for one-to-one conferences and strategy group lessons each week.

Notice in Figure 3.5 that small group time with your below-level readers will be a priority each and every day. You can meet with your on-level and above-level readers less frequently, as they'll benefit from the additional practice time (Connor, Morrison, Fishman, Schatschneider,

FIGURE 3.5 **Planning Small Group Instruction during Independent Reading Time**

Monday	Tuesday	Wednesday	Thursday	Friday
Below Level	Below Level	Below Level	Below Level	Below Level
On Level	Conferring/ Strategy Lesson	On Level	Conferring/ Strategy Lesson	On Level
Conferring/ Strategy Lesson	Above Level	Conferring/ Strategy Lesson	Above Level	Conferring/ Strategy Lesson

& Underwood, 2007; Pressley et al., 2001). These readers can also meet in partnerships or small groups to talk about their books on the days they're not meeting with you. If you have additional instructional support in your classroom, these students might also meet with a paraprofessional, special educator, reading specialist, or volunteer to talk about their texts. Your readers who are below level will also benefit from a "second dose" of reading instruction during the block, assuming you have instructional support available. You will find more information about supporting readers who experience reading challenges in Chapter 11. Also see the "Working and Collaborating" feature in this chapter.

Managing Small-Group Instruction and the Rest of the Class

Teachers often ask, "What are the other students doing while I'm meeting with small groups of students or conferring with individual students?" To answer this question, we see a range of possibilities: First and foremost, your students will be reading at least 30 minutes a day—maybe not the first week of school, but you will build their reading stamina to this minimum level of practice. Beyond that, they can be responding to text in response journals or talking with reading partners. In the primary grades, and particularly if you have support staff or volunteers to make it happen, your young readers will engage in literacy centers like those described in Chapter 6. At any developmental stage, your students will benefit from playing word study games or engaging in extension activities such as those described later in the word study section. Students who are performing below grade level should spend most of their time in small group, teacher-facilitated instruction (Connor et al., 2007; McIntyre, Rightmyer, Powell, Powers, & Petrosko, 2006; Taylor et al., 1999).

Wrapping Up the Workshop: Share Time

At the end of your workshop, you'll gather your students back to the meeting area and invite them to talk about their reading work for the day. You might prompt this reflection by asking, "Take a moment to think about what you learned about yourself as a reader today or this week" or "What's one thing you learned about reading today that you think someone else might like to know?" or "In today's mini-lesson, we learned about . . . [insert a topic]. Several of you said you were going to try it out. How did it go? What did you learn from experience?"

Some days you'll notice something specific during the workshop that you want other students to know about, and you'll ask these students to share. Other times the sharing will be more spontaneous, and still other times you'll share your own observations and reflections from the day. This sharing is a form of closure. It provides an opportunity for students to reflect on their learning, and for you to reinforce this learning as well. It's also a time when students can learn from each other; this is often the richest learning of all. Understandably, your time may be limited, but it's critical to students' long-term retention that you take this opportunity to reflect and share at the end of each lesson (Jensen, 2005; Sousa, 2011).

Writing Workshop: An Overview

Your writing workshop will mirror your reading workshop in that it will have many of the same component parts: a read-aloud or study of a mentor text, a mini-lesson, guided writing, strategy lessons, writing conferences, independent writing practice, and a wrap-up or share time. Several of these component parts are introduced in the sections that follow and more specific examples can be found in the developmental chapters.

Your two workshops will also be connected, whenever possible, by content as well as common structures. A unit on reading informational text, for example, is complemented by a unit on report writing. A unit on using story elements to help students comprehend narrative text is enriched and extended by using story maps as a tool to plan narrative writing in the writing block. Helping students see the reciprocal nature of reading and writing processes strengthens their achievement and enjoyment of both subjects and creates efficiency in your teaching.

Mentor Texts

Your writing workshop will begin as your reading workshop does: with an exemplary piece of text. In writing workshop, we study these texts with "the eyes of a writer" to learn what makes them so effective (Hansen, 2001). Often you'll study the topics or ideas of these texts, other times the structure of them, and still other times you'll study the author's craft—their use of **literary devices** (metaphor, simile, allusion, symbolism, personification, point of view), word choice, or how they develop voice/tone/mood. The mentor texts you use in writing workshop are often the same texts you've used to study vocabulary, comprehension strategies, or text structure in reading workshop. Sometimes you'll use different texts, including your students' writing and other writing you've written collaboratively with your students.

Select your mentor texts with your learning goals in mind. When studying character development in fourth grade, for example, you might study how Kate DiCamillo developed the characters of Opal, her father, and even her absent mother in *Because of Winn Dixie* (2000). When studying setting, you might look at Karen Hesse's masterful development of time and place in *Out of the Dust* (1997). Katherine Paterson's *Bridge to Terabithia* (1977) may be one of the single-best examples of how to develop memorable characters and powerful plots. When studying informational text and different ways to present information, you might study the craft of Tanya Lee Stone and the many different ways she writes and presents information in books such as *The Good, the Bad, and the Barbie: A Doll's History and Her Impact on Us* (2010), *Almost Astronauts: 13 Women Who Dared to Dream* (2009), and *Elizabeth Leads the Way: Elizabeth Cady Stanton and the Right to Vote* (2008). If you are reading *Al Capone Does My Shirts* (Choldenko, 2004) as a companion text, think of some ways it might be used as a mentor text with your students.

Picture books also make incredible mentor texts. We love to use *The Important Book* (Brown & Weisgard, 1949) to teach paragraph construction and description, and *Yo! Yes?* (Raschka, 1993) or *The Girl's Like Spaghetti* (Truss & Timmons, 2007) for punctuation and editing. Throughout the developmental chapters, you'll find lists of picture books that we use to teach genre, the qualities of effective writing, and the habits and dispositions of writers—for instance, *Nothing Ever Happens on 90th Street* (Schotter, 1999), *How to Get Famous in Brooklyn* (Hest & Sawaya, 1995), and *Amelia's Notebook* (Moss, 2006) for older students. Even our youngest writers will imitate the authors and texts you study. Consider authors like Eric Carle, Tomie dePaola, Lois Ehlert, Donald Crews, and Margaret Wise Brown for author studies in preschool and the early grades.

Common Core Connection

Writing Standards: Range of Writing

Mini-Lessons

Your writing mini-lessons will follow the same sequence as your reading mini-lessons: connection, teaching point, demonstration/modeling, active involvement, and link. Like your reading mini-lessons, your writing mini-lesson topics will come from the Common Core State Standards, your local curriculum, and your informal and formal assessments of your students' work, including your observational notes and conference records. Writing mini-lesson topics include procedural lessons, writing process lessons, and craft lessons. Figure 3.6 provides some examples to get you thinking about your future mini-lesson topics.

FIGURE 3.6 Sample Writing Workshop Mini-Lesson Topics

Procedural	Writing Process	Author's Craft
Workshop routines and expectations	Habits of proficient writers	The qualities/traits of good writing:
Keeping a writing notebook or folder	Getting started: Finding topics to write about	• Purpose
Managing time and materials	Writing process lessons:	• Organization
Author's Chair/Share Time	• Planning	• Details/Elaboration
Basic research skills	• Drafting	• Voice/Tone
How to use resources such as dictionaries, thesauruses, and electronic reference tools	• Deciding	• Conventions
	• Revising	Strong leads/endings
How to self-assess	• Editing	Slowing down time/Speeding up time
How to confer with peers	• Publishing	Word choice
	Forms and functions of print	Transitions
	Conventions of print	Developing character, setting, plot
		Using literary devices or text features

Independent Writing Practice

Like independent reading in your reading workshop, independent writing practice is a priority in your writing workshop. Plan for a *minimum* of 30 minutes per day, stretching to upwards of 45 minutes if your schedule allows for it. Writing practice, like reading practice, is the heart of writing workshop.

Your students will especially benefit from writing practice that is purposeful; in other words, your students have clear goals they're pursuing and they have authentic reasons to write. The more you can work to build a community of writers who write for real reasons and real readers, the greater your students' motivation and engagement will be (Calkins, 1994; Hansen, 2001).

Small Group Writing Instruction and Conferring

During your students' independent writing time, you will periodically meet with students in small groups, just as you did in reading workshop. You'll use structures such as guided writing, strategy lessons, and writing conferences to support your students' development. Unlike reading workshop, you will not have to meet with your small groups as frequently. Instead, most of your instruction will come from your mini-lessons and writing conferences. A sample schedule for coordinating small group writing instruction and conferences is found in Figure 3.7. Of course you can adjust these sample schedules to best meet the needs of your students. Flexibility and student-centered decision-making are essential!

Guided Writing

Guided writing lessons, like guided reading lessons, are intended for small groups of students at the same developmental stage. As such, these students have similar instructional needs.

Common Core Connection

Writing Standards: Production and Distribution of Writing

FIGURE 3.7 Planning Small Group Instruction During Independent Writing Time

Monday	Tuesday	Wednesday	Thursday	Friday
Below Level	On Level	Below Level	On Level	Below Level
Conferring	Conferring	Conferring	Conferring	Conferring
Strategy Group	Above Level	Strategy Group	Above Level	Strategy Group

Guided writing lessons are often extensions of the mini-lesson; they scaffold and/or extend students' learning. Other times your guided writing lessons will be more like a group conference. You'll read snippets of your students' writing and talk with them about their progress and then select a teaching point for the whole group. Just like your guided reading lessons, you'll meet more frequently with the students who need additional support and instruction. You'll typically meet with these students at the beginning of the writing block to help them get started successfully.

Strategy Lessons

Strategy groups are heterogeneous groups of children united in one important way: they all have a need for a particular lesson. For example, it may be a lesson on using an editing checklist, adding detail and elaboration, or using informational text features. Whether you're reviewing information that was shared in a previous mini-lesson, or extending children's learning beyond what was taught to the whole group, these groupings usually last for only one or two lessons and they're based on your observations and assessment data. Strategy groups are intended to be short term and based on need.

Conferring

The most powerful instruction in writing workshop may be the one-to-one conversations you have with your writers in writing conferences. Writing conferences, like reading conferences, follow the same research-decide-teach sequence. You'll plan your instruction based on what you observe and talk about during the "research" phase of the conference. Here are some ways to get the conference started (Anderson, 2000):

- How's your writing going?
- What's working really well in your writing?
- What are your next steps or plans?
- Have you thought about trying this idea as another form or genre (for example, writing it as a poem, a report, a letter, an article)?
- Tell me more about why/how you selected this topic.
- Is there a part you're wondering about?
- Have you thought about any parts that you want to revise? Tell me about those.
- Is there something I can do to help you at this point in your process?

Similar to mini-lessons, there are an infinite number of things you might teach in a conference. The best lessons are based on your writers' needs at that moment. Sometimes you'll realize that it's more important to affirm and encourage your writers' efforts than introduce new learning. Only you will know what's best for your students and when. Figure 3.8 highlights some ideas for what you might do or teach in a writing conference.

FIGURE 3.8 The Teacher's Role in a Writing Conference

- Help writers with ideas for their writing.
- Highlight and reinforce students' strengths.
- Ask questions to help uncover and develop the heart of a story.
- Help children articulate and reach their goals for writing.
- Teach and/or reinforce developmentally appropriate conventions of English.
- Develop your students' craft and revision techniques.
- Help your writers with the traits of effective writing: purpose, organization, details/elaboration, voice/tone, and conventions.

Share

Your writing workshop, like your reading workshop, concludes with a share time. Often, students will gather in your meeting area with the drafts they're working on. They may solicit input from peers by reading a sample of their writing to a partner or the class, or they may simply talk about what they're working on as writers, or what they learned about themselves as writers. Not unlike the share time at the end of reading workshop, you may wish to highlight your observations, or intentionally invite specific children to share strategies that will move other writers along in their work as well. Share time is an important part of building a literate community.

Word Study Instruction: An Overview

Word study is an approach to teaching phonics, spelling, and vocabulary. Through word study instruction, you help build children's interest in words and language, their fast and accurate recognition of words when reading, and their fast and accurate spelling of words when writing. You'll also help them better understand the meaning of words and word parts, which will help expand their vocabularies and deepen their comprehension of the texts they read.

Word study instruction is aligned with the five stages of development you learned about in Chapters 1 and 2. Word study begins with a focus on letter–sound correspondence. For example, in the word *cap*, each letter represents one sound: /c/ /a/ /p/. Later, students will compare and contrast long and short vowel sounds in words like *cap* and *cape* to bring their attention to the *pattern* layer of the spelling system. Later still, your students will explore the relationships between the spelling and meaning of words they are studying—words such as *compete* and *competition*. They'll also study parts of words: prefixes such as *un-*, *re-*, and *dis-*, and Greek and Latin roots such as *therm* (heat) and *rupt* (break). This study will help them not only spell words accurately but also learn strategies for using this morphological knowledge to unlock and remember the meaning of unfamiliar vocabulary words when reading.

Three things differentiate word study from other approaches to phonics, spelling, and vocabulary instruction:

1) Word study focuses on children's developmental stage, also known as instructional level.
2) Word study is interactive and hands-on in nature.
3) Word study attends to developing strategic spellers and readers who understand and use the three layers of the spelling system (sound, pattern, and meaning) to help them read, spell, and understand new words.

Common Core Connection

Language Standards: Conventions of Standard English; Vocabulary Acquisition and Use

Word study, like reading and writing workshop, is based on cognitive learning theory (Jensen, 2005; Sousa, 2011); constructivist teaching principles (Bruner, 1996; Vygotsky, 1978); and developmental stage theory (Chall, 1983; Ehri, 1997; 2005; Juel, 1991; Spear-Swerling & Sternberg, 1997; Templeton & Bear, 2011). Through sorting words and discussing theories about how these words work, your students will gain both *general* knowledge of English spelling and *specific* knowledge of the spelling and meaning of words. This knowledge will support their development in both reading and writing (Chall, 1983, Ehri, 2000; Juel, 1991; Spear-Swirling & Sternberg, 1997; Bear & Templeton, 1998).

Your word study block will be a relatively short amount of time: approximately 15 to 20 minutes each day. Many teachers integrate this instruction into their guided reading or guided writing lessons, while others prefer to have a separate block dedicated to word study instruction. Either approach works just fine—so long as you understand that it is critical for you to plan for student-centered, hands-on instruction and meaningful practice each and every day.

Sorting

The brain is a pattern detector; it seeks to find regularity in its environment; it also seeks novelty (Jensen, 2005; Sousa, 2011). Sorting words and pictures are two activities that help students do both: discover patterns about the way words work, and discover exceptions to these patterns, too. We call these patterns **generalizations.**

Note the three columns of words below. How many different ways can you sort them? By the initial letter, number of letters, number of syllables, part of speech, vowel sounds, spelling patterns, rhyming sounds, and even words you like and don't like! There's no limit to the different ways you can sort words. When we give students a list of words such as these and invite them to sort them any way they choose, we call it a **open sort**. Open sorts allow students to creatively categorize, discuss, and come to know their word study words in many different ways. We encourage students to share their categories and their rationale for sorting with one another. After some free exploration and engaging conversation, you'll steer your students to sort their words in a way that helps them understand how they work. Refer to the following word list and see if you can develop a theory about the similarities and differences of these words:

much	*itch*	*teach*
watch	*fetch*	*catch*
rich	*coach*	*sketch*
stitch	*hatch*	*screech*
peach	*reach*	*roach*

After some exploration and conversation among your students, you'll provide them with **keywords** or **key pictures** to help them categorize the words as you intended. In this example, you'd use the keywords *pitch* and *reach*. Write the sort using these key words as headers. Does your sort look something like the one below? Read through each of the words aloud and as you do, see if you can find a pattern of some kind.

pitch		*reach*	
stitch	*itch*	*coach*	*screech*
fetch	*hatch*	*teach*	*peach*
catch	*sketch*	*reach*	*roach*
		*rich	**much*

What did you notice about these words? Compare and contrast them again. What's similar? What's different? What have you discovered about words ending in –*tch* and –*ch*? Did you say that words that end in –*tch* contain short vowels and words that end in –*ch* contain long vowels? If you did, you've made a keen observation and you're developing a theory about how these words work! But what about the words *rich* and *much*? These two words don't fit the pattern, but instead of hiding them, we placed asterisks next to them because we want students to be aware of patterns and their exceptions. (Remember, the brain seeks novelty, too!) Place these exceptions in their own separate category labeled "Oddball." The oddball category can also be a place where students temporarily put words they aren't sure about. Encourage your students to talk about these words and help them reason through which category the word just might (or might not) belong.

When your students have generated a working theory about the words in their sort, encourage them to look for more examples of these patterns in familiar books and texts; this is known as a word hunt. When they find examples, they'll add the words to their lists, including the oddball list. Activities such as word sorts and word hunts help your students deepen their understanding of how the spelling system works and they encourage your students to transfer their learning to a much larger body of words (Bear et al., 2012; Juel & Minden-Cupp, 2000).

Student Talk and Reflection

Student talk and reflection are at the heart of word study instruction. Students need to develop working theories about how words work, and they'll do this through sorting, talking about their sorts with others, and participating in extension activities such as word hunts. As they gain more insight about how their sort works throughout the week, you'll encourage your students to articulate and document the generalizations they're discovering. We call these **reflections,** and your students will write them in their word study notebooks each week. Your students' understandings of how words work allow them to be more strategic when decoding, spelling, and even understanding the meaning of new words. See Figure 3.9 for an example of a fourth-grade student's reflection about the word sort at the beginning of this section.

Different Types of Sorts

Student-centered open sorts may well be one of our favorite ways to sort words, but there are many other ways to sort words, too. In this section, we'll summarize some of these different ways. You'll learn more about sorting words, pictures, and objects by sound, pattern, and meaning in each of the developmental chapters as well.

FIGURE 3.9 **Sample Student Reflection**

Sometimes it's hard to know when to use –tch and –ch because they sound alike! This week I learned that we use the –tch pattern when the vowel sound is short as in the words itch, catch, and fetch. We use –ch when the vowel is long as in the words coach, peach, and screech. I found just a few exceptions to this generalization including rich, much, and such. I also learned that words that have a vowel + r, l, or n, end in –ch, too. Words like mulch, church, and lunch.

Teacher-Directed Closed Sorts

Teacher-directed sorts are the most common way to sort words. These sorts are particularly helpful to novice teachers and students who are new to word study because they follow a predictable routine. This routine, like so many others in the workshop, gradually releases responsibility to the learner through a five-step process known as Demonstrate, Sort, Check, Reflect, and Extend (Bear et al., 2012).

Demonstrate We begin every teacher-directed sort by connecting this week's sort to students' prior knowledge: "Last week we studied the short *i* vowel sound in words such as *bit, hid*, and *fig*. Let's talk about this for a minute." "This week we're going to study some other short *i* word families, including the *–in, –ill*, and *–im* word families."

In a teacher-directed sort, you'll use an enlarged set of word cards or you'll project the words on a screen or Smart Board so all your students can read the words or see the pictures. As you read through each of the words or pictures in the sort, periodically stop to talk about the meaning of the words, particularly words that may not be familiar to your students. When using pictures for your sorts, be sure the students can identify each picture as well as define and describe these words as necessary.

Introduce the categories of your sort. These categories may be letters, pictures, words, or patterns such as the CVC (consonant-vowel-consonant) or CVCe (consonant-vowel-consonant-silent *e*) pattern. These category labels are called **headers**. In the example at the beginning of this section, we used the words *pitch* and *reach* as the headers for each category.

Model for the students how to sort the words by taking a picture or word from the sort, saying it aloud, and comparing and contrasting it to the two (or more) headers. Show the students how to decide which category to place the word or picture into. Repeat this protocol with several words before inviting your students to take turns with the remaining words. Your students will follow the same procedure of naming the words or pictures and comparing and contrasting them to the headers like this:

Comparing and Contrasting Short Vowel Sounds

You would say the following: "This is a picture of *map* – *maaap*. Does it sound like *flag* (*flaaag*) or *truck* (*tru-u-uck*) in the middle? Yes, *maaap* sounds like *flaaag* in the middle. They both have the 'short a,' /ă/ sound, so we'll add the picture to this column with the picture of the flag."

If your students make an error during this guided practice portion of the demonstration, help them self-correct it right away. However, when they practice on their own, patiently wait for them to discover errors when checking their sort with their partners. If they don't recognize their errors, help them discover and self-correct them (as we'll discuss).

Common Core Connection

Reading Standards: Foundational Skills – Phonological Awareness

Sort After your demonstration, students will work together in partnerships to conduct the sort. They'll follow the same protocol you modeled in the demonstration—reading and talking about all the words or pictures first and laying any unknown pictures or words aside. Next, they'll sort by reading each word or naming each picture, then comparing and contrasting each one to the headers, one at a time, before placing them in a column.

Check After students have sorted their words, ask them to check their sorts by reading the words aloud or naming the pictures. As they do, remind them to be thinking about whether or not each word or picture has been placed in the correct column. If your students do not spontaneously self-correct, you might say something like this: "I think there's one word [or picture] in this column that doesn't belong. Can you find it?" Conversely, you might say, "Tell me about why you placed this word [or picture] in this column." Your students' explanations can provide you with valuable insight into the degree to which they understand how the sort and pattern(s) work. After talking with your students about why they sorted the words or pictures as they did, prompt them to self-correct: "Where else might this word go?" and encourage analysis with a prompt such as: "Why does this word fit better in this category?"

Reflect After your students have sorted and checked their words, encourage them to talk with one another about their sort. Prompt them with questions such as:

- What do you notice about the words [or pictures] in your columns?
- How are they alike? How are they different?
- Do you have a hunch about how they work? Tell me about it.
- What do you notice about the sound(s) in these words?
- What do you notice about the spelling patterns?
- How are these words related in meaning?

In the reflection part of the lesson, you're asking students to "compare and declare" (Bear et al., 2012); they summarize their learning, as best they can, in this first lesson. Throughout the week, these reflections will become more precise and include many examples such as the one in Figure 3.9.

Extend Sometimes immediately after the lesson, but more often in the following days, students will continue to practice sorting and studying their words through hands-on activities such word hunts, draw and label, dictionary work, games, or other activities. We will describe these extension activities later in the chapter.

Teacher-Directed Guess My Category Sort

After your students have become comfortable with teacher-directed sorts, they may enjoy a variation of this kind of sort called Guess My Category. When introducing this type of sort, provide your students with two or more headers. These headers may be objects, pictures, or words.

As your students read each word (or identify each picture or object in the sort), they have to figure out which category it belongs to. As they do, be careful not to correct them—part of the fun and learning is encouraging your students to work together to reason their way through the sort and then deduce your categories. Look at the following sort. Can you guess its categories?

cake	_rain_	_play_
lake	_paint_	_tray_
take	_nail_	_day_
flake	_maid_	_stay_

If you answered, "Three ways to spell a long *a*," you're correct! From this initial Guess My Category sort, we could extend the learning in this sort by talking about different ways to spell long *a*, the position of each pattern (in other words, where it falls in the word), and its frequency. As with all sorting activities, be sure your students sort, check, reflect, and then extend their learning throughout the week.

Concept Sorts

Sorting is also great for vocabulary and concept development. Concept sorts can be teacher-directed, open, or a Guess My Category sort. Your concept sorts can be as simple or difficult as you wish: sorting buttons by shape, color, or number of holes, for example, or sorting more sophisticated concepts such as the Five Classes of Animals sort, or sorting vocabulary associated with different battles or causes of the Civil War. At the later stages of development, your students will sort words according to the concepts underlying their Greek and Latin word parts. For example, when studying the Latin root –*spect*–, students would place words such as *spectacle, spectator, inspect,* and *respect* together in a category and talk about how they're all related to looking or viewing.

You'll learn more about concept sorts in the developmental chapters.

Sorting Throughout the Week

Over the course of each week, you'll provide your students with many different opportunities to sort words. In Figure 3.10 you'll find a summary of different ways your students can sort their weekly word study words. When the features you're studying are new to students, consider higher levels of teacher support, such as a teacher-directed closed sort. When they have more background knowledge or experience, an open sort may be more appropriate. As students gain familiarity with words and the features in their current sort, you will vary their sorting experiences across the week to include some of the different forms of sorting as described in Figure 3.10.

Preparing Sorts

When it comes to sorting, two of the most common questions are "How do I know which features my students should study?" and "Where do I get the words for my weekly sorts?" The answer to the first question is easy: This scope and sequence comes from decades of research that examined the development of children's word knowledge. In each of the developmental chapters we identify the scope and sequence for word study at each stage of development: emergent, beginning, transitional, intermediate, and skillful. The answer to the second question is also pretty straightforward. Based on this scope and sequence, you can prepare your own word lists using resources such as *The Reading Teacher's Book of Lists* (Fry & Kress, 2006); *The Spelling Teacher's Book of Lists* (Phenix & Cole, 2003); and *Words Their Way: Word Study for Phonics, Vocabulary, and Spelling Instruction* (Bear et al., 2012). The authors of *Words Their Way* have also prepared weekly

FIGURE 3.10 **All Sorts of Sorts!**

Picture Sorts

Whenever you want your students to focus on the sounds of English, whether it's a rhyme at the end of a word, the initial consonant, a medial vowel sound, or the stress in a syllable, picture sorts will help you achieve your goal. By using pictures or objects instead of print, your students will have to focus their attention on sorting by sound. This awareness of sound facilitates both reading and spelling development.

Pattern Sorts

Students begin to sort words by pattern in the beginning stage of development when they first learn about word families. In the transitional stage, they sort patterns within words such long vowel patterns. Later in the intermediate stage, they begin to look at the spelling and vowel patterns within syllables. And finally, in the skillful literacy stage, they'll sort by words that are related in meaning. Pattern sorts help students generalize spelling patterns beyond the words in their sorts, which helps them read and spell words accurately and quickly.

Buddy Sorts/Partner Sorts

After you've demonstrated a sort, it's typical that you'll have students work as with partners to sort, check, and reflect on the sort at least once on the first day of instruction. Throughout the week, encourage students to continue to sort with their partners, working together to read the words and talk about which category to place them in and why. Buddy sorts can be especially helpful for English learners who have difficulty recognizing the pictures in picture sorts, or the meaning of some words in their word sorts. Your students should always be able to read the words in your sorts, and if they can't, they should set the unknown word aside.

Blind Sorts

Word study buddies are especially helpful for blind sorts. In a blind sort, the partner displays the categories of the sort, shuffles the word cards, and reads each word aloud without showing it to the buddy. The buddy must then select the appropriate category by pointing to it. Together the partners check the sort at the end and reflect on what they're learning about these words.

Blind Writing Sorts

Toward the end of the week, partners can work together as one partner reads each word while the other partner writes the word in its appropriate category. After writing the word, the word is provided and checked for accuracy. After all the words are written, the partners switch roles. Like blind sorts, blind writing sorts engage multiple senses and provide students with much needed sorting and writing practice.

Writing Sorts

When partners are not available, students can still practice writing their sorts by turning over one word at a time, reading it aloud, setting it aside, and then writing the word in its appropriate column. This reinforces their understanding of the big idea of the sort, and provides practice spelling specific words. It's also a multisensory experience. Engaging multiple senses helps students retain their learning better (Sousa, 2011). Be sure to remind your students to self-correct their writing sorts.

Speed Sorts

One of the primary goals of word study is to help students automatically read and spell words. This frees up cognitive resources that allow them to focus on comprehending while reading, and composing their message while writing. All sorting practice helps with this, but speed sorts focus specifically in automaticity and accuracy. Again, partners can work together to time one another while they sort their words and then check the accuracy of their sorting once it's complete. Students also find it motivating to chart their progress throughout the week. Importantly, we emphasize the goal of beating one's own time rather than competing against another student.

word sorts for each stage of development in five companion books and several books with sorts for English language learners. Appropriate words for both spelling and vocabulary are provided in Templeton (2012), too.

Extension Activities

When it comes to word study, accuracy and automaticity are two important goals. When students are accurate and automatic at the word level, it allows them to focus on comprehension while reading, or composing meaningful messages while writing. Extension activities, in addition to repeated sorting, will help your students retain both general and specific information about the words they're studying.

Word Hunts

Word hunts provide students the opportunity to transfer what they're learning about spelling words to the reading of words. This relationship isn't necessarily obvious to students, and so you'll want to help facilitate the connection for them. Word hunts are just one way to do this. To begin, select a piece of familiar text—one they've read many times before—and show them how to search for words that follow the patterns they're studying. Be sure to mention how skimming for words is different from actually reading for understanding. If photocopies of texts are available, your students will enjoy using highlighter pens to note the patterns in different colors. After locating the words, the students will add them to their word study notebooks and/or compile a group chart using the appropriate headings.

Remember, the words students are able to read are more often more difficult than the words they're able to spell. Word hunts, therefore, have the potential to increase the difficulty of students' sorts while also exposing them to richer vocabulary.

Brainstorming

In addition to searching for words in familiar texts, you may encourage students to brainstorm words they think fit the patterns they're learning about. In the beginning stage, this might mean asking children to generate words that rhyme with the word family they're studying and then showing them how they're related in spelling: "If you know the word *hill*, you can read and spell the words *pill*, *fill*, *Jill*, *drill*, and *spill!* Let's look at how to spell them together." At the upper end of the continuum, you might be learning about the Latin root *–port–*. Before sorting their words, or even after, encourage your students to brainstorm words with *–port–* in them: *transport*, *portable*, *import*, *export*, and *deport*, for example. Brainstorming can also help your students discover the meaning of words or roots: For example, you might ask, "What do you think the root *–port–* might mean? Look over your list of brainstormed words. What do the meanings of all these words have in common?" Your students will deduce or look up the meaning of the root to realize it means "to carry." Brainstorming can also help students find exceptions.

Draw and Label

Most students, particularly those in the early stages of development, like to draw and label objects. In the end of the emergent stage and early letter name–alphabetic stage, for example, students might brainstorm and draw pictures of words that start with the consonant *m*. When students label these words, don't expect conventional spelling. You're looking only for the initial consonant sound to be represented accurately because that's what they're studying. Transitional spellers might draw and label homophones as seen in the notebook entry in Figure 3.11. These drawings help students remember the relationship between the meanings of these words and their spelling. Students at the later stages of development also include drawings with labels in their notebooks. Sometimes they extend this activity by noting the word's part of speech or by writing a short definition or meaningful sentence. All of these activities help students see the relationship between spelling and meaning.

Games and Other Activities

In addition to the activities described here and in the developmental chapters, you'll help build students' spelling, reading, and vocabulary skills by including word study games in your weekly

FIGURE 3.11 Sample Notebook Entry

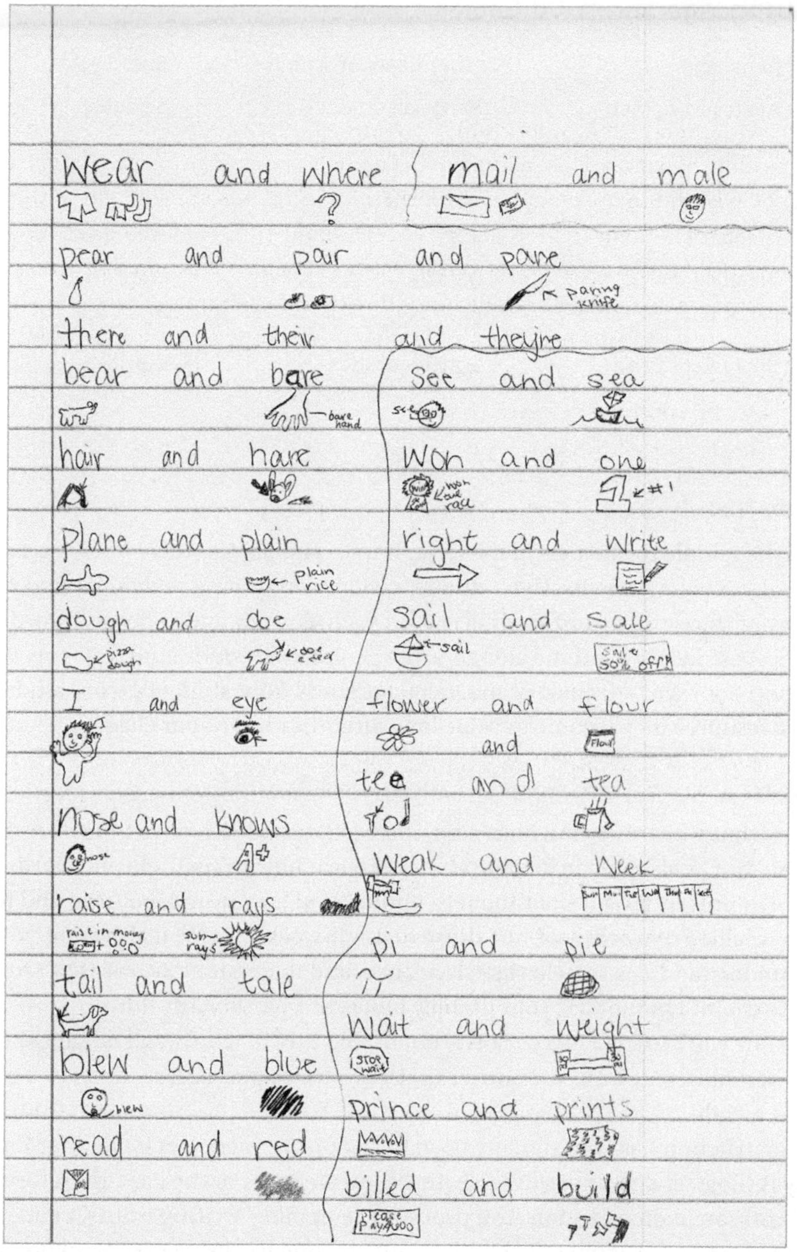

routine. Not only are these games educational but they're also fun! You'll find recommendations and templates for making developmentally appropriate games in *Words Their Way* (Bear et al., 2012) and *Words Their Way with English Learners* (Helman et al., 2012). You may also wish to supplement your teacher-made word study games with some commercially available games, many of which you may have in your closets at home. Figure 3.12 contains some of our favorites. Naturally, you'll select games that are in line with your students' developmental stages and your instructional goals.

FIGURE 3.12 A Sampling of Commercially Available Language and Word Games

Anomia	(The) Game of Things	Sketchy
Apples to Apples	Hangman	Scrabble
Balderdash	Last Word	Scrabble Slam
Bananagrams	Pictionary	UpWords
Bingo	Pop	Who Gnu?
Boggle	Quiddler	Word Thief
Catch Phrase	Rory's Story Cubes	Zingo
Duple Card Came	Scattergories	Zip-it

Word Study Notebooks

Beginning in the middle to late part of the letter name–alphabetic stage, you'll introduce word study notebooks to your students. Here, students will record their weekly sorts and reflections and keep track of their other word study activities such as Draw and Label and word hunts, among others. As students continue along the developmental continuum, you may add a section to students' notebooks for vocabulary and language study. Your students' word study notebooks will become a resource they'll come to value long after they leave your class!

A Final Word about Word Study Games and Activities

You now know that word study is a hands-on, interactive, and reflective time during your literacy block. Your goals include helping students learn how to spell specific words, yes, but perhaps more importantly, you want them to understand how sound, pattern, and meaning are related to the spelling of words, not just those on their weekly list. You also want your students to use these understandings to help them read, use, and understand words that are both familiar and new to them. Throughout your literacy block, but particularly during word study, you will intentionally work to inspire a curiosity about and love of words and language. These goals are probably very different from your own experiences with phonics, spelling, or vocabulary instruction as a child.

Spelling instruction has traditionally been based on the incorrect belief that English orthography is illogical and unpredictable; teaching methods of the past, therefore, relied quite heavily on rote memorization. You probably remember writing words, particularly corrected misspellings, 5 or 10 times each, filling out spelling worksheets or workbooks, alphabetizing spelling words, and memorizing stacks of vocabulary flashcards only to forget the meaning and spelling of these words just days (maybe even hours) later. This wasn't a good use of anyone's time.

When selecting word study activities, think carefully about how the activity can advance the goals you have for your students—goals like those we just shared. If the activity is just busywork, make a different choice. Being aware of how tradition can affect your instructional choices is important. Rather than relying on your own experiences as an elementary or middle school student, turn to the research-based practices shared and throughout this book. The most effective teachers are articulate about their instructional decisions (Mosenthal et al., 2004), and you will be one of those teachers!

Managing Word Study Instruction Across the Week

Your word study block will be easiest to manage when it has a predictable structure each day and across the week. Some teachers find it easiest to extend their guided reading groups by 5 or 10 minutes and embed word study instruction into that structure. In doing so, they extend the reading block by 15–30 minutes each day. Other teachers prefer to have a 15- to 30-minute block exclusively for word study, which is an equally effective arrangement.

As you can imagine, the first day of your word study block requires the most instructional time because you're introducing a new sort to your groups. For this reason, you may have to borrow extra time from other parts of your day to meet with all three groups on the first day of the week. Another possibility is to adopt a cascading or "waterfall" schedule whereby you stagger your five-day lesson plan so each group's "day one" starts on a different day. Figure 3.13 illustrates how this looks over time.

FIGURE 3.13 Sample Cascading Word Study Schedule

Monday	Tuesday	Wednesday	Thursday	Friday
Group A – Day 1	Group A – Day 2	Group A – Day 3	Group A – Day 4	Group A – Day 5
Group B – Day 5	Group B – Day 1	Group B – Day 2	Group B – Day 3	Group B – Day 4
Group C – Day 4	Group C – Day 5	Group C – Day 1	Group C – Day 2	Group C – Day 3

Your Word Study Lesson Plan Sequence

Most teachers like to plan their word study lessons to last for five days, although there's no reason the instructional sequence can't last longer, or be even shorter. In some cases, it may be wise to accelerate the pace; in other cases, students might require a slower pace. These are decisions you'll make once you get to know your students well. For the time being, refer to Figure 3.14 for an example of a five-day lesson plan sequence that works for students at different developmental stages.

FIGURE 3.14 Sample Five-Day Lesson Plan for Word Study Instruction

Monday (Day 1)	Tuesday (Day 2)	Wednesday (Day 3)	Thursday (Day 4)	Friday (Day 5)
Introduce the sort. Students sort at least once with partners. Students discuss their emerging theories about how the sort works.	Students read through the words, sort them once, and try a writing sort. Time allowing, students will work with partners or time themselves on a speed sort.	Begin with a blind writing sort and then return to speed sorting. Include at least one extension activity such as a word hunt or draw and label today.	Begin with speed sorts. Students talk about the week's sort with a partner and write a reflection. Time allowing, students will participate in at least one extension activity, often a blind writing sort.	Do the weekly assessment. Play games and/or add more extension activities.

Word Study Assessment

As you review this five-day lesson plan, you will undoubtedly notice the word *assessment*. When planning your weekly spelling assessments, create an assessment procedure that's reflective of your learning goals. Remember, correctly spelling the words on the week's sort is only one of your many goals. You also want your students to accurately categorize words, and reflect on the big ideas or generalizations they learned each week. Furthermore, you want them to apply these generalizations to words beyond just those on their list. While there are many ways to give a spelling assessment, we like to see assessments that give points for each of these things:

- Spelling words correctly
- Placing words in the correct categories (you can provide the categories or give points to students for labeling the categories)
- A written reflection that reveals the students' understanding of the spelling principles they learned in that week's sort
- Bonus points for applying these principles to words that follow the generalization but were not part of the week's sort. (These words often come from students' word hunts during the week.)

As you might expect, some parents and families will be confused about this kind of assessment. Tradition is a powerful influence on parents and teachers alike. To learn more about how to talk with parents and families about word study instruction, refer to the feature Working and Collaborating in Chapter 8.

Individual Learning Contracts

Students in the upper elementary or middle school grades, and some very mature students in the intermediate grades, are able to manage much of their word study practice independently, especially after you've thoroughly modeled the routines and expectations. You'll still need to meet with students to introduce the sort either the first day of your cycle or the second day after they've had some time to explore the sort on their own or with a partner. After that initial lesson, you can check on their progress through observation, conferring, and assessing their word study notebooks. For students who are ready to manage their work in this way, consider putting together a contract system such as the one in Figure 3.15. Note the focus on word meanings: This particular contract was developed for students in the derivational relations stage. You may choose to use this contract, or you may create your own that will more specifically meet your students' developmental needs and your learning goals.

Comprehensive Core Reading Programs

Comprehensive core reading programs, sometimes called basal reading programs, have been part of the educational landscape for almost 200 years (Templeton, 1996). These programs have evolved over time, yet their purpose has remained relatively constant: to provide teachers and students with a systematic approach and materials to teach with varying types of practice—often including not only reading but also writing and spelling.

Increasingly, today's comprehensive reading programs allow for more differentiation than those of previous generations. They typically include a common grade-level text for all students to read as a whole group, as well as selections for students reading above and below grade level.

FIGURE 3.15 Sample Word Study Contract for Upper-Elementary and Middle-Level Students

WORD STUDY CONTRACT

Name _____ Date _____

Feature of Study _____

Directions: Select activities to earn up to 100 points toward your word study grade. Complete all written work in your word study notebook and turn it in along with this contract for final grading.

Required Activities

_____ Sort, record, and reflect (30 pts)   _____ Work with a partner to complete at least one spelling activity. Partner signs here:_____

Explore Spelling (10 pts each)

_____ Repeat sort 2 times   _____ Sort a different way and record

_____ Blind sort with partner   _____ Word hunt (find at least 5 words)

_____ Blind writing sort with partner   _____ Speed sorts

_____ Play a game with partner   Record times: _____

Explore Meaning (20 pts each—select at least one)

_____ Define 7 words   _____ Brainstorm or hunt for additional words

_____ Use 7 words in sentences   _____ Report etymologies for 7 words

_____ Illustrate 7 words   _____ Make up new words and define them

_____ Create a comic strip using 5 words   _____ Create your own game

_____ Complete a word tree or root web   _____ Other

Total Points _____   Test Grade _____

Source: Bear et al., 2012, p. 77.

These texts are usually accompanied by lesson plans that target instruction in fluency, vocabulary, and comprehension, and, in the early years, phonemic awareness and phonics. They include print, CD-ROM, and online activities for students to complete after each lesson. There are also supplemental teacher and student resources online and on CD-ROMs. In addition, teacher activities and lessons are available for Smart Boards. You will need to use these materials judiciously, keeping in mind the importance of small group instruction, hands-on practice, student discussion, and authentic reading and writing practice.

Comprehensive core reading programs can provide novice and even veteran teachers with very good resources, materials, and support, especially when literacy coaches like Janet Lawton are not available to help you design a research-based reading program. Although they are called "comprehensive core reading programs," these programs are not designed with the expectation that every single activity they include should be taught. Rather, they are designed to be effective resources from which teachers may select the most appropriate activities to use with their particular students. Researchers have found that most teachers do, in fact, pick and choose lessons and parts of lessons that suit their and their students' needs (Grossman & Thompson, 2004; Mesmer, 2006).

Whether you are using a core reading program or not, your ability to make instructional decisions and set priorities for your students is vital. Understanding development and the practices of highly effective teachers will help you create and maintain a vision of what's essential in your language arts block. No program is perfect, and there's also no substitute for well-informed teachers who make decisions based on the needs of their students. You will be such a teacher. Using the principles and practices outlined in this chapter, you'll take advantage of the many resources provided in core reading programs and use them to teach in a developmentally responsive and research-based way. The Reading, Writing, Word Study Workshop provides a framework for you to incorporate as many pieces and parts of the core reading program that make sense for you and your students.

Chapter Summary

Whether you're a novice teacher like Deeni Antonucci, or an experienced veteran like Janet Lawton, it's important for you to identify your instructional priorities and arrange your classroom environment and literacy block to support the things that matter most. The research on highly effective teachers will help you identify many of these priorities, including more small group instruction than whole class instruction, purposeful reading and writing practice, and explicit word study instruction that's connected to reading and writing tasks. These will become your priorities as well.

William James (1958) once wrote, "Teaching is not telling." A corollary to this wisdom may be "Learning is not memorizing." While memory plays a role in learning, you'll work to provide learning experiences for your students that are richer, deeper, and more memorable than rote learning could ever be. Your role is not only to transmit knowledge but also to create environments, instructional routines, and learning opportunities in which your students will be involved in the co-construction of knowledge. This will happen throughout your Reading, Writing, Word Study Workshop. Whether it happens through a discussion of a complex text, during an interesting word sort, or through studying a mentor text with a writing buddy, your students' learning will be active, purposeful, and collaborative.

Holding high expectations and engaging students in appropriately challenging tasks are among the hallmarks of highly effective teachers—teachers such as Deeni Antonucci, Janet Lawton, and you.

Suggested Extension Activities

- Research suggests that students are more likely to read a book if it's recommended by a friend or a teacher. Select some of your favorite picture books and novels for young adults and plan a two-minute book talk to share with your peers or students.
- Whether you're a digital native or a digital immigrant, your students will expect you to incorporate technology in your teaching. Revisit the feature titled Reading and Writing in Digital Contexts and explore some of these online resources. Select one or two to incorporate in your teaching. Write up your plans and share with your peers or a colleague.
- Create a Venn diagram that compares and contrasts your own literacy learning experiences or those you've observed, with the practices outlined in this chapter. How are they alike? How are they different? Look over your notes and identify the things you think will be most challenging to implement. Create a list of goals that you'll refer to as you continue to read, learn, and reflect.

Recommended Professional Resources

Allington, R., & Johnston, P. (2002). *Reading to learn: Lessons from exemplary fourth-grade classrooms.* New York: Guilford.

Bear, D. R., Invernizzi, M., Templeton, S., & Johnston, F. (2012). *Words their way: Word study for phonics, vocabulary, and spelling instruction* (5th ed.). Boston: Pearson/Allyn & Bacon.

Calkins, L. M. (1994). *The art of teaching writing* (2nd ed.) Portsmouth, NH: Heinemann.

Calkins, L. M. (2000). *The art of teaching reading.* Portsmouth, NH: Heinemann.

Denton, P., & Kriete, R. (2000). *The first six weeks of school.* Greenfield, MA: Northeast Foundation for Children.

Diller, D. (2008). *Spaces and places: Designing classrooms for literacy.* Portland, ME: Stenhouse.

Fountas, I., & Pinnell, G. (2001). *Guiding readers and writers (grades 3–6): Teaching, comprehension, genre, and content literacy.* Portsmouth, NH: Heinemann.

Johnston, P. (2004). *Choice words: How our language affects children's learning.* Portland, ME: Stenhouse.

Miller, D. (2002). *Reading with meaning.* Portland, ME: Stenhouse.

Pressley, M., Allington, R., Wharton-McDonald, R., Collins Block, K., & Morrow, L. (2001). *Learning to read: Lessons from exemplary first-grade classrooms.* New York: Guilford.

Taylor, B. M., Pearson, P. D., Clark, K., & Walpole, S. (1999). *Beating the odds in teaching all children to read* (No. 2-006). Ann Arbor, MI: CIERA.

Taylor, B. M., Pearson, P. D., Peterson, D., & Rodriguez, M. C. (2003). Looking inside classrooms: Reflecting on the "how" as well as the "what" in effective reading instruction. *The Reading Teacher, 56*(3), 270–279.

Wong, H. K., & Wong, R. T. (1998). *The first days of school: How to be an effective teacher* (4th ed.). Mountainview, CA: Harry K. Wong Publications.

Online Resources

Annenberg Learner: Part of the Annenberg Foundation

www.learner.org

Annenberg Learner is a multimedia resource for advancing excellence in U.S. schools. As part of this site, teachers will find research, educational videos, and other resources to support their professional development. A special video series on teaching reading and writing workshop can be found under the Literature and Language Arts tab.

Northern Nevada Writing Project: Writing Fix

http://writingfix.com

The Northern Nevada Writing Project has developed an online resource for teachers of writing called Writing Fix. It includes a variety of resources, lesson plans, and information for your ongoing professional development in the area of writing. You will learn more about the writing process, the traits of effective writing, and ways to integrate writing across the curriculum.

Words, Words, Words, and MORE Words

www.wordcentral.com; www.etymonline.com; www.visualthesaurus.com; www.wornikcom; www.allwords.com

Whether you're new to word study or an experienced veteran, you can never find enough online resources for teaching word study, or for your students to access during your Reading, Writing, Word Study Workshop. The above websites are some of our favorites.

Prioritizing Student-Centered Assessment and Instruction

Chapter Outline

» A Brief and Recent History of Assessment and School Reform

» Types and Purposes of Assessment

» The Qualities of a "Good" Assessment

» A Comprehensive Literacy Assessment Program

» Using Ongoing Formative Assessment in Your Classroom

1. How have standards, assessment, and accountability policies changed over time? How might they influence your practice today?

2. Compare and contrast some of the different purposes and types of assessment. How are they similar? How are they different?

3. How are standards, assessment, and instruction related?

4. What makes a literacy assessment a "good" assessment?

5. Explain how screening, diagnostic, progress monitoring, interim/benchmark, outcomes assessments, and the literacy essentials come together to create a comprehensive approach to student assessment.

6. What are some ways you'll include ongoing formative assessment in your classroom? What makes formative assessment so powerful?

P eter Foster is the principal of Main Street School, a relatively small K–8 school located in a large urban setting. One hundred percent of Main Street's students receive free or reduced price lunch, an indicator of poverty in American schools, and more than half of the students are English learners, most of them refugees. The state's commissioner of education recently appointed Mr. Foster to his position when Main Street's students failed to make **adequate yearly progress** *(AYP)* on the state's comprehensive assessment for the third year in a row.

As Mr. Foster prepares for the first staff meeting of the school year, he assembles a group of articles he wants his staff to read. Among them are touchstone articles on the topics of assessment and instruction, including "Less Teaching, More Assessing" (Wilcox, 2006), "Effective Instruction Begins with Purposeful Assessments" (Cobb, 2003), and "Putting It All Together: Solving the Reading Assessment Puzzle" (Farr, 1992). He knows these are sensitive topics for the teachers at Main Street. Despite a lot of professional development and significant gains in their students' test scores, they're still not on track to meet the federal government's target of *all* students being on grade level by 2014—a primary goal of the federal legislation known as No Child Left Behind.

In recent years, members of the press and even local policymakers have called Main Street a "failing school"—a label that cost the former principal her job. Main Street's predicament is not unusual. In this era of **high-stakes testing**, many schools across the country have been labeled by their state departments of education as "needing improvement," and particularly schools that serve diverse and economically challenged populations. Mr. Foster aims to improve student achievement in this school and he believes more assessment is part of the answer, but as you can imagine, it's going to be hard to persuade his teachers that more assessment is the right thing to do, especially since it's their students' test scores that earned them the unwelcome distinction of being in need of improvement.

Mr. Foster begins his staff meeting with some warm and welcoming remarks and then passes out the articles he's selected. He explains that each staff member will read one article closely and then report on the big ideas and his or her reactions in small groups. The school's newest faculty members, first-year teachers Nick Hall, Sarah Davis, and Nina Gonzalez, feel a little anxious, but before long, people are reading and soon conversation fills the room. Nick is the first to share his summary and reaction to "Less Teaching, More Assessing":

"This article really made sense to me. The author explains that ongoing assessment helps teachers identify their students' strengths and opportunities for improvement. Ongoing assessment allows us to share regular and specific feedback with our students so they have clear learning goals in mind; this empowers and motivates them.

"I also learned that feedback is different from praise because feedback is more specific. It communicates to students what they're doing well, what they need more practice with, and how they can improve. When students understand our expectations and how to achieve them, they become partners in their learning. Both regular and specific feedback are critical to students' growth and the effectiveness of our teaching."

Sarah looks over at Nick's group and notices that he's interacting easily with his new colleagues and this helps her feel more at ease. When it's her turn to report to the group, she starts by sharing a quote that she found particularly powerful:

"The author of my article explained the difference between assessment and evaluation in a way that really helped me understand why Mr. Foster thinks we should assess more. She wrote, 'A visit to the doctor's office is to assessment what an autopsy is to evaluation' (Cobb, p. 386). Doctors, like teachers, use assessment to detect and prevent problems.

"Evaluation, on the other hand, is performed at the end of a learning unit, in the same way an autopsy comes at the end of life. Evaluation is commonly called **summative assessment**, or **outcomes assessment**. The author of the article affirms that this kind of assessment is important, but ongoing **formative assessment**, like visiting the doctor's office, better informs our teaching and ultimately leads to better outcomes."

Nina's turn to report came last in her group. Her article helped her understand the big picture of literacy

assessment and the goals of different stakeholders. She explains:

"I never really thought about literacy assessments having different purposes or audiences until I read this article, 'Putting It All Together: Solving the Reading Assessment Puzzle.' I now know that it's important to understand what an assessment does and doesn't offer and to whom. Parents, policymakers, and administrators have an interest and responsibility to ensure that schools are effective. They're more likely to turn to high-stakes tests for that information because it allows them to compare student performance to a norm or a standard. Teachers and administrators can learn some things about an individual student's strengths and challenges from these tests, too, but it's usually more helpful to use these results to reflect on the general effectiveness of the literacy program, and to prioritize ongoing professional development.

"It's regular formative assessment that really helps teachers understand how students are progressing and how to best support their growth and development. When ongoing assessments can identify your students' stages of development, you're more likely to teach students at their instructional level rather than at their frustration level, and this is when learning flourishes!"

Later in the day, Nick, Sarah, and Nina meet for coffee. They share their thoughts from the day, including the staff meeting and the articles. As they talk, they reflect on the importance of (1) ongoing formative assessment, (2) regular and specific feedback to students, and (3) understanding the different purposes and audiences of assessment.

Perhaps most important, they came to realize that assessment and instruction are reciprocal processes and one can strengthen the other. They also learned that no two assessments are exactly alike—they all have different advantages and disadvantages and they're used for different purposes, too.

Nick, Sarah, and Nina recognize they have a lot to learn about literacy assessment, but they're well on their way, just like you are, too! ■

You probably have a lot of feelings about assessment—some may be positive and some may be downright negative! Perhaps you've experienced the high-stakes assessments of No Child Left Behind yourself, or other high-stakes tests such as the Praxis exam, the Scholastic Achievement Test (SAT), or the Graduate Record Exam (GRE). Many students find these assessments simply terrifying, while others have positive experiences with them. Maybe you prefer essay exams, or fill-in-the-blank assessments? Some students, for example, love timed exams; others dread them. As you read this chapter, you'll realize that your own life experiences may affect your feelings toward assessment, and this is probably true about instruction as well. It's important to draw from these experiences but also to move beyond them to consider new and different ways to use assessment in your classroom.

Literacy assessment is a complex topic, and one that is invariably linked to education policy, politics, instructional decision making, and even your professional identity. Before we get into the nuts and bolts of *why* and *how* to assess your students, it's important to contextualize the decisions you'll make in your classroom within the larger policy environment. We begin this chapter with an introduction to the major school reform initiatives of recent decades and how they've led to today's policy environment—one in which high-stakes tests figure so prominently. Understanding this history will help you better understand the perspectives and needs of different stakeholders (students, parents, fellow educators, administrative leaders, policymakers), and the ways in which you can use these insights to better meet your students' needs and improve the effectiveness of your teaching.

A Brief and Recent History of Assessment and School Reform

The field of assessment has changed significantly in recent decades, and the federal government's influence in this change has not been small (McGill-Franzen, 2000; Nichols & Berliner, 2007; Ravitch, 2011; Tyack & Cuban, 1995; Valencia & Wixson, 2000). Today's accountability movement can trace its roots back to the Elementary and Secondary Education Act of 1965 (ESEA) (Public Law 89-10). This act was intended to improve children's access to equitable educational opportunities and to address disparities in the educational achievement of children from differing socioeconomic backgrounds. ESEA called for more rigorous standards in math and science, as well as in foreign language and the liberal arts (Tyack & Cuban, 1995). One of the central goals of ESEA was to restore the United States' global preeminence in science, math, and technology in the post-*Sputnik* era.

Throughout the late 1960s and early 1970s, the standards movement temporarily lost traction as a focus on equity and access took center stage. Issues related to school integration, gender equity, and the inclusion of students with special needs became a significant focus of the public schools. By the mid-seventies, reformers tried to regain control, and in doing so, called for new *minimum* competency standards and tests of basic skills. This back-to-basics campaign was intended to improve the competitiveness and preparedness of the nation's workforce (Amrein & Berliner, 2002).

"A Nation at Risk"

Less than a decade later, in the 1980s, Japan and other nations were gaining a stronghold in the global marketplace, and a considerable number of American jobs were going overseas. The educational system became the scapegoat for the nation's sputtering economy yet again. In response, Congress appointed a national commission to examine the state of education in the United States. The resulting report, *A Nation at Risk* (National Commission on Excellence in Education, 1983), called for the end of the minimum competency standards. The report's authors believed these standards were "dumbing down" the curriculum and holding back U.S. students' achievement.

By the early 1990s, a number of studies revealed that standards-based reform was not affecting student achievement very signficantly, if at all. Researchers found that it was difficult for teachers to translate educational policy, including higher standards, into effective instruction. And commercial school reform programs such as the Coalition of Essential Schools and even innovative assessment and professional development initiatives such as the New Standards Project did little to remedy this problem (McGill-Franzen, 2000; Valencia & Wixson, 2000). The policy pendulum, as some refer to it, was about to swing in a new direction.

The "Reading Wars"

The reform efforts of the mid-to-late 1990s emphasized thinking skills and learning processes more than products or results. The prescriptive standards of earlier reform efforts were replaced during this era with more broadly defined process-oriented standards. States such as California, Michigan, and Vermont led the nation in these efforts. Comprehensive core reading programs, also called basal reading series, were phased out in this decade as literature-based approaches became more popular in the schools (Hiebert, 2005, 2011). "Making meaning" became the primary focus of literacy instruction—an approach often referred to as a **whole-language** approach (Pressley, 2006). There were many positives associated with the whole-language movement, including a focus on fostering children's love of reading, the use of authentic children's literature and informational texts, and process writing. Unfortunately, foundational skills such as phonemic awareness, phonics, and spelling became less prominent in daily instruction. Many believe this was one of the most significant problems with this era of school reform. A successful reading initiative must focus on learning how to read and write, emphasizing these foundational skills, and reading and writing for authentic purposes and audiences (Pressley, 2006).

In the late 1990s, states such as California suffered severe criticism from politicians due to declining test scores, particularly in reading (Allington, 2002). Policymakers responded vigorously in these states and across the nation. More than 100 "phonics bills" were introduced to state legislatures between 1990 and 1997, and phonics instruction soon became associated with the "conservative agenda" (Patterson, 2000, 2002). Congress also got involved and assembled a national commission to put an end to the debate about how to teach reading—a debate commonly referred to as the "reading wars." The resulting report, *Preventing Reading Difficulties in Young Children* (Snow, Burns, & Griffin, 1998), synthesized the available research on early reading instruction. Soon thereafter, Congress appointed a second panel, the *National Reading Panel*. This group was charged with examining the "empircal research" concerning reading instruction—a much narrower slice of the research pie. This meta-analysis of what's come to be known as "scientifically based reading research (SBRR)," focused on *what* to teach rather than *how* to teach it. The "what" included five main topics: phonemic awareness, phonics, fluency, vocabulary, and comprehension.

The final report of the National Reading Panel (NICHD, 2000) created some debate in the field: Many researchers felt the commission overlooked important research methods and findings, while others celebrated its conclusions. Despite the debate, these two congressionally commissioned reports influenced a number of legislative actions and federal grant programs, including the Reading Excellence Act of 1998 (REA), Reading First of 2002, and the reathorization of ESEA, which is now referred to as the No Child Left Behind Act of 2001 (NCLB). The goals of these intiatives are laudable—to address persistent achievement gaps between students of differing racial, ethnic, linguistic, and socioeconomic backgrounds; however, the means by which these goals have been pursued are not without their controversy (Allington, 2002; Elmore, 2002; Meier & Wood, 2004, Office of Inspector General, 2006; Woodside-Jiron & Gehsmann, 2009).

No Child Left Behind and High-Stakes Testing

One of the most concerning aspects of NCLB is its emphasis on high-stakes testing (Bracey, 2000; Nichols & Berliner, 2007; Ravitch, 2011). Students in the United States are now tested annually in grades 3 through 8 and again in high school. Sanctions are imposed on schools that do not make adequate yearly progress—a formula that measures a school's progress toward *all* students meeting or exceeding the standards in key content areas. These sanctions increase in severity the more years a school doesn't make adequate progress and they include a loss of federal grant funding, reorganizations such as the change in leadership at Main Street School, and even school closures. In 2011, nearly half of the nation's schools did not meet the adequate yearly progress targets, and in some states that number is approaching 100 percent (Usher, 2012).

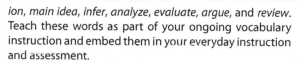

The Language of Your Instruction

Helping Students Succeed with High-Stakes Assessment

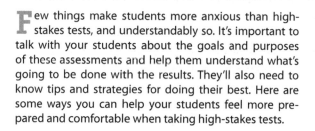

Few things make students more anxious than high-stakes tests, and understandably so. It's important to talk with your students about the goals and purposes of these assessments and help them understand what's going to be done with the results. They'll also need to know tips and strategies for doing their best. Here are some ways you can help your students feel more prepared and comfortable when taking high-stakes tests.

Align Your Curriculum with the Standards

Test preparation should not be the sole focus of your curriculum or your students' learning experiences, but it is important that your instruction be aligned with the standards. When your curriculum is aligned, it ensures that your students are familiar with the content on high-stakes assessments, and this increases their chances for success.

Teach the "Genre" of the Test

Your students will feel more at ease with high-stakes assessment if they're familiar with the "genre" (or format) of the test. To better prepare your students, include tasks that resemble the format of the test in your daily instruction and ongoing assessment.

Teach the Vocabulary of Assessment

Review several sample tests and identify the academic vocabulary your students need to be familiar with on the assessment—words such as *compare, contrast, fact, opin-*

ion, main idea, infer, analyze, evaluate, argue, and *review*. Teach these words as part of your ongoing vocabulary instruction and embed them in your everyday instruction and assessment.

Teach Test-Taking Strategies

Your students will feel more comfortable and confident when they have a repertoire of test-taking strategies. Consider sharing the following tips:

- Read or listen to the directions carefully. Underline key words. Do the sample test item (if there is one) and ask clarifying questions.
- Read the questions carefully and think about the correct answer *before* reading the options. Next, read all the options before selecting the one that makes the most sense. If in doubt, your first instinct is probably correct. If you're still not sure, reread the question and eliminate answers that just don't fit. Select the best choice from what's left.
- When composing a written response, think about your answer *before* writing and create an outline if it's allowed. When you begin to write, explicitly address the question in your topic sentence, provide evidence, and then wrap up your answer with a concluding sentence.
- Be sure you know your purpose for reading *before* you read. Read with that specific purpose in mind. Underline evidence you may use in your written response.

The Misuses and Unintended Consequences of High-Stakes Assessment

The emphasis on high-stakes testing under No Child Left Behind has raised the concern of many scholars and research organizations around the globe. These experts are significantly concerned about policies that use a single test score to determine the quality of a school, a curricular program, a teacher, and/or the learning of individual students (Afflerbach, 2002, 2004, 2010; Maddaus & Russell, 2010/2011; Nichols & Berliner, 2007; Ravitch, 2011; Valencia, 2011). These researchers suggest that high-stakes judgments such as these must be based on a convergence of evidence, rather than a single data point. These same researchers have also identified a number of other concerning effects associated with high-stakes testing and No Child Left Behind, including:

- A narrowing of the curriculum to focus only on those things that are tested
- An increase in the retention of students until they pass their state's test at a given grade level
- An adoption of undifferentiated, "one-size-fits-all" instruction
- An overreliance on commercial programs and products rather than teacher knowledge and professional decision making
- An increase in cheating by administrators, teachers, and even students because the stakes are so very high for these individuals

It's important that you're aware of the pressures these tests and accountability policies exert on the educational system and individuals as well. Perhaps most important, understanding these pressures will help you champion responsible decision making and the highest standards of ethical behavior when it comes to administering and using the results from these and other assessments. High-stakes tests themselves are not necessarily "bad," but their value must be contextualized in the broader landscape of what it means to be "educated" and "effective."

A New Era of Reform: Common Core State Standards

The new Common Core State Standards (Common Core State Standards Initiative, 2010) are the latest iteration of the standards and assessment movement. These standards for "college and career readiness" have been adopted by nearly every state in the union, by the U.S. territories, and by the U.S. Department of Defense schools around the world. With these standards come a new generation of high-stakes assessments: the Smarter Balanced Assessment and the Partnership for Assessment Readiness for College and Career. Both are described in Figure 4.1.

The Common Core State Standards: Challenges and Opportunities

The Common Core State Standards represent a significant increase in the expectations for student learning across the grades (Pearson, 2012; Valencia & Wixson, 2011). Some scholars worry about the standards being too rigorous, but we believe they have the potential to invigorate the curriculum with rich and interesting content—something that has been sorely lacking in recent accountability initiatives. They also set the expectation that literacy will be taught within the content areas.

Given the Common Core's increased rigor and its integrated model of literacy instruction, we see greater opportunity for:

- Collaborative planning among language arts teachers and content-area specialists
- Collaborative reasoning and meaning-making among students

FIGURE 4.1 Examples of High-Stakes Assessments in the United States

Smarter Balanced Assessment Consortium (SBAC) and Partnership for Assessment of Readiness for College and Career (PARCC)

The Smarter Balanced Assessment Consortium (SBAC) and the Partnership for Assessment of Reading for College and Career (PARCC) are state-led groups charged with designing and implementing assessments aligned to the Common Core State Standards. These criterion-referenced assessments will be implemented beginning in 2014 and will effectively replace most other assessments being used as part of *No Child Left Behind*. Information about the development of these assessments can be found at the organizations' respective websites: www.smarterbalanced.org/ and www.parcconline.org/. It's important to familiarize yourself with this new generation of assessment and the Common Core State Standards so you'll be better positioned to help prepare your students for these assessments.

National Assessment of Educational Progress (NAEP)

The National Assessment of Educational Progress (NAEP) is often referred to as "The Nation's Report Card." Started in 1969, NAEP is administered in fourth, eighth, and twelfth grades and is designed to track the achievement of students in key content areas, including mathematics, reading, and writing. Since 1990, NAEP data are broken down by state for the purpose of ranking student achievement in each state. This helps states evaluate the effectiveness of instruction in their state. The NAEP instrument allows policymakers to examine student achievement trends across the country and over time. Its sophisticated design makes it one of the most highly regarded assessments in the field of education. For more information about NAEP, visit http://nces.ed.gov/nationsreportcard/aboutnaep.asp and watch the short video, "Introducing NAEP to Teachers."

- The development of higher-order thinking and reasoning skills
- Rigorous reading and writing experiences for real purposes and audiences

Text Complexity and Teacher Decision Making

In order for students to meet the demands of these new standards, it will be necessary for teachers to expose students to increasingly complex texts, including primary sources in math, science, history/social studies, and the arts. The authors of the Common Core are clear about this expectation and have provided sample titles in the appendix of the document. Some of your students will need more support than others when accessing these texts, and this is where your professional decision making will be critical. The introduction to the Common Core Standards affirms the importance of your critical role: "The Standards define what all students are expected to know and be able to do, not how teachers should teach" (CCSS, 2010, p. 6). The authors also affirm that the one-size-fits-all approaches to instruction will not work; they write, "Instruction should be *differentiated.* . . . The point is to teach students what they need to learn . . . to discern when particular children or activities warrant more or less attention" (CCSS, 2010, p. 15; emphasis added). It will be important that these two powerful ideas—differentiation and professional decision making—not get lost in the rhetoric and the day-to-day realities of this new generation of reform and high-stakes testing.

The Common Core and Assessment

The rigor and complexity of the new Common Core Standards will also necessitate a new generation of assessments, and these assessments will need to be equally sophisticated. It's not practical, for example, to measure students' ability to craft an argumentative essay with a multiple-choice exam. This is good news because sophisticated assessments will exert some pressure on the system to improve, and do so in a thoughtful and hopefully significant way. Given the fact that today's jobs require considerably higher levels of literacy than those of just a generation or two ago (Carnevale, 2001), higher standards are probably necessary and appropriate.

Summing It Up: The Common Core and the Big Picture

The Common Core State Standards are not a silver bullet or panacea. There will be considerable challenges to implementing them well, but we believe they're more meaningful and thorough than the many generations of standards that have come before them. We remain hopeful that the Common Core's vision of integrated literacy will deepen students' engagements with text both *in* and *beyond* the language arts classroom, and will better prepare students for postsecondary education and careers. Perhaps most importantly, the Common Core Standards are intended to help students develop the skills and dispositions necessary to contribute meaningfully to the advancement of democratic ideals, the creation of knowledge, and the common good (CCSS, 2010, p. 3).

While we're cautiously optimistic about the Common Core and this new generation of assessment, we also believe school improvement has its best chance for success when it's embedded as part of a broader policy agenda. Such an agenda should focus on eliminating some of the more profound causes of underachievement, including poverty, unfunded mandates, and under-resourced schools, particularly those that serve students in the greatest need (Books, 2004; Shannon, 1998; Woodside-Jiron & Gehsmann, 2009). The schools alone cannot change the trajectory of all children placed at risk, though they can, as *you can*, make a significant and lasting impact in the lives and literacy achievement of so many children.

Working and Collaborating

Talking with Parents and Families about High-Stakes Testing

Parents and caregivers are important partners in all aspects of education. When talking with families about high-stakes tests, emphasize all the ways you've prepared your students for success. Do your very best to put your students' families and caregivers at ease, and encourage them to support their children each and every day, not just during test-taking seasons. Student success starts at home. When families adopt regular routines and dispositions, there's no need to do anything special on test days. Consider sharing some of the following strategies with families to ensure their children's academic success:

- Create a regular routine for bedtime. Students who are well rested tend to do better in school and on tests.
- Help your child arrive at school on time each day. Some of the most important community building and learning happen in the morning.

- Good nutrition helps children learn better. Keep healthy snacks around the house and provide well-balanced meals.
- Avoid scheduling appointments and vacations during the school day and year. The loss of continuity can be a problem for many students.
- Create a quiet study space for homework completion.
- Create a daily routine that includes reading for at least 30 minutes each day.
- Encourage your child's creativity, inquisitiveness, and persistence. Effort and interest are two important keys to academic success.

Your ongoing positive relationship with families is an essential ingredient in your students' success on high-stakes tests and well beyond.

Types and Purposes of Assessment

As you think back through your many years of schooling, you can undoubtedly recall being assessed many different ways, and high-stakes tests were just one of those methods. As you'll learn in this chapter, there are a number of means to assess student learning and some will be more helpful to you and your students than others. It's important, however, to understand all types of assessment so you can interpret their results responsibly, and purposely select assessments for use in your classroom. In this section we'll review some of the different types and purposes of literacy assessments commonly found in schools today.

Norm-Referenced Assessment

Norm-referenced assessments are formal assessments that are sometimes called **standardized tests**. They are used to compare a student's level achievement to that of other students of the same age, grade, or other demographic. In this way, norm-referenced assessments allow you to compare a student's achievement to a "norm." The Scholastic Achievement Test (SAT) that you may have taken in high school is an example of a norm-referenced test, as is the Graduate Record Exam (GRE). The Woodcock Johnson (Woodcock, 1998) and the Gates-MacGinitie (MacGinitie, MacGinitie, Maris, & Dreyer, 2000) are examples of commonly used norm-referenced reading tests. Figure 4.2 defines several of the key terms and concepts associated with norm-referenced tests.

FIGURE 4.2 Key Terms and Concepts Associated with Norm-Referenced Tests

Raw Score (RS)	The total number of items correct.
Scale Score (SS)	A score that reflects the weight and value of correct answers. Scale scores allow you to compare scores across different forms of a test and different times of administration. Scale scores also allow comparison with other types of tests.
Extended Scale Score (ESS)	An extended scale score is a continuous scale that allows educators to track individual student growth over extended periods of time (including year to year).
Percentile Rank (PR)	Percentile ranks allow you to compare a student's achievement with that of other children the same age who took the same test. Although it's related to percentage, it is not the same as *percent correct*. For example, a child who scores in the 80th percentile scored as well as or better than 80 percent of all students the same age who took the same test; 20 percent of students outperformed this student.
Quartile	One quartile represents one-quarter of the norming group. Student scores are sometimes reported in quartiles. The first quartile is the lowest level of achievement and the fourth is the highest.
Stanine (ST)	As illustrated in Figure 4.3, stanines (a shortened term meaning "standard nines") are nine equally comparable units. The fifth stanine is considered "average," whereas the first through third are "below average," and the seventh through ninth are considered "above average." See Figure 4.3 for more detail about the distribution of scores in each stanine.
Grade Equivalent (GE)	The grade equivalent score is the single most misleading statistic used in norm-referenced assessments. When a fourth-grader takes a norm-referenced test designed for a fourth-grader, his or her score is reported in grade equivalent form. A GE of 6.2 suggests the student read the fourth-grade materials the same way a sixth-grader in the second month of sixth grade would. However, this does *not* mean that the student is reading at the sixth-grade level. All you can say with confidence is that the student is reading above average. To actually determine the student's independent or instructional reading level, you would have to administer more diagnostic assessment that includes text that is actually above grade level. Grade equivalents are so commonly misunderstood that a number of professional organizations recommend not using them.

FIGURE 4.3 Normal "Bell Curve" Distribution

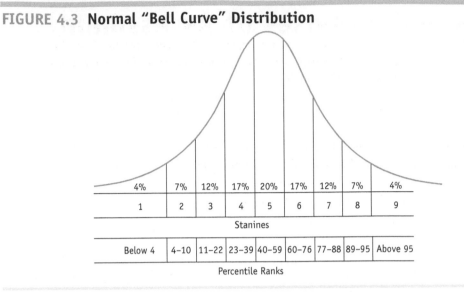

Norm-referenced tests are carefully designed to reflect what's called a *bell curve,* a *normal curve,* or a *normal distribution.* In this way, student achievement is distributed as seen in Figure 4.3. Average performance is indicated by the fifth stanine and fiftieth percentile. As you can see, the vast majority of students will achieve between the fourth and sixth stanines. The fewest percent of students, only 4 percent, will perform at the "tails" of the curve—the first and ninth stanines. Because norm-referenced tests compare student achievement to norms, educators often use these tests to identify students' strengths and learning challenges compared to their age-mates. Comparing the results of two or more subtests on a reading assessment can also help identify areas of concern. If you notice that there's a two-stanine difference between a child's reading comprehension and reading fluency, for example, you can reasonably assume the child is in need of intervention in the lower of the two areas, particularly if it falls below the fifth stanine. A difference of a single stanine, however, is not statistically strong enough to make such a claim. The Total Reading Score is the most accurate overall assessment of your student's performance as a reader, and it's important to consider this when reviewing reports of all your students' achievement.

When analyzing student achievement on norm-referenced assessments, it's also important to realize that these assessments will ask students to read texts or complete tasks that are considered "on grade level." This can be very different from asking students to complete a task at their independent or instructional level. We mention this because anytime you note a concern with a student's level of achievement on a norm-referenced assessment, you will want to do some further testing at the child's independent and instructional levels to better understand his or her strengths and instructional needs.

Criterion-Referenced Assessment

Criterion-referenced assessments, also known as **standards-based assessments** or **outcomes-based assessments,** are increasingly being used in schools as well as by state accountability systems. Criterion-referenced assessments provide comparisons between a student's performance and a predetermined standard. In this way, student achievement can be reported both *quantitatively* through raw scores, scaled scores, and percent of questions answered correctly, and *qualitatively* with labels such as *exceeds the standard, meets the standard, approaching the standard,* or *below the standard.*

Summative Assessment

The high-stakes assessments described in the beginning of this chapter are all examples of summative assessment. Summative assessment comes at the end of a learning unit or grade level. It's intended to assess students' **cumulative** learning. Summative assessments tend to be longer and their stakes tend to be a little higher. The Smarter Balanced Assessment Consortium (SBAC), the Partnership for Assessment Readiness for College and Career (PARCC), and the National Assessment of Educational Progress (NAEP), described in Figure 4.1, are all examples of summative assessments. These tests are also criterion-referenced assessments. As you are beginning to see, there can be overlap between the types and purposes of assessments.

Importantly, summative assessment is not always part of an external accountability system. It can be used in your classroom, too. For example, if you assess a final draft of an essay or a report, or give an end-of-unit test, you're using summative assessment. Appropriately, the grades for these assignments or tests are probably weighted a bit more than drafts or quizzes, which are more formative in nature.

Formative Assessment

Formative assessment differs from summative assessment in that it tends to occur more frequently, the tasks themselves are shorter, and the goals of formative assessment are a little different. You'll typically use formative assessment to provide students with feedback about their progress toward meeting a standard, and you'll share ways they can improve their work based on this assessment (Black & Wiliam, 1998, 2010). Formative assessment also helps with your planning. By looking across student work, for example, you can identify and respond to instructional needs, perhaps adjusting your groupings, the pacing of your instruction, and even the content of what you teach. In all, formative assessment helps you reflect on the effectiveness of your teaching as well as improve your students' learning (Black & Wiliam, 1998, 2010; Hattie, 2009).

Formative Assessment in Your Classroom

Researchers have found that clearly articulated learning goals, ongoing formative assessment, and regular and specific feedback to students are among the most promising ways to improve student achievement (Black & Wiliam, 1998; 2010; Hattie, 2009; Johnston & Costello, 2005). Perhaps most importantly, formative assessment has been found to be most helpful to students most in need of improvement.

Figure 4.4 highlights some ways you might incorporate regular formative assessment in your daily lessons. Other examples of literacy-related formative assessment can be found throughout the chapter and they include the use of teacher observation and conferring, rubrics, running records, portfolios, and self-assessment.

FIGURE 4.4 Ten Quick and Easy Formative Assessment Strategies

The goal of formative assessment is always to deepen and improve learning, as well as for you to assess student learning in such a way that you can provide students with specific feedback about their strengths and opportunities for improvement. Here are 10 ways you might incorporate formative assessment into your daily lessons.

1. **Entrance/Exit Cards**	Provide students with an index card that they'll either turn in as they exit a class, or on their way into the class. Provide open-ended questions, or invite open-ended reflection. For example: • What did you learn about yourself as a reader today? • How have you changed as a writer this week? • Think about the big ideas of today's word study lesson and write a reflection about how this week's words work. Give examples to back up your thinking. • Name the five qualities of effective writing. Describe your strengths and opportunities for improvement in writing.
2. **Asking Questions**	Encourage students to be engaged learners by asking questions that deepen their learning. Invite them to work collaboratively to find the answers and share them with the class or in small groups. With younger students, consider having them finish the prompt: "I wonder . . . " and support and celebrate their inquiries.
3. **Fist to Five/ Green, Yellow, Red**	Periodically survey students on their prior knowledge or understanding of a topic by asking them to rate their knowledge from fist (no prior knowledge) to 5 (very competent). Have them raise their fist for zero or the number of fingers that matches their comfort level with the material. Alternatively, use the colors of a stop light: Green (Got it!), Yellow (Hmm . . . I'm a little unsure/confused), Red (Whoa! I don't understand). Use these techniques to monitor and adjust your instruction as necessary. You can also use this information to group students with more secure knowledge/understandings with students who are less comfortable with the material to get students talking about and (we hope) understanding things better.
4. **Stop and Jot**	Periodically engage students to stop and think, or stop and jot their reflections and/or responses to different learning experiences. Encourage them to share these thoughts or jots. (See Chapter 8 for more about "Stop and Jot.")
5. **Graphic Organizers**	As you're learning about a new topic, help students organize their new knowledge into some kind of graphic organizer such as a concept map, Venn diagram, or flowchart. Have students display their organizers and invite them to conduct a "Gallery Walk" where they observe other people's displays, talk with each other, and then return to revise their own graphic organizer.
6. **Think-Pair-Share**	Periodically stop and invite students to reflect on their learning, pose a problem for them to solve, or ask a question for them to answer. After some think time, invite them to talk with a partner. While the students are talking, you're providing occasional feedback and listening for trends that reveal teachable moments, opportunities to clear up confusions or deepen student learning, and/or identify groups of students who may need additional support or enrichment. To include more students in the conversation, have the pairs "square" and form groups of four.
7. **3-2-1**	In a notebook or on an index card, ask your students to write: • Three things they learned • Two things they're wondering • One thing they're confused about You can change the prompts to suit your specific learning goals or purposes.
8. **Sketch-to-Stretch**	After reading and talking about a text, ask students to represent the big idea or theme in a sketch with limited words. Invite students to share their artistic representations to deepen and broaden their understandings.
9. **Jeopardy**	After learning about a topic for some time, create categories of the big ideas with your students and write them on index cards. Distribute three to five index cards per category and label them with point values. Invite your students to create *Jeopardy*-type answers and questions. Select a game-show host or moderator. Moving in a clockwise fashion, groups of students select a category and the moderator reads the answer. The students have to provide the correct question and when they do, they earn the points on the front of the card. This is a great activity for reviewing material before a summative assessment and a great means to help students reflect on what they still need to learn. It also helps you identify the strengths and needs of the group, which allows you to respond appropriately.
10. **Two or Three Column Notes**	Create a graphic organizer with two or three columns and label the columns in such a way that it supports your goal. For example, when reading informational text, one column may be labeled *Fact*, the next column, *Question*, and the third column, *Response*. As students take notes about their topic, they'll be encouraged to think about these topics by generating questions and responses. When reading fiction, you may have students copy a line of text in one column, and write a response in the other. The options are endless!

Strategies for the Classroom

Planning Assessment *Before* Your Instruction

Backward design is an approach to lesson and unit planning that combines the power of well-planned and aligned assessment and instruction to improve student learning (Wiggins & McTighe, 2005). It's called "backward design" because you begin the planning process by thinking about what you want students to know, understand, or be able to do as a result of your teaching—your learning goals and objectives. After articulating these goals, you'll then identify your activities and instructional approaches. Use the following sequence to help you plan your next lesson, series of lessons, or unit.

1) Identify and articulate your learning goals and the standards you'll address in your lesson or unit. Be very specific. Use active verbs that can be assessed. (Be sure to refer to the "levels of learning" in Figure 2.2 in Chapter 2.)
2) Plan the product, task, and/or assessment you'll use to evaluate your students' learning at the end of the lesson, series of lessons, or unit. Pay careful attention to the verbs you specified in step 1 and revise if necessary. (This is summative assessment.)
3) Plan regular intervals of assessment that will inform your teaching and provide students with feedback

about their progress toward achieving the learning goals articulated in step 1. (This is formative assessment.) These assessments will be carefully aligned to your summative assessment in step 2.
4) Plan your instructional approach, activities, and experiences that will help your students achieve your intended goals.

When planning lessons and units, it might be helpful to think of your teaching as a journey. Like any trip you take, you have to be clear about your destination before you plan your travel route. Think of summative assessment as your destination and formative assessment as signposts along the way. These signs help determine the pacing, grouping, content, and intensity of your instruction. Formative assessment informs your teaching while summative assessment evaluates it (your students' cumulative learning, too). By using backward design, your learning goals, assessment, and instruction are purposefully aligned, and this strengthens not only your teaching but also your students' understanding of the goals and their levels of achievement (Hattie, 2009; Black & Wiliam, 1998, 2010; Wiggins & McTighe, 2005).

The Qualities of a "Good" Assessment

When selecting assessments to use in your classroom or when evaluating the quality of the assessments used by your school or district, there are some important things to keep in mind. This section of the chapter will help you understand some of the qualities of a "good" assessment: reliability, validity, and instructional transparency.

Reliability

A test is considered reliable when it consistently yields the same results under similar conditions. One way to think about reliability is to imagine starting your car each morning. If it starts each and every morning without any difficulty, you might say that it starts *reliably*. **Reliability** is a measure of consistency and it's represented by a decimal. The closer an assessment's reliability gets to 100 percent, or 1.0, the more reliable the test. A reliability of .90, for example, is considered very high. A reliability of .80 is acceptable, but not robust.

The length and complexity of the assessment and the specificity of its administration and scoring protocols affect its reliability. Longer assessments and/or those that require more judgment when scoring are often less reliable, but they may actually be better, more meaningful assessments of student learning (Invernizzi, Landrum, Howell, & Warley, 2005; Valencia, 2011). We'll say more about this in the section titled "Instructional Transparency."

There are many different kinds of reliability (test-retest reliability, equivalent forms, and split-half). **Inter-rater reliability** is the type of reliability that most often concerns the day-to-day work of classroom teachers. It refers to how consistently you score your students' work. Though there are several ways to ensure consistency in scoring, one of the most common ways is to collaborate with colleagues to study and assess student work samples together. You'll know your assessment tools, rubrics, or checklists, for example, are reliable when you consistently get the same score as your peers at least 80 percent of the time (an inter-rater reliability of .80). Again, the closer your inter-rater reliability is to 100 percent, the more reliable the assessment.

If you don't have someone to collaborate with, you can still evaluate the reliability of your assessment tools and the consistency of your scoring by assessing your students' work, putting it away for a week or two, and then rescoring it. If your assessment is reliable, you'll get the same scores *at least* 8 out of 10 times.

Validity

Validity refers to the degree to which an assessment measures what it's intended to measure. By this definition, a test can be reliable without being valid. Consider, for example, the car we judged as being "reliable" in the previous section. Although it started reliably each day, we don't really have enough information to say that it's a "good" car unless, of course, our definition of "good" is simply turning the engine over each morning. Validity expands the definition of a "good" assessment beyond reliability to include the content and intention or goal of the assessment.

Test developers examine the validity of their assessments in highly systematic ways and they often report several different kinds of validity (content validity, construct validity, predictive validity, concurrent validity, and/or consequential validity). For most classroom teachers, the important thing to know about validity is this: A test is considered valid when it measures what it claims to measure. To be sure your teacher-made assessments are as valid as they can be, you'll want to carefully align your learning objectives and goals to your assessment tasks, and consider how you can ensure equal and fair opportunity for success. For more information about creating assessments and even accommodations that ensure **universal access**, visit the Center for Universal Design in Education at www.washington.edu/doit/CUDE/.

Instructional Transparency

Instructionally transparent assessments generally ask students to perform tasks that are similar to the reading, writing, or spelling tasks they engage in as part of daily instruction. Such assessments make it easier for you to use the results immediately to plan instruction for individual students, groups, or the whole class (Invernizzi et al., 2005; Justice, Invernizzi & Meier, 2002). More specifically, instructionally transparent assessments help you:

* Identify your students' stages of development.
* Recognize your students' strengths and instructional needs.
* Identify your students' highest levels of proficiency (their independent level) and their instructional level.

Unfortunately, more often than not, standardized tests do not provide the kind of instructional transparency needed to plan student-centered instruction, nor are the tasks particularly authentic (Buly & Valencia, 2002; Invernizzi et al., 2005; Valencia & Buly, 2004; Valencia, 2011). This is not to say you shouldn't use standardized tests, but you'll just want to be sure they're the best choice for what you wish to measure, and be certain they'll provide you with the kind of information that's most useful when planning instruction and/or intervention for your students. With time and experience, you'll feel increasingly comfortable selecting assessments to suit your needs as well as those of your students.

Accommodating English Learners

Equitable Literacy Assessment for English Learners

Today, English learners account for nearly 20 percent of the public school population in the United States (Helman, Bear, Templeton, Invernizzi, & Johnston, 2012). As you'll learn in Chapter 5, these students' learning needs are similar to those of native English speakers, but they do have some unique needs as well. Assessment is one of those areas where you'll need to make some specific accommodations for your English learners (Garcia, McKoon, & August, 2008; Jimenez, 2004; Lenski, Ehlers-Zavala, Daniel, & Sun-Irminger, 2006). Here are some tips that will help make your comprehensive literacy assessment program more equitable and effective for English learners:

1) Whenever possible, allow students to take assessments in their native language or the language that's most comfortable for them.
2) Allow English learners extra time to complete written, oral, and/or reading tasks. Break longer assessments into smaller pieces and distribute the tasks over time.
3) If permitted, read directions aloud and simplify the language of these directions. This is called **linguistic modification**. After you explain the task, ask your English learners to repeat the directions in their own words to be sure the directions are understood.
4) Use pictures, icons, models, and gestures to support students' understanding of directions and tasks whenever possible.
5) Provide students with sample questions and practice whenever possible.
6) Allow students to answer questions orally rather than in writing. If their native language is preferred, engage the help of a translator or bilingual teacher to allow for this accommodation.
7) Examine test materials for cultural bias. An informal reading inventory (IRI) that includes a passage on Martin Luther King, Jr. or George Washington, for example, may favor students from the dominant culture, as they will likely have more prior knowledge on these topics. Eliminate cultural bias in your assessments as much as possible.
8) Use standardized tests that have been normed for English learners as well as native speakers of English. You may also consider alternative forms that are specifically designed for speakers of other languages.
9) Consult your test administration guides to learn more about allowable accommodations for English learners.
10) Whenever possible, use formative assessment and self-assessment to track students' attainment of goals and specific learning objectives, and to document their growth over time as well as their self-perceptions.

A Comprehensive Literacy Assessment Program

As you begin to make choices about which assessments to use and when, having a vision of what makes an assessment program "complete" or "comprehensive" can be helpful. A comprehensive literacy assessment program enables you to:

- Identify your students' stages of development.
- Determine your students' strengths and instructional needs.
- Monitor your students' progress.
- Assess your students' overall achievement.

To achieve these goals and satisfy the needs of other stakeholders, including parents, educational leaders, and policymakers, it may be helpful to think about your assessment program having five different categories of assessment, as described in Figure 4.5. These categories are most

FIGURE 4.5 A Comprehensive Literacy Assessment Program: Screening, Diagnostic, Formative Progress Monitoring, Interim/Benchmark, and Outcomes Assessment

Screening and Diagnostic Assessment

Screening assessments are usually given in the first week or two of the school year and they're used to identify students' levels of proficiency. Students whose achievement is below grade level on criterion-referenced assessments, or those achieving below average on norm-referenced assessments, are often referred for additional testing. This additional testing is called *diagnostic assessment* and it's intended to illuminate students' specific strengths and challenges, as well as their independent and instructional levels of reading, writing, and spelling. Diagnostic assessments are given on an as-needed basis and they are typically administered in one-to-one settings.

Diagnostic assessments tend to be more time consuming to administer and score than screening assessments, which are often administered to the whole class or in small groups. Many schools and districts choose to use norm-referenced assessments as their screening tools because they can be efficient and inexpensive to administer and score.

Some researchers suggest that students scoring in the bottom quartile on a screening assessment should receive further testing, while other researchers suggest students who perform in the bottom 10 to 20 percent of their class should receive further evaluation (Fuchs & Fuchs, 2006; Morris, 2008). Some screening assessments such as the Phonological Awareness Literacy Screening (PALS) (Invernizzi, Sullivan, Meier, & Swank, 2004; Invernizzi, Meier, & Juel, 2006; Invernizzi, Juel, Swank, & Meier, 2009) set a criterion, or benchmark score, for determining the need for additional assessment and/or intervention. If your school or district does not have a policy for determining which students will receive further diagnostic testing, you can use these guidelines to help you determine the students you'll continue to assess after an initial screening.

Formative Progress Monitoring and Interim/Benchmark Assessment

Formative progress monitoring assessments are those assessments you embed as part of your day-to-day instruction, and the results are used to shape your ongoing instruction. The results of formative assessment also provide students with timely and specific feedback about how they're doing in relation to a standard or learning goal, as well as clear direction for how they can improve. Formative progress monitoring may be included in every lesson or every few lessons. It allows you to reflect not only on your students' learning but also on the effectiveness of your instruction. Formative progress monitoring assessments have more potential to improve student learning than any other assessment method (Black & Wiliam, 1998, 2010; Hattie, 2009).

Interim/benchmark assessment, on the other hand, is strategically distributed throughout the school year (maybe three or four times a year) and used to monitor students' progress toward meeting the standards at a given grade level. These assessments are sometimes called **curriculum-based assessment measures** (C-BAM). It's not unusual for schools to use norm-referenced assessment as part of their interim/benchmark assessment program. School administrators tend to favor these assessments because they provide a quick and easy means for monitoring the ongoing achievement of students. However, their lack of instructional transparency makes the use of interim/benchmark assessment a topic of controversy (Invernizzi et al., 2005; Valencia, 2011). Two recent studies have actually found no statistical difference in students' achievement in schools that use this type of assessment (Henderson, Petrosino, Guckenburg, & Hamilton, 2008; Quint, Sepanik, & Smith, 2008).

If your school uses norm-referenced interim/benchmark assessments, keep an open mind about them and don't overlook the possibility that these assessments may help you identify students in need of additional diagnostic assessment and intervention.

Outcomes Assessment

Outcomes assessment usually refers to assessments given at the end of the school year for the purpose of evaluating students' achievement of grade-level expectations. The PARCC and SBAC described in Figure 4.1 are examples of high-stakes outcomes assessments. Outcomes assessments can also be classroom based. When you create a test of cumulative knowledge or skills, you've created an outcomes-based assessment. Outcomes-based assessment may also be referred to as summative assessment.

FIGURE 4.6 Your Comprehensive Literacy Assessment Program: A Planning Template

	Screening	Diagnostic	Formative/Progress Monitoring	Interim/Benchmark	Outcome
Word Structure					
Fluency					
Vocabulary					
Comprehension					
Writing					
Motivation					

commonly used in schools that use tiered instruction (Gehsmann, 2008; Lipson & Wixson, 2010). (See Chapter 1 and Chapter 11 for more about tiered instruction.)

Assessing the "Literacy Essentials"

In addition to the five categories of assessment described in Figure 4.5, you'll also want to ensure that your comprehensive literacy assessment program appropriately samples the essential elements of literacy you learned about in Chapter 1:

- Word structure
- Comprehension
- Fluency
- Vocabulary
- Writing
- Motivation

In the sections that follow, we'll share examples of literacy assessments that will help you achieve the goals of a comprehensive assessment program, as well as address most of the essentials elements of effective literacy instruction. (Writing assessment will be discussed in a later section of this chapter.) Whenever possible, you'll choose assessments that can satisfy more than one category of assessment as well as more than one of the literacy essentials. Such choices will make your assessment system more efficient, thereby saving valuable time for instruction. As you learn about each assessment, you can use the template in Figure 4.6 to help craft your own comprehensive literacy assessment program.

Word Structure: Pinpointing Development with Qualitative Spelling Inventories

In Chapter 1 and Chapter 2, you learned that children's word knowledge is the bedrock on which their reading and writing development builds. Qualitative spelling inventories help you understand your students' word knowledge through analyzing their spelling of words. These spelling inventories are presented like a typical spelling test, so they're both easy and efficient to administer and score. Perhaps most importantly, they'll help you identify your students' stages of development. The margin box on the right indicates the many different ways spelling inventories can be used.

Qualitative Spelling Inventories

☑ Screening
☑ Diagnostic
☐ Formative Progress Monitoring
☑ Interim/Benchmark
☑ Outcome

When you review spelling inventories such as the Primary Spelling Inventory (PSI), the Elementary Spelling Inventory (ESI), or the Upper Spelling Inventory (USI) (Bear et al., 2012), you'll notice that the words on these lists get increasingly more difficult. On the Elementary Spelling Inventory, for example, the first word on the list is *bed* and the last word is *opposition*. Naturally, most of your students will not get all these words correct, nor are they expected to. The words on these lists are carefully selected to sample specific orthographic features associated with each stage of development. This is one of the significant ways they're different from weekly spelling tests. It's important to explain this to your students so they don't become discouraged when they can't spell all of the words correctly. Also emphasize that you're interested in learning how they spell difficult words so you can learn about the strategies they use when spelling. The spelling inventories mentioned here are from *Words Their Way: Word Study for Phonics, Vocabulary, and Spelling Instruction* (Bear et al., 2012) and they are valid and reliable instruments (Sterbinsky, 2007).

By administering a spelling inventory, you're accomplishing two important things:

1) Identifying your students' stages of literacy development
2) Identifying the phonics and spelling skills your students have mastered and those they're "using but confusing"—an indicator of their instructional level

Since reading and spelling are reciprocal processes, children's spelling is also a reliable predictor of their reading level (Ehri, 2000; Ellis & Cataldo, 1992; Morris & Perney, 1984). With the results of a spelling inventory, you can estimate the level of text your students can read independently and with support. This makes a spelling inventory an especially valuable and efficient assessment. Table 2.1 in Chapter 2 highlights the relationship between a student's spelling and reading level. This information will help you create small, developmentally oriented groups for both word study and guided reading in the first couple of weeks of the school year.

Figure 4.7 will help you select the best inventory for the grades you teach. Naturally, if you have a student who is achieving well below grade level in fourth grade, for example, you can use the Primary Spelling Inventory because it samples more words at the beginning of the developmental continuum, or the Upper Spelling Inventory for a student who is excelling because it samples more words at the upper end of the continuum. Again, your professional decision making and understanding of development are critical when selecting assessments for use in your classroom and with individual students.

Scoring a Qualitative Spelling Inventory

Figure 4.8 shows the feature guide used to score the Elementary Spelling Inventory (ESI) (Bear et al., 2012, p. 320). When analyzing your students' spelling, you'll be less concerned with the number of words correct, and more interested in the orthographic features they represent in their spelling attempts. As you can see on the feature guide in Figure 4.8, there's a place for you

FIGURE 4.7 Selecting a "Just-Right" Qualitative Spelling Inventory

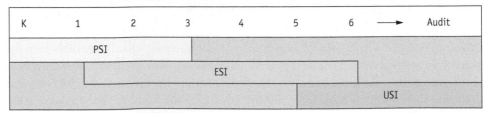

Source: Picard et al., 2011.

FIGURE 4.8 Feature Guide from the Elementary Spelling Inventory

Words Their Way Elementary Spelling Inventory Feature Guide

Student's Name _____   Teacher _____   Grade _____   Date _____

Words Spelled Correctly: ____ /25   Feature Points: ____ /62   Total: ____ /87   Spelling Stage: _____

SPELLING STAGES →	EMERGENT LATE	LETTER NAME—ALPHABETIC EARLY	LETTER NAME—ALPHABETIC MIDDLE	LETTER NAME—ALPHABETIC MIDDLE	LETTER NAME—ALPHABETIC LATE	WITHIN WORD PATTERN EARLY	WITHIN WORD PATTERN MIDDLE	WITHIN WORD PATTERN LATE	SYLLABLES AND AFFIXES EARLY	SYLLABLES AND AFFIXES MIDDLE	DERIVATIONAL RELATIONS LATE	DERIVATIONAL RELATIONS EARLY	DERIVATIONAL RELATIONS MIDDLE		
Features →	Consonants Initial	Consonants Final	Short Vowels	Digraphs	Blends	Common Long Vowels	Other Vowels	Inflected Endings	Syllable Junctures	Unaccented Final Syllables	Harder Suffixes	Bases or Roots	Feature Points	Words Spelled Correctly
1. bed	b	d												
2. ship		p		sh										
3. when				wh										
4. lump	l		u		mp									
5. float		t			fl	oa								
6. train		n			tr	ai								
7. place					pl	a-e								
8. drive		v			dr	i-e								
9. bright					br	igh								
10. shopping			o	sh				pping						
11. spoil					sp		oi							
12. serving							er	ving						
13. chewed				ch			ew	ed						
14. carries							ar	ies	rr					
15. marched				ch			ar	ed						
16. shower				sh			ow			er				
17. bottle									tt	le				
18. favor									v	or				
19. ripen									p	en				
20. cellar									ll	ar				
21. pleasure											ure	pleas		
22. fortunate							or				ate	fortun		
23. confident											ent	confid		
24. civilize											ize	civil		
25. opposition											tion	pos		
Totals	/7		/5	/6	/7	/5	/7	/5	/5	/5	/5	/5	/62	/25

Source: Bear, et al., 2012.

to check each feature a student includes in his or her spelling of a given word. The first column where a student misses two or more features indicates the student's instructional level. The instructional levels are noted along the top of the columns. For example, if your student misses two features in the "Common Long Vowels" column, you would note that he or she is an early *within word pattern* speller.

When you've identified your students' stages of development, use Table 2.1 to help you identify their approximate reading levels. You'll then confirm these levels by using an informal reading inventory, or other assessment of your students' reading accuracy and comprehension. The developmental chapters of this book, Chapters 6 through 10, will describe the reading, writing, and spelling instruction that's developmentally appropriate for your students at each stage of development.

Monitoring Students' Progress with Spelling Inventories

Qualitative spelling inventories can be used as screening, diagnostic, interim/benchmark, and even outcomes assessment. Many teachers administer these inventories several times a year to monitor their students' progress; however, it is important that you not teach any of the words on the inventories directly, as this would invalidate the results.

When analyzing student growth between administrations of a spelling inventory, you'll be looking for improvements in the following categories: total words correct, total feature points, and total points. Although it's possible that you'll see movement within a stage, or into a new stage, not every child will progress that quickly. Some children may stay in a single stage for more than one school year. This is why we look for a variety of indicators of growth rather than focusing on the stage alone. You'll also use your weekly spelling assessments, your observation notes, your assessment of students' word study notebook entries, and the children's writing samples as a means to monitor their progress.

Assessing Foundational Skills: Phonological Awareness Literacy Screening (PALS)

Phonological Awareness Literacy Screening

☑ Screening
☑ Diagnostic
☑ Formative Progress Monitoring
☑ Interim/Benchmark
☑ Outcome

Common Core Connection

Reading Standards: Foundational Skills – Phonological Awareness; Phonics and Word Recognition; Fluency

The Phonological Literacy Awareness Screening (PALS) is a valid and reliable assessment of early reading skills. It's used throughout the country and is the statewide early literacy screening instrument in the state of Virginia. PALS is known for its many strengths, including its ability to predict future reading outcomes, something called predictive validity, and teachers especially appreciate its instructional transparency. The National Center on Response to Intervention rates PALS for kindergarten and grades 1 through 3 quite favorably. (PALS pre-K wasn't reviewed.) See www.rti4success.org/tools_charts/screening.php for more information. Figure 4.9 highlights the skills PALS assesses in preschool, kindergarten, and the primary grades.

Given its many subtests and clear reporting functions (see "Reading and Writing in Digital Contexts" feature), PALS makes it easy to identify students' strengths and challenges, as well as determine their stage of development—two of the most important goals of your assessment program. It also includes interim/benchmark assessments and outcomes assessment, which allows you to monitor students' progress and achievement of learning outcomes. The PALS assessment is quite easy to administer; in fact, many of the subtests can be group administered, which can save precious instructional time.

In addition to PALS being appropriate for screening, diagnostic, interim/benchmark, and outcomes assessment, PALS also provides ongoing formative assessments called Quick Checks. These learning checks are used to periodically monitor the progress of your students' learning

FIGURE 4.9 Overview of the Skills Assessed by PALS

Tasks	PALS PreK	PALS K	PALS 1-3
Print and Word Awareness	X		
Nursery Rhyme Awareness	X		
Name Writing	X		
Rhyme Awareness	X	X	
Beginning Sound Awareness	X	X	
Alphabet Knowledge	X	X	X
Letter Sounds	X	X	X
Concept of Word		X	X
Blending		X	X
Sound-to-Letter		X	X
Spelling/Phonics		X	X
Word Recognition in Isolation		X	X
Oral Reading in Context Accuracy, Fluency, Rate, & Comprehension			X

between the more formal interim/benchmark assessment periods. Beginning in fall of 2014, PALS will be scaled up to grade 8 and include measures of comprehension in informational text as well as a reading vocabulary subtest. A new version of PALS for Spanish-speaking students, PALS *Español* (Ford & Invernizzi, in press), is due out in late 2014.

Assessing Reading Comprehension

Measuring comprehension is no more an exact science than text leveling is. (See Chapter 2 for more about the complexities of leveling text.) Comprehension, as you learned in Chapter 1 and Chapter 2, is the result of a number of things coming together: a student's word reading accuracy and automaticity, fluent expressive reading, prior knowledge, metacognitive strategies, vocabulary knowledge, syntactic knowledge, understanding and use of text features, your student's interest in a topic, memory, motivation, purpose for reading, stamina, and even his

Reading and Writing in Digital Contexts

The Role of Electronic Data Management Systems

In addition to assessing critical foundational early reading skills, PALS offers an online database system that is unusually strong. Simply input your students' scores and you'll find the system can help organize your students into needs-based groups. It also provides information about the kind of instruction that will support these students' ongoing growth and development.

When selecting assessments for use in your classroom, look for assessments that provide this kind of support for grouping students, planning instruction, and monitoring progress over time. Some online database systems offer class-level reporting, grade-level reporting, and even school- and district-level reporting capabilities. A small sampling of such reports can be found in Figures 4.10, 4.11, and 4.12.

FIGURE 4.10 **Sample Student Summary Report: Foundational Skills (Fall, Winter, Spring)**

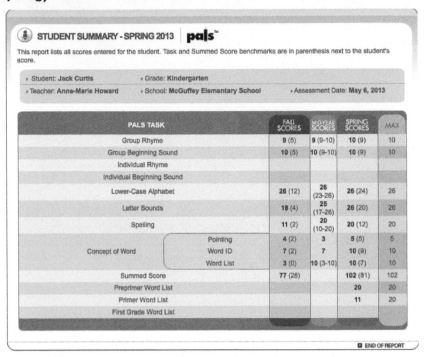

Source: From the PALS Literacy Assessment Series, www.palsmarketplace.com. Used with permission.

FIGURE 4.11 **Sample Student Report: Student Reading Growth Over Time**

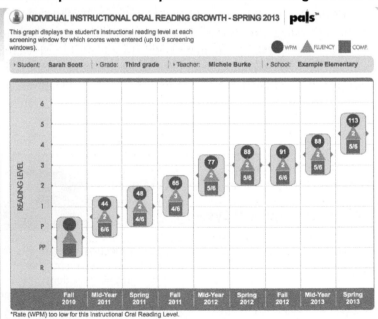

Source: From the PALS Literacy Assessment Series, www.palsmarketplace.COM. Used with permission.

FIGURE 4.12 Class Summary

Source: From the PALS Literacy Assessment Series, www.palsmarketplace.com. Used with permission.

or her engagement with a particular text (RAND Reading Study Group, 2002, Valencia, Wixson, & Pearson, 2011). For these many reasons, using a single measure of comprehension to make judgments about your students' overall reading comprehension is generally not advisable. Instead, you will use your assessment data, the results of both your screening and diagnostic assessment, and your conference notes and observational data, including evidence of students' listening comprehension during read-alouds, to assess their reading and listening comprehension over time.

Although your students' comprehension is difficult to quantify, there are two common ways to go about assessing it. The first is using a norm-referenced assessment such as the Gates-MacGinitie Reading Assessment (MacGinitie et al., 2000), or a criterion-referenced assessment such as Degrees of Reading Power (DRP) (Touchstone Applied Science Associates, 2013). These assessments are often used as screening instruments in grade 4 and beyond. These assessments are appealing because they can be group administered in one class period, they're inexpensive to purchase, and they're efficient to score. The second common way to measure comprehension is to use an individually administered informal reading inventory, also known as an IRI. Each of these assessments has strengths and limitations, which we'll explore in the following sections.

The Gates-MacGinitie Reading Assessment

The Gates-MacGinitie Reading Assessment (MacGinitie et al., 2000) is a norm-referenced test designed to assess students' reading comprehension. In this assessment, students read narrative and expository passages and texts that increase in difficulty, though most of the texts are

Common Core Connection

Reading Standards for Literature and Informational Text: Key Ideas and Details

The Gates-MacGinitie Reading Assessment

☑ Screening
☐ Diagnostic
☐ Formative Progress Monitoring
☑ Interim/Benchmark
☑ Outcome

at the students' specific grade level. Comprehension is assessed through students' responses to literal, "text-based" questions and inferential questions. The multiple-choice format gives it high reliability, though it has some notable limitations. The most obvious of these is this: Unless you are using an **out-of-level test**, students are reading and answering questions about texts and passages that are primarily at their grade level. As a screening instrument, or even as an interim/benchmark or outcomes assessment, this may be appropriate, but it's not sufficient for planning student-centered, developmentally oriented instruction.

When students score "below average" on a norm-referenced test of reading comprehension, it's difficult to know if the primary issue is related to comprehension strategy use, word recognition, fluency, vocabulary knowledge, or gaps in their prior knowledge (among other possibilities). Consider, for example, a fifth-grader who scored at the fifth percentile on the Gates-MacGinitie reading assessment. Do you know why she experienced such difficulty from these results? No. The results probably confirm something you already knew: Your student has difficulty comprehending grade-level text. Only further diagnostic assessment at the child's independent and instructional levels will help you understand your student's strengths, primary area(s) of need, and stage of development.

Informal Reading Inventories (IRIs)
☑ Screening
☑ Diagnostic
☐ Formative Progress Monitoring
☑ Interim/Benchmark
☑ Outcome

Informal Reading Inventories

Informal reading inventories are individually administered reading assessments that are typically used to assess children's word recognition in isolation, reading accuracy in context, and reading comprehension. Some IRIs also include measures of fluency. Informal reading inventories are most commonly used in the primary grades as a screening, diagnostic, interim/benchmark, and

Children's Literature Connection

Doing Your Best: Books about Perseverance and Overcoming Obstacles

Books for the Primary Grades

Bunting, E. (1991). *Fly away home*. New York: Clarion Books.

Bunting, E. (1994). *Smoky night*. New York: Harcourt Children's Books.

Cronin, D. (2000). *Click, clack, moo: Cows that type*. New York: Simon & Schuster Books for Young Readers.

Fraser, D. (2000). *Miss Alaineus*. Orlando, FL: Harcourt.

Henkes, K. (1996). *Lilly's purple plastic purse*. New York: Scholastic.

Hoffman, M. (1991). *Amazing Grace*. New York: Dial.

McCully, E. A. (1992). *Mirette on the high wire*. New York: Puffin.

Polacco, P. (1998). *Thank you, Mr. Falker*. New York: Philomel.

Williams, M. (2005). *Brothers in hope: The story of the lost boys of Sudan*. New York: Lee & Low Books.

Books for Upper Elementary and Middle Level

Anderson, L. H. (2008). *Chains*. New York: Simon & Schuster.

Clements, A. (1996). *Frindle*. New York: Atheneum Books for Young Readers.

Messner, K. (2010). *Sugar and ice*. New York: Walker Children's.

Munoz, P. R. (2000). *Esperanza rising*. New York: Scholastic.

Park, L. S. (2010). *A long walk to water*. New York: Clarion Books.

Roth, V. (2011). *Divergent*. New York: Katherine Tegen/HarperCollins.

Selznick, B. (2007). *The invention of Hugo Cabret*. New York: Scholastic.

Wiles, D. (2005). *Each little bird that sings*. New York: Harcourt.

FIGURE 4.13 Common Informal Reading Inventories (IRIs)

Beaver, J. M., & Carter, M. A. (2006). *The developmental reading assessment (DRA2)* (2nd ed.). Upper Saddle River, NJ: Pearson.

Brozo, W. G., & Afflerbach, P. P. (2010). *Adolescent literacy inventory, grades 6–12*. Upper Saddle River, NJ: Pearson.

Fountas, I., & Pinnell, G. S. (2010). *Benchmark assessment system 1: Grades K–2, levels a–n* (2nd ed.). Portsmouth, NH: Heinemann.

Fountas, I., & Pinnell, G. S. (2010). *Benchmark assessment system 2: Grades 3-8, levels l–z* (2nd ed.). Portsmouth, NH: Heinemann.

Johns, T., & Elish-Piper, L. (2012). *Basic reading inventory: Pre-primer through grade twelve and early literacy assessments* (11th ed.). Dubuque, IA: Kendall/Hunt.

Leslie, L., & Caldwell, J. S. (2011). *Qualitative reading inventory* (5th ed.). Upper Saddle River, NJ: Pearson.

outcomes assessment, and more typically as a diagnostic assessment in the upper elementary and middle school years. A list of commonly used IRIs can be found in Figure 4.13.

Informal reading inventories use graded word lists and leveled passages and texts to:

1) Determine a student's independent, instructional, and/or frustration level of reading.
2) Analyze a student's word recognition skills and strategies in isolation and in context.
3) Better understand a student's comprehension skills and strategies.

As you can see, IRIs are very beneficial, but they do have some notable drawbacks. Because IRIs are individually administered, they can take considerably more time to administer than norm-referenced assessments—perhaps as much as 60 to 90 minutes per child. They also require some training to ensure teachers are administering, scoring, and interpreting the results in a consistent and appropriate manner. With training, IRIs can be reasonably valid and reliable measures of reading (Paris & Carpenter, 2003). Perhaps most importantly, we like IRIs because they provide valuable information that can inform your instruction, particularly for those students experiencing difficulty.

Assessing Word Recognition in Isolation

Children's ability to read words in isolation is highly predictive of their overall reading proficiency (Morris et al., 2010; Rayner, Foorman, Perfetti, Pesetsky, & Seidenberg, 2001; Torgesen, Wagner, Rashotte, Burgess, & Hecht, 1997). For this reason, most IRIs will begin with students reading graded word lists to assess their word recognition skills. The results of this quick assessment are then used to help you match students to appropriately difficult leveled text, which you'll use to assess your students' oral reading accuracy in context as well as their reading comprehension.

Lipson and Wixson (2009, p. 379) recommend the following criteria for interpreting your students' word recognition results:

* *Independent level*: 90–100% recognition of words on graded word lists.
* *Instructional level*: 80–90% recognition of words on graded word lists.
* *Frustration level*: 80% (or below) recognition of words on graded word lists.

Assessing Oral Reading Accuracy

Once you've determined the level at which you'll begin to assess your students' oral reading in context, select a piece of text and briefly introduce it as specified by the administration guide for

Common Core Connection
Reading Standards: Foundational Skills – Phonics and Word Recognition

Common Core Connection
Reading Standards for Literature and Informational Text: Range of Reading and Level of Text Complexity

Common Core Connection
Reading Standards: Foundational Skills – Phonics and Word Recognition

FIGURE 4.14 Formula to Determine a Student's Level of Reading Accuracy

Total Words Read Correctly*	÷	Total Words in Passage	=	Percent Accurate

*This is figured by subtracting the number of errors from the total number of words in the passage/text.

the IRI you're using. This usually includes introducing the title of the text and the gist of the story or the main idea or topic of a piece of informational text. Next, your students will read a specified portion of the text or passage aloud before reading the remainder of the text silently. (At the early levels, students may read the entire text aloud.) While listening to students read, you'll be taking notes about their reading behaviors and **miscues** (reading errors), which you'll analyze later. These notes are called **records of oral reading** or **running records** (Clay, 2000a). Running records can provide you with important diagnostic information. You'll learn more about running records later in the chapter.

There are two primary goals of the oral reading portion of an IRI: (1) to determine the student's level of reading in context: *independent*, *instructional*, or *frustration*, so you can efficiently match students to appropriately difficult books; and (2) to analyze the student's reading behaviors to inform your ongoing reading instruction. When determining your student's level of reading accuracy, you'll need to find the percent of words he or she read accurately. The formula for this is relatively simple and can be found in Figure 4.14.

The administration guide of your IRI will provide guidance about determining students' instructional levels based on their reading accuracy, but many IRIs use criteria similar to, if not the same as, the following:

Independent level:	95–100% accuracy in grades K–3
	98–100% accuracy in grades 4–8
Instructional level:	90–94% accuracy in grades K–3
	95–97% accuracy in grades 4–8
Frustration level:	Below 90% accuracy

Notice from these criteria that as students move along in the grades and their texts become increasingly complex, greater cognitive energy is needed to comprehend them, so the expectations for reading accuracy increase to better support students' comprehension.

Assessing Comprehension with an IRI

After your students complete their reading of a leveled text, they will retell these stories or passages, or answer questions about them so you can assess their comprehension. The administration guide that comes with your IRI will specify the amount and type of support you can provide in these tasks as well as supply directions for how to score students' responses to your prompts and questions. Most IRIs use the following guidelines for determining students' levels of comprehension (Lipson & Wixson, 2009, p. 378):

Independent level:	75–90% correct responses on comprehension tasks.
Instructional level:	60–75% correct responses on comprehension tasks.

In addition to using these guidelines, it's also important for you to analyze the types of questions these assessments ask of your students. All too often IRIs ask literal, "in-the-text"-type questions, which assess only students' basic understanding of text (Applegate, Quinn, & Applegate, 2002). Given the expectations of the Common Core State Standards and your own high expectations for comprehension, you'll want to be sure most of the questions—particularly in the upper elementary and middle school grades—engage your students' inferential and critical thinking skills.

Completing the Assessment

After you complete the oral reading accuracy and comprehension subtests of an IRI at a given level, you will analyze the results to determine your next steps. If your student scores at the independent or instructional level for both oral reading accuracy and comprehension, you will usually administer the next highest level of text. If your student scores at the frustration level on either oral reading accuracy or comprehension, you'll go down a level. Your students will continue to read leveled texts until you find their highest level of independence and their frustration level. Their highest instructional level will typically be the level just below their frustration level. It's valuable to complete this process, as time allows, in both narrative and informational text, with a greater focus on informational text in fourth grade and beyond.

Assessing Fluency

At one time, fluency was considered "the neglected reading goal" (Allington, 1983), but today, perhaps in response to the widely disseminated findings of the *National Reading Panel Report* (NICHHD, 2000), fluency figures prominently in classrooms across the country (Pikulski & Chard, 2005). Unfortunately, not all aspects of fluency are equally valued, assessed, or taught. Most assessments of fluency focus on reading rate, and so fluency instruction has become more focused, unfortunately, on reading quickly rather than reading with expression and a rate that's *appropriate* for the purpose of reading (Rasinski, Reutzel, Chard, & Linan-Thompson, 2011; Samuels & Farstrup, 2006). Just the same, it's important that you know how to assess your students' reading rate, as it can be predictive of their overall reading success across the grades (Morris et al., 2010). Reading expressively, on the other hand, is more predictive of reading success in the later grades (Rasinski et al., 2011).

Fluency Measures
☑ Screening
☑ Diagnostic
☑ Formative Progress Monitoring
☑ Interim/Benchmark
☑ Outcome

Assessing Reading Rate

When measuring oral reading rate, you're typically going to measure your students' Words Correct per Minute (WCPM). The formula for calculating this is noted in Figure 4.15. When using this formula, you'll will need to keep track of your students' reading errors and the number of seconds it takes them to read a given text or passage.

Common Core Connection
Reading Standards: Foundation Skills – Fluency

When using measures of students' reading rate as part of a screening, interim/benchmark, or outcomes assessment, you may opt to have students read grade-level-appropriate text first and compare their results to grade-level norms such as the ones found in Figure 4.16. As part of

FIGURE 4.15 Formula for Words Correct Per Minute (WCPM)

$$\frac{60 \times \text{Number of Words Read Correctly in the Passage*}}{\text{Total Number of Seconds to Read the Passage}} = \text{Words Correct per Minute (WCPM)}$$

*This is calculated by subtracting the number of errors from the total number of words in the passage/text.

FIGURE 4.16 **Hasbrouck and Tindal's Norms for Oral Reading Rate in Grade-Level Text**

Grade	Percentile	Fall WCPM	Winter WCPM	Spring WCPM
1	90		81	111
	75		47	82
	50		23	53
	25		12	28
	10		6	15
2	90	106	125	142
	75	79	100	117
	50	51	72	89
	25	25	42	61
	10	11	18	31
3	90	128	146	162
	75	99	120	137
	50	71	92	107
	25	44	62	78
	10	21	36	48
4	90	145	166	180
	75	119	139	152
	50	94	112	123
	25	68	87	98
	10	45	61	72
5	90	166	182	194
	75	139	156	168
	50	110	127	139
	25	85	99	109
	10	61	74	83
6	90	177	195	204
	75	153	167	177
	50	127	140	150
	25	98	111	122
	10	68	82	93
7	90	180	192	202
	75	156	165	177
	50	128	136	150
	25	102	109	123
	10	79	88	98
8	90	185	199	199
	75	161	173	177
	50	133	146	151
	25	106	115	124
	10	77	84	97

Source: Hasbrouck & Tindal, 2006.

FIGURE 4.17 NAEP Fluency Rubric

Fluent	Level 4	Reads primarily in larger, meaningful phrase groups. Although some regressions, repetitions, and deviations from text may be present, these do not appear to detract from the overall structure of the story. Preservation of the author's syntax is consistent. Some or most of the story is read with expressive interpretation.
	Level 3	Reads primarily in three- or four-word phrase groups. Some small groupings may be present. However, the majority of phrasing seems appropriate and preserves the syntax of the author. Little or no expressive interpretation is present.
Nonfluent	Level 2	Reads primarily in two-word phrases with some three- or four-word groupings. Some word-by-word reading may be present. Word groupings may seem awkward and unrelated to larger context of sentence or passage.
	Level 1	Reads primarily word-by-word. Occasional two-word or three-word phrases may occur—but these are infrequent and/or they do not preserve meaningful syntax.

Source: U.S. Department of Education, 2002.

diagnostic assessment and ongoing formative progress monitoring, you can track your students' fluency rates along with the text levels they're reading at their instructional and independent reading levels. You may also keep track of how your students' rate improves as they reread their guided reading materials as described in the section "Repeated Readings" in Chapter 8.

Measuring Reading Expression: The NAEP Fluency Rubric

Measuring your students' expressive reading is yet another aspect of fluency assessment. Although there isn't a universal standard for measuring expressive reading, the NAEP Fluency Rubric is one measure that's widely used and adapted, and it's as close as we have to a "standard" for oral reading fluency. (See Figure 4.17.) Your IRIs will likely include a variation of this rubric, particularly at the upper levels.

Assessing Vocabulary and Morphological Knowledge

You will informally assess your students' developing vocabulary knowledge on an ongoing and regular basis by observing and noting how the children are using and remembering target vocabulary words in their oral language, writing, and reading. Beginning in the primary grades, you'll also engage your students in self-assessment. For example, when presented with target vocabulary words, they'll indicate for each whether they have "Never heard of it," "Heard it," "Have an idea" what it means, or "Know it well" (Templeton, Bear, Invernizzi, & Johnston, 2010). If they "Have an idea," they will write or draw what they think it means; if they "Know it well," they will write what they know and give examples. These self-assessments give students ownership of their developing word knowledge. With your encouragement, your students will revisit these graphic organizers to add new information as they gain more exposures to and insights about their target words.

You'll also find that it's beneficial for your ongoing formative assessment and summative assessment to be reflective of your instructional techniques. For instance, when learning about

> **Common Core Connection**
>
> Language Standards: Vocabulary Acquisition and Use

homophones *(sail, sale; pear, pair)* students may show their understanding of the spelling–meaning connection with a simple "draw and label" activity. When students are studying "shades of meaning" (words such as *cool, brisk, cold, freezing,* and *frigid*), you can assess their understanding of the meaning of these words by asking them to place the words along a continuum and provide a rationale for each word's placement. Your students can also show their understanding of new vocabulary by using graphic organizers such as concept maps and semantic webs (described in later chapters).

With younger children, you might assess their understanding of new vocabulary by having them engage in a picture sort, or by selecting a picture that best represents a word's meaning and explain why it's the best choice. Students can also show their understanding by providing examples, definitions, or synonyms orally, in writing, through drawing, and even through acting out meaning of words. Your assessment of students' vocabulary learning can be as varied as your instructional methods.

Formal Measures of Vocabulary Knowledge

Two commonly used assessments of vocabulary are the Peabody Picture Vocabulary Test (PPVT) (Dunn & Dunn, 2007) and the Expressive Vocabulary Test (EVT) (Williams, 2006). The PPVT has and continues to be the most widely used, individually administered, norm-referenced vocabulary assessment of vocabulary. The PPVT assesses *receptive* vocabulary by asking the student to select a picture that best represents the meaning of a spoken word. The EVT, as its name implies, similarly measures a student's *expressive* vocabulary. Most often, a reading specialist, special educator, or a speech pathologist will administer these assessments when a language-based learning disability is suspected. Given the relationship between reading achievement and vocabulary knowledge, a formal vocabulary assessment can be an important piece of diagnostic information when readers experience difficulty learning to read. The PPVT and EVT are appropriate for English learners as well as native speakers of English.

Morphological Knowledge

Common Core Connection

Language Standards:
Knowledge of
Language

In addition to assessing your students' vocabulary and concept knowledge, you'll assess their morphological knowledge beginning late in the transitional stage. Morphology, as you recall, underlies students' learning and application of *generative* vocabulary strategies. Although there are formal measures of morphological knowledge such as Carlisle's (2002) Test of Morphological Structure, you can get a good sense of your students' morphological knowledge through informal assessment activities such as the following:

- Present students with several words, and for each word, ask the students to write up to five words that come from that word. For example, *warm* could generate *warmer, warmest,* and *warmly; happy* could generate *happily, unhappy,* and *happiest.*
- Give students several prefixes. For each prefix, they are to write up to four words that have that prefix. Tell them not to include words with plurals. Most frequent prefixes are *un–, re–, dis–, mis–, pre–,* and *non–.* In addition, for each prefix, ask students to write the meaning.
- Provide students several suffixes. For each suffix, they are to write up to four words that have that suffix. Tell them not to include words with plurals. Most frequent suffixes are *–ful, –y, –ly, –less,* and *–ness.* In addition, for each suffix, ask students to write the meaning.

To learn how to assess more advanced morphological knowledge in students—knowledge of both affixes and Greek and Latin roots—and to plan developmentally responsive vocabulary lessons in grades 4 through 12, see *Vocabulary Their Way: Word Study for Middle and Secondary Students* (Templeton, Bear, Johnston, & Invernizzi, 2010).

FIGURE 4.18 Measuring Interest, Motivation, and a Reader's Self-Perception

Elementary Reading Attitude Survey (McKenna & Kear, 1990)
Reader Self-Perception Scale (Henk & Melnick, 1995)
Titles Test (Cunningham & Stanovich, 1992)
Reading Activity Inventory (Guthrie, McGough, & Wigfield, 1994)

Interest Inventories and Motivation Surveys

Your students' motivation and engagement are among the most important factors in their success (Guthrie & Wigfield, 2000). As you learned in Chapter 1, it's difficult, if not impossible, to teach someone to read if he or she doesn't want to learn! Assessing your students' interests and motivation, as well as their self-perception as readers, may be as simple as talking with them and observing their choices and reading behaviors. As you get to know your students, you'll be better positioned to engage your readers and share book recommendations based not only on their reading level but also their areas of interest.

Sometimes it's hard to get to know each and every student, particularly at the beginning of a new school year, or when you're responsible for teaching a large number of students. In these cases, it may be helpful to use a survey or questionnaire to get to know students' interests and perceptions of themselves as readers. Figure 4.18 highlights some interest inventories and motivation surveys that are helpful.

Special Considerations for Emergent and Beginning Readers

Emergent and beginning readers are learning foundational skills that are unique to their stage of development: Skills such as book handling, alphabetic principle, and concept of word in text. For students in these early stages of development, it's important to include assessments of these foundational skills in your comprehensive literacy assessment program.

> **Common Core Connection**
>
> Reading Standards: Foundational Skills – Print Concepts

Concepts about Print

When you select a book to read, you automatically turn to the cover, read the title and author's name, and maybe even turn to the back of the book or the inside flap to read a summary. When you begin reading a book, you intuitively start at the top of the page and read to the bottom in a left to right fashion, attending to the words, punctuation, and the illustrations or text features, but this wasn't always the case. Children in the emergent and early phase of the beginning stage don't necessarily understand how print works. They come to understand it through your modeling and instruction and their own interactions with books at home and at school. Children's print awareness is highly correlated with their success in other areas of early literacy (Clay, 1982).

Concepts About Print (CAP) (Clay, 2000b) is an assessment of children's print knowledge. Through asking a series of questions, you can assess young children's book-handling skills and knowledge of print concepts. The results from this assessment can be used to inform your teaching and to track your students' progress over time. The Phonological Literacy Awareness Screening (PALS), described earlier in this chapter, contains a print and word awareness task in the prekindergarten assessment (Invernizzi, Sullivan, Meier, & Swank, 2004), and the book, *Concepts About Print* (Clay, 2000b) includes guidelines for administering and scoring a stand-alone assessment of CAP. *Concepts About Print* is a valid and reliable assessment of children's early print knowledge (Johns, 1980) and it can be used as a screening, diagnostic, and outcomes-based measure.

Alphabet Knowledge

Alphabet knowledge is a significant predictor of early reading success (Adams, 1990; Snow, Burns, & Griffin, 1998; Speece, Ritchey, Mills, & Hillman, 2003). For this reason, we begin to assess children's knowledge of upper- and lowercase letters beginning in preschool. In addition to both upper- and lowercase forms, we also include the special typewritten font of the lowercase letters *a* and *g*. When assessing students on letter names, we present them out of order, one letter at a time. Letter recognition is a critical skill, but letter-naming fluency—the automatic naming of letters without a second's hesitation—is especially predictive of first-grade reading success (Stage, Sheppard, Davidson, & Browning, 2001).

Concept of Word in Text

As you'll learn in Chapter 6, concept of word in text is a complex task that requires children to orchestrate their growing awareness that print represents speech and letters represent sounds in words. Concept of word in text (COW) is demonstrated by asking children to point to the words as they "read" a piece of memorized text. COW develops over time as children engage in shared reading experiences and begin to learn about initial consonants (Flanigan, 2007; Morris, Bloodgood, Lomax, & Perney, 2003). Achieving a rudimentary understanding of COW is an important milestone that marks the transition from emergent or pretend reading to beginning or conventional reading. The PALS instrument includes a subtest for COW in grades K through 1.

Using Ongoing Formative Assessment in Your Classroom

While there's a lot of attention being focused on high-stakes literacy tests in the policy environment, decades of research have consistently pointed to the potential and power of ongoing formative assessment (Black & Wiliam, 1998, 2010; Hattie, 2009; Valencia, 2011). In this section we will focus on a few ways you can incorporate formative assessment into your daily and weekly instructional routines.

Conferring

Observation and conversation are two of the most powerful and informative ways to assess student learning (Anderson, 2000; Goodman & Owacki, 2002). Reading and writing conferences allow you to observe and analyze your students' reading and writing skills, dispositions, and strategy use in authentic and low-stakes ways. As you observe and talk with your students, you'll not only take note of their strengths and their ongoing instructional needs but also your teaching points. You'll reinforce and encourage their efforts while providing targeted instruction that moves their thinking and skills forward. (For more about conferring, see Chapter 3 and Chapter 8.)

Keeping Records of Conferences

Record keeping is an essential part of conferring, but one that is all too often overlooked. When taking conference notes, use language that describes what your students are doing rather than evaluative language such as "Good job reading!" The goal of record keeping is to inform your teaching as well as document student growth and learning over time.

Consider the difference between "Good job reading!" and the following conference record:

Observations

Josephina is using initial consonants and context clues including the illustrations to help her guess a word that makes sense when reading. For example, she read house for home and bug for beetle.

Teaching Point

Today's instruction focused on initial and final consonant sounds and the importance of looking across a whole word while segmenting each sound before blending it into a word that makes sense in the context of the story. Josephina will continue to practice this strategy in familiar texts and guided reading lessons.

Many teachers like to keep a small notebook for recording their conference notes. Others use address labels to record information quickly and then they transfer these labels to individual student notebooks or folders at a later time. Some teachers we know prefer to use standards-based checklists to guide their observations and to document their students' achievement of various goals. Over time you'll find the record-keeping system that works best for you. The format of your records isn't nearly as important as your commitment to take regular and detailed notes about your observations and instruction.

Records of Oral Reading

Records of oral reading, or running records, are systematic notations of children's oral reading behaviors, including their reading errors, self-corrections, and strategy use (Clay, 1979, 1985, 2000a). Running records can be part of larger assessment, as in the case of an IRI, or they can be done informally any time you listen to a child read. Many people use running records to determine students' oral reading accuracy, but they have the potential to tell us so much more.

> **Common Core Connection**
>
> Reading Standards: Foundational Skills – Phonics and Word Recognition

When using an IRI, take a running record using a typewritten script of the text as in Figure 4.19. As the student reads, take note of her or his miscues and reading behaviors and mark them using the annotations found in Figure 4.19. After the child finishes reading the text, calculate the percent of words read accurately. (See Figure 4.20 for guidance in marking miscues and counting errors.) With practice, you'll be able to take running records informally, too.

Interpreting the Running Record

After taking the running record, study your annotations to look for patterns that can help you plan your instruction. Figure 4.21 summarizes some of the more common trends in children's reading behaviors as captured in running record and the instructional implications of these trends.

Rubrics

Teachers use rubrics to help clarify their own expectations for student learning and to communicate these expectations to students. By definition, using a rubric to score student work makes an assessment both formal and criterion-referenced. Rubrics can also be used as part of your ongoing formative assessment and as a tool to facilitate self-assessment (Skillings & Ferrell, 2000).

FIGURE 4.19 **Completed Running Record**

Count

Source: Beaver and Carter, 2006.

Common Core Connection

Language Standards:
Conventions of
Standard English

One of the most common ways rubrics are used is to assess student writing. Figure 4.22 is an example of a teacher-made rubric used to assess seventh-grade students' personal essays in a language arts class. After reading and analyzing several mentor essays with his students, Mr. Mendenhall and his class developed this rubric before they began drafting their own essays. By involving his students in the process of developing the rubric, his students have internalized the expectations for "meets the standard" work, which is described in the center column (Skillings & Ferrell, 2000). This could also be achieved by using a teacher-made rubric to guide students in reading sample texts "with the eyes of reader."

Common Core Connection

Writing Standards:
Production and
Distribution of
Writing

Throughout the writing process, Mr. Mendenhall confers with his students and together they use the rubric to analyze an essay's strengths and opportunities for improvement. Using the rubric in this way allows students to self-assess, as well as receive specific feedback to achieve their goals. After the students turn in their final drafts, the rubric is then used to assess the essays for a final grade.

Student Self-Assessment and Ongoing Feedback

Self-assessment is very closely related to formative assessment, as described in the example of Mr. Mendenhall's personal essay assignment. Research shows that students as young as age 5 are capable of self-assessment, particularly when the criteria are made clear (Black & Wiliam, 1998,

FIGURE 4.20 Guidelines for Annotating a Record of Oral Reading

Record of Oral Reading Guidelines

Reading Behavior	How to Record Observed Behavior	Annotated Examples	Number of Errors
Accurate Reading	No notation ✓ or check mark	An octopus has no backbone	No errors
Substitution	Record substitution	beginning / tears being to well up	Each substitution is counted as one error*
Repetition	Insert "R" and an arrow to indicate word(s) repeated and underline word(s) repeated	Always looking for a / Mike was thoroughly ᴿ	Repetitions are not counted as errors but impact fluency
Self-Correction	Insert "sc" after substitution	discovered/sc / They described the weather	Self-corrections are not counted as errors
Omission	Circle omitted word(s)	One day, as she and (her) mother	Each omission is counted as one error
Insertion	Use caret to record added word(s)	the / covered in snow and ice.	Each inserted word is counted as one error
Reversals	Use the reversal symbol when words are reversed	She quickly agreed to	A reversal is counted as one error
Sounding Out	Record letter sounds and use slash marks to show how words were segmented	Princess was captivated... / ...uses a funnel for...	Words sounded out incorrectly are counted a one error**
Word Told by Teacher	Insert a "T" above word(s) told	T / many disguises and tricks	Each word provided by the teacher is counted as one error.
Long Pauses	Insert a "W" above the place or use slash marks where student pause or use ⊘ this symbol	⑤ W / They got a bucket / They saw some cashews	Pauses are not counted as errors but impact fluency

*Repeated Substitutions: If the child makes an error (*e.g., run* for *ran*) and then substitutes this world repeatedly, it counts as an error every time. The substitution of a proper name (*e.g., Mary* for *Molly*) is counted as an error the first time only. Substitutions involving contractions count as one error.   Examples: I will   I'll
                                                                                                                                                         I'll   I will

**Words mispronounced due to a speech problem or dialect may be coded but are not counted as errors.
        Examples: get   picture   our
                              git   pitcher   are
Note: Miscues of numerals and abbreviations are not to be counted in the total number of miscues, but they can be noted for future instruction.

Source: Beaver and Carter, 2003.

2010). Using self-assessment combined with formative assessment provides students with three kinds of essential feedback:

1) Recognition of the learning goal/standard

2) A detailed explanation of the student's current level of achievement in comparison to the goal/standard

3) A plan for how to improve the student's work so it meets or exceeds the goal/standard

FIGURE 4.21 Running Records: Common Trends and Instructional Implications

Observation	Instructional Implications
The student's miscues are words that are visually similar.	The student will benefit from reading across the word and segmenting and blending sounds (if mid- to late beginning readers) and/or looking for known orthographic patterns. The student should be encouraged to use the meaning and syntax to confirm the accuracy of his or her reading.
The student inserts words that *are not* in the text and/or omits words that *are in* the text, but the errors do not affect meaning.	By the mid- to late part of the beginning stage, readers need to be encouraged to match spoken words to written words. Over-relying on context can be a sign of a problem with decoding and/or word recognition.
The student repeats words or lines of text and/or self-corrects frequently.	Repetitions and self-corrections suggest that the student is monitoring her or his reading to be sure the reading makes sense and sounds right. This, in itself, is positive, and should be encouraged. However, significant repetitions and self-corrections can negatively affect fluency and comprehension. Be sure the student is matched to appropriately difficult texts and work to build both accuracy and automaticity at the word level.
The student's miscues seem to be guesses not based on letter–sound information and they frequently affect the meaning of the text.	The student's decoding and word recognition skills may need additional practice and support, and the student needs to learn how to use both syntax and the meaning to monitor the reading of words. If the student's reading accuracy is below 90 percent, move to an easier text level for instruction.
The student changes the syntax of the sentence to match the syntactic structure of her or his own oral language.	Both English learners and speakers of different dialects of English can do this, as can children with language-based disabilities. In one sense, they're translating language into a discourse pattern that is familiar, which is a rather sophisticated skill; on the other hand, the child is not using or acquiring Standard English, which is most commonly used in academic settings. Encourage your students to make their reading match the words in their texts.
The student does not attempt unknown words.	The student may not have the skills to decode unknown words. By coordinating your word study instruction with your guided reading instruction and possibly using some decodable texts, you'll help your students gain the skills and confidence necessary to read texts at their independent and instructional levels. Strong book introductions can also help.
The student misses whole lines and/or pages of text.	Teach the student to monitor his or her reading for meaning. Consider using an instructional strategy such as Reciprocal Teaching (see Chapter 8 and Chapter 11).

FIGURE 4.22 Personal Essay Rubric

Personal Essay Rubric

Name _____

Purpose	—Establishes a clear topic; purpose of reflection obvious. —Maintains topic throughout the piece. —Relates each paragraph to the purpose/gist. —Develops a context for the details: related settings, situation, and characters.	❑ Approaching the Standard ❑ Meets the Standard ❑ Exceeds the Standard
Voice	—Uses specific, effective language/vocabulary. —Uses purposeful punctuation—rhythm and flow through effective sentence variety. —Leads with an original or exciting technique. —Concludes the paper powerfully: Creates provocative idea; answers driving question; develops great image; logically connects to or extends the lead.	❑ Approaching the Standard ❑ Meets the Standard ❑ Exceeds the Standard
Organization	—Writes strong lead and wraps that shape paper. —Arranges details and events effectively: "best" order. —Creates effective transitions. —Intentionally paces paper; scenes vary appropriately in length and depth.	❑ Approaching the Standard ❑ Meets the Standard ❑ Exceeds the Standard
Detail	—Uses a variety of strategies: examples, anecdotes, snapshots, dialogue. —Ensures all details develop main idea. —Balances details; uses enough "show" and tell. —Creates relevance for the reader.	❑ Approaching the Standard ❑ Meets the Standard ❑ Exceeds the Standard
Grammar, Usage, and Mechanics (GUM)	—Spelling is correct/conventional. —Sentence control is conventional and uses intentional punctuation. —Correct capitalization. —Viable, logical paragraphs. —Consistent verb tense.	❑ Approaching the Standard ❑ Meets the Standard ❑ Exceeds the Standard

Source: Adapted from D. Mendenhall, 2012. Used with permission.

It's this kind of specific feedback that accelerates learning more than any other teaching strategy (Hattie, 2009).

Like any new tool or strategy, teaching students how to self-assess will require modeling, guided practice, and independent application with ongoing feedback. Self-assessment is a tool as much as it is a topic of study. In other words, you'll work to help students use rubrics and tools not only to assess their own work but also to invite them to analyze and reflect on the accuracy of their self-assessments. Some students will judge their work unnecessarily hard and others will be too generous, so this will become a point of conversation and perhaps a small group strategy lesson for some students. Like most things in your language arts classroom, you'll teach students to back up their self-assessments with evidence from their own work. This will strengthen their understanding of the standards as well as more productively engage them in the assessment process.

Portfolios

Portfolios can be used for many purposes, including showcasing students' best work, documenting students' attainment of standards, and/or documenting students' growth over time (Valencia & Place, 1994). Some teachers and reading specialists also use portfolios for diagnostic purposes (Courtney & Abodeeb, 1999; Lipson & Wixson, 2009); in this way, they collect assessment data and work samples to identify students' strengths and needs so they can plan responsive instruction and monitor progress over time. Other teachers use portfolios to engage students in identifying and documenting the things they "can do"; this becomes a springboard for celebrating growth and accomplishments, and setting future learning goals, too (Cleland, 1999).

Portfolio assessment, particularly when the goals for the assessment are made explicitly clear, engages students in the process of self-assessment and helps them appreciate and celebrate their progress over time (Tierney, Carter, & Desai, 1991). It's this view that helps students set goals for the future and meaningfully engages students in the learning process.

While it's not necessary, most portfolios include some common elements, such as a table of contents, a reflective summary of the portfolio, and a statement of future goals or ongoing work. Portfolios can take many forms. Increasingly, technology is being used to create, store, and display student work. Freeware such as Google Sites, or software programs such as Adobe Pro X, allow your students to scan and save their work samples and arrange them creatively for others to view. These e-portfolios are often used as part of student-involved parent–teacher conferences.

As you can see, portfolios hold a great deal of possibility and reflect some of the best practices of formative assessment, summative assessment, and self-assessment.

Chapter Summary

In this chapter we've explored building a comprehensive literacy assessment system that includes screening, diagnosis, progress monitoring, interim/benchmark assessment, and outcomes assessment for each of our literacy essentials. Having such an assessment system in place, in addition to your deepening understanding of literacy development, will provide you with the strong foundation you need to be most effective.

In the day-to-day world of your classroom, assessment is not separate from instruction; rather, it is fully integrated in the teaching–learning process. Ongoing formative assessment will help you identify what your students know and what they're experimenting with. This insight will allow you to teach in their instructional zones—providing opportunities for modeling and guided practice, ongoing feedback, independent practice, and self-assessment—before more formally assessing their learning again. Figure 4.23 highlights this fully integrated teaching–learning cycle.

Your classroom assessment and instruction exist within a larger policy context in which high-stakes testing figures prominently. Although understanding this context and the needs of different stakeholders is important, you'll find that your ongoing formative assessment is the most powerful and informative assessment you'll use. It is this assessment that will shape the moment-to-moment adjustments in your lessons, the pacing and content of your ongoing instruction, and your instructional goals for your whole class, small groups, and individuals. By inviting your students' participation in the assessment process, you'll stimulate their ownership and engagement in learning. Assessment, when done well, can be a powerful tool and motivator for teachers and students alike.

FIGURE 4.23 Teaching and Learning: Using Assessment to Guide Student-Centered Instruction

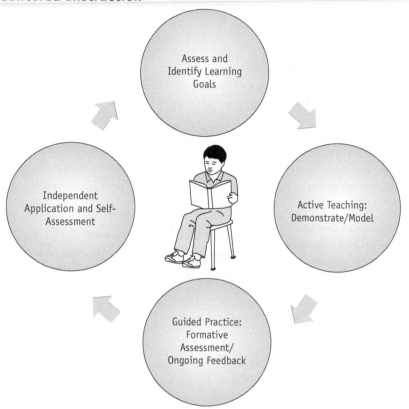

Suggested Extension Activities

- Work with a classmate or colleague to create a timeline from 1950 through present day. Include the major policy and school reform initiatives described in the beginning of this chapter. Next, mark the years you attended elementary school on the timeline and the year you entered the profession. Analyze the policy environment at these times and consider how policy affected both your learning and your teaching.
- Make a copy of the Comprehensive Literacy Assessment Plan template found in Figure 4.6.

Working with a classmate or colleague, develop a plan for assessing each of the essentials across the five categories of assessment.
- Use the NAEP fluency rubric (Figure 4.17) and calculate a child's reading accuracy and words correct per minute. Considering these three pieces of information, determine if this is a "just-right" text for the student and identify an appropriate teaching point for your conference.

Recommended Professional Resources

Calkins, L., Ehrenworth, M., & Lehman, C. (2012). *Pathways to the common core: Accelerating achievement.* Portsmouth, NH: Heinemann.

Clay, M. M. (2000). *Concepts about print: What have children learned about the way we print language?* Portsmouth, NH: Heinemann.

Clay, M. M. (2000). *Running records for classroom teachers.* Portsmouth, NH: Heinemann.

Morris, D. (2008). *Diagnosis and correction of reading problems.* New York: Guilford.

Stahl, K. D., & McKenna, M. (2009). *Assessment for reading instruction* (2nd ed.). New York: Guilford.

Online Resources

High-Stakes Testing

High-stakes testing has become the centerpiece of many school reform initiatives, but it's not without its problems. See what the two leading organizations of literacy scholars and teachers have to say about high-stakes testing by visiting these websites:

IRA Position Statement on High-Stakes Testing
www.reading.org/Libraries/position-statements-and-resolutions/ps1035_high_stakes.pdf

Literacy Research Association's Position Statement on High-Stakes Testing
www.literacyresearchassociation.org/publications/HighStakesTestingandReadingAssessment.pdf

Universal Design

Center for Universal Design in Education
www.washington.edu/doit/CUDE/

Universal design is a set of principles designed to eliminate bias in testing, instruction, and other issues of access.

5

Foundations of Language and Literacy Instruction for English Learners

Chapter Outline

» **The Foundations of Teaching English Learners**

» **Examining Our Dispositions**

» **Characteristics of English Learners**

» **Culturally Responsive and Culturally Inclusive Teaching**

» **Determining Levels of English Learners' Proficiency in English**

» **Literacy Instruction with Your English Learners**

1. What is your own language and cultural background? How might your background impact your teaching of literacy? If your linguistic and cultural background reflects that of the dominant culture, what steps might you take to gain the perspective you need to better meet the literacy and language needs of your English learning students?

2. What are the characteristics of English learners with which you should be familiar as a classroom teacher?

3. How is your literacy instruction for English learners similar to your instruction for native-speaking students? How will it vary, and why?

4. How does knowing something about the spoken and written languages of your English learners assist you in providing the most appropriate literacy instruction for them?

I n her fifth-grade classroom, Kelly Wentrock has a number of students whose home language is Spanish. They are able to read and write quite well in Spanish, and these skills have supported their acquisition of spoken English and their understanding of the ways in which English is written. Their level of English proficiency may be described as intermediate—their receptive vocabulary in English is quite large—but their development in acquiring academic vocabulary will still take a few years to develop more fully. Kelly can accelerate this growth, however, by helping her students develop an awareness of the cognates that Spanish and English share (such as *pentagon* and *pentágono*) and of the ways that understanding their structure can accelerate vocabulary development in both languages (Hancin-Bhatt & Nagy, 1993; Templeton, 2010).

Based on an idea that she found on a vocabulary website recommended by her university mentor (Eddy, 2010—vocabulogic.com), Kelly displays the following word pairs for both her English learners and her native English speaking students:

vacación	conversación	educación
vacation	conversation	education

Kelly asks the students what they notice about the words: How are they alike? How are they different? The students notice that they look a lot alike. Kelly asks if that might be a clue to their meaning: Might words in different languages that are similar in spelling be similar in meaning?

Kelly then displays the following word pairs:

naturalmente	inmediatamente	recientemente
naturally	immediately	recently

She asks the same questions: How are these words alike? How are they different?

Kelly is tweaking her students' word consciousness (Scott, Skobel, & Wells, 2008), helping students become aware that spelling–meaning relationships can exist across languages as well as within a language. When these relationships occur across languages, we refer to them as **cognates**. Cognates, Kelly shares with her students, are words that have the same or similar meanings in different languages, and that are spelled the same or similarly. (We explore this relationship in English, as well as with cognates, more extensively in Chapter 9.)

On another day, Kelly brings her students back to these same word pairs and adds the following pairs:

actividad	responsabilidad
activity	responsibility

This time Kelly asks the students to compare the endings, or suffixes, within each of the Spanish and English cognate pairs. What do they notice? If they are uncertain, she asks a leading question: "If a word in Spanish ends in the suffix *–dad*, what does the English cognate end in?" The students will notice that it's *–ity*. "Do you think that these suffixes have the same meaning in Spanish and English? What makes you think that? How does the suffix affect the meaning of the word?"

By engaging the students in examining the structure of cognates, noting their suffixes, Kelly is helping her students develop a strategy for learning and remembering words—more specifically, academic vocabulary in different languages. Not only may the words look similar but the meaningful word parts look similar as well—and these similarities can be important clues to meaning. ■

The Foundations of Teaching English Learners

We are all English learners, of course. More specifically, however, in education we use the term *English learners* (EL) to refer to students whose first language is not English, and whose proficiency in English has not reached a level at which they can be taught exclusively in English. The reality, however, is that many of these students will receive little if any instruction in their native language. Given this reality, we will expand in this chapter on the principles for accommodating English learners presented in Chapter 3, including the importance of establishing a supportive social context in a learning environment that encourages collaboration and risk taking. Figure 5.1 presents the components of literacy instruction that we will need to address for most English learners.

As we explore the terrain of developmentally based literacy instruction for our English learners, we also build on the instructional foundations we have presented in the preceding chapters. Literacy instruction for English learners is not profoundly different from literacy instruction for

FIGURE 5.1 Major Findings from the National Literacy Panel on Language-Minority Children and Youth (August & Shanahan, 2006)

This major report reached the following conclusions:

- Depending on the level of language and literary proficiency, instruction in one or more of the following clearly benefits language-minority students: phonemic awareness, phonics, fluency, vocabulary, and text comprehension.
- Instruction in these components of reading is necessary but may not be sufficient for language-minority students. Developing *oral* proficiency in English is crucial—but it is all too often overlooked.
- Students' oral language proficiency and literacy competence in their first language can be used to support their literacy development in English.
- Just as with native English speakers, individual differences among English learners significantly affect the development of literacy in English.
- The report found "surprisingly little evidence" that sociocultural variables impacted achievement or development in literacy, but it did find that language experiences in the home can have a positive influence. Apart from this report, however, we do know the negative impact of poverty on both native speakers' and English learners' literacy development (Goldenberg, 2011; Kieffer, 2012).

native English speakers—effective and efficient instruction is consistent regardless of a student's native language. Recall from Chapter 3 Darling-Hammond's observation about the effects of well-prepared teachers on student achievement: "[They] can be stronger than the influences of student background factors such as poverty, language background, and minority status" (1999, p. 38). In order for teachers to have that effect, however, teachers must also be prepared with foundational knowledge about English learners and the characteristics of the languages they represent. We provide that foundational knowledge in this chapter as we set the stage and foundation for the instructional chapters that comprise the rest of this book.

First, however, we begin with You: As Pennington and Sallas (2009) observe, while novice and experienced teachers alike may receive instruction and professional development in how to teach English learners, effective instruction does not usually occur unless teachers also take some time to "attend to their own attitudes and beliefs about language and culture" (Pennington & Sallas, 2009, p. 215). Such attention can be awkward and uncomfortable, but it is necessary.

Examining Our Dispositions

Throughout this book we emphasize that knowledge is *socially* constructed. From time to time it is important to remind ourselves that this of course is true for teachers as well as for our students. The culture in which we have constructed our knowledge also gives us many of our beliefs and attitudes—our *dispositions*—and more deeply, our *identities* (Ladson-Billings, 1999). It is human nature to hold onto what is familiar and comfortable: our knowledge, our attitudes, our beliefs. It is also human nature to compare other cultures, languages, and socioeconomic groups to our own—to assume ours is the "norm" or standard, and to the degree that others vary from what we are familiar with, human nature may also lead us to become more judgmental.

The predominant culture from which almost 90 percent of American elementary teachers come is European American, female, and English monolingual (National Center for Education Statistics, 2012). From this perspective, **cultural diversity** is defined as "perceived deviations from White, middle-class, monolingual backgrounds . . . perceived differences in skin color, language use, linguistic ability, and socioeconomic status" (Dee & Henkin, 2002, p. 25). Regardless of whether you are part of the "almost 90 percent," how does this perspective affect you as you prepare to teach literacy to students from these divergent backgrounds?

Many beginning and experienced teachers are not aware of the subconscious beliefs and attitudes that come with this perspective. Often, they will share that they don't really think of themselves as even *having* a culture (Howard, 2006). They share that they only want the best for their students, that they want their students to learn English and succeed, and that they are in fact "color blind" and don't see racial, ethnic, and/or linguistic differences in their students but rather try to treat all of their students with the same care and respect.

Embedded in this perspective, however, is a "silent curriculum" (Horsford, 1978) that often determines how many teachers view their EL and minority students, and this silent curriculum undermines their efforts to help all students learn (Ladson-Billings, 1998). Many well-intentioned teachers grow anxious when student learning doesn't progress or proceed as rapidly as they hope, and this is often where a subconscious cultural perspective may inadvertently get in the way of providing insightful and effective instruction. These teachers fail to accommodate students' different backgrounds and languages, or if they do and learning still doesn't progress, they blame the students' performance on perceived shortcomings in their backgrounds. At the other extreme, some teachers may overcompensate for these differences in background and language, becoming *too* nurturant and not providing appropriately challenging instruction (Pennington, Brock, & Ndura, 2012).

For example, Pennington and Sallas (2009) describe the case of the caring and dedicated first-grade teacher who, while sharing with another teacher the homework folder from one of her EL children whose home language is Spanish, comments, "I'm worried that these students and their parents just don't get it. I am trying to work on writing in English when they can't even talk in English; how are they going to write in their journals or read at home?" (p. 218). It is not uncommon to hear such a frustrated teacher complain that a community and/or parents in a particular community "just don't value" education the way parents in other communities do. Such frustration may be understandable, but it should not be inevitable: It illustrates an incomplete perspective on the part of some teachers, particularly those from the dominant culture, as they struggle to teach students of diverse language and cultural backgrounds. But parents or adult caregivers who "do not get it" are rare—they definitely "get" how important their child's education is, and they want to be supportive. They may not "get" how their child's teacher is trying to connect with them, however, so we will examine more closely how to bridge that gap.

The following thoughts may help us begin our conversations with ourselves about dispositions—a conversation that frankly most people do not have (Villaneuva, 1993). As a teacher who will work with so many young people from many different cultures, subcultures, and heritage languages, it's a conversation you must have if you are going to be an effective teacher for all your students.

Many teachers may have a worldview that stops "at their country's border. . . . Teachers' lack of knowledge about their students' cultures easily leads to the formation of a protective shield of ethnocentric approaches based on the only frame of reference they possess—their own culture" (Alptekin, 1981, cited in Pennington & Sallas, 2009, pp. 218–219).

The bottom line is this: When teachers are not aware of—much less reflect on—their attitudes, perspectives, where these come and why they exist, they will not be doing all that they can to support their students' learning. As we have acknowledged, we are on delicate ground here: Exploring our own beliefs about language and race can become a minefield (Pennington, 2007). But this is true not only for white European American teachers—this ethnocentric view is often also shared by teachers from nondominant cultures who come from middle-class backgrounds.

So how might we begin this difficult conversation with ourselves, and with other novice or experienced teachers who may or may not share our own cultural background? First, we acknowledge that education—good instruction—can at times be a bit uncomfortable, for it requires us to consider new information and new attitudes and beliefs. And if this new information is at odds with our own dispositions, our first response is often defensive. Again, this is human nature and there is nothing wrong with such a response. But if we—and our students—are to grow, then such experiences are necessary: Good instruction helps students and teachers alike to become aware of worlds and possibilities beyond their own—to be "college and career ready" in an increasingly interconnected world with its hundreds of languages, cultures, and subcultures. The "new" causes us to examine the "known" in a different way, and over time, we understand better and come to appreciate the new. In your classroom, the new will be the other cultures and languages that so many of our students bring. It's up to you to get to know more about these cultures and languages so that you can teach in culturally responsive and culturally inclusive ways (Nieto, 2009).

Second, we examine ourselves and how our language and culture have shaped our own identities (Rodriguez, 1981/2004). The following steps may be helpful in guiding our reflections and, most important, our discussion with others (Marx & Pennington, 2003; Milner, 2003; Pennington, 2007):

- Actively seek information and advice in the community from which your English learners and culturally diverse students come. Consider how you can incorporate and build from their experiences, information, and insights.

- Address the fact that the ways we look at the world—the "reality" we have constructed for ourselves—is in fact shaped by our beliefs and our attitudes. These will affect the ways we think about and teach children from linguistic and cultural backgrounds that are different from ours. This understanding is at the heart of our exploration.
- Talk with fellow teachers who share your cultural and linguistic background as well as teachers who have different cultural and linguistic backgrounds.
- What privileges and/or limitations might we experience because of our race, gender, socioeconomic status, and/or linguistic backgrounds?

These points often lead to defensiveness, sometimes anger, but eventually to an empowering awareness and insight: Your teaching, and your students' learning, will be more rewarding and effective because you have taken this journey to address your own culturally embedded assumptions and perspectives (Marx & Pennington, 2003).

Characteristics of English Learners

Depending on where you will teach, you may have only a handful of English learners, perhaps speaking the same language, such as Spanish or Hmong, or you may have a majority of English learners, with two or more different languages represented. In some larger urban districts there are well over 150 different language backgrounds. Your students may hear a heritage language spoken at home but be exclusively English speakers, though their level of proficiency in English when they first enter your classroom may not be that of your native English-speaking students. Some of your students may be recently arrived immigrants, or, more likely, children born in the United States whose parents are immigrants. Some of your recently arrived students may bring with them solid literacy skills in their home language, which may be used to leverage their learning of spoken and written English (Sparks, Patton, Ganschow, & Humbach, 2012). Many of your English learners' schooling will frequently be interrupted, as with children of migrant workers or children whose families may leave for several weeks to visit the extended family in another country.

The majority of English learners in the United States have some degree of proficiency in English, but because they may not hear much (if any) English spoken in the home, will usually not be at the level of proficiency of their native English-speaking peers. Many English learners will need several years of sustained instruction to approach this level (Freeman & Freeman, 2007). In summary, throughout your teaching career you will probably teach a good many students who represent many different languages, and who will bring with them different levels of proficiency in those languages and in literacy.

In 2005, a little over 10 percent of the student population in the United States were English learners. While over 60 percent of these students are in six states (Arizona, California, Texas, New York, Florida, Illinois), other states had seen their English learner population grow by at least 300 percent in the previous decade. Helman and colleagues (2012) note that in a large study of children in the United States who were English learners, almost half were born in the United States. Among students born in other countries, 15 percent had lived in the United States for five or more years, 22 percent had been in the United States between one and four years, and the balance of English learners had lived in the United States less than a year (Zehler, Fleischman, Hopstock, Stephenson, Pendzick, & Sapru, 2003).

Approximately 180 different languages are spoken by students in U.S. classrooms. Of those languages spoken by English learners in the elementary grades, Spanish is by far predominant (over 75 percent); next are Chinese and Vietnamese (close to 3 percent each), followed by Korean (1.5

Working and Collaborating

Tips for Effective Home-School Communication

Most parents wish to do whatever they can to support their children's schooling and their development in English. To support them, have notes sent home translated into the student's home language. Your school's community liaison will assist with this; if there are any parents who speak and write English, of course, they may also help with this—they can be a real treasure! Show your students how they can work with their families at home (Helman, Bear, Templeton, Invernizzi, & Johnston, 2012):

- Talk with their families about what they are learning in school, and do so in the home language. Involve them in sorting activities—explaining the meaning of words they are learning, for example.
- Ask their parents/grandparents to tell them stories in the home language and to *read* to them in books written in the home language.

percent) and Hmong/Miao, French, German, and Russian (each a little over 1 percent) (Capps, Fix, Murray, Ost, Passel, & Herwantoro, 2005). For recent students who are immigrants, picking up conversational English—the pragmatics, vocabulary, and the syntax—occurs relatively quickly (Nguyen, Shin, & Krashen, 2001). Cummins (1991) refers to this level of language competence as Basic Interpersonal Communication Skills (BICS). On the other hand, learning Academic English—the language and vocabulary—may take from 4 to 6 or 7 years (Cummins, 1991; Thomas & Collier, 2002); you will also see this referred to as Cognitive Academic Language Proficiency (CALP).

Culturally Responsive and Culturally Inclusive Teaching

We would like to share a perspective that is critical not only when we think about English learners but also when we consider all students—your students. As English learners are acquiring knowledge of English, they are bringing their own native languages into the classroom, and this is a wonderful opportunity for native English-speaking students to learn something about those languages. Our increasingly multilingual classrooms are opportunities for language learning to be a two-way street: Students learning English, native speakers learning about other languages. Guided by a knowledgeable teacher, students on this two-way street have the potential to understand the experiences and perspectives of others—a critical skill in the interconnected world of the twenty-first century.

Becoming a culturally responsive teacher begins with learning about the backgrounds and environments of your students. This is critical. If the home language of most of your students is Spanish and you are an English monolingual, then of course taking classes in Spanish will be very helpful, but it does not substitute for being aware of and responsive to the culture of your students. If you have several home languages represented in your classroom, it is not realistic to become even conversationally competent in all of them. But you can learn more about patterns of interaction in these languages and the cultures from which they come. Of course, languages and cultures are complex—the Spanish spoken by your students who come from different regions in Mexico will be different in significant ways, as will the Spanish they speak in contrast to the Spanish spoken by students from Guatemala or Ecuador. One important and effective way to begin learning, as we've mentioned, is to connect with your school's community liaison, usually an individual who comes from the community your school serves and who therefore understands and lives the language and culture. Not only is this understanding important so that you know where your students are coming from, but your community liaison will often be an excellent bridge to share much of the important values and narratives of the community. You will be able to build on these as you support your students' learning of language and literacy (see, for example, Au, 2005; August & Shanahan, 2006; Moll & Gonzalez, 1994).

Effective Instructional Practices

As you are learning about the most significant aspects of your English learning students' home languages (discussed later), you will be applying the following effective *instructional practices* for English learners (Akhavan, 2006; Echevarria, Vogt, & Short, 2012; Freeman & Freeman, 2003; Helman et al., 2012; Krashen, 2003):

Instructional-level teaching. As with native English speakers, most literacy instruction for English learners should be at their instructional level. We will match both tasks and instructional materials to the developmental level of our ELs and to their background knowledge (Calderón, Slavin, & Sánchez, 2011).

Modeling and think-alouds. Provide examples of the task or activity in which the students will be engaged. This may involve a multisensory input. As you "walk through" a task or activity, "talk through" your thinking, making it explicit. These "think-alouds" will be important, supporting your students' understanding of how knowledgeable, perhaps even "expert," individuals make sense of whatever they are engaged with.

Modifying language. Make your input comprehensible (Krashen, 2003): Speak more slowly, face your students, and emphasize important words. Although you will address idioms and idiomatic expressions as part of your language and literacy instruction, avoid using them when teaching content, such as science and social studies. You may also modify your language by paraphrasing, providing examples and simple analogies, and building on your students' responses. For English learners at lower levels of English proficiency, phrase your questions so that their responses "involve pointing, simple yes/no or one- or two-word response, a sentence response, or a more elaborate response" (Templeton et al., 2010, p. 133).

Contextualize instruction. Use "real-life" objects; expressive body language, including gestures; and role-playing.

Build background knowledge. Think about what your readers need to know to be successful when reading a new text. Plan supportive book introductions and build prior knowledge in content-area instruction.

Move from simple to complex. Tasks and activities are broken down into sequenced steps. Over time, move to more complex formats. Provide appropriate feedback as necessary. The Levels of Understanding in Figure 2.2 in Chapter 2, presented in the inverted pyramid, represent the sequence for moving from simpler to more cognitively demanding tasks and formats—from recognizing and recall on through to reorganizing, producing, and reconstructing.

In summary, there is potentially so much for you to work on with your English learners and children who speak a variant or **vernacular** dialect. Where do you begin? What do you focus on?

For Younger Learners

Common Core Connection

Language Standards: Knowledge of Language

In a nutshell, for *younger* learners focus on simpler language based in meaningful experiences. The meaning and the form—the vocabulary and the sentence structure—is foremost. Focusing on *sound* will come along a bit later. A big part of instruction should be building oral vocabulary and encouraging interaction.

FIGURE 5.2 Terms and Topics: The Vocabulary Associated with Teaching English Learners

You will see and hear the following common terms in discussions about instruction with English learners.

Heritage language. In English-speaking countries, this refers to a language other than English that is spoken in the child's home. Because the child is learning English in school and in the community, however, she or he may not fully acquire the heritage language.

Limited English proficient. For several years, this was the more common term for *English learners*. It is used less frequently now because of the less-than-favorable connotation of the word *limited*.

Language-minority students. These are students who hear a heritage language spoken at home, but who only speak English themselves.

Vernacular English. This type of speech differs significantly enough from Standard English to present challenges for students who enter classrooms in which the standard dialect is spoken. Examples are African American Vernacular English, a number of Native American dialects, and Gullah.

Bilingual instruction/programs. Students learn to read and write in their home language while at the same time receive instruction in spoken and written English.

Sheltered English. Students learn subject-matter content through English that is simplified: Sentences are simplified, vocabulary is explicitly defined, and students have opportunities to discuss the content. Grade-level content may be made comprehensible while students are developing their competence in English.

Newcomer programs. These programs support English learners who are recent immigrants. They have very little or no proficiency in English and often have very little schooling in the countries from which they have emigrated. Newcomer programs help students learn basic language skills in English as well as "transition into the new cultural and academic content of their schools" (Helman et al., 2012, p. 2).

For Older Learners

In a nutshell, if your *older* learners are newcomers and not literate in the home language, you begin as you do for younger learners. If they have some proficiency in English, then you may begin to help them focus on more fine-tuned aspects of English—highlighting and keeping a list of irregular verbs to help them with their writing, for example, and learning the pronunciation of high-frequency words that don't follow the expected spelling-to-sound patterns. Academic Language and vocabulary should be simultaneously developed. Figure 5.2 presents the most common terms for referring to the learning and instruction of English learners.

Common Core Connection

Language Standards: Vocabulary Acquisition and Use

Examining Students' Home Languages and Their Literacy Experiences

The following three guiding principles will support your accommodation of English learners and your more effective instruction (Helman et al., 2012):

1) Compare oral languages.
2) Compare written languages.
3) Know what language and literacy experiences your students have had.

Common Core Connection

Language Standards: Conventions of Standard English

To help inform you, invite your students' parents, your community liaison, or perhaps elders in the community, to share and talk about their language. As you think about the differences between spoken English and the languages of your English learners, you will note variations according to the order of words, or syntax. For example, in Spanish (and a number of other Romance languages) adjectives usually come *after* the nouns they modify: *niño enojado* versus *angry child*. You will learn about the differences between the sound systems, or phonology:

Accommodating English Learners

Speakers of Variant/Vernacular Dialects

Many students whose native language is English come from home environments and communities in which a variant, or vernacular, dialect of English is spoken. While speakers of variant and standard dialects are able to understand one another in ways that speakers of different languages are not, the differences between variant and Standard English are significant enough that you will need to be aware of them. There are many regional dialects in American English, and over the years many of these have migrated to other regions of the country. For complex sociopolitical reasons, **African American Vernacular English (AAVE)** has been the variant dialect of American English that has received most attention in U.S. education (Green, 2002; Labov, 1972, 2001; Lanehart, 2001, 2009; McWhorter, 2000, 2001; Smitherman, 1985). Over the last few decades a number of scholars and educators have argued that the dialect *is* a language in its own right (for example Smitherman, 1985). It displays a richness of phonology, grammar, semantics, and rhetorical style, including rhythm, intonation, and articulation that reflects the experiences and subcultures of the African American community across generations. A number of educators have argued that, because of its distinctiveness as a separate language, children who speak AAVE are entitled to be taught in this language in order to acquire literacy and content knowledge while they also would be transitioned, over time, into Standard English.

The implications for your classroom instruction are these: Not only do you need to be aware of the variant dialects your students speak but you must also know that many of the adjustments and accommodations you make for your English learners may in fact also be appropriate for children who speak variant dialects. This is particularly important when you are teaching word recognition and spelling, as well as academic language and vocabulary.

Because of its importance in education and also in the broader cultural makeup of the United States, we will address several characteristics of African American Vernacular English here. Many of these features are shared by a number of other variant and regional dialects, such as Southern American English (McWhorter, 2001). Also referred to as Black English, African American English, and Ebonics, AAVE is often described in terms of how it differs from Standard English—dropping of certain sounds, for example. Although a number of American dialects have the very same characteristics, these features have often led, historically, to a devaluation of the dialect and, unfortunately, to those who speak it (Lanehart, 2001; Van Deusen-Scholl, 2003).

Following are several phonological and syntactic/grammatical features of African American Vernacular English:

Phonological

- Certain sounds are "reduced"; for example, the /oi/ sound in *soil* is pronounced as /aw/: /sall/.
- Certain ending sounds are omitted; for example, *rest* is pronounced /res/; *sand* is pronounced /san/. (In other phonemic contexts, however, certain sounds are *not* omitted: /slant/)
- The initial /th/ as in *that* may be pronounced /d/ as in /dat/.
- In two-syllable words, the sound that *ng* represents at the end of words is pronounced as /n/; for example, *ringing* is pronounced /ringin/. (But at the end of one-syllable words, it stays the same: *ring* is pronounced /ring/). This pattern is found in many other dialects of American English, and is often referred to as "dropping the *g*" in *–ing*. There is no /g/ sound at the end of *ringing*—the letters *ng* stand for one sound; when speakers pronounce the word as /ringin/, they are simply substituting one sound for another.
- In a handful of words, ending sounds are switched: *ask* is pronounced /aks/.

Grammatical

- The verb *to be* undergoes some changes that capture distinctions that Standard English does not make—distinctions that also occur in a number of other languages. For example, *Angie going to school* versus *Angie be going to school* captures the distinction between a behavior or action that is ongoing or habitual in contrast to something that is happening right now.
- The "double negative" structure is used when all negative words in a sentence are negated; for example, *You aren't going anywhere* is expressed as *You ain't goin' nowhere*. (Standard English also does this from time to time: The Academic Language phrase *"It is not unlikely that . . ."* contains a double negative.)
- Different construction of some types of questions; for example, *Why isn't he behaving?* is expressed as *Why he ain't behavin'?*

After this brief overview of African American Vernacular English, we would like to conclude with what linguists emphasize is a critical perspective: A "standard" dialect is the "preferred" dialect not because it somehow expresses ideas better, is more logical, or sounds better or more "refined" than other dialects. It actually is none of these things. It is the standard or preferred dialect simply because it is the dialect spoken by the predominant socioeconomic class in a society. This is where "standard" dialects come from in any society—and it is also why groups that challenge the socioeconomic hierarchy in a society will often use the language of a vernacular dialect to challenge the authority of that hierarchy. Short of outright revolution, however, *changing* a society in any important way involves communicating with the estab-lished power structure in the form of the language it recognizes and, for better or worse, values. For your students whose home language is a variant dialect, you will help them acquire the standard dialect of American English because it will provide the means with which they are more likely to benefit economically and politically in the society (Delpit, 1995/2006).

Languages may not have certain sounds of English. For instance, Arabic does not have the /p/ sound, so native speakers will substitute the sound that is closest: /b/ (Helman et al., 2012). In different languages, intonation patterns across phrases will signal different nuances of meaning as well as of pragmatic or social functions.

In thinking about the writing systems, consider the directionality of the writing: Is it right to left, or perhaps in a column, read from top to bottom? Are sounds represented by an alphabet? Are characters used, as in Chinese? A number of languages that until recently have not been written down are now represented by the Roman alphabet—for example, Hmong and several African languages. If your students' home languages are written alphabetically, explore how the representations compare to English letter–sound correspondences. In Spanish, for instance, the letter *i* sounds like the long *e* in English, the letter *e* sounds more like a rapidly pronounced long *a* in English. So, as they are learning English, Spanish-speaking students may spell *feet* as *fit*, *bake* as *bek*. You'll find a table of common consonant confusions for English learners in Chapter 6.

As we saw in Chapter 2, the English spelling or orthographic system is complex, or *deep*: Letters are combined in various ways to correspond to sound *and* to represent meaning directly—it takes time to learn these correspondences. French is much the same. Spanish, on the other hand, as well as Italian, is a *shallow* orthography: Letters have consistent sounds, and regardless of where they occur in a word, they will consistently represent the same sound. Moreover, there are fewer sounds in Spanish than in English—24 distinct sounds or phonemes compared to 42 to 44 in English, depending on the dialect; and only 5 vowels in Spanish compared to approximately 20 in English. Korean, too, has a shallow orthography—19 consonants and 21 vowels are reliably represented with letters (Taylor & Taylor, 1983). It doesn't take as much time to learn how to spell most words correctly in shallow orthographies (Notarnicola, Angelelli, Judica, & Zoccolotti, 2012).

Chinese is a deep orthography that uses characters rather than sounds. There are thousands of characters, and they must be memorized. Words are constructed by combining these charac-ters. For example, the word for "television" is

in which the first character, which has the meaning of "electricity," is combined with the second character, which means "image" (McBride-Chang, Shu, Ng, Meng, & Penney, 2007). Although there are approximately 40,000 characters in Chinese, in day-to-day writing only about 3,000 are used (Birch, 2002).

As we have noted, students who have learned to read in their home language have a real advantage in learning to read English. The more diverse the language and its writing system are from English, however, the longer it usually takes to learn to read English.

One of the most accessible resources for providing the most significant at-a-glance information about the features of the grammatical, sound, and writing systems of heritage languages spoken in the United States may often be found in the resource materials that accompany a core reading program, if your district has adopted one. The following are additional excellent resources for information about the features of other languages in relation to English:

Birch, B. (2002). *English L2 reading: Getting to the bottom.* Mahwah, NJ: Erlbaum.

Gottlieb, M. (2006). *Assessing English language learners: Bridges from language proficiency to academic achievement.* Thousand Oaks, CA: Corwin.

Peregoy, S. F., & Boyle, O. F. (2012). *Reading, writing, and learning in ESL: A resource book for teaching K–12 English learners* (6th ed.). Boston: Pearson/Allyn & Bacon.

Determining Levels of English Learners' Proficiency in English

As a teacher in a regular classroom, the English language learners who come to you will usually have already been assessed. You will have information about their level of proficiency in English (for example, *Student Oral Proficiency Assessment*, 2000, and *Student Oral Language Observation Matrix* [Rothenberg & Fisher, 2006]) and perhaps of their literacy skills in both their native language (Townsend, Lee, & Chiappe, 2006; Townsend & Collins, 2008) and English. Following are descriptions of levels of proficiency in English. You will see different labels depending on your state and/or the district in which you teach, but the characteristics of each level will almost always be consistent regardless of the labels (Helman et al., 2012; TESOL, 2006; WIDA Consortium, 2011; Zehler et al., 2003). For each of the following levels, we have included the labels from two of the most influential and frequently cited organizations in language instruction for speakers of other languages, *Teachers of English to Speakers of Other Languages* (*TESOL*) and *World-class Instructional Design and Assessment* (*WIDA*):

- **Level 1: Early Receptive Language.** There is very little understanding of spoken English. English learners at this level attempt to communicate primarily in their home language and/or with body language, gestures, and one- or two-word phrases. (TESOL: *Starting*; WIDA: *Entering*)
- **Level 2: Beginning.** Learners show increasing understanding of spoken English and can communicate expressively in short phrases, in contrast to the one- and two-word utterances of Level 1. (TESOL/WIDA: *Emerging*)
- **Level 3: Early Intermediate.** Students may respond with more understanding and confidence to a number of different communication situations. The number and type of phrases they are using is developing more extensively. (TESOL/WIDA: *Developing*)
- **Level 4: Intermediate.** Students' receptive vocabulary is quite large and they use most verb tenses appropriately. However, general academic and domain-specific academic vocabulary are still limited. (TESOL/WIDA: *Expanding*)
- **Level 5: Advanced.** Students' understanding and use of general- and domain-specific academic language and vocabulary has developed significantly. (TESOL/WIDA: *Bridging*)

As you learn about your students' oral and written home languages and the language and literacy experiences they may have had, the following questions will help you put these understandings into effect (Dickinson, McCabe, & Sprague, 2003; Helman et al., 2012):

1) What language, or languages, does the student speak?
2) Does the student use his or her primary language often?
3) Is the student's language common in your school?
4) For how long has the student been learning English?
5) Is the student willing, or hesitant, to start a conversation?
6) Are you able to understand the student when she or he is speaking English?
7) Does the student attempt to use a range of English vocabulary he or she has heard in conversation with others, from the teacher, or encountered in reading?
8) Does the student
   - speak haltingly and with little fluency?
   - use connected phrases when speaking?
   - use more expression in speech?
9) Are there sounds in English that seem to be difficult to pronounce?
10) Did the student receive formal education in her or his primary language? If so, is there information about the level of literacy development in the primary language?
11) Does the student use her or his primary language when writing in classroom activities? Does the student seem to blend the primary language with English?

If you teach at the middle or intermediate grades and you have English learners who have had a strong educational foundation in their primary language, they will be well positioned to learn English as well as to learn to read and write in English. They are also more likely to have developed an awareness of academic language and vocabulary in their home language.

Should you be working with English learners who have not been assessed as to language proficiency, you may find the *Student Oral Language Observation Matrix* (SOLOM) very helpful as you observe your English learners interacting with other students in the regular classroom environment (Bilingual Education Office of the California Department of Education, 2012; Rothenberg & Fisher, 2006).

Literacy Instruction with Your English Learners

English learners follow the same developmental continuum as native-speaking students (Bear, Templeton, Helman, & Baren, 2003; Bear & Smith, 2009). You learned a little about this continuum in Chapter 1 and Chapter 2. Refer to Table 5.1 to review the types of instructional activities that, at each developmental stage, best support your English learners' language and literacy learning. For each stage, the corresponding chapter in this book is indicated; the activities listed at each stage are described and illustrated in that developmental chapter. Within each of these chapters, you'll also find a special feature that focuses on teaching English learners at that specific stage of development.

Although much of your literacy instruction for ELs will be similar to that of native-speaking students, there are special considerations you'll need to make with respect to reading to them, the role of wide reading, purposeful writing, vocabulary instruction, and spelling instruction (Helman, 2009). We will address each of these topics in the following sections.

Common Core Connection
Reading Standards: Foundational Skills – Print Concepts; Phonological Awareness; Phonics and Word Recognition; Fluency

TABLE 5.1 Developmental Stages and English Learners: Reading/Writing and Word Study Activities

Reading and Writing	Word Study
Emergent Stage with English Learners (Chapter 6)	
1. Read to students and encourage oral language activities. 2. Model writing using language experience dictations (one or two sentences in length) and group-dictated charts, usually four or five sentences or lines in length. 3. Encourage "pretend" reading and writing. 4. Teach easy poems and songs in English. 5. Develop *personal reader* activities for language expression and to practice pointing to words as they are read: Levels A–C. 6. Have students draw pictures to support writing.	1. Develop oral language and vocabulary with *concept sorts* of pictures and objects. 2. Play with sounds of English to develop phonological awareness. 3. Plan activities to learn the alphabet. 4. Sort pictures by beginning sound. 5. Encourage finger-point reading of memorized songs, easy rhymes, language experience dictations, and simple pattern books. 6. Encourage *phonic spelling*. 7. Sort pictures by ending sounds.
Beginning Stage with English Learners: Early Letter Name—Alphabetic (Chapter 7)	
1. Read to students and encourage oral language activities. 2. Help students to develop a firm *concept of word in text* by lots of reading in predictable books, song lyrics, dictations, and simple rhymes. Texts should be one or two lines on a page and be highly predictable: Levels C–D. 3. Record and reread individual dictations—four or five sentences in length. 4. Have students label pictures and write in journals regularly; expectations for length of writing is one or two sentences.	1. Collect known words for *word bank*. 2. Sort pictures and words by beginning and ending consonant sounds. 3. Sort pictures and words to help compare and contrast similar sounds between student's home language and English (e.g., *d - t, p - b, b - v*). 4. Study word families that share a common vowel. 5. Study beginning consonant blends and digraphs. 6. Encourage phonic spelling.
Beginning Stage with English Learners: Middle to Late Letter Name—Alphabetic	
1. Read to students and encourage oral language activities. 2. Encourage phonic spellings in independent writing, but hold students accountable for features and words they have studied. 3. Collect two- or three-paragraph dictations that are placed in personal readers and reread regularly: Levels D–G. 4. Engage students in partner reading or cross-age buddy reading to expand opportunities for supported reading practice. 5. Encourage more frequent writing and consider some simple editing procedures for punctuation and high-frequency words. Length of writing can be several lines, up to a page in one sitting.	1. Sort pictures and words by different short vowel word families. 2. Sort pictures and words by short vowel sounds and consonant-vowel-consonant (CVC) patterns. Begin with a single vowel and compare across vowels. 3. Clarify the spelling of vowel sounds that are in contrast with students' primary languages, such as the short *o* and *a* with Spanish speakers. 4. Sort beginning consonant digraphs with pictures and words. 5. Sort beginning consonant blends with pictures and words. 6. Sort ending digraphs and blends, including *ck, ff, nt, nd,* and *mp*. 7. Sort pictures comparing short and long vowel sounds. 8. Collect known words for word bank (up to 200).
Transitional Stage with English Learners: Within Word Pattern (Chapter 8)	
1. Continue to read aloud to students. 2. To work toward fluency (developing speed, accuracy, and expression), engage students in repeated readings and choral readings with poems, and in Readers' Theater. Students may chart reading rate. 3. Guide silent reading of simple chapter books: Levels H–M. 4. Engage students in talking about books each day. 5. Have students write each day during Writer's Workshop. They also will confer, revise, edit, and publish their work for real audiences.	1. Complete daily activities in word study notebook. 2. Sort words by long and short vowel sounds and by common long vowel patterns. 3. Use picture and word sorts to help students attend to and learn to pronounce the vowels of English. 4. Compare words with *r*-influenced vowels. 5. Examine triple blends and complex consonant units such as *thr–, str–, –dge, –tch,* and *–ck*. 6. Explore less common vowel spelling patterns and diphthongs (such as *oi* and *oy*). 7. Explore homophones and homographs for meaning, pronunciation, and spelling. 8. Examine the meanings and pronunciations of plural endings. 9. Study compound words. 10. Explore simple base words and affixes.

TABLE 5.1 *(Continued)*

Reading and Writing	Word Study
Intermediate Stage with English Learners: Syllables and Affixes (Chapter 9)	
1. Continue to read aloud to students. 2. Guide silent reading and literature and content reading discussions: Levels M–S. 3. Include self-selected or assigned silent reading of novels of different genres and of informational texts. 4. Teach simple note-taking and outlining skills, and work with adjusting reading rates for different purposes. 5. Students examine structure and language of narratives and informational texts as models for their writing. 6. Help students develop study skills, including textbook reading, note taking, adjusting reading rates, test taking, report writing, and reference work. 7. Develop students' collaborative reasoning skills through book club conversations and read-alouds.	1. In spelling, study inflectional endings and the grammar and pronunciation underlying suffixes (plurals, past tense, adjectives). 2. For vocabulary, sort and study common affixes (prefixes and suffixes). 3. Study open and closed syllables. 4. Explore syllable stress and vowel patterns in the accented syllable. 5. Focus on unaccented syllables such as *er* and *le*. 6. Explore unusual consonant blends and digraphs (such as *qu, ph, gh,* and *gu*). 7. Focus on two-syllable homophones and homographs. 8. Join spelling and vocabulary studies; link meaning and spelling with grammar and meaning. 9. Explore grammar through word study. 10. For spelling, sort and study common affixes (prefixes and suffixes). 11. For vocabulary, begin to explore most frequently occurring Greek and Latin roots.
Skillful Stage with English Learners: Derivational Relations (Chapter 10)	
1. Provide time for silent reading, fully exploring the genres within literature and informational texts: Levels T and up. 2. Refine study skills, note taking, adjusting rates for different purposes, test taking, report writing, and reference work. 3. Students study the structure and language of narratives and informational texts as models for their writing.	1. Link spelling and vocabulary with grammar and meaning. 2. Explore fully the cognates between English and the home language (for example, there are 10,000–15,000 cognates between English and Spanish). 3. For both spelling and vocabulary, examine common and then less-common Greek and Latin roots, prefixes, and suffixes. 4. For spelling, examine vowel and consonant alternations in derivationally related pairs (for example, *precise-precision*). 5. Explore ambiguous Latin suffix spelling (such as *ence/ ance; –ent/–ant;* and *-ible/-able*). 6. Learn about assimilated or absorbed prefixes (for example, <u>ir</u>responsible and <u>cor</u>respond). 7. Explore etymology and its role in developing vocabulary knowledge.

Source: Adapted from Helman et al., 2012. Used by permission.

Children's Literature Connection

Evaluating Language, Racial, Ethnic, and Culturally Diverse Aspects of Literature

Consider these guidelines as you evaluate the cultural authenticity of literature:

- **Illustrations.** What are the people doing? Do they reflect stereotypes or more authentic scenarios?
- **Narrative.** Do nonmainstream characters need to exhibit exceptional abilities to be successful? Are they—or are mainstream characters—solving the problems? Is power equally distributed?
- **Informational.** Are different perspectives provided? For example, in American history, is the Chinese American perspective on the Exclusionary Acts represented? The Seminole or Navajo interpretation of *resettlement*? (Templeton, 1997)

Reading to Your English Learners: Supporting Language and Literacy Development

When speaking to your English learners, your voice models the rhythm and cadence of spoken English. When you read to them, your voice will also model the rhythm and cadence of written English. Although your English learners who are at a lower proficiency level in English may not grasp the meaning of the text as thoroughly as native speakers, your read-alouds are often opportunities to explain, elaborate, and talk about words and idiomatic expressions that may be unfamiliar. Students' textbooks or other content-area resource material may be read to them as well. Again, you will take time to clarify the most important unfamiliar vocabulary, answer questions, and usually share visuals that support the content.

Common Core Connection

Reading Standards for Literature and informational Text: Integration of Knowledge and Ideas, Range of Reading and Level of Text Complexity

After reading aloud to the whole class, in a smaller group you may have emergent- and beginning-level English learners retell what they learned and remember from the material. As they share, we suggest that you take dictation by writing or typing and projecting their retellings so they can see their language written down. Depending on your purposes, this collaboratively composed informational text may become their instructional-level reading material for the unit. At another time, you might edit it with them, attending to those aspects of English they are ready to explore—verb tense, for example, or plural endings. These compositions may be photocopied for the students so that they can keep them in their journals for rereading. As their English language proficiency develops, these compositions will reflect the students' growing comprehension and thinking skills: description, explanation, and summarization. The discussions that surround these collaborative compositions also develop vocabulary and language knowledge more generally. In this way, read-alouds become the common experience through which you develop a more integrated language and literacy experience: reading, writing, listening, and speaking.

Wide Reading and Purposeful Writing

It is no surprise that, just as with native-English speaking students, our English learners should be immersed in wide reading and purposeful writing. Reading provides the vocabulary and sentence structure; writing provides the opportunity to exercise and develop their vocabulary and syntax.

Wide Reading

While reading widely in English texts, English learners should also have access—if at all possible—to texts in their home language. This is especially important if they are already literate in their home language. For native Spanish speakers, such texts are much more accessible than they were even a few years ago. If your district has adopted a core reading program, it will include texts in Spanish, both hard copy and available on the Web. Not only for Spanish but for many other languages, the Internet is rapidly becoming a rich source for access to texts in a number of languages, including the availability of digital libraries such as the International Children's Digital Library (www.childrenslibrary.org/). For example, you will now find texts, often paired with their English counterparts, printed in Arabic, Farsi, Croatian, Japanese, Russian, and Swahili. The International Children's Digital Library includes texts appropriate for pre-K through the middle grades. These texts will also help native English-speaking students begin to understand other languages and learn a bit about them.

In subject-matter reading, many publishers offer *text sets*, selections at different reading levels that address a single topic (Flanigan, Hayes, Templeton, Bear, Johnston, & Invernizzi, 2012). The "primary" text or selection is made accessible through teacher read-alouds, which are particularly important and provide opportunities to explain and develop vocabulary. This read-aloud may also be available through audiotape, CD, or MP3 player and iPod downloads.

Publishers of core reading programs often provide texts that address the same topic, too, but these texts are at different levels of linguistic and text complexity.

Purposeful Writing

As with native-speaking students, English learners need many opportunities to write. With respect to developing spelling knowledge and vocabulary development, writing allows them opportunities to "exercise" these developing understandings. At the phrase and sentence levels, students can reflect on and apply their developing syntactic knowledge. With respect to correct spelling and other conventions of writing, including punctuation and grammar, the Common Core standards note that for students acquiring English "it is possible to meet the standards in reading, writing, speaking, and listening without displaying native-like control of conventions and vocabulary" (2010, p. 6). The emphasis is on understanding and applying the modes of thinking and reasoning in writing. These will develop out of your reading to the students, their reading, and their discussions about what they are encountering in texts.

> **Common Core Connection**
>
> Language Standards: Conventions of Standard English

Vocabulary Instruction

What we will explore in Chapter 6 for young native-English speakers is equally appropriate for young English learners: We establish a socially interactive classroom environment, share simple stories, and teach vocabulary explicitly. Chapter 6 and Chapter 7 will guide you through a number of activities in which such explicit instruction will unfold. As you saw in Chapter 3, we can gain considerable insight about our younger English learners' vocabulary through picture sorts—naming, categorizing, and discussing with other children. As students develop oral language proficiency and experience literature and informational texts in English, their acquisition of Academic Language and vocabulary will be influenced by these texts. They should continue to have opportunities to try out this developing language and vocabulary in pairs and in small-group interactions.

> **Common Core Connection**
>
> Language Standards: Vocabulary Acquisition and Use

Older English learners, as with younger English learners, need rich discussion opportunities with one another and with native speakers in the context of content instruction (Saunders & Goldenberg, 1999). These engagements will not only help develop your English learners' domain-specific vocabulary, they will also help with concept development and social language skills. Such discussions also provide you with an opportunity to informally assess skills by using the *Student Oral Language Observation Matrix*. See Templeton and colleagues (2010) for more detail about this and other vocabulary-building activities.

Teaching Morphology

With older English learners, the social and language contexts that support your vocabulary instruction are critical, particularly with respect to *morphology*. Your "walking through words" with students, constructing words by combining roots and affixes, and using vocabulary notebooks to record information about words are all important in supporting your English learners' development of both general- and domain-specific academic vocabulary. So often, what our older English learners need is the focus on vocabulary development in general and morphology in particular. It is often the case, however, that even though they are phonemically aware and understanding letter–sound relationships, because they may be determined on an oral language assessment to be Level 1 or 2, they are placed in beginning-level reading programs. These, of course, focus on basic phonics—what they already know (Cobin, Templeton, & Burner, 2011; Lesaux, 2010). This is the case where a more comprehensive literacy assessment program, such as the one described in Chapter 4, in addition to understanding of the unique needs of English learners, will help you better meet your students' language *and* literacy needs.

The Language of Your Instruction

Moving Beyond the Literal: Idiomatic Expressions

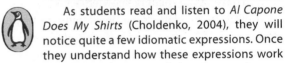

Just about all languages have **idiomatic expressions** or **idioms**. *Idioms* are groups of words that can't be understood by putting together the meanings of each of the words. When we say that someone is "dragging his feet," we of course don't mean that he is actually scraping his feet on the floor; rather, he is moving or working very slowly. Other idiomatic expressions that occur quite frequently are *bite your tongue, hold your tongue, in the blink of an eye, see eye to eye* with someone, *fly off the handle, pull someone's leg,* and she is *all ears.* With English learners, these expressions are learned over time and with some targeted instruction. For example, after explaining the meaning of some common idiomatic expressions in English—such as getting something done "by the skin of your teeth" or "to hit the jackpot," you might invite English learners to share some of the idiomatic expressions from their home languages.

As students read and listen to *Al Capone Does My Shirts* (Choldenko, 2004), they will notice quite a few idiomatic expressions. Once they understand how these expressions work and begin learning the types of situations and experiences they describe, they may enjoy exploring the word-play going on in an expression such as Moose Flanagan's: After Piper's laundry cleaning scam was exposed Moose commented, "I'll tell them about a brown-haired girl who took our whole seventh-grade class to the cleaners" (p. 102). In almost a literal sense, yes, we can say that this actually happened. But it packs an additional chuckle because the idiomatic expression having to do with *taking someone to the cleaners* usually doesn't refer literally to the cleaners, but just to the fact that someone has been really fooled and taken advantage of.

Spelling Instruction

Common Core Connection

Language Standards:
Conventions of
Standard English

In previous chapters we described how your students' spelling errors provide the best insight into what they understand about the structure of words. This understanding is what they draw from as they read and write words. The spelling errors of your English learners who are attempting to spell English words will also yield insights. After having become somewhat familiar with the home language of an EL student, use the following guidelines to gain an understanding of what she or he is attempting to do and understand as knowledge about English is acquired (Helman et al., 2012):

- When trying to spell a sound in English that is not in their native language, ELs often choose letters that stand for the closest sound in their own language. For example, there is no /sh/ sound in Arabic, Chinese, Korean, Spanish, or Vietnamese. A native Spanish-speaking child might spell *fish* as *fich*, because the /ch/ sound is the closest sound to the English /sh/. A Hmong student will perhaps spell *tell* as *teu*, because of the difficulty in pronouncing /l/ in Hmong.
- When English and the student's home language share the same phoneme, ELs will often spell the sound as they would in their home language. For a Spanish-speaking English learner, *spot* would be spelled *espat*, because in Spanish the letter *a* stands for the /ŏ/ sound. The initial *e* in this spelling, by the way, is there because in Spanish an initial /s/ sound is preceded by this vowel.
- Often English learners use a whole word they have learned to spell a word they're not sure about, and that shares some of the sounds of the known word, such as *pick* for *pink*.
- English learners usually do more sounding out. Speakers of Chinese often add a vowel sound between the letters in consonant blends that begin with *s*, as in *simok* for *smoke* (Helman et al., 2012). The child whose home language is Spanish may spell *blade* as *blaede*, sounding it out as *bl – uh – ā – duh*. (This spelling also illustrates the first guideline about using a native spelling for a sound—the letter *e* for the long *a* sound.) Madelon, for example, spelled the words *hive* as *jaif*, *trace* as *chreis*, and *fright* as *ferait*. For native speakers of English, including two vowels when spelling a long vowel sound is usually an indication that they are

Strategies for the Classroom

"Modeling" Academic Language

To facilitate older English learners' understanding of academic language when you are speaking, you may accompany key terms and phrases with gestures (Zwiers, 2008):

- To accompany phrases that set up contrasting examples or ideas—such as *on the other hand*, *nevertheless*, and *even though*—move your hand with palm facing down in one direction, and then move it with palm facing up in the other direction.

- For *thus*, *therefore*, and *for this reason*, use both hands to push forward and out in front of you.
- For *furthermore* and *in addition*, make a rolling motion forward with your hands.
- For *in conclusion*, spread your fingers on both hands, then clasp your hands together.

---

transitional readers and "within word pattern" spellers. With ELs like Madelon, however, two vowels often reveal *how* they are sounding out. Looking at Madelon's spelling of consonants as well as listening to her read aloud will reveal she is still a beginning-stage reader and a middle- to late-letter name–alphabetic speller.

> Applicable to All Stages

- English learners, particularly older students, often show a greater variability in their spelling. This may present a puzzle of sorts, because they often spell correctly words that are more challenging, yet they spell incorrectly words of only one or two syllables. For example, Miguel spells *summer* correctly, but spells *sled* as *slade*. While such students are able to memorize the spelling of several more complex words, their knowledge of English spelling may still be at the letter name–alphabetic stage, requiring examination of simpler one-syllable spelling patterns.
- English learners will often leave out middle and ending syllables in longer words—there is simply too much to try to remember while sounding out, and they may not be pronouncing all of the sounds in longer words. In Spanish, for example, there is no equivalent of the English past-tense *–ed* ending, so learners may not represent it. They might not even perceive the final sound in words such as *reached* and *watched*, spelling them as *reech* and *wach*.

In spelling instruction, like the other literacy essentials, you'll follow the same developmental sequence, but you may adjust the pacing of your instruction and the explicitness of your examples. You'll intentionally focus on both the meaning and spelling of words to support your English learners' dual goals of language and literacy development.

Chapter Summary

Becoming an effective teacher of English learners begins with examining your knowledge and understanding of other cultures and languages, as well as your biases, values, and beliefs. It's helpful and important to remember that English learners' literacy follows the developmental continuum outlined in Chapter 1 and Chapter 2. It's not necessary or even appropriate to postpone teaching literacy skills until certain levels of English are acquired. English learners typically acquire early literacy skills at roughly the same rate as their native-speaking peers. The later reading skills, however, are dependent on vocabulary knowledge and understanding complex syntactic structures—it takes more time for students to learn and progress through these stages.

You will plan instruction based on the assessment of students' oral language and background. The sequence of your instruction in word structure and in levels and complexity of texts will broadly follow the same developmental sequence as for native English speakers, but you will be sensitive to the characteristics of your ELs' home languages that may make learning certain sounds and language patterns more challenging. Activities that are appropriate for native speakers—such as sorting words, generating writing, and learning about the features of different types of texts—are equally appropriate for English learners.

Suggested Extension Activities

- Obtain writings from either primary-age or older English learners. Based on the students' sentence construction, word choice, and spelling, discuss with a partner what you notice about their developing syntactic, vocabulary, and phonological knowledge. As a guide, you may wish to use the *Student Written Language Observation Matrix* available online from the Bilingual Education Office of the California Department of Education.
- Obtain one of the Teacher's Guides for the core reading program that has been adopted in a nearby district. Choose a unit of instruction and carefully evaluate how the Guide supports instruction for English learners. Look beyond the labels. A program may have the label "English Language Learners" displayed prominently and often, but does the instruction to which that label refers actually reflect the effective instructional practices discussed in this chapter? Is it specific enough to be genuinely helpful, or does it only state the obvious (such as, "Adjust instruction appropriately for your English learners")?
- With a partner or small group, begin the conversation described in the "Examining Our Dispositions" section in this chapter. Reflect on your own cultural background and how it has shaped your perspective on other cultures, languages, and on instruction.

Recommended Professional Resources

Calderón, M. E., & Minaya-Rowe, L. (2011). *Preventing long-term ELs: Transforming schools to meet core standards*. Thousand Oaks, CA: Corwin.

Helman, L. A., Bear, D. R., Templeton, S., Invernizzi, M., & Johnston, F. (2012). *Words their way with English learners*: Word study for phonics, vocabulary, and spelling (2nd ed.). Boston: Pearson/Allyn & Bacon.

Krashen, S. D. (1988). *Second language acquisition and second language learning*. Prentice-Hall International.

Online Resources

Colorín Colorado

  www.colorincolorado.org

Available in English and in Spanish, this site provides a wealth of information not only for teachers but also for parents, librarians, and administrators. With links to practitioner information and research, it is one of the most comprehensive sites available that addresses English learners.

The Equity Alliance at Arizona State University

  www.equityallianceatasu.org

The Equity Alliance and its site provide extensive information, links, learning modules, and other types of support for teachers and others concerned with education: administrators, parents, community and school board members, and students themselves.

Center for Research on Education, Diversity & Excellence (CREDE)

  www.crede.berkeley.edu

Emergent Literacy: Engaging the World of Print, Developing Oral Language, and Vocabulary

Chapter Outline

» Overview of the Emergent Stage of Development
» Oral Language Development: The Foundation of Literacy
» Enriching the Language Environment in Your Classroom
» Engaging the World of Print: The Role of Exposure to Written Texts
» Other Texts for Emergent Readers
» Reading to Children: Developing Listening Comprehension and Vocabulary for Emergent Readers
» Developing Concepts about Print: Its Forms and Functions
» Learning the Alphabet and the Role of Letters
» Learning about Units of Print and Units of Language
» Writing in the Emergent Stage
» Putting All the Pieces Together: The Reading-Writing-Language Connection

1. What are the characteristics of emergent readers and writers?

2. How can teachers promote language and vocabulary development in this stage?

3. Explain the importance and the relationship between vocabulary and phonological awareness in the emergent stage and later reading achievement.

4. What kind of instruction is appropriate for emergent readers and writers?

5. How do readers and writers grow and change throughout the emergent stage of development?

The children in Ms. Schwartz's kindergarten classroom are busily engaged in their morning chores and activities when you hear music begin to fill the room. The children immediately finish what they're doing and make their way to the morning meeting area, singing the lyrics of this familiar song:

> The more we get together, together, together
> The more we get together, the happier we'll be
> 'Cause your friends are my friends and my
>   friends are your friends
> The more we get together, the happier we'll be.

Ms. Schwartz sits among the children as a child leads the chorus of voices while pointing to the words of the song on the Smart Board. You immediately feel at ease and join the children as they finish singing. Soon Ms. Schwartz begins the meeting:

"Last week we read a Swahili alphabet book called *Jambo Means Hello*" (Feelings, 1992). As Ms. Schwartz speaks, an image of the book appears on the Smart Board; she continues: "They speak Swahili in Uganda where Salama's family is from." Now a map of the world appears on the screen and the teacher zooms in on Uganda. Salama turns to you and explains that after reading the book everyone was saying "Jambo" to each other and then someone wondered how other people in the world say "hello." Ms. Schwartz asks the group,

"Who remembers some of the different ways we learned to say 'hello'?" When Ruby says that she remembers the word *konnichi wa*, Ms. Schwartz invites Ruby's friends to help her remember where the word comes from. When the children exclaim, "Japan!" Ms. Schwartz selects Japan on the map and *konnichi wa* is displayed in both English letters and Japanese characters. The children become very excited when they see both forms of writing and you can't help but smile, too. Ms. Schwartz explains that languages can be written down in different ways, and she helps the children compare and contrast the two forms of the word *konnichi wa*. Several children comment that they want to learn how to write in Japanese and Ms. Schwartz makes note of this.

Aleha, who was born in Somalia and speaks Arabic at home, adds to the conversation by explaining that Arabic looks different from English, too. Ms. Schwartz quickly looks up how to say and write "hello" in Arabic and then links this new information to Somalia on the interactive map. After some additional sharing and exploration with the map, Ms. Schwartz concludes the conversation by switching to a list of all the different ways they know how to say "hello." She reads each word and the children **echo read** by repeating the word after her and then, using **choral reading**, the whole list together.

Ms. Schwartz models how to greet someone with a handshake and a warm smile: "Jambo, Mitchell," to which Mitchell replies, "Ciao, Ms. Schwartz." Mitchell then turns to the person next to him and continues the greeting, which eventually makes its way all around the circle. You're amazed by how the children can remember the many different ways to say "hello" and the child who greets you even remembers your name! Ms. Schwartz briefly explains that a morning greeting and morning meeting are two important ways to build community and to support children's language and literacy development (Denton & Kriete, 2000).

After the morning greeting, Ms. Schwartz begins to write the morning message on chart paper at the easel: "The first line of our message will be: 'Today is Monday, November 5th.' Where do I begin to write?" Chelsea raises her hand and gestures to the top of the page. "Yes, I start at the top of page on the left side." Ms. Schwartz asks for a volunteer to write the word *today* on the chart. As Lucas comes forward, she hands him the marker. Lucas repeats the word *today* and says, "t-t-t—'T'." As he writes the letter, Ms. Schwartz models and explains how to write the letter *T* in the air and several children copy her motions: "Straight line down and across at the top. This is a capital *T* like in Tonisha's name. We use capital letters in names and at the beginning of sentences. Why are we using a capital *T* here?" She engages the children in stretching out the sounds in the words and invites them to participate by writing in the air as she shares her pen with other students who help her write the message.

As you observe, you realize that Ms. Schwartz keeps the pace of this writing activity brisk and only asks the children to take the pen when it's a task they can successfully complete, such as writing familiar words, letters, sounds, or punctuation marks. She helps them with the parts that are too hard for them right now and breezily uses whiteout tape to "fix up" the mistakes that are an expected part of the learning process.

After writing a complete sentence, Ms. Schwartz reads it to the children while pointing to each word and then invites them to read with her again. When the whole message is written, she reads it to the children in its entirety, pointing to each word and then the children read it back to her while she points. She asks for volunteers to come forward to lead the shared reading by pointing to the words, which the children do with varying degrees of success. Ms. Schwartz seems to expect this and says, "Whoops, I think you ran out of words. Let's try it again." " 'November' is a challenging word because it has three syllables. Let's clap them." After the children respond, Ms. Schwartz asks, "Do you see how it starts with the letter *N*, nnnn—November? How does it end? Yes, with the sound /r/. Where's the last letter of November?" You realize that Ms. Schwartz is scaffolding the children's understanding of how words and print work. You think back to the word *kon-nichi wa* written in Japanese characters and you realize that you've never really thought about how confusing letters and words could be if you didn't already know how to read. You suddenly realize there's a lot to teaching children at the emergent stage and you can't wait to learn more! ■

Overview of the Emergent Stage of Development

The emergent stage of development represents the time before formal reading instruction begins. As you learned from observing in Ms. Schwartz's classroom, children in the emergent stage are developing the knowledge, skills, and dispositions that are considered the "developmental precursors" to conventional reading and writing (Lonigan, Whitehurst, & Anthony, 2004; Whitehurst & Lonigan, 2002). In the early childhood years and throughout preschool, kindergarten, and first grade, children gain many insights about literacy from their teachers, caregivers, and environments, including the following:

1) Print is speech written down.
2) Print conveys meaning and illustrations support print.

3) Print works in a predictable way (in English, top to bottom, left to right).

4) Letters represent sounds in words.

5) Written words correspond to spoken words.

Young children study the language, behaviors, and attitudes of adults in their lives and they imitate these in their play. They enjoy role-playing scenes from their lives and they often include many of the literacy props they notice in these settings. Perhaps you remember this kind of play from *your* childhood? Young children love to use writing materials to make everything from shopping lists and pretend menus, to business cards, make-believe money, and even mail! They do all this long before they can read and write in the conventional sense.

As a teacher, your role is to create environments where emergent readers and writers can role-play as the proficient readers and writers they will become. You will intentionally scaffold their literacy and language experiments with developmentally responsive instruction. This will take careful planning and skill on your part. Understanding the importance of this stage and the expected developmental milestones will help you prioritize your instruction and create literacy-rich environments where emergent readers and writers will flourish!

Oral Language Development: The Foundation of Literacy

Chapter 1 emphasized that the recipe for teaching reading has several ingredients. For young children and English learners, the first ingredient must be adults who engage them in meaningful conversation. Oral language is best developed through authentic interactions as part of daily activities in the classroom and at home (Dickinson & Tabors, 2001). In preschool and the primary grades, and in classrooms with English learners, you will scaffold children's language development and social skills through many structures in your day, including morning meeting, center time, snack and mealtimes, free play, interactive writing, and during read-alouds and shared reading time. While it may appear that you have ample opportunity to develop language skills in the classroom, only the most effective teachers take full advantage of these opportunities (Dickinson, McCabe, & Essex, 2006; Dickinson & Tabors, 2001).

Enriching the Language Environment in Your Classroom

In the early years, conversation is how children build their receptive and expressive vocabularies. As you learned in Chapter 2, vocabulary knowledge influences children's phonological awareness, listening comprehension, and later, their reading comprehension. In general, children from language-rich environments tend to have an easier time learning to read and they learn new words, concepts, and complex syntactic structures more readily, too (Dickinson & Tabors, 2001; Lawrence & Snow, 2011). Teachers play an important role in developing oral language competence, and this is especially critical for English learners and children from high-poverty backgrounds. It's important to remember that it *is* possible to accelerate the language development of children who have not had rich oral language experiences in the early years (Dickinson, McCabe, & Essex, 2006; Lawrence & Snow, 2011).

Density of Talk

When there's a lot of talk in the environment, there's also a greater likelihood that individual words will be repeated in a variety of contexts. This repetition deepens children's understanding of the meaning of words and increases the likelihood that they will be remembered (Carey, 1978). Small group and one-to-one conversations are especially powerful for maximizing children's *exposure to* and *practice with* language (Dickinson & Tabors, 2001). In your classroom you will create opportunities for these more personal conversations to take place throughout each day. Centers, snack and mealtimes, and free play offer particularly good opportunities to engage children in small group conversation.

Common Core Connection

Language Standards: Vocabulary Acquisition and Use

Quality of Talk

You will also work to elevate the *quality* of talk in your classroom by using **novel words**—words more commonly found in written text than in oral language—and **sophisticated words**—words used by mature language users. These types of words reflect the *general academic* and *domain-specific* vocabulary of specific disciplines that children will be developing throughout the school years. For example, when a child remarks that his snack is "yummy," this is a grand opportunity to introduce sophisticated language in response. You might reply, "Is it *scrumptious? Scrumptious* means that it's especially *delicious.* Say 'scrumptious' with me: 'Scrumptious.' What makes your snack so *appetizing* today?" Introducing novel and sophisticated words as part of your natural conversation with children has the potential to increase both the *breadth* and *depth* of their vocabularies while also stimulating word consciousness—the predisposition to learn, appreciate, and effectively use words. Figure 6.1 highlights some additional ways you can integrate sophisticated vocabulary in your everyday interactions with children.

Adaptable to All Stages

FIGURE 6.1 **Sophisticated Words for Daily Interactions**

Every interaction with children is an opportunity to expose them to rich vocabulary. Sometimes this doesn't come naturally, so help yourself by creating lists of sophisticated synonyms for words you frequently use with children. Keep these lists on a clipboard or tape them to the table where you work with children to remind yourself of the importance of elevating the *quality* of talk in your classroom. Here are three examples of such lists:

* When traveling through the hallways or transitioning between activities, you might demonstrate and ask children to *walk, stroll, saunter, trot, meander, glide, promenade, march, stride, jaunt, proceed, skip, prance, hop, tiptoe* or *sashay.*
* When talking about how they'll work together in groups, you might suggest (and explain) that they be *considerate, polite, respectful, participatory, imaginative, conversant, cooperative, determined, collaborative, expressive, orderly, creative, inventive,* or *resourceful.*
* When providing feedback to children about their feelings or behavior, you might use adjectives such as *affable, considerate, apprehensive, collaborative, gracious, delightful, empathetic, anxious, joyous, thoughtful, courteous, inquisitive, creative, athletic, attentive,* and *caring.*

Remember, it's helpful to provide brief and "kid-friendly" definitions or synonyms for sophisticated words as you introduce them in the context of conversation.

The Role of Syntax

Language exposure also helps young children and English learners internalize the structure of language, or **syntax** (for example, how to appropriately use pronouns, verb tense, and sentence structure) (Vasilyeva & Waterfall, 2011). As you remember from Chapter 2, awareness of syntax helps children monitor the accuracy of their early reading attempts. Additionally, researchers have found that syntactic, or grammatical, competence in the early years also predicts later reading comprehension.

One way to influence children's awareness of syntax is to speak in syntactically complex sentences. This is actually easier than it sounds. Complex sentences combine two or more ideas (an independent and dependent clause) and often contain words like *because, after, since, although, that, who(m), which, when,* and *but.* For example, "When we finish snack time, we can go outside for recess"; and "Although I am allergic to hay, I'm still looking forward to our visit to the farm."

Researchers have also found that children benefit from exposure to passive voice, too. Since passive voice is not as common in oral language as it is in written texts, particularly math and science texts, you'll have to make some effort to include the passive form in your talk. When using the passive voice, the subject of the sentence receives the action: For example, instead of saying, "The baseball shattered the window" (active voice) you might say, "The window was shattered by the baseball" (passive voice); instead of "The students added salt to the pretzel dough" (active voice), you'd say "The pretzel dough was salted by the students" (passive voice) (Vasilyeva & Waterfall, 2011).

Children with little exposure to complex sentence structure and passive voice will often have difficulty reading and understanding informational texts, such as content-area textbooks, later on. This difficulty will impede their ability to access and understand rich and interesting content. This is particularly the case with children from high-poverty backgrounds and English learners (Vasilyeva & Waterfall, 2011). Making it a point to use syntactically complex sentence structures, including passive voice, can help children develop their language and comprehension skills.

Scaffolding Children's Syntax

In addition to speaking in varied sentence structures, you can support children's understanding of syntax by scaffolding their grammatical experiments in the course of conversation. For example, a preschooler, kindergartner, or English learner might say, "Me goed to the store with my babysitter." Here, the child is using the objective *me* for the subjective *I,* and overgeneralizing the inflected ending of *–ed* for past tense. A supportive reply corrects one or more of the grammatical errors and provides an opportunity to extend the conversation by asking a *who, what, when, where, why,* or *how* question. For example, "You *went* to the store with your babysitter? *What* did you do there?" In addition to building this child's understanding of how English syntax works, both the regular and irregular features of it, you're also building conversational skills, which lead to improved social competence—an important predictor of school success (Blair, Protzko, & Ursache, 2011; Nelson, 1996).

Authentic and Sustained Conversation

You'll also work to intentionally engage children in *authentic* and *sustained* conversations—this stands in contrast to the more contrived question-and-answer exchanges sometimes found in classrooms. As children talk, purposefully listen to their conversations to learn about their interests and share your own interests and curiosities, too. Encourage conversation by asking open-ended questions, looking in children's direction when they talk, using animated facial expressions, and positioning your body in such a manner that you show sustained interest in what children have to say (for example, leaning forward, bending down, and making eye contact). All of these teacher behaviors are positively associated with children's cognitive engagement and development, as well as vocabulary growth (Dickinson & Tabors, 2001).

Admittedly, it's sometimes hard to sustain a conversation beyond one or two exchanges—it does take some practice! To get started, try these three suggestions for extending and deepening a conversation with young children (or anyone!):

1) Prompt children to **_elaborate_** on their responses: "You said you like Curious George; what do you like about him?"

2) Help children to **_clarify_** their thoughts: "What did you mean when you said Stellaluna was sad?"

> **Common Core Connection**
>
> Speaking and Listening Standards: Comprehension and Collaboration; Presentation of Knowledge and Ideas

> Adaptable to All Stages

Strategies for the Classroom

Building a Tower of Talk

Since vocabulary and language development are dependent on listening _and_ speaking practice, children will benefit from explicit modeling of _how_ to participate actively in sustained conversations. One way to help children develop these skills is to provide a visual representation of an interactive conversation using an instructional strategy called "Building a Tower of Talk."

To model this strategy, select two or three children to work with you while the other children observe. (We call this _fish bowling._) Choose a topic that the class has some interest in and familiarity with—perhaps a recent field trip, the morning's fire drill, or a common read-aloud experience. Explain to the children that the goal of this activity is to work on listening and responding to each other. Each time someone adds to the conversation, they are going to add a Unifix cube to the "Tower of Talk." Pass out two or three Unifix cubes to each participant—be sure each person has a unique color so you can visually note who has and has not contributed. Next, initiate the conversation with a statement: "I learned so much from yesterday's visit to the farm." As you speak, place your Unifix cube down in front of the small group and then, in a whisper, invite the children to reply to your statement with another statement or question. As each child responds to you and each other, a block is added to the tower. Be sure to highlight the importance of taking turns and not speaking over each other.

If children are reluctant to join the conversation, model how to invite them into the conversation by whispering: "I noticed that Alexis hasn't added to the conversation lately so I'm going to ask her a question." In your regular speaking voice engage the student: "Alexis, what was your favorite part of the field trip?" When Alexis replies, she adds a cube to the tower. If Alexis isn't sure how to contribute, whisper a possible comment or question into her ear and encourage her to add it to the conversation. The goal is to keep the conversation going until all the cubes are gone.

After a demonstration, be sure to talk with the whole group about what they noticed from listening to the conversation. Reinforce the importance of adding onto or acknowledging what someone else has said with a question or comment, and then give all the children the opportunity to try out the activity in partnerships or small groups. As you might imagine, the children will take delight in seeing their towers grow and adding their own blocks to it. It won't take long before your students are asking for more and more Unifix cubes so they can grow their own Towers of Talk!

Always remember, the goal of activities like this is to help children internalize the habits of proficient language users. As you celebrate and recognize children's accomplishments, they will aspire to continue practicing these skills in more authentic ways.

3) Engage children in ***explanatory dialogue*** about concepts: Move beyond simple questions like, "What color is your truck?" to more challenging questions and prompts like, "How does the dump mechanism work? Oh, look, do you see this lever? Lift the lever and tell me what happens . . . Why do you think that happens?"

Language and Literacy Development in Meaningful Contexts

Children's vocabulary and language development are optimized when they're supported and developed in the context of their play (Dickinson & Tabors, 2001; Harris, Golinkoff, & Hirsch-Pasek, 2011). Children also learn language skills from interacting with their peers, particularly when children with emerging language skills interact with children whose language skills are more sophisticated (Mashburn, Justice, Downer, & Pianta, 2009). For these reasons, among others, learning centers are a powerful place to support children's oral language development.

To illustrate this point, consider the woodworking center in Ms. Schwartz's classroom. In this setting she introduces words such as *hammer, screwdriver, nail, screw, vise, saw,* and *pliers.* As with all rich conversations about words, her explanations go beyond labeling the objects and she includes descriptions and demonstrations of their functions, too: "A hammer is used to nail things together. See this birdhouse? Where do you see nails? Yes, the sides of the birdhouse are nailed together so they won't fall off. Watch how I use the hammer to nail these two pieces of wood together. Have you ever used or watched someone use a hammer? Tell us about it." Comparing and contrasting words and concepts is also valuable: "How is a hammer like the screwdriver we learned about yesterday? How is it different?" Because children are so actively involved in center play—interacting with materials and each other—they are more likely to use and retain the vocabulary introduced in these experiences.

Children's learning in centers is maximized when you enrich these centers with literacy-related objects such as books, magazines, maps, paper, pens, markers, and crayons, among other things (Morrow & Schickedanz, 2006; Neuman & Roskos, 1992). In the case of the woodworking center, include informational texts such as books with directions for building a simple birdhouse and more complex informational texts about buildings and architecture. Also include storybooks in your centers. One of our favorites for the woodworking center is *Old MacDonald Had a Woodshop* (Shulman, 2002). This book appeals to young listeners because it is based on a familiar song ("Old MacDonald Had a Farm") and it includes many text elements that engage and support young readers, including rhyme, rhythm, repetition, and special print features such as capital letters, italics, and boldface print. The author also does a very effective job defining the woodworking tools by showing their functions in the illustrations, and the sounds the tools make are captured in the text.

It's beneficial to include other manipulatives that stimulate literacy and language development in your centers. For example, in the case of the woodworking center or even a block center, you might include pencils, graph paper, rulers, paper for signs, tool belts, blueprints, and work gloves to stimulate children's role-playing as carpenters and artisans. Teachers who show children how they can interact with one another and the materials during play and center time yield greater and more lasting gains in children's vocabulary learning and language development (Dickinson & Tabors, 2001; Roskos, Tabors, & Lenhart, 2004, 2009). Robust learning is the result of well-planned environments and your intentional scaffolding, instruction, and interactions with children. Figure 6.2 summarizes some guidelines for enriching the language environment for young learners.

FIGURE 6.2 Principles for Enriching the Language Environment

- Quantity of Talk
  - Exposure to a large volume of words
  - Repetition of words in different contexts

- Quality of Talk
  - Novel and sophisticated words
  - Syntactic complexity and passive voice

- Interactive Turn Taking
  - Engaged listening
  - Open-ended questioning/extended response

- Meaningful Settings and Authentic Purposes
  - Relevant to kids' interests and lives
  - Motivating topics and integrated experiences

Strategies for the Classroom

Literacy-Rich Centers

Learning centers are spaces where small groups of children can gather to interact with materials and each other in pursuit of a common goal. Children's learning and enjoyment of centers are enhanced when they are encouraged to role-play and interact with literacy-related objects during their play. What follows is a partial list of the literacy materials you might include to enrich your centers.

Dramatic Play: Dramatic play centers include props for children to enact real-life scenarios: doctor's office, restaurant, house, camping, and so on. Providing students with literacy materials to help them role-play in these different scenarios enriches their play and literacy learning. Consider texts such as menus, cookbooks, books about the human body, telephone books, coupons, maps, and field guides. You'll include other literacy-related materials such as paper for shopping lists, prescriptions, restaurant orders, stationery, postcards, appointment books, calendars, play telephones, and much more.

Writing: Include pens, pencils, colored pencils, gel pens, markers, staplers, hole punchers, white-out tape, address labels, envelopes, and so forth. We also suggest books about people who write such as: *Dear Mr. Blueberry* (James, 1991) or *A Letter to Amy* (Keats, 1968); mailboxes and/or cubbies for each child to send and receive mail; as well as rubber stamps, stationery, lined paper, blank paper, paper with room for illustrations and lines, construction paper, and narrow paper cut for list making. Also include charts with children's names and photos, alphabet models, word walls, and picture dictionaries.

Science/Social Studies: These centers are usually organized around a theme and include many hands-on manipulatives. Enrich the center by including books and other texts (e.g., pamphlets, maps, brochures, charts, graphs, diagrams, photos with captions, and so on) and materials to make such texts. Label the objects and provide index cards and/or address labels for children to label their work and objects as well.

Dramatic Reenactment: Collect props to help young children reenact favorite storybooks: felt boards and magnetic boards, craft stick puppets, or materials to make them.

Library Corner: Books, books, and more books! Organize and sort books by topics, themes, favorite authors, favorite illustrators, and different genres. Create books of environmental print and classmates' names. Include big books and charts of poems, songs, fingerplays, and nursery rhymes. Provide a collection of interesting pointers to encourage children to practice finger-point reading. Highlighter tape and Wikki-Sticks can be fun for children to use when isolating words, letters, or parts of words.

Blocks: When you introduce figures, cars, little people, and/or animals in the block center, you increase the likelihood that children will interact with each other and create narratives to go with their structures. Also include materials to make signs and notes: paper, markers, pencils, pens, craft sticks, clay, tape, cardboard, and so on. Books about buildings and architecture, architectural drawings, and maps are effective, too.

Art: In addition to a wide range of art materials (clay, fabric, watercolors, brushes, crayons, pastels, string, markers, and much more), consider including books about artists and simple how-to craft books. Also include small pieces of card stock so children can write "All About the Artist" descriptions or captions/titles for their art. It's helpful to have materials to make signs to indicate that their work is "in progress" and should not be disturbed.

ABC Center: ABC books, puzzles, rubber stamps, letter tiles, letter stencils, magnetic letters and magnetic boards, pocket chart for making words, ABC sorts and games, ABC charts and desk strips, and handwriting models with arrows—all these serve as wonderful inspirations for children. Include clay to build letters, and sand or rice in trays to write letters. Also provide templates or premade books for children to create their own ABC books with magazine pictures or their own illustrations.

Engaging the World of Print: The Role of Exposure to Written Texts

In addition to oral language practice, an equally important ingredient for emergent readers is having adults read to them and engage them in discussing what is being read—questioning, making predictions, responding to what they are thinking and how they are feeling. Encourage as many adults as possible in adding this ingredient, but the most critical provider will be you! In your classroom you will read to children in both large groups and small, with regular-size trade books and big books. You will engage children in listening to and talking about different genres—poetry, narrative, and informational texts, and the whole palette of **environmental** and **functional print** in your classroom. Over the course of the first few weeks of the new school year, you will increasingly use shared reading experiences to model, teach, and discuss conventions of print and to develop phonological and phonemic awareness. Other times, your read-alouds with narrative and informational books will support children's comprehension and vocabulary development.

Storybook Reading

When we think directly of the impact of stories on literacy development, the implications are powerful! Listening to an adult read a story helps children move beyond their own everyday language and experience. In addition to the rhythm and structure of language, they become aware of experiences and contexts that are not a part of their own everyday worlds, as well as the universality of other experiences and feelings. Equally significant, children gain practice in building and sustaining meanings and mental images over the course of a story—this ability will be critical as they later read and engage in extended texts (Wells, 1986). From these experiences, they will come to learn the symbolic power of language: It creates worlds that do not exist immediately before them, but are constructed in their minds.

Storybook reading is yet another opportunity to develop language and vocabulary. Teachers who read and reread stories—drawing children's attention to novel words and their meanings, as well as complex syntactic structures—yield increases in children's receptive and expressive vocabulary growth, listening comprehension, and, later, their reading comprehension.

Most children take pleasure in listening to stories read aloud. They spontaneously make observations of and connections to characters, the setting, illustrations, and events during reading. They chime, "Again! Again!" when a satisfying story has ended. Reading aloud to children instills a powerful message that reading is simultaneously important and joyful. Notably, there is a positive relationship between children's early storybook reading experiences and their later reading achievement.

Understanding Story Elements and the Language of Stories

Common Core Connection

Reading Standards for Literature: Key Ideas and Details

Storybook reading helps children develop an understanding of the basic elements of narrative text, from the introduction of the characters and the setting, to the development of a problem and a solution and all the events in between. Understanding the elements of narrative text helps young children engage and sustain their attention while listening to stories. It strengthens their listening comprehension skills and helps them acquire the language of storybooks (McGee & Schickedanz, 2007; Sulzby, 1985).

FIGURE 6.3 Great Storybooks for Teaching the Elements of Narrative Text

Alborough, J. (1992). *Where's My Teddy?* Candlewick Press.

Bemelmans, L. (1963). *Madeline*. Viking.

Choi, Y. (2003). *The Name Jar*. Dragonfly Books.

dePaola, T. (1975). *Strega Nona*. Prentice Hall.

Freeman, D. (1968). *Corduroy*. Viking.

Henkes, K. (1996). *Chrysanthemum*. Greenwillow.

Hoffman, M. (1991). *Amazing Grace*. Dial Books for Young Readers.

Hurd, T. (1997). *Art Dog*. HarperCollins.

Keats, E. J. (1964). *Whistle for Willy*. Viking.

Mayer, M. (1968). *There's a Nightmare in My Closet*. Dial Books for Young Readers.

Penn, A. (2006). *The Kissing Hand*. Child Welfare League of America.

Pfister, M. (1995). *Rainbow Fish*. North-South Books.

Pinkney, J. (1999). *The Ugly Duckling*. Morrow Junior Books.

Piper, W. (1930). *The Little Engine that Could*. Philomel Books.

Waber, B. (1965). *Lyle, Lyle Crocodile*. Houghton Mifflin.

Waddel, M. (2010). *Owl Babies*. Candlewick.

Watt, M. (2006). *Scaredy Squirrel Makes a Friend*. Kids Can Press.

Willems, M. (2004). *Knuffle Bunny: A Cautionary Tale*. Hyperion Books for Children.

As you begin to read more and more storybooks yourself, you'll realize that some stories don't include all of the elements of narrative text, while others do, but they may be too subtle for young children or English learners to notice. When selecting a book for the purpose of teaching the elements of narrative text, it's important to select a book that exemplifies the genre, particularly the development of a significant *problem* and *resolution*—two elements that are particularly difficult for young children to recognize. Figure 6.3 highlights some of our favorite books for teaching the elements of narrative text to young children.

> Applicable to the Beginning Stage

Before Reading Children who are frequently read to may implicitly understand the language and elements of narrative text, but most children will benefit from you making these explicit. When reading aloud to children, draw their attention to story elements *before*, *during*, and *after* your reading and encourage them to use their prior knowledge and text-based information to help them predict what may happen next. For example, when reading *Julius, the Baby of the World* (Henkes, 1990), introduce the children to the characters, the gist of the story, and set a purpose for listening: "This is a story about a big sister, Lilly [point to Lilly], and her new baby brother, Julius [point to Julius]. Lilly and Julius are the main characters in this story. Let's look at the picture on the front of the cover; what is Lilly doing? I can't tell if she trying to make her brother laugh or if she is angry with him. What do you think? What makes you say that? Let's read to see what happens." As you read about Lilly and her brother, periodically stop to recap what's happened and invite the children to confirm, reject, or revise their predictions based on the new information in the story. Focusing children's attention on the thinking that goes into making predictions shifts the focus from "being right," to being thoughtful and reflective—two very important dispositions for readers.

During Reading   Elicit children's reactions, connections, and questions through **analytic talk** (Dickinson & Smith, 1994). When reading *Jamaica Tag-along* (Havill, 1989), a story about a little girl whose feelings get hurt when her big brother doesn't let her play, invite your listeners to identify and react to Jamaica's problem. As children share their insights and connections, bring these experiences back to understanding the characters' motivations and the events of the story: "So your experience/connection helps you understand how Jamaica feels. How would you describe that feeling? What do you think she might do next?" Or, "How do you think this problem will be solved? Why?" Encourage children to back up their thinking with evidence from the text and their own experiences: "I think Jamaica will follow her brother to the park *because* she really wants to play with him." Using open-ended questions stimulates elaborated responses and the development of critical thinking skills.

After Reading   Revisit the purpose you set at the beginning of the reading and engage your students in conversation about the story—their reactions, favorite parts, most memorable lines or pictures, and so on. Encourage the children to compare and contrast the story with their lives and other books they've heard; these are called *text-to-life* and *text-to-text connections* (Miller, 2002). After a second or third reading, model and gradually invite children to join you in retelling the story using the language of the text (McGee & Schickedanz, 2007). For example, after reading *Koala Lou* a couple of times (Fox, 1988), show the children how to retell the story by turning the pages and thinking aloud: "This is the story of Koala Lou. In the beginning of the story, Koala Lou was a soft and cuddly baby koala bear and everyone loved her [point to the picture]. Do you remember that part in the beginning? Her mother would smile and say, 'Koala Lou, I DO love you!' [point to the words] and Koala Lou was happy." After some demonstration, invite the children to participate in the retelling: "Over the years, Koala Lou's mother had many more baby koalas and then what? [wait for children's response]. Oh, she didn't have time to tell Koala Lou that she loved her! Yes, I remember—that was the BIG problem in the story. And then what?" Retelling stories helps children actively construct meaning and build **story schema**—the understanding of how narrative text works. Retelling stories also leads to improved reading comprehension later on (Gambrell, Koskinen & Kapinus, 1991; Morrow & Smith, 1990).

Extension Activities   Children's understandings of story elements and storybook language are increased when they have multiple exposures to the stories (Martinez, 1993). For example, after reading a storybook aloud, make it available for children to reread. Show them how to retell from the illustrations and use their memories of the story, too—a mix of retelling and storytelling. It's also valuable to provide props, puppets, or felt-board characters for children to play with while retelling or reenacting the story. These need not be expensive toys. A simple photocopy of the characters and the setting can be made into stick puppets or used on a felt board or magnetic board by affixing Velcro or magnetic tape to the back of the images. When inviting children to retell the story *Strega Nona* (dePaola, 1975), for example, provide a large pot, a wooden spoon, and light-colored yarn. Show the children how they can use these props to dramatize and/or retell stories, and then make the props available for center or free play time. After some initial practice, encourage the children to collect and make their own props for retelling stories. Dramatic reenactments are most powerful when they are initiated by children as part of their play (Martinez, 1993).

Reading Informational Text

Informational text is engaging for children of all ages, including emergent readers! It stimulates curiosity and propels children to make sense of the world around them. It answers questions such as *Where Does the Garbage Go?* (Showers, 1994) and *What Makes a Shadow?* (Bulla, 1994); it explains natural phenomena, as in Tomie dePaola's *The Cloud Book* (1975) and *The Seasons of Arnold's Apple Tree* (Gibbons, 1984); and it can be richly descriptive, too (for example, *Hands!* [Aliki, 1990]).

The Importance of Informational Text in the Early Childhood Years

Despite living in the "Information Age," and in a time when adults read more nonfiction than any other genre (Smith, 2000), storybook reading has surprisingly taken precedence over reading informational text in the early years of school. Duke (2000) found that primary-grade teachers spend an average of about 3.6 minutes a day on informational text—and even less time, 1.4 minutes per day, in schools that serve high-poverty communities. Further, she found minimal informational text displayed on the walls of these classrooms and very few informational texts in classroom libraries.

Your classroom will be different. Informational text builds background knowledge that can improve children's later reading comprehension (Neumann, 2006). It fosters vocabulary development as well as conceptual knowledge. When listening to *Honey in a Hive* (Rockwell, 2005), for example, young children will learn domain-specific words such as *nectar, pollen, drone, queen, mate, antennae, wax, swarm, hive, chamber, honeycombs,* and many more. They will also be exposed to general academic vocabulary that will help them comprehend this and other texts, too (for example, *rapidly, gathering, exhaustion,* and *flight*). Informational text exposes children to transferrable, big ideas and concepts (Smolkin & Donovan, 2001). The book *Honey in a Hive* teaches children about the life cycle of bees, where honey comes from, and the habitat of bees—all concepts that can be applied to studies of other living things.

> **Common Core Connection**
> Reading Standards for Informational Text: Integration of Knowledge and Ideas; Range of Reading and Level of Text Complexity

Informational texts contain text features that are not typically found in storybooks: diagrams, tables, figures, photographs, captions, cutaways, glossaries, indexes, maps, graphs, and many other items. When students learn about these features through listening to and interacting with informational texts, they begin to use them in their own writing and they better understand their functions when reading informational text themselves (Duke, Bennett-Armistead, & Roberts, 2003; Wilson & Anderson, 1986). Perhaps most importantly, reading informational text aloud helps young children appreciate the wonder, excitement, and joy of "reading to learn!"

Reading Informational Text Aloud

When we choose informational text to read aloud, we select texts that are engaging and connected to our thematic studies and/or the interests of the children we're working with. We pay attention to the length and format of the text as well. Some informational texts include graphs, diagrams, or other text features that are better enjoyed up close rather than in a large group. Other texts are just too long to listen to in one sitting, or even more than one sitting. And still others are difficult to read aloud; your oral reading should be fluent, expressive, and free of pronunciation errors, so be sure you're comfortable and well practiced when it comes to reading informational text aloud.

Once you've found the perfect read-aloud, preview the text and consider the needs of your readers *before, during,* and *after* the read-aloud. Plan places in the text to engage children in analytic talk. What follows is a description of how you might use a piece of informational text, *Penguin Chick* (Tatham, 2002), with preschoolers or primary-grade children.

> Applicable to All Stages

Children's Literature Connection

Guidelines for Choosing High-Quality Informational Text

Guiding Principle	Considerations
Accuracy	Does the text represent the most up-to-date information on a topic? Is the terminology correct? Does the author cite resources or provide endnotes to deepen students' understanding of the topic? Is content presented in an unbiased fashion, avoiding stereotypes or unsubstantiated opinions?
Developmental Appropriateness	Is the level of the text suitable to the age group you're working with? Does it use language that is supported within the text with either explanations or other graphic supports? Is there too much technical or specialized vocabulary? Is it an appropriate length for the age group you're working with? Is it best used as a read-aloud, small group lesson, or independent reading?
Matching Text to Goals	Is the text a good match for your teaching goals, considering the content, functions, features, and your overall purpose for reading the text? For example, if your goal is to teach concept of word in text, you would need an enlarged text—a chart or big book with no more than one or a few lines of text per page. If your goal is to teach about the life cycle of a bullfrog, then you'd want a text that shows vivid photos of bullfrogs at different stages of life.
Interest/Motivation	Is the text visually appealing? Is it easy to view from where the children will be sitting? Will your students relate to the content, finding it both relevant and meaningful? Can you envision extension activities that will support their sustained interest in the topic? Will your students like the text? Do *you* like it?
Text Type	Considering the purpose of your lesson, what is the best type of text for teaching the content: a pamphlet, an Internet text, a big book, a trade book, a magazine or an article?
Recommendations	How did you come to learn about this text? Was it recommended by someone? What did this person like about the book? Is it an award winner? Do you know the author? Or series? What do online reviewers have to say about it? Does the text exemplify the genre? What are its pros and cons?

Source: Adapted from Duke, Bennett-Armistead, & Roberts, 2003, pp. 38–39.

Common Core Connection

Reading Standards for Informational Text: Craft and Structure; Range of Reading and Level of Text Complexity

Before Reading When reading *Penguin Chick*, begin by orienting the children to the book and cover illustration: "The title of this book is *Penguin Chick* and it's written by Betty Tatham. She's the author. Look at the cover; What do you see? Yes, two adult penguins and a baby penguin. Maybe they're the baby penguin's parents? Could be. What do you think we call a baby penguin? [pause] How did you know? Oh, the title gave you that information. Nice job using your resources! Have you heard that word before? Yes, a chick can be a baby penguin *or* a baby chicken. Many baby birds are called chicks. Let's think for a minute. What else do you already know about penguins?" As the children share their knowledge of penguins, you'll note their contributions on a "Things We Know about Penguins" chart. When possible, try to keep track of who said what; children love to read their names in print and seeing their own words, even if they cannot read them just yet. This practice helps emergent readers begin to understand the relationship between speech and print. Later, these charts can be added to your thematic centers or your library corner for rereading.

After brainstorming things they know about penguins, you might solicit some questions the children have about the topic and add those to the "Things We Wonder about Penguins" chart. Just like storybook reading, you'll also want to help children develop predictions about the text and model backing them up with evidence from the text, their prior knowledge, or a combination of the two: "I think this will be a book about penguins and penguin chicks *because* the title of the book is *Penguin Chick*." You'll also want to set a purpose for reading: "Today we are going to read *Penguin Chick* to learn about penguins. While I'm reading, I'll stop along the way so you can share something you learned, answer a question from our chart, or ask even more questions!"

During Reading As you're reading, particularly with repeated readings of the text, ask strategic questions to help draw children's attention to important vocabulary introduced within the text: "What's a brood patch again?" Also define new words along the way—for example, after reading the line of text "The mother uses her flippers," point to the illustration: "These are her flippers— they're like arms without hands." You might gesture to props or other teaching aids to help make abstract concepts more concrete. For example, point out Antarctica, home of the Emperor penguins, on a globe and compare and contrast it with where you live. Similarly, it's helpful for children to act out parts of the text: "Can you trumpet like the father penguin? Can you whistle like the chick?" Importantly, you will work to elicit extended student response and analytic talk before, during, and after reading the text. The following are good examples of prompts that may stimulate this kind of talk:

Tell me more about that . . .
What do you mean by . . .?
How do you know?
What makes you say that?

After Reading After your first reading of a piece of informational text, return to your purpose and revisit the "Things We Wonder about Penguins" chart and talk about the questions that have and have not been answered. Chart the answers and anything else learned on a new chart, titled "Things We Learned about Penguins." This entire procedure is referred to as a K-W-L Chart (Ogle, 1986): Things you <u>K</u>now, <u>W</u>ant to know, and have <u>L</u>earned. You might add to this process another chart that captures the children's new questions. This signals that books can stimulate as many questions as they answer—an important discovery. After subsequent readings of the text, it's powerful to model retelling the text and summarizing the main ideas.

> **Common Core Connection**
>
> Reading Standards for Informational Text: Key Ideas and Details

Extension Activities After reading a piece of informational text, it's valuable to provide students with many varied (and exciting!) opportunities to explore the topic. To help children appreciate some of the details from the text you just read, engage them in interactive activities like this one: In a center, or as a class, have the children role-play some of the things they learned from the text. For example, in *Penguin Chick* the children learned that father penguins balance their chicks on their feet to protect them from the cold ground when they're young. To simulate this experience, have the children try to walk around with small stuffed animals or baking potatoes carefully balanced on their feet while they try to complete their normal activities. Relate this experience to what it must be like for father penguin to do this for many weeks! Encourage children to write or draw about this later in the day.

Other Texts for Emergent Readers

Common Core Connection

Reading Standards
for Literature and
Informational Text:
Range of Reading
and Level of Text
Complexity

Applicable to All
Stages

Common Core Connection

Reading Standards
for Literature and
Informational Text:
Craft and Structure

Preschool, kindergarten, and elementary school teachers read aloud to their students several times a day. The purpose of these read-alouds varies as do the texts they use. Although the purpose of your read-aloud should be the most important consideration when selecting a text, you will aspire to achieve "genre diversification," too (Duke & Bennett-Armistead, & Roberts, 2003). Genre diversification simply means that you will intentionally vary the genres you read aloud, the books and texts in your library, and the print in your environment, to roughly achieve:

- One-third narrative text,
- One-third informational text, and
- One-third other genres (poetry, biography, predictable pattern text, and so on) (Duke, Bennett-Armistead, & Roberts, 2003).

Admittedly, it's sometimes difficult to classify a book into just one category. For example, how would you classify *The Story of Ruby Bridges's* (Cole, 1995)? On face value, it's a powerful narrative, but it's also an account of Ruby Bridges's life, so is it classified as a biography or a narrative? How about *Miss Bindergarten Takes a Field Trip with Kindergarten* (Slate, 2003)? In this storybook a kindergarten teacher, Miss Bindergarten, takes her 26 students on an adventure, but there's a catch: Each of her students' names begins with a different letter of the alphabet. Is this an example of a narrative text or an ABC book? At the end of the day, these distinctions are interesting to explore but they're not that important. Your overall goal is to provide a wide variety of texts in both the environment and in your read-alouds. What follows is a description of texts that are commonly used with emergent readers and children in the beginning stage of reading. These texts are in addition to the narrative and informational texts already described. As you will see, these categories are not by any means finite or exhaustive. Our goal in sharing these categories is to help you think intentionally about children's reading and listening experiences and how you might achieve diversification in the texts you read *to* and *with* young children.

Poetry, Fingerplays, Nursery Rhymes, and Songs

The rhythms and rhymes of poetry, nursery rhymes, and songs are the staples of oral and written language that so many cultures have traditionally shared with young children. Do you remember some of your childhood favorites: *The Eensey-Weensey Spider, Humpty Dumpty, London Bridge, There Was an Old Lady Who Swallowed a Fly, Miss Mary Mack, Over in the Meadow,* or Shel Silverstein's *Where the Sidewalk Ends* (1974)? Rhythm and rhyme have deep roots in our psychology and our physical makeup. They are tied to movement, dance, and play. Indeed, because as a species we may be "hard-wired" to respond to rhythm and rhyme, sharing poetry, fingerplays, nursery rhymes, and songs with young children and older English learners supports their literacy development.

As described later in this chapter, an awareness of rhyme and sensitivity to it is critical for young children's development of phonological and phonemic awareness. Poetry, nursery rhymes, and songs are also easily memorized, and they can make good texts for shared reading. They also make for fun transitions between activities and contribute to a positive classroom environment.

Environmental and Functional Print

Long before children can read in a conventional way, they become aware of print in their environment and soon can recognize many signs, symbols, labels, and logos. Parents and caregivers

Children's Literature Connection

Favorite Books and Resources for Poetry, Nursery Rhymes, Fingerplays, and Songs

Poetry

Prelutsky, J. (1984). *New kid on the block.*

Prelutsky, J. (1986). *Read aloud rhymes for the very young.*

Prelutsky, J. (2000). *It's raining pigs and noodles.*

Silverstein, S. (1964). *A giraffe and a half.*

White, M. M., Moore, E., Deregniers, B. S., & Carr, J. (Eds.). (1988). *Sing a song of popcorn: Every child's book of poems.*

Songs

Katz, A. (2001). *Take me out of the bathtub.*

Keats, E. J. (1971). *Over in the meadow.*

Peek, M. (1993). *Mary wore her red dress, Henry wore his green sneakers.*

Peek, M. (1981). *Roll over! A counting song.*

Taback, S. (1997). *There was an old woman who swallowed a fly.*

Taback, S. (1999). *Joseph had a little overcoat.*

Westcott, N. B. (1996). *I've been working on the railroad.*

Westcott, N. B. (1988). *The lady with the alligator purse.*

Zelinsky, P. (1990). *The wheels on the bus.*

Nursery Rhymes

dePaola, T. (1985). *Tomie dePaola's Mother Goose.*

Gustafson, S. (2007). *Favorite nursery rhymes from Mother Goose.*

Lobel, A. (1997). *The Arnold Lobel book of Mother Goose: A treasury of more than 300 classic nursery rhymes.*

MacCuish, I. (2007). *100 best-loved nursery rhymes.*

Fingerplays, Chants, and Rhymes

Cole, J. (1989). *Anna Banana 101 jump rope rhymes.*

Cole, J. & Calmenson, S. (1990). *Miss Mary Mack and other children's street rhymes.*

Delmar, G. (1983). *Children's counting out rhymes, fingerplays, jump-rope and bounce-ball chants and other rhymes: A comprehensive English-language reference.*

Orozoco, J. (2002). *Diez deditos and other play rhymes and action songs from South America.*

---

support this recognition by pointing to words while reading them. Children pick up many words based on the context in which they occur—words such as *Rice Krispies* on a cereal box and *EXIT* on the sign in a public auditorium. Beginning around the age of 2 for some children (Strickland & Snow, 2002), they come to realize that print and symbols represent spoken words and convey meaning. Recognizing the meaning of signs and symbols gives young children a sense of pride and accomplishment. Importantly, these early experiences begin to build the child's identity as a reader.

Concept Books

Concept books help children learn about everyday concepts such as patterns, shapes, colors, numbers, letters, and days of the week. Concept books also help students develop domain-specific vocabulary, too. Some of our favorites include *Freight Train* (Crews, 1993), *Is It Larger? Is It Smaller?* (Hoban, 1985), and *Eating the Alphabet* (Ehlert, 1989). Concept books often expose children to broader topics—culture, food, homes, transportation, families, and so on. Three good examples are *Bread, Bread, Bread (Foods of the World)* (Morris, 1989), *Houses and Homes* (Morris, 1997), and *This Is the Way We Go to School: A Book about Children around the World* (Baer, 1990).

The Language of Your Instruction

Talking with Children about Print in Their Environment

As preschool and primary-grade teachers, you can help develop children's awareness of print by labeling things in the environment and drawing their attention to print. For example, you might label the classroom sink with the word *sink*. Next to the sink you'll create a sign that says *Wash your hands* and include a photograph of your students washing their hands. In small groups you will draw children's attention to the sign by asking, "What is this a picture of? Oh, yes, it's Destiny and Amir washing their hands. This sign says 'Wash your hands' [pointing to each word as you read it]. Now you read it." (You will point to each word while leading the recitation.)

"Nice! Remember to wash your hands [pointing to the words again] when you're at the sink."

Providing children in the emergent stage with picture and environmental cues provides a supportive context for their reading approximations. As you can imagine, reading "Wash your hands" or the word *sink* out of context would not be very likely for children during most of this stage, though a few children will begin to read these words "on sight" at the end of the stage. As children learn the names of letters and some sounds, you will begin to co-construct signs and labels with them, drawing their attention to the forms and functions of print.

Predictable Pattern Books

Brown Bear, Brown Bear, What Do You See? (Martin, 1992) is a concept book, but it's also a great example of a predictable pattern book. Predictable pattern books typically repeat lines of text, words, or questions. These types of books are lots of fun to read with young children and, because they're easily memorized, they can be especially helpful in teaching important early reading skills such as alliteration, rhyme awareness, letter recognition, and concept of word in text.

Predictable pattern books have an important place in the curriculum, but they don't typically provide the same rich language experience of narrative text or the interest of informational text, and they are sometimes overused in early childhood environments. As a literacy teacher, you'll always be thinking about the importance of varying children's exposure to a range of genres as well as the importance of matching text to your instructional goals.

Wordless Picture Books

Wordless picture books are a type of narrative text that tells a story through illustrations rather than words. Some of our favorites include *Pancakes for Breakfast* (dePaola, 1978), *The Snowman* (Briggs, 1978), and *Good Dog Carl* (Day, 1985). These three books are exemplars because they clearly tell a story, the illustrations are engaging, and most young children easily connect with the subject matter.

Wordless picture books help young children develop book-handling skills and their understanding of narrative text as they practice telling a story in sequential order. Telling stories from pictures alone requires a sophisticated level of inference; for this reason, reading wordless picture books supports children's development of comprehension strategies and thinking skills. When telling a story with a wordless picture book, be sure to look through all the pictures and think about how they go together or your story can sound more like a disjointed description of pictures.

Big Books

Big books are enlarged versions of children's books made specifically for the purpose of sharing with a group of children. Many concept books and predictable pattern books have been made into this enlarged format. Using enlarged text allows you to show children:

- How print works—how to begin reading at the top of the page, then read in a left-to-right motion, and return sweep to the bottom of the page;
- How books work—the title, the author/illustrator line, the title page, how to turn pages, and so on;
- The difference between letters and words.

Some big books are better for these purposes than others. When using big books with emergent and beginning readers, choose books that contain just a few lines of text per page and a lot of support from the illustrations. Books that include rhyme, rhythm, and repetition are especially engaging for young children.

Reading to Children: Developing Listening Comprehension and Vocabulary

As you learned in Chapter 3, *you* are the model for the importance of texts in your students' lives (Lane & Wright, 2007; Teale, 2003). *How* you read to children—your liveliness, the tone of your voice, and the gestures you use—are what they will internalize. If you are not comfortable reading aloud, it is time to begin to change that! Regardless of your comfort level, when you first begin reading aloud to children, you should choose books *you* enjoy, and you should practice reading them several times until your reading is fluent and expressive. The following "Children's Literature Connection: Resources for Selecting a Good Read-Aloud" provides some resources to help you get started choosing high-quality books to read aloud.

> Applicable to All Stages

There are many different reasons and ways to read aloud to children, and researchers have studied the practices of teachers and caregivers to identify some "best" practices. Using analytic talk (Dickinson & Smith, 1994; Dickinson & Tabors, 2001), as previously described in the section on narrative and informational text, is one method. Two other "best" practices are *dialogic read-alouds* (Whitehurst, Zevenbergen, Crone, Schultz, Velting, & Fischel, 1999) and *text talk* (Beck & McKeown, 2001). These interactive reading strategies have been found to increase children's listening comprehension, vocabulary knowledge, and overall reading achievement.

Dialogic Read-Alouds

Dialogic read-alouds were first developed as an intervention for children in Head Start preschools. The intent of the intervention was to improve teacher–child and parent–child interactions around text. The approach has three specific goals: (1) to engage children to be actively involved in the comprehension of text, (2) to provide feedback using sophisticated language, and (3) to scaffold children's knowledge and skills through conversation (Lane & Wright, 2007).

Questioning and feedback during dialogic read-alouds begins with basic knowledge questions and progresses to more sophisticated thinking and comprehension skills such as inferring.

Children's Literature Connection

Resources for Selecting a Good Read-Aloud

When selecting books to read aloud, look for texts that are well written, engaging for children, and allow for fluent, expressive reading. These texts should match your instructional goals—whether reading for enjoyment, concept or vocabulary development, and/or the development of comprehension skills. The following resources will help you get started finding the perfect read aloud for your goals.

Books

Allyn, P. (2009). *Stories to read with your child—And all the best times to read them.* Avery Trade.

Anderson, N. (2007). What *should I read aloud? A guide to the 200 best-selling picture books.* International Reading Association.

Fox, M. (2008). *Why reading aloud will change our children's lives forever* (2nd ed.). Mariner.

Lipson, E. R. (2000). *The New York Times parent's guide to the best books for children* (3rd ed.). Three Rivers Press.

Miller, D. (2009). *The book whisperer: Awakening the inner reader in every child.* Jossey-Bass.

Silvey, A. (Ed.). (2002). *The essential guide to children's books and their creators.* Houghton Mifflin Harcourt.

Silvey, A. (2005). *100 best books for children: A parent's guide for your young reader, toddler to preteen.* Mariner.

Trelease, J. (2013). *The new read aloud handbook* (7th ed.). Penguin.

Online Resources

American Library Association: www.ala.org/

Anita Silvey's Book a Day Almanac: http:// childrensbookalmanac.com/

Association for Library Service for Children Caldecott: www.ala.org/ala/mgrps/divs/alsc/awardsgrants/ bookmedia/caldecottmedal/caldecottmedal.cfm

The Center for the Book in the Library of Congress: www .read.gov/cfb/

The International Reading Association's Children's Choice Awards: www.reading.org/Resources/Booklists/ ChildrensChoices.aspx

Jim Trelease's home page: www.trelease-on-reading.com/

Mother Goose Programs: www .mothergooseprograms.org/

Applicable to All Stages

The following are examples of how these questions, comments, and feedback grow increasingly complex over time and repeated exposures to text:

- Begin with simple "what" questions and help children label what they see in the pictures: "What is a . . . ?" or "What's that [pointing to the picture]?" Provide immediate help and praise for children's responses.

- Ask "recall" types of questions; these will help children attend to specific supporting details. Begin with "fill-in-the-blank" statements ("Where did Alexander want to move?") and move to slightly more sophisticated recall questions ("How did Stellaluna get separated from her mother?").

- As children grow in their understandings about storybooks and comprehension strategies, you may provide less support, such as asking them to predict what they think may happen in the story, being sure to follow up on and discuss these predictions: "What do you think the owl babies will do next? Why?"

- Help children make text-to-self connections, but gently guide these discussions back to the text to avoid the run-on monologues many young children are prone to: "Were you once as scared of the dark as Little Bear is? How did you get over being afraid? What do you think Little Bear will do to overcome his fear of the dark?"

- Begin to "stretch" children's thinking with questions that help them draw inferences and understand important main ideas in the text: "Why do you think bullies like Recess Queen act the way they do?" When asking these "stretch" questions, always be prepared to provide support as necessary with specific, recall-type questions: "Do you remember what [the bully] said when . . . ?" and "How might that tell us why she behaves the way she does?" (Lane & Wright, 2007; Whitehurst et al., 1999).

- In storybooks, discuss and use the terms *characters* and *events:* "Which character do you like best? Why?" and "What were the events that led up to the big problem in this story? How was the problem resolved?"

Dialogic read-alouds can be used with any age group and virtually any genre, although narrative text is the most common. The key is to begin with high levels of support in your questions, prompts, and feedback, and then move to more sophisticated and abstract thinking and comprehension strategies—always monitoring students' responses to provide additional support as necessary. Researchers have found that dialogic read-alouds enhance expressive language and emergent literacy skills in as little as four weeks (Whitehurst, Arnold, Epstein, & Angel, 1984; Whitehurst et al., 1999)! The benefits of dialogic read-alouds can be exponentially stronger when implemented over the course of an entire school year.

> **Common Core Connection**
>
> Reading Standards for Literature: Key Ideas and Details; Range of Reading and Level of Text Complexity

Text Talk

Text talk (Beck & McKeown, 2001) is an approach to interactive read-alouds in which the teacher has two main goals: (1) to enhance children's comprehension during reading by asking open-ended questions and (2) to enhance vocabulary development.

> **Applicable to All Stages**

Before Reading

Before reading a text aloud to children, you'll spend some time intentionally previewing it to identify words that may be unfamiliar to children (see "Deciding Which Words to Teach," later in the chapter). In addition to selecting words to teach, you will also plan places to stop your reading so you can engage children in thinking while listening. Here, you can apply the knowledge you acquired from the previous examples of analytic talk in interactive read-alouds and dialogic read-alouds.

Kid-Friendly Definitions   Once you've made your decisions about which words to teach, plan "kid-friendly" definitions of these words (Beck & McKeown, 2001). A kid-friendly definition very simply explains the word's use in accessible language and with examples a child would understand. These definitions often start like this: "[Target word] is when someone . . . ; is when something . . . ; or is when you . . . ." For example, in the book *Make Way for Ducklings* (McCloskey, 1941), you might select the following target words: *enormous, delighted,* and *beckoned.* To make the meaning of these words accessible to children, your definitions might sound like this: "Enormous *is when something* is very, very big; delighted *is when someone* is very pleased or happy; beckoned *is when you* motion for someone to come closer."

During Reading

When reading the story, define each target word briefly within the context, as illustrated here:

> **Reading the Text:**   "'Good,' said Mr. Mallard, *delighted* that at last Mrs. Mallard had found a place that suited her."
>
> **Teacher:**   "Mr. Mallard was *delighted*—that means that he was very pleased and happy—that Mrs. Mallard found a place to live."

As you can see, this parenthetical definition was brief and did not disrupt the flow or comprehension of the story. (In fact, it probably improved the children's comprehension!)

After Reading

After reading the story, expand your vocabulary instruction to include a more elaborated exploration of the targeted words (Beck, McKeown, & Kucan, 2002):

1) *Contextualize* the word by showing where you found it in the story: "In the story *Make Way for Ducklings*, Mr. Mallard was *delighted* when Mrs. Mallard found a home that suited her." (Show the page and illustration.) "*Delighted* is our target word."

2) Ask the children to **repeat** the targeted word so they create a phonological representation of the word: "Say the word *delighted* with me: *delighted*."

3) Next, provide a brief **kid-friendly definition** and example: "*Delighted* means that Mr. Mallard was very pleased or happy. You might be delighted when you're going out to dinner at your favorite restaurant, or when you're doing something you like very much."

4) Elicit **student engagement** with the word: "Can you think of a time when you were *delighted*? You might start by saying, 'I was delighted when _____.' "

5) Wrap up the conversation by asking children to **restate** the target word: "What's the target word we've been talking about? Yes, *delighted* means you are very pleased or happy."

Since children need more than casual exposures to really know a word, it's important that you continue to talk about and provide "meaningful interactions" (Beck et al., 2002; Biemiller, 1999) with your target words in the days and weeks to come. Figure 6.4 provides three examples of ways you might extend this practice after each reading of the text. You will also want to provide

---

FIGURE 6.4 **Three Ways to Extend Your Interactions with Target Words**

Have You Ever?

Have You Ever? is an activity that requires children to think about contexts in which they can apply target words to their own or imagined experiences. Here are three examples of how you would apply this strategy using three target words: *beckoned, delighted,* and *enormous.* Notice how we extend children's explanatory thinking with the prompts *Why?* or *What?* We might also include *How?*

Describe a time you *beckoned* someone. Why did you beckon him or her?
Have you ever *delighted* someone? How? Have you ever been *delighted*?
Describe something *enormous*. What made it *enormous*?

Word Associations

Word associations help students associate new words with known words and phrases. Consider these associations for our target words:

Which word goes with *joy?* (delight) Why?
Which word goes with *a really, really big pile of leaves*? (enormous) Why?
Which word goes with a *gesture*? (beckon) Why?

Always remember to ask children to back up their thinking—for example, "I think *enormous* goes with the word *giant because* . . . ."

Idea Completions

Idea completions require students to use the meanings of the targeted words to complete the sentence; this allows the students to develop a deeper understanding of the target words and the varying contexts in which they may be used.

The teacher *beckoned* her students to . . .
The mom was *delighted* when . . .
The child's jacket was *enormous* because . . .

Beck and colleagues (2002) recommend that at the end of instruction on targeted words, you remind the children of the targeted words and find a way to relate them to one another. In the case of our targeted words, each of them can be expressed through gestures and/or facial expressions so we might demonstrate these as we summarize the meaning of our three target words. (See Beck and colleagues [2002, 2008] for additional ways to extend children's interactions with targeted vocabulary words.)

children with ongoing interactions with previously taught words to ensure they continue to be part of children's speaking and listening repertoire.

Deciding Which Words to Teach

Given what you already know about the correlation between vocabulary and phonological awareness, and between listening comprehension and later reading comprehension, you know the importance of teaching vocabulary directly to emergent learners. While there's no magical number of words per week to teach, the golden rule of vocabulary instruction is this: *"Teach early and teach often!"* (Beck et al., 2002). Here are some tips to get you started in selecting words to teach to emergent learners:

Common Core Connection

Language Standards: Vocabulary Acquisition and Use

1) Select words that have **high utility.** (See discussion about Tier 2 and General Academic Vocabulary words in Chapter 2.) These words can be used in conversation and will likely be encountered in future texts or settings. For a specific reading selection, they are words that children do not currently know but are likely to understand and use in conversation or benefit from knowing when reading or listening to other texts. Given the number of novel words in children's texts, it's likely that this list may be quite long. To narrow the focus, select from three to five words that have the greatest potential to positively affect the children's comprehension of the text *and* have the greatest utility in their spoken language. For example, in *Lilly's Purple Plastic Purse* (Henkes, 1996), the teacher, Mr. Slinger, tells the students to be *considerate. Considerate* is a good example of a word that could be integrated and practiced in daily conversation and it's likely to be found in other texts.

2) Choose words that are **semantically related.** These words can share similar meanings and can easily be connected to words children already know. For example, learning the word *content* is relatively easy because most children readily understand the word *happy.* Learning the word *meteorologist* is not such a leap when children know *weather reporter* or *forecaster.* Teaching words that are related in meaning helps children build networks of words and understand shades of meaning, too (for example, *cool, crisp, chilly, cold, frosty, freezing,* and *frigid*).

3) Teach words that can be **represented in some physical manner.** These words may be taught through acting out, by viewing photos or illustrations, or by hands-on exploration of objects. For example, if you read, "The bear *lumbered* across the meadow," *lumbered* can be acted out. In *Bear Snores On* (Wilson, 2002), Badger arrives in the bear's den with honey-nuts and says, "Let's *divvy* them up," —*divvy* could quite easily be demonstrated.

4) Group and teach words that are **conceptually related.** When reading Byron Barton's *Airport* (1987), for example, children will be enthused to identify and learn about airport-related words (for example, *gates, tickets, baggage, cargo, loaded, checked, passenger compartment, cockpit, runway, pilot,* and so on). Such fertile ground for vocabulary instruction! Conceptually related words will naturally come from your read-alouds and thematic instruction, too, but you'll have to make a conscious effort to intentionally teach these words and their relatedness—something that's easily overlooked.

5) Choose **sophisticated** and **novel words** that high-achieving children just a few years older than your students know and readily use. While teachers should use their judgment about selecting these words, lists such as the "Dale-Chall 3,000 Word List" and Biemiller's *Words Worth Teaching: Closing the Vocabulary Gap* (2010) are very useful resources.

Figure 6.5 summarizes the guidelines for selecting words to teach in the early stages of development.

FIGURE 6.5 Guidelines for Selecting Words to Teach in the Early Stages of Development

Choosing words for direct instruction requires careful planning and thought. Use these guidelines to help you make decisions about which words to teach in the emergent stage of development:

1) High Utility
2) Semantically Related
3) Concreteness—Physically Relatable
4) Conceptually Related
5) Sophisticated and Novel Words

Anchored Vocabulary Instruction

Common Core Connection

Language Standards: Vocabulary Acquisition and Use

Selecting words for instruction is just the start. Teaching the words is the next step. Many well-intentioned teachers think that it's sufficient to read aloud to children and just draw their attention to words and their meanings. It's true that contextualized word learning is important, but it's not sufficient (Beck et al., 2002; Silverman & DiBara-Crandell, 2010). Since most children retain only a fraction of the words they are taught—approximately 40 percent (Biemiller & Slonim, 2001)—it's critical that your vocabulary instruction be explicit and help children develop their understandings of a word's meaning(s), as well as its sounds and what it looks like in writing (Carpenter, 2010; Ehri, 2000; Nagy & Scott, 2000). When we address all of these features, we help "anchor" children's understanding of words and increase the likelihood that they will be remembered (Juel, Biancarosa, Coker, & Deffes, 2003).

Adaptable to the Beginning Stage

Anchored vocabulary instruction is a research-based approach that's proven to increase children's vocabulary knowledge; it also shows promise for developing children's alphabetic and orthographic knowledge (Juel et al., 2003). The protocol is similar to text talk, but it differs slightly in that it focuses not only on the meaning of a word but also on the relationship between the word's spoken form, or phonological representation, and its written form, or orthographic representation. By focusing on so many dimensions or features of words, you increase the likelihood of children effectively storing and retrieving words taught during explicit vocabulary instruction. See the feature box on the next page for an example of anchored vocabulary instruction.

Developing Conceptual Knowledge

Adaptable to All Stages

As you've seen in the context of your interactive read-alouds and thematic units, you will be targeting, defining, and using important concepts and the words that represent them. As previously discussed, learning individual words and the concepts they represent is critical. Equally important is exploring the relationships *among* concepts. Teachers help young children discover these relationships by inviting them to sort objects (for example, buttons, macaroni, keys) and pictures, letters, and eventually words, too.

To illustrate the power of developing conceptual knowledge, consider a concept sort that includes the following pictures: tree, ice cream, airplane, shoe, flower, tomato, apple, hat, banana, orange, toast, map, ring, bagel, beans, stone, pasta, rake, pin, lock, milk, cheese, book, car, and corn. How many ways could you sort these pictures? What does the way you sort these pictures say about their relationships? Consider these possibilities:

Strategies for the Classroom

Anchored Vocabulary Instruction

1) **Associate** the target word with a word the child used or knows: *scrumptious* with *yummy*.
2) Provide a **kid-friendly definition** of the word: "*Scrumptious* is when something tastes really, really yummy."
3) Show the word on an index card or chart paper and draw children's **attention to its orthographic and phonological features**: "This word says *scrumptious* [run your finger along the bottom of the word as you read]. It starts with the letter *s: sssss-scrumptious* [again, pointing to the *s*, ask the children to grab the sound by gesturing in the air and exaggerating the sound of *s*] and it ends in the letter *s*, too: *scrumptious-ssss* [repeat the grabbing of the sound]. Say the letters with me: *s-c-r-u-m-p-t-i-o-u-s* [pointing to each], *scrumptious. Scrumptious* means really, really yummy. Did

you notice that it's a rather long word? How many letters does it have? Let's count them!"
4) Be sure the children **repeat** the targeted word to develop a phonological representation of the word: "What's the word we're learning? Yes, *scrumptious.*"
5) Extend the child's understanding of the word by providing a **new synonym, example,** or **meaning of the word:** "*Scrumptious* is when something is really, really yummy or delicious."
6) As you **revisit** your target words, you'll want to find opportunities to extend children's interactions with words, as noted in Figure 6.5. Pairing semantic information with phonological and orthographic representations helps "anchor" your instruction and increase the likelihood of children remembering and using target words.

Things Found in Nature	Things Made by People

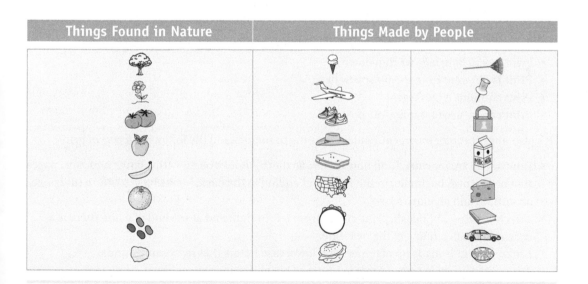

From this example, *Things Found in Nature* and *Things Made by People*, you could re-sort the pictures into two new categories: *Things We Eat* and *Things We Don't Eat.* As children re-sort their pictures, you'll facilitate their awareness that some things we eat are from nature (beans, apples, bananas), while others are made by people (bagel, ice cream, cheese) and not all things in nature are foods (trees, stones, flowers). That said, there may be some debate about these examples as some children will have eaten edible flowers and still others may have eaten bamboo shoots—a type of small and tender tree. You may even find some children debating whether stones can be eaten, particularly if they've read *Stone Soup* (McGovern, 1986)! This is the very kind of conversation we hope to inspire when sorting pictures, objects, and words.

After you've sorted your pictures into these two columns, you may continue to sort and re-sort. In our example, you might help the children sort the pictures of foods into new categories—perhaps *Foods I Like*, *Foods I Don't Like*, or *Fruits*, *Vegetables*, and *Dairy* products. Whichever categories you or the children choose, be sure there is lots of talk about their thinking—explaining why they're placing pictures in each column and how they're related to each other (or not) and the other columns.

Concept sorts help children develop their vocabulary knowledge, conceptual knowledge, thinking skills and language skills, as well as their ability to work well with others. They are especially well suited to children in the emergent stage because all children, including English learners, can participate in a whole-class picture or object sort. As sorts get more complex and include greater focus on letter, sound, or word knowledge, you'll need to differentiate your instruction to better meet the needs of a greater range of learners.

Developing Concepts about Print: Its Forms and Functions

As part of your ongoing interactive read-alouds in preschool, kindergarten, and first grade, you will begin to help children develop concepts about print. These concepts have to do with print's *forms* and *functions*—how print is structured and what it does (Clay, 2000, 2002; Ferreiro & Teberosky, 1981; Storch & Whitehurst, 2002). With your modeling and support children will come to understand the following *functions* of print:

- Print is oral language written down.
- Print is different from the illustrations.
- Print contains a message.
- Print can be used for many purposes.

It's also important for emergent readers to come to understand the following *forms* of print:

- How books are *organized* and how to *handle* them—Books begin with a cover and have pages that are turned, beginning in the front and ending in the back; books have a title, a title page, an author, and an illustrator.
- *Directionality*—In English, print moves from left to right and at the end of a line there is a return to the beginning of the next line.
- *Letters*—Print is made up of upper- and lowercase letters that represent sounds.
- A *concept of word in text*—Words are formed by letters and are separated by spaces.
- Words form *sentences*.
- *Punctuation*—Periods, capital letters at beginnings of sentences and proper nouns, question marks, quotation marks, exclamation marks, and bold print are types of punctuation.

Shared Reading

Adaptable to the
Beginning Stage

Shared reading is a form of interactive read-aloud carefully designed to support children's under-standing of print concepts. Based on the work of Holdaway (1979), shared reading is intended to simulate parent–child interactive reading, but with a larger group of children. Most preschool and primary-grade teachers include at least one, if not several, opportunities for shared reading each day.

One of the things that differentiates shared reading from other forms of interactive read-aloud is the text. Texts used for shared reading tend to be enlarged—big books, charts, or texts projected on Smart Boards or screens. Sometimes children hold their own copy of the text, too. The key points are (1) all children should be able to see the print without squinting or craning their necks, (2) the texts should be just slightly more difficult than what most children can read on their own, and (3) the texts are purposefully selected to advance children's learning of a specific goal or goals. In the case of emergent readers, we often select texts that are predictable. They might include rhyme, rhythm, or the repetition of a line of text, words, or a question, as in *The Very Hungry Caterpillar* (Carle, 1978), *I Went Walking* (Williams, 1989), and *Sheep in a Jeep* (Shaw, 1986). Other times, you may choose very simple repetitive texts like the "I can _____" or "I like _____" type of pattern books. In either case, you'll also want to select texts that have photos or illustrations that support the text and just one or a few lines of enlarged text per page.

Predictable pattern texts make good choices for emergent readers because they are usually easy for young children to memorize and they're fun to read, too! Nursery rhymes, poems, fingerplays, and songs can also great be choices for shared reading. When children can quickly internalize and even memorize the pattern of the text, we can begin to work on more cognitively demanding tasks such as identifying letters, sounds, words, or sentences.

When reading a piece of shared text the first time, think about what children will need to be successful understanding it—remember our *before, during* and *after* perspective. Like other read-alouds, you'll orient the children to the title and author, activate background knowledge, and set a purpose for reading. During and after the reading, you will support children's understanding of the text by briefly talking about the text and new vocabulary words and by engaging the children in making connections, predictions, and retelling the story or summarizing the main ideas at the end. Importantly, you will model fluent and expressive reading and invite the children to participate in reading the text as they begin to pick up the pattern.

On subsequent readings, you will continue to model expressive and engaged reading and begin to explicitly show children how the print works by using a pointer to draw their attention to the forms and functions of print. Over time, we move beyond these basic concepts about print and focus on more sophisticated tasks such as identifying beginning consonants, final consonants, word boundaries, upper- and lowercase letters, punctuation, and so on. Using colored highlighter tape, Wikki Stix, Post-its, and sliding frames can help draw children's attention to these important features.

Print Referencing

Print referencing (Justice & Piasta, 2011) is an approach to shared reading specifically designed to support children's understanding of print concepts. Similar to dialogic read-alouds, print referencing begins with high levels of teacher support and feedback. For example, in exploring the role of author and illustrator, a possible exchange is the following: "The title of the book we're going to read today is *The Recess Queen* [O'Neill, 2002]. Our author's name is Alexis O'Neill [pointing]. We call the person who writes a book the *author*. What does an author do? We call the person who draws the pictures the *illustrator*. What does an illustrator do?" When you're providing high-level support such as this, remember these guidelines:

> **Common Core Connection**
>
> Reading Standards:
> Foundational Skills –
> Print Concepts

1) Provide the child the answer before asking the child a question: "The main character of the story is *Chrysanthemum*. Who is the main character?"
2) After the child answers, be sure to repeat the correct answer, or offer a corrected response: "Right. Kevin Henkes *is* the author."

3) Provide children with explicit support and instruction to ensure high levels of success: "This word says *purse*. We know it says purse because it starts with a *'P' p-p-p-purse*—and there's a picture of an alligator *purse*! How do we know it says *purse*?"

4) Whenever possible, pair your instruction with some kind of interactive or physical support. For example, when reading a chart of *1, 2 Buckle My Shoe*, you might say: "This says, '1, 2, buckle my shoe.' *Buckle* has two syllables. Let's clap them: *buc-kle*. Put your finger on top of my pointing finger and we'll read it together: '1, 2, buckle my shoe.'"

> Adaptable to the Beginning Stage

Over time, you will systematically include instruction that will develop and support a broad range of children's concepts about print, including:

- Print is used to perform different *purposes*—"Let's read to find out how much flour we'll need to add" or, "Let's look to see how cold it is supposed to be today."
- *Directionality*—"Here is where the print begins on this page and where I will start reading. Next, I'll go to this line . . . . Where do you think I should go after that?"
- *Print-Related Language*—"This is a long word—it has eight letters. Let's name them."
- *Sound-Related Language*—"What is the first sound we hear in the word *dance*?"
- *Word Identification*—"Can you find the word *gerbil* in our title? Where else in our text can you find the word *gerbil*? How did you know what to look for?"

Gradually, you'll provide less support and prompt children to apply the knowledge they've developed over time. This is a critical step: the application of knowledge. While it's appropriate to support children when the task is too difficult, you're always intentionally releasing responsibility to the children so they can move your guided practice into independent application. As Justice and Piasta (2011) point out, frequent instruction in print referencing can positively affect children's concepts about print and later word recognition skills, spelling, and even comprehension.

Extensions to Shared Reading Experiences

After many repeated exposures to a text, we often provide children their own copy of the text in either a commercially published "little book" format, or by typing it on a single page to resemble the original text. (*Note:* Be sure to copy the text exactly, including special print and line breaks, or it becomes too confusing for emergent and even beginning readers.) To differentiate one typed poem, story, or chart from another, it's helpful to include a piece of clip art related to the content or theme of the text. Children also enjoy illustrating their personal copies of these familiar texts.

You'll support children's reading of these memorized texts by showing them how to **finger-point read,** or read with their index finger, just as you've modeled with your pointer and enlarged text. Even children who have not actually learned to read the words in the conventional sense can be encouraged to interact with the text by pointing to it while reciting it, and many will enjoy trying to find letters, words, and parts of words they know, too. Little texts provide an ideal opportunity to coach children to apply what you've demonstrated in your shared reading and engage them in one-to-one or small group conversation about the forms and functions of print. These little texts can be stored in children's **personal readers** (Bear, Casserta-Henry, & Venner, 2004) or *I Can Read* folders. These folders contain collections of texts, often memorized or familiar text, that children are encouraged to reread and interact with during free play, center time, and independent reading time.

Independent Reading Practice

In addition to daily read-alouds and shared reading, young children need opportunities to practice their own reading each day. When we talk to emergent readers about independent

Working and Collaborating

Reading with Your Child at Home

Researchers have found strong evidence that parent–child interactive read-aloud experiences can have a positive effect on children's early reading achievement. To help stimulate positive at-home reading experiences, consider sharing some of these tips with parents and caregivers:

1) **Read early and read often.** It's never too early to start reading to your child; and it's never too late to start. Reading for as little as 10 minutes a day can make a positive difference!

2) **Set up a predictable time of day for book sharing.** One of the biggest challenges for busy families is finding the time to start something new. To make sure that your routine sticks, choose a time of day to drop everything (including your electronics!) and read. Some families find first thing in the morning or just before bed the perfect time to cuddle up with a good book.

3) **Tap into your inner child.** Select books you remember loving as a child, or solicit suggestions from friends and family (or from librarians, booklists, or websites). Read with expression and a little drama—ham it up! The more you enjoy a book, the more enjoyable it will be for your child.

4) **Reread favorite books.** Repetition is a good thing for developing minds. When your child chimes, "Again! Again!" pay attention—you're doing something right! Rereading old favorites helps children develop their understanding of narrative text, main idea in informational text, and overall listening comprehension. Perhaps most importantly, it's joyful and helps instill a lifelong love of reading.

5) **Encourage your child's involvement in reading.** Draw your child's attention to the title and author, and discuss the illustrations or pictures on the cover. Ask, "What do you think this book will be about?" During reading, talk about the illustrations and the plot, and ask, "What do you think will happen next?" and

"Why?" After reading, talk about your child's favorite part or character. Allow children to interrupt your reading to talk about the text—this means that they're working to make sense of it, just be sure to bring their talk back to the text if it strays off topic.

6) **Start easy.** For emergent readers, consider concept books (books about numbers, letters, and objects) and books that have lots of rhyme, rhythm, and repetition of words, phrases, or questions. Eventually build up to longer picture books and later introduce simple chapter books. With longer texts, don't be afraid to paraphrase to make the text more manageable for the listener. When you come across tricky words, briefly define them with synonyms or examples your child can relate to. If your child just isn't interested in a particular book, it's okay to stop reading it and find a more engaging text.

7) **Make books come alive!** Connect your child's life experiences to the books you read. Going to the pumpkin patch this fall? Read *Apples and Pumpkins* (Rockwell, 1989). Snow in the forecast? Check out *The Story of Snow: The Science of Winter's Wonder* (Cassino, 2009) or *The Snowy Day* (Keats, 2011). Making blueberry muffins with Grandma? Try *Blueberries for Sal* (McCloskey, 1948). Connecting reading with life experiences stimulates motivation to read!

8) **Be patient.** Not everyone is a natural reader (or listener). Give yourself time to get comfortable with reading aloud. Also be patient with your child; some children have difficulty sitting still or focusing on books. Set small goals—maybe listening for 5 minutes at a time, growing to 10, 15, 20, or 30 minutes a day. If listening to a whole story is too much for one sitting, then talk about the pictures, or try shorter texts like poetry, magazine articles, or informational text. Some children will also benefit from drawing, coloring, doodling, rocking in a chair, or holding a favorite toy or object while listening.

reading, we explain and model that there are many different ways to read books: They can "read" the pictures, "read" from their memory, and read the words, particularly in texts that have been well practiced. We encourage young children to reread "old favorites" (Sulzby, 1985)—familiar books that have been read to them many, many times before and other well-practiced texts from their personal readers. We also show them how to "read the room," which means reading

Adaptable to the Beginning Stage

environmental print and familiar songs, poems, charts, big books, the morning message, the daily schedule, the attendance chart, the alphabet, and any other print in the environment.

Independent reading is rarely independent at the emergent stage; it's actually quite interactive and social. You will facilitate this by assigning reading partners—children of similar abilities who can be coached to support one another's interactions with print. When independent reading is going well at this stage there's a productive "buzz" in the room as children are collaborating and interacting with text.

Learning the Alphabet and the Role of Letters

Letters are the building blocks of print and they help define what words are. When young children learn to identify letters, they are able to focus more clearly on the features of printed words so that they'll be better able to remember those individual words over time. Learning about letters and letter names helps to develop **phonemic awareness** because letters *visually* represent sound. Alphabet knowledge and phonemic awareness are the strongest predictors of *early* reading success (Adams, 1990; Snow, Burns, & Griffin, 1998) and so they're vitally important! Letter-naming fluency is an especially strong predictor of first-grade reading (Stage, Sheppard, Davidson, & Browning, 2001).

Beginning in preschool and on Day 1 of kindergarten, you will teach and explore the alphabet with children, focusing on a new letter each day. On average, most kindergartners are able to recognize and name 12 to 18 lowercase letters at the beginning of the year (Invernizzi, Juel, Swank, & Meier, 2006). Because we know, however, that there will be variability with regard to children's depth and breadth of print concepts, we begin with the whole class and then quickly learn which children know which letters and differentiate our instruction as we move along.

Common Core Connection

Reading Standards: Foundational Skills – Print Concepts

Letters are of course everywhere, and they behave in interesting ways. Their *orientation* is so very important—unlike just about everything else in a child's world. For instance, a tricycle, however one looks at it, will always be a tricycle. Not so with letters—which side of the vertical line the circle is on, and whether it is at the bottom or top, makes a huge difference *(b d p q)*. We will engage children in exploring the names of letters and their shapes—both upper- and lowercase forms—and in writing them, too (Schlagal, 2007).

We begin with teaching the alphabet song on the first day (to the tune of "Twinkle, Twinkle Little Star"), pointing to the letters. Children will eventually learn it by heart—and also come to learn that "ellemenopee" is not one letter! Have an alphabet strip in each child's place—desk, rug, table, wherever. As you focus on a particular letter, model how to write both the upper- and lowercase forms of the letter, and use the terms *uppercase, capital,* and *lowercase,* as opposed to *big* and *little,* as this distinction isn't clear. Show models with numbered arrows that direct children to see how to form these letters early on, and be sure you're modeling the correct way to make each letter (Graham, Harris, & Fink, 2000).

The *function* of letters should also be highlighted from the first day: Use children's names to talk about the letters and their names (Krech, 2000; Cunningham, 2005): "*L* is Lily's letter, *T* is Tonisha's and Terence's letter." Perhaps you can have a "Name of the Day" activity; in fact, this approach allows you to expose children to more letters than is possible in the traditional "Letter of the Day" activity (Bear, Invernizzi, Johnston, & Templeton, 2010). For each child, prepare a card in which her or his name is written beginning with a capital letter and the remaining letters in lowercase. Use a large gift bag in which all the children's names are deposited. Each day, draw a new name and place it in a pocket chart. Over time, the names will be arranged alphabetically. Names may be compared to one another; for example:

"Both *Sam* and *Sasha* begin with the letter *S*."

"*Marika* and *Fabiola* end with the letter *A*."

"*Damon* and *Chris* both have five letters in their names."

"*Mary* has four letters in her name. What other children have four letters in their name?"

Short sentences may be constructed using **alliteration**—the same beginning sound repeated—to reinforce letter names and sounds. For example, *Sam* and *Sasha see* the *sand*. This will also support your beginning consonant instruction, as discussed later in the chapter.

When it comes to learning the letters of the alphabet, it's important to realize that young children have a lot of information to work out (Ehri & Roberts, 2006; Justice, Pence, Bowles, & Wiggins, 2006). Here are just a few of the details:

- There are upper- and lowercase forms for each letter (*Aa, Bb, Cc, Dd,* and so on). Letters whose uppercase forms match their lowercase forms are easier to learn (letters such as *Cc, Oo,* and *Ss*).
- Most letter names provide clues to the sounds they represent *(B = bee, D = dee, K = kay, Z = zee)* and the names of vowels *A, E, I, O, U* are their long sounds). These letter sounds are easier for children to learn than letter names that start with vowel sounds *(F = ef, M = em, N= en)* or letter names that do not have beginning sound association *(H = aich, W= doubleyoo, Y = wie)*.
- Letters share similar shapes (vertical and horizontal lines, diagonal lines, up-down motions, circular shapes, and a mix of circular and vertical lines). These shapes affect how they're written. And letters with similar shapes (such as *M, N, W, Z*) are easily confused, as are letters that are commonly represented in fonts that do not match their handwritten forms (for example, lowercase *g* and *a*).
- Letters with similar sounds (for instance, voiced and unvoiced pairs) and those with similar points of articulation are also easily confused. (See discussion about beginning consonants later in this chapter.)

Recognizing the complexity of acquiring alphabet knowledge will help you plan well-sequenced, clear, and supportive learning experiences for young children and English learners. (See *Words Their Way for PreK–K* by Johnston, Invernizzi, Bear, Helman, and Templeton [in press] and *Words Their Way Letter and Picture Sorts for the Emergent Stage* by Bear and colleagues (2010) for additional suggestions and activities.)

Reading and Writing in Digital Contexts

Resources for Evaluating Learning Applications

A number of applications, or apps as they are more commonly called, are available that support learning the alphabet, letter names, and tracing and writing the letters. Others present simple texts and songs, such as "Wheels on the Bus," that are quite engaging and very interactive. As the availability of apps grows exponentially, it is important to evaluate them and to provide information for parents to do so, too. Two informative websites are:

- **Parents' Choice:** This is the nation's oldest guide to high-quality children's toys and media. The website

provides up-to-date information and reviews on children's books, software, apps, educational games, video games, websites, and toys. www.parents-choice.org

- **Common Sense Media:** This independent nonprofit advocacy group specializes in evaluating children's media. The website provides reliable tools for evaluating the quality of online media for children. www.commonsensemedia.org

Alphabet Books

A large number of alphabet books are available, and more are being published all the time. They are not all created equal, however, and you will want to have on hand those that include both upper- and lowercase forms as well as pictures that clearly represent the sound each letter stands for. That said, don't be afraid to share great alphabet books that are not perfect; a book that has rich vocabulary and engaging photos or illustrations may be worth reading even if the author uses an occasional word such as *chimney* or *cereal* to represent the sound of *C*. While it is preferable to find texts that clearly represent the most common letter–sound correspondences, when you come across a picture or word that is not an exemplar in that way, explain that some letters represent more than one sound. Focus most of your attention on pictures and words that most clearly represent the letter–sound correspondence you're teaching. When your emergent readers become beginning readers and even transitional readers, they'll enjoy going back through these alphabet books and hunting for the different sounds letters represent.

As you read an alphabet book, show the children how to use such books. Point to and name each letter: "Here is an uppercase *M* and a lowercase *M*." Point to the illustration(s) or note that "*M* is for *moon, moon* begins with *M; man* starts with *M*." This type of "mentioning" of how these letters occur at the beginning of these words prepares children for the more explicit examination of beginning consonant sounds. Interestingly, it has been shown (Justice & Piasta, 2011; Smolkin, Yaden, Brown, & Hofius, 1992) that reading alphabet books to children affords more print-specific discussion than does storybook reading!

Handwriting Instruction

As part of your alphabet instruction, you will model how to *write* both upper- and lowercase letters. When teaching letter formation, begin with gross-motor activities such as having the children form the letters with their bodies or write them in the air with large sweeping motions. Then move to activities on a smaller scale, perhaps painting the letters with a big brush and paint on an easel pad, or writing them on a large chalkboard or the side of a building with a wet brush or sponge. It's also good to engage fine-motor skills and encourage letter formation using clay or Wikki Stix and writing in rice, sand, or shaving cream.

Most children will naturally be drawn to write on paper. We offer young children a range of writing utensils and types of paper to nurture their interest in written expression: chubby crayons and markers, pencils and pens, and paper cut in different shapes (narrow paper for lists, folded paper for cards, pre-sized paper for assembling books, lined and unlined paper, paper with boxes for illustrations, and so on). Writing is a particularly effective way for children to practice alphabetic principle because it slows down the processing of letters and sounds (Clay, 2002).

When modeling how to form letters, we use consistent language (for example, "straight line down" and "around and back down") and show models of the letters with numbered arrows that direct children to see how to form these letters correctly. Children's later writing fluency will be dependent on their understanding of letter–sound correspondence and their automatic formation of letters (Graham, Harris, & Fink, 2000).

Beginning Consonant Sounds and Letters

In addition to teaching the names and forms of letters, we also begin teaching children the sounds that letters represent. We begin by focusing on the initial consonants in words and we do this systematically, beginning with letters that represent **continuant sounds** such as *M* and *S*. Continuant sounds can be isolated and elongated without distorting the sound the letter represents (for example, *mmmman* and *ssssit*). We contrast letters with continuant sounds with

FIGURE 6.6 Pronunciation Guide for Consonant Sounds

Unvoiced	Voiced	Nasals	Other	Place of Articulation
p	b	m		lips together
wh	w			lips rounded
f	v			teeth and lips
th (the)	th (thin)			tip of tongue and teeth
t	d	n	l	tip of tongue and roof of mouth
s	z		r	tongue and roof of mouth
sh			y	sides of tongue and teeth
ch	j			sides of tongue and roof of mouth
k	g	ng		back of tongue and throat
h				no articulation—breathy sound

Source: Bear et al., 2012, p 112.

letters that represent **stop sounds**, or sounds made with a burst of air that cannot be continued without adding the **schwa** sound (for example, /b/ and /k/ rather than an exaggerated "buh" or "kuh"). Stop sounds can't be elongated, but they can be bounced (/k/-/k/-/k/) and this sometimes helps children isolate the sound and associate it with the letter.

Applicable to the Beginning Stage

When teaching initial consonants, we are careful to contrast sounds that not only sound different (/m/ and /s/) but that also feel different when they're articulated: /b/ and /r/. The sound of B, /b/-bat, is made with your lips together, whereas the sound of R, /r/-rug, is made with your tongue close to the roof of your mouth. Because these sounds are articulated so differently, they make good contrasts. The letters F and V, however, would *not* make good contrasts when children are first learning about letter sounds because they are articulated in such a similar manner: Make the sound of F (/f/) and now V (/v/). Did you notice how these letters are formed with your teeth on your lips? Now make the sound again and put your fingers on your larynx. What do you notice? The sound for V caused your vocal cords to vibrate, didn't it? But they didn't vibrate when you made the sound for the letter F. We call these sounds **voiced** (as in /v/) and **unvoiced** (as in /f/) pairs and they can be quite confusing for emergent and beginning readers. Figure 6.6 shows how to pronounce each of the consonant sounds of English.

EL Connection

Understanding how letter sounds are articulated can help you understand children's early spellings of words like VN for *fun* or BT for *bed*. It can also help you make choices about the sequence of your letter–sound instruction. While there's no perfect order, research suggests that the following sequence is effective:

m, s, b, r
t, g, n, p
c, h, f, d
l, k, j, w
v, y, z

Beginning Sound Sorts

When teaching letters and beginning sounds, we begin with a short piece of text in either shared reading or small-group instruction. We purposely select this text to ensure that it highlights the most salient sound of the letters we're working with. For the letters *M* and *S*, we might select a familiar rhyme, perhaps *Sam, Sam the Baker Man,* or a longer text such as *No More Monkeys Jumping on the Bed.* When first reading the text, we help children comprehend and enjoy it. On subsequent readings, and as children have come to memorize the text, we shift our focus to print-referencing skills and, more specifically, to interactions with letters and sounds: "This word is *Sam* and it starts with a capital *S* because it's a person's name. Let's highlight that letter so we don't forget it. What's the letter we're studying? Yes. It's *S* like the name *SSSSam.* Get your mouth ready to say the word *Sam, SSSSam.* When you make the sound for *S* /ssss/ did you notice how your tongue reaches toward the top of your mouth? Try it again: /ssss/—*Sam.* Let's see if we can find another word that starts with the letter *S.*" You will repeat this kind of dialogue for both letters, reinforcing the big idea: "The letter we're learning about today is *S,* like in the word *Sam. S* goes with the sound /ssss/." Always remember to reread your selection in its entirety (or a portion if it's very long) before closing the lesson.

Immediately following your shared reading, or sometime later during word study, you will provide students with a picture sort that reinforces your introduction to the initial consonants you're studying. In our current example, we might have pictures of a man, mop, match, mitten, moon, monkey and sack, soap, sun, sock, soup, sink. We begin by showing the children a card with a capital and lowercase *Ss* and another with a capital and lowercase *Mm* and reinforce the sounds they represent by making connections to the children's prior experiences with the letters and sounds. Next, we engage children in a teacher-directed sort. (See Chapter 3 for more on teacher-directed sorts.)

With initial sound sorts, be careful to emphasize both the letter name and the sound it represents: "This is a picture of a match—*mmmatch. Match* begins with the letter *M. Match* goes with the word *man.* They both begin with the letter *M*—*mmmmatch* and *mmmman.*" After sorting, encourage the children to read down their columns to check their work. Inevitably, some children will have difficulty sorting the pictures and/or self-correcting, and when they do, make note of it and gently help them along: "Hmmm . . . , I think there's a picture that tricked you in this column. Can you find it and fix it up?" or "Check these two pictures: *ssssoap* and *mmmmoon.* One of them doesn't belong. Which one do you think it is? . . . What makes you say that? . . . Okay, try it again. . . . Were you right?" Close your sorting activity by eliciting or providing a statement that reinforces the big idea of your sort.

Extensions

Throughout the day and week, you'll continue to engage children in interactions with text and letters and sounds. Depending on the children in your group, they may like to draw and label pictures of *M* and *S* words in their own ABC book. Others will prefer to cut pictures out of a magazine and then label them. Encourage children to find examples of the letters and sounds they're learning, particularly in the beginning position in words.

Learning about Units of Print and Units of Language

It is critical that young children explicitly understand the alphabetic principle—the understanding that letters represent sounds that are arranged left-to-right within a word. Your teaching of the alphabet and the names of the letters facilitates this understanding, but it is equally

Accommodating English Learners

Predictable Consonant Confusions for English Learners

B	The voiced *B* may should more like the unvoiced *P*.	C	Hard *C* is often confused with hard *G*. Many languages do not have a hard *C*.
D	Often sounds like the /th/ in Spanish (*dog as thog*)	F	Easily confused with *V*, especially in Arabic. In Japanese, it may be pronounced like /h/.
G	Hard *G* may be confused with *K* by speakers of Arabic, French, or Swahili.	H	Silent in Spanish. In Chinese it sounds more like /kh/ as in *loch*.
J	In Spanish represents the /h/ sound; *J* may also be pronounced like /ch/.	K	May be confused with /g/ by Spanish speakers, such as *gangaroo* for *kangaroo*.
L	May be confused with *R*; final *L* may be difficult.	M	May be dropped at the end of words.
N	Speakers of Chinese may not pronounce this sound and confuse it with *L*. It may be dropped at the end of words.	P	Easily confused with *B* because they are both formed with the lips and only differ in the vocal cords.
R	Rolled in Spanish; confused with *L* in Asian languages.	S	Difficult to perceive in final position.
T	May be substituted with /d/ by Spanish speakers and not pronounced at the ends of words.	V	May be confused with *B* in Spanish and Korean. It does not exist in many languages and may be substituted with /f/.
W	Spanish speakers may pronounce this with more of a /gw/ sound, saying *gwen* for *when*.	Y	This sound may be more like /ch/ in Spanish, as in *chew* for *you*.
Z	May be pronounced like the /s/ sound in Spanish and not voiced.		

Source: Bear et al., 2010, p. 111.

important that you guide children's awareness and understanding of *how* that relationship between letters and spoken language "works." Connecting phonological and phonemic awareness activities to your word study and shared reading and shared writing activities will help children develop this understanding, as well as advance their development of early reading and writing skills.

> EL Connection and Applicable to All Stages

Phonological Sensitivity and Awareness of Words

Phonological awareness, or sensitivity to the sound structure of English, begins with children's exposure to oral language. Since fluent speakers do not speak in a word-by-word fashion, it's actually quite difficult for children to segment spoken words from running speech. To simulate what it's like for children to identify words from speech, imagine this: You're at a busy restaurant and the couple sitting next to you is speaking in a language that's foreign to you. You may be able to identify the language based on its prosodic features (that is, its rate, rhythm, pitch, and intonation), but unless you have some more specific knowledge of the language, each word will run into one another, making it very hard for you to determine where one word begins

Common Core Connection:

Reading Standards:
Foundational Skills –
Phonological
Awareness

or ends. In English, when we say, "Let's go to the park," it actually sounds like "Letsgotothepark." As children develop semantic representations for words in the first year of life and as toddlers, they begin to segment some words from speech, but not all words. They first notice words that are frequently repeated in their environment (for example, *dog, car, bye-bye*) and they remember the high-frequency words that are personally relevant to them (such as *bottle, blankie, mommy, daddy*), but they don't yet have a conscious awareness of words themselves. This comes in preschool and the primary grades as children begin to learn about texts, letters, and sounds. Through these experiences, children come to notice the spaces between written words—but this doesn't just happen; rather, it requires instruction and practice. By the end of the emergent stage, children will have developed at least a rudimentary understanding of what's known as concept of word in text.

Awareness of Syllables

On a tacit or subconscious level, it's theorized that the brain identifies and stores words based on their phonological features beginning with **syllables** (for example, *cupcake* is stored as *cup-cake; lady* as *la-dy*) (Goswami, 2001; Metsala, 2011). With support, young children are capable of becoming aware of spoken syllables within words. We talk in terms of "Let's listen to hear how many parts our names have. Deshawn [clap while saying 'De-Shawn']. How many times did I clap? How many parts does Deshawn's name have? How about Allie . . . Connor . . . Lytania . . . Zack? We call those parts syllables. How many syllables do we hear in Amir? Salvadore? Anahita?"

Rhyming

It's hypothesized that words that share similar sounds form "neighborhoods" in the brain and they are stored and retrieved more readily (Goswami, 2001; Metsala, 2011). This lexical reorganizing coincides with preschoolers' engagement with language play, alphabet instruction, instruction in initial consonant sounds, and their conscious awareness and interest in rhyming words. We capitalize on this interest by playing rhyming games with children's names—"Letisha Bonisha," "Tiffany Miffany" (McGee & Richgels, 1990)—and by sharing nursery rhymes, jingles, and chants. We also draw their attention to rhyme in our shared reading experiences and by introducing rhyming sorts during word study. Reading and interacting with texts that rhyme, including nursery rhymes, and engaging children in rhyming picture sorts will be helpful in developing an explicit understanding of "rhyme."

Awareness of Onset-Rime

As preschoolers acquire more and more words in their receptive and expressive vocabularies, their brains are under increased "developmental pressure" to quickly recognize and store these words. Consequently, the brain becomes increasingly sensitive to smaller speech units: onsets and rimes (Goswami, 2001; Metsala, 2011). In addition, our instruction in rhyming is happening simultaneously with our instruction in letter names and initial consonant sounds, laying the groundwork for children's explicit awareness of onsets and rimes.

Learning about beginning consonants provides a gateway for breaking syllables into onsets and rimes. As we saw in Chapter 2, an onset is the initial consonant letter sound or consonant cluster in a syllable (*b-, dr-, s-*) and the rime is the vowel sound and letter sounds that follow it in a single syllable word (or single syllable). For some children, identifying the onset—the initial consonant sound—may be easier than supplying the rime, particularly in the case of

Strategies for the Classroom

Shared Reading, Print Referencing, and Rhyme

As children experience success with rhyming activities, such as identifying rhymes in familiar texts, they'll begin to spontaneously offer words that rhyme. You can stimulate children's interest in the sounds of language by reading predictable texts that include rhyme, rhythm, and repetition—for example, *Sheep in a Jeep* (Shaw, 1986), *Silly Sally Went to Town* (Wood, 1994), *I Can't Said the Ant* (Cameron, 2003), and *Oh, a-Hunting We Will Go* (Langstaff, Parker, & Parker, 1991; Kellogg, 1998). From these shared reading experiences, you'll extend children's practice with print concepts and phonological awareness, too. One way to do this is by copying a favorite part or a refrain onto sentence strips or chart paper like this one:

> **Down by the Bay**
>
> Down by the bay
> Where the watermelons grow
> Back to my home
> I did not go
> For if I do
> My mother would say
> "Did you ever see a _____

Kissing a _____?"
Down by the bay.

Given the rhythmic and repetitive nature of this text and others like it, children will readily memorize it and when they do, you'll encourage them to generate their own creative rhymes or use pictures from their rhyming picture sorts to rewrite these favorite songs and texts: "Have you ever seen a *moose* kissing a *juice*? Down by the bay." They'll find this immensely fun! Children's awareness of rhyme and their later awareness of onset-rime will help them begin to think about individual letter sounds, too—an important precursor to conventional reading.

Your phonological awareness activities will be well planned and follow a developmental sequence from larger sound units (words and syllables) to smaller sound units (phonemes). However, you'll also capitalize on children's intrinsic motivation to play with language and sounds throughout your whole day—in your literacy block, during transitions, and well beyond. Language play and oral language exposure are two critical contributors to early reading success.

---

low-frequency rimes (for example, *-ud* or *-id* versus higher-frequency rimes like *-at* or *-it*). Once children experience some success with syllable awareness, we draw their attention to onsets and rimes in single-syllable words: "In the word *bed,* the first sound is *b-* and the last part is *-ed, b-ed, bed.*" We make these observations in our shared text and then manipulate these sounds using letter tiles or letter cards in pocket charts. These manipulations strengthen children's understanding of onsets, or initial consonant sounds, and rimes, or the vowel and what follows.

> Adaptable to the
> Beginning Stage

The terms *rime* and *rhyme* can be confusing for us (not to mention the children!). This is why we avoid using the terms "onsets" and "rimes" with children. But because these terms have emerged prominently in literacy instruction over the last ten years, it's important for *teachers* to know them. The following explanation may help you understand the distinction between the concepts underlying *rime* and *rhyme*: The term *rime* applies to a unit within *single* words—for example, *–it* in the word *sit*. The term *rhyme* applies to *two or more words*—if words contain the same rime units they are said to rhyme—for example, *sit, bit, hit*.

Awareness of Phonemes

As you learned in Chapter 2, a phoneme is the smallest unit of sound in a language, and in English there are approximately 44 of them. Children become increasingly aware of phonemes in words as they learn about beginning consonants in words. *Phonemic awareness* refers to children's ability to hear, identify, and manipulate these sounds. In its purest sense, phonemic awareness is strictly an oral activity, but researchers have found that phonemic awareness training is optimized when it's combined with letters (NICHD, 2000).

FIGURE 6.7 Scope and Sequence for Phonemic Awareness Training in the Primary Grades

Phoneme Isolation:	Recognizing individual sounds in words (beginning with initial consonants, then final consonants, and ending with medial vowels): **Teacher:** What's the first sound in *top*? **Child:** /t/
Phoneme Identification:	Recognizing the same sound in different words: **Teacher:** Which sound is the same in the words *boy, bus,* and *bake*? **Child:** /b/
Phoneme Categorization:	Recognizing the word that doesn't belong in a group of 3 or 4 words: **Teacher:** Which word doesn't belong: *toe, take, tub,* or *ring*? **Child:** *ring*
Phoneme Blending:	Children listen to a sequence of spoken phonemes and blend them into a single word: **Teacher:** What word is /b//a//t/? **Child:** /b//a//t/ is bat. **Teacher:** Let's write the sounds of *bag:* /b/, write b; /a/, write a; /g/, write g. Let's read the word: *bag.*
Phoneme Segmentation:	Segmenting or breaking a word into its individual sounds (often by pushing sounds using sound chips or pennies): **Teacher:** How many sounds in the word *thin*? **Child:** /th//i//n/ Thin has three sounds. Let's write the word *thin:* /th/, write th; /i/, write i; /n/, write n. Let's read the word: *thin.*
Phoneme Deletion:	Recognizing the part of the word that's left when you remove a phoneme: **Teacher:** What's *truck* without the /t/ ? **Child:** *ruck*
Phoneme Addition:	Making a new word by adding a phoneme to an existing word: **Teacher:** What do you have when you add /s/to the beginning of *mile*? **Child:** *smile*
Phoneme Substitution:	Substituting one phoneme for another to make a new word: **Teacher:** The word is *fun.* Change the /f/ to /b/. What's the new word? **Child:** *bun*

Source: Adapted from Armbruster, Lehr, and Osburn, 2006.

Applicable to
Beginning Stage

Phonemic awareness is most effective when it focuses on only one or two types of phoneme manipulation at a time (NICHD, 2000), and segmenting and blending tasks provide the most immediate application to reading and spelling words. Phonemic awareness, like phonological awareness, is a means to an end: the automatic recognition and production of words in reading and writing. When children read words accurately and effortlessly, their cognitive resources are freed up to focus on meaning making—the goal of literacy instruction. Figure 6.7 highlights a typical scope and sequence for phonemic awareness.

Throughout the emergent stage, children will begin to more consciously notice how the beginning sound of *bat, /b/* and *mat, /m/* are different and the words themselves have different meanings. This more conscious awareness is often the result of children's increased knowledge of letter names (Treiman, Tincoff, Rodriguez, Mousake, & Francis, 1998). Throughout the emergent stage, children are learning how to map speech sounds to print. This mapping of phonemes to graphemes, or sounds to letters, is called *alphabetic principle* and it is the very beginning of phonics instruction.

Phonics

Awareness of initial consonant sounds and rimes helps children as they begin to read and write phonologically similar words. For example, if a child knows how to write or read the word *sit*, then reading or writing the words *pit, fit, lit,* and *kit* will not be such a stretch *if* they are phonemically aware (that is, they are sensitive to the similarities and differences in the sounds of these words) and have a good understanding of initial consonants and onset-rime. Beginning readers will move beyond their recognition of initial consonants and rimes and come to identify and segment each individual sound, or phoneme, in a word beginning with initial consonants, then final consonants, before attending to medial vowels. When children can fully segment and blend a one-syllable word (/k/ - /i/ - /t/), they can begin to make even more new words by substituting a single phoneme in the initial, final, or medial positions (for example, *kit, sit, sip, sap, soup,* and so forth). Segmenting and blending of phonemes, or sounds, can be done as an oral activity, but it should always be brought back to contextualized reading and writing experiences. When we move from oral practice to print, we shift from phonological awareness and phonemic awareness to phonics.

Common Core Connection

Reading Standards:
Foundational Skills –
Phonics and Word
Recognition

Phonological Awareness and Language: A Strong Foundation

It's important to remember that there is a reciprocal relationship between vocabulary development and phonological awareness. In other words, the more words children know, the greater their sensitivity to the sounds of language and vice versa (Lawrence & Snow, 2011; Roth, Speece, & Cooper, 2002). Vocabulary development in the early years and with English learners begins with oral language exposure and practice. Enriching the verbal environment and explicitly teaching vocabulary are two important ways you can improve children's phonological sensitivity. You will also heighten children's awareness of the sound structure of English through

- shared reading and shared writing
- language play
- teaching the alphabet and beginning consonant sounds
- sorting letters and sounds, and later on, sorting words

Phonological and phonemic awareness are predictors of early reading success, particularly phonemic awareness. Children who experience challenges with early reading often have difficulty analyzing the sounds of language; it may appear that they cannot "hear" onsets and rimes and phonemes in the same way children without disabilities can (Scarborough, 2002; Stanovich & Siegel, 1994). Moreover, children who have difficulty with phonological awareness may also have difficulty recognizing, storing, and retrieving words that are typically acquired from conversation. Not surprisingly, this puts them at increased risk for reading difficulties. In Chapter 11, we will address the special needs of these students. In the meantime, it's important to remember that phonological and phonemic awareness are important, but they are a means to

FIGURE 6.8 The Relationship Between Print and Spoken Language

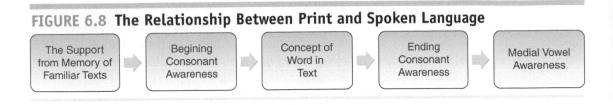

an end. Researchers suggest that typically-developing children need roughly 20 hours of training in phonological and phonemic awareness in the early years (NICHD, 2000). This means that 5 to 7 minutes of language play per day is usually sufficient in preK through grade 1. This exploration is *in addition* to your shared reading and shared writing instruction and other instruction with sound/symbol correspondences.

Concept of Word

Common Core Connection

Reading Standards: Foundational Skills – Print Concepts

As proficient readers we take many things for granted. The concepts of letters, sounds, and words are among them. While emergent readers have heard the term *word* a great deal, it's not until they begin to learn about initial consonants that words begin to "stand still" for them (Flanigan, 2007; Morris, Bloodgood, Lomax, & Perney, 2003; Smith, 2012). Before this, looking at print was about as clear as listening to a stream of speech—all the black marks on the page sort of blended together much like the utterance, "Letsgotothepark." Figure 6.8 illustrates the general scope and sequence of children's understanding of the relationship between print and units of language.

At the beginning of the emergent stage, children read words in their environment much like they would logos or signs: They use context and the overall shape of the word to help them recognize it. As they acquire alphabet knowledge and awareness of beginning consonant sounds in words, they begin to note the spaces in familiar text, and this is strengthened as they learn about final consonant sounds. This awareness of word is also heightened by your pointing to and referencing text during shared reading.

Like most skills, concept of word in text follows a developmental progression beginning with children gesturing to print to suggest that they understand it has something to do with the story. They might touch the print rhythmically as they've observed their teachers and caregivers do. In the middle of the emergent stage, children begin to point to text in a more precise manner, often touching the page once for every syllable rather than each word. For example, in the rhyme "1, 2, Buckle My Shoe," a child might point like this: 1 / 2 / buc / kle / my / shoe. When the child says the second syllable of *buckle,* she would be touching the word *my.* Toward the end of the emergent stage, children will have acquired considerably more letter knowledge and practice with finger-point reading and concepts about print. They begin to self-correct their finger-point reading based on the available words in a line of text, and when they notice that they've run out of words, but there's still more to recite, they go back to the beginning of the line to try to match their voice to the print. They also begin to use their alphabet and sound knowledge. For example, in "1, 2, buckle my shoe," the child would come to realize that the word *shoe* cannot be the word *my* because it doesn't start with the letter *m.* This would cause the child to reread and self-correct her pointing of *buckle* so *my* could be the next word in the recitation. When children can recite a piece of memorized text while maintaining fairly accurate finger-point reading, we say that the child has developed a **rudimentary concept of word.** This typically happens by the end of the emergent stage and it's an important sign that children are beginning the transition to beginning reading.

Writing in the Emergent Stage

Emergent writers can be industrious and creative, going through reams of paper while they busily narrate stories and talk with each other. Children's early writing samples will provide you with valuable insight into their understanding of print. Figure 6.9 shows the developmental progression of written expression in the emergent stage. As you can see from Frame A, early writing is characterized by random marks and scribbles that bear little resemblance to print (Schickedanz, 1986). Children will often "read" these scribbles as their stories as this child did, "All the birdies." As children develop greater fine-motor control, they begin to create representational drawings that replace the scribble forms. Children's drawings now "tell" the story and they begin to include letterlike forms in their writing, as in Frame B. This type of writing is referred to as "mock linear writing" (Clay, 1975) because it looks like an imitation of adult cursive with its organized squiggly marks. This writing is usually formed in a left-to-right fashion.

Later in this stage, children's writing, as noted in Frame C, often includes letters and numerals that may or may not have any phonetic or semantic relationship to the story. Their inclusion, however, signals a greater awareness of conventional print. In this frame, we see how Cameron writes her friend Jasmin's name by representing the two most salient sounds, *J* and *M*, accurately, and she includes other random letters to complete the word. This is quite common at this stage of development.

FIGURE 6.9 Progression of Writing Development in the Emergent Stage

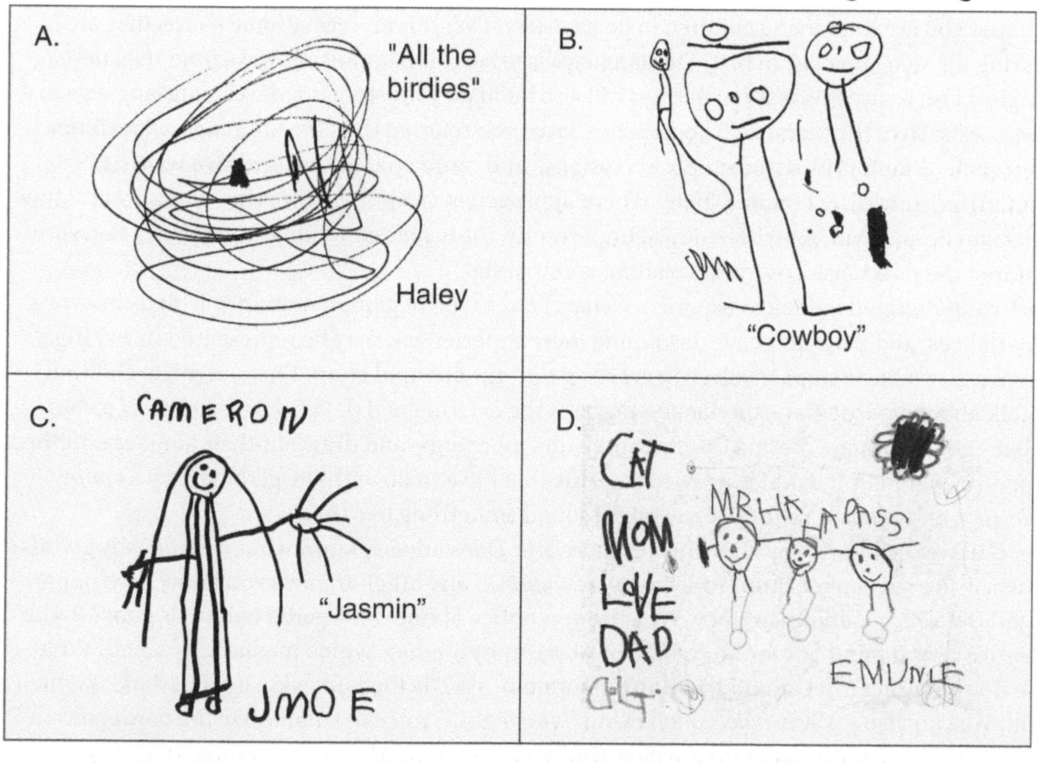

Source: Bear et al., 2012, p. 11.

In the late part of the emergent stage and in the early part of the beginning stage, as noted in Frame D, most children can write their name, or many letters of their name, and some sight words *(cat, dog, Mom, Dad)*, and they can also represent the most salient sounds in words. Some educators call this **invented spelling**, but we know it's not invented as much as it reveals children's growing understanding of alphabetic principle, so we prefer to use the term **phonic spelling** (Invernizzi & Hayes, 2004).

Children are often very motivated to write because they've observed writing in their environments—grocery lists, greeting cards, letters to Grandma, e-mail, notes for the babysitter, reminders on Post-its, and so on. The motivation to communicate through writing can grow even stronger as children learn to write their names and gain increased awareness of the names and sounds of letters. When children begin to stretch the sounds of words to help them identify the most salient or prominent sounds, they're practicing and reinforcing alphabetic principle and the understanding that print is speech written down—the two critical insights necessary for reading *and* writing. For many children, writing is the gateway to reading because it slows down the processing of letters and sounds.

As with reading, children need daily opportunities to practice their writing. Journal writing and writing during center play are two activities that provide young writers the opportunity to express themselves in writing *and* to practice critical emergent literacy skills.

Putting All the Pieces Together: The Reading-Writing-Language Connection

Common Core Connection

Writing Standards: Text Types and Purposes

Because you are immersing children in poetry, narratives, and informational genre, they are hearing the rich language of text. This language is different in important ways from the language of everyday conversation. But you will also build on your students' developing language to *create* texts. Over the years, such approaches have been referred to as the **language-experience approach** (Stauffer, 1970), or simply "dictations," and more recently, **interactive writing** (McCarrier, Pinnell, & Fountas, 1999). These approaches model (1) how print works and (2) how what can be said can be written down. Importantly, these guided writing experiences also show children the relationship between reading and writing.

Group-dictated language-experience charts are a type of guided writing in which children's experiences, and their language describing these experiences, may be represented in writing. There are two basic steps involved in creating a group-dictated chart: Encourage the children to talk about a particular experience—perhaps the exciting and delightful discovery of a clan of baby gerbils when entering the classroom one morning—and draw out their language. In the process, you might introduce a few new words that have to do with the gerbils, such as *pups*, *pale*, *tiny*, and *squeak*. Your dialogue might sound something like this:

"Can we see how many gerbil babies there are? Does anyone know what we *call* baby gerbils? I wasn't sure so I looked it up—they're called *pups!* Do any other animals you know have pups? Right! Dogs have puppies or pups. What do you notice about these gerbil babies or pups? Right; they are very small. They are so small that we say they are *tiny*, which means 'very small.' What else do you notice?" If the children don't mention it, ask, "Is the pups' skin light or dark? Right; it's light. We can also say it is *pale*, which means 'very light.'" You can summarize the conversation by saying, "Our little gerbil pups are pale, tiny, and they squeak!"

After several minutes of talk, you'll then bring the children around the easel on which rests a large pad of chart paper: "We're now going to write about our new gerbil babies." It is important

FIGURE 6.10 **Language-Experience Chart**

Gerbil Babies Are Called Pups

Rachel said, "They are tiny."

Fadila said, "I think they're cute."

Daren said, "Dogs have pups, too."

Taylor said, "They are pale."

Wendy said, "Mama Gerbil looks tired."

Lebron said, "When they grow up and run all day on wheels I want to take them home."

that the children see your actual construction of print, so if you use an interactive white board instead of an easel pad, you still will write by hand so that formation of your letters and words is clearly visible to the children. Begin by helping the children focus on what they have already said, but if new observations and comments come up, that's fine. At first, the composition should be no longer than a page or a single screen with a sufficiently large "zoom," so that it will be easier for children to remember what they and others dictated, as in Figure 6.10. Not all the children will be able, or want to, contribute, but they will still be paying attention. The following are the kinds of guiding questions you'll ask, with the focus of each in italics:

"Rachel, *do you remember what you said* about the size of the pups?"

"Who remembers the *new word* we used to describe how very light the pups' fur is?"

"Is there *anything else* that we might say and write about our pups?"

"Boys and girls, *what would be a good title* for our composition?"

By beginning each child's contribution with her or his name, you're providing an anchor for the child to locate more easily what she or he contributed. A bit later on, you might write a continuous text about the gerbils. You may also engage the children in helping you actually write the message. This "sharing of the pen," or "interactive" writing (McCarrier, Pinnell, & Fountas, 1999) begins as children have started to acquire some alphabet and initial consonant knowledge. What did you (the teacher) model in the creation of this chart?

- What someone says can be written down exactly as it is said.
- How print works: Left to right, return sweep, top to bottom.
- The end of a line is not always the end of what was said.
- As each word is pronounced, the children see it being written.
- How letters are formed.
- The relationship between letters and sounds.
- How punctuation works: The functions of periods, commas, quotation marks, apostrophes, and capital letters at the beginning of sentences and in proper names.

After the composition is complete, read it back to the children, using a pointer to point to each word; invite the children to read it with you, leading with your voice as necessary, backing off when they seem to be taking the lead. You may ask children to come up and read what they contributed (children who did not contribute may also read if they wish), and you might also follow up by asking the children to point to the first word in their contribution and read it, the last word, and a word in the middle of their sentence. In such fashion, you are able to assess on the spot the development of the children's concept of word in text (Morris & Slavin, 2003; Templeton, 1995). You can also work to develop and informally assess children's print-referencing skills:

> Adaptable to the
> Beginning Stage

"Whose name is longer? Tonita's or Jeff's? Right! It looks like Tonita is longer. To be sure, let's count the letters in each name" or "Here is the letter *D*. It's a capital *D*. It begins the word *Dogs*, and that word is the first word in the sentence, so it's capitalized."

These types of language-experience/interactive writing activities give teachers considerable insight into children's literacy knowledge, language development, and behavior. For instance, which children felt comfortable contributing to the discussion and to the composition? Which were able to sustain attention throughout the activity, children's concepts about print, and alphabet knowledge? (For more extensive discussions and applications of these types of language-experience activities, see Bear and colleagues [2010] and Templeton [1995, 1997].)

After taking a dictation, you will post the chart in an easily accessible place so that children can reread it together, pointing to and touching the words. You might also make copies for each child's personal reader. Encourage the children to illustrate the dictation and practice their finger-point reading. Some children will want to highlight letters or words they know, too.

Whether called language-experience approach, interactive writing, shared writing, or guided writing, writing *with* children is an important part of your daily instructional plan. Shared writing provides a rich opportunity to integrate oral language with children's developing knowledge of alphabetic principle, concepts about print, and concept of word while building their emerging identities as readers and writers.

Chapter Summary

The emergent stage of development is a time of remarkable growth and discovery. Children begin the stage imitating readers and writers and by the end of the stage, they've acquired critical insights into how language and print work and they are beginning to approximate conventional reading and writing. There are two essential understandings that support this transition from *emergent* to *beginning* reading:

1) The understanding that letters represent sounds (alphabetic principle) as demonstrated in children's spelling of words

2) The understanding that a spoken word matches a written word as demonstrated by children's ability to accurately point to words while reading familiar text (concept of word)

Achieving these important insights requires alphabet knowledge, phonological and phonemic awareness, and print awareness. Figure 6.11 summarizes children's growth in these skill areas across the emergent stage of development.

FIGURE 6.11 Characteristics of Children in the Emergent Stage

	Reading	Writing	Word Study
Early "All the birdies" Haley	• Engages in pretend reading • Basic book-handling skills (for example, turns pages front to back) • Identifies signs and symbols in the environment	• Writing resembles scribbles and random marks • Children tell their stories while scribbling and marking the page	• May identify a few letters' names, particularly from own name • Working to identify and manipulate sounds in syllables • Beginning to acquire alphabet knowledge

FIGURE 6.11 *(Continued)*

Middle 	• Reads from memory and uses storybook language • Developing concepts about print (for example, directionality and awareness that print and illustrations are separate)	• Directionality becoming evident in writing • Writes a mix of letters and numerals and letter-like forms • Writing and illustrations are now separate	• Knows many uppercase letters and some lowercase letters • Starting to learn beginning consonant sounds, alliteration, onset-rime, and can identify rhymes
Late	• Rudimentary concept of word when reading familiar text, including child's own writing • Notices many initial consonants in words when reading • Beginning to know some words on sight • Retells narrative text with prompting	• Rudimentary concept of word in writing (for example, beginning to use initial consonants and some final consonants and spaces; periods or slash marks may start to appear between words) • Labels pictures and begins to write simple sentences • Forms many letters correctly	• Knows most upper- and lowercase letter names and sounds • Represents the most salient consonant sound(s) when spelling words • Some confusions about letters that look alike, sound alike, and feel the same when articulated

Suggested Extension Activities

• One of the big ideas of this chapter was the importance of enriching the language environment. To translate this theory into practice, collect a language sample of teacher–child interactions in a preschool or kindergarten classroom (or your own classroom). Study the transcription with a partner or small group. Identify both the strengths of the current language environment and the opportunities for improvement. Write three specific recommendations based on guidelines for enriching the language environment in this chapter.

• Using the criteria from the chapter, select an exemplary piece of narrative or informational text and plan an *interactive read-aloud* with a focus on both comprehension and vocabulary development. Explicitly plan how you will engage children in analytic talk and select three to five target words for your vocabulary instruction. Explain how you will support children's vocabulary and comprehension development before, during, and after your reading.

Recommended Professional Resources

Allyn, P. (2009). *Stories to read with your child—And all the best times to read them.* Avery Trade.

Anderson, N. (2007). What *should I read aloud? A guide to the 200 best-selling picture books.* Newark, DE: International Reading Association.

Bear, D., Invernizzi, M., Johnston, F., & Templeton, S. (2010). *Words their way: Letter and picture sorts for emergent spellers* (2nd ed.). Boston: Pearson/Allyn & Bacon.

Bear, D., Invernizzi, M., Templeton, S., & Johnston, F. (2010). *Words their way: Phonics, vocabulary, and spelling instruction* (4th ed.). Boston: Pearson/Allyn & Bacon.

Ericson, L., & Juliebo, M. F. (1998). *The phonological awareness handbook for kindergarten and primary teachers.* Newark, DE: International Reading Association.

Fox, M. (2008). *Why reading aloud will change our children's lives forever* (2nd ed.). New York: Mariner.

Helman, L., Bear, D., Invernizzi, M., Johnston, F., & Templeton, S. (2008). *Words their way: Emergent sorts for Spanish speaking-English learners.* Boston: Pearson/ Allyn & Bacon.

Johnston, F., Invernizzi, M., Bear, D., Helman, L., & Templeton, S. (in press). *Words their way for preK–K.* Boston: Pearson/Allyn & Bacon.

Lipson, E. R. (2000). *The New York Times parent's guide to the best books for children* (3rd ed.). New York: Three Rivers.

McCarrier, A., Pinnell, G., & Fountas, I. (1999). *Interactive writing: How language and literacy come together, K–2.* Portsmouth, NH: Heinemann.

McGill-Franzen, A. (2006). *Kindergarten literacy: Matching assessment and instruction in kindergarten.* New York: Scholastic.

Miller, D. (2009). *The book whisperer: Awakening the inner reader in every child.* San Francisco: Jossey-Bass.

Richgels, D. (2003). *Going to kindergarten: A year with an outstanding teacher.* Lanham, OH: Scarecrow.

Schickedanz, J. (1986). *More than ABCs: The early stages of writing.* Washington, DC: National Association for the Education of Young Children.

Silvey, A. (2005). *100 best books for children: A parent's guide for your young reader, toddler to preteen.* New York: Mariner.

Silvey, A. (Ed.) (2002). *The essential guide to children's books and their creators.* Boston: Houghton Mifflin.

Trelease, J. (2006). *The new read-aloud handbook* (6th ed.). New York: Penguin.

Online Resources

International Reading Association Position Statement on Preschool Literacy

www.reading.org/General/AboutIRA/ PositionStatements/PreschoolLiteracyPosition.aspx.

"High-quality preschools embrace appropriate early literacy experiences delivered by well-prepared, knowledgeable, caring preschool teachers. High-quality preschools can ensure that all children are prepared for school and are developing literacy skills. This position statement highlights:

* The importance of preschool
* The nature of language development and literacy-based instruction in quality preschools
* What to aim for in preschool teachers' preparation and professional development
* Recommendations for preschool educators, early childhood and elementary educators, public school boards, teacher educators, policymakers, and community leaders."

Joint Position Statement of the International Reading Association and the National Association of Young

Children: Learning to Read and Write: Developmentally Appropriate Practices for Young Children

www.reading.org/General/ AboutIRA/PositionStatements/ DevelopmentallyAppropriatePosition.aspx

"The International Reading Association and the National Association for the Education of Young Children agree that experiences throughout early childhood affect the development of literacy. Those who teach young children—parents and child care providers as well as teachers in preschool and early elementary settings—need to support the literacy development of children in their care." This position statement emphasizes the importance of developmentally appropriate practice.

National Early Literacy Panel Report: Developing Early Literacy: Report of the National Early Literacy Panel

http://lincs.ed.gov/publications/pdf/NELPReport09.pdf

On this website you will find a synthesis of the research on early literacy development and interventions for children at risk for learning difficulties.

7

Beginning Conventional Reading and Writing

Chapter Outline

- » **Overview of Beginning Readers, Writers, and Letter Name–Alphabetic Spellers**
- » **Word Knowledge: The Linchpin of Literacy Development**
- » **Word Study: Phonics, Spelling, and Vocabulary**
- » **Small Group Reading Instruction for Beginning Readers**
- » **Beginning Fluency: From Automaticity to Expressive Reading**
- » **Reading *To* and *With* Children: Guiding Comprehension Development**
- » **The Beginning of Conventional Writing**

Focus Questions

1. What are the characteristics of beginning readers and writers?
2. How do teachers develop children's word knowledge in this stage?
3. Explain the relationship between word knowledge and beginning reader's fluency and comprehension.
4. How can teachers develop sophisticated vocabulary, thinking skills, and comprehension in the beginning stages of reading?
5. How do readers and writers grow and change throughout the beginning stage of development?

You arrive for your visit to Ms. Johnston's first-grade classroom just a little earlier than planned and she motions for you to come in and take a seat behind the children who are sitting in the meeting area. Ms. Johnston seems to be wrapping up a mini-lesson on story elements: "So readers, today during independent reading, you're going to be looking for that 'Oh, no' moment—that 'big problem' that needs to be resolved. Not every book will have a big problem, but a lot of them will, just like our read-aloud did today. When you find a problem in your book, mark it with a Post-it note so you remember to talk with your partner about it during share time. After you mark it, read on to find out *if* and *how* the problem gets resolved. Turn to your partner now and talk about your job during independent reading today."

After a few minutes of conversation, Ms. Johnston calls the children back together for a quick recap and then dismisses them to their "book nooks" where they immediately settle in and begin their independent reading. As the children read and share their books with their partners, you join Ms. Johnston at a table in the corner. Here, she's assembled a small group of readers and she's holding a little book, "Max Rides His Bike" (Giles, 2000). She begins, "Readers, this story is called 'Max Rides His Bike' and the author is Jenny Giles." Ms. Johnston points to each word as she reads it. "This is a

story about a little boy named Max. Let's read the title together: 'Max Rides His Bike.' Look at the picture on the cover, what do you see?"

The children eagerly describe the scene: Max is riding a bike with training wheels as an older gentleman, probably his grandfather, looks on. They predict that the book will be about Max learning to ride a two-wheeler and one child begins to hypothesize what the "big problem" might be. Ms. Johnston seems delighted with this and asks the child to back up her thinking using the word *because*, which she does: "I predict Max will fall off his bike *because* learning to ride a bike is hard and I fell off my bike a lot of times when I was first learning." Ms. Johnston acknowledges that when readers predict, they use clues from the text and their own experiences to think about what might happen next. Just then she turns the page for the children to see that their first prediction was indeed correct: The grandpa *is* taking the training wheels off Max's bike. Ms. Johnston draws their attention to the word *Grandpa* and shows them how to segment and blend the word. She tells the children that this is a word they'll practice and will add to their **word banks** later in the week.

Ms. Johnston then continues to orient the children to the gist of the story by turning the pages and talking about the pictures and the developing plot. She draws their attention to some other words along the way— often showing them the word written on her white board, talking about its meaning, and then showing them how to segment and blend the word before reading it together. After that, she prompts the children to find the word in the text and they read it together in context. She selects several words to teach in this way: *bike, ride, riding, little, went, down,* and *shouted.* When she teaches the children the word *bike,* she begins by showing them the familiar word *like* and highlights how they're the different in only one way—the initial consonant sound. Ms. Johnston affirms that if they can read *like,* they can read *bike.* Then several children add to the conversation by offering other rhyming words such as *hike, trike,* and *Mike.* You notice that Ms. Johnston routinely builds from what the children already know and links this prior knowledge to their new learning—something you've only read about until now.

Ms. Johnston leads the picture walk right up to the "big problem" of the story and the children confirm that Ruby's prediction was indeed correct: Max falls off his bike. After a brief conversation, Ms. Johnston invites the children to continue their picture walk with their partners to see *if* and *how* the problem is resolved. As the children begin talking about the pictures, Ms. Johnston turns to you and mentions that young children often have difficulty identifying the problems and solutions in stories and so she explicitly teaches them about this cause/effect relationship. As you think about this comment, you realize that recognizing problems and solutions is critical to understanding most narrative

text, and you begin to appreciate that there's a lot to think about when teaching reading.

As the children start to read the story independently, Ms. Johnston gets up from her seat to listen to and take notes about each child's reading. If someone is stuck on a word, she prompts that child by asking questions rather than revealing the word: "What's the part you know? What could you do to help yourself?" or "Use your finger to help say the sounds slowly. Now put them together quickly." After everyone's read the story at least once, they talk about the parts that were hard, and Ms. Johnston affirms their observations. Then they look at some of the confusing words (such as *come* and *came*) together. After this, they briefly discuss the plot and practice retelling the story—first she models the retelling and then the children retell the story to each other by turning the pages and recounting the events, including the big problem and its resolution.

Ms. Johnston closes the lesson by reminding the children of the new words they learned in the story. She hands each of them their own copy of words and they practice reading them right away. When Ms. Johnston is sure these words are familiar to the children—in other words, they can read them without much hesitation— she'll let them add them to their word banks. The children will practice reading these words and their new book in the days to come. All this in 20 minutes' time—you're amazed by Ms. Johnston's efficiency and planning! ◼

Overview of Beginning Readers, Writers, and Letter Name-Alphabetic Spellers

Ms. Johnston is keenly aware of the varying needs of children in the beginning stage of development, and she knows their needs change throughout the stage, too. In the early part of the stage, beginning readers are still firming up their understanding of alphabetic principle—their awareness that letters represent sounds in words. They demonstrate this growing insight in both their reading and writing behaviors:

In reading, they are able to finger-point read predictable and memorized text, matching their voice to the words on the page. When reading these familiar texts, it's not uncommon that their pointing gets a little off track, especially when they attempt to read words with two syllables. Early beginning readers can also have some difficulty identifying individual words in context. These two reading behaviors suggest that early beginning readers have a *rudimentary concept of word.* This concept of word will become more stable as they continue to develop letter–sound knowledge, and your instruction and modeling in shared reading and shared writing will also help.

When writing, children in the early phase of the beginning stage will write many of the most prominent sounds in words—typically the initial consonant sounds as well as some final consonant sounds. They're called "letter name–alphabetic spellers" because they use the names of the letters to represent the sounds they're trying to spell, especially in the early phase of the stage: GF for *drive* will become JRIF in the middle of the stage and DRIV later in the stage. Early beginning writers are able to read their own writing by pointing to the words, and they read them with surprising accuracy. As you follow along, you see the logic of their spelling attempts and this is exciting to you as well!

Children's growing awareness that letters, sounds, and words have an order to them is a critical insight, yet one that can initially bring them some concern. Beginners, particularly in the early phase of the stage, replace their carefree enthusiasm for reading and writing tasks with a temporary, yet often intense, preoccupation for doing things "right" (Sulzby, 1985). Your response to them will be key! It will be tempting to give them quick answers to the questions they ask (for example, "How do you spell . . .?" or "What's this word?"), and sometimes it's okay to do so, but more often your job will be to coach children to strategically use what they already know to improve their reading and spelling skills. In time and with your support and instruction, beginning readers' caution will be replaced with feelings of empowerment and pride. The beginning stage of development is a time of remarkable and rewarding growth. As you will see throughout this chapter, your knowledge and understanding of this stage of development will help shape your instructional priorities and the effectiveness of your instruction.

Word Knowledge: The Linchpin of Literacy Development

The goal of reading and writing is the construction of meaning. Whether reading a sophisticated piece of literature or a menu, writing a personal letter or a scientific report, the goal of proficient readers and writers is the same: to understand and communicate through the written word. Becoming literate is a dynamic and complex process but one that is dependent on a handful of foundational understandings. Among them is *word knowledge*. Proficient readers and writers rely on the fast, accurate *recognition* of words when reading, and the fast, accurate *production* of words in writing. Automaticity at the word level frees up children's cognitive resources to focus on the broader goal of literacy: meaningful engagements with text (Duke & Carlisle, 2011; Rasinski, Reutzel, Chard & Linan-Thompson, 2011; Samuels, 1974).

For children in the early phase of this stage, you will facilitate their development of word knowledge by continuing to focus on many of the skills you learned about in the emergent stage: alphabet knowledge, phonemic awareness, print concepts, especially concept of word, and oral language development. As children progress through the stage, you will focus more intentionally on phonics and word recognition—the gateway to fluency and comprehension.

Alphabet Knowledge

Children's alphabet knowledge and phonemic awareness in the emergent years *predict* their success with early reading (see Adams, 1990; Snow, Burns, & Griffin, 1998; NICHHD, 2000). Researchers explain that these two features are *causally related*—meaning beginning reading is dependent on letter and sound knowledge. Children's ability to accurately and automatically name the letters is yet another strong predictor of early reading success (Stage, Sheppard, Davidson, & Browning, 2001). For these compelling reasons, you'll begin teaching the alphabet and letter–sound relationships in the emergent stage, focusing on a new letter each day and then combining many familiar letters at once. In the early phase of the beginning stage, most children can readily identify all the letters of the alphabet and most of the sounds (Snow, Burns, & Griffin, 1998), though some children will need additional review. When teaching letter–sound knowledge, you'll build from what children already know—connecting new learning to their prior knowledge to ensure a lasting effect. If you're unsure of your students' alphabet knowledge, consider administering an assessment such as the Beginning Consonant Assessment found in Figure 7.1. This assessment can be administered one-to-one, in a small group, or to your whole class.

As you review the children's work, you'll quite likely notice that some children are accurately representing initial *and* final consonants in words, while others are including some medial vowel sounds, too. This information will be useful as you consider where children are along the developmental continuum *within* (or beyond) the beginning stage of reading. As you'll learn throughout this chapter, understanding children's word knowledge allows you to effectively differentiate your instruction.

> **Common Core Connection**
>
> Reading Standards: Foundational Skills – Print Concepts and Phonological Awareness

FIGURE 7.1 **Beginning Consonant Assessment**

Administration guidelines. Name each of the pictures one at a time. Use the word in a sentence and then repeat the name of the picture again. Be careful not to accentuate or elongate any of the sounds. Speak slowly but naturally. Encourage the children to label each picture, spelling the words as best they can.

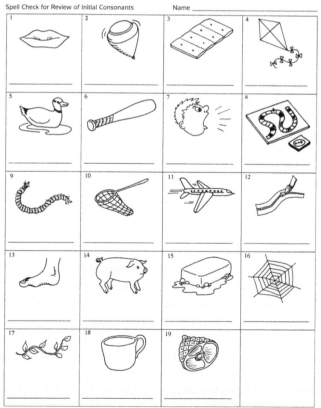

Source: Johnston et al., 2009.

Phonological and Phonemic Awareness

Phonological awareness begins in the emergent stage and its development continues through the beginning stage. To be phonologically aware, children need to consciously reflect on the sounds of language—its "pieces" and "parts" beginning with spoken words, syllables, rhymes, onsets and rimes, and finally, phonemes, which are the smallest unit of sound. Because phonological awareness requires children to recognize their own awareness of sounds, researchers call it a **metalinguistic skill**.

Phonemic awareness is a subset of phonological awareness. The term refers to children's ability to recognize, identify, and manipulate phonemes—the smallest unit of sound. Phonemic awareness, like phonological awareness, is an oral language activity; however, children's phonemic awareness is advanced and strengthened through its reciprocal relationship with letters. It's through children's understanding that letters have names and represent sounds, that they become increasingly aware of the sounds of language and concept of word in text (Flanigan, 2007; Morris, Bloodgood, Lomax & Perney, 2003, Smith, 2012).

In the beginning stage, we first focus on segmenting and blending tasks, as they have the most immediate utility when it comes to both decoding and encoding—the reading and spelling of words. Later, we focus on phoneme substitution tasks to help children apply their awareness of onsets and rimes by helping them hear the similarities and differences among words such as *kit, bit,* and *sit*. Over time, they will come to learn that if they know how to read the word *fit,* then reading (and writing) words like *pit, lit,* and *hit* will not be such a stretch (Leslie & Calhoon, 1995; Treiman, Goswami, & Bruck, 1990). Later still, as children learn to segment words by their individual phonemes, you will teach them to substitute sounds in other positions, such as the final consonant or the medial vowel. For example: the chain of words *cap, sap, lap,* and *tap* differ by only a single phoneme, the initial consonant, but substituting a single phoneme in a different position (a final consonant or medial vowel) can make even more words: *lot, let, pet,* and *put*.

Alphabet knowledge and phonemic awareness activities help ensure children's early reading success. It's important to remember, however, they are a *means* to an *end*: the automatic and accurate processing and production of words in reading and writing. Embedding phonemic awareness tasks in your word study instruction and in reading and writing activities will help advance children's understanding of letter–sound relationships and how they can strategically use this information to read and spell. The "Strategies for the Classroom" feature on page 225 illustrates just a few examples of how you can explore the relationship between letters and sounds within your word study or guided reading lessons.

Concept of Word in Text

Common Core Connection

Reading Standards: Foundation Skills – Print Concepts

Concept of word in text develops as children's understanding of letter–sound knowledge becomes more robust. By the middle of the stage, most children have achieved *full concept of word,* meaning they can read text without pointing to each word, and they can accurately find individual words in familiar text when prompted. Children with full concept of word can read many words both in and out of context, although the latter may be harder for them.

Children in the early phase of the beginning stage continue to benefit from shared reading and shared writing activities that focus on developing concept of word in text. When rereading newer or less familiar texts, you'll invite the children to repeat a line or lines of text after you've modeled reading them—this is called **echo reading.** In more familiar texts, you'll invite the children to read along with you in unison—this is known as **choral reading**. As you read, you'll carefully point to each word. It's also helpful for early beginners to see how the initial and final

Strategies for the Classroom

Hearing and Representing Sounds

Segmenting sounds in words is one of the most complex tasks beginning readers will attempt, and it's a critical and necessary skill that will help them not only read words but also spell them. Russian psychologist Daniel Elkonin (1973) recognized the importance and difficulty of phoneme segmentation and developed a now widely used phonemic awareness activity known as *Elkonin boxes,* or *sound boxes.* Sound boxes can be embedded as part of your phonics or spelling instruction for emergent and beginning readers.

Toward the middle of the beginning stage, children will begin to segment more complex words, including short vowel words with digraphs, blends, and, later, nasal sounds. These sounds are more difficult to discriminate and some of these sounds are represented with more than one letter. Over the course of the beginning stage, you'll help children gain the awareness that the relationship between letters and sounds is not always a one-to-one correspondence.

Procedures

Select a picture or word from the children's word study lessons, guided reading, shared reading, or interactive writing. Say the word and model how you segment it into its individual sounds by pushing a coin or plastic chip that represents each sound into a sound box like the one below. For example:

"This is a picture of the sun: /s/ /ŭ/ /n/, sun. Let's see how many sounds are in the word sun. *Push and say the sounds with me:* sss-u-u-u-nnn. *How many sounds in the word* sun?*" (3)*

After pushing the sounds, be sure to write the letters in each box to emphasize the important relationship between letters and sounds:

Variations

Segmenting and blending are critical skills for beginning readers and spellers, as is phoneme substitution. You can enrich your phonics and spelling instruction by showing children how a single phoneme substitution, beginning with the initial consonant, can change a word. Using letter tiles, or letters in a pocket chart, show the children how knowing one word can help them learn others through simple letter–sound substitutions.

"This is the word map: /m/ /ap/. If you can read the word map, you can read the word sss - ap. What's the word? That's right! Sap. If you can read sap, you can read other words. Who can make a new word?

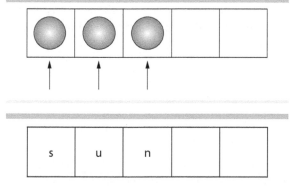

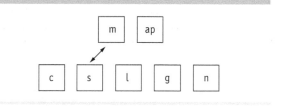

consonants work together to create word boundaries or spaces *between* words. When words with two syllables trip them up, you'll show them the initial and final consonants in the word and you'll help them clap the syllables, while affirming that it's just one word. Children in the middle of this stage will be able to focus more intentionally on automatic word recognition, and both groups of children will benefit from a focus on comprehension. Figure 7.2 illustrates how you might address all three goals as part of your daily shared reading experiences.

FIGURE 7.2 A Five-Day Shared Reading Lesson Plan: Developing Concept of Word in Text, Comprehension, and Sight Word Vocabulary with Beginning Readers

Concept of word is often taught through whole class shared reading experiences, particularly when a majority of the children would benefit from instruction in this skill. In cases where only a small number of children need continued work with concept of word, you might bring this instruction to your smaller and developmentally oriented guided reading groups. What follows is Ms. Johnston's five-day sequence for teaching her students about concept of word using the book *The Carrot Seed* (Krauss, 1973).

Day 1: Book Introduction and Reading

Ms. Johnston gathers her students around the easel and an enlarged copy of *The Carrot Seed*. As part of her planning, she's already previewed the text and anticipated the parts that might provide the children with some challenge. She's also identified the sight words she plans to emphasize: *come, came, little, mother,* and *father.* Here's how she introduces the book: "Readers, today we're going to read a book that goes along with our study on how plants grow. The book is called *The Carrot Seed* by Ruth Krauss and it's a narrative. Turn and talk with your partner about what makes a book a narrative." When Ms. Johnston reads the title, she points to each word and talks about the illustration: "Here we see a little boy on the cover. What do you think he's doing?" "What kind of seed do you think it is?" "What made you say that?" "Oh, who can find the word *carrot* in the title?" "How did you know that word said 'carrot'?" Through these well-planned questions, Ms. Johnston activates children's prior knowledge, engages them in the plot, and emphasizes letter–sound correspondence and concept of word. She frames the word *carrot* and shows them how to read across the word, emphasizing all the sounds and ending with the letter *t* and the /t/ sound. She reminds them that *carrot* has two syllables, but it's only one word. She repeats this process with the word *seed,* a single-syllable word. Next, Ms. Johnston begins to preview the text. As she turns each page, she paraphrases the story and draws the children's attention to what's happening in the picture and the text: "Here we see the little boy's mother. Let's read this page: 'His mother said, "I'm afraid it won't come up." ' " As she reads the words, she points to each one and then asks some follow-up questions: "Where do you think it says 'mother'? How do you know?" Ms. Johnston briefly shows them how to read all the sounds in the word *mother.* As she previews the text, she helps the children read some words many of them already know by sight: *his, it, up, the,* and *day.*

Ms. Johnston previews the text to the point where the big problem is revealed: "Everyone kept saying it wouldn't come up," and then she asks the children to use their knowledge of how seeds grow to predict what might happen next. After a brief conversation, she sets the purpose for listening: "Today while I'm reading, listen to see *if* and *how* this big problem gets resolved and be ready to talk to your partner about it at the end." Ms. Johnston reads the text through from the beginning. This time she points only to the new sight words for emphasis and focuses on the children's understanding and enjoyment of the text. The children turn and talk periodically, and when the book is done, they talk about their predictions and the problem's resolution. Ms. Johnston also facilitates their retelling the text by turning the pages and referring to the written text from time to time. If time allows, she rereads the shared text at least once more on the first day. This whole activity takes about 15 minutes.

Day 2: Rereading and Print Referencing

Ms. Johnston knows that early beginning readers need many opportunities to reread text so they can memorize it. Using memorized text supports their efforts to productively apply their knowledge of letter–sound correspondence to develop concept of word. These scaffolded experiences also help children begin to recognize words on sight—a critical skill for beginning readers.

On day 2, Ms. Johnston rereads the text all the way through and the children join in and read the parts that are becoming familiar. As she reads, she points to each word. While reading for the second time this day, she provides additional practice with text referencing: identifying letters,

FIGURE 7.2 *(Continued)*

sounds, and words—particularly the sight words she's emphasizing this week and other familiar words, too. Children find these words and Ms. Johnston uses highlighter tape to underline them in the text. She also shows them how to decode these words, or the parts of these words that are phonetically regular, thereby putting their knowledge of letters and sounds to work. (See Chapter 6 for more information on print referencing and elsewhere in this chapter for information about teaching sight words.) After a couple of rounds of rereading, the children take turns coming to the easel to lead their classmates' reading by pointing to the text as they read aloud.

Day 3: Reading and Retelling Practice

On day 3, Ms. Johnston shares the story in a new form: She's copied it onto sentence strips and in doing so she's paid careful attention to each line break and the words to be sure they're an exact match. The children compare and contrast this version of the story with the big book. After some practice reading the new text using echo reading, the class reads it chorally and then children take turns leading the finger-point reading. Ms. Johnston also introduces a few props for the children to use when retelling the story. After modeling one retelling, she invites partners to retell the story to each other. She places the props in a retelling center for additional practice during center time.

Ms. Johnston concludes the lesson by providing the children with an exact copy of the text on an 8½ × 11-inch piece of paper. They read this personal copy of the text with their reading partners. As they read together, Ms. Johnston takes note of their voice–print match and then encourages them to find words they know—both familiar sight words and the newly introduced words. The children and teacher underline these words with highlighters. Ms. Johnston then tells the children to add this text to their personal readers for additional reading practice during independent reading time. She also makes copies of the book available in the library corner, and there are even a few copies of the book and a recording of it in the listening center.

Day 4: Sentences to Words

The children revisit the sentence strip version of the text and practice rereading it several times. When Ms. Johnston notices their improved fluency and voice–print match, she knows they've sufficiently memorized the text. Today, she helps the children identify sentences in the text and reminds them about capital letters at the beginning of sentences and periods at the end—a Common Core standard. She asks the children to count the number of words in some sentences—again, emphasizing concept of word in text.

> A little boy planted

> a carrot seed.

After talking about the sentences, words, and various text features, Ms. Johnston takes the first sentence (above) and cuts it into individual word cards and she and the children read the sentence as it's cut apart: "A – little – boy – planted – a – carrot – seed." Next, they read each word in isolation, but still in the order of the sentence. They then reconstruct the whole sentence and read it yet again. Finally, they scramble the words and work together to read them out of sequence and then reconstruct the sentence—a task that's considerably more demanding than you might think.

(Continued)

FIGURE 7.2 *(Continued)*

When Ms. Johnston is confident that the children can read the sight words she's emphasized throughout the week, she gives them a copy of the words for their word banks. They will continue to practice reading these words each day and they'll play games such as Go Fish and Concentration with them, too. The children also enjoy making sentences with the word cards and their other sight words in the days and weeks to come. Ms. Johnston adds these words to the word wall and encourages the children to refer to this resource or their word bank whenever they're unsure how to spell them. She clearly communicates her expectation that the children apply what they're learning about words to their authentic reading and writing experiences.

| little | come | came | mother | father |

Day 5: Written and Artistic Responses

On the last day of the week, Ms. Johnston and the children read the story one last time and they talk about its meaning. Because the children already have a solid understanding of the plot, she works to help them determine if there's a "big idea" or theme in this text. One child mentions that the little boy had to be patient and believe in himself. Another child suggests that it's important to believe in yourself even when others don't. Yet another child says, "Vegetables take time to grow and you have to take care of them." Ms. Johnston captures the children's ideas on a chart—sharing the pen with them as they write the sounds and words they know. The chart will be added to the library corner for rereading during the children's center time.

Sometimes Ms. Johnston uses this time on the fifth day to dictate sentences, or she asks the children to write a response to the text using some of the words they've been learning. In both cases, she reinforces the spelling of words that are at the children's developmental level and encourages them to spell familiar sight words correctly, too. Today's shared reading lesson concludes with children drawing pictures to go with their reflections.

Sight Word Vocabulary

Sight words are words that children can read automatically "on sight" in less than a second. Throughout the beginning stage of development, children gain upwards of 150 sight words. We refer to this bank of words as a child's **sight word vocabulary**. Many children in the same stage of development will share some common sight words, but not every word will be the same. Children are most likely to remember words that have personal relevance and high utility for them (for example, names of friends, family members, and sports teams, and other topics they frequently read, talk, and write about). One first-grader had these words in her store of sight word vocabulary: *Grammy, Ashley, gymnastics, beagle, Vermont,* and *family.*

Sight words are sometimes confused with **high-frequency words**—the most commonly occurring words in print. These are words such as *the, of, and, a, to, in, is,* and *you.* Although there will be some overlap between children's collections of sight words and high-frequency words, their sight word collections are not limited to words found on high-frequency word lists such as Fry's Instant Word List (Fry & Kress, 2006). High-frequency word lists can be a helpful resource when you're considering which words children need to know automatically, but you will teach children to read many kinds of words in the beginning stage, not just high-frequency words. You'll also come to realize that many high-frequency words are encountered so often that they may not require much, if any, instruction at all. Others will need to be taught directly and multiple times. Listening to children's reading miscues—the words they misread—and observing their spelling attempts will help you determine which high-frequency words require your instruction.

Many years ago it was common practice for teachers to teach sight words through rote memorization. Perhaps you remember this from your own childhood? Today we're careful to teach words in a more meaningful and contextualized way—beginning with a piece of text—either a guided reading book, a text used in shared reading, or even a text you've written with the children. Here, the children see the utility of the words because they are in their natural state. Without this context, learning sight words would be a lot like trying to memorize all of the numbers in the phone book. It's clearly much easier to remember the ones that mean something to you, or the ones you dial frequently, isn't it? Context is especially important for learning "function" words—words that do not form a mental image—words such as *the, that, which, where,* and *of.* Certainly, context helps children learn words by sight, but context alone isn't enough.

When strong beginning readers approach new words, they strategically use letter–sound correspondence and familiar spelling patterns to accurately decode new words (Cunningham, Perry, & Stanovich, 2001; Cunningham, Nathan, & Schmidt Raher, 2011). High-frequency words are no different! It's true that some high-frequency words are so irregular they must be learned as whole units (for example, *of*), but most high-frequency words can be decoded, at least in part, using letter–sound knowledge. The word *from,* for example, is 75 percent regular (three letter sounds are regular; only one, *o,* is not); *did* is 100 percent regular; and even the word *said* is two-thirds regular! We show the children how to use their decoding skills when reading these words and we help them see the parts that aren't regular, too. Our goal in teaching high-frequency words in this manner is to increase children's automaticity with reading these words, yes, but also to reinforce how to decode unknown words.

As readers work to decode a new word using phonics and/or familiar spelling patterns, the brain is simultaneously searching its "mental dictionary," or its lexicon, to determine if the word is a known word. This confirmation is more likely to occur in children who have larger vocabularies and in those who have had more practice reading (Lesaux, Koda, Siegel, & Shanahan, 2008; Helman & Burns, 2008). These children may be able to learn to read as many as five or more words from each new book. This would probably be too many for children with limited English proficiency—either English learners or children with language-based disabilities. Special considerations for these students can be found in the next feature, "Accommodating English Learners."

> **Common Core Connection**
>
> Reading Standards: Foundational Skills-Phonics and Word Recognition

> EL Connection

Word Banks

Word banks are collections of known words that have been explicitly taught in small group-guided reading, shared reading, or shared writing instruction (Bear, Invernizzi, Templeton, & Johnston, 2012; Stauffer, 1980). In the opening vignette and in Figure 7.2, Ms. Johnston demonstrated how to teach specific words first in context and then more explicitly out of context before returning back to meaningful reading and writing activities. Researchers have found that learning words first in context, and then examining their spelling features, talking about how to pronounce them, and discussing the meaning of these words improves the likelihood that children will learn and retain them over time (Ehri & Wilce, 1980; Ehri & McCormick, 1998; Johnston, 2000).

Each child in the beginning stage has his or her own personal word bank. These words are read each day as part of daily reading practice and they are stored in plastic zipper bags or recipe

Accommodating English Learners

Building Sight Vocabulary

Word recognition requires the automatic engagement and integration of phonological knowledge, orthographic knowledge, and children's familiarity with words, sometimes referred to as **lexical knowledge**. This means that when beginning readers approach an unknown word, they look at the letters and think about the sounds they represent and then attempt to segment and blend the word until it's recognizable. English learners (ELs) are no different in how they approach word recognition tasks (August & Shanahan, 2006), but they do experience some unique challenges (Helman & Burns, 2008). Given their often limited vocabulary knowledge, they cannot always confirm that their reading attempts "sound right" and they're also not always sure if they "make sense" in the context of their reading (Lesaux et al., 2008). Further, their working memory can be quite taxed learning letter–sound correspondences in their new language. For these reasons, English learners and children with limited language proficiency will need some special considerations when learning sight word vocabulary:

Differentiation

While children in the beginning stage of development may share many similar characteristics, the needs of ELs may differ from their native speaking peers or even from other ELs who have differing levels of oral language proficiency. English learners with medium to high levels of English proficiency seem to acquire sight word vocabulary more readily and similar to their native-speaking peers, so grouping them together may be just fine. Students with limited English proficiency, however, will likely need additional practice, fewer words to learn at once, and more support for oral language development (Helman & Burns, 2008). Researchers Helman and Burns recommend the following strategies for teaching sight word vocabulary to ELs, particularly those with limited English.

Initial Instruction

1) Whenever possible, introduce words that have high utility and those that will appear frequently in the children's reading. Referring to Fry's Instant Word List may be a good place to start, as well as finding words that are personally important to the children and/or their understanding of the text they're reading. Three new words can provide sufficient exposure without overloading children with limited English proficiency. As their oral language proficiency improves and as they acquire more sight words, you can reconsider the number of new words they're learning at a time.

2) When introducing a new word, provide a written representation of it, talk about how to pronounce it, how to read it, and what it means. Supplement the children's vocabulary development by using photos, objects, or physical gestures or movements to help reinforce the meaning of new words.

3) Contextualize the words by reading them in and out of context. Encourage the children to generate sentences using the words—both orally and in writing.

4) Encourage conversation and questions about the meaning of the words—linking these new words to children's prior knowledge and, when possible, connecting these words to their primary language.

Practice and Extension

All children need multiple exposures to facilitate the automatic and accurate reading of sight words, and English learners are no different. To encourage this extra practice and exposure, consider some of the following suggestions (adapted from Helman & Burns, 2008):

1) Purposefully select guided reading texts for additional exposure to high-frequency words and other words from your word study lessons. Minimize exposure to lower-frequency words that take ELs' attention away from building automaticity and accuracy at the word level.

2) After introducing ELs to new sight word vocabulary in either guided reading or word study activities, create word cards for children to practice reading each day. Encourage children to interact with these words in the same way described in the section on sight word vocabulary in this chapter. Additionally, encourage the children to occasionally sort their collections into two categories: words I can read and words I cannot read, or word meanings I know and word meanings I don't know. This provides the springboard for conversation and additional practice and instruction. Words that are not readily identified with some consistency may need to be removed from the collection until they can be reintroduced in guided reading or word study.

3) Provide daily opportunities to read independent-level text and instructional-level text with support. Additionally, have students reread and talk about familiar texts to encourage oral language development, word recognition, fluency, and comprehension.

boxes. The words are written on $1'' \times 3''$ cardstock paper so they will last over time. As seen in Figure 7.3, when children are first acquiring their sight word vocabulary, it's helpful to annotate each card with a code to indicate the chart, poem, song, or book the word came from so the child can return to the original text in case the word is forgotten.

In addition to rereading these words during independent reading time, encourage the children to revisit their word banks during word study to find examples of words that fit (or don't fit) the feature or pattern under study. Children also enjoy sorting these words and playing "Guess My Category" (see Chapter 3), or creating silly or interesting sentences with them. Some teachers provide children with a traveling dictionary in which they write these words for quick reference during independent writing time; others encourage the children to keep their words in alphabetical order so they're easily accessible reference during writing time.

Word banks do take some time to prepare and maintain, but they are well worth the effort, particularly for children who are having some difficulty acquiring a sight word vocabulary. For these children, word banks can provide a much-needed reinforcement that their reading is improving (Johnston, 1998). As children's word banks grow, so does their confidence. Some teachers even graph children's progress with sight word acquisition. As a new word is added to the collection, the child will color a bar graph to mark his progress. When the word banks grow to about 150 words, the children will be approaching the transitional stage of reading and their word banks are usually replaced with word study notebooks. Word banks are usually kept with children's personal readers (see Figure 7.3).

FIGURE 7.3 **Word Banks and Personal Readers**

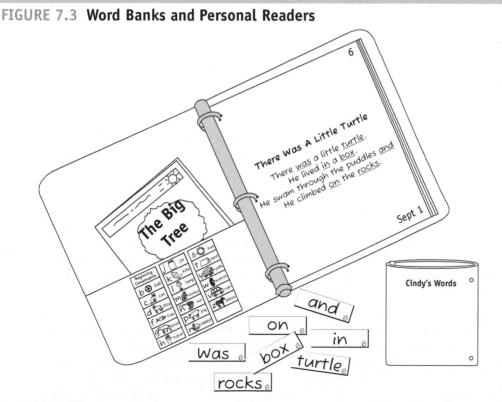

Source: Adapted from Bear et al., 2012.

Word Walls

In addition to word banks, some teachers display **word walls** in their classrooms (Cunningham, 2008; Cunningham & Allington, 1999). Word walls can take many forms, but the most common form in the emergent and beginning stage is a display of alphabetically arranged high-frequency words. Some teachers organize their word walls by word families, or spelling features such as digraphs, blends, or vowel patterns. Other teachers use word walls like a thesaurus, where they display synonyms for common words such as *said*, *nice*, or *fun*. Whatever form your word wall takes, you'll want to display it at children's eye level and be sure the size and clarity of the font makes it easily readable from some distance.

Word Study: Phonics, Spelling, and Vocabulary

Your word study instruction will help beginning readers and writers become more automatic and accurate when reading and spelling words. And your vocabulary instruction will help broaden and deepen children's understanding of word meanings, as well as provide helpful strategies for "unlocking" the meaning of words.

Phonics

Phonics is the study of letter–sound relationships. Beginning readers use their phonics knowledge to begin reading words in early readers and familiar text. These children are said to be "glued to print" (Chall, 1995), meaning they have to concentrate very intentionally to decode and read each word, and this typically results in them reading in a word-by-word fashion (Bear, 1992). As their letter–sound knowledge improves, they are able to segment words by their individual phonemes: the word *cat*, for instance, is sounded out as: /c/-/a/-/t/. Mapping sounds onto these letters and blending them into recognizable words takes a great deal of effort. This is especially true for English learners who typically do not have the same store of words as native speakers, and this makes it harder for them to confirm the accuracy of their reading attempts.

With practice and your ongoing word study instruction, beginning readers will move from segmenting and blending words by their individual sounds, to recognizing **word families**, or **phonograms**. These are words that share the same rimes (for example, words with *–at*, words with *–it*). These beginners soon come to realize, with your instruction, that *cat, hat, bat,* and *sat* all have the same part. The mapping of phonological information to spelling patterns creates efficiency for readers in the middle to late phase of the stage. This type of instruction is called **analytic phonics,** or **analogy phonics** (NICHD, 2000), and children with strong phonological skills tend to do better with these analogies (Leslie & Calhoon, 1995; Treiman, Goswami, & Bruck, 1990). Figure 7.4 highlights the most common phonograms in English with examples.

As children continue to accumulate reading and writing experiences, it will be important for them to move beyond their recognition of common word families to understand the basic consonant-vowel-consonant (CVC) short vowel pattern (Bear & Barone, 1997). Although CVC short vowel pattern and word families are clearly related, there is a difference between the two skills. Consider, for example, asking a child if *sit* and *fit* sound the same in the middle. What about *sit* and *fin*? As you can imagine, the latter example would present a greater challenge, but

FIGURE 7.4 **Most Common Phonograms in Order of the Number of Words They Form with Examples**

— **ay** say, day, play	— **ot** pot, not, got	— **op** mop, pop, flop	— **ob** job, rob, knob
— **ill** will, fill, spill	— **ing** sing, ring, thing	— **in** pin, win, thin	— **ock** sock, lock, block
— **ip** dip, ship, trip	— **ap** cap, map, trap	— **an** can, Dan, than	— **ake** cake, Jake, brake
— **at** cat, sat, flat	— **unk** bunk, junk, trunk	— **est** best, rest, pest	— **ine** line, fine, shine
— **am** ham, ram, Sam	— **ail** pail, nail, snail	— **ink** sink, pink, drink	— **ight** light, night, fright
— **ag** rag, sag, flag	— **ain** rain, main, chain	— **ow** low, grow, snow	— **im** him, Kim, brim
— **ack** sack, black, Jack	— **eed** seed, need, freed	— **ew** new, few, grew	— **uck** duck, luck, truck
— **ank** bank, sank, drank	— **y** my, by, try	— **ore** more, tore, store	— **um** gum, hum, drum
— **ick** sick, pick, quick	— **out** pout, trout, shout	— **ed** bed, fed, bled	
— **ell** bell, fell, yell	— **ug** rug, bug, shrug	— **ab** cab, flab, crab	

Source: Adapted from Fry, Kress, & Fountoukidis, 2000

its significance should not be overlooked. Children's awareness of the CVC short vowel pattern is important because it will

- enable beginner readers to decode and spell considerably more words than word families alone
- help them read novel or low-frequency words, and
- help them in later stages of development as they learn to decode and spell long vowel patterns and polysyllabic words.

Phonics instruction and the application of phonics skills are embedded in nearly everything you do in the beginning stage of development. It will be part of your shared reading and shared writing instruction, your small group guided reading and guided writing instruction and your word study instruction, as well as children's daily reading and writing practice. While we advocate for this integrated approach to phonics and spelling instruction, it's important to note that your teaching cannot be haphazard (NICHD, 2000). These skills are too important to leave to chance! Your goal will be to teach letter–sound relationships and orthographic patterns in a systematic and developmental sequence *and* in a way that engages young learners. Table 7.1 summarizes a common scope and sequence of word study instruction in the letter name–alphabetic stage (Bear et al., 2012). (See *Words Their Way: Word Sorts for Letter Name-Alphabetic Spellers,* 2009, by Johnston, Bear, Invernizzi, and Templeton for a more complete scope and sequence, and sample lesson plans for letter name–alphabetic spellers.)

> **Common Core Connection**
>
> Reading Standards: Foundation Skills: Phonics and Word Recognition

Letter Name–Alphabetic Spellers

When letter name–alphabetic spellers write, particularly early in the stage, they use the names of letters to represent sounds in words (Read, 1975). For example, *when* might be spelled YN because the letter name of "Y" (*wie*) sounds like the beginning sound in *when; jeep* might be spelled GP because the name of the letter "G" (*jee*) sounds like the first sounds in *jeep*. Some letter names such as "H" (*aich*) and "W" (*doubleyoo*) are not as helpful when trying to spell, but

> **Common Core Connection**
>
> Language Standards: Conventions of Standard English

TABLE 7.1 **Scope and Sequence for Letter Name–Alphabetic Spellers**

Early Letter Name–Alphabetic	Middle Letter Name–Alphabetic	Late Letter Name–Alphabetic
• Initial Consonant Sound Sorts with Pictures (e.g., *m/r/s*)	• Mixed Vowel Word Families (e.g., *at/ot/it*)	• Short Vowels in CVC Words (e.g., *a/o*)
• Same-Vowel Word Family Sorts (e.g., *at/an, op/ot/og*, etc.)	• Picture Sorts for Short Vowels (e.g., *a/o*)	• Short Vowels with Blends and Digraphs (e.g., **tr**ot, **fl**ag, **sh**ip, mu**ch**)
• Mixed Picture Sort: Digraphs and Initial Consonants (e.g., *c/h/ch*)		• Preconsonantal Nasals (e.g., *an/ant, in/ing*)
• Mixed Picture Sort: Blends and Initial Consonants (e.g., *s/t/st*)		• R-Influenced Vowels (e.g., *a/ar, o/or*)

some children will find a way to use them in their writing: for example, it's not uncommon for a child early in the stage to use "H" (*aich*) to represent the digraph *ch* as in "chocolate" (HKLT).

Figure 7.5 highlights the names of the letters. As you review them, read them aloud so you can begin to appreciate how early beginners may use these letter names to represent sounds in their writing.

Spelling Vowels

Before long, letter name spellers attempt to represent the vowel sounds in their spellings, though it's common that they will continue to confuse these vowel sounds throughout the middle and even into the late phase of the stage. As you learned in Chapter 6, the root of this confusion is related to how these sounds are articulated. Vowel sounds are made with the lips, tongue, and jaw. As you say the following vowel sounds, notice how you articulate each one: /ē/, /ĭ/, /ā/, /ĕ/, /ă/, /ī/, /ŏ/. You probably noticed that the long *e* sound was formed in the front of our mouth with your lips in the shape of a slightly parted smile, and as you made each sound your jaw lowered and your lips rounded. If you didn't notice this, try it again. You might also find it helpful to look into a hand mirror while forming the sounds—this can help you as well as the children identify how sounds are related to the way they are formed in the mouth.

Other vowel sounds are made in the back of the mouth, such as: /ū/, /ō/, and /ŏ/. Short *u* is formed in the central part of the mouth. Sounds that are formed close to one another are easily

FIGURE 7.5 **Names of the Letters of the Alphabet**

A *ay*	H *aitch*	O *oh*	V *vee*
B *bee*	I *ie*	P *pee*	W *doubleyoo*
C *see*	J *jay*	Q *kyoo*	X *ecks*
D *dee*	K *kay*	R *are*	Y *wie*
E *ee*	L *el*	S *es*	Z *zee*
F *ef*	M *em*	T *tee*	
G *jee*	N *en*	U *yoo*	

Source: Bear et al., 2012, p. 155.

FIGURE 7.6 Common Short Vowel Confusions

a for short *e* (*bad* for *bed*)
e for short *i* (*shep* for *ship*)
i for short *o* (*hip* for *hop*)
o for short *u* (*bot* for *but*)

confused: sounds like long *a,* as in the word *late* (spelled LAT), is commonly confused with the sound of short *e* as in the word *let* (also spelled LAT by middle letter name–alphabetic spellers).

When spelling long vowels, children can rely on the letters' names, but when spelling short vowels, middle letter name spellers more often rely on the long vowel sound that's closest to where it's pronounced – its **point of articulation** (Read, 1971). Over time and with daily word study instruction and practice reading conventionally spelled short vowel words, beginners at the end of the stage are able to read *and* spell these words with greater accuracy and automaticity. Figure 7.6 highlights some common short vowel confusions for beginning readers and writers. Common consonant *and* vowel confusions for ELs can be found in the feature "Accommodating English Learners" in Chapter 6.

EL Connection

Other Orthographic Features of the Letter Name–Alphabetic Stage

Toward the middle of this stage, letter name–alphabetic spellers will also learn to spell short vowel words with digraphs and blends. A digraph, as you may recall, is a single sound that's spelled with two letters. Examples of digraphs taught at this stage include: *ch, sh, th, wh,* and *ph* (Bear et al., 2012). Blends are a little more difficult for children to learn because each of the letters retains its sound, but it's joined with the sound of its neighboring consonant or consonants (in the case of three letter blends), making it harder to segment and identify each phoneme. Perhaps you can appreciate this difficulty when saying and thinking about the blends in these words: ***plus, tree, skunk,*** and ***queen.*** Blends taught at the beginning stage include: *s*-blends: *st, sp, sc, sw, sn, st, sp, sk, sm; l*-blends: *pl, bl, gl, sl, cl, fl; r*-blends: *fr, br, gr, pr, tr, dr, cr,* and blends with the /*w*/ sound, too: *qu* and *tw* (Bear et al., 2012). Later, you will teach children how to read and spell digraphs and blends at the beginning *and* the end of single-syllable short vowel words (for example, ***shop, dish, stop,*** and ***past***).

Picture sorts help children focus intentionally on the sounds in words, which is a critical first step at this stage of development. Because learning and understanding digraphs and blends takes time, children will probably find it helpful to compare and contrast pictures that begin with each of the consonants in a digraph or blend with pictures that actually contain the blend or digraph (for example, *t – top, r – rake,* and *tr – tree*). Pushing and saying these sounds and then spelling them in Elkonin boxes can also help children see the relationship between letters and sounds in words. (See the feature titled "Strategies for the Classroom" on page 238 for more detail.) Figure 7.7 shows an example of a sort used for introducing the digraph *ch* and another for the blend *st.*

Preconsonantal Nasals   Some final blends can be especially challenging for children to discern, particularly **preconsonantal nasals**. Preconsonantal nasals are made with the nasal sounds /*n*/, /*m*/, and /*ng*/. Try making these sounds: /*n*/, /*m*/, /*ng*/. Now try making them while holding your nose. You can't, can you? These sounds are made in the nasal cavity of your mouth, hence the reason they are called *nasal sounds.* The term *preconsonantal* is not nearly as difficult as it sounds. It simply means nasal sounds that come before the consonant, as in ***hand, dump, pink,*** and ***sing.***

FIGURE 7.7 Sample Introductory Sorts for the Digraph *ch* and the Blend *st*

SORT 14   *C, H,* and *CH* Digraph   SORT 18   *S, T,* and *ST* Blend

Source: Johnston et al, 2009, pp. 38, 42.

Preconsonantal nasals are difficult for beginners because they don't feel the sound the same way they do for other consonants. This is because the air flows through the nasal cavity rather than the mouth. You might show the children how this works by having them say these words aloud and then repeat them while gently holding their noses. It's also helpful to contrast words that have sounds and those that do not. As children strengthen their phonemic awareness through your word study instruction and reading and writing practice, spelling words with preconsonantal nasals becomes more consistent, but this typically doesn't happen until the end of the stage.

Consonants That Influence Vowel Sounds   The position of consonants can influence not only other consonant sounds but vowels, too. Consider and say these word pairs: *fat, far; sap, saw;* and *back, ball.* What do you notice about the sound of the vowel in these pairs? It's different, right? Both groups of words follow the CVC short vowel pattern, but the vowel in the second word of each pair is quite clearly influenced by the consonant *r, l,* or *w.* These sounds are articulated more like vowels because they change the shape of the mouth or tongue. This is in contrast to other consonants that are formed with a burst of air that is obstructed or modified somewhere between the throat and lips.

The sounds /r/ and /l/ are called **liquid** sounds. Liquids affect the sounds of vowels and they can present letter name spellers—and even within word pattern spellers—some challenge. Toward the end of the letter name–alphabetic stage, we focus children's attention on how these special consonants affect the vowels in word families such as *–ar, –or, –aw, –all,* and *–ill.* Later still, in the within-word pattern stage, we'll examine other *r*-influenced patterns such as *–ear, –are,* and *–eer,* and *–ur, –ir,* and *–ire.*

Summing It All Up: Spelling Development across the Stage

Children in the letter–name alphabetic stage gain tremendous insight into how words work throughout this stage—beginning with initial consonants, to short vowel patterns, all the way through *r-*, *l-*, and *w*-influenced vowels. To better appreciate and understand this growth, let's consider how a letter name–alphabetic speller would spell the word *lump* across this beginning stage of development: Early in the stage, the letter name–alphabetic speller would spell it LP, in the middle of the stage it would be LOP, and then LOMP or LUMP at the very end of the stage. Take a moment to consider the underlying logic of these spelling attempts and then review this explanation:

Common Core Connection

Language Standards: Conventions of Standard English

- Early letter name–alphabetic spellers represent the most salient or prominent sounds in words—often the initial and final consonants and only occasionally vowel sounds.
- Middle letter name–alphabetic spellers begin to experiment with short vowel sounds in words. As they experiment, they confuse these vowels with the names of long vowels that are articulated in close proximity; they might also notice the short vowel sound in these letter names, which can contribute to their confusion.
- By the end of the stage, letter name spellers more consistently represent short vowels in words and are able to represent digraphs and blends, including preconsonantal nasals, more readily. This is the result of their fully developed phonemic awareness, your ongoing word study instruction, and their practice with reading and writing.

Importantly, you will also help children come to understand that single-syllable words with blends and digraphs still maintain the CVC short vowel pattern. The number of consonants that fall before or after the vowel does not change the short sound of it, but the letters *r*, *l*, and *w* do influence and change the sound of that vowel.

Vocabulary Development

As you've discovered, much of your word study instruction in the beginning stage focuses on helping children develop automaticity and accuracy when reading and writing easy single-syllable words, including some high-frequency words. However, this focused instruction can't be at the expense of vocabulary development. Children's early language experiences significantly affect their later reading achievement (Roth, Speece & Cooper, 2002; Storch & Whitehurst, 2002), so you'll continue to support their understanding of increasingly sophisticated vocabulary and complex syntactic patterns.

Common Core Connection

Language Standards: Vocabulary Acquisition and Use

In addition to being mindful of the quality of your oral language when talking with children, you'll intentionally teach the meanings of a wide variety of words through your read-alouds and content-area explorations. As you recall from the emergent stage, there are five guidelines for selecting words to explicitly teach in the early stages:

1) High Utility
2) Semantic Relatedness
3) Concreteness
4) Conceptual Relatedness
5) Sophisticated and Novel Words

In the later stages of development, you'll more intentionally select words based on their morphological relatedness.

Throughout the beginning stage, children will start to read and listen to increasingly complex narratives and informational texts. As these texts gain in complexity, the vocabulary and syntax

Strategies for the Classroom

Word Study in Practice: A Sample Five-Day Lesson Plan

flag	slip	glad
clip	brag	flat
plan	dril	clap
grip	trap	grab
cram	flip	drip
crab	slid	drag
slam	slap	brat
grill	skip	spin

Source: Johnston et al., 2009.

Day 1: Introduce the Sort

This late letter-name sort comes after two weeks of sorting easy short vowel words *(cup, bed, pig, sock, cat)*. This week we've added familiar initial blends to short *a* and short *i* words. We start with these two short vowels because they're easier for children to discriminate and compare and contrast. Sounds like short *a* and short *e*, for example, would be much harder to compare and contrast because they sound so similar. We'll add all the vowel sounds together in a later sort.

Because this sort combines familiar concepts (short vowels and blends), this provides a good opportunity for the children to work in partnerships and explore the words with an open sort. You'll probably find that the children will sort the words many different ways: by the short vowels *a* and *i*, *r*-blends, and/or *l*-blends. Some children may also sort by word families. Examples include *–ip*, *–ap*, *–ad*, *–id*, and *–ag*. You'll encourage the children to *sort*, *check*, and *reflect*—sorting the words different ways and talking about their sorts and what they're learning. You'll facilitate this talk by asking open-ended questions:

- Tell me about your sort.
- How did you decide to create those columns? or How did you decide to put that word in that column?
- Can you sort these words a different way?

You'll also encourage self-correction if it's needed:

- I think there's a word/picture that doesn't belong in this column. Can you find it?
- Why do you think it doesn't belong? Where might it go? Why?

- Is there part of this sort that is difficult or confusing? What's challenging about it?

Depending on your goals, you may conclude the lesson with asking the children to sort a specific way.

Day 2: Practice and Reflect

As you well know, beginners benefit from extended practice in reading and writing words. Today, you'll encourage the children to sort their words into short vowel patterns (short *a* and short *i*) and then by *r*-blends and *l*-blends. After checking their sorts with partners, have them record the sorts in their notebooks and write a short statement of reflection about what they're learning from each sort. You can facilitate this reflection by asking guiding questions such as these:

- Do you have a hunch about how these words work?
- What's the same about these words? What's different?
- What do you notice about the sounds? What do you notice about the patterns?
- How would you describe the "big idea" in this sort?

You might also scaffold the task by providing a frame for their writing: Today I learned _____. An example of this is _____.

You'll also have students conduct a speed sort today. This provides them with a "time to beat" the next day. When speed sorting, remember to remind the children to read each word aloud. This ensures that they are indeed reading the words and not just moving words around quickly.

Day 3: Extension Activities

Each day we begin with sorting and today is no different. We also encourage buddy sorting and speed sorting, but we're careful not to let peers compete against each other in a speed sort. You'll emphasize that the goal of speed sorting is to beat one's own time. We like to see students complete three speed sorts in one sitting.

In addition to these activities, we'll extend children's practice with words by getting them started with a word hunt. Working in partners, they'll revisit familiar texts to find words that follow the patterns they're studying—short vowel *a* and *i* words with the *r*-blends and *l*-blends at the beginning of words. After they've created their own lists, they'll work together to add to their lists by sharing one another's examples. Here, we emphasize that knowing one word pattern can help a child read and spell many, many more words!

Day 4: Building Automaticity

Today, the children will sort their words again—first alone and then with partners, and they'll even continue to try to beat their time with speed sorting. Partners will also work together to complete a blind writing sort. Here, one partner will call the words while the other writes them—not only spelling them correctly but also placing them in the correct categories. Partners may opt to include new words from the word hunt, too. This emphasizes the importance of being able to generalize patterns beyond the list of 20 or so words in a given week.

Day 5: Games and Assessment

You'll find many simple file folder games that you can make to accompany your weekly word sorts in the back of *Words Their Way* (Bear et al., 2012). Children will enjoy playing these games with this week's words and even previous week's sorts, and in doing so, they benefit from the additional practice reading and writing these words. If you haven't had a chance to make some of these games just yet, you could provide some commercially available word games for their enjoyment and reading and writing practice. Some favorites for beginners include: *Boggle Jr., Scrabble Slam* (card game), *Zingo*, and *What's Gnu?* You may administer your weekly assessment to each group as the other students enjoy some additional practice and fun with the word study games.

will no longer resemble the informal discourse of oral language, but rather the more formal discourse of written English. As this shift occurs, you'll notice that guidelines 2 through 5 will help you identify much of the *general academic vocabulary* and even *content-* or *domain-specific academic vocabulary* appropriate for instruction at this stage.

General Academic Vocabulary

General academic vocabulary—words such as *opposite, merriment,* and *delicate*—may be introduced and taught in the context of your interactive read-alouds. Since these words are often more difficult than what beginners can typically decode or spell, you won't expect them to read these words accurately or recognize them by sight, much less spell them correctly. Our goal in teaching these words is to elevate both the quantity and quality words in children's receptive and expressive vocabularies. Focusing on developing children's vocabulary will improve their listening comprehension skills now and their reading comprehension and word recognition skills in the years to come. Let's look at what these interactions with general academic vocabulary might look like in your classroom.

After reading an informational picture book such as *Painting Word Pictures* (Bauman et al., 2012) you may select *combination, ease, important,* and *rhythm* as target vocabulary words for explicit vocabulary instruction (Templeton, 2012). As you read these words in context, you'll share accessible, "kid-friendly" definitions (Beck, McKeown, & Kucan, 2002) and talk about the meaning of these words in the context of this book. You'll also extend children's understanding of these words by asking meaningful and engaging questions such as "Which are *combinations* of foods—carrots and peas *or* apples?" "What are some things you can do with *ease*?" "What are two things that are really *important* to you? Why?" "When do you hear *rhythm*—when books fall off the shelf or when you hear a song? Why?" Including the word *why* in your questioning is especially important because it stimulates descriptive and explanatory talk, which leads to children's deeper thinking about words and increases their opportunities for oral language practice (Dickinson & Tabors, 2001). You'll also use the instructional strategies you learned about in Chapter 6: strategies such as dialogic read-alouds, text talk, and anchored vocabulary instruction.

Adaptable to All Stages

Content- or Domain-Specific Academic Vocabulary

In both the emergent and beginning stage of development, young children are particularly excited to learn about the world around them. Through your thematic units and various interactions with informational text, you will have ample opportunity to expose children to *content-* or *domain-specific academic vocabulary.* Consider Ms. Johnston's current study of seeds and plants. What a rich opportunity for vocabulary development! You're already beginning to think about the possibilities, aren't you? Words like *root, stem, stamen, pollen, seedpod,* and *herbivore* can be introduced and discussed. Just like other words we want children to learn, we begin by teaching domain-specific academic vocabulary through text. In the case of Ms. Johnston's class, she begins this unit with several read-alouds, including *Seeds Get Around* (White, 1993), *The Tiny Seed* (Carle, 1970), *From Seed to Plant* (Gibbons, 1991), and *The Reason for a Flower* (Heller, 1983). As she reads these texts over and over again, she facilitates conversation about the vocabulary and concepts in them. She uses these books to initiate a whole-class vocabulary notebook on several pieces of chart paper. Writing this glossary becomes a great opportunity for shared writing. The children help her write the words and definitions while also including drawings and labels that extend their learning of these words and concepts.

Ms. Johnston knows children need many, many exposures to learn new words and so she looks for other meaningful ways to extend children's interactions—for example, she asks engaging questions before, during, and after reading: How does the wind *disperse* the seeds? What are some other ways seeds are *dispersed*? If you feel a tickle in your nose, is it *pollen* or *nectar* that makes you want to sneeze? She also invites her students to draw, label, and write in their journals about what they're learning, which they love to do. Many children create their own glossary of terms, while others access the class chart to spell these words correctly when writing them in sentences or stories.

During center time, Ms. Johnston organizes materials for concept sorts in the science center. Here, children discuss the similarities and differences among fruits and vegetables and they sort pictures of the two according to their understandings. They also sort types of seeds by size and color and other attributes—often sorting by two or more attributes at a time as suggested by the Common Core Standards. These many, varied, and engaging interactions with words and concepts significantly increase the likelihood that children will develop deep and lasting understandings of them (Bear et al., 2012; Beck, McKeown, & Kucan, 2002).

Morphological Analysis

In the beginning stage of reading, we also introduce children to early morphological analysis by breaking familiar words apart into their meaningful elements, or their *morphemes.* This helps children at the beginning stage become aware of *morphology.* This awareness builds children's sensitivity to words and to their meanings, enriching the concepts that underlie words and building a foundational understanding that will develop in later stages into a powerful generative vocabulary strategy. This generative strategy involves applying knowledge of word formation processes in English—how prefixes, suffixes, roots, and root words combine—to figure out unfamiliar words independently. Beginners' dawning awareness of morphology also develops their appreciation of and curiosity about words, often referred to as "word consciousness" (Scott, Skobel, & Wells, 2008)—another important aspect of vocabulary development.

Since they were preschoolers, beginning readers use a number of words that were created through morphological processes, but they rarely think about the morphemes or meaningful parts within these words—for example, *looked, looking, teacher, helper, careful, joyful,* and *colorful.* In spoken language, inflectional morphology develops earlier and is more prevalent in beginners' speech. It involves adding the endings *–ed, –ing,* and *–s/–es,* and *–er/–est* to root words. The role of plural endings is easy to talk about: Add an *s* to *dog* and now you have *dogs,* which means "more than one dog." But it is difficult to talk about what *–ed* and *–ing* actually *mean* and how they affect words to which they attach. Fortunately, children subconsciously pick up these meanings as they acquire language. Later in the beginning stage the children will need to learn to decode words that have these endings. So we may address inflectional endings in the context of sentences such as the following, in which we can talk with children about how the word *look* changes across the sentences:

> I look out the window.
> Charlie look*s* out the window.
> Charlie look*ed* out the window.
> Charlie was look*ing* out the window.

The comparative *–er* and superlative *–est* may be illustrated in sentences such as the following:

> I run fast.
> Tonisha runs fast*er*.
> Bernadette runs the fast*est*.

Simple derivational morphology is easier for beginners to understand because, unlike most inflectional endings, derivational suffixes and prefixes are more concrete in their meaning: *joyful*, *unhelpful*, *slowly*. So, using such known words, we guide children's exploration of how these morphological processes work:

> Chuck is slow when he walks.
> Chuck walks slow*ly*.

> Gloria likes to help.
> Gloria is help*ful*.
> Gloria is *un*help*ful*.

When you're teaching children about derivational affixes, write the sentences so the root words line up as seen in the examples above. This helps children see directly how a root word can "grow" through the addition of suffixes and/or prefixes. To extend this study, consider adding derivational affixes like *un–*, *–ful*, and *–ly* to children's word banks where they can continue to explore how they change the meaning of root words and sentences.

Small Group Reading Instruction for Beginning Readers

Teaching reading in the primary grades will be one of your most important priorities and it will probably take more instructional time than any other content area. Certainly, we are sensitive to competing priorities in your day, but the research on the importance of this topic is rather sobering: Children who fall behind in early years rarely catch up (Foorman, Francis, Shaywitz, Shaywitz, & Fletcher, 1997; Juel, 1988; Stanovich, 1986). It's critically important that you provide young children with the best possible start. Although a strong start doesn't guarantee they won't experience reading difficulties later, it significantly improves the odds of their success.

The most effective primary-grade teachers teach reading to children in smaller, developmentally oriented groups. Not only do these children learn more but they are also more likely to retain the learning over time (Connor et al., 2011; Morris, Blanton, Blanton, Nowacek & Perney, 1995; Pearson, Clark, & Walpole, 2000; Wilson, 2008). In a touchstone study of highly effective teachers, Taylor and colleagues (2000) found that the most accomplished primary-grade teachers spend more than two hours a day teaching literacy. Their students spend approximately half that time in small group instruction and about 30 minutes in independent reading practice. (That's a lot of time!)

Guided Reading

Adaptable to All Stages

Guided reading is a method for teaching children how to read in small, flexible, and developmentally oriented groups (Calkins, 2001; Fountas & Pinnell, 1996). The overall goal of guided reading is to provide children with the skills and strategies necessary to read and understand increasingly complex text. Through strong book introductions and your ongoing coaching and support, children will read instructional-level text in these groups—texts that are just slightly beyond what they can read on their own. With your well-planned instruction, today's *instructional*-level text will be tomorrow's *independent*-level reading.

As you learned in Chapter 4, there are three important parts to every guided reading lesson:

1) Book selection and introduction
2) Reading practice, teacher observation, and coaching
3) A teaching point and link

We'll explore each of these parts in the sections that follow.

Book Selection and Book Introductions

When selecting a text for guided reading, consider books that are neither too difficult nor too easy. Instructional-level texts in the primary grades are usually texts children can read with 90 to 94 percent accuracy after a brief book introduction. We intentionally use texts that are just a little bit beyond what children can read independently because we want them to practice their phonics and word recognition skills, as well as their thinking skills and comprehension strategies. If the texts are too easy, children won't get much practice with word-solving strategies or maintaining meaning while reading. On the other hand, if the texts are too hard, the children will feel overwhelmed and will have great difficulty maintaining any kind of fluency or comprehension. In addition to a text's difficulty level, you'll also want to consider the interests of the children in your group and the needs of your readers, as well as the genre of the text, making sure you provide equal opportunities to read literature—stories and poetry—and informational texts.

When you've selected an instructional level text, preview the book to note the structure of the language. Does the syntax sound natural or is it more contrived? Is there a pattern to the text? Does the pattern change? Maybe there's dialogue or special print or punctuation? What kind of support will your readers need to comprehend the book? Importantly, you'll also consider the kind of support your young readers will need to be successful decoding the words, keeping in mind some words will be so far beyond your readers' decoding skills that you'll help them use context and one or two features of the word to help them read it. As you recall from Chapter 2, young children's guided reading books have increased in complexity in recent decades (Hiebert, 2005, 2011). This makes these books especially difficult for beginners, English learners, and children who experience early reading challenges. Depending on the needs of your students, you may look for books that provide repeated exposure to high-frequency words, particularly if the children are having difficulty acquiring a sight word vocabulary. You may also consider using decodable text, which is described in a later section.

When introducing a new book to children, be sure to prepare a brief introduction to the book—approximately two or three sentences that capture the gist of the story. You'll also introduce the structure or syntactic patterns within the text, words that may be beyond your students' ability to decode, and/or new vocabulary words. Figure 7.8 shows the template Ms. Johnston uses to prepare for her daily guided reading lessons. You'll see a lesson she prepared for readers in the late phase of beginning stage.

> Adaptable to the
> Transitional Stage

FIGURE 7.8 Guided Reading Planning Template

Name: *Humpback Whales* (Kijak, 1996) **Level:** Guided Reading E/DRA 10 **Word Count:** 72

Teacher Previewing

What do you notice about the language/structure of the text?

This book is set up in a question/answer format (for example, "What is that? It's the tail of a whale" pp. 4–5). There is a diagram/map of how far the whales swim and a diagram of a whale's body parts and special print on the last page: "WE DO!" (p. 15).

What do you notice about the words?

There are some easily confused question words: *what, where, who.*

Many known sight words: *it, is, of, they, in, the, do, likes, we*

General or domain-specific vocabulary: *humpback, whales, ocean, krill, blowhole, mouth, flippers, tail, eye*

Other words that may be challenging: *kind, live, eat, watch*

What is the gist of the story? Are there any confusing parts that need support/scaffolding?

The reader follows a family on a whale watch—something that is probably unknown to many students so it will require explanation. The passengers ask the tour guide questions. The text follows a predictable format until page 9, when the question appears on the righthand page and the answer is found in two places: pages 10 and 11. This might be confusing to the readers. This text is also something of a hybrid because it looks like a story with its color illustrations, but it's also a piece of informational text. The Common Core calls these texts "literary nonfiction." This concept is worth exploring with the children if time allows.

The Lesson Plan

Before Reading

Introduction:

"Readers, today we're going to read a new book called *Humpback Whales* by Anna Kijak. Let's look at the title together. The word *humpback* has two syllables, clap them with me. It's also a compound word. A compound word is two words that come together to make a new word. What are the two words? Right!" Write *hump + back = humpback* on your white board. (Discuss the meaning of *hump* and *back* and show the children a picture and the diagram on page 16. Read each of the words and talk about how "blowhole" is another example of a compound word.)

"In this story, *Humpback Whales*, this little girl [point to the cover illustration] is going on a whale watch. A whale watch is when you take a boat ride on the ocean to see whales. On this boat there's a tour guide who answers the passengers' questions about whales. Have you ever gone on a whale watch?"

Picture Walk/Orientation to the Text:

"Let's look at the first page. What do you see? . . . People are on the boat looking at the whales. What kind of whales are they? . . . They are 'humpback whales.' Where would you expect it to say 'humpback whales'? (pp. 4–5).

(Continued)

FIGURE 7.8 *(Continued)*

"Here, the people are watching one of the humpback whales and someone asks, 'Where do humpback whales live?' The tour guide says, 'They live in the . . . —let's look at this word, it starts with the letter *o*—get your mouth ready for that first sound /ō/. Think about the story—what could that word be? . . . Yes, the word is *ocean.* (pp. 6–7).

"On this page the guide is showing the passengers a map that shows how far the whales swim (p. 10) and here's a close-up of that map" (p. 11).

Set the Purpose:
"Readers, today while you're reading, I want you to be thinking about what you're learning about humpback whales. When you're done reading, we'll talk about what you learned. If you finish reading before others, practice rereading to make your voice sound smooth like talking and find something special to share. Who can tell me your job today?"

During Reading

Coaching/Conferring:
As the children read independently in whisper voices, you'll circulate around the group listening to children read and recording your observations in your conferring log. Be sure you have a copy of "Prompts to Encourage Readers to Be Strategic" on hand to help you coach your readers to be strategic word solvers. (See the "Language of Your Instruction" feature in this chapter.)

As you listen and observe individual readers, you're looking for a trend—the one teaching point that could really move this group of children forward in their reading.

After Reading

Debriefing/Comprehension Discussion:
Here, you'll refer to the purpose you set at the beginning. Today, the students will talk about the things they learned about humpback whales.

Teaching Point:
Your teaching point will come from observing the readers and identifying the one thing that will advance their reading skills; however, it's good to have a teaching point prepared in case a trend doesn't present itself. In today's book, it might be interesting to ask the children to discuss their thoughts about whether this text is a narrative or informational text. Ask the children to back up their thinking with evidence. (It will be important that they know there's not one correct answer to this question—it's their rationale that's important.) Explain that there is an integrated genre called "literary nonfiction."

Sometimes it's helpful to solicit input from the children when deciding a teaching point: "I noticed that there were places where you felt really, really strong as readers. Can you tell me about some of those times and places in the book? . . . What did you do to help yourself feel strong? . . . Can we hear what it sounded like? . . . Was there a place where it was kind of difficult or confusing? . . . Will you show us that place? . . . What was challenging about it?" As you listen to their reflections, think about how you'll build from their strengths and connect their new learning to their prior knowledge. Your teaching point will include modeling and guided practice.

Link:
Link your teaching point to their independent reading practice—be sure to teach for transference: "So readers, today when you go back into independent reading, you're going to try . . . , or remember . . . , or think . . . " [choose one teaching point].

Reading Practice, Teacher Observation, and Coaching

After you've introduced the new book or text, invite the children to read the text in its entirety. When reading the text, they will do so independently and quietly, but not silently. It's not until later in the transitional stage of reading that children are able to consistently read silently, "in their heads," as opposed to aloud. Toward the end of the beginning stage, some children may be able to whisper read, particularly a familiar or easier text. Until then, they need the auditory feedback reading aloud provides, as it helps focus their reading of words and it supports and reinforces their decoding attempts, too.

As the children read, you will move around the group and listen, sometimes crouching next to an individual child to listen to him read. As you learned in Chapter 3 and Chapter 4, you'll record the reading behaviors you're noticing, both the children's strengths and their challenges. While observing, you'll be especially interested in noting specifics about *how* the children are reading—their accuracy, their rate, their phrasing, and what they do when they're stuck on a word (their strategic problem-solving skills). You'll also notice whether or not (and how) they're self-correcting their miscues. As necessary, you'll coach children to use three different types of knowledge, which you learned first learned about in Chapter 2:

- Phonics knowledge—letter–sound correspondence; later, children will rely on using familiar orthographic patterns to readily identify words
- Syntactic knowledge—the structure or order of words within sentences
- Semantic knowledge—the meaning of individual words and word parts—together with the overall gist the story, which can be inferred from both the illustrations and reading the text itself

Proficient readers use all three of these types of knowledge when reading; however, beginners are typically "glued to print," and with your instruction and practice, they become quite efficient with decoding and word recognition—two important goals for this stage. When children overrely on syntax or meaning to "guess" what words say, it's a signal that you must draw their attention back to print and word-solving strategies (Ehri, 2005; Stanovich, 1980). In "The Language of Your Instruction," you'll find prompts to help encourage your beginning readers to become more strategic. You'll also find suggestions for instruction based on your students' miscues.

> Applicable to Other Stages

Your Teaching Point and Link

After your readers have completed their first reading of the text, you'll pull them back together for a teaching point—a very brief lesson that will advance their reading not only of this text but other texts, too. You'll use your observation notes to look for a trend across the group. Was there something specific that challenged them? Are they experiencing difficulty with decoding or word recognition? Are they monitoring their reading and self-correcting their miscues? Perhaps they could be coached to read without their finger now? Ask yourself, "What's the one thing I could teach these readers that would improve their reading skills not just in this book but beyond?"

Sometimes it's hard to find the perfect teaching point for all of the children. At times like these, it can be helpful to engage them in a discussion about the reading. Consider using open-ended prompts such as "Tell me about a place where you did some really great reading work today." After talking about their strengths and affirming their use of strategic reading skills, ask the children if there was a part that was challenging or a part that confused them. Most children will quite readily go back to those parts even if they didn't slow down and try to fix them while reading the text the first time. When they identify these challenges, take the opportunity to ask

The Language of Your Instruction

Prompting Readers to Be Strategic

All readers benefit from instruction that prompts them to be self-reliant and strategic. After you've provided sufficient modeling and guided practice, it's appropriate to coach beginners to use their knowledge of print concepts and word recognition strategies, and you'll encourage their monitoring and self-correction of miscues, too. What follows are some prompts you can use to encourage children to become independent and strategic readers.

Encouraging Voice-Print Match

Use your finger to point to each word.

Did it match?

Start here and try that again.

Do you have enough/too many words?

Let's try that again.

Encouraging Strategy Use (When the Reader Is Passive)

Hmm . . . . What could you try? (Okay, try that now.)

You might try . . . .

Is there a part you know?

What would make sense?

What would sound right?

Encouraging the Use of Phonics Knowledge to Accurately Read Words

Is there a part you know?

Get your mouth ready for the first sound.

Check across the word—let's say the sounds slowly. Now say them quickly. Do you know a word like that?

Does part of this word look like a word you know?

Is there a familiar pattern?

Try it another way (often switching long/short vowels).

You said _____. Does that match the letters? The pattern? What else could it be?

Encouraging Monitoring and Self-Correction*

Hmm . . . . Did something confuse you in that sentence (on that page)?

Does that match? Does that look right?

Try that again and think about what would match the letters; sound right; make sense. (Choose one based on the information the child needs to attend to.)

Could it be that?

Are you right? How do you know?

That makes sense (or sounds right) but it doesn't match the letters. Let's try again.

Is that a real word? Does it sound right?

Does it make sense? What could it be?

Encouraging the Use of Context/Meaning Clues to Affirm Word Reading Accuracy*

Look at the picture and think about the story and then look at the letters. What could it be?

Think about what would make sense in this story.

You said _____. Would that make sense in this story?

Hmm . . . . Is that a real word? Would that make sense?

Just a minute. . . . I think I'm confused.

Help me understand what's happening in the story.

Encouraging the Use of Syntax to Affirm Word Reading Accuracy*

You said_____. Does that sound right?

Hmm . . . . Does that sound like talking?

Think about what would sound right. Okay, try it.

*Use thoughtfully with English learners. It's possible that they may not have the oral language skills necessary to verify the accuracy of some of their reading attempts, particularly new speakers of English. The greater the language need, the more you must support readers in your book introductions and vocabulary instruction.

them how they might have helped themselves solve these challenges. If they're not sure, model a strategy that might have helped and then have them try it while you watch. Your teaching points should include modeling and guided practice.

As you wrap up your teaching point, emphasize how your readers can apply what they're learning in guided reading to their independent reading as well as other reading—this is called the "link." You might say something like this: "Readers, today when you go back into independent reading, you're going to try . . . [insert the strategy you demonstrated] when . . . [insert the times when they're likely to use this strategy]. You'll encourage the children to reread their new book alone or with a partner for extended practice. Repeated oral readings can lead to increased word recognition skills, fluency, and even comprehension.

Adaptable to Other Stages

You'll also look for opportunities for the children to continue their reading practice beyond the school day. The feature titled "Working and Collaborating" will help you work with families and after-school personnel who may be willing to provide children with additional reading practice.

What Beginning Readers Can Read Themselves

Reading and spelling develop simultaneously and in "synchrony" (Bear & Templeton, 1998). Spelling is a "conservative" measure of children's word knowledge because children can read words that are just slightly more advanced than what they can spell (Bear, 1992). You can understand this yourself: There are words you are able to read but you may be uncertain about

Working and Collaborating

Paired Reading

Paired reading is a form of reading practice where an adult or a more skilled reader chorally reads an instructional- or independent-level text with a beginning reader. As the beginning reader gains confidence and positive momentum, the skilled reader drops back and allows the child to read independently. If the child becomes stuck on a word for more than a few seconds, if the child misreads a word, or if fluency and/or comprehension begins to break down, the partner steps back in and the two begin to read chorally again. This technique is especially effective when the text is read multiple times. Paired reading has been found to improve children's word recognition skills, fluency, and reading comprehension (Rasinski et al., 2011).

Getting Started: Guidelines for Parents and Reading Partners

Before Reading:

1) Select a piece of text that is close to or at your child's independent reading level. For best results, allow the child to choose from a small collection of familiar books or other texts.
2) Create a comfortable and positive environment free from distractions.
3) Before reading, talk about the title of the story and preview the text.

During Reading:

1) Begin reading together in unison, not too fast and not too slow. Try to approximate a pace just a little slower than talking and a little faster than your child can read independently.

2) Let your child take over the reading as you see an increase in confidence and reading fluency.
3) If your child pauses at a word for more than a few seconds or reads a word incorrectly, read the word correctly, encourage your child to repeat it, and continue reading together again until your child regains momentum.

After Reading:

1) Talk about the story—its setting, characters, problem and solution, or what you learned in informational text. Discuss your favorite parts and make connections to your child's life, other books, and the world.
2) Praise your child's efforts to:
   - Figure out words independently.
   - Read words accurately.
   - Catch and fix reading mistakes.
   - Read like talking.
   - Remember the important details from the story or informational text.

Other Tips:

   - Set a regular time to read together each day (10 to15 minutes of this kind of reading is probably sufficient).
   - Keep paired reading time positive and fun.
   - Don't worry about teaching your child to decode the words that provide challenges—just provide the word and maintain your child's positive reading momentum.

spelling—words such as *sacrilegious* or *allegiance*. With this in mind, we look at children's independent word knowledge through their spelling. We then select texts that include features they are "using but confusing" in their spelling, but which they'd likely be able to read quite readily. For example, the child who spells *train* as TRANE or *sleep* as SLEPE is probably comfortable reading many words with long vowels. The child who spells *train* as JRN or *ship* as SEP would be better placed in text that includes more high-frequency words, simpler sentences, and some short vowel words, too.

As a novice or even an experienced teacher, it can be hard to know where to start when it comes to selecting texts for beginning readers. This is where "qualitative" measures (see Chapter 2) such as text leveling systems—for example, the Developmental Reading Assessment (DRA) (Beaver, 2006; Beaver & Carter, 2003) and Guided Reading Levels (Fountas & Pinnell, 1999)—can be helpful. Over time, you'll begin to internalize the many factors that make texts complex (for example, the length of the text, the difficulty of the words, the syntactic complexity of the sentences, the size and placement of the text, the content, the vocabulary, and the genre, to name but a few), and when you do, you will rely less on these leveling systems when choosing books for teaching children how to read. In the meantime, it's appropriate to use these leveled texts and your own good judgment to find books your young readers *can* read and *want* to read. In the section that follows, we share some guidance for matching books to readers *within* the beginning stage of development.

Common Core Connection

Reading Standards for Literature and Informational Text: Range of Reading and Level of Text Complexity

Early Beginning Readers

Children in the early phase of the beginning stage are still working on the voice–print match and can get overwhelmed with a lot of text on the page. Sometimes they read books with just one or two words per page. Other times early beginners can read slightly longer texts, particularly when they follow a predictable pattern and have been introduced well.

In general, when selecting books for early beginners, look for books with these features:

* Clear distinctions in the placement of the print and illustrations
* Consistent placement of text (the text appears in exactly the same place on each page)
* Strong picture support (the illustrations will help with word identification, particularly words that are beyond children's ability to decode)
* A repetitive, predictable pattern in the text (for example, "I can walk. I can jump. What can you do?")
* Syntactically simple sentences
* High-frequency words (for example, *the, and, is, can, do, like*)
* Very few words on the page (sometimes as few as one or two words)
* Very low total word count

These features are most commonly found in guided reading levels C and D or Developmental Reading Assessment (DRA) levels 3 or 4.

Figure 7.9 shows an excerpt from a book that's appropriate for early beginning readers. This book, *The Wet Pet* by Jacklyn Williams and Linda Clark-Ford (2000), is a DRA level 3. Here we see a simple story about a kitty who has fallen into a pool and needs to be rescued. The story contains some dialogue and the language is a little unnatural because the author is emphasizing the –*et* word family. Fortunately, the picture support and repetition make it accessible to early beginning readers. This book is the perfect complement to teaching the –*et* word family or the short *e* vowel pattern.

FIGURE 7.9 Excerpt from *The Wet Pet* (Williams & Clark-Ford, 2000)

"Get the jet," said the vet.

"Get the net," said the vet.

4

5

Middle Beginning Readers

Children in this phase of the stage have acquired quite a number of sight words, perhaps as many as 50 to 75 words. While their word recognition is improving, they still read new texts in a word-by-word fashion with some two- to three-word phrases in more familiar texts. By this point, children's concept of word in text is strong enough that they rarely need to finger-point as they read, although they may revert back to finger-point reading when they lose their place or come across a difficult word or unexpected change in sentence structure. Children in the middle part of this stage will have increased stamina for reading, too. When selecting books for these readers, we look for books that have:

- Increased amounts of text per page and/or smaller font size
- Strong picture support, but the distinction between the illustrations and text may not be as defined as in earlier levels and the location of the text may not be as consistent
- More narrative elements (such as characters and a simple plot) and the informational texts now provide children opportunities to learn information beyond their immediate life experiences
- More general academic vocabulary
- Some two- and even three-syllable words
- More words in total

These features are most commonly found in guided reading level E and DRA text levels 6–8.

In Figure 7.10 we have an excerpt from *The City Cat and the Country Cat* (Miranda, 1996), a DRA level 8. This story is modeled after the classic fable *Country Mouse, City Mouse* and it's a good example of the kind of text children in the middle of the beginning stage can read. As you can see, this book contains many features of narrative text: characters, setting, problem, and later a resolution. Although the illustrations are related to the text, the children will need to go beyond their literal comprehension to understand the story. Consider, for example, the text and illustration on page 9 of the book. Here, we see the city cat packing and the text explains that he didn't like the country. The reader must then *infer* that the city cat is packing to go home. This is a noticeable shift from earlier texts, and an appropriate one. As your students become more efficient at the word level, they will have more cognitive resources available for comprehending increasingly complex text, but they will also need your instruction

FIGURE 7.10 **Excerpt from *The City Cat and the Country Cat* (Miranda, 1996)**

and support in this area, too. Efficient word reading is not enough to guarantee comprehension (Duke & Carlisle, 2011; Pressley, 2005).

Figure 7.11 provides a good example of informational text that's appropriate for beginning readers in the middle of the stage. Here, we see a level 8 text called *Eyes Are Everywhere* (Peterson, 1996). The text includes more sophisticated and varied sentence structure than earlier levels of text. This shift requires the reader to not only to stay "glued to the print" but she must also be thinking about the meaning of the text. Similar to the narrative text in Figure 7.10, the reader must consider the text and the illustrations in a more integrated way to fully understand the author's intention.

Late Beginning Readers

Children in the late phase of the stage have developed a full concept of word in text. They no longer use their finger as an aid in reading and they are beginning to read in longer phrases, sometimes as many as three- and four-word phrases, especially in familiar texts. They are aware of the role of punctuation and understand dialogue, though reading with expression can still be difficult, especially in unfamiliar texts. This difficulty will persist into the early and middle phase of the transitional stage, when children's sight vocabularies increase exponentially and they're

FIGURE 7.11 **Excerpt from *Eyes Are Everywhere* (Peterson, 1996)**

able to read new words with considerably greater efficiency, thanks in part to their increased awareness of spelling patterns.

Late beginning readers may read as many as 50 to 60 words correctly per minute and they have increased stamina when reading, too. It would not be unusual to for these readers to sustain their independent reading for 30 or more minutes at a time. Early and middle beginning readers may benefit from sharing some of that "independent" reading time with a partner—breaking it up into two 15-minute chunks: 15 minutes of independent reading and 15 minutes of partner reading.

The books that children read at the end of the beginning stage tend to reflect written English more than spoken language. They also include a greater range of genres such as realistic fiction, fantasy, folktales, and informational text, including sequential pieces (also called "how-to" books or procedural pieces) and descriptive texts (commonly called "all-about" books). Other characteristics include:

- Longer sentences and more text per page
- More pages per book (sometimes 25 or more pages)
- Increasingly diverse and specialized vocabulary
- Complex characters and plots in narrative text
- More sophisticated and less familiar concepts in informational text
- Difficult high-frequency words and polysyllabic words
- Less support from illustrations

These characteristics are most commonly found in guided reading levels F and G and DRA levels 10–12. They may be seen in Figure 7.12, an excerpt from *Sparky's Bone* (Daniel, 1996).

Decodable Text for Beginners

Decodable texts provide early readers repeated exposure to phonics elements and they advance children's phonics and word recognition skills. *The Wet Pet* in Figure 7.9 is a good example of a decodable text that focuses on the word families *–et* and *–at*. This would be an especially good text to use when teaching about these word families in word study. Early readers would find the predictability of the text structure and the repetition of the word families supportive, and these repeated exposures can accelerate some readers' early reading success.

FIGURE 7.12 **Excerpt from *Sparky's Bone* (Daniel, 1996)**

"Who stole my bone?" asked Sparky.
Then she saw Frog.
"Frog, do you have my bone?" asked Sparky.

"No," said Frog.
"But I have a pretty green bug.
Do you want that?"

"No, thanks," said Sparky.
"I want my bone."
And off she went.

Decodable texts also have some limitations. The vocabulary, for example, is limited to only those phonics skills that have been introduced. This can also lead to some rather unnatural syntactic structures—for example, "A fat cat sat on a mat." Because the language in decodable texts can be quite unnatural, reading them exclusively can negatively affect some children's motivation to read, particularly children with strong oral language skills.

In sum, decodable texts have a specific role in supporting beginning readers' decoding skills. Using them judiciously and integrating them thoughtfully with other more interesting and more challenging texts will likely yield the best results for most children.

Beginning Fluency: From Automaticity to Expressive Reading

Common Core Connection

Reading Standards: Foundational Skills – Fluency

Fluency is said to be the "bridge" from decoding to comprehension (Pikulski & Chard, 2005). In order for children to become fluent readers they must be able to process words both accurately and efficiently *and* read with appropriate expression (Duke & Carlisle, 2011; Rasinski et al., 2011; Samuels & Farstrup, 2006). In the previous two sections of this chapter, we explored how children come to recognize words through a developmental process beginning with alphabet knowledge, an understanding of letter–sound relationships, and then the recognition of spelling patterns, but what about expressive reading? There's less research on this topic compared to phonics and word recognition, but it's clear that expressive reading requires children to notice the prosodic features of language: its varying rate, rhythm, stress, pitch, and intonation. In doing so, and with your modeling and instruction, they learn to group words into meaningful phrases and they also begin to attend to punctuation. This facilitates reading in a manner that makes meaning clear and sounds more like talking.

When practicing fluent reading, the difficulty of the text should be related to the level and kind of support available. When a reader is well supported, you may use instructional-level text for fluency practice (books children can read with 90 to 95 percent accuracy); with less-supported reading practice, be sure the children are using independent-level texts (95 percent or greater accuracy).

As children near the late phase of the beginning stage and certainly when they're in the transitional stage, their word reading will be automatic enough that they'll be able to apply more of their cognitive energies toward reading with expression and greater comprehension. Interestingly, when children better understand the texts they're reading, their fluency and word recognition also improve. Researchers recognize that fluency has a reciprocal relationship with comprehension (Duke & Carlisle, 2011; Rasinski et al., 2011; Strecker, Roser, & Martinez, 1998). With this in mind, you may come to see fluency as a "two-way bridge," as seen in Figure 7.13.

Fluency Instruction for Beginning Readers

Fluency development in the beginning stage of development is nurtured though many instructional approaches, perhaps most notably in word study instruction (Templeton & Bear, 2011) and repeated oral readings (see NICHHD, 2000, and Kuhn & Stahl, 2004). Repeated oral readings allow children the opportunity to practice their automatic processing of words through repeated exposure to the orthographic representations of these words (Ehri, 2005; Samuels, 1979) and, importantly, it also increases children's sensitivity to the syntactic and prosodic features of

FIGURE 7.13 Fluency: A Two-Way Bridge

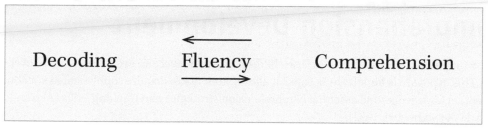

language (Schreiber, 1987; Schreiber & Read, 1980). Although there are many variations of repeated oral reading, we highlight three in this chapter: paired reading, which was described in the feature called "Working and Collaborating: Paired Reading"; fluency-oriented reading instruction (FORI) described below; and technology-assisted reading, which is described in the feature titled "Reading and Writing in Digital Contexts."

Adaptable to
All Stages

Fluency-Oriented Reading Instruction (FORI)

Earlier, you read about a five-day shared reading lesson plan in the feature called "Strategies for Your Classroom." The FORI five-day repeated reading protocol is very similar. It was designed to intentionally support children's reading of on-grade-level texts—texts that may be a little (or a lot) harder than what they can read independently (Stahl, Heubach, & Holcomb, 2005). On the first day of the protocol, the teacher reads the text aloud to the children as they follow along in their own copies. The teacher supports the children's comprehension by talking about the text with them, retelling it, or discussing the big ideas in informational text. In the days that follow, the children reread the text several different ways, including choral reading, echo reading, and partner reading. Students are also expected to read the text at home for an additional 15 to 30 minutes a day. This intense focus on supported repeated readings and comprehension have been proven to improve students' word recognition, fluency, and comprehension of on-grade-level text.

Reading and Writing in Digital Contexts

Technology-Assisted Repeated Readings

Technology-assisted repeated readings can aid in developing students' fluency, as well as leading to improvements in their word recognition and comprehension (Rasinski et al., 2011). As children listen to and read along with recorded readings of appropriately difficult passages and texts, they begin to see the relationship between letters and sounds, and even spelling patterns. This leads to greater accuracy and efficiency, which results in more automatic word recognition. Listening to models of fluent reading also helps children read more expressively. Automatic word recognition and fluent reading influence children's overall understanding of what they're reading.

Although many children will be drawn to reading this way, technology-assisted repeated readings should not be seen as a substitute for reading instruction; rather, technology should be seen as a valuable supplement to high-quality small group instruction.

Reading *To* and *With* Children: Guiding Comprehension Development

Common Core Connection

Reading Standards for Literature and Informational Text: Range of Reading and Level of Text Complexity

We use interactive read-alouds to expose children to grade-level and even above grade-level texts. This exposure is important because it allows students to acquire sophisticated vocabulary, conceptual knowledge, and essential comprehension strategies and thinking skills (Alexander & Jetton, 2000; Stanovich, 1992).

When planning an interactive read-aloud, we think about the readers' needs *before*, *during*, and *after* the reading and these become the focus of our instruction. A big part of your instruction during interactive read-alouds will be related to comprehension strategies. When teaching these strategies, we begin with modeling a single strategy and being explicit about *how*, *when*, and *why* to use it, next we provide guided practice; and finally, independent practice. This *gradual release of responsibility* (see Chapter 1), has been proven effective in comprehension strategy instruction (Pearson & Gallagher, 1983). As new strategies are learned and related to reading specific types of genres, you will model how to use these strategies flexibly and as needed.

Before Reading: Activating Prior Knowledge, Previewing, Predicting, and Setting a Purpose

As you've undoubtedly noticed from the chapter vignettes, each time we engage children in a reading task, we orient them to the gist of the story or the topic of a piece of informational text. In doing so, we activate children's prior knowledge and connect it to the new learning: "What do you know about whales?" or "What was it like for you when you first learned to ride a bike?" Activating prior knowledge improves children's engagement with text and helps them remember what they're reading (Duke & Pearson, 2002). When introducing a new book we also talk about the title, the author, the illustrations or text features, interesting or difficult words, challenging syntactic constructions, and the overall structure of the text (Clay, 1991; Fountas & Pinnell, 1996). These introductions orient children to the task of reading or listening and help them generate plausible predictions about what may happen or what the text may be about (Hansen & Pearson, 1984).

Children's predictions *before* and *during* reading are generated from two sources: the clues in the text itself and their prior knowledge, including their previous reading experiences. Familiarity with text structure also helps young children anticipate how stories or informational text work. For example, when introducing a narrative text, children who have had lots of experience reading books, listening to books, and talking about books will come to expect at least one, if not many, problems in a story (Morrow, 1985, 1986). Informational text is a little harder to predict because there are so many different forms and they often overlap (cause/effect, problem/solution, compare/contrast, sequential/"how-to books," and description/"all-about" books), but the title of the text, and your introduction and previewing of the text will help the children generate plausible predictions (see Meyer & Rice, 1984, for a review). We focus on the word *plausible* here because the point of predicting isn't necessarily to be right but to engage in the meaning-making process—to actively think while reading. As you read this, you might be thinking that predicting is a lot like inferring, and you're correct. Predictions, like inferences, will vary based on children's prior knowledge and experiences with different types of text. This is another reason we're so interested in the rationale for children's predictions.

In addition to previewing a text and generating predictions about what might happen and why, you'll also want to support children's construction of meaning by helping them identify a purpose for reading. In the chapter-opening vignette, Ms. Johnston wanted her readers to read *Max's Bike* to find out how the problem was solved. In a later feature box, Ms. Johnston directed her readers to find one thing they learned about humpback whales and be prepared to share it after reading. The purpose you set for your readers will depend on your goals for them at that time, as well as the type of text you're using, and the standards at your grade level. One of your most important goals, therefore, will be for your young readers to develop the habit of previewing texts and identifying a purpose for reading them (Duke & Pearson, 2002).

During Reading: Monitoring and Questioning

As you read aloud to children, or as they're reading themselves, you'll teach them to confirm, reject, or revise their predictions based on new information in the text. In doing so, they are monitoring their understanding, thinking about what's happening in the text, what they're learning, and what may come next. Children who monitor their predictions get more from their reading and, in general, have stronger comprehension (Fielding, Anderson, & Pearson, 1990; Hansen & Pearson, 1984). As children monitor their understanding of text, they're also adjusting their rate of reading—slowing down when meaning starts to break down, or when they need to read something more carefully. This change in rate is often based on their purpose for reading and their prior knowledge (Rasinski et al., 2011). As readers become more proficient, they will often read selectively and speed up their reading when it disinterests them or when it's not related to their intended goals (Rasinski et al., 2011). This speeding up doesn't typically happen with beginning readers, but you will notice that beginners sometimes read right through their errors without realizing that their words don't match the text, make sense, or sound right. When this happens, it's a grand opportunity to model how to monitor one's reading to be sure it matches the letters, sounds, and patterns in words *and* makes sense and sounds right. The earlier feature, "The Language of Your Instruction," will help you facilitate children's monitoring of their reading attempts.

While reading with or to children, you will ask them questions to help engage them in the meaning-making process. Asking children questions while reading not only shapes their thinking about the book being discussed but it also creates a habit of mind that they'll hopefully bring to other reading or listening experiences (see Anderson & Biddle, 1975). For example, children who are asked factual, recall-type questions tend to read for those details. Conversely, beginning readers who are regularly exposed to open-ended, higher-order questioning tend to develop higher-order thinking skills and read with deeper comprehension (Duke & Pearson, 2002; Pressley, Allington, Wharton-McDonald, Collins Block, & Morrow, 2001; Taylor et al., 2000). With this information in mind, you'll intentionally work to vary your questioning techniques to include some factual/recall-type questions because these help children notice the important details that provide the foundation for literal comprehension. You'll also ask more challenging open-ended questions that require higher-order thinking and reasoning skills.

Figure 7.14 illustrates the type of questions you might pose to your readers when reading the picture book, *A Chair for My Mother* (Williams, 1982), or the Spanish version, *Un sillón para mi mama* (Williams, 1994). As you look at this figure, you'll notice how the questions grow increasingly more sophisticated, from the more basic recall questions at the bottom, to questions that stimulate synthesis and evaluation at the top. The lightly shaded inverted triangle in the

FIGURE 7.14 **Asking Higher-Order Questions in Scaffolded Reading/Listening Tasks**

Increasingly Sophisticated Questions	**Synthesizing**	• What do you think the author's message is in this text? What's the big idea or theme? • Look at our collection of books by Vera B. Williams. What do you think she's trying to express with this body of work? • How might you live differently if you took the theme of this book seriously? • What kind of messages or lessons do you want readers of your writing to learn?
	Evaluating	• What did you notice about how the author marks the passage of time? Was it effective? • Think back to the dedication page. How does Vera Williams draw from her life experiences when she's writing? How do you think this affects the quality of her writing? • What kind of person was the main character? Defend your opinion with evidence from the text.
	Analyzing	• Have you ever wanted something very, very much? How does that text-to-life connection help you understand how the main character feels? • Compare this text to *Music, Music for Everyone* (Williams, 1984). How have the character's lives changed over time? How have they stayed the same? • Discuss the importance of the chair in this book. What does it symbolize or represent?
	Applying	• How could you earn money to save for something you really wanted? • How could you use what you learned from this main character to help you solve a problem of your own? • What "craft moves" can you borrow from this author?
	Understanding	• Why do you think it takes a long time for them to fill a big jar? • The text says, "Some days she has lots of tips. Some days she has only a little. Then she looks worried." Why do you think the mamma looks worried on those days?
	Remembering	• Where does the little girl's mother work? • How does the little girl earn her own money?

Adaptable to All Stages

background reminds us of the importance of incorporating more higher-order questions when talking with children about text. Naturally, these are just examples and we wouldn't ask them all at once; you will plan questions that align with your learning goals, the needs of the children in your classroom, and the specific text you're sharing.

Researchers have noticed that the most proficient readers generate their *own* questions *before*, *during*, and *after* reading (Raphael & Pearson, 1985; Yopp, 1988) and so we explain *why* this is important and show children *how* to generate their own questions while reading. Questioning propels readers forward into the text in the same way predicting does; questions stimulate motivation and help readers find a purpose to keep reading. Sometimes the answers can't be found in the text, and this stimulates conversation and curiosity to pursue new learning. We encourage children to share their wonderings during read-alouds and mini-lessons, and in guided reading groups, too; each of these structures provides a grand opportunity to reinforce and shape their thinking and comprehension strategy use.

At first, children's questions will sound just like yours and this is okay. Cognitive psychologists call this kind of imitation "rehearsal" (Sousa, 2011). Eventually, as children have more opportunities to listen to you share your thinking aloud, and they have more opportunity to practice questioning themselves, you'll strategically shift the responsibility for constructing meaning to them. As you do, their questions will become more personal, more authentic, and more spontaneous; this is called "elaborate rehearsal" (Sousa, 2011). In Chapter 9 we will further explore the relationship between questions and their answers and ways to categorize questions and answers with a strategy called *Question-Answer Relationships* (QARs). In the meantime, the feature box, "Children's Literature Connection," will provide you with a short list of texts that can help stimulate authentic questioning in your primary-grade classroom.

After Reading: Retelling

When reading or listening to narrative text, young readers often focus on the things they personally relate to and they miss the more subtle details such as a character's motivation or the cause/effect relationship in problem generation. In informational text, beginning readers (readers at other stages, too!) often get sidetracked by interesting details and miss the big ideas (Alexander & Jetton, 2000; Lipson, Mosenthal, & Mekkelson, 1999). While we periodically stop and scaffold children's understandings *during* their reading of the text, it's often unclear what children have truly understood about a text until the reading is complete. For this reason, we often engage children in retelling the story, at the end of a reading or listening episode, and when we do, we explain the task like this: "Tell the story/text/book in your own words as if you were telling it to a friend who has never heard it before. Start at the beginning and tell all the important parts right up to the end." It will be important for you to model the qualities of a "good" retelling many times before expecting the children to retell stories and informational texts themselves.

Children's Literature Connection

Texts That Stimulate Children to Ask Questions

Abercrombie, B. (1990). *Charlie Anderson*. M. K. Elderry.
Bunting, E. (1991). *Fly Away Home*. Clarion Books.
Bunting, E. (1989) *Wednesday's Surprise*. Clarion.
Cameron, A. (1981) *The Stories Julian Tells*. Panthenon.
Campbell Pearson, T. (2002). *Where Does Joe go?* Farrar Strauss Giroux.
Cherry, L. (1990). *The Great Kapok Tree: A Tale from the Amazon Rain Forest*. Harcourt Brace Jovanovich.
Crews, D. (1992). *Shortcut*. Greenwillow.
Davies, N. (2001). *One Tiny Turtle*. Candlewick.
Garland, S. (1993) *The Lotus Seed*. Harcourt Brace Jovanovich.
Grindley, S. (1997). *Why Is the Sky Blue?* Simon & Schuster Books for Young Readers.
Hazen, B. S. (1979). *Tight Times*. Viking.

Hearne, B. G. (2000). *Who's in the Hall? A Mystery in Four Chapters*. Greenwillow.
Rylant, C. (1996). *An Angel for Solomon Singer*. Orchard Books.
Van Allsburg, C. (1986). *The Stranger*. Houghton Mifflin.
Wiesner, D. (1991). *Tuesday*. Clarion.

Series Books

Eyewitness Books. Knopf.
First Discovery Books. Scholastic.
I Can Read All About . . . Troll Publishers.
If You . . . Series. Scholastic.
The Magic School Bus Series. Scholastic.
Rookie Readers—Read About Science Series. Children's Press.

Children's understanding of text structure can help them assemble meaning *during* reading and *after*, too (Goldman & Rakestraw, 2000). Providing children with graphic organizers—a story map, for example—can also help them better understand the structure of different forms of writing, which, in turn, aids their comprehension and their ability to retell. Some teachers complete graphic organizers with the children's help after reading a text and then invite them to complete them on their own, as seen in Figure 7.15. These organizers can help children orally retell stories, write retellings, and write responses to text, too—another effective way to improve and assess their comprehension (Duke & Pearson, 2002; Morrow, 1996).

Retelling Narrative Text

If you plan to ask a child to retell a story at the end of a reading or listening episode, be sure to set this expectation from the beginning of their listening or reading experience because, as you now know, comprehension is shaped by the reader's or listener's purpose. When children retell stories, we listen to see if they remember to include all the elements of narrative text:

- An introduction
- Characters (by name)
- Setting
- Plot (in sequential order)
    In the beginning,
    Then . . .
    Next . . . (and so . . .)
    After that . . .
    And finally . . .
- Problem
- Resolution
- Conclusion

You'll also listen to see if they use language from the text, such as "Once upon a time . . ." or a repetitive phrase like "In a dark, dark wood . . ." (Carter, 1991), or "I think I'll move to Australia" (Viorst, 1972). A good retelling sounds like the child is telling the story, as opposed to a summary that captures the gist or big ideas of a story or piece of informational text in just a few sentences (Kletzien, 2009). Summarization is a considerably more difficult task because it requires children to determine the most important parts of a text. While we may model summarization in the emergent and beginning stages, we don't typically teach it explicitly until the early phase of the transitional stage.

As you listen to children's retellings, consider what they do well and what needs improvement. For example, children will often use pronouns when retelling—for example, "He got gum stuck in his hair." Don't be afraid to ask them to *clarify*: "You said, 'He' got gum in his hair. Who is *he*?" Or when they leave out important parts, scaffold their retelling by prompting them to *elaborate*: "You said, 'Lilly cried and cried when she got home.' Can you say more about that part?" You will also ask them to *explain* unclear parts of their retellings, too: "You said Patricia was *mad*. What did you mean by that?" You will intentionally turn the responsibility for asking these questions over to the children and encourage more student-to-student conversation about books over time.

Improving Retellings: Character Motivation and Problem Identification   As you listen to children's retellings, pay careful attention to the depth and sophistication of their understandings. Do their retellings illuminate their understanding of characters' motives and the cause/effect relationship that inherently causes tension in narrative texts, or is their retelling more

FIGURE 7.15 Events in *Frog and Toad Are Friends* (Lobel, 1979)

literal or superficial? What about the organization of their retellings? Are they able to sequence events accurately? Sequencing events is a skill that will be critically important for them to develop as they read and listen to longer and more complex texts that often have to be read in more than one sitting.

Understanding characters' motives, problems and resolutions, and the passage of time are important aspects of comprehending narrative text, and effective retellings will reflect these understandings. When children are having difficulty with these, consider scaffolding the task with graphic organizers such as Somebody-Wanted-But-So (Macon, Bewell, & Vogt, 1991).

Somebody-Wanted-But-So is a graphic organizer (see Figure 7.16) intended to help children better understand character's motives, problems, events, and resolutions. It can be completed while reading a text or afterwards. Like all strategies and tools, you'll want to model how to use this graphic organizer prior to asking the children to use it. You'll also want to be clear about how they can use graphic organizers to deepen their comprehension, improve their retellings, or create written responses to text. Graphic organizers are intended to be a *means* to an *end*, rather than an end in themselves.

FIGURE 7.16 **Somebody-Wanted-But-So Graphic Organizer**

Somebody (character)	wanted (motive)
but (problem)	**so. . .** (resolution)

Retelling Informational Text

Common Core Connection

Reading Standards for
Informational Text:
Key Ideas and Details;
Range of Reading
and Level of Text
Complexity

Whenever we teach a comprehension strategy (predicting, questioning, retelling) or thinking skill (analysis, synthesis, evaluation) in one genre, it's important to think about how that skill or strategy might transfer to another genre. This is particularly significant when we're thinking about retelling narrative text versus informational text. Retelling informational text can be especially challenging because of its many different forms and because children often lack experience and familiarity with it (Duke & Bennett-Armistead, 2003; Goldman & Rakestraw, 2000).

When teaching retelling in informational text, begin with one of the easiest forms to retell: either a "how-to" procedural piece, or an "all-about" descriptive piece. These are easier because they tend to be more similar to narrative structure. Some of the other forms, notably compare/contrast and cause/effect, are more challenging to retell because young children often have difficulty understanding these relationships, much like understanding character motivation is hard for them, too. Over time, and with your support and instruction, they will be able to identify and understand these more subtle yet important elements in both narrative and informational text. When they do, you'll capitalize on their growing insights and think about how you can build on them in your writing instruction, too. The more intentional you are about connecting your reading and writing, the more efficient and effective your instruction will be.

As you can see, in addition to your guided reading experiences with children, it's critical that you engage them in daily interactive read-alouds as well. These read-alouds are where they are exposed to grade-appropriate and even above-grade-level text. It is also the time of day where they'll receive the most exposure to academic vocabulary and complex syntactic structures (Hiebert & Mesmer, 2006) and they'll learn *how*, *when*, and *why* readers use various comprehension strategies (Duke & Pearson, 2002).

The Beginning of Conventional Writing

Common Core Connection

Writing Standards:
Text Types and
Purposes

Beginning writers are keen observers and grand imitators! They've been watching others write for several years and they've been experimenting with their own writing, too. They've come to realize that writing is used for many purposes and they've also learned about many different genres and forms of writing along the way: labels and signs, cards and letters, stories, poetry, songs, and informational text. When these beginners were in the emergent stage in preschool and kindergarten, they drew pictures and narrated them with great enthusiasm, gradually adding print to their stories. Whether in the form of scribbles, symbols, pictures, or conventional letters, they used writing to express themselves (Bear et al., 2012; Schickedanz, 1986; Sulzby, 1985).

Late in the emergent stage and early in the beginning stage, writers start to focus more of their attention on actual writing rather than illustrations. These young writers are very proud of their writing and will eagerly read it to you or anyone else who will listen. However, as their awareness of conventional writing increases, they can become preoccupied with spelling things correctly, and the pace of their writing slows even more as they try to get everything "right." This can be discouraging to early beginners and some may even become even a little disinterested in the task they once loved (Sulzby, 1985). Early beginning writers need lots of encouragement!

Getting Started with Writing Workshop

One of your primary jobs in the beginning stage of writing is building children's esteem as writers. If you model the joy of storytelling and writing, your young writers are more likely to see the value and importance of these activities, too. They'll also come to appreciate the habit of writing through your modeling of writing and by listening to stories in which the main character writes or tells stories. (See Figure 7.17 for a suggested list.) Children love the book, *The Stories Julian Tells* (Cameron, 1981), and the adventures of Julian's little brother Huey, too (Cameron, 1995). What's not to love about a barn full of cows writing persuasive, if not demanding, letters to Farmer Brown in *Click, Clack, Moo: Cows That Type* (Cronin, 2000), or a worm that keeps a diary (Bliss, 2003)? And then there's their beloved animated friend, Arthur (Brown, 1996), who teaches them that they don't need to invent outlandish tales when writing narratives—just writing about one's everyday life is exciting enough! The characters in each of these texts and those in Figure 7.17 serve as important role models to beginning writers and you'll refer to the lessons found in these books throughout the year.

As you launch your writing workshop, you'll want to impress on your beginning writers that writing isn't something they'll just do in school, but something that's part of their whole lives. One way to make this point is to organize opportunities for your young writers to interview older students and adults about their writing lives. Encourage the children to collect examples of other people's writing, too, and display these artifacts in your writing center—things like maps and directions, letters, recipes, e-mails, stories, reports, shopping lists, newspaper articles, journal entries, instructions for doing or fixing things, and "to-do" lists, among other things.

> Adaptable to All Stages

FIGURE 7.17 Books with Main Characters Who Write or Tell Stories

Auch, M. (2010). *Plot Chickens*. Holiday House.

Bliss, H. (2003). *Diary of a Worm*. Joanna Cutler.

Brown, M. T. (1996). *Arthur Tells a Story*. Little, Brown.

Cronin, D. (2000). *Click, Clack, Moo: Cows That Type*. Simon & Schuster Books for Young Readers.

Duke, K. (1992. *Aunt Isabel Tells a Good One*. Dutton Children's Books.

Hest, A. (1995). *How to Get Famous in Brooklyn*. Simon & Schuster Books for Young Readers.

James, S. (1991). *Dear Mr. Blueberry*. M. K. McElderry.

Keats, E. J. (1998). *A Letter to Amy*. Viking.

Lester, H. (1997). *Author: A True Story*. Houghton Mifflin.

Lowry, N. J. (1988). *If You Were a Writer*. Four Winds.

Schotter, R. (1997). *Nothing Ever Happens on 90th Street*. Orchard Books.

Spinelli, E. (2008). *The Best Story*. Dial Books for Young Readers.

These examples inspire children to think about the many forms and functions of print, as well as giving them tangible examples of things they might write when writing a whole story feels too daunting.

You'll also do your best to invite members of the literary community into your classroom. Perhaps there's a local storyteller who could visit, a librarian who knows a lot about children's books and authors, or maybe even a local author who would be willing to talk about his or her writing life. If you don't have access to such people, don't worry! Publishers and authors often have websites to support your author studies. Two particularly good websites for planning your next author study are the U.S. Department of Education's *Reading Rockets* website (www.readingrockets .org) and the International Reading Associations' *readwritethink* website (www.readwritethink.org).

What Should I Write About?

One the most common questions children ask is, "What should I write about?" Others may grumble that they don't have *anything* to write about. Fortunately, most authors of children's books expect children to ask where they get their ideas for writing and they usually address this question on their websites. Marc Brown, for example, talks about his sister being the inspiration for the character Francine in his *Arthur* series. He also displays a photo of himself from the third grade and asks his readers if he bears resemblance to any of his characters, and of course it's Arthur. (Your beginning writers will love this!) Gail Gibbons explains on her website that she has always been fascinated with asking "Why?" questions. Her wonderings have led her to publish more than 170 books! Over time, children will come to value these mentor authors not only for their insights about where to get ideas for writing but you'll help them learn craft moves from their writing, too (Calkins & Hartman; 2003; Fletcher & Portalupi, 2007).

Since getting started with a piece of writing is often the hardest part for young writers (maybe all writers!), you'll help your beginning writers by generating a list of topics they *could* write about. These are usually topics and memories from their everyday lives or topics they know a lot about. You'll invite families to help with this task, too, by asking them to collaboratively prepare a list of potential writing topics with their child. You may also suggest that they send in small items that might inspire their child's writing: a photograph of a favorite object or person, a postcard from a favorite place, a ticket stub from an amusement park or movie, or a piece of sports memorabilia. These items can be taped to the children's writing folders as reminders of all the things they could write about. You'll also have a class-generated list of topics and types of writing in case children need any additional inspiration.

It's important to emphasize that items they bring in may be quite ordinary. Many children's families are not able financially to go to the movies often, much less take a trip to Disney World or even an amusement part across town. As we've noted, many children have never been farther than six blocks in any direction from their home. A photograph, a locket, an action figure—any item can be an inspiration, capable of generating a description or narrative treasure.

Getting Started with Narrative Writing

Storytelling and narrative text are believed to be a natural part of how humans make sense of their world (Fischer, 1989). When teaching children about different genres, we usually start with narrative text because it's the genre they're most familiar with and is typically the easiest for them to learn (although we're open to the possibility that some children, especially boys, may be more open to and comfortable with informational writing; see below). Because beginners can be apprehensive about writing, you'll thoughtfully and intentionally model how to compose simple narratives as part of your daily mini-lessons, particularly in the early part of the year. You'll show

FIGURE 7.18 Books about Everyday Experiences

Brinckloe, J. (1986). *Fireflies*. Aladdin.

Crews, D. (1996). *Shortcut*. Greenwillow.

Crews, D. (1998). *Bigmama's*. Greenwillow.

Frazee, M. (2003) *Roller Coaster*. Harcourt Brace Jovanovich.

Hesse, K. (1999). *Come on Rain*. Scholastic.

Keats, E. J. (1962). *The Snowy Day*. Viking.

Keats, E. J. (1998). *Peter's Chair*. Puffin.

Penn, A. (2007). *The Kissing Hand*. The Child Welfare League of America.

Pilkey, D. (1999). *Paperboy*. Scholastic.

Rylant, C. (1986). *Night in the Country*. Bradbury.

Viorst, J. (1972). *Alexander and the Terrible, Horrible, No Good, Very Bad Day*. Atheneum.

the children how you "write down your life" by picking a single episode or memory to draw and describe. Noted writing expert, Lucy Calkins, calls these "small moments" and refers to them as the "seeds" of narrative writing (Calkins, 1994; Calkins & Oxenhorn, 2003). (See Figure 7.18 for a list of sample texts about everyday experiences.)

As you're creating a quick sketch of the setting of your story, tell your story in storybook language, keeping it simple yet interesting. Perhaps your story will be about finding a four-leaf clover, the first time you met your new baby sister, or your favorite birthday. Whatever the topic of your story, you'll show the children how to move from sketching to writing a few lines of text. As you model your writing, explicitly show the children the strategies you use to organize your writing, spell unknown words, choose descriptive adjectives (without using the label yet), and use punctuation. At first, your narratives will mostly describe single moments in your life; later, the stories will build with multiple episodes. As children enter the late phase of the stage and move into the transitional stage, you'll teach them how to use story maps and other planning tools to develop their characters and plot before they start writing. In the beginning stage, oral rehearsal—talking about their topics— and sketching their illustrations before they start writing are usually sufficient prewriting strategies for narrative text.

Writing to Inform: Procedural "How-To" Writing, "All-About" Texts, and Persuasive "Argument" Writing

Young children are naturally inquisitive about the world around them. They're forever asking "Why?" and "How come?" They also love to collect small things from nature: rocks, acorns, flowers, sticks, and so on. Perhaps you remember having similar collections when you were young. Most children are naturally curious about the world around them and this often stimulates informational writing.

As described in Chapter 6, about one-third of your read-alouds will be informational text. Sometimes these books will be related to your science, social studies, or health themes; other times you'll just share them because they're great books for children to enjoy. There are times, too, when your read-alouds will become "mentor texts" that you'll study with your beginning writers to learn more about a genre or an author's craft. Figure 7.19 lists some possible mentor texts for descriptive "all-about" writing, sequential "how-to" books, and persuasive "argument" texts—three forms of informational text specified in the Common Core.

Common Core Connection

Writing Standards: Text Types and Purposes

FIGURE 7.19 Mentor Texts and Authors for "All-About" Books, "How-To" Books, and Persuasive "Argument" Writing

"All-About Texts"
David Adler (biographies)
Aliki
Gail Gibbons
Ruth Heller
Anne McGovern
Seymour Simon
Tanya Lee Stone

"How-To" Texts
Chauffe, E., & Chauffee, E. (2009). *Kids Show Kids How to Make Balloon Animals*. Casey Shay.
Craighead, G. J. (2000). *How to Talk to Your Dog*. HarperCollins.
Gibbons, G. (1990). *How a House Is Built*. Holiday House.
Gibson, R. (1999). *I Can Draw People*. Usbourne.
Holub, J. (2001). *The Pizza We Made*. Viking.
Lin, G. (2002). *Kite Flying*. Knopf.

Persuasive "Argument" Texts
Hoose, P. (1998). *Hey Little Ant*. Tricycle.
Kaufman, O. K. (2004). *I Wanna Iguana*. Putnam.
Kellogg, S. (1971). *Can I Keep Him?* Dial.
Layne, S. (2003). *My Brother Dan's Delicious*. Pelican.
Viorst, J. (1990). *Earrings*. Atheneum.
Wells, R. (2008). *Otto Runs for President*. Scholastic.

The Writing Process

The Common Core's Writing Standard for Production and Distribution of Writing emphasizes the importance of students using the writing process. This process includes planning and prewriting activities, drafting, revising, editing, and publishing and sharing one's writing. Each step of the writing process for beginners is described in the following sections.

Planning and Prewriting

Common Core Connection

Writing Standards: Text Types and Purposes; Research to Build and Present Knowledge

When teaching children to retell informational text they read or listened to, you might show children how to use a web to keep track of the big ideas and details in a piece of descriptive text. After introducing a web as part of reading comprehension, you might then use such a tool for planning a piece of descriptive writing. In Figure 7.20, you'll see how Ms. Johnston begins her first "all-about" descriptive writing of the year with a web entitled "Me." She chooses this as the topic for the children's first report writing so they can learn the form without worrying about conducting research. Similarly, the children will write their first procedural pieces about something they know how to do quite well—maybe making waffles or feeding the dog. When they plan these pieces, they'll use a sequence chart. Later in the year, she'll work with small groups of writers to research and write "all-about" reports about animals

FIGURE 7.20 Webbing as Part of Planning an "All-About" Book

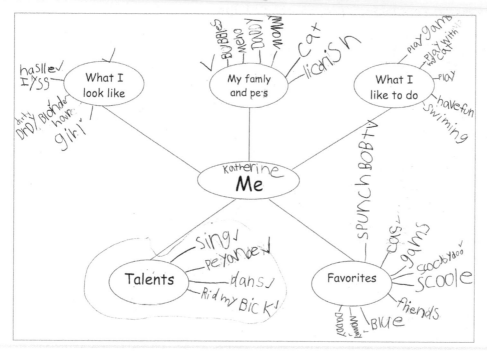

and their habitats, and when they do, they'll create concept maps before they write. Content-area writing addresses the Common Core's *Research to Build and Present Knowledge* standard.

Drafting

Ms. Johnston models using a web for planning her writing. She begins by thinking aloud and telling the children about her talents, family, pets, and "favorites" as she makes notes on the graphic organizer. After modeling how to use the web to plan, the children complete their own webs and then she models how to draft a paragraph from each of her "big ideas." After modeling, the children turn to their writing partners and discuss their writing plans for the day before they begin to write their own descriptions of themselves. In the writing sample in Figure 7.21, we see Seth's writing: "My head is fat. I have a crooked toe. I have brown eyes." Notice how Seth uses the word wall to spell some high-frequency words such as *my, have, is, brown, eyes,* and he relies on his letter–sound knowledge to spell *fat* FAT and other unknown words, too: *head* HED and *crooked* CRICID.

Revising, Editing, and Publishing

As the children finish the first draft of their "All about Me" pieces, Ms. Johnston revisits some of her own writing while doing a think-aloud: "Writers, after reading this chapter of my book, I'm realizing that I started every sentence with the same words, 'I am . . . .' And I was thinking: that's not very interesting. I wonder if there's another way I could write some of these sentences. Turn and talk to your writing partner and see if you can come up with some suggestions for me to revise my work." Ms. Johnston explains to the children that revising is part of the writing process and it means that they are re-visioning their writing, or seeing it again through new eyes, to make it better. After talking about different ways she could vary her sentence structure, she takes out a red pen and shows the children how to mark up their drafts as they revise. Seth revises his piece to add the word *also* to the last sentence.

FIGURE 7.21 First Draft of an "All-About" Book

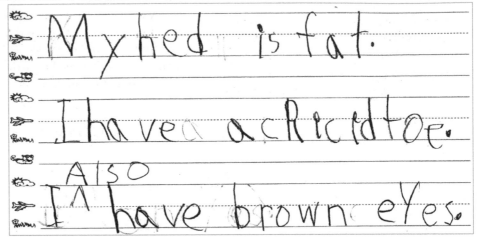

In the days to come, Ms. Johnston will show the children how to add text features such as a table of contents, chapter headings, and captions for their illustrations. Then she'll introduce an editing checklist that's based on the Conventions of Standard English Standards in the Common Core. This won't be the first time the children have seen or used this checklist. Ms. Johnston first introduced it during interactive writing (McCarrier, Pinnell, & Fountas, 1999), and they often use it when writing their morning message, too. Just the same, she'll model how to use it in this new context and she'll begin by editing her own writing, which has a few intentional mistakes in punctuation and capitalization so she can demonstrate how to effectively use the tool. After the children self-assess, they'll share papers with their writing buddies who will also edit their work using the checklist. After that, their work is turned into the Editor in Chief: Ms. Johnston herself.

Sometimes you'll want to help edit children's work so it is polished and free of errors, but most of the time, their errors are developmentally appropriate. Correcting children's approximations risks sending the message that their efforts are not "good enough" and this can inhibit future risk taking—something you certainly wish to avoid. When displaying work that is not completely "conventional" in terms of spelling or punctuation, consider a subtle disclaimer that acknowledges that the students' work is "under development," "in progress" or "under construction" so that readers will understand that you honor where children are along a continuum and you're not expecting perfection even in final drafts.

Common Core Connection

Language Standards:
Conventions of
Standard English

Common Core Connection

Writing Standards:
Production and
Distribution of Writing

Chapter Summary

The beginning stage of reading and writing is a time in children's development when they first read and write in the conventional sense. They begin the stage with two critical insights that supported their transition from *emergent* reading to *beginning* reading:

- The understanding that letters represent sounds (alphabetic principle), as demonstrated in children's spelling of words, and
- The understanding that a spoken word matches a written word, as demonstrated by children's ability

to accurately point to words while reading familiar text (concept of word in text).

Throughout the stage, children's reading, writing, and word study instruction elevate these early understandings, and before long, children are reading and writing texts with increasingly elaborate plots and interesting information. They're reading more words by sight, and with this developing automaticity, they're able to focus more of their cognitive resources on comprehension. Beginning writers use what they've learned about text structure in reading workshop, as well as what they've learned in writing workshop about different genres. Table 7.2 summarizes children's growth in reading, writing, and spelling across the beginning stage of development.

TABLE 7.2 Characteristics of Children in the Beginning Reading Stage

	Reading	Writing	Word Study
Early bed – *bd ship – *sp float – *ft drive - *gf *Text Levels:* DRA Level 4 Guided Reading Level C–D	• Rudimentary concept of word when reading familiar text • Reads dictated sentences fairly accurately • Notices many initial consonants in words when reading, but still relies on memory and predictable/patterned text • Beginning to know some words on sight (about 20) • Reads aloud in a word-by-word fashion	• Rudimentary concept of word in writing (beginning to use initial consonants and some final consonants) • Labels pictures and begins to write simple sentences that the child can accurately read, as can adults who understand letter–name logic • Still relies on pictures to tell much of the story • Forms many but not all letters correctly	• Knows most upper- and lowercase letter names and sounds • Represents the most salient consonant sounds when spelling words • Some expected confusions about letters that look alike, sound alike, and feel similar when articulated
Middle bed – *bad ship – *shep float – *fot drive – *jriv *Text Levels:* DRA Level 6–8 Guided Reading Level E	• Self-corrects when finger-point reading; gets off track (especially in two-syllable words) • Sight-word vocabulary growing to approximately 50–75 words • Beginning to use analogy to learn new words • Reads aloud	• Writing is focused on letter–sound correspondence with the majority of effort directed toward spelling • Writes simple stories to go with pictures • Is beginning to experiment with different genres	• Spells words phonetically and includes initial and final consonant sounds in most words • Experiments with medial vowels and may confuse these with the names of the vowels and/or their point of articulation
Late bed – correct ship – correct stick – *stik float – *flot drive – *driv *Text Levels:* DRA Level 10–12 Guided Reading Level F–G Rate: Approximately 50–60 WCPM	• Full concept of word • Can identify short vowel words and many high-frequency words both in and out of context • Reads with some phrasing and expression in well-rehearsed text • Reads about 150 words by sight • Can make plausible predictions and retell stories read independently • Improved stamina when reading • Can whisper read	• Writes several paragraph stories, reports, and procedural pieces, but writing requires a great deal of effort • Beginning to edit own writing and self-correct spelling errors in single-syllable short vowel words and some high-frequency words • Begins to revise own writing • Letter formation is more automatic and accurate • Improved stamina and motivation when writing	• Spells words phonetically • Accurately spells many high-frequency words and words with the CVC short vowel pattern • Spells many words with digraphs and two-letter blends and is beginning to use preconsonantal nasals and r-influenced vowels accurately • Has generalized the CVC short vowel pattern beyond word families

Suggested Extension Activities

- **Interactive read-aloud.** Plan an interactive read-aloud focused on comprehension and vocabulary instruction. Be sure to plan your book introduction, select your target vocabulary words, and identify what you'll do before, during, and after reading to support children's comprehension.

- **Guided reading.** Plan two guided reading lessons for children in the beginning stage of reading using both narrative and informational text. Describe the characteristics of your group and how you selected your texts. Use the guided reading planning template found in the chapter as a model.

- **Leveled Text.** Gather a collection of narrative and informational texts from levels 3 through 12. Review texts and sort them according to the levels. Study the texts and look for how they change as they get progressively more complex. Create your own list of characteristics. Use this list, as well as the ones in this chapter, to attempt to estimate the levels of some of the trade books typically found in a classroom library. As you learn the factors that contribute to text complexity, you'll be less dependent on commercially published leveled text.

Recommended Professional Resources

Calkins, L. (2003). *Units of study for primary writing: A yearlong curriculum.* Portsmouth, NH: Firsthand.

Duke, N., & Bennett-Armistead, S. (2003). *Reading and writing informational text in the primary grades: Research-based practices.* New York: Scholastic.

Fountas, I., & Pinnell, G. S. (1996). *Guided reading: Good first teaching for all children.* Portsmouth, NH: Heinemann.

Helman, L., Bear, D., Invernizzi, M., Templeton, S., & Johnston, F. (2008). *Words their way: Letter name-alphabetic sorts for Spanish speaking–English learners.* Boston: Pearson/Allyn & Bacon.

Hoyt, L. (2006). *Interactive read alouds, grades K–1: Linking standards, fluency and comprehension.* Portsmouth, NH: Firsthand.

Hoyt, L. (2008). *Revisit, reflect, retell: Time-tested strategies for teaching reading comprehension in the primary grades.* Portland, ME: Stenhouse.

Johnston, F., Bear, D., Invernizzi, M., & Templeton, S. (2009). *Words their way: Word sorts for letter name-alphabetic spellers* (2nd ed.) Boston: Pearson/Allyn & Bacon.

McCarrier, A., Pinnell, G., & Fountas, I. (2000). *Interactive writing: How language and literacy come together, K–2.* Portsmouth, NH: Heinemann.

Miller, D. (2002). *Reading with meaning: Teaching comprehension in the primary grades.* Portland, ME: Stenhouse.

Pressley, M., Allington, R., Wharton-McDonald, R., Collins Block, K., & Morrow, L. (2001). *Learning to read: Lessons from exemplary first-grade classrooms.* New York: Guilford.

Online Resources

Phonological Awareness Literacy Screening (PALS)

http://pals.virginia.edu/tools-activities.html

PALS is a statewide early literacy screening in the state of Virginia. The PALS office, in conjunction with the Curry School of Education at the University of Virginia, have created this website to support the instruction and assessment of emergent and beginning readers. Here you will find activities, teacher resources, and helpful information to share with parents.

Reading Rockets, U.S. Department of Education

www.readingrockets.org/

This online clearinghouse of information on teaching reading and writing includes lesson plans, research, recorded interviews with authors, tips for author studies, and countless other resources. The site has special portals for different stakeholders: teachers, parents, librarians, and school leaders. The information is available in both English and Spanish.

readwritethink.org, The International Reading Association

www.readwritethink.org

A joint venture between the International Reading Association and the National Council of Teachers of English, this website is a free online resource for reading and language arts lesson plans and professional development. Resources for community partners including daycare professionals and parents can also be found on this site.

Transitional Reading and Writing

Chapter Outline

» Overview of Transitional Readers, Writers, and Within Word Pattern Spellers

» Within Word Pattern Spellers: Moving from Sound to Pattern

» Vocabulary Development: Spelling Instruction and Beyond

» Interactive Read-Alouds: Developing Engaged Listeners and Deep Thinkers

» From Talking Well to Writing Well: Written Response to Text

» Books for Transitional Readers: Independent and Small Group Reading Practice

» Developing Transitional Readers' Fluency and Comprehension: Research-Based "Best" Practices

» Reading and Writing Connections: Helping Transitional Writers Write Well

8 Focus Questions

1. What are the characteristics of transitional readers and writers, and within word pattern spellers?
2. How do teachers develop children's word knowledge in this stage?
3. How can you support transitional readers' and writers' critical engagements with complex text?
4. How will you teach transitional readers to *read* with fluency and comprehension?
5. How will you help transitional writers *write* with fluency and intention?
6. What are some ways reading and writing instruction can be integrated in the transitional stage of development?

Today you're visiting Mr. Garcia's second-grade classroom to learn about fluency instruction with children in the transitional stage of development. As you enter the classroom, you're excited to see the children so engaged in their reading. Most are reading silently, but a few are reading quietly and talking in partnerships. Before long, you notice Mr. Garcia working with two students in the library corner and you join him there. He briefly introduces you to the two boys he's conferring with and they politely welcome you, but they're eager to get back to their discussion. The children are holding copies of *The Little Red Hen* (Galdone, 1973) and they're debating whether it's fair that the hen keep the bread all to herself. As they talk, you notice how Mr. Garcia introduces sophisticated words into the conversation quite naturally: "So you're saying that the Little Red Hen was selfish—egoísta—because she wouldn't share the bread with the other animals?" Jax replies, "Sí!" and in a mix of English and Spanish, he explains his reasoning and he points to the pictures and rereads lines from the text to make his point. He's clearly disappointed with the Red Hen's decision not to share the bread. Ramon disagrees with his friend: "I see it differently," he explains. "I think she's trying to teach her friends a lesson." Mr. Garcia probes, "So you think she's wise, Ramon, and not selfish?" Ramon agrees with Mr. Garcia's assessment and builds on it: "She's just like the tortoise was in *'The Tortoise and the Hare'.*" "How

so?" inquires Mr. Garcia. Ramon explains that reaching your goal takes hard work and both the Little Red Hen and the tortoise had to stay focused on their goals and they both achieved them.

Mentioning the tortoise and the hare gets two other students' attention and they move closer to eavesdrop. You notice that they're each holding a copy of *The Tortoise and the Hare* (Stevens, 1984) and this makes you smile. Before long, the two sets of partners are comparing and contrasting the characters and lessons from their two stories and Jax offers a new perspective: "Okay, maybe the hen isn't selfish, but her friends sure are lazy and the rabbit is definitely a show-off!" Everyone laughs and Mr. Garcia has a satisfied look on his face. You begin to stand because you think the conference is over, but Mr. Garcia leans forward and this causes you to hesitate. He says, "Readers, you've done a marvelous job analyzing these characters and the big ideas in both of these texts. I love that you all have different opinions and those opinions are being shaped by the texts, your own beliefs and prior knowledge, and what you hear other people saying, too."

Mr. Garcia continues, "After listening to all of you talk this morning, I came to realize that opinions are a lot like predictions: Having an opinion isn't really about being right or wrong, but backing your opinions up with evidence makes them strong—just like predictions. And just like predictions, your opinions can change as you read, think, and listen to others."

The children listen attentively and when Mr. Garcia finishes speaking, they talk about predictions they've had before and how they've been right sometimes and how they've had to revise or abandon them other times. You're amazed by how aware they are of their strategy use and you remember this is called "metacognition," an important part of comprehension instruction (Baker, 2000).

Mr. Garcia concludes the conference by saying, "Let's use the time we have left today to reread your books and continue thinking about your opinions, and evidence to back them up. Use these Post-its to jot down some ideas or mark pages in your book where you can find evidence to back up your opinions and we'll talk about your ideas again tomorrow." With that, the four children return to their texts and continue to talk among themselves. You notice that two of the children swap books and you realize that Mr. Garcia is masterful at creating a community of readers and thinkers. Even you want to reread these classic tales!

At the end of the workshop, you have a few minutes to debrief with Mr. Garcia. You're not sure where to begin, but since your assignment was to observe fluency instruction, it seems like you'd better ask him about that because you didn't see what you expected. Mr. Garcia smiles when he hears your question. He explains that some people see fluency through what he calls "a very narrow lens" and this can unfortunately lead to some rather dull experiences for children. He sees fluency instruction as a small piece of a much bigger puzzle; he explains that children need access to books they *can* read and *want* to read (Guthrie, Wigfield & Perencevich, 2004). When they read texts with high levels of accuracy, they're more likely to read with better fluency and comprehension, too (Negrete, 2010; Rasinski, Reutzel, Chard, & Linan-Thompson, 2011; Sinatra, Brown, & Reynolds, 2002).

Mr. Garcia continues to explain that talking about books also stimulates reading engagement and deepens children's comprehension (Anderson et al., 2001; Palinscar & Brown, 1986; Waggoner, Chinn, Yi, & Anderson, 1995). These conversations inspire children to revisit and reread their books again and again. You're intrigued by this comment because you know repeated readings are an important way to build fluency. He explains that when children reread texts, especially texts they understand, they're more likely to read with expression and with an appropriate rate, too (Kuhn & Stahl, 2004; Rasinski et al., 2011).

As you listen, you realize this makes a lot of sense and you wonder what he'll do in reading workshop tomorrow. Mr. Garcia explains that he'll gather these four children together into a small guided reading group and introduce *The Little Red Hen: A Play* (Young, 1996). They'll read it as a guided reading selection first, and then throughout the week the children will practice reading and rereading their parts until they're ready to read the play to their peers. This, he explains, is called **Readers' Theater** and it's an effective way to improve oral reading fluency with transitional readers.

You're impressed by how Mr. Garcia integrates fluency instruction into the broader goals of literacy instruction: reading comprehension and enjoyment, too. You're impressed by how many Common Core Standards he addressed in one short reading conference and you can't wait to tell your classmates all about it! ■

Overview of Transitional Readers, Writers, and Within Word Pattern Spellers

For most children, the transitional stage of development begins in the middle to end of first grade or early second grade, and it can stretch into the middle of fourth grade for some and sometimes beyond for some others. If you're thinking this is a long period of time, you're right! The English language has more vowel sounds than many languages, and learning the relationships between these sounds and the letter patterns that represent them is the main focus of word study in this stage of development. It often takes time for children to develop the understandings necessary to accurately read and spell the many different vowel sounds of English. Admittedly, it can be tempting to rush children through the within word pattern stage, particularly when they are progressing slowly, or when you feel some external pressure to move them to the "next level," but it's not advisable to do so. All too often, children who struggle with literacy in the later years do so because they have not gained the critical insights of transitional readers and writers (Flanigan et al., 2011). That said, it's important to monitor children's progress and adjust the pacing of your instruction based on their rate of learning and their needs. Some children will be able to move more quickly; others will need additional time and practice with some sorts. Monitoring student learning and adjusting your instruction are important in all stages of development. (See *Words Their Way: Word Study for Phonics, Vocabulary, and Spelling Instruction* by Bear, Invernizzi, Templeton, & Johnston, 2012, for specific pacing suggestions.)

Your understanding of the importance of this stage of development will help you stay focused on providing developmentally oriented instruction to your transitional readers and writers. It's this child-centered focus that will yield the most powerful and lasting results.

Throughout this chapter, you'll come to see the transitional stage of development as something of a bridge between beginners' deliberate and concentrated efforts to read and write words, and intermediate readers' critical engagements with complex text. It's these critical engagements with text that are necessary for children to succeed in middle and high school, as well as in college and in their later careers (CCSS, 2010; Kamil, 2003). While we explicitly model and practice critical thinking and reasoning skills through our read-alouds and guided reading experiences, it's not until the intermediate stage where children are able to more independently initiate and sustain these kinds of robust engagements with text themselves (Sticht & James, 1984).

Children in the transitional stage are becoming more efficient when reading and writing words; they are beginning to see patterns *within* words and they can read a number of words by sight—starting with about 150 words and growing to nearly 400 words later in the stage. Because transitional readers are becoming more efficient at the word level, they also begin to read in more meaningful phrases and with expression. Their reading rate improves from 50 to 60 words correct per minute to 100 words (or more) by the late part of the stage. They're also learning that reading "fast" isn't necessarily the goal, but that reading thoughtfully and for meaning are most important. They'll come to understand that proficient readers vary the rate of their reading and the volume of their reading for dramatic effect. They'll also learn that they can vary their rate as a means of monitoring their reading comprehension. Importantly, as children's fluency improves, you'll also observe improvement in their motivation and engagement, stamina, and comprehension (Duke & Carlisle, 2011; Rasinski et al., 2011). We see similar effects in writing: As children become more automatic in spelling words and forming letters, you'll see improvements in the length and quality of their compositions as well (Abbott, Berninger, & Fayol, 2010; Graham, Harris, & Fink, 2000).

Understanding how children develop and grow throughout the within word pattern stage will allow you to identify their individual needs, differentiate their instruction, and deepen not only their word knowledge but also their understanding and enjoyment of reading and writing activities.

Within Word Pattern Spellers: Moving from Sound to Pattern

We begin this chapter with a focus on word knowledge. We do so because it's this focus on reading and writing words accurately and automatically that allows transitional readers and writers to access more complex text and engage in more sophisticated writing tasks beginning in this stage and well beyond (Bear et al., 2012; Chall, 1996; Duke & Carlisle, 2011; Rasinski et al., 2011).

FIGURE 8.1 Spelling Samples of Early, Middle, and Late Within Word Pattern Spellers

Mackenzie	José		Amber	
1. fan	1. fan	14. friht (fright)	1. fan	14. fright
2. pet	2. pet	15. chewed	2. pet	15. chewed
3. dig	3. dig	16. crall (crawl)	3. dig	16. crawl
4. rob	4. rob	17. wishes	4. rob	17. wishes
5. hope	5. hope	18. thorn	5. hope	18. thorn
6. wate (wait)	6. wait	19. shouted	6. wait	19. shouted
7. gum	7. gum	20. spoyle (spoil)	7. gum	20. spoyl (spoil)
8. sled	8. sled	21. groul (growl)	8. sled	21. growl
9. stek (stick)	9. stick	22. thurd (third)	9. stick	22. third
10. shaine (shine)	10. shine	23. campt (camped)	10. shine	23. camped
11. dreme (dream)	11. dream	24. trys (tries)	11. dream	24. trys (tries)
12. blad (blade)	12. blade	25. claping (clapping)	12. blade	25. claping (clapping)
13. coche (coach)	13. coach	26. rideing (riding)	13. coach	26. rideing (riding)
14. frite (fright)				
15. chood (chewed)				
16. crall (crawl)				
17. wishis (wishes)				
18. thorn				
19. showted (shouted)				
20. spol (spoil)				

Within word pattern spellers vary quite considerably across the transitional stage of development. This is probably best illustrated by looking at children's writing samples or their spelling attempts on a spelling inventory. To illustrate this point, consider the spelling samples in Figure 8.1. Here, we meet three children from Mr. Garcia's second-grade class: Mackenzie, José, and Amber. All three children are in the transitional stage of development, yet a close look at their spelling on the Primary Spelling Inventory (Bear et al., 2012) reveals some qualitative differences in how they approach spelling words with various vowel patterns. Take a few minutes to analyze the children's spelling by using the scope and sequence in Table 8.1 to help you identify what they are able to do independently and the first place they begin to "use but confuse" spelling features (Invernizzi, Abouzeid, & Gill, 1994). This is their *zone of proximal development* (Vygotsky, 1978) or *instructional level* (Bear et al., 2012). Take a moment to jot some notes about your observations before reading the analysis that follows.

Characteristics of Early, Middle, and Late Within Word Pattern Spellers

Our first student, Mackenzie, demonstrates an understanding of single-syllable short vowel words as you see in her correct spelling of *bed, pet, dig,* and *fan.* She also demonstrates her understanding of many blends and digraphs as in ***sled, stick, dream, fright, coach, wishes,*** and ***thorn.*** Mackenzie sometimes relies on sound when she's unsure of a spelling, as we see in the word *stick,* which she spells as STEK—confusing the short *i* sound with the short *e* sound, and representing the /k/ sound at the end of the word with the letter *k* rather than the digraph *ck.* She'll revisit this skill later in the within word pattern stage.

As we continue down the list, we notice that Mackenzie is starting to think about sound and pattern when writing words with long vowels. You see that she's overgeneralizing the *consonant-vowel-consonant-silent e* long vowel pattern (CVCe) in her spelling of *wait* (WATE), *dream* (DREME),

TABLE 8.1 **Scope and Sequence of Word Study Instruction in the Within Word Pattern Stage**

Early Within Word Pattern	Middle Within Word Pattern	Late Within Word Pattern
Long and Short Vowel Studies	R-Influenced Vowel Patterns	Other Vowel Sounds
Long and short vowel picture and word sorts (CVC and CVCe) Final –k, –ck, ke	R-Influenced Vowels (ar, or, ir, er and ur)	Diphthongs and other ambiguous vowel sounds (e.g., oi, oy, $\overline{oo}$, $o\overline{o}$)
CVVC and CVV long vowel patterns (ai, oa, ui, ee, ea, ay, ow, ew, ue, gh, y) VCC in il, in, ol, os	R-Influenced /a/ sounds (ar, air, are)	Complex Consonant and Consonant Clusters Silent beginning consonants (kn, wr, gn) Triple r-blends (scr, str, spr) Consonant digraphs plus r-blends (thr, shr) Hard and soft c and g Final e (ce, se, ve, ge) Complex consonant clusters dge/ge and tch/ch
	R-Influenced /e/ sounds (er, ear, eer)	
	R-Influenced /i/ sounds (ir, ire, ier)	Other Features Homophones Inflected endings for plurals and past tense endings Contractions
	R-Influenced /o/ sounds (or, ore, oar)	
	R-Influenced /u/ sounds (ur, ure)	

Source: Adapted from Bear et al., 2012.

and *coach* (COCHE). This tells us two things: First, she's aware that the vowel sound is long, so we know she can discriminate between long and short vowels, and second, we also know that she understands the CVCe is used when vowels are long—a keen insight! It's clear that Mackenzie is an *early within word pattern speller* and she will benefit from instruction that builds on her understanding of long and short vowels and the CVCe pattern. You'll begin her word study instruction by comparing and contrasting long vowel words with the CVCe pattern and those with the *consonant-vowel-vowel-consonant* (CVVC) long vowel pattern.

José, another student from Mr. Garcia's classroom, is a *middle within word pattern speller* and we know this because he consistently spells the features of the letter name–alphabetic stage correctly: short vowels, blends, and digraphs. He also writes many long vowel words correctly, particularly those with the CVCe pattern such as *hope, shine*, and *blade*. You probably also noticed that he's accurately representing some other common long vowel patterns such as the CVVC long vowel pattern in words such as *dream* and *coach*.

José first shows some difficulty with *r*-influenced vowels, as seen in the word *third* (THURD), and other vowel patterns such as the *–ight* in *fright* (FRIHT) and the *–aw* in crawl (CRALL). From these observations, we realize that José is ready for instruction in the middle part of the scope and sequence. You'll begin his instruction with *r*-influenced vowels first, moving to less common vowel patterns, including diphthongs and ambiguous vowel patterns later.

Finally, we turn to Amber's spelling inventory and we see that she is spelling long vowel patterns correctly and most other vowel patterns, too, with the exception of the diphthong *oi* in the word *spoil*—this is to be expected of *late within word pattern spellers*. She is also beginning to experiment with inflected endings as in the words *tries* (TRYS), *clapping* (CLAPING), and *riding* (RIDEING). You notice that she spelled *camped* correctly and this suggests that she has some understanding of the different sounds of the suffix *–ed*: /d/ as in *played*, /t/ as in *baked*, and /id/ as in *needed*. Revisiting diphthongs and other ambiguous vowels as well as working with inflected endings will be the focus of Amber's word study instruction as she begins her transition to the syllables and affixes stage.

From these three examples of children's spelling on the Primary Spelling Inventory, you can see how assessment data can help you determine not only children's stage of development but also your instructional priorities. In the section that follows we share some of the spelling features you'll teach throughout this stage of development. For more information about word study and within word pattern spellers, see *Words Their Way: Word Study for Phonics, Vocabulary, and Spelling* (Bear et al., 2012) and *Words Their Way: Word Sorts for Within Word Pattern Spellers* (Invernizzi, Johnston, Bear, & Templeton, 2009). You'll also find additional support and resources for teaching word study to English learners in *Words Their Way with English Learners: Word Study for Phonics, Vocabulary, and Spelling* (Helman, Bear, Templeton, Invernizzi, & Johnston, 2012).

Studying Vowels in Single-Syllable Words

EL Connection

Children in the early part of the within word pattern stage have achieved full phonemic awareness and are beginning to become more efficient when reading and writing words. This efficiency is related to their growing awareness of spelling patterns (Bear et al., 2012; Cunningham, Nathan, & Schmidt Raher, 2011). At first, within word pattern spellers focus on the CVCe long vowel pattern and before long they will come to understand that vowels are spelled in different ways. They will also realize that this has to do with a number of things, including a word's origin, where the vowel sound falls within a word, how the surrounding letters affect the vowel, and how the meaning of a word affects its spelling. Learning all the vowel sounds of English can take some time, especially for English learners whose primary language may not have as many different vowel sounds or spellings for vowels (Helman, Bear, Templeton, Invernizzi, & Johnston, 2012).

Common Long Vowel Patterns

The most common long vowel patterns are the CVCe, CVVC, CVV, and CV patterns as in *cape, soap, day,* and *so.* As you can see from these examples, there are times when long vowel sounds are represented with more than one letter. We call these other letters **vowel markers**. The silent *e* in *cape,* the *i* in *rain,* and the *y* in *day* are all examples of vowel markers. Through your daily word study instruction, children will come to understand these different long vowel markers and patterns, as well as the frequency of each. Figure 8.2 highlights some of the more common and less common long vowel patterns in English with examples.

R-Influenced Vowel Patterns

R-influenced vowels are sometimes referred to as *r-controlled vowels.* In words with *r*-influenced vowels, the letter *r* affects the sound of the vowel that precedes it. To illustrate this point, read these words aloud: *car, her, sir, fort,* and *fur.* Can you hear how the *r* influences the vowel sound

---

FIGURE 8.2 Long Vowel Patterns in English

Common long *a* patterns:	*a-e (save), ai (drain), ay (may)*
Less common:	*ei (freight), ey (they)*
Common long *e* patterns:	*ee (feet), ea (dream), e (be)*
Less common:	*ie (field), e-e (eve)*
Common long *i* patterns:	*i-e (site), igh (flight), y (dry)*
Less common:	*i* followed by *nd (bind)* and *ld (mild)*
Common long *o* patterns:	*o-e (phone), oa (boat), ow (tow)*
Less common:	*o* followed by two consonants *(most)*
Common long *u* patterns:	*u-e (rude), oo (spoon), ew (few)*
Less common:	*ue (argue), ui (fruit)*

Source: Adapted from Bear et al., 2012.

FIGURE 8.3 Transitional Writing Sample with *R*-Influenced Vowel Sounds: "The Weird Life of Birdy the Best" by Adam

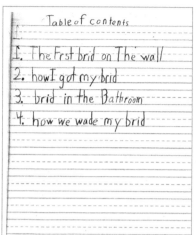

in each word? You probably also noticed that the sounds of *ar* and *or* are easier to distinguish than *ir, er,* and *ur.* For this reason, we teach them first. The vowel sounds in the words *her, sir,* and *fur* all sound the same; this is referred to as a *schwa + r* pattern. When we teach this pattern, we begin by comparing and contrasting it with words that have *ar* and *or,* and this helps reinforce all three sounds and spelling patterns. As children sort and explore words with the *schwa + r* pattern, they'll come to realize that *ur* and *ir* are the more common spelling patterns in single-syllable words. Importantly, they will also realize that they cannot rely on sound alone when spelling the *schwa + r*-influenced vowels.

Some words with *r*-influenced vowels are also homophones—words that sound the same but are spelled differently: *bear/bare, dear/deer, fur/fir.* Children will come to realize they cannot rely on sound or pattern alone when spelling them, but the meaning of homophones provides an important clue to their spelling: *Deer,* spelled *d-e-e-r,* refers to a four-legged animal, whereas *dear,* spelled *d-e-a-r,* is a greeting or salutation as in "*Dear* Sir," or a term of affection as in "my *dear* friend." We'll discuss homophones in more detail later in this chapter.

When spelling words with *r*-influenced vowels, early transitional spellers sometimes omit the vowel because the *r* sound is so dominant; they may spell, for example, *bird* as BRD. Other times they confuse *r-blends* with *r-influenced vowels*: *girl* might be spelled GRIL. Figure 8.3 illustrates these points beautifully. Notice how Adam spells words like *bird* (BRID) and *first* (FRST). We can help within word pattern spellers like Adam recognize the position and spelling of *r*-influenced vowels and *r*-blends by creating sorts that contrast initial *r*-blends such as *gr, tr,* and *fr* with words that have the *r*-influenced vowels such as *er, ir,* or *ur.*

In addition to the above-mentioned examples, children in the middle phase of this stage will also learn about *r*-influenced long vowel patterns such as *–air, –are, –eer, –ear, –ire, –ier, –ore, –oar,* and *–ure.* Here, we create sorts with simple *r*-influenced patterns (*ar, er, ir, or,* and *ur*) and we compare them with words that include these *r*-influenced long vowel patterns. See Figure 8.4 for an example of such a sort.

Diphthongs and Other Ambiguous Vowels

In addition to short vowels, long vowels, and *r*-influenced vowels, there are two other types of vowels in the English language and they are neither long nor short. They are called *diphthongs* (*spoil* and *house*) and *ambiguous vowels* (*talk, fault, paw,* and *cough*). In the case of diphthongs, you'll notice how the sounds of the vowels "glide" from one vowel to the other. The /*oi*/ in *boil* is a good example,

FIGURE 8.4 Long *R*-Controlled Vowel Sort

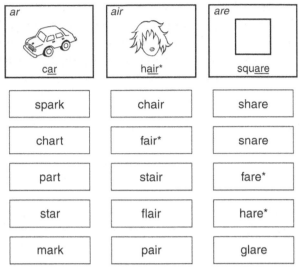

ar	air	are
car	hair*	square

spark	chair	share
chart	fair*	snare
part	stair	fare*
star	flair	hare*
mark	pair	glare

* homophones

Source: Flanigan et al., 2011, p. 108.

as is the /*ou*/ in *mouth*. Say them slowly. Do you hear (and feel) how the first vowel sound glides into the second? Ambiguous vowels are a little different and these sounds are often influenced by surrounding letters such as *l* or *w*, as in the words **talk** and **wash**. Other examples of ambiguous vowels include the /*oo*/ sound in *moon*, the /*oo*/ sound in *book*, and the /*ô*/ sound of *dog*. These vowels will be explored later in the stage. Figure 8.5 illustrates a sample sort for the diphthongs *ow* and *ou*.

When teaching the less common vowel sounds of English, you'll compare and contrast them with more regular long or short vowel sounds and patterns. Doing so reinforces how vowels are represented and helps children generalize both patterns to a larger body of words. Because the decoding and spelling of vowel sounds of English do take some time and practice to learn, you'll want to be sure you're connecting children's word study lessons to their reading and writing

FIGURE 8.5 Sample Sort for Ambiguous Vowels

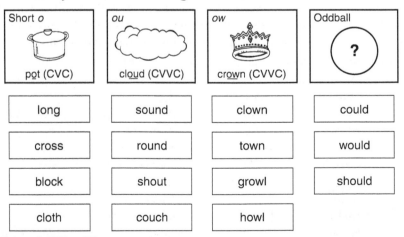

Short *o*	*ou*	*ow*	Oddball
pot (CVC)	cloud (CVVC)	crown (CVVC)	?

long	sound	clown	could
cross	round	town	would
block	shout	growl	should
cloth	couch	howl	

Source: Flanigan et al., 2011, p. 109.

practice, too. Some ways you might do this include having children: read books with the words and features they're studying; go on word hunts and then document their findings in their word study notebooks; create traveling word walls of different vowel patterns; write meaningful sentences using words from their sorts or other words that follow the pattern; or edit their own writing or their peers' writing to ensure that they're accurately using the patterns they've learned about in word study. Given the complexity of the vowel sounds of English, children need considerable exposure to and practice in reading and writing words with the vowel patterns they're studying.

Summing It Up: Teaching the Vowel Spellings of English

Since there are many possible options for spelling the vowel sounds of English, it can be helpful to provide children, particularly English learners, with a visual representation of the various sounds of each vowel. The feature called "Accommodating English Learners" includes a graphic (Figure 8.6) that illustrates the sounds of *long a* in a very simple way. Such a visual helps children not only recognize different sounds of *a* but also know when they might use each spelling pattern. For example, the child who is trying to write the word *pain* could consult this chart and realize there are three possible options for representing *long a* in this word. On closer examination, it becomes clear that the *–ay* spelling of long *a* typically comes at the end of a word, therefore reducing the number of options to two. In this particular example, *pane* and *pain* are homophones and so the meaning of the word determines its spelling.

EL Connection

Other times the child will have to think about which option is most likely—and here's where children's understanding of the frequency of spelling patterns can help. For example, when spelling the word *cake*, the child contemplates the choices CAKE and CAIK, and when he does, he recognizes that the CVCe pattern is much more common. In fact, the child cannot think of a single example of the *–aik* word family and so he chooses to write the word as CAKE. Teaching children to strategically use their knowledge of phonograms will help them spell and read unknown words more accurately and more automatically (Cunningham, Nathan, & Schmidt Raher, 2011; Leslie & Calhoon, 1995; Treiman, Goswami, & Bruck, 1990). As you recall from the beginning stage, this is called *analogous phonics*.

Studying Consonants in Single-Syllable Words

In addition to studying vowel patterns in the within word pattern stage, we explore three-letter blends such as *school*, *throw*, and *stripe*. We also teach children about silent initial consonants as in *knife*, *gnat*, and *wrench*, and complex consonants clusters such as *–dge* in *edge* and *–tch* in *catch*. With your instruction, children will come to understand that the spelling of these complex consonant clusters is affected by the vowel sounds and letters closest to them. For example, study the following word sort and see if you can identify a generalization for the use of *–dge* and *–ge* (Invernizzi et al., 2009, p. 100).

-dge	*-ge*	*r, l, n + ge*
edge	cage	large
badge	stage	charge
lodge	rage	bulge
ledge	huge	change
hedge		sponge
ridge		plunge
pledge		range
fudge		surge
judge		

Accommodating English Learners

Teaching the Vowel Sounds of English

Vowel sounds are especially difficult for students to learn because there are so many of them and they are spelled using many different patterns. English learners find vowels particularly challenging to learn because their home languages often have fewer vowel sounds or a more linear, one-to-one relationship between letters and sounds (Helman et al., 2012). Spanish, Italian, and Polish, for example, are considered **shallow orthographies** because each letter represents a specific sound, which makes decoding and spelling words much easier. English is a **deep orthography**, which means the letter–sound relationships are more complex and less direct. There are 26 letters in English and approximately 44 different sounds!

Short vowels tend to be easier for English learners because there is more of a one-to-one relationship between the vowel sound and the letter that represents it. We see this in the *consonant-vowel-consonant (CVC)* short vowel pattern. Long vowels, on the other hand, can be represented a number of different ways, and this can be especially overwhelming to children who are learning the sounds, patterns, *and* meanings of words simultaneously.

One way to help English learners understand the different sounds of vowels is to create a visual representation such as the one shown in Figure 8.6. Here, we see the many different sounds of *a*. This visual is particularly effective because it includes labels, pictures, key words, and an explanation of the different patterns. As you teach your students the many sounds of a vowel, you'll add to the chart and you'll have your students create their own charts in their word study notebooks, too. These visuals become valuable resources for these learners during reading, writing, and word study time.

FIGURE 8.6 **The Big Picture**

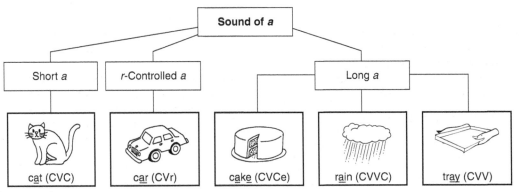

Source: Flanigan et al., 2011.

Common Core Connection

Reading Standards:
Foundational Skills –
Phonics and Word
Recognition

Common Core Connection

Language Standards:
Conventions of
Standard English

After studying this sort, you probably determined that we use –*dge* in words where the vowel is short: *edge, badge,* and *smudge;* we use –*ge* in words where the vowel is long: *page, stage,* and *huge;* and we use –*ge* after the vowel markers *r, l,* and *n* as in *large, bulge,* and *change.*

In the late phase of the stage, you'll teach children about other complex consonants such as hard and soft *g* and *c* and words that seem to be "oddballs"—words that look like they follow the long vowel pattern but they don't—words such as *dance* and *have.* With these words, you'll help children come to understand that the silent *e* is associated with the consonant rather than the vowel. The *e* in *dance* makes the *c* soft; the *e* in *have* goes with the letter *v* because words in English don't end in *v.* These discoveries reinforce the understanding that sounds are often affected by letters that are nearby.

Working and Collaborating

Talking with Families about Word Study Instruction

Most parents and caregivers are not familiar with word study instruction. When they think back to their own experiences learning to spell words, it's likely that memorization was their primary strategy for learning words, and perhaps this was true for you, too. People who learned to spell through more traditional methods may have come to believe that good spellers are "born" because they see the English language as illogical. (From reading Chapter 2, you know better!) These people may also believe that memorizing words is the only way to learn them. (Again, you know better.) Since word study will be so central to your literacy instruction, it's good to help families better understand *what* word study is and *how* they can support their children's development at home.

What follows are some typical questions we've heard from parents and caregivers over the years and our answers may help you envision how to talk with families about your word study program.

What is word study?

Word study is a research-based approach to teaching phonics, spelling, and vocabulary. Word study lessons are planned with each child's stage of development in mind, so the words children study are "just right" for them. Word study lessons are interactive and designed to help children understand words and the influence of the three layers of spelling: sound, pattern, and meaning.

Why does my child sort words?

As children sort words, they begin to understand how letters, sounds, and spelling patterns work. Children test these theories by looking for words that confirm their ideas and words that may be exceptions, or "oddballs." This practice helps children identify generalizations about how words *do* and sometimes *do not* work. It's these generalizations that help extend their knowledge beyond the 20 or so words they study as part of their weekly word sorts to a larger body of words. Word knowledge is important because it helps children become better readers, writers, *and* spellers!

Why are there pictures in some sorts?

Picture sorts help children focus on the sounds in words (**b**at versus **m**at, or c**ă**p versus c**ā**pe). As children develop their awareness of sound, they come to learn the letters that represent these sounds (b for /b/ and m for /m/) and the patterns associated with these sounds (the short vowel pattern: *consonant-vowel-consonant* and a common long vowel pattern such as *consonant-vowel-*

consonant-silent e). As children learn more about spelling patterns, you'll start to see a mix of pictures and words in their sorts and eventually their sorts will contain only words. When your child's sorts contain only words, he will continue to think about sounds *and* patterns when sorting.

Should I correct my child's spelling?

It's important that children take risks when writing. We want to encourage them to use the words that best communicate their message rather than just use words they know how to spell. When young children write, we encourage them to say words slowly and do their best to match letters to the sounds they hear. Sometimes children will use the name of letters to help them spell, spelling *jeep* as GP because the letter name of *G* is "jee." When children are first beginning to write words it's not unusual that they leave vowel sounds out—and when they start to include them, they are not always correct. This is also expected.

As children are able to represent each sound with a letter, they'll start to think about "chunks," or groupings, of letters in words—for example, –*at* in words like *cat, bat, sat,* and *mat*. These words are part of the –*at* family. Still later, they'll focus on long vowel patterns such as the *consonant-vowel-consonant-silent e* (CVCe) pattern. Encourage your child to make connections between letters, sounds, and patterns he or she knows: "The word *sad* is a lot like another word you know. Can you think of one? Yes. If you can spell *dad*, you can spell *sad*. Which part is the same? Which part is different? How do you represent that sound?

As children participate in developmentally appropriate word study instruction, their spellings will come to reflect conventional or correct spelling of words over time.

What should I say when my child asks me to spell a word?

Encourage your child to write parts she knows. The following prompts may help encourage your child to strategically spell unknown words:

- What do you have so far?
- What's a part you know? What's another part you know?
- Say it slowly. What sounds do you hear?
- Is that word like another word you know? Which part is the same? Which part is different?

If you do provide a word that's clearly beyond your child's stage of development, consider writing it on an index card that can be put in a container for later reference. Your goal is to help your child become an independent and resourceful speller.

What can I do to help my child be a better speller?

When your child brings home words to sort, read the words and talk about them together. As your child sorts, ask him to explain how and why he sorted the words the way he did. Encourage your child to check his work, too. Talk about different ways you might sort the words; this is called *open sorting*. Ask your child to tell you about sound sorts, pattern sorts, speed sorts, writing sorts, blind writing sorts, and buddy sorts.

When you're reading familiar books together, look for pictures and words that match the sounds and/or patterns your child is studying and talk about them. When your child writes, encourage him to use what he knows when spelling words with familiar patterns or sounds. You can also encourage your child to edit his writing, but don't expect him to correct spelling features or patterns he has yet to learn.

In your free time, play word and language games such as *Boggle, Apples to Apples, Scrabble,* and *Up-Words* among countless others. Introduce sophisticated words and concepts into your daily conversations and help your child notice vocabulary and language in the world around him.

Vocabulary Development: Spelling Instruction and Beyond

> Adaptable to Other Stages

As children become proficient in reading and spelling the more common spelling patterns of English, they're ready to start exploring the meaning layer of language through their word study lessons. We begin this study with homophones, homographs, and other meaning-based features in the late phase of the within word pattern stage. Naturally, vocabulary development is a priority across all stages of development and so, in addition to vocabulary study as part of spelling instruction, we continue to teach children *general academic vocabulary* and *domain-specific vocabulary*, too.

The intent of all vocabulary instruction is to build children's word knowledge. However, there are important differences between vocabulary instruction as part of word study versus vocabulary instruction that help develop children's general academic and domain-specific academic vocabularies. When we teach vocabulary as part of word study, we expect children not only to understand the words but also to grasp the spelling-meaning connection, particularly as they progress along the developmental continuum (Bear et al., 2012; Templeton, Bear, Invernizzi, & Johnston, 2010). We also expect them to spell the words correctly. When teaching academic vocabulary, we focus intentionally on the meaning of these words, and when we look at their phonological or spelling patterns it is usually to aid children's pronunciation, reading, and understanding of them. Unless these words include spelling patterns the children already know, or are currently studying, we do not hold them accountable for spelling these words accurately.

In this section, we'll discuss the kinds of words transitional readers study as part of word study instruction and those they study as part of the broader goal of vocabulary development.

Homophones, Homographs, and Other Features of Late Within Word Pattern Stage

Homophones are words that sound alike but are spelled differently (*dear/deer, bear/bare*), and homographs are words that are spelled the same but have different meanings (*park* a car in the garage, or visit a *park* on a sunny day) and/or pronunciations (*lead* a group; pencil *lead*). Although children will come across many homophones during the study of long vowel patterns (*pain/pane* and *sail/sale*), and the study of *r*-influenced vowels (*fare/fair; pear/ pair/ pare; wear/*

ware/where; and *heard/herd*), your more intentional study of homophones and homographs won't come until late in the within word pattern stage. It's at this time that children have a better understanding of the many different vowel patterns in English and they're able to focus more fully on the meaning of these words.

When teaching children about homophones, you'll explain how the meaning of these words affects their spelling: For example, when teaching the children about the words *sale* and *sail,* provide easily understood definitions: "*Sale* means something is being sold at a lower price, or at a discount, and we spell it *s-a-l-e.* That's very different from the word *sail,* which is a large piece of cloth that catches the wind to make a boat move. This is spelled *s-a-i-l.*" After comparing and contrasting the meaning and spelling of these words, you'll encourage children to draw and label and even define these words in their notebooks. Some children will also enjoy crafting meaningful sentences that include both words: I bought a new *sail* for my *sail*boat on *sale* at the marina. (See Figure 8.7 for an example.)

Late in the within word pattern stage, you will help children explore words they have been reading for quite some time: irregular verbs and their spelling and pronunciation changes (*stand/stood; swim/swam; drink/drank, lead/led*), and contractions (*I will/I'll; do not/don't*).

FIGURE 8.7 Word Study Notebook Example

The sail for the sailboat is on sale.

Shades of Meaning: Synonym and Antonym Lines

One of the hallmarks of skilled readers is their ability to understand nuanced meanings; this takes some time to develop. Studying the relationships among words and concepts helps children learn about the "shades of meaning." The Common Core State Standards emphasize shades of meanings, word relationships, and nuanced meanings beginning in kindergarten.

One way to help children think more deeply about the relationships among concepts is an activity called Synonym and Antonym Lines (Templeton, 1997; Templeton et al., 2010). Because analyzing character traits, feelings, and motivations is a common activity for transitional readers, you might consider taking "emotions" as an overarching category of discussion. From this broad topic, your students would brainstorm and discuss the words and concepts that are a part of the "emotions" domain and arrange them along a continuum. You'd begin with those emotions that they believe are the farthest apart (antonyms), then decide where to place the other words next to one another and closer to one end of the continuum or the other. Cunningham (2009) gives us the following example with the words *despondent, happy, glum, euphoric, elated, sad,* and *unhappy:*

despondent   glum   sad   unhappy   happy   elated   euphoric

As with most focused discussions, students' justification about *why* they have arranged the words the way they did is especially powerful. The students not only "unpack" their underlying, developing understandings for each word, but they extend and elaborate those understandings as they are compared and contrasted with the other words. In the earlier stages, you might select concepts that are more concrete, such as words that describe the taste or feel of things, and then move to slightly more abstract words, such as words that describe the weather, for example. Talking about words, their meanings, and their relationships helps children develop conceptual knowledge. It's these understandings that help them become readers who notice the subtleties of language in more sophisticated text. With your support, they will also incorporate more precise language in their *writing.*

Generative Vocabulary Instruction: Early Morphological Awareness

Adaptable to All
Stages

Morphological analysis provides children an important strategy for understanding words by breaking them into meaning units, or their morphological parts. This strategy not only helps them decode longer words but it also assists them in strategically "unlocking" the meaning of these words. We begin our study of early morphological awareness with words that are easy for children to read and understand—words with inflected endings (*-ed, -s, -es,* and *-ing*) and words with common prefixes (*un-, re-, in-,* and *dis-*). Interestingly, these few prefixes (*un-, re-, in-,* and *dis-*) account for more than half of all words with prefixes in English (White, Stowell, & Yanagihara, 1989); this makes studying them first a particularly helpful and wise choice! Refer to the following "Strategies for the Classroom: Teaching the Prefix 'un-' to Transitional Readers" to see how you'll teach prefixes like these in the transitional stage of development.

In addition to the most common prefixes in English, late transitional readers will study the meaning of other common prefixes and suffixes such as the ones found in Table 8.2. A more intensive study of prefixes and suffixes will be part of children's word study instruction in the intermediate stage of development.

Compound Words

When you combine two words to make a new word, you've created what's known as a *compound word*—for instance, *cup + cake = cupcake; snow + man = snowman.* Children in the middle and late phases of the within word pattern stage really enjoy reading, studying, and playing with

TABLE 8.2 Sequence of Instruction for Core Affixes: Transitional-Level Students

The following prefixes and suffixes are studied in the primary grades. Because of their frequency, they will continue to be addressed in the intermediate and middle grades as they combine with the words and roots that are appropriate at those levels.

Prefixes			Suffixes		
un-	not, opposite	unlock	-y	like	lacy
in-	not, without	incorrect	-ly		gladly
im-		impossible	-er	comparative	colder
re-	again, back	remake	-est	superlative	coldest
dis-	not, opposite	disagree, dislike	-less	without	penniless
	apart	disconnect	-ness	condition	happiness
non-	not	nonfiction	-ful	full of, like	hopeful, careful
mis-	badly, wrongly	misfortune, misfire	-er	people who	teacher
pre-	before	preview, preseason	-or	do things	actor
uni-	one	unicycle	-ist		pianist
bi-	two	bicycle			
tri-	three	tricycle			

Source: Adapted from Templeton, 2004.

Strategies for the Classroom

Teaching the Prefix "un–" to Transitional Readers

When introducing prefixes to transitional readers, such as the prefix *un–*, you'll want to plan several interactions over the course of a few days. The following is a template for teaching prefixes in the transitional stage of development:

Day 1

1) Write the following words:
   selfish
   fair
   Read and discuss what each word means. You might invite children to "turn and talk" with a partner to stimulate collaboration and conversation and then engage them in "meaningful interactions" using the words (Beck, McKeown, & Kucan, 2002): For example, "How would you describe someone who is *selfish*? Can you share an example of acting in a *fair* way?"

2) Add the prefix *un–* to each word. Ask: "How do you think adding the prefix *un–* to these words affects their meanings?" Again, encourage student-to-student conversation, group discussion, and extended interactions with the words.

3) Write the following words on the board, and talk about how *un–* affects the meaning of each:
   unpack
   unwrap
   unbutton
   under
   In this example, *under* is the exception, or "oddball," and including it here helps students realize that the letters *un* are not always a prefix.

4) Next, explore the meaning of the prefix: "So, how do you think we should define the prefix *un–*? What meanings do you think it has?" This discussion is important: While some students will identify the meaning "not," by talking about the words *unpack, unwrap*, and *unbutton*, you will lead them to the understanding that it also usually means the "opposite" or "reverse" of the word it's attached to. Write down the definition you decide on in simple terms. (Avoid complex dictionarylike definitions.)

5) Help the children become accountable for the learning by having them create a permanent record of it in their word study notebooks: "There are two things we're going to do in our Word Study Notebooks today: First, write down our *un–* words. Then, write down our definition for *un–*."

Day 2

1) Display the words from Day 1. Ask students: "What is our definition of the prefix *un–*?"

2) Write the new words:
   unable
   unfinished
   "With a partner, determine the meaning of each word, write a sentence for each word, and then write your sentences in your Word Study Notebook."

3) Create opportunities for children to extend and transfer the learning of this prefix: "Today and tomorrow, keep your eye out for words that contain the *un–* prefix. They could be anywhere—in our reading, on billboards, in newspapers, or in conversations you are having or listening to! Record or write the words down in your Word Study Notebooks. If you find any oddballs, write those down in a separate column. We'll share what you find over the next two days." When you follow up with the children in a couple of days, ask, "What are some *un–* words you've found? Were you able to figure out their meaning?"

4) Again, to extend the learning and stimulate excitement and "word consciousness," consider this activity as well: Hang a chart on the wall or some prominent surface in the classroom. Invite the children to add to the chart as well as their notebooks throughout the week. Say to them: "I'll put up an *un–* chart here, and any *un–* words you find that are really interesting, write them on our chart and I'll do that as well!" As children add to this mini-word wall, provide positive and public feedback—this will stimulate engagement and enjoyment as well as affirm the importance of the activity. As the week goes on, check the chart with the students from time to time to see how it's coming along. You'll continue to display the chart over time so children can use it as a reference when thinking about words' meanings and spellings, too.

End of the Week

Based on what the children found and recorded in their word study notebooks and on the class chart, talk about the meanings of the many *un–* words they have found. Review the meaning of *un–*: "not," "opposite," or "reverse." Also encourage the children to share some of the sentences they have written with *un–* words. If a child is not certain about the meaning of a word she found, this is a good opportunity to talk about the word with the class and try to tease out its meaning. It's also a grand opportunity to model how to confirm their hunches by using a print or online dictionary. The transitional stage of development is an appropriate time to introduce some basic dictionary skills. See Chapter 9 for some suggestions how to introduce children to print and online dictionaries.

compound words. It's motivating for them to read these longer words, and it's especially fun to study their meanings and origins. Sometimes you'll find students inventing their own compound words and we love that, too!

As children talk about the meanings of words, even seemingly simple words such as *cupcake*, they're compelled to start asking questions. What exactly *is* a *cupcake*? Where did this word come from? Questions like these can inspire research about words' origins and help build curiosity and interest in vocabulary—something researchers call *word consciousness* (Stahl & Nagy, 2006).

So where *did* the word *cupcake* come from? Well, the word first appeared in mid-nineteenth-century America where cupcakes were invented. Food historians debate two theories about the word's origin: It was either the result of these little cakes being baked in cups rather than cake pans, which makes sense, or it may have been related to the actual recipes used to bake the little cakes—one cup of butter, two cups of sugar, three cups of flour, and so on. Because cupcakes were made from these very simple recipes, they were once referred to as *numbercakes*.

Baking in the mid-nineteenth century was done in beehive ovens—a heat source that was pretty hard to regulate. For this reason, cupcakes cooked more evenly than the larger cakes that often burned on the outside before cooking all the way through. Cupcakes are said to have revolutionized baking during this time period. Fascinating! Oh, wait; you're wondering what a beehive oven is, aren't you? This is exactly the kind of curiosity your word study instruction will inspire! So what *do* you think a beehive oven is? (*The Oxford School Dictionary of Word Origins: The Curious Twists and Turns of The Cool and Weird Words We Use* (Ayto, 2009) is a great resource for this kind of study of word origins.)

The study of compound words will continue well into and beyond the intermediate stage of development where children will study these words in relation to their growing understanding of syllable juncture, word meanings, and the origins of words. Children's expanding vocabulary knowledge, sight word knowledge, and dictionary skills will help them deepen their experiences with these words in the later stages. For now, the study of compound words and simple affixes stimulates transitional readers' early morphological awareness and heightens their word consciousness. These activities, in addition to teaching general and domain-specific vocabulary as part of read-alouds and content-area learning, will provide children in the transitional stage with many rich experiences learning specific words and learning *about* words, as well as strategies to "unlock" the meaning of unknown words. (Refer to Chapter 7 and Chapter 9 for additional suggestions for teaching general and domain-specific vocabulary.)

Interactive Read-Alouds: Developing Engaged Listeners and Deep Thinkers

Interactive read-aloud is the time of day where you'll expose children to sophisticated literature and informational texts that are typically *at* or *above* their current grade level. It's through your daily read-alouds that you'll model fluent reading, expand and deepen children's vocabulary knowledge, and show children how to construct meaningful responses to text through active thinking and collaborative reasoning. Part of children's "active thinking" concerns comprehension strategy use. In this stage, like others, you'll continue to model and help children practice using comprehension strategies flexibly and as needed with specific genres, noting the importance of different strategies *before, during*, and *after* reading (predicting, questioning, monitoring, retelling, and summarizing). You will also begin to model more analytic and critical thinking skills (comparison, interpretation, inference, evaluation, and synthesis). Using the gradual release of responsibility (Pearson & Gallagher, 1983), you'll show children how to use these skills by thinking aloud as you read—making your thinking and strategy use transparent and inviting children to co-construct the meaning of text.

Interactive read-alouds build on the **transactional model of reading** (Rosenblatt, 1978). In this model, a reader's response to text follows a continuum from an **efferent stance**, in which the reader focuses on acquiring and taking away information, through an **aesthetic stance**, in which the reader attends to connotations, nuanced meaning, and more personal and affective connections. A reader's stance is related to her purpose for reading. Prior knowledge, critical thinking skills, motivation, engagement, and thoughtful reasoning all come into play when the reader transacts with a text. This continuum of efferent through aesthetic response forms the basis of **Reader Response Theory**.

When children are responding to text, they are interpreting it. Sometimes that interpretation results in a basic retelling, which would be appropriate for transitional readers who are reading text independently; this is a more efferent response—one in which the reader is reading for specific information or a given purpose. A reader who reads a piece of text and comes to appreciate the author's craft, or is moved in a personal or emotional way, is experiencing and interacting with the text in a more aesthetic way. Importantly, it's possible for a reader to have both an efferent and aesthetic stance when reading a piece of text. It's also not uncommon for students to experience and respond to a text in a new way when they reread it. You've probably experienced this yourself when you've revisited favorite texts from your childhood or adolescent years.

Reader Response Theory in Action: Supporting Comprehension Development

As readers develop, and as you continue with your support and instruction during interactive read-alouds, you want their interpretive strategies to become more sophisticated and to include:

> Adaptable to All Stages

- Making meaningful connections to other texts, their lives, or the world
- Exploring character traits, motivations, and feelings through what characters do, what they think, what they say, and what others say about them
- Examining the narrator's point of view and comparing and contrasting it with their own point of view, or that of various characters
- Noting and evaluating author's craft and the use of techniques such as literal and figurative language, dialogue, and/or text features
- Inferring the author's bias, purpose, and/or determining the theme of a text

It's important to realize that the more interpretive or aesthetic a response is, the more subjective it becomes. By nature, aesthetic responses are deeply personal interpretations that are based on the reader's prior knowledge, beliefs, and experiences. This means aesthetic responses cannot be judged as "right" or "wrong"; rather, we evaluate them based on how compellingly the reader can "argue" his interpretation or "stance" (Newell et al., 2011; Reznitskaya & Anderson, 2002). Naturally, this argument must be plausible. In other words, it cannot be solely dependent on the reader's prior knowledge; it must reflect the interaction of the reader's schema and evidence from the text (Williams, 1993). With this in mind, you'll encourage your students to think about their purposes, intentions, and/or goals when they read.

Many of the interpretive strategies noted here are reflected in the Common Core State Standards beginning as early as kindergarten. Figure 8.8 highlights some of the standards most relevant to these strategies and children in the transitional stage of reading. By way of this

FIGURE 8.8 Sample Third-Grade Common Core Standards Related to Response to Text

Reading Standards for Literature	Speaking and Listening Standards
Key Ideas and Details	**Comprehension and Collaboration**

1) Ask and understand questions to demonstrate understanding of a text, referring explicitly to the text as a basis for the answers.
2) Recount stories, including fables, folktales, and myths, from diverse cultures; determine the central message, lesson, or moral, and explain how it is conveyed through key details in the text.
3) Describe characters in a story (e.g., their traits, motivations, or feelings) and explain how their actions contribute to the sequence of events.
	1) Engage effectively in a range of collaborative discussions (one-on-one, in groups, and teacher-led) with diverse partners on grade 3 topics and texts, building on other's ideas and expressing their own clarity.
	  a. Come to discussions prepared, having read or studied required material; explicitly draw on that preparation and other information known about a topic to explore ideas under discussion.
	  b. Follow agreed-on rules for discussion (e.g., gaining the floor in respectful ways, listening to others with care, speaking one at a time about the topics and texts under discussion).
	  c. Ask questions to check understanding of information presented, stay on topic, and link their comments to the remarks of others.
	  d. Explain their own ideas and understanding in light of the conversation.
	2) Determine the main ideas and supporting details of a text read-aloud or information presented in diverse media and formats, including visually, quantitatively, and orally.
	3) Ask and answer questions about information from a speaker, offering appropriate elaboration and detail.

Reading Standards for Informational Text	
Key Ideas and Details	
1) Ask and answer questions to demonstrate understanding of a text, referring explicitly to the text as a basis for the answers. 2) Determine the main idea of a text; recount the key details and explain how they support the main idea. 3) Describe the relationship between a series of historical events, scientific ideas or concepts, or steps in technical procedures in a text, using language that pertains to time, sequence, and cause/effect.	
Writing Standards	**Presentation of Knowledge and Ideas**
Text Types and Purposes	4) Report on a topic or text, tell a story, or recount an experience with appropriate facts and relevant, descriptive details, speaking clearly at an understandable pace. 6) Speak in complete sentences when appropriate to the task and situation in order to provide requested detail or clarification.*

1) Write opinion pieces on topics or texts, supporting a point of view with reasons.
  a. Introduce the topic or text they are writing about, state an opinion, and create an organizational structure that lists reasons.
  b. Provide reasons that support the opinion.
  c. Use linking words and phrases (e.g., *because, therefore, since, for example*) to connect opinion and reasons.
  d. Provide a concluding statement or section.	

*Numbering reflects those of the original source and are used intentionally.

Source: *Common Core State Standards*, www.corestandards.org, pp. 12, 14, 20, 24. Retrieved on March 12, 2010.

example, we're highlighting the third-grade standards, but you will adjust your instruction and expectations for children's response based on the grade level you teach (Gehsmann & Templeton, 2011/2012; 2013). Standards such as these are helpful because they provide a vision for the kind of interactions and responses you'll need to plan for and explicitly teach.

Over time and with your instruction, children will begin to transfer the dispositions and strategies you've modeled in read-alouds to their own independent reading. This transfer will be further supported and advanced though small group structures such as guided reading, conferring, reading partnerships, and later though literature circles or book clubs as well as "close readings" of exemplar texts. By the intermediate and skillful stages of development, children will more independently engage with text in critical and analytical ways, thereby deepening their comprehension and enjoyment of literature and informational text.

Talking Well, Thinking Well: The Power of Talk in the Development of Comprehension

We carefully select our read-alouds to stimulate thoughtful dialogue among our listeners. Our goal is for the students to bring their own background knowledge, or schema, to these listening experiences and then co-construct a deeper understanding of the text through collaborative reasoning with their peers (Anderson et al., 2001; Reznitskaya & Anderson, 2002). Your role is to facilitate this reflective thinking and collaboration among the children by not only selecting texts that will stimulate authentic conversation but also by strategically modeling *your* thinking, scaffolding interactive discourse patterns for the children, and planning opportunities for them to stop and talk at strategic moments when listening to text (Anderson, Chinn, Waggoner, & Nguyen, 1998). Through these experiences, you'll prompt children to:

Common Core Connection

Language Standards: Speaking and Listening

Adaptable to All Stages

* Become aware of their thoughts while listening and then share them with others by using sentence starters such as "I think . . . ," "I noticed . . . ," "I predict . . . ," " I wonder . . . ," or "I didn't really understand the part when . . . ."
* Develop and share their opinions in a compelling way using words and phrases such as *because, for example, and so,* and *therefore*—all words that signal a logical, well-reasoned argument.
* Actively listen to and build on one another's comments: "I agree with what you're saying . . . ," "Another way to think about that . . . ," "I have another example of that . . . ," or "I have a connection to what [name] just said . . . ."
* Question and challenge one another's ideas in a respectful manner using language such as, "Could you say more about . . . ," "Can you give an example of . . . ," "I'm not sure I understand . . . ," "What did you mean by . . . ," "Have you ever thought . . . ," or "I hear what you're saying and I see it another way . . . ."
* Develop conclusions: "I think the author is trying to say . . . ," "My thinking changed when . . . so now I think . . . ," "The moral/lesson of this story is . . . ," "The big thing I learned from this text is . . . ," or "I think the author's message is . . . ."

As our examples of teaching children how to talk well and think well illustrate, we're careful to make children's conversation during read-alouds as authentic as possible. This is why we explicitly teach children the art of listening and ways to add onto a conversation, even how to challenge or disagree with someone's thinking in a respectful and productive manner. We teach and develop these skills by focusing on them one at a time, starting with teaching children to share their thoughts, then how to back them up with evidence, and finally, how to deepen a conversation by adding onto or questioning what someone else has said.

After the children have learned how to "turn and talk" and sustain a thoughtful conversation for several volleys back and forth, we'll support their working collaboratively to draw conclusions about text. Since these responses are likely to be slightly more aesthetic than some of their other responses, it will be especially important for them to practice their active listening skills so they can encourage, challenge, and deepen one another's conclusions in a thoughtful manner.

As you can see, there are two parallel curriculums at work here: *what* to talk about and *how* to talk about it. Both will need your modeling and support as well as your patience. Not all children will develop these skills at the same rate.

Supporting Children's Conversations about Books

One way you'll support children's participation in these conversations about text is to create anchor charts that summarize ways to initiate, sustain, and/or deepen a conversation. Some teachers even create bookmarks with the previously mentioned sentence starters on them to encourage children to use the language of readers' response.

Children's Literature Connection

Interactive Read-Alouds for Developing Critical Thinking in the Transitional Stage of Development

Literature

Babbitt, N. (1975). *Tuck Everlasting*. Farrar, Straus and Giroux.

Burnett, F. H. (1962). *The Secret Garden*. Lippincott.

DeGross, M. (1994). *Donavon's Word Jar*. HarperCollins.

Howe, D. & Howe, J., *Bunnicula Series*. Atheneum.

MacLachlan, P. (1985). *Sara, Plain and Tall*. Harper & Row.

Napoli, D. J. (1992). *The Prince of the Pond*. Penguin.

Rylant, C. (1997). *Poppleton*. Blue Sky.

Rylant, C. (1985). *Every Living Thing*. Bradbury.

Scieszka, J. (2008). *Knucklehead: Tall Tales and Mostly True Stories about Growing Up*. Viking.

White, E. B. (1952). *Charlotte's Web*. Harper & Row.

Picture Books

Baumgartner, B. & Hall, A. (1998). *Good as Gold*. DK Publishers.

Brown, M. W. (1949). *The Important Book*. Harper.

Bunting, E. (1990). *The Wall*. Clarion.

Bunting, E. (1994). *A Day's Work*. Clarion.

Garland, S. (1993). *The Lotus Seed*. Harcourt Brace Jovanovich.

Martin, R. (1998). *The Rough-Face Girl*. New York: G. P. Putnam's Sons.

Polacco, P. (1998). *My Rotten Redheaded Older Brother Ralph*. Aladin Paperbacks.

Rappaport, D. (2001). *Martin's Big Words*. Hyperion Books for Children.

Rumford, J. (2008). *Silent Music*. Roaring Brook Press.

Steig, W. (1971). *Amos & Boris*. Farrar, Straus and Giroux.

Stone, T. L. (2008). *Sandy's Circus*. Viking.

Yolen, J. (1987). *Owl Moon*. Philomel Books.

Van Allsburg, C. (1990). *Just a Dream*. Houghton Mifflin.

Wiles, D. (2001). *Freedom Summer*. Atheneum Books for Young Readers.

Informational Text

Bass, H. (2009). *The Secret World of Walter Anderson*. Candlewick Press.

Greenburg, J. (2002). *Action Jackson*. Roaring Brook Press.

Hoose, P. M. (1993). *It's Our World Too! Young People Making a Difference, How They Do It—How You Can Too!* Joy Street Books.

Rappaport, (2008). *Lady Liberty: A Biography*. Candlewick Press.

Simon, S. (1997). *Lightning*. Morrow Junior Books.

Stone, T. L. (2010). *Elizabeth Leads the Way: Elizabeth Cady Stanton and the Right to Vote*. Henry Holt and Co.

Poetry

Fletcher, R. J. (2005). *A Writing Kind of Day: Poems for Young Poets*. Wordsong/Boyds Mills Press.

Fleischman, P. (1998). *Joyful Noise:* Poems for Two Voices. Harper & Row.

Poems for Two Voices. Harper & Row. Fleischman, P. *(2000)*.

Big Talk: Poems for Four Voices. Candlewick Press.

Graves, D. (1996). *Baseball, Snakes, & Summer Squash*. Wordsong/Boyds Mills Press.

Greenfield, L. (1978). *Honey, I Love, and Other Poems*. Crowell.

Heard, G. (2002) *The Place I Know: Poems of Comfort*. Candlewick Press.

Janeczko, P. (2005) *A Poke in the I: A Collection of Concrete Poems*. Walker Books.

Roessel, D. & Rampersad, A. (Eds.) (2006). *Poetry for Young People—Langston Hughes*. Sterling Publishing Co. Wilson, E. G. (Ed.) (2007). *Poetry for Young People: Maya Angelou*. New York: Sterling.

We advocate for some temporary scaffolding of children's talk during interactive read-alouds, but we want to emphasize the importance of these supports being *temporary*. The goal is for these conversations to be as natural as possible, which means you'll have to resist the urge to overuse supports such as sentence starters. You'll also want to be wary of the **I.R.E. cycle** in your discussions, too (see Cazden, 1988). The I.R.E. cycle refers to a discourse pattern in which the teacher *Initiates* a question, such as: "Why do you think Moose's mother lies about his sister's age?" Then the child *Responds* to the question: "Because she's embarrassed about her behavior." And then the teacher *Evaluates* the response: "Good thinking." Regrettably this discourse pattern is all too common in literacy classrooms and it usually discourages active thinking, engagement, and the kind of collaborative construction of meaning we're advocating. Instead, you'll encourage children to turn and talk, sitting "eye-to-eye, knee-to-knee" (Miller, 2002). They'll share their thinking with "talk partners" and together they'll work to sustain their conversation for several minutes. Whenever you call the children back to a whole class conversation, try to limit hand raising and the calling of children's names, as this will also constrain the authenticity and richness of the conversation (Reznitskaya & Anderson, 2002).

Common Core Connection

Speaking and Listening Standards: Comprehension and Collaboration; Presentation of Knowledge and Ideas

When talking as a whole group, it will be important for you help facilitate rich student-to-student conversation, but it's also important that you not be the "discussion director"—and this can be a challenge! To really encourage the children to engage and "own" the conversation, it may be helpful for you to remove yourself from the circle altogether and sit behind the children as they talk. If this is uncomfortable for you, you might continue to sit in the circle, but let them know you won't be participating very often. Some teachers—Mr. Garcia, for instance—find it helpful to take notes while listening to the children talk. (See the feature titled "The Language of Your Instruction: Collaborative Reasoning in Action" for a description of this.) If you think this practice can work for you, be sure to let the children know the kinds of things you're writing and why. This helps alleviate any anxiety some children may feel about you writing while they're talking.

Collaborative Reasoning and Argument Schema

When you focus so intentionally on helping children respond to text and form opinions about text, you're helping them understand that reading is really about thinking. This focus on analysis and interpretation also helps children develop what researchers call *argument schema* (Newell et al., 2011; Reznitskaya & Anderson, 2002). Argument is a way of thinking and reasoning that results in a discourse pattern that is highly valued in academic settings. While the term *argument* does not appear in the Common Core until grade 6, seeds of this genre are found in earlier standards where students focus on developing opinions, backing them up with evidence from the text and presenting them orally to groups. (See the Reading, Writing, and Speaking and Listening Standards in Figure 8.8.)

The Language of Your Instruction

Collaborative Reasoning in Action

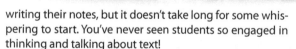

Ms. Novak, a fourth-grade teacher in Mr. Garcia's school, has just finished reading Chapter 4: American Laugh-Nosed Beet in *Al Capone Does My Shirts* (Choldenko, 2004). As she closes the book, the students erupt into conversation, each talking over one another and sharing very impassioned opinions. Ms. Novak looks pleased by their enthusiasm, but not so pleased with their discourse pattern. She interrupts in a soft-spoken voice, "Friends, this was a very engaging chapter and I'm interested in what you have to say, but I can't hear what you're saying when everyone is talking at once. Let's take a moment to collect our talking points. On your pad of Post-it notes, *stop and jot* one opinion that you'd like to share and at least two pieces of evidence to back up your thinking. If you have more than one opinion to share, write it and your evidence on another Post-it. In approximately two minutes, we'll start our conversation." The children dutifully start

writing their notes, but it doesn't take long for some whispering to start. You've never seen students so engaged in thinking and talking about text!

After a couple of minutes, Ms. Novak joins the students on the floor and says, "Today when you're sharing your opinions about the text, I want you to work on two goals: First, when you share your opinion about the text, be sure to back it up. What are some words we say when we're backing up our thinking?" The students respond in a polite fashion without raising their hands and they say that they'll use words such as *because* and *for example*. Ms. Novak affirms these as great choices and writes them on the chart paper. Then she shares her second goal: "Readers, sometimes you're so excited to share what you have to say, that you forget to listen to what others are saying. Please remember to listen as much, if not more, than you talk. I'll know you're being engaged listeners when you build on what others have said. What are some and you're deepening the conversation?" Ms. Novak adds these words to the chart and then turns to the group and asks, "Who can get us started in a conversation?"

Words to Back Up Your Opinion	Words that Deepen the Conversation
• Because • For example • One thing that makes me think this is . . .	• I agree . . . • I see it differently . . . • That makes me wonder . . . • What is one example of what you're saying?

Sergio: I don't think it was right for them to send Natalie away to the school. She obviously doesn't want to go because she sat down on the floor of the boat and wouldn't move and then Moose had to trick her to get off the boat.

Micah: I hear what you're saying and I see it differently. They moved their whole family to Alcatraz Island so Natalie could go to this really good school. They wouldn't do that if they didn't care about her.

Sergio: I didn't say they didn't care about her, I just don't think people should force someone else to do something they don't want to do.

Hugh: Isn't it true that sometimes it's important for people to help you do things you don't want to do? Remember in the book *The Story of Ruby Bridges* (Coles, 1995) how people were against integration and if those kids didn't have the courage to go to the "White school" we might still have segregated schools today?

Jane: Hugh, you just gave me a new thought. It's weird how they would send Natalie to a special school, isn't it? That's like segregation, too. Why didn't she go to the same school as Moose and all the other kids?

Aman: Doesn't this story take place before the Civil Rights Movement? [The students turn and talk for a minute and Aman takes the book from the easel.] Yes, it says right here, "January 6, 1935." The Civil Rights movement didn't really begin until the 1950s.

Hugh: I don't know if it's segregation if it's a special school for kids like Natalie.

Selma: Well, if this is a good thing, why does Moose feel sick to his stomach and why is his mom crying?

Ms. Novak can sense that there's a lot of excitement about this question and she asks the students to turn and talk and share their thoughts in smaller groups. After some time, the whole class comes back to together and the students have moved from this topic to analyzing both

Moose and his mom. As they talk, Ms. Novak captures their thoughts and evidence on the chart (see below). She'll continue to add to these notes throughout the book and together as a class they'll study how the characters stay the same, how they change over time, and how the students' opinions of them change, too.

Chapter 4: Character Analysis

Moose

Character Trait	Evidence
Considerate	• He always asks Natalie about the sun in the morning because she gets upset if he doesn't.
Troubled	• He wants to stop reading the index but he doesn't. He says, "This is the right thing to do, I tell myself. But I don't believe it."
Cunning and Funny	• He tricks Natalie into getting off the boat by reading the index wrong to be funny and getting her to correct him and follow him off the boat.

Conversations in which students work together to interpret texts help them deepen their comprehension and engagement with reading. When students develop and share opinions that can be supported using evidence from the text, they're learning how to take a stance on a topic. This is an important literacy skill, certainly, but it is also a life skill that is necessary for individuals to productively contribute to the vibrancy of a democratic society (Bomer & Bomer, 2001; Johnston, 2012).

At the end of this discussion, Ms. Novak will ask the students to reflect on the effectiveness of their conversational skills—noting what they did well and what they might try to improve on in their next group discussion. She'll support their reflections by sharing specific evidence of their strengths and opportunities for improvement from her notes about the discussion. In asking the students to self-assess, she's not only empowering them to "own" both the content and the process, but she's also giving them an opportunity to internalize a rubric for effective book discussions. Later in the day or week, she may provide the students with an opportunity to revisit any of the topics from today's conversation, or one of their own, in a written response to text.

Children learn how to develop the thinking and reasoning skills of argumentative discourse when they participate in group discussions (Anderson et al., 2001; Kuhn, Shaw, & Felton, 1997). The quality of talk is said to have a "snowball effect" on children who are initially reluctant to talk. By listening to others engage in collaborative reasoning, these children acquire the discourse pattern and thinking to support their interpretation of text (Anderson et al., 2001). For this reason, we intentionally provide regular opportunities for such discussion during our daily read-alouds and in guided reading groups, too. The feature called "The Language of Your Instruction: Collaborative Reasoning in Action" will help you see how to put reader response theory, collaborative reasoning, and the development of argument schema into practice. In this example we see how collaborative reasoning can be applied in a fourth grade classroom with older transitional readers. This same method could be used with with younger transitional readers using a more developmentally appropriate read-aloud.

Adaptable to All Stages

From Talking Well to Writing Well: Written Response to Text

In the opening vignette and in the previous feature, "The Language of Your Instruction: Collaborative Reasoning in Action," both Mr. Garcia and Ms. Novak's students took a moment to "stop and jot" their thoughts about text. Figure 8.9 highlights one student's two Post-it notes about the chapter in *Al Capone Does My Shirts* (Choldenko, 2004).

Despite having multiple opportunities to turn and talk, Devon, like many children in the class, did not have a chance to talk about all of her opinions. Written response to text gives children the opportunity to continue to reflect on their reading and further develop their responses to text. One of the most efficient and productive ways to facilitate this kind of reflection is through quick writes.

Quick Writes

Quick writes are informal opportunities for children to respond to text or other topics in short writing blocks, each lasting only 5 to 10 minutes. The goal of quick writes is to help children develop their thinking skills and ultimately improve their engagement with and comprehension of texts and ideas. Because quick writes are informal, they are usually ungraded, and it's optimal to do them several times a week so children can realize improvements in their thinking skills as well as writing skills.

Adaptable to All Stages

We generally recommend using quick writes as a way for children to continue to explore their thinking after participating in a **grand conversation** about a piece of text or a topic, or after children have collected several *stop and jot notes* and are ready to analyze them further, but these notes may also be used to prepare for a group conversation. In some cases, you might find that it's more appropriate to provide a prompt for the children to respond to, which is also fine—just be sure your goal is not to assess their thinking as much as it's to give their thinking a place to grow and flourish. Children will return to these writing samples when it's time for them to write a more structured and elaborated response, so it's a good idea for them to keep them in a folder, portfolio, or response notebook.

FIGURE 8.9 Devon's "Stop and Jot" Notes

I think Moose has a lot of responsibility in the family because his dad says,

"We can't do this without Moose." And when Natalie refused to get off the boat his dad says, "Moose, can you get her up?"

I think Natalie loves her brother because:

- Her feelings were hurt the day he didn't wish her good morning by saying "The sun get up okay today?"

- She grabs his hand as she gets off the boat.

Reading and Writing in Digital Contexts

Blogging in Response to Text

Blogging is a great way for children to engage in response and it can be an interesting alternative or supplement to quick writes. Children are often motivated to participate in blogs because online writing is freer from some of the conventions of more formal academic writing, and there's also the promise that someone will read and respond to their work!

Beginning in third grade, the Common Core Standards suggest that children should "use technology to produce and publish writing (using keyboarding skills) as well as interact and collaborate with others" (2010, p. 21). Blogging is one way to accomplish both goals! Be sure to help students safeguard their personal information and right to privacy by using secure, password protected blogs.

From Quick Writes to Response Essays

Common Core Connection

Writing Standards: Text Types and Purposes

After reading and discussing a picture book, a piece of poetry, a novel, informational text, or even after engaging in content-area learning that may or may not be text based, teachers like Mr. Garcia and Ms. Novak routinely provide time for children to talk about their learning and share their thoughts. After many of these conversations they invite children to document their thinking in some low-stakes kind of way. Stop and jot notes and quick writes are two ways they might do this. Sometimes graphic organizers are better for the task: webs, two-column notes, or diagrams can be especially helpful tools. Other times an artistic response is the best way to go. You'll strategically vary the methods of response so they best match the goals of your instruction and sometimes you'll even let your students choose which form of response works best for them.

Like Mr. Garcia and Ms. Novak, you'll have students keep track of their responses over time. There will come a time when you'll invite the children to look through their work to select one topic they'd like to revisit and develop into a more elaborate and structured essay.

When teaching children about response, we refer to the writing standards of the Common Core for guidance about what needs to be taught at each grade level. You can refer to the standards for written response in Figure 8.8 as an example of these standards.

The Gradual Release of Responsibility in Action

Adaptable to All Stages

Mr. Garcia and Ms. Novak facilitate children's learning of new text structures such as response essays using a gradual release of responsibility (Pearson & Gallagher, 1983). They begin by having children read a model text, also called *menor text,* an *exemplar,* or an *anchor text.* Until you have the opportunity to collect your own students' work as benchmarks, Appendix B of the Common Core State Standards can be a good resource for sample texts (CCSS, 2010). With your students' involvement, you'll talk about the content, structure, and craft of benchmark pieces and then take notes about these observations in the margins of the text. From this experience, you'll often create an anchor chart or graphic organizer that helps define the structure and characteristics of the type of text you're studying. If you and your students were studying narrative text structure, for example, you might create a story map and highlight words to mark the passage of time, a Common Core Standard. When it comes to writing a response essay, children in the transitional stage will need to express an opinion, identify evidence to back up their opinion, and write a conclusion to their essay.

After studying the structure and qualities of an effective response, you'll model how to write a response essay using a topic you and your students know a lot about. As you talk about *what* to write and *how* to write it, your students are developing an internal rubric for what makes an effective essay. Sometimes Mr. Garcia and Ms. Novak actually invite the children to co-construct such a

FIGURE 8.10 Constructed Response Scoring Rubric, Grades 2–4

Score	Writing (Purpose, Organization, Details)	Understanding of the Text	Conventions
4	Meets Score 3 PLUS one or more of the following: • elaboration of details • reflection on evidence • extension/conclusion (the so what)	Meets Score 3 PLUS one or more of the following: • evidence of deep thinking • shows understanding of multiple perspectives	No score for exceeds.
3	• restates question • organized ideas • 2-3 pieces of evidence from the text • concluding statement	• correct response • evidence is relevant • understands main idea • understands author's craft (if applicable)	Control at grade level conventions is evident. • applies spelling knowledge • punctuates correctly • capitalizes words correctly
2	Responses MAY include: • partial restating of question • confusing organization • only 1 piece of evidence from the text • reference(s) to text that are too general or not relevant	Responses MAY include: • misunderstanding the question • minor inaccuracies • over-reliance on personal connections • unclear understanding of the text's central idea	Control of grade level conventions is inconsistent. • occasional misspellings • inconsistent punctuation and capitalization
1	• missing focus • general and/or inaccurate evidence • may be repetitious • simple structure	• incorrect response • misunderstandings and confusion • lacks basic understanding of text	Control of grade level conventions is minimal.

Source: Hajdun, 2012. Used with permission.

rubric, but other times they just provide a teacher-made rubric like the one found in Figure 8.10. After the class collaboratively drafts, revises, and edits their essays, they work in partnerships to self-assess them and this helps the children further understand the expectations for the assignment. Extensive planning, modeling, and collaboration between students, and the students and their teacher, are the hallmarks of an effective writing program (Pritchard & Honeycutt, 2006).

In Figure 8.11 we see how Sloane, a second-grader and early transitional reader, responds to *Invaders* (Edwards, 2003)—a text about invasive species. His teacher, Mr. Garcia, poses a question for him to respond to: *Why are invaders such a problem?* Sloane begins with a controlling idea or thesis statement: "Invaders are such a problem because they have no/few enemies." He goes on to provide additional evidence:

- Because they lack enemies, they continue to grow.
- They can clog water pipes and then people won't get any water.

Sloane concludes his essay by saying: "That's why when you see an invader try to kill it or dig it up." If Sloane were your student, you'd acknowledge his many strengths by highlighting them on the rubric and talking about them in a conference. You'd also select one thing for Sloane to continue working on to continue. While there are many great options, focusing your instruction on sentence construction or elaboration are two ways you could help Sloane improve his work. As a first draft, this is a solid piece of writing! Since this is such a solid piece of writing, you might also, with Sloane's permission, project his essay for the whole class see to discuss. Students are more comfortable volunteering

FIGURE 8.11 Early Transitional Writer's Response to Text

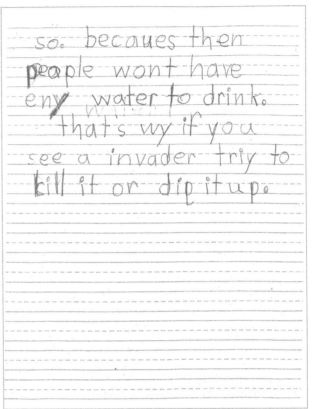

Name Sloane   Date 2/2/12

Response to Text

We read the book Invaders, by Karen Edwards. Invaders are plants or animals that have moved into a place where they don't belong. The book tells about many different kinds of "invaders" and the problems they cause.

Why are invaders such a problem?
Use evidence from the text to back up your answer

invaders are such a probem becaues they have no few enimies so. but if they doht have enimis they just keep growing. also invaders are such a prodrem is they glog pipes so water cant get throo

so. becaues then peaple wont have eny water to drink. that's wy if you see a invader triy to kill it or dip it up.

for this when they are immersed in a rich writing environment. Earlier in the school year, you might use an example from a former student.

In Figure 8.12 we see how responses change over the course of this stage. Here, we see a late transitional/early intermediate writer's response to a topic she learned about in health class: obesity in Vermont. Even though this is just a quick write, we see that Summer, a student in Ms. Novak's class, has a pretty good handle on the structure of an effective response essay as outlined in the Common Core Writing Standards. Instead of responding to a teacher's question, she begins with a thesis statement she generated on her own: "Obesity in VT [Vermont] is very common." She goes on to detail the concern and potential solutions to the problem. She finishes the essay with a conclusion and extended commentary: "All of these organizations and more hope to end obesity in Vermont. With a lot of support and help we can help achieve their goal."

As the children in your class gain experience writing these short response essays, you'll encourage them to return to one of their favorites to fully revise and edit it for publication. Some late transitional writers will be ready to move beyond a single-paragraph essay to an essay of three or four paragraphs in which they will provide more evidence to back up their thinking. If most of your students are ready for this kind of writing, you will teach it in your mini-lessons. If only a few are ready, you'll use smaller guided writing groups.

When the children have taken their work through the writing process as best they can, Ms. Novak creates a class book of their pieces, titled *This Makes Me Think Of . . . .* She publishes the book in print copies for the classroom and school library, and she also puts them on her class

FIGURE 8.12 Sample Response to a Special Topic: Obesity in Vermont

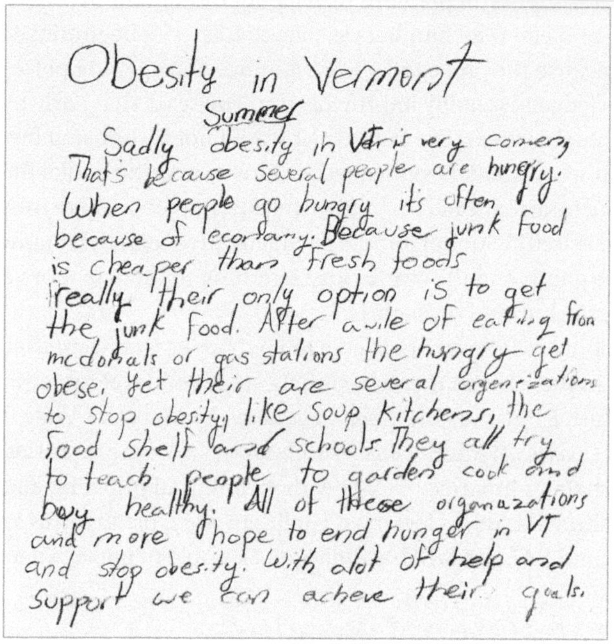

Obesity in Vermont

Summer

Sadly obesity in Vt is very comen, That's because several people are hungry. When people go hungry its often because of ecomany. Because junk food is cheaper than fresh foods really their only option is to get the junk food. After awile of eating from mcdonals or gas stations the hungry get obese. Yet their are several organizations to stop obesity like soup kitchens, the food shelf and schools. They all try to teach people to garden cook and buy healthy. All of these organizations and more hope to end hunger in VT and stop obesity. With alot of help and support we can acheve their goals.

webpage as well as the school's library page. The book becomes an interesting and valuable resource for children to find recommendations for books and topics to study, and the essays become models for other students who are learning to write response essays. Writing experiences like these help children develop their thinking and writing skills, and they help create a community that values reading, writing, inquiry, and response.

Books for Transitional Readers: Independent and Small Group Reading Practice

Transitional readers are eager to engage in rich content and complex text, especially when it's read aloud to them. When they read on their own, much of their attention is still focused on reading the words accurately, particularly in the early phase of the stage. As their reading accuracy improves, so does their fluency, and they begin to develop stronger comprehension skills, too. Transitional readers continue to benefit from daily small group reading instruction where you'll intentionally provide books they can read with high levels of accuracy—at least 90 to 94 percent after a book introduction. As we described in Chapter 4, in unsupported reading practice, children will be reading text with an even higher rate of accuracy—95 percent or better. This is called **high success reading** (Allington, 2009) or **independent level** text (Fountas & Pinnell, 1996). Children are more successful comprehending texts in which their reading accuracy is above 95 percent (Sinatra, Brown, & Reynolds, 2002). In the following section, we'll discuss the kinds of texts and instruction children need in the early, middle, and late part of the transitional stage.

Common Core Connection

Reading Standards for Literature and Informational Text: Range of Reading and Level of Text Complexity

Early Transitional Readers

Early transitional readers still prefer to read aloud, though they're increasingly comfortable with whisper reading and can read familiar text silently. They're beginning to read words more efficiently in part because they recognize word families and spelling patterns more readily and their sight-word knowledge is steadily improving, too. The texts that early transitional readers read have a greater volume of text. For example, it would not be unusual for their books to have 6 or more lines of text per page. The sentences are longer, and the books themselves are longer, too.

When reading informational text, early transitional readers are introduced to new places, experiences, and scientific understandings. In narrative text, the characters are beginning to have a little more depth and the stories are beginning to include more elements of narrative text (characters, setting, and problem/solution).

Early transitional readers are now able to read books that were their favorite read-alouds when they were in the emergent and beginning stages of development: books such as *The Carrot Seed* by Ruth Krauss (1973), *Goodnight Moon* by Margaret Wise Brown (1947), and Tomie dePaola's (1988) *Cookie's Week*. Because the children know these stories so well, these become great books for them to practice reading with meaningful phrasing and expression. Books that make early transitional readers feel most confident are typically DRA levels 14 to16 or guided reading levels H and I. Figure 8.13 highlights an example of narrative text at level 14.

Middle Transitional Readers

Children in the middle of the transitional stage are reading in short phrases and know around 200 to 300 words by sight. Their increased fluency helps them better monitor their reading, so they're more likely to notice when their comprehension begins to break down, or when they need to correct a misread word. Transitional readers in the middle part of the stage are beginning to read early chapter books such as the *Henry and Mudge* series (Rylant) and the *Nate the Great* series (Sharmat & Sharmat). These early chapter books are longer—upwards of 50 to 60 pages in length—so middle transitional readers must learn how sustain their interest and comprehension over time. These books are usually DRA levels 18 to 20 or guided reading levels J and K.

When reading informational text, transitional readers will also need to learn ways to keep track of the big ideas and important details of text. Graphic organizers can help them do this, as can turning to talk periodically with reading partners. Other response techniques are stopping

FIGURE 8.13 Sample Text for Early Transitional Readers

In the winter, the tractor pushed the snow off the driveway.

Vroom-vroom-vroom

Grandpa kept the tractor in the shed. He put a blanket and a rope on the tractor.

Time went by, and the farm got bigger. The little tractor could not do all the jobs anymore.

to jot some quick notes while reading, or comprehension routines such as **reciprocal teaching** (described later in this chapter). In narrative text, transitional readers will start exploring some of the elements of setting such as *place* and *passage of time*. These two elements of narrative text can be particularly challenging for transitional readers as their stories can now take place in multiple settings and over a span of time that's longer than a few moments or a day. Their stories may also start to include literary elements such as flashbacks or foreshadowing, which can provide a new challenge for transitional readers who are accustomed to a more linear sequence of events.

Common Core Connection

Reading Standards for Literature: Key Ideas and Details and Craft and Structure

To help children in the middle of the transitional stage successfully comprehend and enjoy early chapter books texts, you'll want to thoroughly study these books before you introduce them to the children so you can anticipate those aspects that may be challenging for them. Whether it be words that are difficult to decode or understand, unusual text features, or craft techniques such as flashbacks or figurative language, you'll want to identify these challenges and plan how you'll scaffold children's understanding in their guided reading lessons. It is important that you teach your young readers how to be strategic so they can be successful when they encounter these challenges when reading on their own.

Using Series Books to Support Students' Comprehension and Positive Engagements with Text

Since the cognitive demands of text are increasing for transitional readers in the middle part of the stage, you might find that they feel strongest when reading series books—for example, *Nate the Great* (Sharmat & Sharmat), *Horrible Harry* (Kline), or *The Boxcar Children* (Chandler-Warner) series. Series books are a particularly supportive for children who are just starting to read longer texts. This is because series books have a predictable structure to them, and this allows transitional readers to focus more of their attention on deepening their comprehension and applying the interpretative strategies they're learning about in your interactive read-alouds. With your support and instruction, they will be able to engage in character analysis, the study of author's craft, comparing and contrasting texts, and even analyzing the important or "big" ideas of informational text. As you can see, your guided reading instruction in the middle part of this stage will strategically shift to focus more explicitly on reading for meaning in both fiction and informational text.

The Language of Your Instruction

Teaching Children to Infer

Comprehension strategy use follows a developmental progression that is dependent on children's word knowledge, their background knowledge, and their cognitive development (Duke & Carlisle, 2011; Paris, Wasik, & Turner, 1991). In order for children to infer, they need to consider the words and illustrations in texts and combine these with their background knowledge to be able to think beyond the literal interpretation of text. Children in what Piaget termed the **concrete operations** stage of cognitive development (Piaget & Inhelder, 1969, Wadsworth, 2003) are more likely to go beyond literal understanding to form a more reasoned and sophisticated interpretation of text.

The concrete operations stage generally spans ages 7 through 11—the typical ages of transitional readers and writers. Children in this stage of development are capable of understanding concepts like time, volume, quantity, and symbols. They have come to realize that ideas are separate from objects and they're more capable of understanding and using language to represent more complex ideas. This makes comprehension strategies such as predicting, inferring, and monitoring comprehension more accessible.

When teaching about inference, we use the gradual release of responsibility model (Chapter 1) (Pearson & Gallagher, 1983) as illustrated in the following lesson:

Explain *what* the strategy is, *why* we use it, and model *how* to use it.

When introducing inference to transitional readers using a specific text, you might say something like this:

"Readers, you know it's important to think about what you already know about a topic, an author, or a genre before, during, and after you read. We call this background information *schema,* and it helps you enjoy and understand your texts more because you make connections to your life, other texts, and the world. Schema also helps you 'read between the lines' of a text. Reading between the lines means you're thinking about the message the author is trying to give you even though it might not be written in the words of the text. Sometimes it's fun to imagine that the important messages are written in invisible ink between the lines of text and your job is to think like a detective or spy to try to figure out what these messages are! When you 'read between the lines' of text, you're inferring the author's message. Today I'm going to show you how to infer using the book, *William's Doll* [Zolotow, 1972]."

As you read the story aloud, you'll show the children how you combine your schema with the pictures and text in the story. For example, on page 11 when William's brother calls him a sissy, you'll explain to the children how you inferred that William's feelings were hurt even though the author doesn't say so in the text. Or on page 12, when William's father buys him a basketball instead of a doll, you infer that maybe his dad isn't comfortable with his son playing with dolls because he wouldn't buy him one when he asked.

Guided practice

After you model how to combine your background knowledge with the clues the author and illustrator leave in the text, you'll periodically stop at strategic points and invite the children to "turn and talk" about their inferences. Sometimes it's helpful to prompt this thinking with a question. For example, on page 23, William's grandmother comes for a visit and we see a picture of William with his arms wrapped around her and his cheeks are flushed pink. Here, you might ask the children to infer how William feels about his grandmother and why. You might then ask them to predict what they think will happen next and why. (Yes, predictions are a form of inference!) When William's grandmother buys him a doll and explains to his dad why having a doll is important for young boys, you might ask the children to infer how the dad is feeling now and why.

As you've noticed, children's answers to the question *Why?* are as important, if not *more* important, as the inference itself. Like predictions, inferences can be confirmed, modified, and abandoned. This is all part of monitoring one's reading for understanding—a metacognitive strategy that is critically important to your readers' success. You will want to impress on your readers that the plausibility of a prediction or inference—is it *reasonable*?—is more important than being "right."

Link to independent practice

After modeling and guided practice, you'll encourage your readers to practice inferring during independent reading time. You might ask students to jot on a Post-it a place where they inferred during reading practice and have them bring it back to share time later in the workshop. Alternatively, you may have them jot some notes about inferring on a graphic organizer like the one shown here. The key is that you want to encourage your readers to practice the strategy and then, over time, integrate it with other comprehension strategies so they use it flexibly and as needed.

What it said in the text:	What I inferred:

Learning comprehension strategies, particularly interpretative strategies such as inferring, or metacognitive strategies such as monitoring, takes a lot of modeling and practice.

Late Transitional Readers

Common Core Connection

Reading Standards for Informational Text: Craft and Structure

Readers in the late phase of the transitional stage are beginning to read texts that are considerably more challenging. The stories and ideas are more complex and often more abstract. Fantasy, historical fiction, and biographies are now more accessible to these readers, though they will likely need support in reading these new genres. Series books also continue to popular with late transitional readers. Among their favorites are the *Cam Jansen* series (Adler), the *Magic Tree House* series (Osborne), the *Pinky and Rex* books (Howe). In addition to an increase in the length of the text, you'll find less picture support, longer and more complex sentence structures, more challenging vocabulary, and greater sophistication in the plots and concepts. Also, the literary elements such as figurative language, word play, and similes and metaphors become more common. These literary elements will become an instructional focus in your small group instruction in this late phase.

Informational texts are becoming increasingly sophisticated at the end of this stage. Books such as *Young Thurgood Marshall: A Fighter for Equality* (Carpenter, 1996), *Dinosaur Days* (Milton, 1985),

FIGURE 8.14 Sample Informational Text for Late Transitional Readers

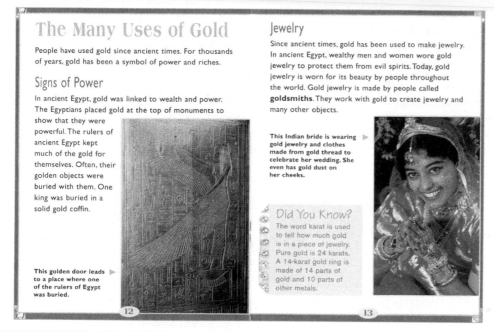

The Many Uses of Gold

People have used gold since ancient times. For thousands of years, gold has been a symbol of power and riches.

Signs of Power

In ancient Egypt, gold was linked to wealth and power. The Egyptians placed gold at the top of monuments to show that they were powerful. The rulers of ancient Egypt kept much of the gold for themselves. Often, their golden objects were buried with them. One king was buried in a solid gold coffin.

This golden door leads to a place where one of the rulers of Egypt was buried.

Jewelry

Since ancient times, gold has been used to make jewelry. In ancient Egypt, wealthy men and women wore gold jewelry to protect them from evil spirits. Today, gold jewelry is worn for its beauty by people throughout the world. Gold jewelry is made by people called **goldsmiths**. They work with gold to create jewelry and many other objects.

This Indian bride is wearing gold jewelry and clothes made from gold thread to celebrate her wedding. She even has gold dust on her cheeks.

Did You Know?

The word karat is used to tell how much gold is in a piece of jewelry. Pure gold is 24 karats. A 14-karat gold ring is made of 14 parts of gold and 10 parts of other metals.

12   13

From Wax to Crayon (Nelson, 2003), or *Planets around the Sun* (Simon, 2002) are quite popular choices. To fully access all of the information in these texts, or to "read around them" for specific information, late transitional readers will need to understand **informational text features**.

Figure 8.14 is a good example of the kind of informational text children in the transitional stage will read. It comes from a book called *Gold* (Schwartz, 2002). In order for transitional readers to be successful reading this text, they will need to understand the role of headings to signal importance, captions to describe pictures or illustrations, and boldface print to highlight important words that can also be found in the glossary. They'll also learn how interesting facts are often found in inserts such as the "Did You Know?" feature box. All of these text features aid readers' comprehension, and you'll teach your transitional readers how to use them to improve their understanding and enjoyment of informational text.

When Mr. Garcia teaches his second-graders about informational text features, he and his students study benchmark texts to find examples of these features and then they create an anchor chart like the one in Figure 8.15. The children also keep *text feature notebooks* where they name, describe, and include an example of each text feature they study (Miller, 2002). These notebooks become references for the children when they conduct their own research during reading workshop or theme time, and when they write informational text in writing workshop. As children progress through the transitional stage of development, there are increasing opportunities to integrate reading, writing, and content-area instruction.

FIGURE 8.15 Informational Text Features Anchor Chart

Common Core Connection

Reading Standards
for Literature and
Informational Text:
Range of Reading
and Level of Text
Complexity

Late transitional readers are often most comfortable reading books at DRA levels 24 to 28 or guided reading level M. Of course, each individual reader's background knowledge and interests are important when we match children to text, and this becomes increasingly true as we progress through the stages. Concepts and content unfamiliar to them will likely require more support than texts that address content for which they have more background knowledge.

When possible, consider offering students choices not only in their independent reading materials but also in the books they read in guided reading. Choice is an important motivator for readers (Guthrie, Wigfield, & Perencevich, 2004). As the books they read are increasingly longer and complex, your late transitional readers will need to commit a considerable amount of time and effort to the task of reading. Offering choices, even if they're controlled choices (for example, inviting the children to choose one book from a small collection of books that are "just-right" for them), can improve their engagement, motivation, stamina, and even fluency and comprehension.

Children's Literature Connection

Other Books for Transitional Readers

The Common Core State Standards identify specific genres appropriate for children in second through fourth grades, including folktales, fables, and myths. A summary of each genre and sample titles is included here.

Folktales

Folktales are simple stories that have been handed down through generations by way of storytelling. Many folktales have since been written down and made into books.

Traditional folktales typically highlight the struggle between good and evil, the weak and the powerful, or the rich and the poor. They can also explain how things in nature came to be (e.g., why the sun sets or the reason for the seasons).

Folktales often include repetitive elements or rhyming verses: "Run, run as fast as you can . . ." or "Mirror, mirror, on the wall . . .". They frequently include repetitive sounds, too: "mek, mek, mek" and "kaa, kaa, kaa" (Aardema, 1975).

Folktales entertain readers and listeners by exposing the folly and goodness of man. Characters often have to overcome obstacles (three trials), magic can figure prominently (three wishes), as can trickery. Good examples of folktales include *Anansi the Spider* (McDermott, 1972); *Mufaro's Beautiful Daughters* (Steptoe, 1987); *The Fisherman and His Wife* (Grimm & Grimm, 1980); *Rumplestiltskin* (Lanning & Grimm, 1983); *Strega Nona* (dePaola, 1975); *Yeh-Shen* (Young, 1982); *Stone Soup* (McGovern, 1986); and *Rapunzel* (Isadora & Grimm, 2008).

Folktales can be great vehicle for learning about culture and storytelling traditions. Comparing and contrasting different versions of folktales can help your students develop their analytical skills. Folktales, like fables and myths, help children go beyond their literal interpretation of text to understanding the author's purpose.

Fables

Fables are very short tales in which animals, and sometimes natural elements (the wind, sun, or trees), speak and act. Fables are intended to teach the reader a moral or lesson through a very fast-moving plot. Extracting the moral from these stories can be difficult for children in the early part of the stage, but over time and through collaborative reasoning, most children are able to move beyond their literal interpretations to access the more sophisticated lessons of these stories.

Aesop's fables are probably among the best well-known fables in the Western World. Modern versions of these old tales include *Town Mouse, Country Mouse* (Brett, 2003); *Seven Blind Mice* (Young, 2002); *Fables* (Lobel, 1983); *Aesop's Fables* (Pinkney, 2000); and *Mice, Morals & Monkey Business: Lively Lessons from Aesop's Fables* (Wormell, 2005).

Myths

Myths are yet another type of traditional literature that attempt to explain natural phenomena and human nature. Sometimes their purpose is to celebrate a hero or heroine. Immortal gods and goddesses with supernatural powers figure prominently in these classic tales. Myths, like folktales and fables, provide readers a window into other cultures and beliefs about human nature. Greek myths are among the most popular of this genre.

Some favorite titles include *Keepers of the Earth: Native American Stories and Environmental Activities for Children* (Caduto & Bruchac, 1998); *Greek Myths* (Williams, 2011); *Greek Myths for Children* (Amery, 2009); *Mythlopedia: Oh My Gods* (Bryant, 2009); *Mythlopedia: She's All That* (Bryant, 2009); and *Mythlopedia: All in the Family* (Bryant, 2010).

Developing Transitional Readers' Fluency and Comprehension: Research-Based "Best" Practices

Transitional readers' interactions with text change quite considerably throughout this stage of development. In the early part of the stage, their reading is becoming more accurate and they may read in some two- or three-word phrases, but much of their reading is still word by word. Efficient and expressive reading will take more time to develop. Through developmentally grounded word study instruction and your coordinated guided reading lessons, transitional readers gain increased accuracy and automaticity through the middle and late part of the stage. And, as their word knowledge improves, they're able to focus more of their cognitive energies on reading expressively and comprehending text. These are two important and related goals.

In this section, we'll share a few strategies for increasing children's fluency, particularly their ability to read with expression. We'll also explain how a comprehension routine called **reciprocal teaching** (Palincsar & Brown, 1986) can improve the reading comprehension of transitional readers.

> **Common Core Connection**
>
> Reading Standards: Foundational Skills – Fluency

Wide Reading

If you want to get better at something (nearly anything!), then one word comes to mind: *practice*. Developing reading fluency is no different. Children need ample opportunity to read for concentrated amounts of time each day. The term **wide reading** refers to children reading a variety of texts and genres every day—as much as possible. The keys to successful reading practice are threefold: (1) children need to read for a reason—they should be purposeful and intentional in selecting their books; (2) children need to read with specific goals and purposes in mind (Duke & Pearson, 2002); and (3) children should be reading books in which they have very high levels of accuracy (Kuhn, Schwanenflugel & Meisinger, 2010; Reutzel, Jones, Fawson, & Smith, 2008; Sinatra et al., 2002). Allington (2009) emphasizes that all readers, particularly those who struggle, need daily opportunities to practice this kind of "high success reading."

Wide reading is positively correlated with children's reading fluency as well as their comprehension and improvements in word recognition (Kuhn, Schwanenflugel, & Meisinger, 2010; Kuhn et al., 2006; Rasinski et al., 2011). Student choice is an especially important motivator for engaged reading (Guthrie, Wigfield, & Perencevich, 2004).

Repeated Reading

In the beginning reading stage, you learned about the importance of repeated oral reading. In contrast to wide reading, repeated reading is just that—rereading the same text over and over again. Researchers have found that repeated oral reading, yields improvements in children's word recognition, fluency, and comprehension (National Reading Panel, 2000; Rasinski et al., 2011). (See Chapter 7 for an overview of various methods of repeated reading.)

One of the primary goals of fluency instruction in the transitional stage is to focus on reading with appropriate phasing, rate, volume, and expression. Expressive reading is an important goal because there is a very strong and positive relationship between expressive reading and silent reading comprehension (Daane, Campbell, Grigg, Goodman, & Oranje, 2005; Rasinski, Rikli, &

> Applicable to All Stages

Johnston, 2009; Raskinski et al., 2011). While we continue to teach transitional and even intermediate readers strategies for decoding longer and more challenging words, we simultaneously focus on developing children's expressive reading and comprehension. Readers' Theater and other forms of performance reading are two important and motivating ways to teach expressive reading.

Readers' Theater

Readers' Theater is a form of repeated reading whereby children read scripts intentionally prepared for reading aloud. Readers' Theater is different from putting on a play: There's no need for children to memorize lines or create costumes or scenery. Instead, children work together, and with you, to read a script with expression and understanding.

We often introduce children to a Readers' Theater script during guided reading, as Mr. Garcia explained in the opening vignette. We introduce it the same way we might any other text: by providing necessary background information, previewing the text, talking about the gist of the story, looking at the text's structure and illustrations, and making predictions. After reading it through once or twice and discussing the meaning of the play, you'll assign children different roles and you'll model how to read these parts in a way that makes their meaning clear. With your help, the children will study the text to determine where to pause and which words to group together and stress while reading. You'll help children also use the punctuation to inform *how* they read the text.

In the days following the introduction, the children will work individually and together to practice reading the play with expression. Many children find this practice incredibly motivating! After several days of practice, and when the children have achieved the desired level of fluency, they read it for their classmates. Readers' Theater is an effective means of engaging children in repeated reading practice (Martinez, Roser, & Stecker, 1999).

Other Forms of Performance Reading

Some forms of writing are just meant to be performed: poetry, speeches, announcements, newscasts, and songs, for example. It's exciting to listen to and study how professionals read these texts and then attempt to imitate their fluent reading. Sometimes your students will read along with the recordings as a way to develop their reading skills. This is called *technology-assisted repeated reading* and it has the same benefits as other forms of repeated reading or performance reading (Rasinski et al., 2011).

Performance reading, whether in the form of Readers' Theater, in-class newscasts, or reading picture books aloud to younger book buddies, improves children's reading fluency, word recognition, and comprehension, not to mention their engagement and motivation to read!

Comprehension Routines: Reciprocal Teaching in Action

Common Core Connection

Speaking and Listening: Comprehension and Collaboration; Presentation of Knowledge and Ideas

Reciprocal teaching is a comprehension routine that incorporates four key comprehension strategies—predicting, clarifying, questioning, and summarizing (Palincsar & Brown, 1986)—and it supports children in their efforts to orchestrate using multiple strategies at a time. It has a very deep research base and is one of the most effective means of improving students' comprehension (NRP, 2000; Rosenshine & Meister, 1994). Reciprocal teaching can be used in whole class read-alouds, guided reading groups, and intervention lessons.

Reciprocal teaching begins with the teacher modeling how to use all four comprehension strategies after reading a short piece of text—a paragraph, a page, or a chapter—the length depends on how much support your students need. After some modeling, the teacher invites a student to become "the teacher" for the next section of text, hence the name "reciprocal teaching." All the students read the new section of text and then the new teacher leads the think-aloud by asking a

FIGURE 8.16 Stop and Think: Reciprocal Teaching in Action

Predict	**Clarify**
I think . . . because . . .	One part that was confusing for me . . .
I predict . . . because . . .	I'm not sure I understand the part . . .
I have a hunch that . . . because . . .	The author lost me when . . .
I expect . . . because . . .	I didn't understand . . .
	What did you/the author mean when . . .
Summarize	
This section was about . . .	**Question**
The important ideas in this section are . . .	Why . . .
The gist of this section is . . .	What do you think . . .

question or two of the group, often a *How?* or *Why?* question. This teacher summarizes the passage, asks for clarifications, and then predicts and solicits predictions about what may come next. The language of these four comprehension strategies can be found in Figure 8.16.

At first, the children will take turns in the role of teacher and before long they will spontaneously share the role. As they gain proficiency integrating and using all four strategies, their talk can become more organic and slightly less structured, moving in the direction of the book club conversations described in Chapter 9. Reciprocal teaching gives children a predictable routine for orchestrating multiple comprehension strategies to deepen both their engagement and comprehension of text.

The Language of Your Instruction

Conferring with Transitional Readers and Writers

Carl Anderson wrote, "To teach writing well—to confer with student writers well—we must be affected by our students and the details of their lives" (2000, p. 189). Anderson reminds us that conferring is about listening attentively to what our young readers and writers say, the things that matter to them, and noticing what they do. After listening to a child's reading of text or their own writing, and listening to him talk about the things he's working on, your job is to find the one thing that will move this child forward—this becomes your teaching point. The key to an effective conference is your willingness to listen intently and respond thoughtfully.

Reading and writing conferences last around five minutes and they have three distinct parts: research-decide-teach (Calkins, 1994, 2000; Anderson, 2000). A description of each part follows.

Research: Gathering Information

During the first part of a conference, you're gathering information that will help you identify a child's strengths, interests, and opportunities for improvement. If the child is reading when you approach her, ask the child to "turn up her volume" so you can listen to how the reading is going. You might take this opportunity to take an informal running record, which will help you notice the child's strategic reading behaviors.

When there's a natural place to stop reading, shift the conference toward a conversation about the child's reading work. With fluent readers, you might ask the child to summarize what's happening in the text. If the child is writing, you might ask her to read and talk about her piece of work. It's wise to have a brief conversation with the child about the things she is currently working on and her goals. Asking open-ended questions allows the child to reflect on her work and intentions. There's no limit to the kinds of questions you might ask, but here are a few that we've found helpful over the years:

- Tell me about your reading/writing today.
- What's something you're working on in your reading/writing? How's that going?
- Is there something that you'd like to work to improve your reading/writing?
- I noticed that you . . . . Tell me about that.
- Have you ever tried/thought/wondered/considered . . . .
- How have you grown as a reader/writer? What are some of your new goals?

- The last time we conferred we talked about . . . . How's that going now?

Decide: Contemplating Your Instructional Focus

After you've gathered some information from and about the child as a reader or writer, you'll select *one* thing to teach or reinforce. You'll intentionally build on the child's strengths and help her stretch her skills beyond her current level of independence. It's important that your teaching point be something the child will be able to transfer to other reading or writing activities. Lucy Calkins often says, "Teach the reader, not the book." Some possible teaching points include:

- Selecting a "just-right" book
- Keeping track of your thinking while reading (stopping to think, talk, or jot)
- Applying decoding strategies to longer words
- Selecting a topic to write about
- Adding details, dialogue, or text features
- Writing strong leads or conclusions
- Improving fluency and building stamina for reading or writing for longer periods of time

Teach: Connect, Model, Guided Practice, and Link

When you've selected your teaching point, you'll teach it using the gradual release of responsibility (Pearson & Gallagher, 1983):

Begin with a *connection*: "I noticed you were reading the words in phrases like we talked about last time, like right here: (read a section of text where the child did a nice job breaking the text into meaningful phrase units). Tell me about that . . . ." "One other thing I noticed is there's a lot of dialogue and special print in this text, like right here (point out some places where there's dialogue and special print)."

Next, you'll *model* the teaching point: "Authors include dialogue and special print because they want the reader to read these words with expression. For instance, (select a section to read and show the child how to read it expressively)." After modeling, invite the child to try out the strategy. In this case, it might be good to try some echo reading. Be sure to discuss with the child how understanding a text affects how she reads it aloud and how reading with expression will help deepen her understanding and enjoyment of the text, too.

At the conclusion of the conference, summarize the learning and then *link* it to the child's reading life: "So, whenever you're reading, you'll remember to notice when characters are talking or there's special print. When you see these things, the author wants you to read the words with expression. When you read with expression, it means you're thinking about the meaning of the text and that's your goal! You get started and I'll listen . . . ." "The next time we confer, I'll be looking to see that you're working on reading with phrasing *and* expression."

Reading and Writing Connections: Helping Transitional Writers Write Well

Transitional writers tend to be more prolific than beginning writers because improvements in their handwriting fluency and word knowledge have made the task of writing more efficient (Abbott, Berninger, & Fayol, 2010; Graham, Harris, & Fink, 2000). Children in this stage are also reading with improved accuracy and comprehension, and for these reasons, they're able to access a greater variety of texts and genres such as fantasy, biography, and other forms of informational text. Exposure to a variety of texts helps children envision new possibilities for *writing*, too. You'll teach your transitional writers about text structure and author's craft by rereading familiar texts with the "eyes of a writer" (Hansen, 2001) as Ms. Novak did when teaching her students to write a response to text earlier in this chapter. Like her, you'll use mentor texts, either student-authored or professionally published, and the gradual release of responsibility to teach other forms of writing.

Transitional writers write a number of things, including poems, narratives, reports, and persuasive essays. In the section that follows, we'll look at the writing samples of three transitional writers to understand the characteristics of writing at this stage, as well as the instruction that's necessary to help them compose well-organized pieces of writing.

Narrative

Children's narrative writing follows a developmental progression beginning in the emergent stage where children describe memorable events such as a birthday party or a special trip while pointing to their markings on the page. Their stories include elements of storybook language such as "They lived happily ever after" (Sulzby, 1985; Nelson, 1981), but they rarely include all of the elements of narrative text. Since their writing is not yet conventional, the children often have difficulty retelling the same story twice.

Common Core Connection

Writing Standards:
Text Types and
Purposes; Production
and Distribution of
Writing

Beginning writers' narratives are also inspired by their own experiences, but they begin to include more of the elements of narrative text: characters, setting, and usually a problem (Bruner, 1991). Transitional writers elaborate on these elements and sometimes include more than one problem in their stories. They also reveal more about their characters' feelings and goals, and the story's problem usually gets resolved by the end of the story. By the middle and late part of the transitional stage, children's writing is longer and reflects their growing understanding of narrative text structure (McKeogh, Palmer, Jarvey, & Bird, 2007).

Prewriting and Planning Narrative Text

While studying narrative text in reading workshop, children are ready to explore further how to write narrative text in writing workshop. Some teachers encourage children to talk a lot about their story as a way for them to rehearse or plan their writing. Talking and sharing their writing with peers is a unique motivator for young writers (Pritchard & Honeycutt, 2007). Other teachers encourage children to plan their narratives using a story map. Still others recommend a combination of both. The five-step planning process noted here is a good example of how you may combine both techniques—oral rehearsal and the use of a graphic organizer (Graham & Harris, 2007):

Step 1: Invite students to brainstorm ideas for a story with each other.

Step 2: Encourage the children to "let their minds be free" so they can think about many different ideas for each part of the story. Again, this process is maximized when they share these ideas with peers and talk through the story plan.

Step 3: Prompt the children to answer the following questions before drafting. This structure is called, W-W-W; WHAT; HOW.

Who is the main character; who else is in the story?

When does the story take place?

Where does the story take place?

What does the main character want to do; what do the other characters do?

What happens when the main character tries to do it; what happens with the other characters?

How does the story end?

How does the main character feel; how do the other characters feel? (Graham & Harris, 2007, pp. 131–132)

- **Step 4:** Students draft their stories using their notes as a guide.
- **Step 5:** As students write, they're encouraged to reread their texts to be sure they make sense and are interesting! They're also encouraged to elaborate and revise their stories to make them more engaging for the reader.

Researchers have found a significant improvement in the quality of children's narrative writing after learning how to use a planning process like the one described here (Harris & Graham, 1996).

In Figure 8.17, we see Colin's story about his missing cat in the book, *Car Cat*. This story describes the day Colin lost his cat—the big problem of the story. He describes his feelings: He was scared and worried. He explains how he sat at his computer for a bit when he couldn't find

FIGURE 8.17 Sample Transitional Writer's Narrative Text, *Car Cat*

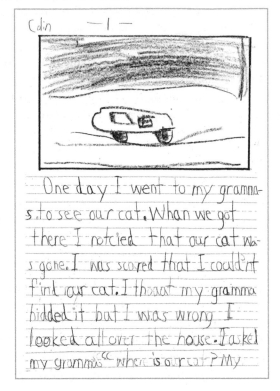

Colin — 1 —

One day I went to my grammas to see our cat. Whan we got there I noticed that our cat was gone. I was scared that I couldint find our cat. I thoaat my gramma hidded it but I was wrong. I looked all over the house. I asked my grammas "where is our cat? My

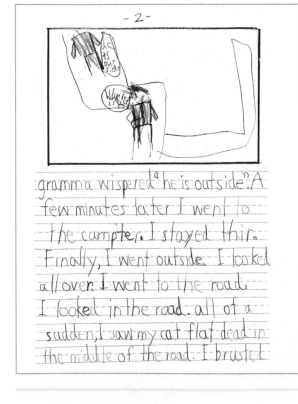

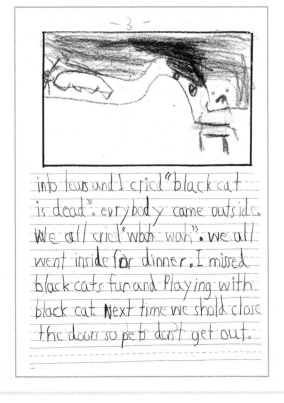

- 2 -

gramma wispered "he is outside". A few minutes later I went to the campter. I stayed thir. Finally, I went outside. I looked all over. I went to the road. I looked in the road. all of a sudden, I saw my cat flat dead in the middle of the road. I brustet

~3~

into tears and I cried "black cat is dead". evrybody came outside. We all cried "wah wah". we all went inside for dinner. I missed black cats fur and Playing with black cat. Next time we shold close the doors so pets don't get out.

his cat, and we can infer that he just didn't know what to do. After a short time, he went outside to look for his cat and found it dead on the road (the sad resolution to the problem). Colin demonstrates his growing understanding of narrative text structure when he adds dialogue to his writing, "Black cat is dead," and the sounds of everyone's reaction, "wah, wah." Colin also includes great transition words such *finally* and *all of a sudden*. These are among the characteristics that differentiate transitional writers' work from that of beginners (McKeough et al., 2007).

Colin goes beyond retelling his story when he elaborates and reflects at the end: "I miss black cat's fur and playing with black cat." He also reveals that he understands narratives sometimes teach lessons when he writes, "Next time we should close the door so pets don't get out." Colin's narrative writing is representative of children in the transitional stage of development.

Research and Reports

After listening to her teacher read *Freckle Juice* (Blume, 1971) aloud, McKenna, a bouncy second-grader with blonde hair and freckles, became completely fascinated with freckles and where they come from. This propelled her to do a little research on the topic and when she did, she wrote a report about what she learned. Her report is called "Human Leopards" (see Figure 8.18).

McKenna's teacher, Mr. Garcia, had recently completed a unit on reading informational text where McKenna learned about the structure of reports and informational text features. We see evidence of McKenna's understanding of these features on her first page where she has two pictures with captions and a text box that describes the main idea of the text.

McKenna's writing begins with a solid lead that hooks the reader and signals the "controlling idea," or topic, of the report: "Did you know people aren't born with freckles?" McKenna informs the reader that the sun and melatonin in your skin make freckles, and people with fair complexions or red hair are more prone to getting freckles. As required by the standards, McKenna wraps up her report with a conclusion: "I learned people with freckles need to be careful and use sunscreen so they don't get burned. Now I know how me and my mom got freckles."

Mr. Garcia supported McKenna's report writing by working with her in the prewriting/planning stage, too (see MacArthur, Schwartz, Graham, Molloy, & Harris, 1996). Here, he asked McKenna a few questions:

1) What do you want to learn?
2) What do you already know about the topic?
3) What questions to do you have about the topic?
4) What is your response to what you've learned?

After talking about the answers to these questions, McKenna created a concept map to help organize her research questions and report. As she learned the answers to the questions, she added them to the map.

When McKenna gathered all her research, she conferred with a writing partner and asked advice about how to sequence her report. After considering the advice and her own thoughts on the matter, she added numbers to reflect the order she planned to write the report. Once the planning was complete, she began drafting. The writing in Figure 8.18 is her final draft.

Persuasive Pieces: The Seeds of Argument

Children are motivated by interesting topics and authentic and meaningful writing experiences (Boscolo & Gelati, 2007). Few writing activities are more engaging and authentic as writing persuasive essays. Persuasive writing encourages writers to look at a complex issue and take a stand it. In doing so, they need to build a case for why their position is right.

> **Common Core Connection**
> Writing Standards:
> Research to Build and
> Present Knowledge

FIGURE 8.18 Sample Transitional Writer's Report, "Human Leopards"

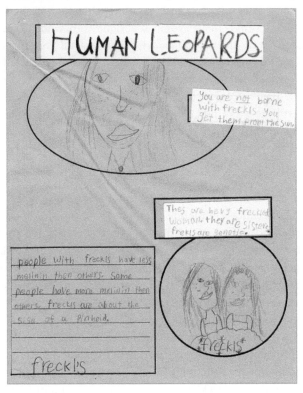

HUMAN LEOPARDS

by Mckenna Raymond   2-1-11

Did you know people arnt borne with freckles? acshaly your body makes freckles. The sun on your skin makes freckles. I bet you did not know that.

people with freckles have less melanin. melanin is made by skin cand melanocyte it helps proteckte you from uv-rays.

Everyone has melanin. Some people have more melanin then others. Melanin gathers in spots on your skin.

people with fair skin or red hair usatly have more freckts. You inherit your skin tipe. I lernd people with frekis have to be carfelt puting sunskrean on so they do not get bernd. Now I know how me and my mom got fizzris.

FIGURE 8.19 Transitional Writer's Sample Persuasive Letter

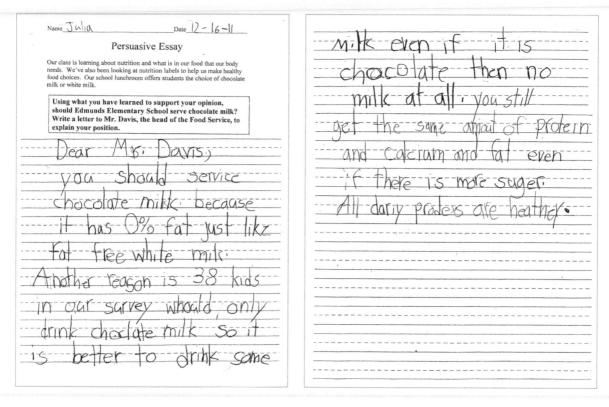

The children in Mr. Garcia's second-grade classroom did just that. After learning about the nutritional needs of children and the nutritional value of different kinds of milk that's served in the cafeteria, the children were asked to take a position on whether the school should serve chocolate milk. The children were taught to develop their argument using the *DARE* strategy (Graham & Harris, 2007, p. 138):

Develop a topic sentence.
Add supporting details.
Reject arguments from the other side.
End with a conclusion.

Figure 8.19 shows one transitional writer's letter trying to persuade the Director of Food Services to add chocolate milk to the menu.

In this letter we see how Julia states her case in a topic sentence, "You should serve chocolate milk because it has 0% fat just like fat free milk." She goes to support her position that the school should serve chocolate milk for a variety of health reasons. She anticipates the objection that chocolate milk has more sugar by asserting that it has the same protein as other milks and she concludes with a strong statement "All dairy products are heathey [healthy]."

Persuasive essays are made stronger when children understand the overall structure of a good argument, and the DARE mnemonic can help them plan and write a convincing essay. As children transition into the intermediate stage of writing, their persuasive essays will come to reflect a more sophisticated form of writing called an *argumentative essay*, which you'll learn more about in Chapter 9. Until then, written responses to text and persuasive essays provide transitional writers with developmentally appropriate practice with this important form of writing.

Chapter Summary

The transitional stage of development is marked by tremendous improvements in reading and writing fluency, as well as an increase in children's comprehension and interpretative skills. By the end of the transitional stage, children have gained the critical understanding of how vowels work and they're beginning to explore the spelling–meaning connection. They've also learned important connections between reading and writing different forms of narrative and informational text. Their understanding of text structure improves not only their comprehension of texts but also their writing of texts. Investing time in planning and prewriting activities significantly improves the quality of transitional writers' compositions and

provides them with critically important habits and understandings of text structure that will help them over time.

As transitional readers and writers move into the intermediate stage of development, they're well positioned to more independently engage with complex text in sophisticated and critical ways. They're also ready to expand their repertoire of revision techniques and craft moves in writing. The transitional stage of development is a relatively long stage, but it provides children with a strong foundation from which they can continue to build their skills. Figure 8.20 summarizes children's growth throughout the transitional stage of development.

FIGURE 8.20 Characteristics of Children in the Transitional Stage

	Reading	Writing	Word Study
Early when – correct jump – correct float – *flote* train – *trane* Text Levels: DRA Level 14-16 Guided Reading Level H-I Rate: Approximately 50–60 WCPM	• Can identify short vowel and many long words and many high-frequency words both in and out of context • Reads with some phrasing and expression in well-rehearsed text • Reads about 150 words by sight • Predicts, generates questions, and retells stories read independently • Improved stamina when reading • Can whisper read	• Writes several paragraph stories, reports, and procedural pieces, but writing requires a great deal of effort • Beginning to edit own writing and self-correct spelling errors in single-syllable short vowel words and many high-frequency words • Letter formation is more automatic and accurate	• Spells some words phonetically • Accurately spells many high-frequency words and words with the CVC short vowel pattern • Spells many words with digraphs and two-letter blends, preconsonantal nasals, and some *r*-influenced vowels accurately • Has generalized the CVC short vowel pattern beyond word families and is overgeneralizing the CVCe long vowel pattern

FIGURE 8.20 *(Continued)*

Middle float – correct train – correct stick – correct fright – *frite* table – *tabul* Text Levels: DRA Level 18–20 Guided Reading Level J–K Rate: 60–80 WCPM	• Prefers silent reading to oral reading • Reads in meaningful phrases • Reading longer texts and sustaining their attention and comprehension over time • Is beginning to employ interpretive strategies collaboratively • Beginning to independently monitor reading and employ strategies to fix comprehension or reading miscues	• In narrative text, students write "bed to bed" stories that chronicle a whole day in their lives • Learning the structure of response essays, reports, and persuasive essays • Engages in process writing: drafting, revising, editing, and publishing • Uses writing for a variety of purposes • Writing is less labored	• Uses common long vowel patterns such as CVCe, CVVC, CVV, and CV correctly • Beginning to learn about less common vowel patterns including *r*-influenced vowels, diphthongs, and ambiguous vowel patterns
Late bright – correct spoil – *spoyle* chewed – *chood* switch – *swich* smudge – *smuge* color – *coler* Text Levels: DRA Level 24–28 Guided Reading Level L–M Rate: 80–100+ WCPM	• Is beginning to employ interpretive strategies more independently • Beginning to understand literary devices in narrative text and text features in informational text • Monitors reading comprehension and employs fix-up strategies when meaning breaks down • Reads with accuracy, appropriate rate, and improved phrasing and expression • Self-corrects miscues	• Increased writing fluency, stamina, engagement, and clarity in written expression. Beginning to use "craft moves" such as dialogue and text features • Revisits and revises work to clarify meaning and add details • Aware of various text structures • Beginning to view writing as means to deepen one's understanding of text or topics	• Spelling most common and less common vowel patterns correctly • Beginning to learn about inflected endings, homophones, complex consonant units, and contractions • Beginning to accurately use common prefixes and suffixes

Suggested Extension Activities

• Plan a sequence of word study instruction for a within word pattern speller using the scope and sequence in Figure 8.1 and the sample five-day lesson planning template for the primary grades found in Chapter 3.
• Plan a guided reading lesson by selecting one piece of leveled text for a small group of readers in the early, middle, or late phase of the transitional stage. Study the text and determine the support your transitional readers will need to successfully read it. Remember to plan your instruction in such a way that you're supporting transitional readers in being strategic problem solvers and co-constructors of meaning.
• Study the Exemplar Texts for your grade level in Appendix B of the Common Core State Standards. With your colleagues or classmates, create a "kid-friendly" rubric for four genres: narrative, response, report, and persuasive writing.

Recommended Professional Resources

Bear, D., Invernizzi, M., Templeton, S., & Johnston, F. (2012). *Words their way: Word study for phonics, vocabulary and spelling instruction* (5th ed). Boston: Pearson.

Calkins, L. (2003). *Units of study for primary writing: A yearlong curriculum.* Portsmouth, NH: Firsthand.

Duke, N., & Bennett-Armistead, S. (2003). *Reading and writing informational text in the primary grades: Research-based practices.* New York: Scholastic.

Flanigan, K., Hayes, T., Templeton, S., Bear, D., Invernizzi, M., & Johnston, F. (2011). *Words their way with struggling readers: Word study for reading, vocabulary, and spelling instruction, grades 4–12.* Boston: Pearson/Allyn & Bacon.

Helman, L., Bear, D., Templeton, S., Invernizzi, M., & Johnston, F. (2012). *Words their way with English learners: Word study for phonics, vocabulary, and spelling* (2nd ed.). Boston: Pearson/Allyn & Bacon.

Hoyt, L. (2008). *Revisit, reflect, retell: Time-tested strategies for teaching reading comprehension in the primary grades.* Portland, ME: Stenhouse.

Invernizzi, M., Johnston, F., Bear, D., & Templeton, S. (2009). *Words their way: Word sorts for within word pattern spellers* (2nd ed.) Boston: Pearson/Allyn & Bacon.

Miller, D. (2002). *Reading with meaning: Teaching comprehension in the primary grades.* Portland, ME: Stenhouse.

Oczkus, L. D. (2010). *Reciprocal teaching at work: Powerful strategies for improving reading comprehension* (2nd ed.). Newark, DE: International Reading Association.

Rasinksi, T. V. (2003). *The fluent reader.* New York: Scholastic.

Ray, K. W. (2002). *What you know by heart: How to develop curriculum for your writing workshop.* Portsmouth, NH: Heinemann.

Online Resources

Annenberg Learner: Part of the Annenberg Foundation
www.learner.org

Annenberg Learner is a multimedia resource for advancing excellence in U.S. schools. As part of this site, teachers will find research, educational videos, and other resources to support their professional development. A special video series on teaching reading and writing workshop can be found under the Literature and Language Arts tab.

National Writing Project
www.nwp.org

The National Writing Project is a teacher-led organization dedicated to improving writing instruction and schools through ongoing professional development. With more than 200 local sites in the United States, the National Writing Project has a strong presence across the country. Research shows a positive connection between teachers who are engaged in the National Writing Project and their students' achievement.

The Knowledge Loom
http://knowledgeloom.org/index.jsp

The Knowledge Loom is an interactive online community dedicated to sharing research and promising practices for improving children's achievement. The site is managed by the Education Alliance at Brown University and provides resources on a range of topics, including elementary literacy, adolescent literacy, culturally responsive education, and teaching with technology. You will find resources, guidebooks, and answers to some of your most pressing questions here.

Intermediate Reading and Writing

Chapter Outline

» **Overview of Intermediate Readers, Writers, and Syllables and Affixes Spellers**

» **Developing Comprehension and Understanding of Texts**

» **Developmental Word Knowledge**

» **Fluency: The Bridge to Comprehension**

» **Writing**

1. Compare and contrast the characteristics of transitional and intermediate readers and writers.

2. How does intermediate students' understanding of text structures support their comprehension of and critical engagements with literature and informational texts?

3. How are teachers able to guide intermediate students' close, deep readings of texts?

4. Why is the teaching of morphology in spelling and vocabulary so critical for intermediate students?

5. How may reading and writing instruction be integrated in the intermediate stage of development?

Kari Nordsen has eagerly responded to your request to talk with her about how she incorporates the book club format within her integrated unit on the Depression Era and World War II (1929–1945), as well as observe her class when she introduces *Al Capone Does My Shirts*. Most of the students in Kari's fifth-grade classroom are at the intermediate stage of literacy development; a handful is still either transitional or skillful. Kari has selected *Al Capone Does My Shirts* (Choldenko, 2004) as one of the titles available for book club during this unit because of its historical setting and because it addresses coming of age, which is a dawning reality for many 11- and 12-year-olds. She won't talk about this directly with the students, of course, but she knows they will recognize themselves and others to varying degrees as they experience the book.

Set in 1935 during the Great Depression, *Al Capone Does My Shirts* reflects the overall feeling and sense of what life was like for so many people during that time. What is unique, of course, is the experience of being 12 years old and living on the island of Alcatraz—the location of the maximum-security prison where the most dangerous convicted criminals were sent. The book complements Christopher Curtis's *Bud, Not Buddy*, also set in the Depression, in 1936 (and a Common Core exemplar text), which Kari has also shared with her students—most of them either read it on their own or read, with support, after Kari had finished reading each chapter aloud.

When the six students who will be reading *Al Capone* first meet, Kari asks them to discuss briefly what they are learning about the Great Depression and what life was like during that time. She then passes out copies of the book, and after the students examine the front cover she asks them to look at the back cover. Though they can read it themselves, Kari still reads it aloud to model fluency, exaggerating a bit as if she were the voice of a movie trailer while they follow along. Many students will notice the reviews on the back cover as well; the fact that Louis Sachar is mentioned is enough to get immediate "buy in" from students who have recently read *Holes* or remember Sachar's *Wayside School* books from previous years.

Next, Kari has the students turn to the two-page spread of the labeled photograph of Alcatraz at the front of the book and talk about it: Talking about the appearance of Alcatraz and the different areas that are labeled helps establish expectations for characters and plot structure.

Kari knows that her students will come to learn and understand more about the hard times in general and about U.S. society in particular during the midst of the Depression as seen through Moose Flanagan's eyes. They will come to talk about, and understand better, why life is so hard, frustrating, and challenging at times—but that people can learn how to respond to that complexity. ■

Overview of Intermediate Readers, Writers, and Syllables and Affixes Spellers

Students at the intermediate stage of literacy development are poised to explore the genres and themes of literature in more depth, and will be reading and writing more broadly in informational genres. Their foundational skills—their knowledge of how words work at the alphabetic and pattern levels—are more secure. This in turn enables their reading and writing behaviors to be more fluent, which supports their more thoughtful and reflective engagement with texts of increasing complexity. The number of words correct per minute (WCPM) increases from around 100 at the early intermediate stage to 120 at the middle intermediate, to approximately 145 in the late intermediate stage. Literacy, nested within the social contexts in which you are embedding your literacy instruction, begins to become a powerful tool with which students at this level extend their awareness, understanding, and engagement with the broader world. Students have the cognitive potential to "step outside" themselves and understand other points of view, from both their day-to-day worlds and from a historical perspective. Their reading will also become a major vehicle for developing vocabulary knowledge, which in turn is further expanded through the development of morphological knowledge.

You will be developing your students' potential for comparing and contrasting themes across literature and informational texts. They will learn in greater depth how literature and informational texts each have their own similarities in their structure and in their language (Fisher, Frey, & Lapp, 2012). While you will teach procedures for writing in different genres and for different purposes, it's important to bear in mind that your students' developing abilities to write will primarily be informed by the amount and range of reading they do. They will be better able to "orchestrate," or manage, the many cognitive demands of writing—able to encode more fluently at the word and sentence levels, while sustaining focus and intent. Their writing has the potential to reflect greater complexity. For example, they may craft an essay that develops a central idea with support from examples and information drawn from different sources. With this degree of immersion in texts, you will guide their research writing, in turn reflecting the characteristics of the texts and sources they are reading. In both reading and writing, students at this level are developing the "staying power" to be engaged with reading and writing texts over more extended periods of time.

Later in this stage, students have the potential to explore the nuances of language, particularly literary language, more extensively. They may learn how literature more precisely allows understanding of different cultures and historical periods. This insight can extend to science and the arts as well. They are able to understand in more depth how the histories of words, or *etymology*, contributes to present-day meanings. They are also able to understand how words and ideas are connected *across* languages: You will support their exploration of **cognates**, words in different languages that are spelled the same or similarly and have the same or similar meanings (for example, English/Spanish *information/información, solve/solver*). Students in the intermediate stage are also developing the language and cognitive resources for exploring and understanding in greater depth the differences between literal and figurative language.

At this stage, your students' use of the conventions of writing—including grammatical form, spelling, and punctuation—will be informed by their extensive reading. You will build on this immersion with lessons that address these conventions, including word study that will support those aspects of learning to spell words of two or more syllables, and words with simple affixes and roots.

Developing Comprehension and Understanding of Texts

The Types of Text chart in Chapter 2 (Figure 2.5) displays the range of texts that students in the intermediate stage will be expected to read. *Literature* includes a range of genres—stories, drama, and poetry—and *Informational* includes literary nonfiction and domain-specific texts.

Strategies for Approaching Texts: Predicting, Questioning, Clarifying, Summarizing, Extending

You will teach, model, and gradually release responsibility of your students' *active* engagement before, during, and after the texts they read. You will build on strategies taught during the transitional stage—or if they haven't learned them previously, teach and develop them for the first time during this stage. The students' approach to reading literature or informational texts will involve:

- Thinking about the genre, which will determine *how* they read, and what they do before, during, and after the reading
- Thinking about what they are likely to encounter, given the title or focus of the text
- Previewing the text if it is informational
- Questioning the text as they move through it
- Clarifying ideas and information that may be confusing
- Summarizing what is read, and capturing the gist and why it is important (if it's literature, insights will relate to humanity; if it's informational, insights will relate to the nature of the world; and the insights from each will combine for greater overall understanding).

Teaching these strategies supports increased understanding, particularly for your students in the intermediate grades who may be struggling (Cross & Paris, 1988). You will teach and support students' learning and *application* of these strategies with specific texts rather than spending time teaching strategies in and of themselves.

These basic strategies, applied to the high-quality texts that students are reading and listening to, will support their ability to read critically—questioning the author, questioning the commonplace, questioning power and class, questioning gender roles, and seeking alternative perspectives.

Common Core Connection

Reading Standards for Literature and Informational Text: Range of Reading and Level of Text Complexity

Types of Texts and Approaches to Reading

Effective reading is strategic reading based on understanding the structure of the text to be read. In this section we will explore the structure and nature of the major text genres students will be reading: informational and literature.

Strategies for the Classroom

"Reading with a Pencil"

As we explore the ways into reading and discussing texts, **written response** and **note taking** become more systematic at the intermediate stage. When your students take notes while reading literature or informational texts—using Post-it notes is the most practical way to do this—to a greater extent, they are more likely to slow down, process, and interact with what they are reading. They are able to reflect on the author's language and word choice. Students begin to develop this habit as transitional readers (Chapter 8) when they "Stop and Jot," but they now have the potential to grow this into a lifelong strategy. Fisher, Frey, and Lapp (2012) refer to this as "Reading with a Pencil." As students work online with files—for example, those in PDF formats—they can use the "Sticky Note" feature in Adobe to respond and annotate.

Ryan Delacroix is reading Newbury Award–winning *Maniac Magee* by Jerry Spinelli to his fifth-grade class, and displays the page on the screen as he reads. When he reads the chapter in which Maniac is teaching the old ballplayer, Grayson, how to read, Ryan models his own reaction to the language and emotion conveyed at the end of the chapter when Grayson is able to read the sentence "I - see - the - ball" all by himself. Spinelli writes, *His smile was so big he'd have had to break it into sections to fit it through the doorway.* "A golden line!" Ryan exclaims. "Ladies and gentlemen, this image says it all for me! [He writes 'Golden line!' on a Post-it and slaps it onto the page.] Yes, Spinelli is using a bit of hyperbole here, but he *really* captures the joy and pride that Grayson feels after having read that simple sentence all by himself. Can you imagine what it would be like to have lived for decades and not be able to read a single word? I'm going to get my reaction down here in just a few words." [On the Post-it Ryan writes "Hyperbole—but such joy, pride—just like I felt when I got my first hit in Little League!"]

Angie Gutierrez teaches English/Language Arts and Social Studies at Traner Middle School; most of her students are intermediate-level readers. At the beginning of each week she passes out short news stories or opinion pieces she has downloaded from CNN's website that have to do with issues the class has been addressing. Students pull out their Post-it notes and respond as they read. Angie first modeled this earlier in the year on the whiteboard. After they read and respond, the students turn to a partner to compare and contrast their reactions. Angie then brings the whole class back together for a summary discussion.

Informational

Informational texts have basic underlying **patterns** or **text structures: description, temporal/sequential, cause/effect, compare/contrast,** and **problem/solution.** These patterns are *signaled* by particular words and phrases, and are a critical part of *academic language*:

Description	Temporal/ Sequential	Compare/ Contrast	Cause/Effect and Problem/Solution
For example	Before	However	Therefore
For instance	After	On the other hand	Because
Most important	When	Either . . . or	As a result
	First, Second, . . .	Although	As a consequence
	Next	Unless	Thus
		Similarly	If . . . then

In Joy Hakim's *Making Thirteen Colonies* (1999), the chapter on Ben Franklin begins "Some people had problems with Benjamin Franklin . . ." (p. 109). We may be set up to expect a problem/solution pattern right away, but as we move through the first paragraph—as well as subsequent paragraphs—we see a definite comparison/contrast pattern. As we read the following two pages, we see how Franklin not only "helped with the ideas that made this country special," but, probably because of his humorous and engaging personality that endeared him to the French, "got the French to help pay for the revolution that made us free" (p. 109).

The science article *Tornadoes Strike—1974: A Super Outbreak* (Baumann et al., 2012) appears in a magazine format and describes a devastating series of storms and tornadoes that swept through the part of the United States referred to as "Tornado Alley." It begins: "Few things in nature are more powerful than tornadoes. Their winds rage. They can strike quickly without warning and destroy everything in their path. In early April of 1974, a series of events occurred that illustrated their deadly power."

We read the article first because its flow pulls us along, reading about the devastation each successive series of tornados is causing. But then we go back, as we often share with students, "to see how the author does it." This brings us deeper into the reading and understanding, and provides models for our own writing. In this case, part of the author's craft is to use primarily a temporal/sequential pattern, but to a lesser extent comparison/contrast patterns are evident and important. The temporal/sequential pattern effectively propels the text along while explaining the science behind the devastation. The temporal/sequential pattern is found in the phrasing "a series of events . . . , On April 3 and 4 . . . , the greatest number of tornadoes in a single 24-hour period in history . . . , the outbreak began . . . , about an hour later . . . , then, around 3:30 in the afternoon . . . ." The comparison/contrast pattern is evident when the author explains that, although weather prediction was not sophisticated enough in 1974 to forecast tornadoes in specific areas until they were actually visible, today the technology does allow us to be better prepared, farther in advance.

As we'll see later in this chapter, when students are reading informational texts, learning the types and functions of **signal words** and the patterns they represent, they will be applying this developing understanding in their informational *writing* as well.

Reading Informational Texts

Students' reading in science, math, and social studies increasingly occurs in online digital formats. These formats allow more rapid negotiation among ideas and multimedia *but* much of informational reading will still be focused on books in print-based format, either hard copies or presented on the screen. Figure 9.1 lists types of informational text features that characterize many informational texts but that are particularly apparent in textbooks (Fisher, Frey, & Lapp, 2012). They should be explicitly examined at the beginning of the school year, and then applied in reading informational texts, whether skimming and scanning for specific information or engaging the text more critically.

Content Directed Reading Activity

When you engage your students in a **Content Directed Reading Activity** you are facilitating their application of how text features support their reading—moving them toward their independent application of the features. This activity rests on decades of basic research in educational psychology that tells us:

- Before we begin reading an informational text in which we are going to be expected to learn and apply information, we ask questions of the text.
- As we read through the text, section by section, we periodically stop to see if our questions are being addressed.

FIGURE 9.1 Text Features and Their Functions

Type of Element	Text Features
Elements That Organize	• Chapters • Titles • Headings • Subheadings • List of figures
Elements for Locating Information	• Table of contents • Indexes • Page numbers
Elements for Explanation and Elaboration	• Diagrams • Charts and tables • Graphs • Glossary
Elements That Illustrate	• Photographs • Illustrations
Elements That Notify	• Bolded words • Italics and other changes in font

Source: Fisher et al, 2012.

Common Core Connection

Reading Standards for Informational Text: Integration of Knowledge and Ideas

- When we finish it, we explicitly check and reflect on the questions and information we have picked up.

Throughout this process, we make active use of the text features to support our reading and scaffold our broader understanding. Our initial focus is on the *process,* so it is important that the selection we use—chapter or article—is well organized and constructed. Follow these steps:

1) When conducting a Content Directed Reading Activity for the first time, tell the students *why* they're doing it. Just as with reading a story, they are thinking about the information they are likely to find in the reading. Thinking about what they *do* know about the topic will help them read and remember new information much better than if they simply read through a chapter from the first to the last page.

2) *Preview* the selection. After reading the title, go through the selection, reading each heading and the captions for any illustrations or diagrams.

3) After the preview, use the title, headings, and subheadings to make *predictions* about the information that may be found in each section. For example, ask students, "What information do you think we'll find in a section with the heading 'The Komodo Dragon's Terrible Teeth'?" If they respond (and at first they will!) with something like "We'll learn about the Komodo Dragon's teeth!" you follow up with: "What *about* those teeth, specifically? *Why* might those teeth be described as 'Terrible'?" Turning a heading into a question makes a huge difference in a reader's level of engagement with whatever is being read. Write students' predictions so that they can see them *and* be able to refer to them.

4) Go back and *read* the first section under the first heading. After finishing it, review the predictions—confirming, rejecting, or modifying as necessary. Ask the students if there is any important new information they might add to their predictions.

5) Continue with this procedure: Read each heading for the section, make predictions, read, check predictions, and add new information.

6) When you have finished reading the chapter or selection or an appropriate part, *review* the major points that were addressed.

Most print and digital textbooks usually include a list of objectives and/or prereading questions that help students focus on important information. These may provide a foundation for the predictions that students will make. We point these out when we discuss the features of a textbook, but we also tell students that there is still room for their own questions and predictions, right along with those in the text.

Common Core Connection

Speaking and Listening: Comprehension and Collaboration

When you first introduce the Content Directed Reading Activity, students might complain that it takes more time to read this way. Be honest with them about this. Tell them that, yes, at first, it *does* take longer! Eventually, though, they may find that they will wind up *saving* time by reading this way: They will understand more and remember the information longer. (And let's be honest with ourselves, too: A lot of us, as college students—and for that matter, as classroom teachers—have never gotten into the habit of reading this way. We need to prove the value of this approach to *ourselves* in order for our students to buy into it—they know when we're really walking the walk rather than just talking the talk.)

Questioning the Author

In *Questioning the Author*, Beck, McKeown, Hamilton, and Kucan (1997) suggest *initiating* and *follow-up* queries that may be applied to informational texts (see also Beck & McKeown, 2006):

- *Initiating* queries may be phrased as "What is the author trying to say here?," "What is the author's message?," "What is the author talking about?," and "*Why* is the author telling us this?"
- *Follow-up* queries are "What does the author mean here?," "Did the author explain this clearly?," and "Does this make sense with what the author told us before?"

Strategies for the Classroom

Accountable Talk

There are three main components to *accountable talk:* Students and teachers are accountable to the classroom community, to the knowledge base, and to reasoned logic (Fisher, Frey, & Lapp, 2012; McConachie & Petrosky, 2010). This type of talk involves discussing, clarifying, and questioning among students. As they do so, they learn how to provide evidence, disagree in a considerate manner, and work to develop solutions with one another (Michaels, O'Connor, & Resnick, 2008). Fisher, Frey, and Lapp (2012)

describe how **sentence frames** may be used to help students become aware of and use accountable talk:

- I agree that _____, a point that needs emphasizing since so many people believe that _____.
- Though I concede that _____, I still insist that _____.
- While I don't agree that_____, I do recognize_____.
- The evidence shows that _____.
- My own view, however, is that _____.

FIGURE 9.2 Question/Answer Relationships (QARs)

IN-THE-BOOK QUESTIONS   **IN-MY-HEAD QUESTIONS**

Right There The answer is in the text, usually easy to find. The words used to make up the question and the words used to answer the question are right there in the same sentence. 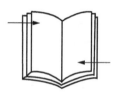	Author and You The answer is *not* in the text. You need to think about what you already know, what the author tells you in the text, and how it fits together. 
Think and Search The answer is in the text, but you need to look in different parts of the text to find it. Words from the question and words for the answer are *not* found in the same sentence. They come from different parts of the text.	On My Own The answer is *not* in the text. You may or may not need the text to answer the question. You need to use your own experience and prior knowledge. 

Question–Answer Relationships

A powerful approach for helping students learn about the different sources of information in a text are *question–answer relationships (QAR)* (Raphael & Pearson, 1985; Raphael & Au, 2005). The QAR approach helps students become explicitly aware of the differences among *literal, inferential,* and *critical* comprehension of a text, and do so in relation to the questions that are asked based on that text (see Figure 9.2). For this reason, QARs are also very effective in helping students understand the "test genre"—specifically, the questions that are used to test their comprehension of a text.

Following is an example of how you might introduce QARs. The text example is from *Explorer Books: Jungles & Rain Forests* (Andrews, 1991, p. 6):

Common Core Connection

Reading Standards for Literature and Informational Text: Key Ideas and Details

Layers of Life

When you first enter a rain forest, it looks like a tangled green mess. But it's really a well-organized garden. Rain forests are divided into three distinct layers. Each layer has its own community of plants and animals. The top layer of the rain forest is called the canopy. It is formed by the thick, leafy tops of giant trees as tall as 15 flagpoles, or 300 feet. Monkeys, anteaters, birds, and most of the other animals in the forest live in the canopy.

First, read the text displayed on the screen aloud. Then, present each of the following questions, one at a time:

> Into how many layers are rain forests divided?
> Is the *canopy* part of the "well-organized garden"?
> Do *mammals* live in the rain forest?
> Would you like to go on an expedition in which you would explore a rain forest?

Speaking to the students, you might say, "With this first question in mind, let's skim back over the paragraph to search for the answer. Ah! It's *right there*: In the paragraph it actually *says* that 'Rain forests are divided into three distinct layers.' The words *divided* and *layers* are in the question, and we've found them in the text. This is called an 'In the Book' question.

"For this next question, we can't find where the text actually *says* that the canopy is part of the well-organized garden, but by *thinking and searching* we may be able to figure it out. The text says that a rain forest is really a well-organized garden, and a little farther into the paragraph we see this sentence, 'The top layer of the rain forest is called the canopy.' So, by putting the information that the rain forest is a well-organized garden *together* with the information that the top layer of this rain forest is called a canopy, we are able to answer the question: Yes, the canopy is part of the well-organized garden. This question is also an 'In the Book' question.

"For this next question, I'm going to skim for the word *mammals* in the text. Hmmm . . . . Can't find it. But has the author given me enough information so that, together with what I already know, I can answer this question?" At this point, you might ask the students to turn to a partner to figure this one out. Then, as a whole class, talk about what information the author provided that helped the readers answer the question: monkeys, anteaters. You might say, "This information fits together with the information in your head—monkeys and anteaters are mammals—to provide the answer to the question. This kind of question is an 'Author and You' question. I can read the book all day long, but unless I know what *mammals* are—information that is in my head—I won't be able to answer it.

"And how about this last question? Of course, the author does not know you personally, so she is not talking about you showing up in the rain forest at all. You are only able to answer the question by thinking about what you have learned about rain forests in relation to yourself and what you might like or not like. This is an 'In My Head' type of question, but you're really on your own in answering it."

Reading Literature: Narrative Fiction

Although settings, plots, and events in a story or narrative are addressed during the transitional stage, intermediate-stage learners will explore them in more depth. As we will see later, narrative writing is not always fictional—aspects of narrative appear in informational texts, too. At this level, students will also explore more deeply the nature of characterization and theme.

Narrative Directed Reading Activity

In the **Narrative Directed Reading Activity** we guide students in combining their prior knowledge with information in the story they are reading to make predictions and then confirm or revise those predictions. It also affords students the opportunity to apply their developing decoding strategies. Originally conceived by Stauffer (1969, 1975) as the Directed Reading-*Thinking* Activity, it addresses both comprehending and thinking critically about narratives.

Establish a Purpose for Reading the Story Read the title and the first one or two paragraphs of the story: "What do you think this story is going to be about? If we know something about the author and the types of stories or books she usually writes, does that give us any additional clues?" Write down students' predictions. We often share with students that, just as investigators on the *CSI* TV shows use clues to solve crimes, when we read we also use clues to help us figure out what is going on and what might happen in the story.

Read to a Predetermined Stopping Place   For example, you might say to the students, "Read the next two pages, then stop and, keeping your place with your finger, gently close your book. If there are any words you don't know, apply your decoding strategy, but if you still can't figure a word out, go on and keep reading. We'll check it later." You'll check on those words after you finish reading the story.

Stopping early in a story allows for a quick check on the predictions that the students made: "Well, what do we think *now*?" and "Why do we think so?" This second question requires students to justify their thinking with evidence from the story. We may cross out any predictions that have turned out to be off the mark, and put a question mark by any that are still possible.

Depending on the length of the story, you may stop once or twice more—at points where the suspense or excitement is at a high level. At first, this might be slightly irritating to the students, but they also realize they are most invested in debating their predictions and impressions at these points. Take just a minute or two, and then return to the reading.

After-the-Story Discussion   Students justify their final predictions, again with evidence from the story. You will follow with just a few questions that will engage the students in thinking more deeply about the story.

Discuss Any Unknown Words   This is your opportunity to go back and ask students how they tried to figure out a word. If at first no one volunteers, you may ask about a particular word: "Look back on page 37. In the first paragraph there's that word that begins with *ex*. How'd you figure that out? Was it a familiar word when you sounded it out, or was it a brand new one? What did you think it meant? Why?"

As you guide students' deeper explorations of narratives, the exemplar questions in Figure 9.3 will draw them into the narratives while connecting with the significance of these explorations and themes in their own lives and in the broader world. These questions may be addressed both orally and in writing.

Narrative Directed Reading Activities move students into closer, deeper reading of texts. This is also an emphasis of the Common Core State Standards. Such an emphasis on close reading, however, is not new. Templeton (1996) described "intensive" reading—the type of deep and critical reading that both engages and stretches students. For many years, scholars have provided guidance for teachers in engaging students at all levels in deep discussions, and these engagements have been described with a variety of labels—for example, book clubs, literature circles, and grand conversations (Calkins, 2001; Daniels, 1994; Peterson & Eeds, 2007; McMahon, Raphael, Goatley, & Pardo, 1997). We'll use the term *book club* here. Recall that we began the chapter with a glimpse at how Kari Nordsen initiated a book club with one group in her fifth-grade classroom.

Common Core Connection

Reading Standards for Literature: Integration of Knowledge and Ideas

Reading Literature: Poetry

Poetry, like narratives, resonates in a deep place in our psyches (Templeton, 1996). Because it is tied to rhythm—at least, the poetry that students first experience in the elementary grades—poetry surrounds them in the music and lyrics they hear. Yes, most students are astonished to learn that lyrics are a type of poetry as well! Poems move well beyond rhyme—they also tap into images, feelings, and emotions. Their power lies in their saying so much, usually in so few words.

When we explore poetry with students, we also are able to address different aspects of language use: *similes*, *metaphors*, *alliteration*, *personification*, and so forth. Because many of the

(continued on page 329)

FIGURE 9.3 **Exemplar Questions for Narratives**

Use of the following questions, together with your follow-up requesting evidence to support and justify your students' responses, models the same type of "accountable talk" that your students may use when discussing narratives with one another (Hammond & Nessel, 2011; Templeton, 1996, 1997)—as, for example, during Book Talk (see below).

Characterization

If you could be any character in this book, who would you be? Why?

Which characters seemed like real people? How did the author make them seem like real people? Did you feel you were really inside them—feeling, thinking, and seeing the way they did?

Who is the real hero in this story, and why? Who is the real villain? Why?

Setting

If the story had taken place in a different setting, would that have changed the plot? If so, how?

What words or phrases did the author use to make you feel you were really in the story? How did the author put you in a certain mood right away?

Plot

Does the author tell the story in a sequential order? Why or why not?

What does the author do to make you want to keep reading?

Sometimes stories leave you with the feeling that there is more to tell. Did this story do that? What else do you think might happen?

Theme

What do you feel is the most important word, phrase, sentence, passage, or paragraph in this story? Explain why it is so important.

What is this story *really* about?

Why do you think the author wrote this story? What is the author trying to tell us?

Do you think the title tells the truth about the story?

Style

How did the language of the story work for you?

Which scene was *really* vivid to you? What did the author do to create that?

(If students have read several different authors' work in the same genre): How does their style seem the same? How is it different?

Point of View

Why did the author have ____ tell the story?

Did the point of view switch back and forth? Why?

General Questions

In addition to these questions that focus on specific narrative elements, there are some general questions you may pose about the narrative and its author (adapted from Fisher, Frey, & Lapp, 2012):

What do you know about the author, and why do you believe the author wrote the story?

Does this story tell us anything about the author?

If the author wanted to know what you thought could be improved in this story, what would you tell him or her?

Have you read similar stories? How is this the same or different from those?

How did the language that the characters used affect you? Was there anything about their language that you particularly liked or disliked?

Now that we've talked about this story, is there anything that someone said that made you think differently about the story?

Strategies for the Classroom

Book Clubs

Overview of Book Clubs

Book clubs are usually long-term ability-based groups of readers who meet regularly to talk about their reading experiences. In most cases, book club members read the same book at the same rate, planning stopping and talking points. Book club members prepare for their meetings by jotting ideas for conversation in their notebooks or on Post-its. When the groups get together, each person shares a thought/idea and the students try to build on each other's ideas through active listening and providing examples from the text. After sharing everyone's ideas, the group returns to one "big idea" and attempts to unpack it a bit more, growing a so-called Tower of Talk (see Chapter 6). Book club members usually write a longer response (at least a page) once a week. Importantly, *book clubs often don't get under way until the second half of the school year.* This is so teachers and students have time to develop their "close reading" skills, including asking and responding to questions with evidence and justification. Teaching students to work with reading partners is a good way to ease into book clubs. You'll know they're ready for book clubs when you notice:

- They can prepare for partnership talk and take turns—sharing their thinking but also listening and responding to one another to focus in on one issue to deepen their understanding of it;
- They can reliably cite evidence from the text and not stray away from the book when talking;
- They complete reading homework and/or work independently on reading assignments, including preparing talking points for conversation; and
- They use Post-its or other forms of notes to prepare for partnership meeting times. (Calkins, 2001, pp. 404– 405)

Getting Started

The Basics

Club Membership You will need to decide who will be in the club. Some teachers put two partnership pairs together to form a group of four. Other teachers ask students to identify three or four friends they do good reading work with, and then create the groups using student feedback and their own judgment. Book club usually works best with an even number of students (four or six).

Choosing the Books The books are often student-selected from a small group of texts provided by the teacher. It's important that the students can read the words of these texts rather effortlessly and can comprehend the text with minimal help, at least at a basic level of understanding. It's even better if they can begin to analyze and interpret the text on their own. They will work together to construct a deeper understanding of the text during meeting times.

Pacing The book club will need a calendar to plan their reading commitments and meeting dates/times. Sometimes the teacher provides a calendar that sets out the meeting times based on her availability and sets an expectation about when the book will be completed (usually within two to three weeks). Partnerships may check in with each other daily during partner reading time and the larger book club group may meet only once or twice a week. It's important that the teacher attend at least one of these meetings each week.

Club Rules Some teachers help the students establish a Club Compact or Contract. This agreement specifies the "rules" or expectations of their club. For example, rules might include the group's expectations for talk, expectations for completing reading, and goals for accountable talk. Some teachers develop rubrics for students to self-assess the quality of their group work.

Launching the Club

Students often select books after hearing brief book talks or "infomercials" about them. In the first meeting, the teacher facilitates a book introduction by helping students read through the summary, title, and chapter titles in the table of contents. The club may chart their predictions and questions. After reading the first chapter or two, the group may reconvene to attempt to confirm, reject, or elaborate on their predictions, and answer initial questions as well as develop new ones. It's important that students get off to a strong start.

Before students begin book clubs, make sure you have already modeled your expectations by using shorter texts, reading closely and deeply, and showing students how to prepare notes. You'll also demonstrate how to start a conversation and how to nurture it through active listening and responding. Some teachers like to assign specific roles for students when first introducing book clubs (described later).

In the beginning, you might also set a purpose for students' work. For example:

- "Readers, today while you are reading, I'd like you to be using your schema for narrative text and be prepared to provide a summary of the chapter when we get together tomorrow."

Strategies for the Classroom (continued)

- "Readers, it seems as though you've been noticing that the main character is changing. Please read the next two chapters and be prepared to give evidence of how and when the character is acting 'out of character.'"
- "Readers, when you're finished with your assignment, please select from one of these articles or picture books related to our topic. Be prepared to discuss your text-to-text connections."

Eventually we expect students to be more self-directed and set their own purpose, but it's important that they have a repertoire of ideas from which to draw.

Building on that repertoire of ideas, as your students become more familiar with book club, you can provide guidelines for their journal entries about their reading (Scott, Skobel, & Wells, 2008, p. 81). As a chapter is completed, you might assign one of the following roles—the roles will rotate with each successive chapter. We like to use these roles as a temporary scaffold to help students internalize the kinds of topics and roles they might integrate in a more authentic and organic conversation about text.

Discussion Director Write about one or more of the following:

Questions about what is occurring in the chapter/story
Do you have any predictions you want to share?
Is there something that happened in this chapter that your book club group needs to discuss?

Connector Write about connections you make between the chapter and your own life, other texts, and the world:

Have you ever felt like the protagonist—the main character—in the book?
Have you ever been in a situation similar to the one in which the main character is involved?
Make a connection with another book you've read or another situation in the real world that you know about.

Word Hunter Record any words or phrases that are "Golden Words" or "Golden Lines" that really grab you while you read. Write the page number(s) where you find them:

Why do these words reach out to you?
Were there any words you came across that were new? How did you figure them out? What do they mean?

Friend of the Characters Write about any of the characters in the chapter:

What are they experiencing, and how are they feeling about it?
Why do you think they are behaving as they are?

Elevating the Quality of Talk in Book Clubs

The following activities should help to elevate the quality of talk in your students' book clubs:

- Consider videotaping some book club meetings and ask the students to watch themselves and identify the things they're good at and the things they could improve. Make an action plan for the next book or meeting.
- Consider taping a book club conversation and typing a transcript for students to analyze. A primary goal here is to help students see if their talk is moving from literal to inferential.
- Try "fish bowling" a group during a meeting, minilesson, or share time to study what the group is doing. Other students may use a checklist or rubric to provide feedback.
- Plan a series of mini-lessons that support students in improving the quality of talk in their clubs. Topics may include:

How do you get a conversation started?
How do club members disagree respectfully and productively?
How do we find evidence in the text to back up our thoughts?
How do we ask questions of each other?
What does good talk sound like in the middle of the book club meeting? At the end?
How do we bring out each person's voice?

- While observing book clubs, try to employ the research-decide-teach method of conferring (Calkins, 2001). Start by studying the group; next, develop a hunch; and then provide the group with a gem of wisdom—a teaching point. Hold the students accountable for the teaching point.

Issues and Mini-Lessons for Book Clubs

Calkins identifies a handful of predictable issues with book clubs (2001, p. 420). This list helps us anticipate the tricky parts and helps us be proactive by planning minilessons that address these issues before they become problems.

- Completing homework/reading assignments
- Staying connected to the text and using evidence from the text to back up your opinions
- Encouraging all group members to participate in the conversation
- Going beyond the literal "right there" understanding of text to deeper analysis and interpretation
- Studying the author's craft—asking, "How did the author decide to write it *this* way?" "How else might he or she have written it?"
- Learning to agree and disagree with each other in polite and productive ways

- Learning to listen to one another
- Taking a moment in the middle of a book talk to reflect by "stopping and jotting" notes to clarify one's thinking before retuning to the conversation
- Making connections to and between other texts
- Learning to extend and deepen conversations between meeting times

Deepening Students' Engagement with Texts after Reading

As your book clubs and reading partnerships become more sophisticated, encourage your students to linger with books after they are done reading them. Calkins (2001, p. 485) provides suggestions for lingering with a book:

- Think about a passage or passages in the text that moved you in some way: Maybe it made you feel happy, angry, melancholy, or confused. Maybe it was a place where the description of the setting or a character was particularly vivid. Return to these places that evoked a response and think about how they contributed to the overall message of the story.
- Think about the author's purpose. What is this book saying all together? How is it similar to or different from other books you know? Is there a line or passage that best reflects the theme or big idea?
- How does the organization of the text (its overall structure) and the author's craft—word choice, details, the use of figurative language—contribute to the overall message of the book?
- How did the author "hook" the reader, keep him or her engaged, and conclude the book? How might he have done this differently? Why do you think he made the choices he did?
- How has this book affected your thinking? In what ways might you live differently if you took the message of this book seriously? In what ways has this book changed you as a reader or as writer?

poems to which students are exposed in the intermediate grades are not very lengthy, they provide ready and accessible examples of these different aspects. They also invite rereadings, discussion, and, in many cases, memorization. For example, consider the metaphors in Valerie Bloom's poem *Time*, which you may hear her read on www.poetryarchive.com:

Common Core Connection

Speaking and Listening: Comprehension and Collaboration

> *Time's a bird, which leaves its footprints*
> *At the corners of your eyes,*
> *Time's a jockey, racing horses,*
> *The sun and moon across the skies*
> *Time's a thief, stealing your beauty,*
> *Leaving you with tears and sighs,*
> *But you waste time trying to catch him,*
> *Time's a bird and Time just flies.*

You might introduce the poem by asking the students about the words they've probably heard quite often: "Time flies." What does that mean, exactly? Do all of the poet's metaphors suggest that time flies—that time goes by very quickly? Does time always fly? When doesn't it seem to? After reading the poem, students may discuss with partners their first reactions to the poem. You might find that you want to reread it again. Have different pairs take different metaphors and unpack them: Bird, jockey, thief . . . Why does Bloom begin and end with the metaphor of time being a bird? What does it mean to say that "you waste time trying to catch him"? Another possible question involves the gender of time: *him*. Couldn't time be female? If so, what do the students think: Would that affect the poem? If so, how?

Common Core Connection

Reading Standards: Key Ideas and Details; Integration of Knowledge and Ideas; Craft and Structure

Let your students know there is no "one right answer" to such questions. Students at this level often wish there were, but they are also venturing out to cognitive levels where they can notice and come to understand ambiguity and different possibilities. This is a critical part of "growing up" at this stage. Poems can encapsulate the ambiguities and possibilities in a very small space—"deep" readings and questions may be explored without reading several pages.

We reiterate that you should not begin your exploration of poetry with students with a bunch of questions. Rather, over time, ease into these deeper, closer readings. Just like you wait until well

Young Adult Literature Connection

For Middle School Students at the Intermediate Stage

Students in sixth, seventh, and eighth grades will, of course, be able to listen to and discuss more challenging texts. If their independent or instructional reading level is at the fourth- or fifth-grade level, however, we want to be sure they are having opportunities to read texts at these levels on their own and have a sense of more comfortable, fluent reading. *Graphic novels* are excellent, and often incredibly motivating for students. The *Bluford* series, written by a number of different authors, has the common connection of life in an urban setting, with attendant issues of race, self-esteem, and love. A number of short narratives that lend themselves to profound realizations and insights may be found online, such as Langston Hughes (*Thank You, Ma'am*, a fourth-grade reading level), Sandra Cisneros (*Eleven*, *The Read Sweater*), Richard Peck (*Priscilla and the Wimps*), and Gary Soto (*7th Grade*).

Common Core Connection

Reading Standards for Literature: Craft and Structure and Reading: Foundational Skills

into the year to begin book club, you should wait to begin these explorations as well. But *enjoying* poetry should get under way right away with the rhythm, humor, and word-play of poems such as Shel Silverstein's *Sarah Sylvia Cynthia Stout*, Jack Prelutsky's *Be Glad Your Nose Is on Your Face*, and Jane Yolen's *Dinosaur Dances*. Reading and rereading poetry also supports the development of *fluency*. At this level, students begin to develop the habit of *memorizing* favorite poems (a habit that is encouraged in the CCSS)—these short, simple poems lend themselves to that.

Two excellent poetry websites for elementary students are www.readingrockets.org/calendar/poetry/, which includes links to a number of other excellent websites, with original poems and poets reading their work, and www.poetryarchive.org/childrensarchive/home.do.

Developmental Word Knowledge

Intermediate students extend their understanding of *pattern* as they explore the spellings of polysyllabic words, and learn how syllables may also be morphemes that key the meaning of unfamiliar words they encounter in reading. This understanding of meaningful elements in words is central to growing a rich vocabulary.

Spelling: Exploring Syllable Patterns and Morphology

Common Core Connection

Language Standards: Conventions of Standard English

Learners in the intermediate stage of literacy development have developed a fairly solid foundation in understanding the spelling patterns within single-syllable words, and are ready to examine the spelling patterns in polysyllabic words. Most of their study will address two-syllable words such as *human* and *summit*, and learning the conventions that determine the spelling where syllables join, called *junctures*: Are there one, two, or more consonants at these junctures, and why? Some of students' learning, however, will be with words of more than two syllables: Root words to which affixes have been added, such as *uncovering* and *mistakable*. As at earlier stages, your students should already be able to read the words they'll be learning to spell correctly, and exploring these words will help them generalize important principles about syllable juncture patterns.

Table 9.1 presents the scope and sequence for spelling instruction at the intermediate stage. Begin with inflectional endings: "What happens when these suffixes are added to a word: Do we

The Language of Your Instruction

Spelling Features at the Intermediate Stage

Open and closed syllables. Open syllables end with a long vowel sound, and closed syllables end with a consonant sound—we say they are "closed" by the consonant:

| Open: | *be* | *so* |
| Closed: | *bed* | *sod* |

Closing a syllable with a consonant usually makes the vowel sound short. Understanding open and closed syllables helps students learn about the syllable juncture spelling patterns in longer words. For example, consider the words *diner* and *dinner*:

| Open: | *di/ner* |
| Closed: | *din/ner* |

Even though there is a single consonant sound in each of these words where the syllables join, we need two consonant letters to tell us we've got a closed syllable in *dinner*. Otherwise, it would be *diner*—a different word.

Syllable juncture patterns. There are five basic syllable juncture patterns (see Table 9.3). These patterns represent the pattern of vowels and consonants on both sides of the syllable juncture—for example, the vowel-consonant-vowel (V/CV) pattern in *hu/man* and the vowel-consonant-consonant-vowel (VC/CV) pattern in *rab/bit* and *bas/ket*.

Ambiguous vowels. Vowels that are not long or short are called *ambiguous vowels*. These include (1) diphthongs such as /oy/ (de*stroy*, *poi*son) and /ow/ (*thou*sand, *cow*ard); (2) r-controlled vowels such as in *har*vest and com*pare*, and (3) sounds such as /aw/ that are spelled with different vowel digraphs, as in *laun*dry and *awk*ward.

Schwa. The *schwa* is the least-accented vowel in a word of two or more syllables. For example, the schwa sound is represented by the boldfaced letters in the words **a**bout, moun**tai**n, and defini**ti**on. In the pronunciations of words in dictionaries, the schwa is represented with the symbol /ə/.

simply add –*ing*, or do we double a final consonant, or do we drop a final *e*?" Other inflectional endings –*ed*, –*s*/-*es* are then examined. As revealed in her spelling inventory in Figure 9.4, Carrie, an early intermediate student, reveals her readiness to explore these aspects. While there may still be a little bit of attention given to some late within word pattern features (*smuge/smudge*), she is ready to explore primarily syllables and affixes features.

Appropriate for students in the early intermediate stage, the following sort explores adding –*ing* to words with one or two consonants. This sort helps students become aware of why we need to add another consonant to a root word in some words before adding an inflectional ending.

• Use the words *run* and *rest* as headers. Leaving some space in between the columns on the Smart Board, sort the remaining words under the appropriate header with the students:

TABLE 9.1 Scope and Sequence Spelling Instruction in the Syllables and Affixes Stage

Early	Middle	Late
Adding plural endings –*s* and –*es* Adding inflectional endings –*ed* and –*ing*	Open and closed syllables and syllable juncture patterns VCCV doublet: *summer, cotton*	Final unaccented syllables: *traitor, private*
Compound words: *downcast, sandstone*	VCCV different consonants: *basket, plastic* VC/V open with long vowel: *open, baby* VCV closed with short vowel: *magic, punish* Vowel patterns in unaccented syllables: *maintain, shadow*	Reduced vowels in unaccented syllables: *civilize, definite*

FIGURE 9.4 Carrie: Early Intermediate Spelling

1. switch		11. sailer	(sailor)
2. smuge	(smudge)	12. vialeg	(village)
3. traped	(trapped)	13. disloyal	
4. scraped		14. tunel	(tunnel)
5. notted	(knotted)	15. humer	(humor)
6. shaving		16. confidents	(confidence)
7. squrt	(squirt)	17. furternet	(fortunate)
8. pounce		18. visabul	(visible)
9. scratches		19. soscoufens	(circumference)
10. crater		20. sivlasen	(civilization)

swim, stand, ask, sit, yell, put, pass, get. Tell the students that you'll use the term *root word* to refer to these words, because you're going to be adding inflectional endings to them. The completed sort would look like this:

run	*rest*
swim	yell
get	ask
sit	stand
put	pass

- Now write the labels CVC above *run* and CVCC above *rest*. Remind the students that these stand for the spelling pattern in the root words (these labels had been introduced to students at the within-word pattern stage). Ask students if they notice anything about all the root words. If they are hesitant, ask, "What vowel sound do you hear in all of the words?" (short) Then, place the *–ing* form of each root word next to it. Pointing to the CVC + *–ing* words, ask the students what happened to the root word *get* before the *–ing* was added. Ask the same question with several other words in this column. Share with the students: "When a root word ends in one vowel and one consonant, we need to *double* the final consonant before adding *–ing*." Place the label *Double* at the top of the *running* column. Ask students, "What do you notice about the *–ing* words in the *resting* column?" If they don't notice it at first, ask them if anything happened to words in the *rest* column when *–ing* was added. Then, add the label *Don't Double* above this column. Your sort will look something like this:

CVC	Double	CVCC	Don't Double
run	**running**	**rest**	**resting**
swim	swimming	yell	yelling
get	getting	ask	asking
sit	sitting	stand	standing
put	putting	pass	passing
		jump	jumping
		pick	picking

- Students will now repeat the sort as you observe. When they finish, ask them to turn to their partners and see if they can come up with a rule that tells them when they double a final consonant when adding *–ing*. Then bring the group back together and discuss what they noticed. You will find it helpful to begin a chart with these syllable juncture rules, beginning with this generalization: *When adding an ending to a word that contains a short vowel, there need to be two consonant letters after the short vowel.* The power in this lies in the students

TABLE 9.2 Changes to Root Words When Adding Inflectional Endings or Other Suffixes That Start with a Vowel

Root Words	+ *ing*	+ *ed* (or *er*)	+ *s*
1. CVVC, CVCC Ex: *look, walk*	No change Ex: *looking, walking*	No change Ex: *looked, walker*	No change Ex: *looks, walks*
2. CVC* Ex: *bat*	Double final letter Ex: *batting*	Double final letter Ex: *batted, batter*	No change Ex: *bats*
3. CVCe Ex: *skate*	Drop final *e* Ex: *skating*	Drop final *-e* Ex: *skated, skater*	No change Ex: *skates*
4. Words that end in a consonant+y Ex: *cry*	No change Ex: *crying*	change *y* to *i* Ex: *cried, crier*	change *y* to *i* and add *es* Ex: *cries*
5. Words that end in a vowel+y Ex: *play*	No change Ex: *playing*	No change Ex: *played, player*	No change Ex: *plays*
6. Two-syllable words accented on second syllable Ex: *admit, invite, apply, destroy*	Follow rules for 1–5 Ex: *admitting, inviting, applying, destroying*	Follow rules for 1–5 Ex: *admitted, invited, appalled, destroyed, destroyer*	Follow rules for 1–5 Ex: *admits, invites, applies, destroys*
7. Words that end in a c Ex: *mimic*	Add a *k* Ex: *mimicking*	Add a *k* Ex: *mimicked*	No change Ex: *mimics*

*Words ending in *x* and *w* do not double (e.g. *boxed, chewed*). Words that end in *ck* avoid having to double a final *k* (*blocked, blocking*). Words that end in *ve* avoid having to double a final *v* (*loved, loving*).

Source: Adapted from Bear et al., 2012.

using their own language to express the rule. This chart will grow as you move through different patterns with the students.

- When they return to their seats after meeting with you, the students will record this sort in their Word Study Notebooks. They will also record the rule that they came up with. Throughout the week, routines presented in our discussion of word study in Chapter 3 will extend the students' exploration and understanding. They will encounter oddballs, and these should be entered in an *Oddball* column in their notebooks. Later in the week, you may want to give the students some additional words and have them apply their generalization:

drop tick   squish   drag   mess   stir   blink   press

Table 9.2 presents the types of changes to root words when suffixes are added.

After examining the Double versus Don't Double patterns, students may contrast "doubling" with "e-drop" patterns—adding inflectional endings to VC and VCe spelling patterns in the root words. Consider the following sort:

hoping	hopping
using	clapped
riding	running
chased	telling
liked	sitting
hiding	stopped
	pulled
	spilled

In the first column, we drop the *e* when adding endings that begin with a vowel because the *e* is no longer needed: The vowel-consonant-vowel juncture is what tells us the first vowel is long.

TABLE 9.3 Types of Syllable Juncture Patterns

Label	Type	Examples
VCCV	Closed	*skipping, button, rubber* (doublets) *chapter, window, garden* (two different consonants)
V/CV	Open	*lazy, coma, beacon, bacon*
VC/V	Closed	*river, robin, cover, planet*
VCCCV	Closed	*laughter, pilgrim, instant, complain*
VV	Open	*create, riot, liar*

In the second column, if students don't notice it, point out that two consonants are necessary in words like *hopping*—they keep the vowel short.

Exploration with inflectional endings lays the groundwork for learning about *syllable juncture patterns* in English spelling. There are five syllable juncture patterns (see Table 9.3). The most reliable syllable juncture pattern for vowels and consonants in spelling is the vowel-consonant/consonant-vowel (VCCV) pattern: *dinner* and *tender*. This pattern tells us that the first syllable in a word is "closed" by a consonant sound, signaling a short vowel in that syllable. A variation of this pattern is the vowel-consonant-consonant-consonant-vowel (VCCCV) pattern, as in *gamble*.

Henderson (1985) commented, "One remembers only things one has attended to . . . . Syllable-sorting tasks develop the habit of looking where it counts" (p. 150). The following sort helps students "look where it counts" by building on the "doubling" principle first developed when they examined the addition of inflectional endings. It reinforces the understanding of why we often need two consonant letters at syllable junctures even though we hear only one consonant sound.

Using the words *dinner* and *diner* as headers, ask the students to sort words according to whether there is one or two consonants at the syllable juncture. The completed sort will look like this:

diner	dinner
super	supper
silent	kitten
pilot	lesson
fever	cotton
later	traffic
paper	ribbon
crazy	penny
tiny	summer

When the sort is finished, you may introduce the labels *VCV* and *VCCV*: Write the words *diner* and *dinner*, then underline the letters *i, n,* and *e* in *diner* and *i, n, n,* and *e* in *dinner*. Then, label each letter:

VCV   VCCV

di̲n̲e̲r   *di̲n̲n̲e̲r*

JeQuette's spelling inventory (Figure 9.5) shows us in words 3 through 15 that she has learned much about adding suffixes and syllable junctures. Her errors in these words illustrate the need for students in the middle intermediate stage to examine vowel patterns and spellings within stressed syllables and in unaccented final syllables (*creater/creator, disloul/disloyal*). Her writing reveals additional errors with *ambiguous vowels*—for example, *fawcet* for *faucet*. Students first explore these vowel patterns in single-syllable words as transitional readers and writers.

FIGURE 9.5 JeQuette: Middle Intermediate Spelling

1. switch	11. sailer	(sailor)
2. smudge	12. village	
3. trapped	13. disloul	(disloyal)
4. scraped	14. tunnel	(tunnel)
5. knotted	15. humer	(humor)
6. shaving	16. confidence	
7. squirt	17. forchinet	(fortunate)
8. pounce	18. visable	(visible)
9. scratches	19. cercomfrence	(circumference)
10. creater (crater)	20. silveliesatin	(civilization)

Although there are few "rules" that explain which spelling of the /aw/ sound to use, it is the reading, writing, categorizing, and examining of these words from a variety of perspectives that will, over a few days' time, lock in the correct vowel spelling:

au	aw	al	oddball
saucer	awful	also	laughed
author	awkward	always	all right
August	lawyer	almost	
autumn	awesome	although	
laundry	gnawed	already	
caution	gawking		
faucet	flawless		
sausage			
auction			
haunted			

In the late intermediate stage, students explore the spellings of unaccented syllables as in *cable, tunnel, vital* and *savor, dollar, weather.* The vowel sound in these syllables is the *schwa (/ə/),* and because it is spelled several ways, students will explore those generalizations that help them remember its spelling. They will also need to learn which spelling of the schwa goes with a particular word. Conducting several sorts with the same group of words, sorting according to different criteria, will support memorization of these particular words. Students will also learn that some spellings for the schwa will occur far more often than others—just as transitional children come to learn that certain vowel patterns in one-syllable words occur with far greater frequency. Knowing this will help intermediate students apply a "best guess" strategy when uncertain about a spelling during writing.

For example, if the students wish to use the word *tattle* but aren't certain about whether the last syllable is spelled –*el* or –*le*, they should go with the odds: –*le* occurs far more often than –*el*, –*il*, or –*al*, so go with –*le* and check later. If uncertain whether *commuter* ends with –*or* or –*er*, go with –*er* because it is much more common than the –*or* ending. Students will learn that final /ər/ in comparative adjectives such as *madder* and *tastier* will always be spelled –*er* (Johnston, Templeton, Invernizzi, & Bear, 2009). Students will also examine morphology more systematically as well as two-syllable homophones (*absents/absence*) and homographs (*permit* [noun] versus *permit* [verb]). Students are much more likely to learn and retain the spellings of individual words through the depth of exploration that categorization activities afford, but the payoff is broader than simply better spelling: It is the depth of thinking about words more generally that occurs *during* these activities as students sort, think, and talk about what they are noticing. Refer to our discussion in Chapter 3 about the nature and organization of word study in your class-room—these guidelines apply equally and as effectively for intermediate learners as for beginners and transitional learners.

Vocabulary Development

Common Core Connection

Language Standards:
Vocabulary Acquisition
and Use

The intermediate stage is the developmental level during which learning vocabulary from reading far outpaces learning vocabulary from listening, and this will continue to be the case from this stage onward. Wide reading and purposeful writing are critical to this growth, as is the rich, word-consciousness-oriented oral language classroom environment (Scott, Skobel, & Wells, 2008; Stahl & Nagy, 2006). In addition to developing and facilitating this context, you will be directly addressing (1) *generative* vocabulary instruction—of which morphological processes are the primary focus (Anglin, 1993; Nippold, 2007; Templeton, 2012) and (2) strategies and activities that develop and extend the depth and breadth of students' vocabulary growth (Beck, McKeown, & Kucan, 2008; Graves, 2006).

How do you know which words you should teach? Before teaching a selection or a unit, ask:

Which words are critical to address in depth *before* moving into the unit/selection?
Which words are critical to address only briefly *before* moving into the unit/selection?
Which words are critical but might lend themselves to students' problem solving *during* their reading? You may follow up on these *after* the students have read.

Lesson plans that accompany the texts and selections in your reading/language arts curriculum and in your subject matter curriculum usually have targeted the important vocabulary words most students will need to learn. These plans can be a very helpful guide, but you should still ask the preceding questions of those targeted words. Why? Lesson plans often will not make a distinction between "in depth" and "only briefly" types of instruction because text-created lesson plans of course cannot target *your* particular students—only you have this insight.

Generative Vocabulary Instruction: Morphology and Greek/Latin Roots and Affixes

We've seen that morphological development in language begins in the preschool years and grows throughout the beginning and transitional literacy stages. It is possible for children at those stages to begin to develop an awareness of more advanced morphological features and processes, including those involving Greek and Latin roots (Mountain, 2005). But it is not until the intermediate stage that more systematic, in-depth exploration of these features takes off. So, you'll plant the seed with transitional children, but those early understandings will not really flourish until students have sufficient words in their reading vocabularies to begin productive analysis, which in turn may be applied to *generate* understanding of new words encountered in their reading. This is because there are a great many more words in the texts that students are reading that reflect these morphological features and processes than in texts at the primary levels.

Scope and Sequence of Morphology Instruction
Instruction in morphology really takes off at the intermediate stage. Students' understanding of morphology—how *prefixes*, *suffixes*, and *roots* combine—is the engine that will drive their learning of, quite literally, thousands of words over the course of their school years and beyond. Most students, however, do not discover the pieces and patterns in morphology unless you point them out and walk students through them.

Table 9.4 presents the scope and sequence for morphological elements that you will be teaching at this level. When you begin your instruction early in the year, you may set the stage by sharing the following:

(continued on page 338)

TABLE 9.4 Sequence of Instruction for Core Affixes and Roots: Intermediate-Level Students

The following prefixes and suffixes have usually been introduced in the primary grades, but they should be addressed in the intermediate and middle grades as they combine with the words that are appropriate at these levels.

Prefixes			Suffixes		
un-	not, opposite	unreasonable	-y	like	faulty
in-	not, without	inaction	-ly		cowardly
im-		improper	-er	comparative	bolder
re-	again, back	regroup	-est	superlative	boldest
		recall	-less	without	meaningless
dis-	not, opposite	disadvantage	-ness	condition	effectiveness
		discredit	-ful	full of, like	faithful
	apart	disconnect			forgetful
non-	not	nontraditional	-er	people who	reporter
mis-	badly, wrongly	mistreat	-or	do things	legislator
		misinterpret	-ist		artist
pre-	before	preseason			
		prejudge			
uni-	one	uniform			
bi-	two	biennial			
tri-	three	triangle			

The following prefixes and suffixes are introduced in the intermediate grades.

Prefixes			Suffixes		
com-	together, with	compress	-al	like, characterized by	national
con-		conjoin			natural
co-		co-occur	-ous	possessing, full of	courageous
cor-		correlate	-ment	result, action, or condition	excitement
sub-	under	submarine			development
		suburban	-ion*	action, process of, or result	inspection
de-	remove, opposite	defuse	-ic	of, relating to, or	angelic
		detract		characterized by	formulaic
post-	after	postgame	-able	capable of, likely to	profitable
		postseason			detachable
inter-	between	intercontinental	-ible		credible
		interrupt			legible
		interstate	-ant/-ent		performing or causing
intra-	within	intrastate			an action
		intramural			confident
trans-	across	transport			observant
		transcontinental	-ance/-ence	action or process	observance
anti-	against	antifreeze			confidence
		antiprejudice			

			Suffixes		
			-ity	quality, condition	
				acidity, morality	
			-an/-ian	relating to, specializing in,	Chicagoan music
				belonging to	Canadian politician

*-ation -ition -sion -tion: These four suffixes are all variations of -ion. Which spelling is used depends on the root to which the suffix is attached.

(continued)

TABLE 9.4 (Continued)

The following Greek and Latin roots occur frequently in literature and informational texts beginning in the intermediate grades:

Greek Roots		Latin Roots	
-tele-	far, distant	-aud-	hear
	television, telegraph		audible, audience
-therm-	heat	-dict-	say
	thermometer, thermostat		predict, dictate
	exothermic	-spec-/-spic-	look spectator, inspect
-photo-	light		conspicuous
	photograph, telephoto	-vis-/-vid-	see vision, invisible
-gram-	thing written		video, revise
	diagram, monogram	-port-	carry import, export
	telegram		report, transport
-graph-	writing	-struct-	build construct
	telegraph, autograph		structure
	biography, digraph	-rupt-	break* interrupt, eruption
-micro-	small	-fract-	break* fracture, fraction
	microscope, micrometer	-tract-	drag or pull
-scop-	target, view, see		extract, tractor
	telescopic, periscope	-gress-	go progress, regress
-phon-	sound	-mot-	move
	telephone, symphonic		motion, motivate
	homophone	-scrib-/-script-	write transcribe,
bio-	life		transcription
	biology, biography, biome		prescribe, prescription
auto-	self		
	autograph		
	autobiography		

*Occasionally, more than one root from Latin with a similar meaning has come down to us, as is the case with *rupt* and *fract*. More often, however, it is the case that a root from Latin and a root from Greek have come to us with the same meaning.

Source: Adapted from Templeton (2004) and Templeton, Bear, Invernizzi, & Johnston (2010).

This year, we're going to be learning more about the most important prefixes, suffixes, and Greek and Latin roots in the language. Greek and Latin were languages spoken over 2,000 years ago, and if you know the word parts that came from these languages, you will be able to read, figure out, and use thousands of words in English!

Root Words and Affixes As at every developmental level, teach prefixes and suffixes first with familiar words, not unfamiliar ones. This ensures that your students will understand the *process* of word formation as they are learning about a new prefix or suffix. *Then*, you can show how understanding this process helps to figure out unfamiliar words in print. You will walk through the process with students, both *building* words and *taking them apart*.

If appropriate, share the following information with your students: The meaning of the prefix *in–* and its other spellings is most often "not," "opposite," or "reverse." The *next*

Strategies for the Classroom

Teaching Morphology at the Intermediate Level with Root Words and Affixes

The following two lesson examples illustrate how you may walk through this critical process, addressing prefixes, suffixes, and root words.

Prefixes *dis– (opposite, not)* and *mis– (badly, wrongly)*

Day 1

1) Write the following words:

   disappear   misplace
   disagree   misbehave
   disrespect   misjudge
   disobey
   dishonest

   Ask the students, "What do you notice about these words?" They will probably mention that the words in each column begin the same. "If something di**s**appears, what does that mean? If you di**s**agree with someone, what does that mean? If you di**s**respect someone, what does that mean?" Continue the same type of question with the *mis–* words. If the word *misjudge* is unfamiliar, use the following sentence and discuss what the word might mean: *Sometimes we mi**s**judge someone when we think they will behave in a certain way and then they behave very differently.*

2) Ask, "So, what might we say the prefix *dis–* means? [not, the opposite of] How about the meaning of *mis–* ? [badly, wrongly] Knowing what we know about the meaning of *mis–*, how might we spell the word *misspell*?" Because this word is frequently misspelled, discussing the meaning of *mis–* and what it means when combined with *spell* is an important and valuable insight for students.

3) Tell the students, "There are two things we're going to do in our Word Study Notebooks today: First, write down our *dis–* and our *mis–* words. Then, write down our definition for *dis–* and for *mis–* ."

Day 2

1) Display the words from Day 1. Ask the students, "What is our definition of the prefix *dis–* ? What is our definition of the prefix *mis–* ?"

2) Write the following words on the board/overhead/Smart Board:

   disconnect   miscopy
   discontinue   mispronounce
   displease   mistreat
   displace

   Say, "With a partner, figure out the meaning of each word. The two of you will then choose one of the *dis–* words and one of the *mis–* words, discuss a sentence for each word, and then write your sentences in your Word Study Notebook."

3) "Today and tomorrow, keep your eye out for words that contain the *dis–* or *mis–* prefix. They could be anywhere: As we saw last week, they could be in our reading, on billboards, in newspapers, on the Web, or in conversations you are having or ones you overhear. Record or write them down in your Vocabulary Notebooks. If you find any oddballs, write those down in a separate column. We'll share what you find over the next two days."

4) "I'll put up a *dis–* and *mis–* chart on the wall, and any words you find that contain these prefixes and are really interesting, write them on our chart. I'll do that as well!"

Day 3

1) Based on what they've found and recorded in the Word Study Notebooks and wall chart, ask, "What are some *dis–* and *mis–* words that you have found? Were you able to figure out the meaning? Did one of the prefixes have more examples than the other? Which one?" [It will probably be *dis–* .] Review the meaning of *dis–* (*opposite, not*) and *mis–* (*wrongly, badly*).

2) Share a few sentences that the students have written. If a student is not certain about the meaning of a word he found, this is a good opportunity to talk about the word with the class and try to tease out its meaning. If students can share the source of the word, that provides an excellent context for the discussion of the meaning.

Strategies for the Classroom (continued)

The Suffix –*ion* ("act" or "process")

Day 1

1) Write the following word pairs on the board:

    suggest   invent
    suggestion   invention

2) Tell the students, "We're going to examine the suffix –*ion* and see how it affects the root words it attaches to." Pointing to the *suggest/suggestion* word pair, ask the students, "How are the meanings of *suggest* and *suggestion* alike? How are they different?"

    Have the students turn to partners and talk about which word in each pair is the *noun* and which is the *verb*. Encourage students to cast the words into sentences; this will also highlight the similarities and differences. Do the same with the *invent/invention* pair.

3) Then, write the following words:

    instruction   interruption   eruption

    Say, "What is the root word of *instruction*? Right, *instruct*. [Write *instruct* underneath *instruction*.] What is the root word of *interruption*? Right, *interrupt*. [Write *interrupt* underneath *interruption*.] What is the root word of *eruption*? Right, *erupt*. [Write *erupt* underneath *eruption*.] What do you notice about these words?" If necessary, ask more specific questions, such as "What happens to the root words when the –*ion* suffix is added? How are the root word and its suffixed form alike? How are they different?

    "What meaning do you think the suffix has? Let's check it in the dictionary. [Type –*ion* into the online dictionary for elementary students, www.wordcentral.com, visible on the whiteboard.] Okay, it says it means 'act' or 'process.' So an *interrup-*

tion would be the 'act' or 'process' of interrupting someone. A volcanic *eruption* would be the 'act' or 'process' of erupting."

4) "Okay! In your Word Study Notebooks today, here's what we'll be doing: Label one column 'Verb' and one column 'Noun,' and write today's words in the appropriate column. Check with your partner to compare."

Day 2

1) Write the following words on the board:

    illustrate   explode
    division   imitation
    explosion   intrude
    intrusion   illustration
    imitate   divide

2) Ask the students, "Any ideas about the meaning of *intrude* or *intrusion*? If you know the meaning of one, does that give you clues to the meaning of the other?" Check their ideas with a dictionary.

3) Next, say, "In your Word Study Notebooks, decide which root word and suffix forms go together, and then add them to the 'Noun' or 'Verb' columns you began in your notebooks yesterday. For example, *illustrate* would be matched with which word? Right. It would be matched with *illustration*."

Day 3

Have students go on a word hunt, looking for words that end in –*ion*. If they can identify the root word, have them write it next to the word they found in their Word Study Notebooks. You may also post an "–*ion* chart" to which students may add words.

Day 4

Share some of the words students found on their word hunt, and discuss which column they placed them in.

most-often-occurring meaning is "into." Explain to the students that this will be helpful to think about when they are trying to analyze an unknown word in their reading that begins with this prefix. First, try the meaning of "not," but if that doesn't seem to help, then try the meaning of "into." When the prefix *dis*– is introduced, its most frequent meaning is "not," but its next-most-frequent meaning is "apart."

Greek and Latin Roots Greek and Latin roots usually cannot occur by themselves as words, but they are the meaningful cores of hundreds of thousands of words. From a single word root, we're able to "grow" dozens, sometimes hundreds, of words. We're able to "dig up" and find the roots by taking away all of the prefixes and suffixes that we think are in a word, and if what is left is not a word, then we've found the word root!

In her fourth-grade class, Darcie Mesieres introduces her exploration of Greek and Latin roots with the following type of lesson:

"Ladies and gentlemen," Ms. Mesieres begins, "we know we've probably found a Greek or Latin root in a word when we take off all of the prefixes and suffixes we can, and are left with something that doesn't look like a word. For instance, let's look at these two words:

unbreakable
invisible

"With *unbreakable,* we can take off the prefix *un–* and the suffix *–able,* and we have the word– *break.* [She draws a line through each affix as she reads them.] With *invisible,* we can take off the prefix *in–* and the suffix *–ible* and what do we have left? Right! Just *vis.* Is *vis* a word? No, it isn't, so we've found the word root!

"Roots usually have the same meanings they had back when people spoke classical Latin and Greek. In ancient Rome, where they spoke Latin, *vis* meant 'to see.' Let's look at *invisible* again: We know what the prefix *in* means, don't we? Right! It means 'not.' So, if something is 'not visible,' what does that mean?" [It cannot be seen.]

Applying What They Are Learning: Decoding and Learning Longer Words in Reading

This is a strategy that you should walk through quite often with your students:

"When you come to a word you don't know, first look *inside* the word and then look *outside* of it—at the context. Looking inside the word first helps you to *pronounce* the word to see if it's one you already know. If it isn't, looking inside the word helps you decode the *meaning* of the word.

"Examine the word for its meaningful parts—the root word, prefixes, and suffixes:

- "First take off the affixes to find the root word. Do you know it?
- "Put the word back together, thinking about the meanings of the root word, the suffix, and the prefix. This should give you a more specific idea of what the word is." [Very often, this is all that you need to do: You'll either recognize the word as one you already know in spoken language or the meaning will be pretty obvious.]
- "Try out the meaning of the word in the sentence. Does it make sense in the context of the sentence and the larger context of the text that is being read?
- "If sounding it out and looking for meaningful parts doesn't work, then use *context clues*— look around the word."

This strategy will take more time at first, yes, but the payoff is that students eventually will internalize it and become flexible in applying it. This flexibility includes those times when students take off prefixes and suffixes, and what's left doesn't look like a root word they know. When that happens, we tell them to try to pronounce the syllable or syllables that they see "in the middle," and then blend them together with the affixes (Roberts, Christo, & Shefelbine, 2011; Shefelbine, 1990). The ability to identify, pronounce, and blend these syllables is supported by your spelling instruction at this stage, which is addressing syllables and affixes.

Work by Baumann, Blachowicz, and Manyak (2011) offers excellent guidelines for supporting students' awareness and understanding of how context clues, together with morphological analysis, can support students' independent vocabulary learning. Here's how you can develop this strategy with your students:

> **Common Core Connection**
>
> Reading Standards:
> Foundational Skills

(continued on page 344)

Strategies for the Classroom

Teaching Morphology at the Intermediate Level with Greek and Latin Roots

As the following two lessons will illustrate, your "walk through" of how these word roots combine with affixes to create the meaning of each word is *very* important. You are providing a model for thinking about more complex word structure. It will help students decode unfamiliar words, but even more important, *learn* and *remember* the meaning of new words.

Lesson 1, Greek Roots

–micro– ("small")   *–tele–* ("distant")

–phon– ("sound")   *–photo–* ("light")

–scop– ("to look at")

Day 1

1) Introduce the topic of Greek roots to the students: "This week we're going to be looking at a handful of Greek roots. Like most roots, they usually do not occur by themselves as words, though on occasion some of them may do so. As I've said, learning the meaning of a number of these roots and understanding how they combine to form other words will be extremely helpful in learning and reading *new words*."

    Write the following two words on the board or whiteboard, and read them with the students:

    microscope

    microscopic

    Ask, "How are these two words alike?" After discussing this, point to a microscope and say, "Let's look at the Greek roots that make up these words: *Scope* comes from a Greek word that means 'to look at,' and *micro* means 'small.' So, when we put them together, we get the meaning 'to look at something small.' A *microscope,* of course, is an instrument for looking at very small or tiny things. If we say that something is *microscopic,* what does that mean?" [Students discuss.]

2) Now write the following two words on the board:

    telescope

    telescopic

    "Let's look at their Greek roots: We already know that *scope* means what? Right! It means to look at.' What do you suppose *tele* means?" If necessary, go ahead and tell the students that *tele* means "distant": "A *telescope* is an instrument for looking at distant objects. Okay. Let's try this word: *periscope*."

If no one identifies it, say, "We know it has something to do with looking at something, right? [Underline *scope*.] How about this part? [Underline *peri*.] You know, there's a word we've learned in math that has this same root, *peri*. [Write *perimeter*.] What's it mean . . . ? Right! The border or boundary of a figure. It has the word *meter*, which means 'measure,' and this same root, *peri*. When we figure out the *perimeter* of something, we 'measure [underline *meter*] around' it [underline *peri*]. So, *periscope* means . . . [at this point at least one student usually says something like, "Oh yeah! A periscope like on a submarine!"] Now you're on to something! So, what does a periscope help you do if you're in a submarine . . . ? Yes! 'Look around' . . . Because you're underwater, you need to be able to see what's around you on the surface of the water."

3) "Now, how about these words? Turn to your partner and talk about how the Greek roots combine to create the meaning of each word."

    television

    telephone

    "Did you talk about how a *television* delivers visions from a distance? What do you think *phone* means?" If no students have an idea after their partner talk, tell them that *phone* comes from a Greek word that means "sound." Say, "So, *telephone* is 'sound that comes from a distance.'"

4) Ask, "How about this word?"

    microphone

    "When we put the roots together, we literally mean 'small sound.' Of course, a microphone is not literally a small sound, but it picks up sounds that would otherwise not be heard very well."

5) "In your Word Study Notebooks, write our words just as I have done, one underneath the other. That helps us remember how they are alike in meaning and what their roots mean."

Day 2

1) Write the following words on the board/whiteboard:

    telemetry

    telephoto

2) Tell the students, "With your partner, talk about what *telemetry* and *telephoto* might mean. We

know what *tele* means; how does it combine with the rest of each word? We haven't talked about their meanings, but you might recognize them!"

3) It may be necessary to discuss *telephoto* with the students. They may have heard the word in the context of a telephoto *lens* but not thought about the meaning. Tell them that *photo* means "light." This may lead to a productive discussion about the literal meaning of *telephoto*—"light from a distance." Does that make sense when they think of a "telephoto lens"?

Day 3

1) "Ladies and Gentlemen, in your Word Study Notebooks, write each Greek root that we've been learning about, then write its meaning next to it. If you need to refresh your memory, check with a partner. Here is an example."

micro = small

2) "With your partner, using any of these Greek roots, create a word. It may be a real word, or it may be a word that does not yet exist in English! In your Word Study Notebook write the word, a definition for it, and—if it can be illustrated—include the illustration, too."

Day 4

New words that the students generated on Day 3 may be shared. This is a good point at which to post a chart labeled "Words That Don't Exist but Could," on which students may record their made-up words.

Lesson 2, Latin Roots

–vis–/–vid– (see) and –dict– (say or speak)

Day 1

1) Introduce the students to the topic of Latin roots: "This week, we'll begin looking at roots that come from Latin. Let's begin by looking at this word."

predictable

"If something is *predictable,* what does that mean? If we take the suffix *–able* off, what's left? Right: *predict.* Do you see a prefix in *predict*? Yes, there's *pre–.* What does *pre–* mean? Right: It means 'before.' If we take *pre–* off, we're left with *dict,* which is not a word—so *dict* is the root of *predictable.* It comes from a Latin word that means 'to say or speak.' To 'predict' that something will happen literally means that you *say* it will happen *before* it happens."

The students have already begun learning about Greek roots, so if you feel they don't need such an explicit walk-through, ask them, "What do you think the root *dict* means? If you *predict* that

something will happen, what does that mean? How does combining the root and the prefix lead to the meaning of *predict*?"

2) Write the words *vision* and *revision* on the board. Say, "*Vision* has to do with seeing, right? What about *revision*? We use this word when talking about our writing, don't we? Turn to a partner, and talk about what you think *revision* has to do with 'seeing' as it applies to writing. When you *revise* something that you've written, what does that mean?" [This discussion should help students understand that *revision* literally means "to see their writing again."]

Day 2

1) Display the words from Day 1. Ask students, "What is our definition of the root *–vis–*?" Display the following words:

visit	*dictate*
visor	*dictionary*
visibility	*contradict*
supervise	*dictionary*

2) "With a partner, talk about how the meaning of each root works in each of these words. For example, how does the meaning of *say* or *speak* work in *dictionary*? When you *contradict* someone, what does that mean? With your partner, compose a sentence using the words *visor* and *supervise*, or *dictate* and *contradict*. [Underline these words as you read them.] Write your sentences in your Word Study Notebook." If you have students look up *visit* in an unabridged dictionary they may be surprised to realize that the word literally means to "go see" someone: *it* actually is a root than means *go*! (And yes, that's why the word *exit* literally means "to go out"!)

Day 3

1) Have students volunteer to share their sentences.
2) You might wish to post a "golden sentences" chart or charts on which students may write their favorite sentences with the word containing the root underlined.

Day 4

"Using any of the prefixes we have explored so far together with either *vis* or *dict*, create a word. Quite a few of you did a neat job with creating words with Greek roots! In your Word Study Notebook write the word, a definition for it, and—if it can be illustrated—include the illustration, too." (The students' new words can be shared later or on the next day.)

"When we first talk about how to use context clues—the words and sentences around an unknown word—we model our thinking:

- "Look for context clues both before and after a word you don't know.
- "Clues may be close to a word, in the same sentence, or farther away, in other sentences or paragraphs.
- "Clues may be strong or obvious, or they may be weak."

Let's look at two examples showing how you might model contextual analysis:
On page 39 of *Al Capone Does My Shirts*, the Warden tells Moose,
"You can never trust a con. Nobody came here for singing too loud in church. Do you know what the word *conniving* means?"
" 'Sneaky, tricky,' I say.
"That's right. Remember that, Mr. Flanagan. Conniving men with no sense of right or wrong."
(p. 39)

In this example, neither trying to sound the word out nor looking for meaningful parts seems to help, so we rely on the context clues. In this instance, the context clues are *strong*—the words close by as well as those not too far away. While Moose's understanding of *conniving* is not exactly a dictionary definition, it's close enough, and the Warden's elaboration on what he says provides a fuller sense or connotation of the word. As you display this segment of text on the whiteboard, underline the words and phrases that provide context clues as you model your thinking: *sneaky, tricky, no sense of right or wrong.*

On page 9 of *Al Capone*, the author writes, "When Moose first steps into his room in the small apartment on Alcatraz, he says, 'It smells like the inside of an old lunch bag in there. My bed's a squeaky old army cot. When I sit down, it sounds like dozens of mice are dying an ugly death. There's no phonograph in this apartment. No washing machine. No phone . . . no radio.'

Say to the students, "Things that Moose clearly thinks are important are missing—things that we come to learn he had before his family moved to Alcatraz. How might we figure out what a *phonograph* is? Well, when we look for meaningful parts, we see two Greek roots, *phone* and *graph,* and we've probably learned that they mean 'sound' and 'writing.' But that's not too much of a help at first. So let's think about possible context clues: First of all, a phonograph is something Moose thinks is absolutely necessary in a home [underline *No washing machine, No phone, no radio*] and that means it's a good thing to have around. And it has to do with sound and/or writing. And that's about as far as we can get—the context clues are pretty *weak* in this example. So we'll follow up by checking it in the dictionary, where we'll also find a drawing or photograph of it."

After you model the strategy of how to think about surrounding contextual clues, it's helpful to bring in the labels that best distinguish different types:

Definition. The author explains the meaning of the word right in the sentence or selection: "It is earth's only natural *satellite*. A satellite is an object that travels around another object."
Synonym. The author uses a word similar in meaning: "A glove is the *fundamental*, or basic, tool of an outfielder in a baseball game."
Antonym. The author uses a word nearly opposite in meaning: "Cindy found this to be *tedious* work—very different from the almost constant excitement when she was river rafting."
General. The author provides several words or statements that give clues to the word's meaning: "Antonio felt like an *outcast* in his new school. No one sat close to him at lunch or asked him to join in any sport."

Using the Dictionary

As many teachers are realizing, online dictionaries and dictionary apps have the potential to bring students into the exploration and appreciation of words more than ever before. It is a tremendous convenience not having to physically turn pages, skim guidewords at the top of pages and entry words on the pages. However, our instruction in (1) how to use the dictionary and (2) how it is organized, is best accomplished with the print version. Projected on a screen or a whiteboard, we walk through the features with the students. Such a walk-through provides the larger context for the features and insights that a dictionary provides.

All major educational publishers offer dictionaries for different levels: from "pictionaries" for preschoolers and kindergartners, through primary, intermediate, middle, and secondary. Although you should have an unabridged dictionary in your classroom—yes, the big fat one that weighs a ton!—for intermediate-level students the intermediate-level dictionaries are appropriate. If there are not enough copies for every student, there should be several easily accessible copies in the classroom. Your intermediate dictionary will have two to three pages at the beginning that address "How to Use This Dictionary," and provide the labels (guide words, entry words, and so forth) as well as the definitions for these features. It will present the pronunciation guide, which will also appear on every two pages throughout the dictionary for easy reference (see the bottom of the sample dictionary page in Figure 9.6). The introduction will highlight special feature boxes that address aspects of words and language; for example, synonyms and "Word Builders" (morphology: affixes, roots, and their combinations). Synonym boxes will usually point out antonyms as well. Some intermediate dictionaries also provide "Spelling Note" features, which address morphology through pointing out the spelling–meaning relationships among, for example, a root word such as *clean* and its many derivatives (*cleanse, cleanly*) (*American Heritage Children's Dictionary,* 2009; *Longman Study Dictionary of American English,* 2006).

After the general organization of the dictionary is addressed, walk through how the entry for a word is structured: pronunciation, part of speech, definition(s), and often, words that are derived from the entry word through the addition of affixes. Level-appropriate dictionaries use language that is accessible to most students, providing definitions and context sentences that help students make the important distinctions for multiple-meaning words. At this point, you may also share an online entry for a particular word, such as that for *barometer* (Figure 9.6); online dictionaries and apps are based on the print version of the dictionary. Their advantage is the inclusion of a "speaker"-type icon that, when clicked or tapped, provides the pronunciation of the word. Two of our favorite online dictionaries for intermediate students are www.wordcentral.com and www.longmandictionariesusa.com, both of which also include etymological, or word history, information about most words.

It is important that you walk through and model the process of checking a "best guess" meaning of a word in reading with the definition(s) in the dictionary. For example, at a promising point in *Al Capone*—given all of the challenges in trying to get Natalie accepted at the Esther P. Marinoff School—Moose describes his mother as *radiant.* Contextual clues are strong here: Both what has happened in the book up to that point *and* the sentence that follows about Natalie's interview with Mr. Purdy—"Natalie was wonderful"—confirms that *radiant* has to do with joyous feelings and appearance. Now, turning to the dictionary, there will be two meanings for *radiant*: "giving off light or heat" and "filled with love or happiness, glowing." Talk with the students about which meaning captures the book's use of *radiant.* This type of modeling and discussion, by the way, also supports an important point about language and words: Although the dictionary may begin with a literal meaning—the first dictionary entry for *radiant* provides this—it is the second entry that metaphorically extends the first meaning and captures the sense in which Gennifer

FIGURE 9.6 Longman Study Dictionary of American English

ba·rom·e·ter /bəˈrɑmətər/ *noun* 🔊

an instrument that measures the pressure of the air around us and shows what the weather will be like. When the air pressure is low, the weather will be rainy. When the air pressure is high, the weather will be fine.

[ORIGIN: 1600-1700 From the Greek words *baros* and *metron*, which mean "weight or pressure" and "measure."]

Source: From Longman Study Dictionary of American English, by permission of Pearson Education UK.

Common Core Connection

Reading Standards for Literature: Craft and Structure

Choldenko chose to use it. This explicit talk about how literal meanings shade into metaphorical meanings is very important: You are addressing and modeling the ways of thinking about the *nuances* of a word's meaning, both in dictionary meanings and in how those meanings are captured and reflected in context.

Systematic Instruction in *General Academic* and *Domain-Specific* Vocabulary

The research into the effective teaching of vocabulary supports the following practices:

Common Core Connection

Language Standards: Vocabulary Acquisition and Use

Activate background knowledge. Through discussion and preassessment (see Chapter 3), determine what your students already know about the words and the concepts the words represent. When possible, relate this to familiar concepts and newer concepts they have recently learned. Usually there is a range of understandings among your students, so getting them involved in discussion is very important.

Use a variety of activities. Choose activities that involve students in discussing words, thinking about their meaning, and using them.

- Effective and engaging Questioning
- Categorizing/Sorting the words
- Vocabulary notebooks

Graphic organizers. Graphic organizers and charts or diagrams support your explanations and discussions. When introducing a new chart or diagram, you will walk through its construction in a whole-class context first; in subsequent lessons, students may construct these as they work in small groups and in pairs.

- Word or concept maps
- Venn diagrams
- 4-square diagrams
- Webs
- Semantic feature analyses
- Antonym/Synonym continuum

Teach *generatively*!

- Reinforce how the structure or morphology of the words—affixes, root words, and Greek and Latin roots—provides clues to their meaning.
- Think of words that are *related* morphologically.

Use the words. Make a point of using the words often yourself.
Review. Periodically review the words.

Questioning   We're always asking questions, of course, to facilitate our students' thinking and concept development, but as we've seen it's the *quality* of our questions that is so important. When we are focusing on developing and extending the concepts that underlie important vocabulary words, our questions should aim to help students "unpack" their developing understanding, comparing and contrasting the features of concepts (Beck, McKeown, & Kucan, 2008). For example, students who are developing understanding of the math terms *vertex, prism, cylinder, sphere, circle,* and *face* could do a turn-and-talk and address the following questions:

Which would be more dangerous: Being poked by the *face* of a box or the *vertex* of a box? Why?
Would you rather play catch with a *sphere* or a *rectangular prism*? Why?
Would you pour water into a bottle shaped like a *cylinder* or a *circle*? Why?

Concept Sort   In an Earth Science unit addressing the four earth systems, vocabulary terms will be sorted according to the earth system of which they are examples: the *atmosphere*, the *biosphere*, the *hydrosphere*, and the *lithosphere* (Templeton, Bear, Invernizzi, & Johnston, 2010). You select the important new vocabulary (such as *hydrogen, oxygen,* and *organisms*) and incorporate terms that will be familiar to your students (*water, air*). You have already introduced the major earth systems, and for this concept sort you use them as category headers by displaying them on the whiteboard. Talking about the words is an opportunity for students to apply what they have been learning about Greek and Latin word roots:

hydrosphere: hydro = "water," as in *hydroplane*
biosphere: bio = "life," as in *biology*

Lithosphere will probably be a puzzle but they may be able to figure it out after seeing the terms that remain after the sorting into atmosphere, hydrosphere, and biosphere is completed—and then they can check in the dictionary to confirm, discovering that *litho* means "rock." Have the students work with a partner or a small group. Remind them that if there are words they are not sure about, set them aside in a "Don't Know" pile.

After the students have completed the sort, discuss it with them and try to reach agreement about where the terms are categorized. Wrap up the activity by explaining that the students will encounter these words in their reading and throughout the unit, and they should pay careful attention to them.

Vocabulary Notebooks   Students enter definitions of important terms along with examples of their use outside of class (seeing, hearing, or using). They may write or record any webs or diagrams they have created either individually or working with others.

Word or Concept Map   Important concepts are explored deeply by responding to and recording insights about what is concept is, what it is like, and identifying some examples of it. Figure 9.7 presents a partially completed map for the concept of *renewable resource*.

Venn Diagrams   When comparing and contrasting two important concepts, the Venn diagram format *visually* makes the similarities and differences distinct. Using two types of galaxies as an example, Figure 9.8 presents the same type of comparison as a Venn diagram, but more explicitly and distinctly: It lists the features that are being contrasted as well as those that are shared by the two types of galaxies.

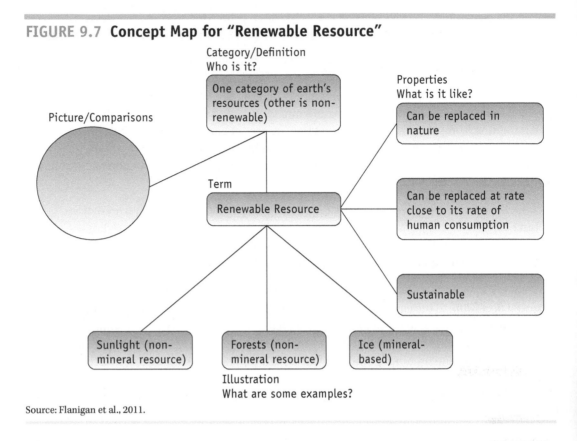

FIGURE 9.7 **Concept Map for "Renewable Resource"**

Source: Flanigan et al., 2011.

4-Square Diagram By constructing this type of diagram as they discuss a target word, students develop a *deep* understanding of a word and its underlying concepts. One of the words you may select from *Al Capone Does My Shirts* is *recommendation*. It first appears on page 155 in the sentence "Mrs. Kelly says Natalie is really improving. She's going to write her a flying-color recommendation" (see Figure 9.9).

Webs The example shown in Figure 9.10 provides a comprehensive exploration of the concepts underlying the verb *saunter*, and it also gets students thinking about the nuanced meaning of the verb through exploring its shades of meaning. While such a word may be learned by young children (see Chapter 6), older students are able to "dig deeper," elaborating and extending their understandings by thinking and talking about the word and its relationships within a wider web of meanings and uses.

Semantic Feature Analysis When you construct this type of a graphic, you arrange the target vocabulary terms across the top, and list the defining characteristics that will be distinguished down the left-hand column. Figure 9.11 presents a semantic feature analysis for the three different types of government (Flanigan & Greenwood, 2007; Templeton, Bear, Invernizzi, & Johnston, 2010). Taking the first term, *dictatorship*, students will read the features in the left-hand column, and those that they agree are a characteristic of a dictatorship they would indicate by writing "+" in the appropriate box underneath *dictatorship*. If a characteristic does not define *dictatorship*, they would write "–". If they are not sure, they would write "?" and then follow up by referring to source material or checking with you. They would continue in this fashion for *direct democracy* and *representative democracy*.

FIGURE 9.8 Venn Diagram and Compare/Contrast Table: "Types of Galaxies"

(A) Venn Diagram

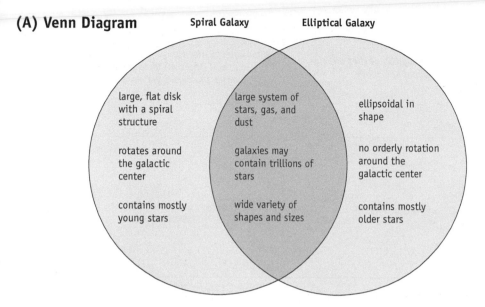

(B) Compare/Contrast Table

Spiral Galaxies	FEATURE BEING CONTRASTED	Elliptical Galaxies
large, flat disk with a spiral structure	SHAPE	ellipsoidal in shape
rotates around the galactic center	MOVEMENT	no orderly rotation around the galactic center
mostly young stars	AGE OF STARS	Mostly older stars
FEATURES IN COMMON		
large system of stars, gas, and dust		
galaxies may contain trillions of stars		
wide variety of shapes and sizes		

Fluency: The Bridge to Comprehension

Fluency is the ability to read orally with appropriate rate, accuracy, and expression. While intermediate students definitely read words more rapidly and accurately, they are still developing their ability to read with *expression*. This ability involves making the text sound "natural" by grouping phrases together, and is an expectation of the Common Core State Standards. We know that the expectations of the CCSS are for all students to read more complex, demanding texts with fluency. Although the standards state that students should read *on-level* informational texts and literature, we also know that the criteria for determining "on level" are being raised.

FIGURE 9.9 **Four-Square Diagram for** *Recommendation*

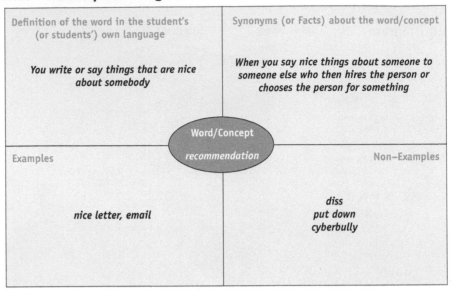

Definition of the word in the student's (or students') own language	Synonyms (or Facts) about the word/concept
You write or say things that are nice about somebody	*When you say nice things about someone to someone else who then hires the person or chooses the person for something*

Word/Concept
recommendation

Examples	Non–Examples
nice letter, email	*diss* *put down* *cyberbully*

FIGURE 9.10 **Web for the Verb** *Saunter*

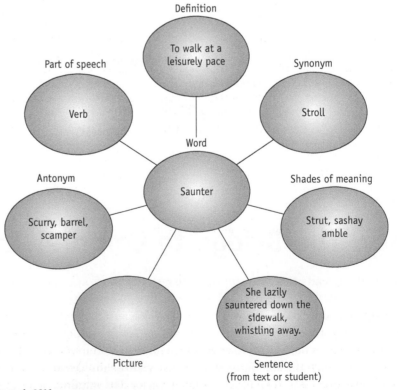

Source: Flanigan et al., 2011.

FIGURE 9.11 Semantic Feature Analysis for Types of Government

	Dictatorship	Direct Democracy	Representative Democracy
Citizens have voting rights			
Citizens elect leaders			
Limit to leaders' term of office			
Representatives are elected by citizens			
All decisions voted on by people			
Decisions can be made quickly			

Source: Templeton et al., 2010.

Accommodating English Learners

Awareness and Understanding of Cognates

At the beginning of Chapter 5, we saw how Kelly Wentrock introduced *cognates* to her students. Cognates—words that have the same or similar meanings in different languages, and that are spelled the same or similarly—are a rich resource that can support students' learning the vocabulary of another language (Bravo, Hiebert, & Pearson, 2007; Hancin-Bhatt & Nagy, 1994; Templeton, 2010). In recent years, a number of states have mandated that textbook publishers for the elementary and middle grades include attention to cognates—primarily English–Spanish—in all content areas as well as in English Language Arts.

In supporting students' awareness of cognates, we begin with cognates that are spelled the same or almost the same and that stand for the same concept—for example, *important/importante*, *initial/inicial*, and *office/oficina*. We next move to cognates whose spelling is not as similar, but "close enough" so that a visual connection may still be made—such as *stamp/estampa*, *study/estudiar*, *state/estado*.

Instruction may eventually address terms in which the word order is reversed in one language when compared with another—for example, the math concepts *compatible numbers/números compatibles*, and *place value/valor de posición*.

For our older English learners, we want to help them realize that, with longer words in reading, trying to *pronounce* them to figure them out is not a productive strategy. On the other hand, paying attention to their *structure,* or their *visual* features, *will* be a productive strategy. And, by the way, understanding cognates is as important for English-only speakers as it is for English language learners. (See Helman, Bear, Templeton, Invernizzi, & Johnston, 2012, for additional examples and more in-depth exploration of cognate instruction.)

So it is important to emphasize that these new expectations for accessing more complex texts and working toward reading them fluently should still be grounded in our developmental model: We know that students develop fluency primarily through the reading of texts that are at their independent or instructional level, and we must provide time for them to read comfortable, "just right" texts every day. We will be providing appropriate word study for them. *All* these factors build fluency. But we also know from the research that some "stretching" is appropriate

Common Core Connection

Reading Standards: Foundational Skills; Range of Reading and Level of Text Complexity and can contribute to fluency. We emphasize *some;* we do not mean "a lot." In this section we will discuss ways to develop fluency in on-level and above-level texts.

Modeling Fluent Reading

The first component of effective fluency instruction is the teacher: You must continue to read to your students. And as you read to them, follow the author's cues—punctuation, word choice, stance toward the topic, situation, the story. Adjust your reading rate and intonation according to how the author has punctuated the text. Practice these read-alouds ahead of time. If you are uncomfortable reading orally and/or realize you yourself tend to read aloud in a monotone, then arrange to sit in and observe a school librarian or a classroom teacher as she or he reads aloud to students of different age levels, noting how they adjust their reading. You might also listen to writers themselves read their work, or actors who've recorded audio versions of children's and young adult literature. In a whole-class context, you may find the following structured shared-reading approach helpful for most of your students in a whole-class context; for those students who may be struggling, we will discuss later how to adjust appropriately.

Bridging from Read-Alouds to Students' Reading of Anchor Texts

At the beginning of the week, you read the selection to the students. Over the next two days, *partner read*, and on the last day, *whisper read*. With each rereading, provide a new purpose that students will keep in mind. On occasion, you may elect to have the students *choral read* the selection with you. Other times, you may skip this first phase because you believe the students are able to engage the selection without modeling.

For *partner reading*, the students will alternate reading aloud to each other, perhaps one page or for a certain amount of time. The "silent partner" will follow along in the text and provide feedback if a word is misidentified. A variation of this partner reading format is matching students by reading levels—those students who are slightly better readers are matched with those performing not quite as well (McMaster, Fuchs, & Fuchs, 2006); this is an effective means of providing support and feedback for those whose instructional levels are below grade-level expectation (see Chapter 11). If partners are not available, having students read along while listening to a recording of the text can provide the same benefit. This can be especially beneficial if you don't have partners who match up in terms of reading levels and/or personalities.

During *whisper reading*, all students will be reading the selection at the same time, but in a quiet voice. When they finish, they may respond in their reading logs to the question or purpose they kept in mind during this final rereading; they may also turn to their partner and discuss their thoughts.

Writing

The act of writing—by hand, on a keyboard, on an electronic tablet, or on a smart phone—involves the encoding of thoughts and information. E. M. Forster's classic insight is no less true

FIGURE 9.12 Characteristics of Common Writing Genres

Text Type	Genres	Features	What Students Need to Be Able to Do
Opinion/Persuasive (argument)	Essays, speeches, editorials, letter to the editor	• State an opinion or point of view and provide reasons and information • Seek to convince a reader about the validity of a position or action	• Define a position • Offer supporting evidence using primary and secondary sources • Address concerns of the reader
Informative/Explanatory	Report of information summary Technical literary analysis	• Give a factual report containing information or observations • Restate briefly a text's main ideas • Provide instructions and procedures	• Use multiple sources and document sources • Refrain from expressing opinions • Identify sequence accurately • Use correct format for document
Narrative	Autobiography, Biography Creative Fiction, Memoirs	• Use time as a deep structure • Have a narrator • Establish a situation and sequence	• Inform, instruct, persuade, or entertain • Use monologue or dialogue, visual details, and actions

Source: Fisher and Frey, 2013.

in the digital age than when he wrote in the earlier age of paper, pencil, and manual typewriters: "How do I know what I think until I see what I say?" In this section we will explore the development of intermediate level students' understanding and growth in the uses and types of writing.

Immersed in reading, students at this level will have many models of text language and structure. We share with them, however, that those texts did not spring effortlessly from the minds of their writers. What students see was crafted over time, and they will be approaching their own writing the same way: trying out the voices and structures in those texts, getting feedback, and fine-tuning. The way in which we teach writing attempts to support this approach. Otherwise, the "number of things that must be dealt with simultaneously in writing [would be] stupendous: . . . spelling, punctuation, word choice, syntax, textual connections, purpose, organization, clarity, rhythm . . . the possible reactions of various possible readers . . . to pay conscious attention to all of these would overload the information-processing capacity of the most towering intellects" (Scardamalia, 1981, p. 81).

Figure 9.12 presents the common genres of writing and the characteristics of each. Before any of these can be meaningfully explored, however, your students need to get the "feel" of writing as they begin the new school year. They need to have a reason to write—one that is personally meaningful to them. Of course, much of their writing throughout the school years will not have this personal connection and motivation. But the students will not learn how to do that type of writing—the kind that ultimately helps them *learn*—unless they have realized at a personal level what writing feels like, what it requires, and the gratification it can convey. You must connect with your students at this level first. In order to do this, at the beginning of the school year you may get your students' thoughts flowing and the writing out on the page by asking them to think about what they know a lot about, what they're an expert in. Then have them make a list, write a sentence, or write several sentences. Explain to your students that this is how to get the "feel" of the writing process flowing.

Standards have rarely emphasized students' writing of poetry. However, simply because poetry writing is not required or assessed in the CCSS should not mean students don't have opportunities to write poetry if they wish. Students are of course expected to *read*, respond to, and memorize poetry. As with narratives/stories and informational texts, *writing* poetry immerses students in its myriad forms and rhythms. It can focus their sensitivity to the aspects and nuances of words and language such as simile and metaphor. As with other forms of writing, trying out in one's own writing the form and language of a favorite poem can lead to the types of deep understanding and appreciation we are attempting to develop.

The Writing Process in the Intermediate Stage

You must write. You will model for your students, and whenever possible, model using your own "real writing." It may be an assignment for a graduate or in-service class, a memo or report to a committee, a letter home to parents—any composition you are working on. Teachers often "liberate" themselves in their writing when they begin to model for their students (Calkins, 1983, 2001; Routman, 2007). If you model, you will often find you will get more buy-in from your students. They are more likely to engage in effortful, thoughtful writing attempts. Your walk-through of the writing process will support these attempts and their development as writers.

Prewriting

This first phase of the writing process involves students doing whatever they need to do to get thoughts out of their heads and onto a page or screen. The purpose of prewriting is to generate ideas for later use and development. Whatever they write at this point—words, phrases, using a graphic aid such as a concept map—is part of the process. It is important, though, that you think about what you want your students to learn or believe as a result of reading their writing. Dipping back into a text that they've read may be a critical part of this step—it can serve as a mentor text for structure, ideas, and/or craft. This is also the place to think about including multimedia/digital options if that's allowable in an assignment, from simple images—imported or created—to including links or videos.

Drafting

Most of the writing is generated during this phase, often called the *composing* phase. There is an "inner ear" that students will develop to guide them during this phase, although it usually takes some time to develop. It grows out of the feedback from other students, from you, and from the texts they have read and are reading. Most of the time, the drafting phase involves *first* drafts; students understand that they are not writing "final copy." These first drafts are tentative, so students should try out language and feel free to take risks. First drafts are usually messy—we cross out, insert, and write in the margins. Composing with a word processor may also be messy if students use the "track changes" option—which they *should*. What they delete today they may wish to use tomorrow, and it will be there for them in the "markup" feature.

Show them how to use the "strikeout" feature, too, so that they have the option of keeping their deletions in the document itself rather than in a "deletion" box in the margin. As with hard copy, keeping previous work in the context of word processing will be invaluable in the *revising* phase.

Revising

A little bit of revision unavoidably goes on during first drafts, but the *revising* phase is a significant reworking or "seeing again" of the first draft. In fact, when we talk about the steps in the writing process, we often make the link for our students with our instruction in morphology when we take apart the term *revise:* The Latin root *–vis–* means "to see" and the prefix *re–* means "again." Students see their own writing again, through a different lens—a lens that's been crafted from the feedback of others and from their own thoughts about the composition since they completed the first draft and walked away from it for a day or two. In teaching about this step, we usually focus on one or two aspects of the writing, rather than everything. Depending on our purpose, we may address word choice or sentence fluency or overall organization. Remind students that writing is thinking, and our thinking never stays in one place, so as they "re-see" their writing, they are "re-thinking" it as well, keeping their purpose and audience in mind so that their writing will have the effect they wish it to have.

Clearly, your students' writing will have a broader audience than the "audience of one" that has traditionally been the teacher. As your students share their writing with one another, in peer conferences and with you, the purpose of revision will become quite concrete. This broader engagement develops the sensitivity to audience that is critical for effective thinking—and therefore effective writing. This is also usually the point at which students make final decisions about digital/multimedia content they want to include.

Editing

The last step, editing, will be critical: Students need to ensure that their message will reach its mark. That's the process of fine-tuning or *editing* their composition—spelling, usage, and punctuation. *External* punctuation involves periods, question marks, and exclamation marks; *internal* punctuation involves commas, apostrophes, quotation marks, and semicolons. This step deserves almost as much attention as each of the initial planning, drafting, and revising steps, for if students don't attend to it, their writing will *not* reach its mark. "The only way to keep someone from noticing a surface is to make it 'disappear'. . . . The only way to . . . keep the surface of your writing from distracting readers away from your message—is to make it right" (Elbow, 1999). Particularly at the intermediate level, your students will come to realize that "spell check" and "grammar check" are not all they have to do to edit their writing—if for no other reason than that "spell" and "grammar" options rarely catch all errors, and often turn a correct spelling or subject/verb agreement into an incorrect one!

Publishing

You will share your students' writing within the class, of course, but frequently beyond. This is much easier with the Internet. Some of your students will become webmasters for the class's website, developing and maintaining the site. This is the most obvious venue for disseminating your students' writing more broadly. Your students will also have the potential to move their writing throughout and beyond the whole class, to the World Wide Web. If the published writing is going beyond a simple presentation—written or word-processed pages—then students will want to consider design features such as page layout and how text interfaces with illustration. If published in a digital/multimedia format, how will text, images, sound, and video be balanced? Where will hyperlinks be inserted for optimal effects?

The Language of Your Instruction

Writing Traits

We have frequently commented on how the terminology in education changes over time, but that the underlying concepts that the terms represent often remain the same or change little. This is the case with writing traits. Teachers you will work with who are familiar with the Six Traits Model will see how those traits are still reflected in the CCSS Writing Standards and criteria. The following comparison applies broadly to both informational and narrative compositions:

CCSS Writing Standards Terminology ➡	Which "Six Traits" Address These?
Purpose	Idea Development & Organization
Organization	Organization
Details/Elaboration	Idea Development
Voice and Tone	Sentence Fluency & Word Choice
Conventions	Conventions

The Traits of Writing

Common Core Connection

Writing Standards:
Production and
Distribution of
Writing

For decades, writing educators have described the characteristics and the teaching of writing in terms of **traits** (Diederich, 1974; Koslow & Bellamy, 2004; Murray, 1982; Spandel, 2008). In recent years, these descriptions have included insights into how these traits develop in children and older students over time. The "Six Traits Model" has been the most prevalent and widely applied of these perspectives, and the traits and indicators of trait development teachers have learned in the Six Trait Model are evident in the CCSS writing criteria you will be teaching and assessing.

Most students in grades 4 and 5 will be at the intermediate stage of literacy development. Figure 9.13 presents the CCSS traits and criteria for opinion (persuasive) pieces based on texts in fourth and fifth grades. Rubrics are being developed for the Common Core Writing Standards criteria (Hess, 2011), and students' writing will be assessed according to whether it reflects *Novice*, *Apprentice*, *Practitioner*, or *Expert* characteristics. The *Practitioner* category represents grade-level expectations for students, so we have included those criteria in Figure 9.13.

Let's consider three examples of student writing from students in the intermediate stage. Figure 9.14 (p. 358) shows Summer's opinion piece based on the topic of "Friends." She shows us she has learned about the structure of an opinion-persuasive composition: She clearly states and reiterates the focus of her piece, provides supportive details, and offers a clear conclusion. With continued reading, writing, and attention to developing this type of writing, Summer's informational compositions will appear less like they are written to a formula. Although the necessary structure will be there, her description and elaboration will develop further, reflected by her vocabulary and more complex sentence structure.

Common Core Connection

Writing Standards:
Text Types and
Purposes

In Figure 9.15 (p. 359), Kaitlyn's constructed response to an informational text addressing the *Valdez* oil spill demonstrates her ability to address questions about the disaster. She includes specific information that documents the extent of the tragedy in both the ocean and on land and includes responses to the situation. She begins and ends with explicit statements about the problem.

FIGURE 9.13 Example of CCSS Traits and Criteria

Compose Opinion Pieces about Informational or Narrative Texts/ Persuasive Writing, Grades 4 and 5	
Writing Criteria	**Practitioner Level**
Purpose • Context • Focus/controlling idea (opinion) • Evidence of understanding the text • Reflections/connections are related to text/theme • Analysis of selected elements of the text (e.g., plot, character change, author's craft, theme, opinion stated in text)	Context includes name of author and title of text Focus/controlling idea (opinion) is clearly stated Responds directly to the text with short summary and analysis/ reflection
Organization • Overall coherence • Information presented in a logical, cohesive fashion • Transitions connect ideas (e.g., compare/contrast, description, cause/effect, problem/solution, proposition/support)	Has coherence and organization: intro, body, and concluding statement or section support the focus Sequences and groups related ideas Transitions appropriately connect text and support reasons

Details/Elaboration
• Specific concrete details with
  • Appropriate references to/citations from text to support writer's viewpoint
  • Comparisons
  • Analogies
  • Examples, facts, definitions
	Uses references to text, citations/quotes, and/or concrete details, facts, definitions to support focus
	Reasons are elaborated on using relevant descriptive details

Voice and Tone • Authoritative person • Vocabulary—Precise language • Sentence structure • Sentence variety	Voice/tone is of an authoritative person supporting persuasive viewpoint Appropriate use of vocabulary & some variety of sentence structure (simple, compound, complex)
Conventions of Standard English • Grammar • Usage • Mechanics (spelling, capitalization, punctuation)	Uses resources to edit Minor errors in grammar, word usage, or mechanics do not interfere with reader's understanding

Figure 9.16 (p. 359) is the beginning of a co-authored first draft of a narrative based on the mystery genre in which two middle-to-late intermediate stage students had been immersed. Their beginning reflects the nature of this genre: fairly normal, everyday setting with just a hint, or foreshadowing, of more serious events to come ("I still think there's going to be some kind of a crime around here soon. I can feel it in my bones. . ."). The students are also picking up the language of narrative (". . . and then he fell silent"). They have learned how the seeds of surprise can be planted ("Jonathan Henry," mentioned early in the story, isn't heard from again until the end of the story, when it is discovered that he is the murderer of Mr. Gunman).

Such narrative writing—in structure, language, and length of episodes—is a clear reflection of the volume of reading in which intermediate students may be engaged.

FIGURE 9.14 Opinion-Persuasive Composition

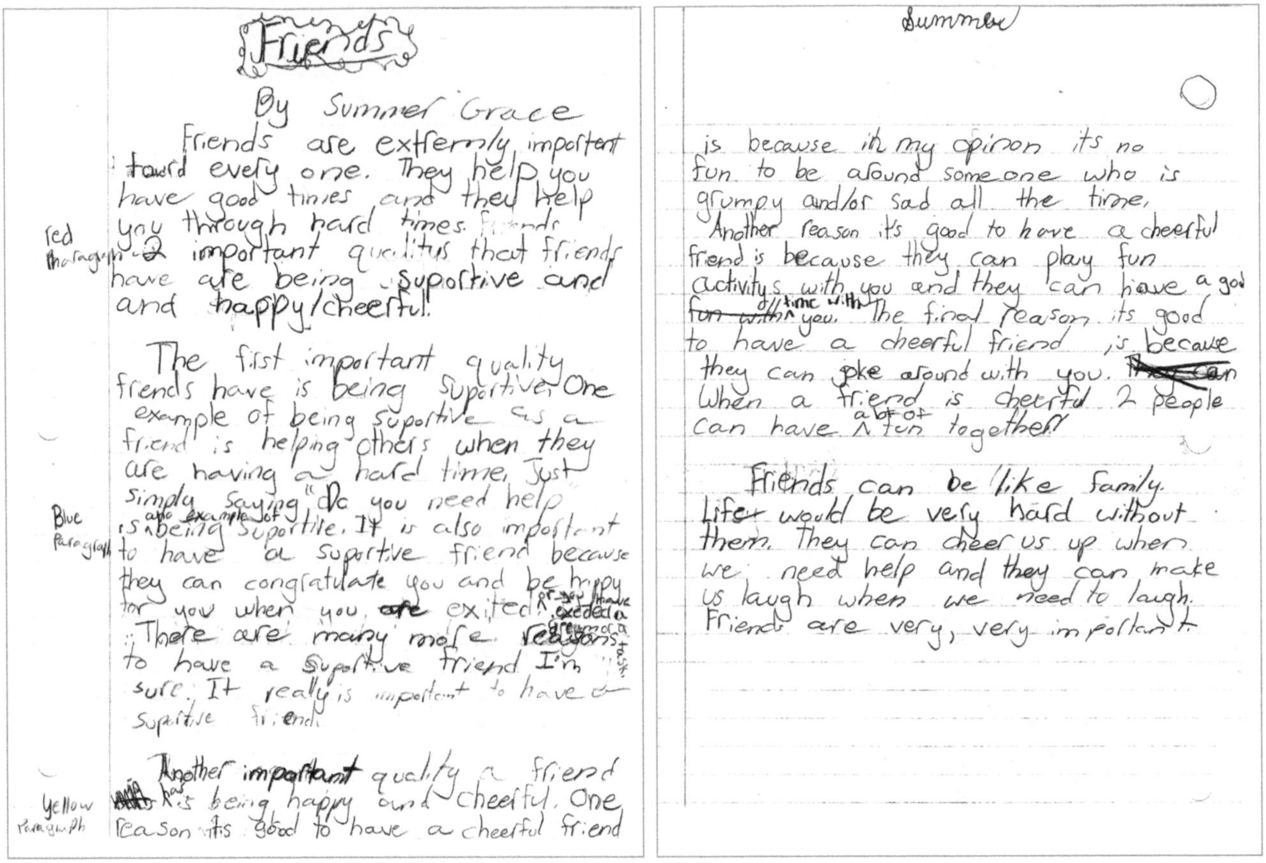
Friends
By Summer Grace
Friends are extremly important toward every one. They help you have good times and they help you through hard times. Friends 2 important qualitys that friends have are being suportive and and happy/cheerful.
Red Paragraph
The first important quality friends have is being suportive. One example of being suportive as a friend is helping others when they are having a hard time. Just simply saying "Do you need help" is another example of being suportive. It is also important to have a suportive friend because they can congratulate you and be happy for you when you exited or you have exceded a greatness. There are many more reasons to have a suportive friend I'm sure. It really is important to have a suportive friend.
Blue Paragraph
Another important quality a friend has is being happy and cheerful. One reason its good to have a cheerful friend
Yellow Paragraph
Summer
is because in my opinon its no fun to be around some one who is grumpy and/or sad all the time. Another reason it's good to have a cheerful friend is because they can play fun activitys with you and they can have a good time with you. The final reason its good to have a cheerful friend is because they can joke around with you. When a friend is cheerful 2 people can have a lot of fun together.
Friends can be like family. Life would be very hard without them. They can cheer us up when we need help and they can make us laugh when we need to laugh. Friends are very, very important.

Getting Under Way with Informational Writing: RAFT Papers

Common Core Connection

Reading Standards for Informational Text: Integration of Knowledge and Ideas

RAFT papers are a motivating means of moving students into informational writing (Santa, Havens, & Valdes, 2004). RAFT stands for the four basic components that writers address in any composition, regardless of genre: Role, Audience, Format, and Topic.

Role of the writer. Who are you? A 12-year-old girl fighting in the Revolutionary War? An equilateral triangle? The nucleus of a cell?
Audience. Who are you writing to? Your worried parents? An isosceles triangle? A mitochondrion floating by?
Format. In what genre will you write? A letter? A persuasive essay?
Topic and a strong verb. What is your topic? Your purpose in writing? Is it to reassure your parents or convince them that you have made a wise decision? To make the case that you are an example of geometric perfection? Or, more considerately, to assure the isosceles triangle that if she just keeps trying she might one day become an equilateral triangle? To compel the mitochondrion to work harder to generate energy?

(continued on page 361)

FIGURE 9.15 Constructed Response: Informational Text

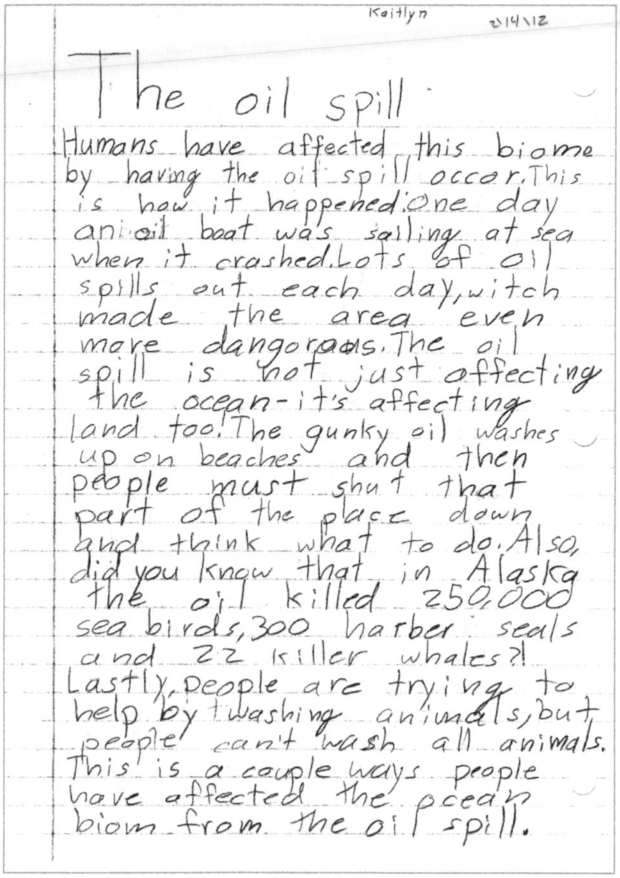

Kaitlyn 2/4/12

The oil spill

Humans have affected this biome by having the oil spill occor. This is how it happened. One day an oil boat was sailing at sea when it crashed. Lots of oil spills out each day, witch made the area even more dangoraos. The oil spill is not just affecting the ocean-it's affecting land too! The gunky oil washes up on beaches and then people must shut that part of the place down and think what to do. Also, did you know that in Alaska the oil killed 250,000 sea birds, 300 harber seals and 22 killer whales?! Lastly, people are trying to help by washing animals, but people can't wash all animals. This is a couple ways people have affected the ocean biom from the oil spill.

FIGURE 9.16 Beginning of Narrative: Middle- to Late-Intermediate Level

The Mystery of Mr. Gunman's Death

One day, Jimmy Gordon was sitting on the front porch steps with his sister, Katie Gordon.

"I'm bord," said Jimmy. "Me, too!" said Katie. "Nothing exiting happens around here any more. Jimmy agreed. "That is unless you're counting the time when Mrs. Waterman had the minnows coming out of the kitchen faucet!" Jimmy said. "No" said Katie. "I mean like a safe cracking or something." Jimmy said "We haven't had one of those since 1924! And I don't think we'll have one of those for a long time. Because the guy, I think his name was Jonathan Henry or something like that, served a 20 year sentence in prison!"

"Well, I still think there's going to be some kind of a crime around here soon. I can feel it in my bones," said Katie.

"Don't get your hopes up," said Jimmy. "And besides, Christmas is coming so we'll have something to play with."

Just at that moment there mom came out. "Jimmy and Katie, it's almost dinner time." Jimmy and Kate both said together "Oh, mom." Jimmy said "By the way, what is for dinner?" His mom answered "We're having pizza . . . "Goodie!" Jimmy and Katie interupted.

"Wait, let me finish" said their mom. "Your father and I are having pizza, and your having liver." "Yuck!" said Jimmy and Katie. "Can't we skip dinner tonight?" said Jimmy.

"No, but I suppose you could have a couple of pieces of pizza," said there mom. Jimmy and Katie looked relieved. And right at that point they heard a cry of pain from next door, Mr. Gunman's house. Jimmy and Katie rushed over to help him. "Wait!" cried their mom. "Come back it might be dangerous!"

"Danger's my middle name!" said Jimmy. They heard the cries get softer but they were getting closer and closer. They heard a soft "help" and looked down. And they saw Mr. Gunman laying on the floor. Jimmy asked "What happened?"

Mr. Gunman said nothing except "Find the cause of my death," and then he fell silent.

Strategies for the Classroom

Author's Craft Lessons

Author's craft lessons show students *how* writers do what they do, and support students in becoming writers in their own right. In your author's craft lessons you will model and explore techniques for students who are developing the craft—for example, generating appropriate and effective word choice and figurative language.

Barbara Cuitino plans to model for her fifth-graders how effective writers "grab" their readers (http://writingfix .com/Chapter_Book_Prompts/Watsons_Leads3.htm). In narratives—real or fictional—there are a number of ways to do this. To illustrate an effective lead, Barbara uses as a mentor text Christopher Paul Curtis's (1995/2000) *The Watsons Go to Birmingham–1963*. Her plan is to read the first chapter in which Kenny's older brother, Byron, winds up with his lips stuck to a frozen side mirror on the family car. She then has the students discuss how Byron felt: How would they feel if they were in the identical situation? During the next several days, the students will be writing their own narrative, exploring the theme of "Most Embarrassing Moment." First, however, Barbara explores the different possible ways they might grab their readers' attention if they were going to write a narrative based on Byron's embarrassing moment. Writers may open with:

- A question
- A quotation
- A riddle that makes the reader think
- A personal experience
- Personal feelings
- A movement
- A close-up of a character

After exploring these possibilities in their Writing Notebooks, the students are going to write personal narratives about their own most embarrassing moments, trying out the different possibilities for leads. Barbara models how they can set this up in their notebooks: They will *summarize* their embarrassing moment in four (or fewer) sentences, illustrate it if they wish, then write five possible leads for their narrative. Before they move to discuss this with a writing partner, Barbara shares on the screen the page from her own Writer's Notebook. Her summary reads:

> At a teacher conference, one of my favorite authors was signing books. I bought the book I wanted to have signed, stood in line, and waited 25 minutes to get to the front. When I presented the book to the author, he said, "I didn't write that one!" He ended up giving me one of his actual books . . . signed!

Beneath her summary, Barbara shares a few ideas for leads she's already written; she will discuss with the class which they like best. She will also ask them if *they* have any suggestions for leads:

1) "That's actually *not* my book, Ma'am," he said.
2) Who made a fool of herself in front of her favorite author? Me!
3) My cheeks turned beet red as he pulled his pen back and shook his head.
4) I placed the book on his table. The wrong book.

Source: Adapted from the Northern Nevada Writing Project. www.writingfix.com.

Reading and Writing in Digital Contexts

Connecting Content Learning and Technological Literacy

We know that students' inquiry and learning increasingly is occurring on the Web. As Ikpeze and Boyd (2007) note, "The new literacies of the Internet enable learners to search for, retrieve, and critically evaluate Internet resources; collaborate; and construct new knowledge" (p. 645). These authors go on to observe that *WebQuests* are a way in which students can be engaged in focused, purposeful informational writing while learning how to negotiate the world of information and communication technologies. WebQuests provide an important scaffold between domain-specific learning and technological literacy. Ikpeze and Boyd offer an excellent exploration of the possibilities of Web-Quests, discussing both short- and long-term engagements. We suggest you begin with short-term projects, because they reflect the CCSS focus on providing students at this level with practice in short, focused research projects. As Ikpeze and Boyd demonstrated in a fifth-grade classroom, with a clear topic and purpose—such as "Why Is Environmental Protection Important?"—and your guidance, students can learn how to explore, understand, evaluate, and respond knowledgeably to multimodal ways of learning. These include icons, animated symbols, different types of audio/video clips, and streaming video.

These explorations lead in turn to an appreciation of different perspectives on the topic. Along the way, students learn how to search and retrieve appropriate information as well as develop their hypertext reading skills (Ikpeze & Boyd, 2007, pp. 647–648). Students' Web-based explorations tie back to other literacy engagements in the classroom, often in surprising ways: Readers' Theater as students transform Web-based texts, and poetry reading and writing as they discover a website devoted to the environment (www.planetpals.com).

Students learn how to evaluate the resources they discover on the Web; questions they might explore are:

What can you learn from a site's URL?
Who sponsored this site, and why?
How can you tell if the site is kept current and updated?
Are you able to verify whether the information is authentic?

Do the links on the page work? Are they helpful? Does the design of the site support easy navigation and access to information, or does it get in the way?

Inevitably, students will reach a point where they experience information overload. You can address this by reminding them to apply their skimming and scanning skills, as well as chunking information in a way that makes it easier to manage (Ikpeze & Boyd, 2007; Vidoni & Maddux, 2002). Students deal with a chunk of the information—a paragraph or a single webpage, for example—at one time, rather than feeling they have to navigate within and between several sites.

Ikpeze and Boyd (2007) address distraction head-on: Students wind up checking email, for example, when they first log on before getting into the WebQuest assignment (an issue not only with fifth-graders!). You may want to share your own strategies for disciplining yourself: scheduling a certain time of day to check email, for example, or to play games. Be up front about this: Almost all of us who go online to do particular tasks are seduced by the other possibilities. We need to let students know how we, as teachers, handle this in our own lives. (Like your teaching of writing, this is another area in which you will be learning how *better* to do it as you share with your students how you do it- yet again, "walking the walk"!)

Here's how you can get the RAFT process under way (Flanigan, Hayes, Helman, Bear, & Templeton, 2013):

1) Provide some examples of possible papers. For example, in a fifth-grade history unit on the Revolutionary War, the *Role* in a persuasive RAFT paper may be played by the quill pen that Thomas Jefferson used to write the Declaration of Independence, the *Audience* are the divided colonists, the *Format* may be a letter, and the *Topic* is to convince (your strong verb) the colonists why the Declaration is necessary, and justify (another strong verb) the arguments made in the Declaration.
2) Distribute a number of texts in a particular subject-matter area to groups of students. Have each group identify in a text the role, audience, format, and topic.
3) The first RAFT paper assignment, as Flanigan and colleagues suggest, may be the same for all students. As students become more familiar with this approach, you may allow them more leeway in choosing some or all of the components. The target vocabulary for a unit should also be used in the paper.

Importantly, RAFT papers involve students in examining the structure and content of different informational genres, and in applying their developing knowledge of that structure in their own writing. Such application supports close reading of texts at the same time as it supports effective writing.

Chapter Summary

The intermediate stage of development is a time during which students read more texts, building stamina to support reading of longer texts and for longer periods of time. Cognitive and language growth are accelerating significantly, allowing for closer, deeper reading of and reflection on texts. Reading interests expand, and students' wide reading, coupled with vocabulary growth developing in part through wide reading and in part through direct instruction and morphological analysis, support deeper, closer, more extensive reading. These developmental criteria also support students' growth in *writing*—they are better able to balance the demands presented by attention to topic, genre, and conventions. Figure 9.17 summarizes growth across the intermediate stage of development.

FIGURE 9.17 **Characteristics of Learners in the Intermediate Stage**

	Reading	Writing	Spelling
Early Text Levels: DRA Level 30–38 Guided Reading Level Level N-O-P Rate: 100 WPM	• Reads with good fluency and expression; prefers silent reading as it is now faster than reading aloud; students self-select reading materials and can independently prepare for literature discussions	• Written responses are more sophisticated and critical • Begins to explore longer pieces of writing in a variety of genres • Revision and editing come to play bigger roles • Begins to write for a wider variety of purposes, including note taking and outlining • Uses author's craft techniques such as dialogue, special print, metaphor • Writes plays using a more significant role in the development of knowledge	• Spells most single-syllable words correctly, though ambiguous vowels continue to be addressed • Makes some errors at the juncture of syllables and in unaccented syllables crawl — *crall* shopping — *shoping* amazing — *amazzing* serving — *surving* bottle — *botel*
Middle Text Levels: DRA Level 40–50 Guided Reading Level Q-R-S Rate: 120 WCMP			Vowel Patterns in Accented Syllables Unaccented Final Syllables correspond — *coraspond* damage — *damige* parading — *peraiding* fortunate — *forchinet* opposition — *opacizion* civilization — *civalasation*
Late Text Levels: DRA Level 50–60 Guided Reading Level T-U-V Rate: 145 WCPM Rate: 145 WCPM			Morphology: Root words + affixes Two-Syllable Homophones and Homographs Vowels in Unaccented Syllables dominance — *dominace* opposition — *opisision* criticize — *critisize* civilization — *civilazation*

Suggested Extension Activities

- Plan to conduct a Narrative or Content Directed Reading Activity. Depending on your selection, plan to ask a few of the questions provided in "Reading Literature" or "Reading Informational Texts" section.
- Based on what the students are ready to explore, plan to teach "Day 1" and perhaps "Day 2" of one of the morphology lessons in this chapter. Immediately afterward, make notes: Did all the students seem to "get it"? Were there some who

didn't—along the way or even toward the end? If so, how did you attempt to adjust?

- Obtain the spelling inventory and the first draft of a composition for a fourth- or fifth-grade student. Compare spelling inventory results with errors in the first draft of a composition: Do they confirm each other? If there are fewer errors in writing, do you have the impression that the student is playing it safe, avoiding words that you believe he might otherwise use?

Recommended Professional Resources

Ayto, J. (2009). *Oxford school dictionary of word origins: The curious twists & turns of the cool and weird words we use.* Oxford: Oxford University Press.

Common Core Curriculum Maps in English Language Arts, Grades K–5. (2011). San Francisco: Jossey-Bass.

Crutchfield, R. *English vocabulary quick reference: A comprehensive dictionary arranged by word roots.* Leesburg, VA: LexaDyne.

Fine, E. H. (2004). *Cryptomania! Teleporting into Greek and Latin with the Cryptokids.* Berkeley, CA: Tricycle. (Also see the website: http://www.cryptokids.com)

Fisher, D., & Frey, N. (2012). *Common Core English Language Arts in a PLC at work, grades 3–5.* Bloomington, IL: Solution Tree.

Kennedy, J. (1996). *Word stems: A dictionary.* New York: Soho Press.

Knight, M. (2009). *Percy Jackson and the Olympians: The ultimate guide.* New York: Disney/Hyperion.

Morrow, L. M., Wixson, K. K., & Shanahan, T. (Eds.). (2012). *Teaching with the Common Core Standards for English Language Arts: Grades 3–5.* New York: Guilford.

Rasinski, T., Padak, N., Newton, R. M., & Newton, F. (2008). *Greek & Latin roots: Keys to building vocabulary.* Huntington Beach, CA: Shell Educational Publishing.

Templeton, S., Bear, D. R., Invernizzi, M., & Johnston, F. (2010). *Vocabulary their way: Word study with middle and secondary students.* Boston: Pearson/Allyn & Bacon.

Templeton, S., Johnston, F., Bear, D., & Invernizzi, M. (2009). *Words their way: Word sorts for syllables and affixes spellers* (2nd ed.). Boston: Pearson/Allyn & Bacon.

Online Resources

Common Core Curriculum Mapping Project
   http://commoncore.org/maps/

This site is an ongoing project that provides teacher-constructed units and lessons that address the Common Core standards. We have referenced the print publication that included the elementary units, but you will find new tools continually being posted. The curriculum maps are offered for grades K–2, 3–5, and 6–8. A lot of information is available free of charge; access to all of the resources, however, requires a subscription.

Cooperative Children's Book Center (CCBC)
   www.education.wisc.edu/ccbc/

The **Cooperative Children's Book Center (CCBC)** is "a unique and vital gathering place for books, ideas, and expertise in the field of children's and young adult literature." Based at the University of Wisconsin, this

was one of the very first children's literature websites. It is continually updated, and does a particularly good job of providing information, titles, reviews, and links. Its coverage of multicultural literature is excellent.

Northern Nevada Writing Project
   www.nnwp.org

This National Writing Project site is internationally recognized for the quality and extent of its online resources, as well as for its published materials available on the website. In addition to excellent writing support at all grade levels, it provides a wealth of writing projects based on particular anchor texts, reflecting the emphasis in the Common Core on writing critically in response to literature and informational texts, and using these anchor texts as models for generating students' original compositions.

Skillful Literacy

Developing Critical Engagements with Texts, Language, and Vocabulary

Chapter Outline

- » **Overview of Skillful Readers, Writers, and Derivational Relations Spellers**
- » **Characteristics of Texts for Skillful Readers**
- » **Developing Comprehension and Understanding: In-Depth Critical Engagements with More Complex Texts**
- » **Developmental Spelling Knowledge: Derivational Relationships**
- » **Vocabulary Development**
- » **Writing in the Skillful Stage**

10

10 Focus Questions

1. Compare and contrast the characteristics of intermediate and skillful readers and writers.

2. The issues that middle school students deal with are challenging. How can reading and discussing potentially controversial subjects/topics help them in their personal lives? In their interactions with other students and adults?

3. How does the exploration of morphology and word histories, or *etymology*, contribute to students' reading and writing?

4. What is the difference between writing an *argument* and writing a *persuasive* piece?

5. Most of our students will not need to write stories in college or in their careers—so why is there still emphasis on narrative writing in the middle grades?

Elaine Rangierri, seventh- and eighth-grade language arts teacher at Traner Middle School, begins a word study lesson by explaining a common spelling error for skillful readers at this level. In so doing, she also sets up a vocabulary lesson: reinforcing students' understanding of how *Latin word roots* work in words:

"Ladies and gentlemen, this is what I call a very good spelling error! [She writes *circumfrence* on the board.] I've noticed this type of error in a number of your drafts lately—and there's an easy way to clear it up. But first, what do you notice about this misspelling?" Some students will probably mention that it's missing an *e*. "Correct! *Where's* the *e* missing?" After students indicate that it's after the *f,* Elaine asks, "Thank you! Why do you think there is an *e* there?"

Jenelle responds, "Well, it's because we <u>say</u> *cir-cum-fer-ence,* so the spelling shows us that."

"Yes! Thanks, Jenelle! And the dictionary pronunciation shows us that, too. [She pulls up the entry for *circumference* on the online dictionary so everyone can see. She points to the schwa symbol – ə – and continues]. That vowel sound in the third syllable is the problem, because its sound isn't a good clue to its spelling. That's why a lot of very good readers and writers actually misspell words like *circumference*—that unaccented

vowel sound can be spelled any number of ways. And you know what? A lot of us, when we're talking and not thinking about how we're pronouncing words, don't really *say* that third syllable—we say 'cir-cum-frence,' just like this misspelling [points to *circumfrence*].

"There's something else going on in that third syllable of *circumference*—the spelling *f-e-r* not only stands for a syllable, it stands for a *word root.* Let's look at the etymology for *circumference* [points to the displayed dictionary entry]. We see right at the end of the entry where it shows us that the word is composed of *circum-* plus this Latin root [points to *–ferre–*], and it tells us this word means 'to carry around,' from combining *circum* with *ferre*. It also gives us the meaning of *–ferre–,* 'to carry.' You've all learned how to figure out the circumference of a circle, but it's fascinating to know that originally this word simply had something to do with going around a circle.

"Okay, what does this have to do with spelling? That Latin root *–ferre–* now turns up as *–fer–* in *circumference*, and in a lot of other words as well . . ." Elaine writes the following words in a column:

    inference

   conference

    reference

"Let's check it out: In every one of these words we have the Latin root *–fer–*, meaning 'carry' [she underlines *fer* in each word]. It can also mean 'to bear' something, which is another way of saying you're *carrying* something, like when you 'bear a burden.' Let's look at *inference.* We've talked about *inferential* comprehension when you read—how the meaning is not right there on the page but how you have to *carry* [points to *–fer–*] your own background knowledge *into* [points to *in–*] what you are reading.

"What about *conference* [points to the word]? When you have a *conference* with someone, you are 'carrying' a conversation '*with*' that person [points to the prefix *con–*]. Turn to your partner and discuss: How does the meaning of *carry* function with the prefix in *reference* to suggest the core meaning of the word? [When we make a *reference* to something or someone we are 'carrying back' our thinking or attention to them.]

"So a way of fixing a high-level misspelling like *circumfrence* as well as [writes the misspellings *refrence* and *confrence*] is to pay attention to and remember those meaningful chunks or parts of words—in this case, the root *fer*—and think about its meaning. Remember our spelling–meaning connection? 'Words related in meaning are often related in spelling as well, despite changes in sound.' Words like *circumference, inference,* and *conference* all are related by their common root *–fer–*, and whenever we see this root we will know it means 'carry' or 'bear.'"

At this point, Madison asks a question. She and her group are investigating the *suffragette* movement in social studies—the campaign during the late nineteenth and early twentieth century in Great Britain, the United States, and a number of other countries for women to have the right to vote. Madison says, "I just realized that the word *suffrage* might come from *suffer* . . . is that right? I mean . . . if you were a woman and you couldn't vote . . . you would be suffering, right?"

"Wow! Great question, Madison! Let's see. . . ." The teacher types *suffrage* into the *American Heritage Dictionary* online. "Okay, *suffrage* does refer to the right to vote, and when we look at the etymology at the end of the entry for *suffrage* it says it's from Latin and means 'the right to vote'—from this Latin word [points to *suffrāgārī*], which means 'to express support.' That all makes sense, but it doesn't mention the root *–fer–* anywhere, so *suffrage* must come from a different Latin root than *suffer.* Hmmm . . . .

"Do you notice, right at the end of the etymology, it says 'see this root [points to *bhreg–*] in Indo-European roots'? Remember last week when we were talking about the Indo-European language—that language spoken almost 8,000 years ago and that has contributed words to over half of the world's languages today? Well, it looks like *suffrage* also has its roots in Indo-European. We don't have time to track that down at the moment, but perhaps one of you 'word nerds' can follow up on this later! What is the root in *suffrage*, and what's the story behind it—how in the world did it wind up meaning 'the right to vote' in Latin and English?"

After the lesson, Elaine shares with you that as the year progresses she introduces these students to resources that address etymology, or word histories. You'll learn a number of these in this chapter. She instructs her students in their use and helps them learn how to think and talk about the evolution of the meaning of words and how to use this knowledge in expanding their vocabularies and supporting their reading and writing. The challenge she mentioned to these students—Who can track down the root of *suffrage*?—may be addressed by exploring the entry in the Indo-European dictionary more closely or by checking one of the word history books she has shared and keeps within handy reach on a bookshelf.

Elaine leans back, sighs, and says, "Last year was the first time in my teaching that I engaged those students who really were ready for this exploration. I used to think it was 'stretching'—but I realize how important it is to look at words, vocabulary, at *language* this way. By the end of last year, we had explored the books and dictionaries I've shared with you, as well as the online *Oxford English Dictionary* and the *Online Etymological Dictionary.*" Elaine pauses and laughs, spreading her arms wide as she exclaims, "Not too long ago, I wouldn't have even *attempted* to pronounce 'etymological' in public!"

Elaine goes on to explain that for most of her career she had never thought about words this way, much less about teaching to this depth. She says that a professional development workshop gave her the beginnings of a foundation and the courage to begin trying it out. She realized she didn't need to have taken Latin, or to have been in Honors English in high school—all of those little fears that kept her from exploring Latin and Greek elements, as well as etymology. She shares with you a couple of books written for teachers that provide more information, model lessons, and ways of talking about words with students at this level. You'll find these titles listed in the Professional Resources section at the end of the chapter. ■

Overview of Skillful Readers, Writers, and Derivational Relations Spellers

You may recall how in Chapter 3 literacy coach Janet Lawton summed up a beginning-of-school conversation with the very wise observation: "There's no shortage of great ideas, approaches, and strategies for teaching literacy; the issue isn't finding more of them, but selecting those that create predictable routines [for students to] become independent and purposeful readers, writers, and thinkers." Skillful readers are independent readers, and they certainly have the potential to be purposeful writers and thinkers, but often they do not realize this promise. You will be modeling ways of asking questions and thinking about texts and—as Elaine Rangierri has modeled—about words that will help all readers at this level realize these types of deep engagements as they read and write.

The strategies and skills that intermediate readers develop in the upper elementary grades support their reading and writing at the middle grades. As they encounter increasingly sophisticated content and texts, however, those strategies need to become adjusted—they may work in one content area or *discipline* but not very well in another (Shanahan & Shanahan, 2008). The middle school years are a time when intermediate readers can begin to grow into skillful readers, learning how to adjust and adapt their abilities to the more specific ways of reading and thinking in particular disciplines. This adaptation includes their ability to identify and understand multiple viewpoints and perspectives in the texts they read—analyzing, evaluating, summarizing, and applying information and ideas in literature and informational texts. Chall (1983/1996) described this reading stage at which students understand and appreciate multiple perspectives as developing in high school and extending into the early years of college. In the present educational context, the Common Core State Standards are emphasizing the need to develop these multiple perspectives in the middle grades.

Disciplinary literacy is the term you will increasingly see applied to learning and communicating the specific information, ideas, and ways of thinking that characterize each discipline or subject-matter area: English/language arts, the sciences, mathematics, and the social sciences/history. If students can develop these more specialized strategies and skills, they will be better able to read and write in particular disciplines (Shanahan & Shanahan, 2008). If you teach at the elementary level, you are already laying the foundation for helping your students think the way a scientist or historian thinks; middle school teachers will build on that foundation.

Derivational relations spellers focus primarily on spelling–meaning connections—how *morphology* supports both advanced spelling knowledge and generative vocabulary development.

> **Common Core Connection**
>
> Reading Standards for Literature and Informational Text: Integration of Knowledge and Ideas

Characteristics of Texts for Skillful Readers

Much of the literature and literary informational texts that middle school students will explore reflect the following three characteristics (Crumpler & Wedwick, 2011):

- **Power relationships in the real world:** People and institutions have "varying levels of power" over young adolescents—protagonists in literature struggle to understand themselves in this context.

- **The reality of social injustice:** Individuals, however, are able to struggle to overcome it.
- **Sexuality:** In literature, sexuality is usually addressed as innocent and harmless. "The potential of its power is not fully understood" (Crumpler & Wedwick, 2011, p. 67).

In literature, students may explore "Higher level themes of moral dilemma, social criticism, government control, war and hunger" (Kansas Department of Education, 2012). Students' developing awareness of these characteristics is also reflected in their keen interest in *dystopian* novels—those that are set in societies, often in the future, in which there is extreme oppression and misery. Examples are Suzanne Collins's *The Hunger Games* (2008) and P. J. Haarsma's *The Softwire* series (2008). Some novels—such as Lois Lowry's *The Giver* (1993) and Madeline L'Engle's *A Wrinkle in Time* (1962)—challenge students to debate whether a society is utopian or dystopian.

Critical literacy will develop significantly during the middle school years (Busching & Schlesinger, 2002; Kretovics, 1985). In its broadest sense, critical literacy identifies power relationships and uses language in effective ways to change society. Freire (1970) originally spoke about this as "reflecting and acting upon one's society and the larger world in order to transform it" (p. 36). We noted earlier that literature and informational texts for young adolescents address this issue, and you can draw on these texts to help students develop frameworks for reading, identifying, and engaging issues in the real world. What are the authors—of *any* text, written or visual—trying to say, and how are they trying to say it? Close reading and evaluation of these texts will help your students understand better how to think and craft their own purposes for reading and writing knowledgeably and critically. This is empowering in its own right, and will help them understand and apply strategies as they, as individuals and collectively, begin to transform their worlds—and ours.

McLaughlin and DeVoogd (2011, p. 279) offer the following questions that develop and support reading from a critical perspective:

Whose viewpoint is expressed?
> What does the author want us to think?
> Whose viewpoints are missing, silenced, or discounted?
> How might alternative perspectives be represented?
How would knowing about viewpoints included and not included contribute to your understanding the text from a critical stance?
Where do the Internet links lead you and what does that mean?
What action might you take based on what you have learned?

These questions develop and support *viewing* from a critical perspective:

Who is in the video/photograph?
Why are they there?
What does the videographer/photographer want you to think?
Who/what is missing from the video/photograph? (silenced? discounted?)
What might an alternative video show?
What might an alternative photograph look like?
How would that contribute to your understanding the video or photograph from a critical stance?
What action might you take based on what you have viewed?

Many texts prior to this level may be characterized as **academic**, but this characteristic evolves significantly at this level, and continues on through high school and beyond. Specifically, most texts that students will read at this level are characterized by **academic language**. Nagy and Townsend (2012) note "Academic language is the specialized language, both oral and written, of academic settings that facilitates communication and thinking about disciplinary content" (p. 92). Academic language occurs at the word, sentence, and paragraph levels. We will

(continue on page 371)

Young Adult Literature Connection

The Uses of Mythology

There are many references in literature, as well as in informational texts, to Greek and Roman mythology (see Figure 10.1). Someone opens a *Pandora's Box*, is stuck in a situation in which they feel like *Sisyphus* pushing that rock uphill, or has a job so challenging it is like *cleaning the Augean Stables*. Students reading *Anne Frank: The Diary of a Young Girl* (Frank, 1991/2001), may notice that she refers to Peter's "Danaidean" appetite, alluding to the Danaids and their punishment for killing their husbands—for all eternity, pouring water into a vessel filled with holes. Peter's appetite will never end, either—and Anne has found "just the right" adjective to describe a very large appetite! If students do not mention it, you may point out that Anne has been studying mythology, and this is one example of how she applies this developing knowledge to inform her choice of words in writing.

The *Percy Jackson and the Olympians* book series (Riordan) does an excellent job of introducing a new generation of students to the Greek myths, heroes, and deities. As students learn about Greek mythology, they are surprised to find out how many of these aspects of mythology appear in graphic novels, video games, movies, and on TV—they are all reflections of the ideas, issues, and challenges faced by the Classical Greeks. Students also discover similarities in myths from different cultures such as those from the Middle East and the Anasazi of the American Southwest. Words from myths—their ideas and connotations—are a significant part of the academic vocabulary your students will learn.

Some excellent resources for exploring the Greek myths are:

Isaac Asimov's *Words from the Myths* (1961; although it is out of print, it is available in most libraries and on out-of-print book websites)

Bernard Evslin's *Heroes, Gods, and Monsters of the Greek Myths* (1996/2005). New York: Scholastic.

Megan Bryant's *Oh My Gods!* (2007). New York: Scholastic.

FIGURE 10.1 Words from Classical Myths and Legends

Greek names are listed first. Those changed in Roman mythology are listed second, slightly indented. Names are listed in approximate chronological order of their appearance in the myths.

Chaos The raw material of the universe—a great, dark, confused mass in which air, earth, and water were all mixed together.
Chaos • chaotic • chasm • gas

Cosmos The opposite of chaos—things with form and shape; in order, good arrangement.
Cosmic • cosmopolitan • cosmetic

Gaia, also **Gaea** (JEEuh) Goddess of earth; Greek word for earth. *geography • geology • geometry • geode*

Terra
territory • terrain • terrestrial • terrace • terrarium

Uranus God of sky, heaven.
uranium • Uranus (the planet)

Gigantes Children of Uranus and Gaea, ferocious beings of tremendous size and power.
giants • gigantic

Cyclops Children of Uranus and Gaea, they lived on the island of Sicily and made thunderbolts for Zeus; from a Greek word meaning "round-eyed"—monstrous giants with one eye in the forehead.
cycle • cyclone

Titans/Titanesses Offspring of Uranus and Gaea, these were a race of giants who ruled the world before the Greek gods and goddesses took over. They warred with the gods and lost; their fate was eternal punishment of some type or another.
Titanic • titanium

Cronus Most powerful of Titans; because of the similarity to the Greek word *chronos*, he is often mistakenly referred to as the god of time.
chronological • synchrony • synchronous

Oceanus (oh-*see*-uh-nus) Oldest of the Titans; symbolized water that encircled the land of the world.
ocean • oceanic

Atlas One of the Titans, Atlas's punishment was to support the world on his shoulders. A picture of this was often included in early books of maps, so over time such books came to be called atlases. *atlas • Atlantic • Atlanta • Atlas* Mountains (the god Atlas turned to stone)

Zeus God of the sky, king of the gods.

Jupiter or **Jove**
jovian • jovial

Luna Goddess of the moon. At one time people believed the moon had the power to drive some people out of their minds.
lunar • lunacy • lunatic

Hypnos God of sleep.
hypnosis • hypnotic • hypnotism

Somnus
insomnia • somnambulate

Mt. Olympus Where the Greek gods and goddesses lived.
Olympian

Aphrodite Goddess of beauty and love.
aphrodisiac

Venus Her symbol, a looking glass, became the symbol for female.
Venus (the planet) *• venusian • venerate • venerable*

(continued)

FIGURE 10.1 *(Continued)*

Eros God of young love.
erotic *erog*enous

  Cupid
    *cupid*ity

Psyche A maiden who fell in love with Eros. Her name means "soul."
*psych*ology • *psych*iatrist

Nyx From Chaos, goddess of darkness or night.

  Nox
    *noc*turnal • *noc*turne

Lethe Daughter of Eris, the goddess of discord. Her name means "forgetfulness." Lethe is the river in Hades where the spirits of the dead drink and then forget their former life and become listless ghosts.
*leth*argic • *leth*al

Europa She lived on the Asiatic coast of the Mediterranean and was the first person on the continent of Europe. Zeus turned himself into a white bull and Europa jumped on his back. She rode him to the continent of present-day Europe.
Europe • *Europe*an

Apollo God of prophecy, poetry, medicine, and music.
Apollo Theater (in Harlem) • *Apollo* (moon program) • *Apollo*nian

Athena Daughter of Zeus, goddess of wisdom, knowledge, arts, war and peace.
Athens • *Athen*ian

Minerva

Ares God of war.

  Mars His symbols, the shield and the spear, became the universal symbol for "male"; also means "bloody." *Mars* (the red planet) • *March* • *martial* arts

Phobos Son of Ares, the god of war. His name means "fear."
*phob*ia • *phob*ic

Demeter Goddess of grain and the harvest.

  Ceres
    *cere*al

Pan God of fields, forests, wild animals. Part man/part goat, he often caused serious trouble. The belief that he was nearby often caused people to run in terror.
*pan*ic • *pan*demonium • *pan*demic

Faunus God of woodland life.
fauna

Iris Goddess of rainbows, she was also Zeus's messenger.
iris (the flower, part of the eye) • *iri*descence

Helios God of the sun.
*heli*um • *helio*centric

  Sol
    *sol*ar • *sol*ar system • *sol*arium • para*sol*

Hermes Messenger of the gods; was also thought to be related to Thoth, the Egyptian god of astrology and magic.
*herme*tic (sealed off) • *herm*it (one who is "sealed off" from society)

  Mercury
    Mercury (the planet) • *mercur*ial

Mnemosyne Mother of muses, goddess of memory.
*mnemo*nic • *amne*sia • *amne*sty

Hygeia Goddess of health.
*hygi*ene • *hygi*enist

  Salus
    *salu*te • *salu*tation • *salu*tory • *salu*brious

Charites The Graces, three sisters who were goddesses of all that is charming in women.
*char*ity

  Gratiae
    *grac*e • *grac*eful • *grac*ious

The Muses Nine daughters of Zeus, they are the goddesses primarily of the arts.
*mus*ic • *mus*eum

Nemesis Goddess of retribution, justice, or vengeance
nemesis

Tantalus Human son of Zeus. He boasted of his friendship with the gods, so Nemesis followed him and had him punished by a lifetime of standling in water up to his neck with grapes not quite within reach; when he bent to drink, the water receded.
*tanta*lize

Echo A mountain nymph, she offended Zeus's wife, Hera, because she talked so much. Hera condemned Echo to haunt the mountainsides, being able only to repeat the last few words of the person speaking.

Echo was in love with Narcissus; after he died, she wasted away until nothing was left but her voice.
echo *echo*lalia

Narcissus A young man who fell in love with his own reflection in a pool of water.
*narciss*ism

Heracles The strongest of the Greek heroes. Heracles had to perform several seemingly impossible tasks (for example, one was the slaying of a nine-headed monster, the Hydra; when one of its heads was severed, two grew in its place).

  Hercules We often speak of *hercule*an tasks, which means they are very difficult and trying.

Hydra A water serpent that was slain by Heracles.
*hydr*aulics • *hydro*phobia • *hydr*ant

Odysseus The Greek king whose attempts to sail home after the Trojan War took him far away from home.
odyssey

  Ulysses

Orpheus Poet-musician with magic musical powers.
*orph*an • *orph*ic

Ambrosia The food of the gods.
ambrosia

Nectar The drink of the gods.
nectar • *nectar*ine

Marathon A plain located 25 miles from Athens on which a battle was fought between the Greeks and the Persian. A Greek courier ran to Athens to tell the city of the Greek victory and then died.
marathon

Romulus and **Remus** Twin brothers who were raised by a she-wolf, Romulus was the legendary founder of Rome.
Roman • *roman*tic • *roman*ce

Janus Roman god of doors—entrance and exit—who had two faces.
*Janu*ary • *jan*itor

Laconia A part of Greece where the Spartans lived. The Spartans were warlike but not given to boasting. They spoke few words and in few sentences.
*lacon*ic

Source: Adapted from Templeton et al., 2010.

address the word level in the "Vocabulary Development" section later in this chapter, and the sentence and paragraph levels in the "Informational Texts and Academic Language" section. A common and unfortunate misperception about the structure and vocabulary of academic language is that it is used only to maintain certain power relationships between groups and individuals. In other words, we could say the same thing, express the same ideas, with simpler language and shorter sentences. The truth, and what we help students understand, is that *all* the registers of a language have their own set of nuances and complexity, and the linguistic features of each register serve specific functions and purposes (Townsend, 2011).

Because many—often most—students in the middle grades are still in the intermediate stage of literacy, this may influence their ability to "cold read" many complex texts independently. However, they are still able to begin to *think* at the levels required by these more complex texts, and be influenced by and learn the academic language of these texts. A significant difference between intermediate readers at the middle grades and those at the upper elementary grades are the themes and ideas the middle grade students are able to read about, think about, and explore—these become more sophisticated and psychologically complex.

Developing Comprehension and Understanding: In-Depth Critical Engagements with More Complex Texts

Throughout the middle grades, students will be expected to read literature from many different perspectives—connecting with history, sciences, and the arts; exploring themes and literary elements more deeply—character development, for example (perhaps beginning with a work of contemporary realism like Neil Shusterman's *The Schwa Was Here* (2006) before moving into more complex texts), and examining the role that *setting* plays in developing a character and determining the development of a narrative. Through this exploration of more complex themes—psychological and moral, for example—students will gain "insight into human existence" (*Common Core Curriculum Maps*, 2012). Reading Yeats's *Song of Wandering Aengus* (1956) becomes a springboard for exploring the theme of survival in the wild, and Gary Paulsen's *Hatchet* (1987) and *The River* (1991)—often read in the intermediate grades—may be revisited. The book *The Hunger Games* (Collins, 2008) may be introduced and read (including a comparison/contrast with the movie). Toward the end of exploring this theme, students again read *Aengus*, and realize why they now have a deeper understanding of the poem. Robert Frost's *The Road Not Taken* (1916/1968) can bookend a theme exploring the nature of personal choice: Where does it come from, and to what degree are we in control of it?

Students explore primary sources including firsthand narratives such as *Anne Frank: The Diary of a Young Girl* (Frank, 1991/2001) and other related informational texts. The juxtaposition of literature and informational texts, just as it was in the elementary grades, will continue to be a powerful framework for deeper explorations.

Common Core Connection

Reading Standards for Literature and Informational Text: Integration of Knowledge and Ideas

Literature

Students will explore *themes* more deeply—for example, what distinguishes childhood from adulthood and the important related "coming of age" developmental benchmark in these years. Moose Flanagan in *Al Capone Does My Shirts*, for example, struggles to understand the increasingly complex world in which he finds himself—both personally and emotionally—and in the significantly new environment of Alcatraz. His father tells him, "Nobody knows how things will turn out, that's why they go ahead and play the game, Moose. You give it your all and sometimes amazing things happen, but it's hardly ever what you expect" (p. 34). As we've just noted, the idea of sports as a metaphor for life is strong in literature, and it is a current that runs throughout *Al Capone*. Moose loves baseball, and at the end of the book, Moose's father observes, again, "Life is amazing, isn't it? You can't ever tell what will happen. Nobody knows until they go ahead and play the game" (p. 214).

The author of *Al Capone Does My Shirts*, Gennifer Choldenko, "bookends" Mr. Flanagan's observations, and these observations are, of course, essentially the same. What has changed in between is Moose's understanding of his increasingly complex world. Moose is growing up: From the black-and-white world with its clear distinctions between right and wrong, good and bad, to learning that life is full of grays. Yes, life is complicated, and students at this level are learning why, and, importantly, learning more every day about dealing with those complications. Other themes that emerge from the literature students read at this level include:

A person can be both good and bad

People are capable of changing

Trusted individuals are sometimes capable of betrayal

Older individuals are often wiser (in the *Star Wars* movies, Yoda is an "archetype" of the wise elder)

Using one's intellect or cleverness is often more effective than using physical force

Freedom is a right

Survival—the individual versus nature/ the individual versus others

The willingness of some to ignore truth

The power of the storyteller (good or evil, again!)

The Language of Instruction

Provoking a Persuasive Stance

"Students like to argue," Jeff Zwiers points out, "and they like to be right" (2008, p. 57). By asking provocative questions and situations in every discipline, you engage your students in critical thinking, using academic language and vocabulary. As they respond, in discussion and/or in writing, students must provide evidence from a text or texts. Here are some examples of questions and statements to provoke your students' critical thinking:

- In *Al Capone Does My Shirts*, Moose's father talks about "Playing the game." Do you agree with the statement "It's not whether you win or lose, but how you play the game"?
- On page 74 in *Al Capone Does My Shirts*, Moose is thinking about Piper and observes, "I stare at her right through her pretty brown eyes. There's something true in those eyes and something false too." This shows that Moose is still learning about young women and doesn't understand them. Do you agree?

- "Humans are born evil" (Zwiers, 2008).
- Love at first sight exists.
- "Genuine poetry can communicate before it is understood." (T. S. Eliot in Kermode, 1975)
- "We are tempted to think that our little 'sips' of online connection add up to a big gulp of real conversation. But they don't. E-mail, Twitter, Facebook, all of these have their places . . . . But no matter how valuable, they do not substitute for conversation." (Sherry Turkle)

From the different disciplines, Zwiers (2008, p. 57) suggests the following possibilities:

- Statistics often lie.
- You cannot divide by 0.
- Columbus Day should not be a holiday.
- Volcanic eruptions are helpful.

Engagements with Narratives

As students explore the elements of narratives—setting, plot, characterization—and think critically about how authors develop these elements, the following framework for a narrative analytical essay will guide this exploration. This example focuses on *characterization*, but it can be adapted for analysis of setting, plot, and theme. The underlying structure will be essentially the same across the elements. As your students move beyond analysis of a single narrative to compare and contrast two or more narratives, this structure may also be adapted—your students are always committing to a thesis statement, supporting it with reasons and evidence:

> *Introduction:* A "Hook" and the Thesis Statement
> *Body of the Essay:*
> > What are the reasons for your thesis statement? These will be your topic sentences.
> > What is the evidence that supports your reasons? Explain how your evidence supports each reason/topic sentence.
> *Conclusion:* Why has the author included this character? You are going beyond your thesis statement and the narrative here. What does this character help us understand about life more generally?

A student who chooses to analyze the character of Piper Williams, the Warden's daughter in *Al Capone Does My Shirts*, might hook the reader with the following excerpt: "Piper waves like she is the sweetest girl next door. For a second I almost believe her. That's how good she is. And then I realize she *is* the girl next door . . . the girl next door to Al Capone" (p. 41). The thesis statement might be "Although mischievous, Piper Williams has a caring heart." Supportive reasons might address: (1) She understands Moose's challenges in caring for Natalie and (2) she understands and cares for Natalie more than she usually shows.

There is one episode in which evidence for both of these reasons is touchingly apparent: When Piper and Moose discover Natalie holding hands with a convict, Moose is both confused and terrified. He is confused because Natalie doesn't like to hold hands with anyone (there are only two times in his life when Natalie allowed him to hold her hand), and terrified because he has continually been worried about her physical development into a young woman and the convicts who may notice this. As he struggles not to cry and is unable to call out to Natalie, Piper simply says, "It's okay." And at that point, as he stands still, shaking, Moose thinks:

> Natalie is holding hands with a man convicted of some awful crime. It's so strange, so awful and so . . . normal. Natalie doesn't look weird. She's my older sister. A sixteen-year-old girl holding hands with a man not much older than she is.
> > This is terrible.
> > This is good.

With her simple reassurance—"It's okay"—Piper leads Moose to this insight and acceptance.

Figure 10.2 presents questions that facilitate students' thinking about and responding to narratives to those deeper levels we wish to explore (Hess, 2011). You may wish to compare/contrast these questions with those presented in Figure 9.3 to get a feel for how these questions build, and extend in important ways, those questions. In your classroom, over the course of the year, perhaps you'll address most or all of these questions. At any one time, for a particular narrative, you might assign different questions to different groups, or have group presentations to the whole class.

The Diary of Anne Frank: A Play by Frances Goodrich and Albert Hackett (1956) is one of the exemplar drama texts in the *Common Core State Standards*. Students should read, discuss, and watch the play performed, but this should not be the only version of the *The Diary of*

Common Core Connection

Speaking and Listening: Comprehension and Collaboration

Common Core Connection

Reading Standards for Literature: Integration of Knowledge and Ideas

FIGURE 10.2 Questions to Facilitate Critical Engagement with Narratives

- Are characters from all social levels represented equally? Explain.
- Is there a class of "virtuous" people? What makes them so?
- Are problems in the narrative caused by an individual or by a group? Are the solutions addressed by an individual or by the group?
- What values contribute to positive change in society? What seems to be valued most—going along with the status quo or resisting?
- Who is actually "civilized" in the book? Who is the most primitive?
- What view of the family is portrayed? Do the relationships among the family members change in the story/novel?
- Compare and contrast the society in the narrative to our society. How similar/different are they?
- Are there any strong beliefs expressed or represented? For example, belief in one or more supreme beings? The power of nature (Mother Nature, natural disasters) or of "magical" places such as lakes or sacred rocks?
- Examine for "Hero" archetypes: The quest in which the hero (male? female?) goes on a journey and addresses challenges—perhaps impossible tasks—to save his or her people. What characterizes the phases of the quest/journey—the initiation, the separation, how the hero is transformed, and the nature of his or her return at the end of the journey? Is the hero a "scapegoat" or "victim" (he or she must die so that others may live)?
- (If a novel): Is each chapter "a novel in miniature"? Does each chapter describe only one major event? Why or why not?
- Is the narrative evenly divided among different settings, or is one setting given more space? Why would the author do this?
- Does the point of view help or hinder your understanding of the narrative? Why did the author choose this point of view, or multiple points of view? Is the narrator or narrators reliable?
- If the author chose another character to narrate the story, who might be an effective narrator? Why? What would *not* get told? What would receive greater emphasis? Would this change anything?
- How does the author develop the characters? Do we learn about them through direct description, how events play out, through the eyes of other characters, or some combination of these?
- Does the author's character development work for you? Why or why not?
- Is the fictional world like the actual world, or is it a fantasy? Is it realistic? Why or why not?
- Are cause and effect clearly linked, or are the incidents and events unrelated? Do there seem to be too many "coincidences"?
- Does the ending convey a sense of closure? What is the ending's significance?

The following questions may be applied to narratives in general that students read:

- What roles are most often assigned to women/men?
- What characteristics are tied to certain behaviors and certain types of women/men, young women/ young men? (For example, in fairy tales beauty is almost always associated with being chosen, becoming rich, getting married, and being happy "ever after." External appearance reflects inner value. Does this happen only in fairy tales?)
- What have you been noticing: How and why do female/male characters succeed? How do they fail? If they receive a reward, what kind of reward is it?
- How are "femininity" and "masculinity" defined? What is a "woman"? What is a "man"?

Anne Frank that they experience. We would argue that students at this level should read the book on which the play is based, Anne Frank's own diary—specifically, the Definitive Edition (edited and translated by Frank, Pressler, & Massotty, 1991/2001). This edition includes material that was originally left out of the diary when it was first published by Anne's father, Otto, in 1947: descriptions of individuals that Otto felt would be too hurtful or embarrassing, as well as Anne's writing about her own developing sexuality. She was the same age when she wrote her diary as present-day middle school students, so her unedited diary is especially appropriate and compelling for this group. *Anne Frank: The Diary of a Young Girl* is a documentation of life under the specter of the German occupation of the Netherlands and the Holocaust. Eight individuals hid in a house in Amsterdam, never leaving, never going outside, windows covered, for over two years. It is also a compelling coming-of-age story, as Anne becomes a young woman, experiencing all that this entails, during this period of suffocating confinement. Elaine Rangierri, the teacher you met at the beginning of this chapter, observed that throughout the diary, Anne's voice could just as easily be that of any of the young women in her classes today.

The Diary of a Young Girl is a work of literary nonfiction, so in one important aspect it falls in the "Informational" text category. We discuss it here, however, because of its underlying *narrative* structure; because of this structure, it may be read in conjunction with other narratives in the historical fiction genre. Spector and Jones (2007) describe how a critical perspective may be brought to this literary work by comparing and contrasting the play, the definitive edition, and edited video clips from the 2001 television documentary *Anne Frank: The Whole Story.* The television presentation addressed Anne's probable experiences during her deportation to and imprisonment in three concentration camps—Westerbork, Auschwitz, and Bergen-Belsen—and her death at Bergen-Belsen less than two months before the liberation of the camp. Anne's diary has been used as an example of the resilience of humanity and the power of optimism. Spector and Jones, however, address how critical readings and discussions across these different texts will engage students in going beyond the almost fairy-tale–like version that is prevalent in the culture, due in large part to the popularity of the play. Students will think about the reality of the Holocaust as they consider challenges Anne faced after she could no longer record her reflections in her diary, and was experiencing the horror of the camps herself.

For a number of reasons, *The Diary of a Young Girl* is an excellent exemplar or mentor text for students at this level because of the close reading and writing it affords as well as the potential number and nature of thematic and disciplinary connections:

- Students reflect on the *processes* of reading and writing.
- *How we read* primary *sources:* Students become aware of how their own experiences and background knowledge contribute to their perspective. Once they are aware, however, they are better able to deliberately seek other perspectives, points of view, and interpretations.
- *Writing process*: Anne's deliberate revisions were made later on, especially after she realized she hoped her writing would eventually be read by others. Tragically, she did not imagine others reading her diary after her death. She imagined she would be alive, and was primarily concerned about how her writing might reflect on herself as well as those with whom she lived—one reason why she used several pseudonyms for the occupants of the house.
- Becoming aware of, and understanding how, *The Diary* is a microcosm of human behavior and dynamics.
- The underlying *theme* of courage in the context of resistance/powerlessness.
- The magnitude of the *historical period* the text reflects.
- *Figurative language:* Anne's deliberate use of simile and metaphor.
- Anne's references to *classical mythology.*
- *Point of view:* The voice of a young adolescent, reflecting an awareness of her own perspective and making the effort at times to step beyond it, to try to understand others in the contexts of their situations, attitudes, upbringings.

After reading *The Diary* closely, Elaine provides the option of reading one of the following: Jane Yolen's *The Devil's Arithmetic* (1990) or Art Speigelman's graphic novels *Maus: A Survivor's Tale* (*Volume 1: My Father Bleeds History*, 1986; *Volume 2: And Here My Troubles Began,* 1993). Speigelman was a pioneer in the graphic novel genre; the publishing world really didn't know how to describe what he had done when he first published these works. His effort, however, brought the reality of the Holocaust—before, during, and after life in the concentration camps—to a much wider audience, and with a very powerful impact. Speigelman later was awarded the Pulitzer Prize in literature for *Maus*. Elaine will guide her students' experiences and responses to *Maus* and to *Devil's Arithmetic* in the context of reading texts critically, with support and with care. She has discussed how to use these texts with her fellow English language arts teachers, and with Sansée Chandram, the social studies/history teacher. She draws from the list of critical questions in Figure 10.2. Importantly, Elaine's students compare and contrast the additional narrative they are reading with *The Diary*: Jane Yolen closes the fictional *The Devil's Arithmetic* with a short chapter titled "What Is True about This Book." Yolen's concluding lines observe: "Fiction cannot recite the numbing numbers, but it can be that memory. A storyteller . . . can point to the fact that some people survived even as most people died. And can remind us that the swallows still sing around the smokestacks" (pp. 169–170). Art Spiegelman's father was a survivor. Did his experience reflect the spirit of hope expressed in popular culture's interpretation of *The Diary*?

Elaine has also worked with Sansée to coordinate readings on the Holocaust and on other genocidal events since that time. Their combined purpose is not to dwell on these other events and issues, but rather to facilitate students' awareness. They want their students to realize that, unfortunately, no civilization, no society, is exempt from the conditions that can lead to genocide. Excellent books, intended for young adolescents, may be found on the educational websites of the Anti-Defamation League (www.adl.org); www.echoesandreflections.org addresses the Holocaust, and the following offers works not only on the Holocaust but Cambodia, Rwanda, Bosnia, and Iraq: www.adl.org/education/curriculum_connections/spring_2005/bibliography.pdf. See also Paula Stedman, *Investigating the Holocaust: A Collaborative Inquiry Project* at www.readwritethink.org/classroom-resources/lesson-plans/investigating-holocaust-collaborative-inquiry-416.

Figure 10.3 provides a suggested list of just a handful of high-interest/issue-oriented literature.

FIGURE 10.3 Suggested High-Interest/Issue-Oriented Literature for the Middle Grades

Literature
Blume, Judy. (1975/2007). *Forever*. Gallery Books. First love for a 14-year-old girl, and the reality of dealing with both the emotions and the issue of sexual involvement.
Compestine, Ying Chang. (2007). *Revolution Is Not a Dinner Party*. Henry Holt. A fictional account of the very real tragedy of the Chinese cultural revolution, seen through the eyes of a naïve young woman who eventually comes to realize what is happening. A coming-of-age story in the harshest of times.
Dickinson, Peter. (2001). *The Ropemaker*. Delacorte. Almost forever, it seems, the Valley has been safe from invasion. When the magic that protects it begins to fail, Tilja and her grandparents set out to find the ropemaker, who might restore the magic of protection. This journey evolves into Tilja's search for her own identity.
Flake, Sharon. (1998). *The Skin I'm In*. Hyperion. Maleeka Madison is bright, creative, and a math whiz, but is considered "too black" by many of her fellow students who are African American. This novel connects powerfully with middle grade students—regardless of race and ethnicity—about issues of self-respect and self-esteem.

FIGURE 10.3 *(Continued)*

Hijuelos, Oscar. *Dark Dude*. (2008). Simon & Schuster. Rico leaves Harlem, where he was accused of being too light-skinned, for rural Wisconsin—and a different set of issues—but still based primarily on the color of his skin.

Jaramillo, A. (2006). *La Línea*. Roaring Brook. Two teenagers, 15-year-old Miguel and his 13-year-old sister, Elena, travel from Mexico to join their parents in the United States. Their journey—emotionally and physically—reflects what countless immigrants have experienced, and helps readers understand that laws and the bitter politics of a nation and society will never extinguish the basic dream of a good and meaningful life.

Jinks, Catherine. (2009). *The Reformed Vampire Support Group*. Houghton Mifflin Harcourt. A more "realistic" and savvy exploration of vampires—an engaging counterpoint to the more romantically oriented nature of this genre for young adults.

Katcher, Brian. (2008). *Playing with Matches*. Random House/Delacorte. A young man, considered a "loser," is changed through his relationship with a girl who has been badly burned. He comes to struggle, however, with the possibility of a different kind of relationship.

Marillier, Juliet. *Cybele's Secret*. (2008). Random House/Knopf. A mystery evolves into an other-worldly fantasy in Istanbul.

Pixley, Marcella (2007). *Freak*. Farrar, Straus and Giroux. A social outcast at school, verbally gifted seventh-grader Miriam's complex relationship with her older sister, and a boy with whom they share common but also different relationships, lead to a wide palette of emotions and complications—but ultimately, to hope and resolution.

Stork, Francisco X. (2009). *Marcelo in the Real World*. Scholastic/Arthur A. Levine Books. A young man with Asperger's syndrome discovers how to negotiate the "real world" his father believes he should experience.

Woodson, Jacqueline. (2008). *After Tupac and D Foster*. Putnam. Three girls from very different backgrounds find their worlds and relationships turned upside-down.

Woodson, Jacqueline. (2009). *Peace, Locomotion*. Lonnie Motion is a foster child, separated from his younger sister who is living with another foster family. "Locomotion," as he is known, writes letters to his sister that document his life—which becomes more challenging when his foster parents' son returns from war, seriously injured. Locomotion turns his gifted mind to Peace, within himself, his world, and in the broader world.

Informational

Bruchac, Joseph. (1998). *Bowman's Store: A Journey to Myself*. Dial Books. Bruchac was raised by his grandparents, who were Abenaki Indians. He was a bright child who was often the victim of bullying when he was young. This is a powerful memoir about family, childhood, and being true to oneself. Middle grade students will see themselves, and a good part of their emotional lives, in this book.

Jackson, Donna. (2009). *Extreme Scientists: Exploring Nature's Mysteries from Perilous Places*. Houghton Mifflin Harcourt. The lives of a hurricane tracker, a microbiologist who explores underwater caves, and a scientist who pursues organisms in tall-crown trees are all described.

Oppenheim, J. (2006). *Dear Miss Breed: True Stories of the Japanese Incarceration During World War II and a Librarian Who Made a Difference*. Scholastic Nonfiction. This book shares letters to a librarian in San Diego, California, from Japanese American students who, with their families, were incarcerated in an internment camp in the Arizona desert during World War II.

Partridge, Elizabeth. (2009). *Marching for Freedom: Walk Together, Children, and Don't You Grow Weary*. Viking. Presented here are the narratives of young people who worked, marched, and suffered in the battle for voting rights in Selma, Alabama, in 1965. Partridge conveys the timelessness of this truly historic period.

Thimmesh, Catherine. (2009). *Lucy Long Ago: Discovering the Mystery of Where We Came From*. Houghton Mifflin. This is a compellingly described and illustrated account of how scientists and artists worked to identify, portray, and understand the skeleton that came to be named Lucy—perhaps the earliest ancestor of humankind.

Independent Reading: Motivating and Engaging Readers with Self-Selected Reading

Teachers need to keep in mind that students who are skillful readers and who are expected to engage texts deeply still need to read texts of their own choosing just for fun. It is not uncommon for students who were avid readers in the elementary grades to fall away from reading for enjoyment in the middle grades and beyond, simply because of the coursework demands that accelerate in the middle grades. English/language arts teachers will keep titles on hand such as Jennifer Holm's *Middle School Is Worse than Meatloaf* (2007), Roald Dahl's *The Twits* (1980; as delightful for middle grade readers as for intermediate), Eric Elfmann's *Almanac of the Gross, Disgusting, and Totally Repulsive* (1994), and graphic novels (see http://graphic-novelreporter.com/ for a comprehensive resource). If you are a recreational reader—which may be difficult because your own life and study demands take so much time—you at least read something you personally enjoy at bedtime. Your students are no different. They, too, need a break. We often hear students say that they need a break from all of the "important" reading they are required to do. Even though the reading may include engaging books, they need a break from always reading, thinking about, talking about, and writing about those significant themes.

Engagements with Poetry

Poetry extends language, word nuance, and themes from literature, often provoking and providing powerful new awarenesses. For skillful readers, and for other middle school students who deserve the exposure, reading—and writing—poetry may usher in compellingly different ways of perceiving and thinking about their experiences and their lives. While it often begins with renewed appreciation of the lyrics of songs, awareness can springboard to poetry that, in text, creates its own rhythm of sound and of thought—whether metered or not, rhymed or not.

Students may be surprised to learn that probably the most famous "nonsense poem" in English, "The Jabberwocky," is considered to be "great literature." Appearing in the first chapter of Lewis Carroll's *Through the Looking Glass, and What Alice Found There* (1872/1963), the poem begins with these two stanzas:

> 'Twas brillig, and the slithy toves
> Did gyre and gimble in the wabe;
> All mimsy were the borogoves,
> And the mome raths outgrabe.

> 'Beware the Jabberwock, my son!
> The jaws that bite, the claws that catch!
> Beware the Jubjub bird, and shun
> The frumious Bandersnatch!'

The entire book, *Through the Looking Glass*, is a play on language and possible meanings. Humpty Dumpty, for example, tries to explain the poem to Alice, specifically the meanings of the words. Alice is quite confused, of course, but tries to be ever so polite:

> "It seems very pretty," she said when she had finished it, "but it's rather hard to understand!" (You see she didn't like to confess, even to herself, that she couldn't make it out at all.) "Somehow it seems to fill my head with ideas—only I don't exactly know what they are! However, somebody killed something: that's clear, at any rate."

Young Adult Literature Connection

Literature for LGBTQI Students

Throughout history, marginalized populations have been underrepresented in texts that are available to readers: ethnic groups such as African Americans, Latina/Latino Americans, Asian Americans, Native Americans; groups with various language, learning, and physical disabilities; and groups of immigrants that are not distinct from each other but that often overlap. With time, as social movements for civil rights lead to legislative action, attitudes in the broader culture shift significantly and what was once marginalized moves into the mainstream. Unfortunately, however, there still remain biases and prejudices, the roots of which run deep in some subcultures. In such cases, education has not had the impact or the appropriate reach into such communities. So, even when once marginalized groups are in the mainstream, members of these groups will still encounter bias and prejudice. In the meantime, however, literature that represents these groups has become more available and widespread.

Such is the case with literature written to represent and engage lesbian, gay, bisexual, transgender, questioning, or intersex (LGBTQI) students in the middle and secondary grades (Blackburn & Clark, 2011; Vega, Crawford, & Van Pelt, 2012). This literature addresses not only issues of identity but of straight students' awareness of and insights into LGBTQI communities in general and the lives of friends who are members of these communities.

You will find the following resources very helpful as you reflect on and plan for literature experiences—in the classroom and out—that reflect LGBTQI communities.

Resources for Teachers

Blackburn, M. V. (2005). Co-constructing space for literacy and identity work with LGBTQ youth. *Afterschool Matters, 4*, 17–23.

Blackburn, M. V., & Buckley, J. F. (2005). Teaching queer-inclusive English language arts. *Journal of Adolescent & Adult Literacy, 49*(3), 202–212.

Blackburn, M. V., & Clark, C. T. (2011). Becoming readers of literature with LGBT themes. In S. A. Wolf, K. Coats, P. Enciso, & C. A. Jenkins (Eds.), *Handbook of Research on Children's and Young Adult Literature* (pp. 148, 163). New York: Routledge/Taylor & Francis.

King, J., & Schneider, J. (1999). Locating a place for gay and lesbian themes in elementary reading, writing, and talking. In W. Letts & J. Sears (Eds.), *Queering Elementary Education* (pp. 61, 70). Lanham, MD: Rowman and Littlefield.

Wiest, L. R., Brock, C. H., & Pennington, J. L. (2012). Exploring educational equity for GLBT students and teachers. *Teacher Education & Practice, 25*(1), 119–130.

Resources for Young Adults

Bass, E., & Kaufman, K. (1996). *Free Your Mind: The Book for Gay, Lesbian, and Bisexual Youth—And Their Allies.* New York: HarperCollins.

Bauer, M. D. (Ed.). (1995). *Am I Blue? Coming Out from the Silence.* New York: Harper Teen.

Herron, A. (Ed.). (1995). *Two Teenagers in Twenty: Writings by Gay and Lesbian Youth.* Boston: Alyson.

Levithan, D., & Merrill, B. (Eds.). (2006). *The Full Spectrum: A New Generation of Writing about Gay, Lesbian, Bisexual, Transgender, Questioning and Other Identities.* New York: Knopf. (LGBTQ writers between the ages of 13 and 23)

Marcus, E. (2007). *What if Someone I Know Is Gay? Answers to Questions about What It Means to be Gay and Lesbian.* New York: Simon Pulse.

Singer, B. L. (1993). *Growing Up Gay/Growing Up Lesbian: A Literacy Anthology.* New York: New Press.

The poem can be explored from multiple perspectives—simple word coinage, grammatical structure, possible etymological keys to word meanings (see "Vocabulary" section), and beyond. Without even exploring beneath the surface of the words, however, the poem offers an excellent template for noting parts of speech and their labels—*brillig* has to be a noun, *slithy* an adjective, *toves* another noun, and so forth.

Students at this level may develop a keen sense of word consciousness—being interested in words, appreciating their nuances, and motivated to apply this sensitivity in oral and written language. The categories of **clipped** and **blended** words offer rich terrain to

Common Core Connection

Reading Standards for Literature: Craft and Structure

explore. *Clipped* words are those such as *gym* (from *gymnasium*), *memo* (from *memorandum*), and *recap* (*recapitulate*). *Blended* words are sounds and/or syllables from different words that have been blended together to form a new word, such as *smog* (blending parts of *smoke* and *fog*), and *cyborg* (*cybernetic organism*).

A large proportion of words in "The Jabberwocky" are blended and clipped words, and exploring a few will give students a keen sense of how the sounds and senses of words may be combined. Here is just a handful:

gyre (related to *gyroscope*)   *frumious* (fuming + furious)
chortle (chuckle + snort)   *mimsy* (flimsy + miserable)
slithy (lithe + slimy)   *frabjous* (fair, fabulous, and joyous)
                                         outgrabe (Humpty Dumpty tells Alice that "'outgrabing'" is something between bellowing and whistling, with a kind of sneeze in the middle")

As we share and engage students in reading and responding to poetry, the following procedure works well when we want them to explore a poem deeply (Fisher, Frey, & Lapp, 2012):

1) Read the poem to yourself. Mark any words or phrases that are unclear.
2) Discuss with your *partner*: What does each stanza mean?
3) Discuss with whole *class*: Share your, or your partner's, interpretation of the poem.
4) First Teacher Reading: Students follow along as the teacher reads. Partners then read the poem to each other, following the teacher's model.
5) Second Teacher Reading: The teacher thinks aloud, modeling how she is making sense of, interpreting, the poem—for example, how she finds out clues about the writer/narrator of the poem. Students follow along in the poem as the teacher reads. Based on Robert Frost's *The Road Not Taken*, for example, the teacher might say:

   The first line talks about a "yellow wood" which means it is in the fall. But I know that in poetry there's lots of symbolism. It reminds me about the autumn years of a person's life. I'm thinking that the narrator is in his late middle age, like maybe he is about fifty or so.
   . . . So here's what I have noted about the narrator. I think he's middle-aged, and he's by himself. And I am thinking that he's not so confident about his choices, like that he has some doubt or some regret. By paying attention to the narrator, I am beginning to get to the poem's less obvious message. (Fisher, Frey, & Lapp, 2012, p. 130)

6) Students read the poem and address teacher-provided questions that will help them dig deeper into what the poet may have intended the poem to mean.
7) Write in Notebook/Journal: Students record their understanding of the poem—for example, comparing and contrasting the conventional and the "subversive" meanings of *The Road Not Taken*.

Fisher, Frey, and Lapp (2012) provide an excellent example of applying these steps in their analysis of *The Road Not Taken*, which is usually interpreted as supporting the wisdom of following your own dream, no matter the paths down which that might take you. The last three lines of the poem read:

   Two roads diverged in a wood, and I—
   I took the one less traveled by,
   And that has made all the difference.

In their example, the teacher begins the lesson by telling the students, "The purpose of our lesson is to discover why Robert Frost called this a 'tricky poem' and a 'wolf in sheep's clothing'" (p. 127). There is a "subversive" message that Frost may be conveying, and the students will be looking for it. After the teacher guides her students through the next several steps, here are just a few examples of the questions Fisher, Frey, and Lapp suggest students explore in Step 6 above:

> Why do you believe so many people incorrectly call this poem "The Road Less Traveled" than its correct title?
>
> What words or phrases does Frost use to signal regret?
>
> Frost uses the word "sigh"—Is this a sigh of regret, or relief? Use evidence from the text to support your opinion.

Despite the importance of reading closely and with increasing insight, it is important that students not be turned away from the larger objective of enjoying poetry for its own sake. So we balance our "deep" explorations of poems; you may wish to share something like the following perspective with your students early in the school year:

> "The poems that I will be sharing with you this year and that we will be reading and discussing deeply are poems that each generation feels are truly important and powerful. Sometimes we learn what the poet herself or himself intended the poem to 'mean'—as Robert Frost shared—and other times the poet leaves us no clues except the poem itself. Most of the poems that you will read on your own probably will not be read to this depth. Some poems will speak to you in a certain way, but if you were to share that with a few others, you might discover they came up with an entirely different meaning. By sharing your meanings, you and others will come to understand and appreciate the poem more deeply than if you had not shared.
>
> "By thinking through a few poems together this way, we'll be learning ways of approaching and thinking about poetry on our own. Remember, as we discussed last week, poetry often 'communicates before it is understood'!"

You will find the following resource to be an excellent exploration and summary of poetry that includes attention to young adults:

Apol, L. & Certo, J. L. (2011). A burgeoning field or a sorry state: U.S. poetry for children, 1800–present. In S. A. Wolf, K. Coats, P. Enciso, & C. A. Jenkins (Eds.), *Handbook of Research on Children's and Young Adult Literature* (pp. 275, 287). New York: Routledge/Taylor & Francis.

Students are often confused about what poetry is and is not. So many of the "great" poems follow rhyme schemes and have a definite meter—but then others do not. *Free verse* is an example of the latter. For an excellent example of modeling and facilitating middle school students' appreciation of the power of free verse, the lessons in the following link explore how to adapt the words of Cesar Chavez to this form:

www.readwritethink.org/classroom-resources/lesson-plans/writing-free-verse-voice-777.html

These two volumes offer compelling examples of poems written by young adults:

Franco, B. (Ed.). (2001). *You Hear Me? Poems and Writing by Teenage Boys.* Cambridge, MA: Candlewick Press.

Franco, B. (Ed.). (2001). *Things I Have to Tell You: Poems and Writing by Teenage Girls.* Cambridge, MA: Candlewick Press.

Informational Texts and Academic Language

Chapter 9 explored how the structure of informational texts supports the development of ideas and information. For skillful readers and for most students in general at the middle grade level, teachers should build on that foundation through a more in-depth exploration of how informational texts represent the *academic language* of each content area or discipline. In this section we explore academic language at the sentence and paragraph levels (Nagy & Townsend, 2012; Schleppegrell, 2004; Zwiers, 2008), focusing on domain- or discipline-specific texts, *not* on literary texts within the different disciplines. As Wong-Fillmore & Fillmore (2012) note in discussing these texts, "The language demands are such that many students . . . need instructional support from teachers to discover how to gain access to the ideas, concepts, and information that are encoded in the text" (p. 6).

In most disciplines, the common characteristics of sentence-level and paragraph-level academic language are fairly constant (Nagy & Townsend, 2012). At both levels, information is densely packed (see Figure 10.4):

- **Sentence level.** Sentences are often long, containing multiple clauses, with many cohesive words and phrases (Townsend, 2011; see Figure 10.5).
- **Paragraph level.** Arguments and reasoning are constructed and developed from one paragraph to the next. More abstract and technical ideas are referenced across many sentences.

Common Core Connection

Reading Standards for Informational Text: Range of Reading and Level of Text Complexity

Academic language and the kinds of *thinking* involved vary across disciplines, however, so students may be skillful readers when reading and understanding history, for example, but not skillful in reading and understanding mathematics. Following are the characteristics of reading and thinking within each discipline:

- **Mathematics.** "Close reading" is extremely important—literally reading and rereading *every* word. Function words are critical—*the* or *a* signal very different relationships. Vocabulary is very precise and exact—there are very few "multiple meaning" words. The *exact* meaning of terms in fact needs to be memorized; "gist" or connotative meanings simply are not acceptable. Learning and often memorizing specific mathematical strategies is critical. Specifically, there is a major emphasis on *error detection* (Shanahan & Shanahan, 2008)—how to look for and identify where in a computation an error may have occurred.

FIGURE 10.4 **The Nature of Academic Language**

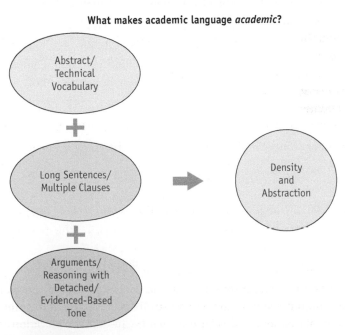

Source: Townsend and Templeton, 2012.

FIGURE 10.5 Cohesive Words and Phrases

Adding/Comparing	Contrasting	Summarizing
also	although	all in all
and	and yet	altogether
besides	but at the same time	finally
equally important	despite that	in brief
finally	even though	in conclusion
furthermore	for all that	in other words
in addition	however	in particular
in the same way	in contrast	in short
likewise	in spite of	in simpler terms
moreover	instead	in summary
next	nevertheless	on the whole
second	notwithstanding	that is
similarly	on the contrary	therefore
still	on the other hand	to put it differently
too	regardless	to summarize

Source: Townsend, 2011.

- **History.** History texts present primarily cause/effect relationships, but these are not always clearly stated. In order to identify them, readers must learn how to determine the reasons for events and their outcomes. They need to attend to the structure of the *arguments* in the history text—that is, how the writer/historian is presenting, interpreting, and judging actions and events (Schleppegrell, 2004). Students need to read more than a single source and to evaluate information across *several* sources (Wineburg, 1991, 2001). In so doing, they learn that simply because information is presented in a text, it is not necessarily "fact"—history is as much about who writes it and how the writer interprets it.

- **Science.** Scientific texts are technical and the information they present is dense, tightly packed, and interconnected. These interconnections are hierarchical: *topic* supported by *subtopics* supported by *details*. Scientific writing is characterized by considerable *nominalization*. Nominalization is when a specific process—for example, *salinize*—is turned into a noun, *salinization*, and that noun is more abstract and adds complexity. There is more that students have to "unpack" because the concept takes on and takes in additional features (Schleppegrell, 2004). Experiments and processes are described with *procedural* terms: *measure, record, predict, examine,* and *align,* for example (Zwiers, 2008). In contrast to scientific literary texts, there is no room for opinion—scientific texts are written and presented as *fact*.

The role that *graphics* play in informational texts is also different across the disciplines. In science, attending to pictures, graphs, charts, and diagrams is absolutely critical in understanding the information presented. In history, such information can elaborate and help explain, but is not as critical as in the sciences. Learning how to read diagrams in mathematics is critical.

Common Core Connection

Reading Standards
for Informational
Text: Integration of
Knowledge and Ideas

Following is the first paragraph of the *Invasive Plant Inventory* (California Invasive Plant Council, 2010). The Inventory is a type of technical text in science that the Common Core uses to illustrate the nature of such texts and the demands they place on the middle school reader.

> The Inventory categorizes plants as High, Moderate, or Limited, reflecting the level of each species' negative ecological impact in California. Other factors, such as economic impact or difficulty of management, are not included in this assessment. It is important to note that even Limited species are invasive and should be of concern to land managers. Although the impact of each plant varies regionally, its rating represents cumulative impacts statewide. Therefore, a plant whose statewide impacts are categorized as Limited may have more severe impacts in a particular region. Conversely, a plant categorized as having a High cumulative impact across California may have very little impact in some regions.

In this paragraph, just the idea of "negative ecological impact" is complex: Its partition into High, Moderate, or Limited is carried across the sentences. And there are other factors that may contribute to negative ecological impact, but these are not assessed. But then "High" and "Limited" impacts are qualified—"Limited" can be "High" in some areas, "High" can be "Limited" in others. It is important to note this, and that's why the writers used the word *conversely* to signal this important distinction.

We often begin by showing students how we can "unpack" a paragraph, one sentence at a time. In fact, at first, we may walk through and "think aloud" how we are comprehending a single sentence—and that's as far as we go on one day (Wong-Fillmore & Fillmore, 2012). Figure 10.6 illustrates how a teacher can walk through such a sentence in a science text. Such explicit examination of text structure and academic language will not only advance your students' reading comprehension, but their writing of a variety of texts, too. This is important for all learners, but it's critical for English learners and readers who struggle. These students often have the least amount of experience with Academic Language and therefore need the most support (Schleppegrell, 2004).

EL connection

Developmental Spelling Knowledge: Derivational Relationships

At this stage of development, most word study is focused on vocabulary. Spelling is not nearly as much of an issue because most students at this level are correctly spelling most of the words they use in their writing. It is fair to say that the few types of errors that remain are really higher-level errors. Learning how to correct them, however, will expand students' understanding of morphological processes and of the deeper semantic and historical relationships among words. As we will see here, vocabulary development at this level will also explore these deeper relationships among words, using the spelling of the words as the compass to guide this exploration.

The type of word knowledge that students at this level reveal through their spelling is termed *derivational relationships*. They have the foundation to explore higher-level aspects of how words are *derived* from roots and the relationships among words that are derived from the same root. Although most of their spelling is indeed correct, skillful readers are often not aware of those conventions that determine those spellings. They will be exploring the conventions that govern the correct spelling of words that they have learned earlier as new vocabulary words and which they have learned to read. Focusing on spelling or word structure at this level will also develop further students' continuing reading ability. Over the years, they will become even better readers

FIGURE 10.6 Sentence-Level Sample Think-Aloud

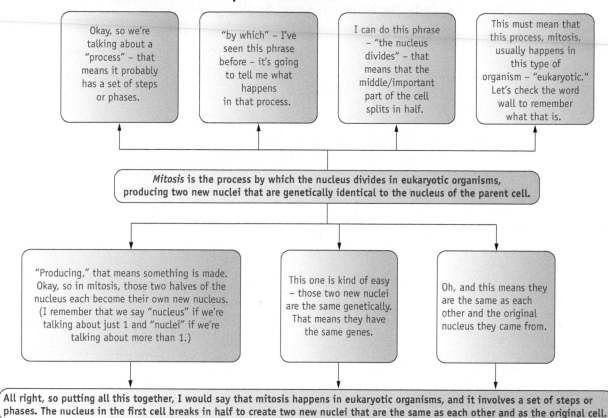

Okay, so we're talking about a "process" – that means it probably has a set of steps or phases.

"by which" – I've seen this phrase before – it's going to tell me what happens in that process.

I can do this phrase – "the nucleus divides" – that means that the middle/important part of the cell splits in half.

This must mean that this process, mitosis, usually happens in this type of organism – "eukaryotic." Let's check the word wall to remember what that is.

Mitosis is the process by which the nucleus divides in eukaryotic organisms, producing two new nuclei that are genetically identical to the nucleus of the parent cell.

"Producing," that means something is made. Okay, so in mitosis, those two halves of the nucleus each become their own new nucleus. (I remember that we say "nucleus" if we're talking about just 1 and "nuclei" if we're talking about more than 1.)

This one is kind of easy – those two new nuclei are the same genetically. That means they have the same genes.

Oh, and this means they are the same as each other and the original nucleus they came from.

All right, so putting all this together, I would say that mitosis happens in eukaryotic organisms, and it involves a set of steps or phases. The nucleus in the first cell breaks in half to create two new nuclei that are the same as each other and as the original cell.

Source: Townsend, 2011.

as they encounter more complex texts. *Even for college students* who are skilled readers, examining the spelling of words and the logic underlying this spelling supports their further development as readers (Hersch & Andrews, 2012).

Students at this level have considerable experience with the words they will be examining, so they will have the necessary foundation to understand the derivational spelling patterns they will be discovering (Templeton, Bear, Invernizzi, & Johnston, 2010):

1) They sharpen their focus on the connection between the spelling of words and their meanings.
2) They learn how to use the *spelling–meaning connection* as a *strategy* for remembering problematic spellings.
3) They realize how an understanding of the spelling–meaning connection can expand their vocabulary by establishing links between known words and new words.

Figure 10.7 shows Ethan's performance on the *Upper Level Spelling Inventory* (Bear, Invernizzi, Templeton, & Johnston, 2012). Based on what he has spelled correctly and the errors he has made, we can determine that Ethan is a derivational-level speller. He has mastered those syllable juncture features that are studied at the intermediate stage of literacy development, as well as spelling–meaning relationships represented by words such as *confidence* (derived from the root word *confide*). His first error is in the word *circumference*. Some of his other errors occur in words that he knows the meaning of and that he is able to read—such as *dominence* and *iliterate*. From this point on, these types of errors will be addressed by the teacher "walking through" with students the more advanced aspects of morphology. As you read this section, you may find

FIGURE 10.7 Early Derivational-Level Spelling Knowledge

1.	switch	17.	fortunate
2.	smudge	18.	visible
3.	trapped	19.	circumfrence
4.	scrape	20.	civilization
5.	knotted	21.	monarchy
6.	shaving	22.	dominence
7.	squirt	23.	correspond
8.	pounce	24.	iliterate
9.	scratches	25.	emphasize
10.	crater	26.	opposition
11.	sailor	27.	clorine
12.	village	28.	commotion
13.	~~traitor~~ disloyable	29.	medicinal
14.	tunnel	30.	irresponsible
15.	humor	31.	succesion
16.	confidence		

Source: Johnston et al., 2009.

yourself firming up and possibly extending some of your own understanding of how and why the way words are spelled captures morphological and historical information.

The spelling features that students at this level will explore include:

- The interplay of sound and meaning across morphologically related words such as *resign*/*resignation*, *suppose*/*supposition*, and *seren*/*serenity*.
- The consistent spelling of *Greek and Latin roots* across words: A Latin root in *circumference* is –*fer*–, which means "to bear, carry." Gaining this insight will help Ethan fix his misspelling of *circumfrence*, as well as explicitly connect with other words that contain the same root: *transfer* (carry across), *aquifer* (bearing water), *inference* ("carry [meaning] into" what you read). This study will also include those specific spellings that come from Greek—the *ch* for the /k/ sound in *chlorine*, for example (note Ethan's spelling of *clorine*).
- The different spellings for related *suffixes*: –*ent*/–*ence* and –*ant*/–*ance,* for example (note Ethan's misspelling of *dominence*); the –*ion* suffix; and when to use –*able* or –*ible*.
- *Assimilated* or *absorbed prefixes* and the consonant doubling they involve: *correspond*, *irresponsible*, *illiterate* (note Ethan's spelling of *iliterate*).

The different types of investigations and sorting activities we share here illustrate the most common spelling challenges for skillful readers. For additional types of sorting activities, see Templeton, Johnston, Bear, & Invernizzi, (2009).

Adding the Suffix –ion. A number of higher-level errors involve adding –*ion* to a root word, as Ethan's spelling of *succesion* reveals. Sorting root words and their derivatives that include these suffixes will reveal some logical patterns:

collect	oppress	prevent
collection	oppression	prevention
detect	impress	invent
detection	impression	invention
subtract	confess	
subtraction	confession	

These words illustrate that, when –*ion* is added to a large number of root words, the resulting spelling of the /*shun*/ sound doesn't change the spelling of the root at all. So, after your students examine word pairs such as these, you'll ask them what they notice about the spelling when –*ion* is added. Nothing changes! You may follow up by saying, "If you're not sure how to spell the /*shun*/ sound when –*ion* is added to a root, well, for a large number of words there *is* no change in spelling!" You may make a request of students: "Keep a log of words like *detect–detection* and *confess-confession*—notice how often the spelling remains exactly the same."

Of course, in many words the spelling of the root *does* change when –*ion* is added. If you have students arrange words in the following way, however—again matching up root word and suffixed word—predictable patterns will emerge:

decorate	invade	comprehend	admit
decoration	invasion	comprehension	admission
create	conclude	expand	commit
creation	conclusion	expansion	commission
relate	divide	suspend	submit
relation	division	suspension	submission

Tell students that the pattern in the last syllable of the root word provides a clue to the spelling of –*ion*. As they discuss the words in each column, the "rules" should emerge:

If the root word ends in –*te*, drop the *e* and add –*ion*.
If the root word ends in –*de* or –*it*, drop the *de* and add –*sion*.
If the root word ends in –*nd*, drop the *d* and add –*sion*.

Students often ask about /*shun*/ being spelled –*ian*. What's up with that? Show them the following word pairs:

electric	music	politics
electrician	musician	politician

The –*ian* spelling for /*shun*/ is used to signal that a person is usually involved—someone who "does" whatever the root word refers to: An electric**ian** works with electricity, a music**ian** plays music, and so on.

Silent-to-Sounded Consonant Alternation Patterns. We point out a number of spelling–meaning relationships to students at the intermediate stage, but we can expect skillful readers to spell these words correctly on closer inspection:

si**g**n	colum**n**	resi**g**n
si**g**nature	colum**n**ist	resi**g**nation

For most students (and adults!), seeing this "silent-to-sounded" consonant alternation pattern may cause a light bulb to go on—it's an illuminating insight for them. Most individuals, however, do *not* notice this type of spelling–meaning connection unless a teacher points it out. We can share with the students that "Very often those 'weird' spellings that have 'silent' letters in them—like *sign* and *bomb*—make sense when we think of related words like *signature* and *bombard*." As students at this level read more deeply and widely, they will encounter this pattern in less familiar words, and it should help them learn and remember those words (for example, *paradigm/paradigmatic, assign/assignation,* and *corpuscle/corpuscular*). They will also begin to notice relationships among some known words and wonder how they developed, as in the words *design* and *designation.*

(Continued on p. 390)

Reading and Writing in Digital Contexts

Critical Literacy in Action on the Web

While studying the suffragette movement, Madison found the photo in Figure 10.8A online. She had already learned that a number of suffragettes, particularly in Britain, supported violence as a means of advancing the cause of women getting the vote. In fact, she discovered that, for many people during the early twentieth century, the term *suffragette* referred to those who supported violence, whereas the term *suffragist* referred to those who did not—a distinction that, Madison found out, dictionaries do not make. She wondered about the name "Sir Rufus Isaacs" on the picket sign, and why he "justifies violence." Did Isaacs *himself* believe in violence and justify it, or did his *actions*, in the opinion of the suffragettes, justify *their* violence? Searching for his name on the Web led to Madison accessing a story in the *Boston Evening Transcript* dated May 15, 1912 (see Figure 10.8B) that described Isaacs's prosecution in England of two suffragettes for "conspiring together" and for acts that would lead to "malicious damaging of property" and "anarchy."

Madison became fascinated, which drove her to extend and refine her online search. She found reference to *Herland*, a utopian novel from 1915, written by Charlotte Perkins Gilman. Madison read that the book is about an isolated society of women. Until three explorers—who happened to be men—discovered their isolated civilization, they had never seen men. The society the women created was far superior to existing societies—there was no war, and everyone got along with one another. Madison realized the book would not be a major resource for her project, but she was intrigued enough to want to check it out and read it on her own time. She was also intrigued by the author, Gilman, who was described on several websites as a writer, social critic, and feminist. Although the entry in Wikipedia came up first in her search for Gilman, Madison skimmed a few other sites, the URLs for most of which contained university names.

Why didn't Madison settle for Wikipedia? Her teacher, Mrs. Rangierri, had told the class that Wikipedia, although helpful for a quick overview of a topic, may not be as reliable for more focused research. Her science teacher, Mr. Braddock, had also shared the same advice with the class. But students were also told, and reminded, that there's also the possibility that the website from one professor at one university may represent a particular perspective, and another's would provide a different perspective. Madison and her fellow students are learning how to look for information that is consistent across a number of websites—that is more likely to be "settled" information (although not always!). From there, students can then see where various sources may differ regarding facts and interpretation. In the case of literature, science, and the social sciences, while there is certainly common ground in so many areas, there are also controversy and different perspectives.

As we think about helping students learn to do research on the Internet, what are some lessons we can draw from Madison's experience? Madison's ability to access and think about what is useful information, and to ask critical questions about that information, was learned first in the context of exploring particular texts in depth—not by surfing and skimming through different websites. *That* ability, informed by Madison's critical perspective, underlies the following lessons:

- The skills we use to do research on the Web are in some ways much like doing research the "old-fashioned" way—like pulling different books off the library shelves and spreading them out on the table, comparing and contrasting different perspectives and conclusions drawn, taking notes, *however . . .*
- Many of the websites—even those of professors at universities—do not have to be evaluated as rigorously as most publications by respected book publishers and journals. Most websites are not

FIGURE 10.8A Suffragette in London: Online Caption Says Circa 1910

Courtesy of George Eastman House, International Museum of Photography and Film.

"peer reviewed" by other knowledgeable scholars in that subject/discipline. Such review does not guarantee that we are getting the best information. But such peer-reviewed print sources—and the websites from which we can download those peer-reviewed publications—are the best way of getting as close as we can to informed consensus about any subject. Madison became aware of this distinction between print- and web-based resources in the fourth and fifth grades (Ikpeze & Boyd, 2007; see Chapter 9).

- On the Web we can access *more* resources *much* more quickly. Before the Internet, Madison may have found some pictures such as the one in Figure 10.8A, but it would have taken a great deal more time and effort to access the scans of contemporary newspapers as in Figure 10.8B, as well as of so many primary sources. Now, many historical documents and government reports, for example, are available on the Web. This is an incredible advantage over libraries, even those that did have microfiche resources available.

- One interesting link leads to another! Madison saw a link on one of the websites to *Herlands*, which in turn led her to websites about Charlotte Perkins Gilman. Although she didn't dig more deeply at

FIGURE 10.8B *Boston Evening Transcript* dated May 15, 1912

SUFFRAGETTE LEADERS
ARRAIGNED IN COURT

MRS. PANKHURST AND MRS. LAW-
RENCE CHARGED WITH CONSPIR-
ACY IN ENGLAND

London, May 15—Mrs. Emmeline Pankhurst, leader of the militant suffragettes,
and Mrs. Pithwick Lawrence, joint editors
of Votes for Women, were arraigned today
at the Old Bailey sessions on the charge
of conspiring together and also with Chris-
tabel Pankhurst to incite their followers to
malicious damage of property. All of the
defendants pleaded not guilty. There was
a big array of counsel. Attorney General
Sir Rufus Isaacs prosecuted and in the
opening averred that the defendants had
deliberately planned a campaign which, if
it had succeeded, means nothing less than
anarchy.

that moment, she did make a note to read the book, and probably go back to some of these websites at a later date. As we noted earlier, like other students in the middle grades, Madison is becoming aware of power relationships in society, and her potential to negotiate those relationships, so she realizes a figure such as Gilman might be a helpful role model. Prior to the Web and the ease of following references, Madison would probably have not pursued a passing reference to Gilman in print. However, students need to learn how to "monitor" themselves as they explore links, to keep in mind the time frame for their assignment, assignments from other classes, and their own personal schedule. This will help them learn how to decide what's important to explore and read *right now*, and what—like Madison's discovery of Charlotte Perkins Gilman—should be noted, book-marked, and returned to at a later time.

- It's often easier to note, and evaluate, inconsistent information on the Web. For example, the caption accompanying the photo in Figure 10.8A reads "Circa 1910." That's important because it means whoever posted the picture on the Web is not certain of the exact date when the photo was taken, but the person's best estimate is that it was "around" (circa) 1910. But Madison is able to see right away, from the newspaper article she found, that Isaacs didn't prosecute the suffragettes until 1912. Is 1912 "around" 1910? Is it close enough to be acceptable? Does it matter? Why? (Would you want someone many years from now to think that the 9/11 attacks were "around 2003" or would you want them to know the exact month, day, and year [2001])? Would it matter? Why?) These are all issues and questions with which scholars as well as students have dealt for a very long time, but the Web makes the identification, pursuit, and evaluation of these questions considerably easier than in pre-Web times.

The promise of the Web is that it enables *critical literacy* to be exercised across a much grander scope than ever before. The flip side of that promise is that there is so much more that our students—from the intermediate grades through college and/or their careers—will need to be critical *about*. For this reason and so many others in the new Digital Age, the importance of reading and writing "the world" and doing so critically, lies in the words of Antonio Machado, the Spanish poet: "Traveler, there is no road. The road is made as you walk" (cited in McLaughlin & DeVoogd, 2011). You are providing students with the strategies and tools to build those roads themselves, with confidence and determination.

Exploring Vowel Patterns across Related Words. Again, have students sort words by grouping root words and their derivatives together:

athl*e*te	ign*i*te	rev*i*se	ser*e*ne
athl*e*tic	ign*i*tion	rev*i*sion	ser*e*nity
n*a*ture	cr*i*me	m*i*ne	def*i*ne
n*a*tural	cr*i*minal	m*i*neral	def*i*nitive

For each of these word pairs, the long vowel in the root word changes to a short vowel in the related word when the suffix is added. Remind students how the spelling preserves the meaning relationships that these word pairs share.

The Secret to Spelling the "Schwa" Sound. Spelling the *schwa* sound (as in the word *admiration*) will be problematic *unless* you show students how attention to the spelling–meaning connection can explain so many "schwa" spellings. Share the following with students:

Many spelling errors occur when we're trying to spell the *schwa* sound, represented by the symbol /ə/ in the dictionary. It sounds like an /*uh*/ sound with no 'oomph' behind it, and it occurs in unaccented syllables of words with two or more syllables. It is the first sound you hear in ***above***. Sound is no clue to the spelling of the schwa—it can be spelled many different ways—so that is why these spelling–meaning patterns are helpful to study.

For example, have you ever had to stop and think about how to spell a particular word, such as *similar* or *admiration*? Thinking of a related word may provide a clue. With *admiration*, think of the root word *admire*, with the long *i* sound in the second syllable. That will help you remember the spelling in the second syllable of *admiration*. With *similar*, thinking of the related word *similarity*, with its accented third syllable, will help you remember the spelling of the third syllable in *similar*.

Students can follow up on your explanation by examining the following word pairs and discussing how one of the words in each pair is the clue to the spelling of the schwa in the other:

comp*o*se	inv*i*te	leg*a*l
comp*o*sition	inv*i*tation	leg*a*lity
opp*o*se	comb*i*ne	met*a*l
opp*o*sition	comb*i*nation	met*a*llic

Exploring the Relationship between Spelling and Vocabulary. The following exploration of word pairs illustrates the overlap between developing both spelling knowledge and vocabulary. These words will extend students' understanding of how they may apply the spelling–meaning connection as a strategy: A spelling problem in a *known* word can be fixed by pointing out a related but *un*known word. When we help students with this, we do two things: First, we clear up the spelling error, and second, we expand their vocabulary.

Ask the students to talk about what it means to say that someone has a *genial* personality. Then, write *geneal* and *genial*. Ask students which is the correct spelling. There will probably be disagreement! Next, write the word *geniality* underneath *genial*, and ask if that gives them a clue. Have they ever seen the word *geniality* before? Probably not. Do they have an idea about what it means? Look at *genial* for the clue! Does the pronunciation of *geniality* provide a clue to remembering how *genial* is spelled? Tell them that learning the word *geniality*, in which the vowel sound in the third syllable is clearly short *a*, will help them remember the spelling of the schwa sound in the unaccented final syllable of *genial*.

In addition to providing a clue, though, the relationship between a related unfamiliar word and a misspelled word may often be more abstract. For example, to clear up the misspelling of *presadent,* we relate it to the word *preside*: Although students may have some knowledge of the meaning of *preside*, the relationship between *preside* and *president* is not immediately obvious. So, you explain to the students, "One can 'preside' over a meeting *or* over an entire nation, as in the case of a president." To clear up the misspelling *manditory*, show students *mandate*—for most, it is probably an unfamiliar word. Talk about the meaning of *mandatory*—if something is *mandatory*, it must be done; it has been *mandated*. "So," you ask the students, "How can the spelling of the word *mandated* help you remember the spelling of *mandatory*?"

Have students match up the following word pairs according to their similarity in spelling. For any words in a pair that they may not be familiar with, have them discuss how the meaning of the familiar word may be a clue to the meaning of the unfamiliar word. Talk about how this awareness may also help them remember the spelling of the familiar word.

cust*o*dian	central	mob*i*le	lab*o*r
cust*o*dy	centr*a*lity	mob*i*lity	lab*o*rious
proh*i*bit	frag*i*le	rig*i*d	
proh*i*bition	frag*i*lity	rig*i*dity	

Assimilated Prefixes: Spelling and Meaning Clues. Assimilated prefixes are often misspelled. When students explore them closely, however, they not only fix most of these prefix spelling errors, but they also extend their vocabularies. The following word sort investigates prefixes that are attached to root words. Ask your students to sort words by the spelling of the prefix *in–*, *im–*, *il–*, or *ir–* (Templeton et al., 2010).

in–	*im–*	*il–*	*ir–*
incorrect	immobile	illegible	irreplaceable
inactive	immoral	illegal	irresponsible
inescapable	immeasurable	illiterate	irreducible
incapable	immature	illogical	irregular
innumerable	immortal	illegitimate	

Talk about the meanings of some of the words: *Incorrect* means "not correct," *immobile* means "not mobile." Follow up by saying, "Now we're going to explore *why* the spelling of the prefix *in–* changes.

"Look over the words in each column, and talk with your partner: *Why* do you think the spelling changes from *in–* to *im–*, *il–*, and *ir–*?" Students often notice that the spelling of the first letter in the root words might be a clue. Follow up on that by asking them to try pronouncing several of the words in the *im–*, *il–*, and *ir–* columns as though they began with *in–*: *in-measurable, in-legitimate, in-reducible*. Discuss how that feels awkward as their tongues have to move quickly from the /n/ sound to the sound at the beginning of each word. Historically, this awkwardness led, over time, to the assimilation of the sound of /n/ into the sound at the beginning of the word to which *in–* was attached. Eventually the spelling of *in–* changed to reflect this change in sound.

Subsequently, your students can explore assimilation of other prefixes such as *ad–*, *sub–*, and *com–* with Greek and Latin roots (see Table 10.1). The word *assimilated* itself contains an assimilated prefix, and when we break the word down, it means "similar to." In this case, the sound of the prefix is "similar to" the sound at the beginning of the root that it is attached to. In the word *assimilate*, the assimilated prefix *as–* started out as *ad–* (meaning "to" or "toward") and, over time, became assimilated into the sound at the beginning of the root (*ad*similate is hard to say!). The word *support* comes from *sub–* (under) + *port* (carry), literally meaning "carry from beneath"—but *subport* was difficult to pronounce, so *sub* became assimilated to *support*.

Sorting Out –able and –ible. The *–able*/*–ible* suffixes are frequently confusing. The following completed sort, in which words are categorized according to whether they end in *–able* or *–ible*, may yield an exciting insight for your students:

–able	*–ible*
dependable	credible
adaptable	audible
profitable	indelible
attainable	legible
predictable	feasible
cherishable	plausible
perishable	compatible
decipherable	

- If the suffix is attached to a root word (*adapt*) it is usually spelled *–able*.
- If the suffix is attached to a Greek or Latin word root (*aud*) it is usually spelled *–ible*.

(continued on p. 394)

TABLE 10.1 Scope and Sequence for Greek/Latin Roots and Affixes

As students read within and across different genres and content areas in the middle grades, they encounter an increasingly large number of root words and Greek and Latin roots that combine with the following prefixes and suffixes.

Prefixes			Suffixes		
super–	over; greater	*supervise, supernatural*	*–logy/ –logist*	science of, scientist	*geology, geologist*
counter/ contra–	opposing	*counteract, contradict*	*–phobia/ –phobic*	abnormal fear	*claustrophobia, aquaphobic*
ex–	out	*exit, excommunicate excise*	*–ism/*	condition, belief	*autism, capitalism*
e--		*erupt, emit*	*–ist*	one who does, believes, specializes	*pianist, capitalist podiatrist*
ex–	former	*ex-president*	*–crat/ –cracy*	rule	*autocrat, democracy*
fore–	before	*foreword, foreknowledge*			
pro–	in front of, forward; in favor of	*proactive, prospect* *pro-American, pro-development*			
in– im– il– ir–	in, into	*indent, implode illuminate, irradiate*			
en–	cause to be, in, on	*encourage, enable, encircle*			

TABLE 10.1 *(Continued)*

Assimilated Prefixes		
The process of assimilating or "absorbing" prefixes is examined explicitly:		
in– not, in/into		*in* + *m*ediate = im*m*ediate *in* + *l*iterate = il*l*iterate *in* + *r*ational = ir*r*ational *in* + *p*ort = im*p*ort

Additional Roots: Middle Grades					
–pos–/–pon–	put, place	com*pos*e, ex*pos*e, op*pos*e, *pos*ition com*pon*ent, ex*pon*ent, op*pon*ent	*–ced–/ –ceed–/ –cess–*	go	pro*ceed*, pro*cess*, ex*ceed*, ex*cess*, inter*ced*e
–duc–/ –duct–	lead	pro*duc*e, pro*duct*, re*duc*e, re*duct*ion	*–ven–/–vent–*	to come	inter*ven*e, circum*vent*, co*ven*ant, *ven*ue
–vers–/ –vert–	turn	re*vert*, di*vert*, intro*vert*, *vers*atile	*–clud–/–clus–*	close	ex*clud*e, ex*clus*ion, con*clud*e, con*clus*ion
–ject–	throw	pro*ject*, re*ject*, e*ject*, inter*ject*, ob*ject*	*–jud–*	judge	pre*jud*ice, *jud*icious, ad*jud*icate
–leg–	law	*leg*al, *leg*islate, *leg*itimate, privi*leg*e	*–fac–*	make	*fac*tory, *fac*simile, satis*fac*tion, *fac*ilitate
–leg–	read	*leg*ible	*–fec–*		in*fec*t, ef*fec*t, af*fec*t
–fer–	bear, carry	trans*fer*, in*fer*, acqui*fer*, de*fer*	*–fic–*		*fic*tion, ef*fic*ient, bene*fic*ial
–bene–	good, well	*bene*fit, *bene*ficial, *bene*factor, *bene*volent	*–fy*		beauti*fy*, falsi*fy*, satis*fy*, personi*fy*, objecti*fy*, classi*fy*
–corp–	body	*corp*oration, in*corp*orate, *corp*ulent, *corp*se, *corp*oreal			
–sta–/stit–	stand	*sta*ble, *sta*tic, *sta*tistics,	*–man–*	hand	*man*ual, *man*age, *man*ufacture, *man*acle
–stit–		con*st*ant, con*stit*ution	*–mis–/*	send	*mis*sion, *mis*sile, di*smis*s,
–cred–	believe	*cred*o, *cred*ible, in*cred*ible, *cred*ence, in*cred*ulous, *cred*itable	*–mit–*		pro*mis*e, trans*mit*, e*mit*, re*mit*

Additional Prefixes: Middle Grades					
mal–	bad	*mal*function, *mal*adjusted, *mal*content, *mal*aria	*dia–*	through	*dia*gnose, *dia*gram, *dia*rrhea
				across	*dia*meter, *dia*chronic, *dia*spora
a–/an–	without, not	*a*part, *a*moral, *an*emia, *an*archy	*retro–*	backward,	*retro*spect, *retro*active, *retro*gressive
pi–	upon, on, over, near, at, before, after	*epi*center, *epi*demic, *epi*dermis	*per–*	through, thoroughly	*per*spective, *per*ennial

(continued)

TABLE 10.1 *(Continued)*

Additional Prefixes: Middle Grades *(continued)*					
ab–	off, away	absent, abduct, abstract, abnormal	*ana–*	**up back/ backward**	*ana*tomy, *ana*lyze (loosen *up*) *ana*chronism, *ana*phora, *ana*thema
meta–	beyond	*meta*morphosis, *meta*phor		**again**	*Ana*baptist (baptize *again*)

Assimilated Prefixes		
a*d*–	to, toward	a*d* + *c*ount = a**cc**ount a*d* + *f*irm = a**ff**irm a*d* + *g*ress = a**gg**ress(ion) a*d* + *p*oint = a**pp**oint a*d* + *s*ign = a**ss**ign a*d* + *t*end = a**tt**end
co*m*– co*n*– co– cor–	together, with	co*m* + *e*ducate = **co**educate co*m* + *i*ncidence = **co**incidence co*m* + *o*perate - **co**operate co*m* + *c*lude = **con**clude co*m* + *d*uct = **con**duct co*m* + *g*ress = **con**gress co*m* + *r*upt = **cor**rupt co*m* + *s*pire = **con**spire co*m* + *t*ract = **con**tract co*m* + *v*ene = **con**vene
sy*n*– syl– sym–	together, with	sy*n* + *d*rome = *syndrome* sy*n* + *l*ogistic = *syllogistic* sy*n* + *b*ol = *symbol* sy*n* + *m*etrical = *symmetrical* sy*n* + *p*honic = *symphonic*

Source: Templeton et al., 2010.

This is a rule that works most of the time, although your verbally talented students may investigate those times when it doesn't (Templeton et al., 2009)—they will discover explanations for those exceptions! (For example, with *navigable*, we'd expect *–ible*, because *navig* cannot stand by itself as a word. Actually, though, for words like *navigable* and *irritable*, the root word ends in *–ate*: *navigate*, *irritate*—but when adding *–able*, the *–ate* is dropped.)

Vocabulary Development

Students' development of *academic vocabulary* really takes off at this level. Academic vocabulary is part of *academic language* more broadly, and students' understanding of this language will be critical from this point on. While English/language arts teachers will continue to teach *general* academic vocabulary—those words that occur across all content areas—they will increasingly have their own domain-specific vocabulary as well. And with respect to those words that occur across most or all areas, you will explore with students how the ways in which the words are *used* in each discipline will often vary. The words *product* and

Strategies for the Classroom

Skillful Readers with "Spelling Issues"

We all know students who seem to be skillful readers but whose spelling is not as advanced as we would expect. Administering an upper-level spelling inventory (Bear et al., 2012) will help target where they are and where we should begin spelling instruction. And we *should* definitely address spelling instruction. Traditionally, spelling has not been taught in the middle grades and beyond. As an English/language arts teacher at the middle school level, how might you accommodate students who still need spelling instruction?

- Just as for your intermediate-level spellers, plan for a few minutes of spelling instruction at the beginning of the week. Present word lists, selected based on the results of your assessments, and talk about the patterns.
- Ideally, students will also do a word sort—if not in class, then for homework (recorded in their vocabulary notebook). Along with the sort, they will in their own words write the rule or generalization that

applies to the words and the patterns the words represent.

Until this time, these students have been learning to read words and comprehend by bringing a lot of background knowledge to the task, but they have not been paying that much attention to words. As teachers, we often think that because they are such good readers they don't need word-specific instruction. But they do. By providing appropriate instruction for your skillful readers whose spelling ability lags behind their reading ability, you will find that their spelling performance should pick up rather quickly. This will be motivating to them as well, because now they are coming to see the logic that underlies spelling patterns. You'll find the following resource very helpful in providing and adjusting spelling instruction for your skillful readers:

Johnston, F., Invernizzi, M., Bear, D. R., & Templeton, S. (2009). *Words Their Way: Word Sorts for Syllables and Affixes Spellers*. Boston: Pearson/Allyn & Bacon.

---

function, for example, have quite different meanings when we look at their use in the social sciences and in math.

To illustrate the nature of Academic Vocabulary, let's look again at the *Invasive Plant Inventory* we introduced earlier. Please notice the following:

- The connectors that represent relationships among ideas—important features of academic language—are capitalized.
- The *general* academic vocabulary words are italicized; the *domain-specific* vocabulary words are in boldface.
- Words that occur in general academic vocabulary but that also have domain-specific meanings are both italicized and boldfaced.

> The Inventory *categorizes* plants as **High**, **Moderate**, or **Limited**, *reflecting* the level of each **species'** *negative* **ecological** *impact* in **California**. OTHER *factors*, such as **economic** *impact* or difficulty of **management**, are not included in this **assessment**. It is important to note that EVEN Limited **species** are **invasive** and should be of concern to **land managers**. ALTHOUGH the impact of each plant *varies regionally*, its *rating represents cumulative* impacts statewide. THEREFORE, a plant whose statewide impacts are categorized as Limited may have more *severe* impacts in a particular region. CONVERSELY, a plant categorized as having a High *cumulative* impact across California may have very little impact in some regions. (California Invasive Plan Council, 2010)

Advanced Generative Vocabulary Instruction

Skillful readers will expand and extend their understanding of derivational relationships among roots and words derived from those roots. They will explore Greek and Latin *bound morphemes*—roots and affixes—particularly in different academic domains or subject areas. They will also examine in depth the etymology underlying them and that may be learned and explored during the middle grades (Flanigan, Templeton, & Hayes, 2012). Table 10.1 presents the scope and sequence for Greek and Latin affixes and roots at this level. The order they appear in the table is the suggested order in which they may be taught.

Skillful readers may extend and appreciate relationships among words and within words that are not as concrete or obvious. In so doing, they are growing their vocabulary. For example:

- How are *custody* and *custodian* related? Discuss with your students how *custodian* refers not just to an individual who takes care of the condition of a school—but it has a broader application, referring to anyone who has custody of or "takes care" of something, including ideas ("*custodians* of democracy").
- How are *sage* (someone, or describing someone, who is very wise) and *sagacious* related? *Presage*? If someone exhibits *sagacity*, what does that mean?
- If someone is *pugnacious* (from the root *–pugn–*, meaning "fight"), what does that mean? Would they behave with *pugnacity*? If someone *impugns* your reputation, what does that mean? How could the meaning of *impugn* come from a root meaning "fight"? Many years ago, boxers were referred to as *pugilists*.

On occasion, words that look similar are *not* related in meaning—*admiral* and *admire*, for example. When this happens, it usually means that the words came from different languages. Checking each in the dictionary will reveal the origins. *Admire* came into English from French, and meant "to wonder" (containing the root *–mir–*, meaning "wonder," and related words are *miracle* and *miraculous*, which also have to do with "wonder"). *Admiral* comes from Arabic and meant "commander."

When you engage students in thinking about relationships among words at this level, you are helping them develop a sensitivity to words that applies well beyond the particular words being analyzed. This sensitivity will help them develop a whole new level and habit of thinking about words in general. This is the essence of *generative* vocabulary learning.

Templeton, Bear, Invernizzi, and Johnston (2010) provide comprehensive lists of generative roots and affixes in science, mathematics, and social studies/history.

Sorting Words by Their Latin or Greek Roots

Common Core Connection

Language Standards:
Vocabulary
Acquisition and Use

We can facilitate deep and nuanced thinking about words and the Latin and Greek roots they contain by categorizing words according to their roots. The following "root sorts" illustrate the thinking you want to model and encourage among your skillful readers.

This first sort focuses on two roots that have opposite meanings. The students will first sort the words by their root, *–bene–* or *–mal–* (*mal–* is often categorized and taught as a prefix). We have listed it as a prefix in Table 10.1, but as this sort will reveal, it also functions as a root. Begin your discussion by asking the students which words they think they know, and discuss these. Make sure the students understand that *benefit* has to do with "good." Discuss *malfunction*—if something *malfunctions*, does it function well or poorly? Then discuss *benefactor*: Do the students recognize another root they may have recently explored (*–fac–*, "to make")? A *benefactor* is literally someone who "makes good," who may be *beneficial* and *benevolent* (which literally means "good will": *–vol* means "will"). Contrast *benefactor* with *malefactor*. The word *benediction* also contains two roots, *–dic–* ("say") and *–bene–*, meaning "good." So, *benediction* literally means "good saying" and usually refers to the blessing at the end of many religious services.

–bene–	*–mal–*
benefactor	malefactor
beneficial	malevolent

benefit	dismal
benevolent	malaria
benediction	malcontent
	malfunction
	malice
	malicious
	malediction

After the words have been sorted, have the students discuss how the meaning of the affixes and roots combine to generate the meaning of the words. Those they are uncertain about may be looked up in the dictionary. In so doing, they will learn that *dismal*, for example—which might appear to mean "not bad"—originally meant "evil day."

You would conduct the following sort farther along in the scope and sequence for exploring roots and affixes. It explores roots that have to do with the body:

–cap– "head"
–dent–, –dont– "tooth"
–ped–, -pod- "foot"
–corp– "body"

Because this sort involves six roots and the words that contain them may be sorted several different ways, you will plan to conduct this sort over two or three days. It should involve a back-and-forth dynamic between the information you are providing and the thinking about the words and roots that your students will be doing.

- On the first day, address *–cap–* and *–ped–/–pod–*. Have students sort the words according to the word root. Ask students what *decapitate* means. Their mentioning of "head" allows you to discuss *capital* and *capitol*—two words that have to do with being the "head" of government and that share the root *cap*. Students will usually realize that a *cap* is worn, of course, on the head! And the word *recapitulate* refers to stating again (*re–*) the main points, or *headings*, of a report or argument.

- As you discuss *–ped–* and *–pod–*, which both refer to "foot," remind the students of the words *monopod, tripod,* and *quadruped*. Based on analyzing their structure, most of the *–ped–* words are understandable, but discuss them with students to be certain. *Pedicure* contains a second root, *cure*, which means "care." *Expedite* means to speed up or accelerate. You may wish to share—or have the students do the detective work—that the Latin word for *expedite* meant "to free from entanglements." This originated from the meaning "to free [one's foot] from a snare," *–ex–* meaning "out," plus *ped* meaning "foot." Similarly, *impede* has evolved to mean "obstruct the progress of" something (the prefix *im–* meaning "in," and the word originally meaning "to put *in* fetters, to shackle").

- As you discuss *dentist* and *orthodontist*, ask students what orthodontists do, and then mention that *ortho–* means "straight or correct." Show the word *periscope*, and ask what *peri–* means ("around"). So, *periodontal* means "around the teeth," as in *periodontal* disease, a disease of the gums. *Indent* is interesting: If you bite on something, you might leave a dent. The word *dent* means to notch or bend inward. When we *indent* a paragraph, in a sense, we bite into it.

- The meaning of *podium* and *pedestal*, "base," evolved from "foot." Because the students have learned that *ortho* means "straight" or "correct," ask them to speculate about the meaning of the word *orthopedic*. Based on what they know about dentists and orthodontists, what might a podiatrist do? *Podiatry* means "the healing of" (*–iatry*) the foot. A *podiatrist* practices *podiatry; –iatry* occurs in a number of words, and refers to healing.

- On the second day, address the root *–corp–* by first discussing *corpse*—quite literally a body. Move then to *corps,* which can be a military "body," or a "body" of individuals such as a press corps. Then discuss how *corporal* and *corporation* reflect the concept of "body." Students are usually surprised to learn that the first dictionary entry for *corporal* has to do with the body— the next entry is the more familiar one, a particular rank in the military.

–cap–	*–corp–*	*–dent–/–dont–*	*–ped–/–pod–*
decapitate	corpse	dentist	pedal
capitol	corps	orthodontist	pedicure
capital	corporal	periodontal	pedestal
capitalize	corporation	dentures	centipede
captain		indent	impede
			orthopedic
			podiatrist
			pedestrian
			podium

In summary, here are the steps you may follow for supporting and extending your students' deeper exploration of roots through sorting activities:

1) Read and discuss the meaning of the words that contain the roots. Identify those that may be unfamiliar. These are the ones for which a later analysis of the root and affixes may reveal the meaning.

2) Have students categorize the words by their common roots. This usually involves sorting more than once, because many of the words contain more than one root.

3) Select a few words to discuss. How does their meaning result from the combination of their root(s)?

4) At first, you will provide more background information. As your students learn more about the etymology of words and understand better how their meaning results from the combination of their roots and affixes, however, you will balance providing background information with having the students speculate about how the meanings of the words result from these combinations.

After reading through that last root sort, you may have felt just like Elaine Rangierri described in the opening vignette, before she took that professional development workshop on *how* to teach about words at this level. She referred to some professional resources; we list them below. These resources will be very helpful in sequenced activities with Latin and Greek roots and affixes. They will also provide you with much of the background etymological information about words:

Danner, H. G., & Noel, R. (1996). *Discover It! A Better Vocabulary the Better Way*. Occoquan, VA: Imprimis Books.

Templeton, S., Johnston, F., Bear, D. R., & Invernizzi, M. (2009). *Words Their Way: Word Sorts for Derivational Relations Spellers* (2nd ed.). Boston: Pearson/Allyn & Bacon.

Templeton, S., Bear, D. R., Invernizzi, M., & Johnston, F. (2010). *Vocabulary Their Way: Word Study with Middle and Secondary Students*. Boston: Pearson/Allyn & Bacon.

The Role of Etymological Knowledge in Growing and Deepening Vocabulary Knowledge

Why the emphasis on *etymology*? Wilfred Funk (1950/1998) offered a very simple reason: "To know the life history of a word makes its present meaning clearer and more nearly unforgettable"

(p. 2). C. S. Lewis, author of *The Lion, the Witch, and the Wardrobe* (1950/2000) and other *Chronicles of Narnia* tales, wrote about how words have a "semantic biography." Readers and writers who develop a sense of these "biographies" may construct deeper, more developed meanings as they read and write, connecting with deeper affective and cognitive roots as well (Templeton, 1996).

For example, earlier this year Elaine Rangierri piqued her students' curiosity when, after discussing the Latin root –dec–, which means "ten," she wrote the words *decimal* and *decade* on the whiteboard. She talked with the students about how the root –dec– stood for "ten" in each of them. She then wrote the word *decimate* on the board and asked, "Could *dec* possibly have the same meaning of 'ten' in the word 'decimate'? Well . . . , let me tell you a story! Back in Roman times, when soldiers in the army were about to desert or mutiny, the commander selected, by lot, one of ten soldiers. That soldier was executed to set an example. The origin of the word *decimate* literally came from 'killing a tenth'! We've learned that, if we give a word a lot of time, over many years its meaning can grow and become extended. Nowadays, of course, *decimate* means much more than 'killing a tenth,' but unfortunately, the sense of 'death' is still a part of the meaning of the word."

On another occasion, Elaine asks, "And what about *December*? *Dec* means 'ten,' and what about those other months? *October* has the root *oct*, meaning 'eight,' and what do you think? Does *sept* mean 'seven'? Quick—check it out in the dictionary!" When students confirm that *sept* indeed means "seven," Elaine asks, "So why do we have the last four months of the year—the ninth, tenth, eleventh, and twelfth—named after seven, eight, nine, and ten? Use your dictionary or word history reference books—let's see what we can find!" Students discover that these months *were* the seventh through tenth months in the old Roman calendar, because the first month in the old Roman calendar was March. So, counting forward from March, the names for these months made sense.

Exploring further, students learn that when the Romans adopted the Greek's calendar, they realized they needed to begin their new year two months earlier, so they had to come up with the names for two new months. *January* came from *Janus*, in Roman mythology the god of doorways—he had two faces looking in opposite directions, so he was thought to look back to the old year and forward to the new year. The original name for the month was *Januarius mensus* (month of January) and was later changed to January. *February* came from *Februa*, the name of a festival held during that time of the year. (Be ready, by the way: Students—usually young women—who learn that *mensus* means "month" may realize the link between *mensus* and *menstruation*. If this comes up in the middle school classroom or, on occasion, in the upper elementary grades, you might respond simply by reminding students that, "Yes, the more we learn about roots, the more often we find them in words we're already familiar with.")

The following resources will be excellent guides and references in developing your own deeper background in words and their origins:

Asimov, I. (1960). *Words from the Myths*. Boston: Houghton Mifflin.

Ayers, D. M. (1986). *English Words from Latin and Greek Elements* (2nd ed., rev. by Thomas Worthen). Tucson: The University of Arizona Press.

Ayto, J. *Dictionary of Word Origins*. New York: Arcade.

Funk, W. (1950/1998). *Word Origins: An Exploration and History of Words and Language*. New York: Wings Books.

Merriam-Webster New Book of Word Histories. (1991). Springfield, MA: Merriam-Webster.

Moore, B., & Moore, M. (1997). *NTC's Dictionary of Latin and Greek Origins: A Comprehensive Guide to the Classical Origins of English Words*. Chicago: NTC Publishing Group.

How Word Meanings Grow over Time

The meaning of words grows metaphorically—someone once said that each word began as a picture. Show your students how the "core" or original sense of a word grew metaphorically from its concrete, picturable meaning. *Metaphor* means "carry beyond," and when you share with your students how a word has been "carried beyond" the years, growing the scope and range of its meanings along its journey, you help them gain a sense of control, power, and respect for the legacy that each word brings when it is used in speech or print. These legacies underlie the power that words convey. Like Elaine Rangierri felt for many years, you may not be used to thinking about words this way, but you can initiate your students' understanding and learn a lot right along with them.

Elaine laid the groundwork for such an exploration when she explained the spelling of *circumference*. Later, she took advantage of her students' reading of Suzanne Collins's *The Hunger Games*. She asked the students how they would describe Katniss's behavior at the end of the book when she is crowned by President Snow, and then during the interview she and Peeta have with Caesar. The students felt that Katniss was very careful, worrying about saying the wrong thing or behaving in a way that could lead to her death. Elaine then told the students, "You've just described the meaning of this word [writes *circumspect*]. Actually, *circumspect* comes from two roots—*circum* and *spect*. *Circum* means what? Thank you! Yes, it means 'around.' And *spect* means . . . Yes, thanks! It means 'look.' So, *circumspect* literally means 'to look around.' What in the world does that have to do with how Katniss behaved? Well, when she first arrived and saw Peeta, after being separated from him for much too long, she 'looked around' to see who was there and what seemed to be going on. She didn't want to behave in a way that would have unfortunate consequences! So, while *circumspect* has the literal meaning of 'look around,' that meaning has grown to include not only looking around but also thinking about what might happen if you're not careful."

After this type of explanation, Elaine supports her students in becoming etymological detectives:

"We've learned that the Latin root *rupt* means 'break,' and that a common meaning of the prefix *dis-* is 'away, apart.' Let's say someone barges through the door and starts hollering at me—we might say that person would *disrupt* the classroom. Turn to your partner and discuss this: When you combine *rupt* and *dis*, what is their literal meaning? How does that meaning apply to a situation where someone *disrupts* a classroom or something that is going on?" Her students realize that *disrupting* a classroom literally causes someone to break (*rupt*) away (*dis*) from what they are doing.

"If you *differ* with someone, what does that mean? Now check the morphemes in *differ*—with your partner, discuss how the combination of the prefix and suffix apply to a situation where you *differ* with someone." This is a bit more of a stretch, but it's exactly the kind of thinking that Elaine wants to nurture and develop. Even skillful readers may need to draw on the etymological entry in a dictionary, but with Elaine's explanation, they will realize that *differ* contains the root *–fer–*, meaning "carry," and the assimilated prefix *dis–* which, just as it did in *disrupt*, means "away" or "apart."

"So," Elaine summarizes, "if you *differ* with someone, you have an opinion that you 'carry away' from them!"

Systematic Instruction in General Academic and Domain-Specific Vocabulary

In Chapter 9 we discussed those practices that support effective teaching of important vocabulary throughout the grades. For skillful readers and writers, and for most students at the middle grade level, we build on these practices with vocabulary that is appropriate at these levels. You will continue to engage students in looking at words from a *variety* of perspectives, discussing them, and applying the developing understanding of them in meaningful engagements with texts.

Concept Sorts

As at earlier developmental levels, *concept sorts* facilitate the types of discussion and thinking that support learning new vocabulary. In a Western Civilization unit on the Reformation and its effects, for example, the specific target concepts may be classified according to whether they refer to the Reformation, Counter-Reformation, or to both movements, as shown here:

Reformation	Counter-Reformation	Both
Self-government	Jesuits	New World colonization
Indulgences	Council of Trent	Erasmus
Martin Luther	St. Ignatius of Loyola	
John Calvin	Catholic Church	
95 Theses		

Four-Square Diagram

The comparison/contrast mode for learning significant new concepts continues to be supported at this level by Four-Square Diagrams. Figure 10.9 illustrates such a diagram for math. Rather than putting the definition in students' own words, however—an effective practice in English/language arts and history, for example—the *precise* definition is used.

FIGURE 10.9 **Four-Square Diagram in Math**

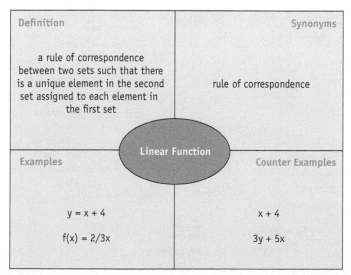

Source: Templeton et al., 2010.

Semantic Maps

Semantic maps provide support throughout a unit. They focus on the important target vocabulary and involve collaborative construction:

1) In science, for example, the teacher displays the topic of the unit: *Alternative Energy.* Students brainstorm words that come to mind when they think about alternative energy.

2) The teacher adds words to the list that are the most significant target concepts in the unit.

3) The teacher guides a discussion in which students categorize the words on the list.

4) As students move through the unit, they may reorganize and add categories and terms to the map.

Figure 10.10 illustrates the form of a semantic map at the conclusion of the Alternative Energy unit.

Vocab-O-Grams

Common Core Connection

Speaking and Listening: Comprehension and Collaboration

The Vocab-o-gram is a vocabulary/classification activity usually based on the structure or components of a narrative (Blachowicz & Fisher, 2009). Figure 10.11 is an example of a Vocab-o-gram based on Cynthia Rylant's (1992) short story, *Checkouts* (Templeton et al., 2010). Students make predictions about how the author will use key vocabulary words in developing the narrative. Vocab-o-grams help to tap into and engage background knowledge and generate interest in the narrative.

The teacher passes out copies of the activity (Figure 10.11) to student groups (3 to 5 students per group). At first, the teacher walks the students through the activity; once they are comfortable with it, the teacher may display the vocabulary words and the students will draw the Vocab-o-gram chart in their vocabulary notebooks, after which they fill in the words. The teacher discusses the directions with them, then asks them to discuss the following:

1) What do they think each word means?

2) How does the author use each word to develop the narrative? In the left-hand column, students will classify the words according to the story element they believe each word may be used to develop. The words may be placed with more than one element. Unfamiliar words are placed in the "Mystery Words" category.

FIGURE 10.10 **Semantic Map in Science**

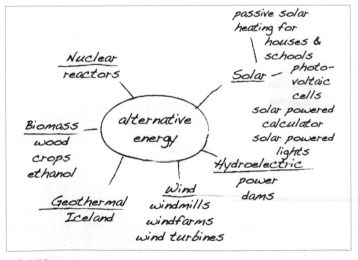

Source: Templeton et al., 2010.

FIGURE 10.11 Vocab-O-Gram: Cynthia Rylant's *Checkouts*

Discuss what you know about each of the words. Think about how Cynthia Rylant might be using the words to develop her story and write the words where you think they will be used to develop each story element. The words may be used more than once. If there are words that your group is not sure about, list them as Mystery Words. Use the vocabulary words to make predictions about "Checkouts" and write your predictions in the right-hand column next to the words.

| intuition   solitary   distract   lapse   impulse   bland   shards   dishevelment | |
reverie meditation depression witty grocery cocky deftly	
Setting	
Characters	
Problem or Goal	
Actions	
Resolution	
What Question(s) Do You Have?	
Mystery Words	

Source: Templeton, et al., 2010.

3) In their groups, based on the words they have placed with each element, students will make predictions about how they think the narrative will develop. They write their predictions in the right-hand column.

4) Students list questions they have about the narrative. These questions will emerge from their discussion about the meanings of the words and how the words might be used to develop the elements of the story, and from their predictions. These questions become *purposes* for reading.

5) Groups share classifications, predictions, and questions. The teacher then decides if any of the words need additional discussion. Quite often, words that are listed as "Mystery Words" become clarified in the context of the whole-class discussion.

6) Students read the story. When they are finished, the teacher guides their discussion of the predictions and questions, perhaps revising some. The words are also discussed.

Vocabulary Notebooks

Vocabulary notebooks are the repository for much of the information about words, definitions, and usage that students are acquiring. Ideally, the habit of keeping a vocabulary notebook will become ingrained and students will continue the practice of maintaining one—handwritten or digital—throughout their student careers and beyond.

Students will use vocabulary notebooks to record word sorts and concept sorts, as well as other vocabulary activities. These notebooks may also be used to record information about new and interesting words students encounter in their reading. It is a reasonable expectation to require students at this level to collect from 5 to 10 such words per week. Yes, these will be above and beyond the required vocabulary words they are also studying, but the way in which students think about these words will reinforce *generative* word knowledge as well as specific target vocabulary words. Spiral-bound notebooks and 3-ring binders work best, though some online vocabulary sites are developing this capability (for example, search the Internet for the vocabulary site developed by Thinkmap, *www.vocabulary.com.*).

When students do sorts with target words, they record these in columns in the notebook. They write what they learned about the words: their meanings and the meanings of roots and affixes. When there are spelling generalizations that may be generated from the words—such as determining –*ent* or –*ant*, –*ence* or -*ance* spellings—students may write these rules in their own words.

Encourage students to be alert to words that really "leap out" at them as they read:

1) While reading, circle the word. If you cannot mark in the book, mark the word with a sticky note. When you are through, go back to the word(s).

2) Record the word in your notebook, along with the sentence in which it was used. Write down the page number and the title—if it's a long one, an abbreviation will do. If the sentence is really long, record enough of it to give a sense of the context in which the word occurred.

3) Write down any words that you think may be related through spelling–meaning/ morphology to the target word(s). Write them underneath the part of the word that is similar.

4) Find the word in the dictionary. If there is more than one definition, find the one that applies to the word as it's used in your sentence. Look at the origin of the word, and add the most important part of it to your to your entry.

5) Over the next several days, if you encounter the word anywhere else, record where this occurred.

Strategies for the Classroom

Reading Workshop Mini-Lesson: Author's Craft

At this level, students are guided into more nuanced thinking about choice and the use of words in their writing. The reading that they are doing, of course, nourishes that insight. You will guide your students in their awareness, understanding, and application of this word knowledge. How do writers of powerful and engaging narratives use and arrange words to achieve the effects they wish to have on their readers?

In his seventh-grade English/language arts class, Matt Derrick is using a passage from Susan Cooper's *Over Sea, Under Stone* (2007) to illustrate Cooper's use of words and language to establish a particular mood. The book is in the *fantasy* genre and is the second in Cooper's *The Dark Is Rising* series. The fantasies are set in England and Wales, yet they seem real, believable, and especially chilling because they develop out of the everyday lives of the characters in which true evil lurks in very ordinary places, situations, and people. The students have been discussing how Cooper draws readers into the world of the book, feeling deep down the terror that arises from this evil.

Matt wants to provide an example of how he thinks as he reads, and pull his students into the conversation.

He displays the following passage (Cooper, 2007, p. 196) on the screen and engages his students in a discussion:

And then, like the sudden snapping of a bow, the noise came.

Into the air over their heads, a dog howled: a long weird note so unexpected and anguished that for a moment they all stopped dead. It echoed slow through the harbour, a freezing inhuman wail that had in it all the warning and terror that ever was in the world."

Matt pauses before continuing. "We've been talking about how authors establish the setting and the mood of a narrative in literature, and I think we've all agreed that Susan Cooper has a way of doing this *par excellence*!

"How about this first line: '. . . like the sudden snapping of a bow . . . ' Quick check: Simile or metaphor? [Students chorus, "Simile!"] Why? ["The word "like"!] Very good! But *what* a simile! '. . . like the sudden snapping of a bow, the noise came.' What is happening when a bow 'snaps'? [Students discuss—the sudden sound when the string is released, sending the arrow flying.] Yes, it's the sudden snapping that sends the arrow flying—but where? Toward us or away? How do you know? [Students discuss—the word *came* suggests "toward"; otherwise, Cooper would have written *went*. And, the next line, 'into the air over their heads.']

"Yes," Matt agrees. 'Into the air over their heads'—this does suggest the noise, like an arrow, is shot toward them. Then, Cooper shows us *what* the noise is: the howl of a dog: 'long, weird . . . unexpected . . . anguished . . . .' I don't know that I've ever heard a dog's howl that sounded quite like that. It caused Barney and the others to stop dead. And while they're standing there, the howl 'echoed slow through the harbour'—and it's not just that unearthly sound that is echoing, but Cooper goes on to describe it as [Matt pauses for a couple of seconds, then reads in as low a voice as he is able] 'a freezing inhuman wail that had in it all the warning and terror that ever was in the world.'

"How does that description make you feel? Remember a few pages earlier when Mr. Hastings told Barney, ever so softly, 'You will find, Barnabus Drew . . . that the dark will always come, and always win'? Remember how we said that at that point many of us felt the hair stand up on the back of our necks? We've been talking about *foreshadowing*—Well, wow! Hastings's warning was fore-shadowing this howl, and all that it represents. As for me, it makes the hair stand up all over again!

"Why is this description working so well? A dog's 'howl' connotes unhappiness, but Cooper tells us it's more than this—it's *anguished*. Then, the howl *echoes* and becomes 'a freezing inhuman wail'—'inhuman' here suggests more than just the fact it's coming from a dog—it's like it's from another world—a very evil other world."

This type of thinking about words—how and why a writer selects and combines them in certain ways—slows down and focuses students' thinking more explicitly on this process. It is part of reading more deeply, experiencing a text more deeply, getting underneath and moving beyond simply "what happened." Matt encourages his students, now that they've talked about Cooper's word choice, to try this out in their own writing—a piece that they're currently drafting or revising.

Writing in the Skillful Stage

Students' writing at this stage may develop and reflect their close readings: how the core ideas in a text are determined and analyzed, and how critical supporting evidence is summarized. Students' developing sense of the nuances of narrative may also inform their writing, both narrative in its own right as well as narrative in support of informational writing. As an example of the potential of young adults to engage and write about narrative, Figure 10.12 shares a portion of Ashley's response to *Warriors Don't Cry: A Searing Memoir of the Battle to Integrate Little Rock's Central High* (Beals, 1994). Ashley illustrates her integration of analysis and response, and as part of her response, she has written brief poems. Although not required to do this in her response paper—only to excerpt powerful lines and comment on them in this assignment—the degree to which Ashley was engaged and moved by the book elicited this level of response, both poetic and rhetorical. By way of providing you some background for this work, here is an excerpt from Melba Patillo Beals' Author Note at the beginning of her memoir:

> Some people call me a heroine because I was one of nine black teenagers who integrated Central High School in Little Rock, Arkansas, in 1957. At the age of fifteen I faced angry mobs, violent enough to compel President Eisenhower to send combat-ready 101st Airborne soldiers to quell the violence. I endured a year of school days filled with events unlike any others in the history of this country. (p. xvii)

> **Common Core Connection**
>
> Writing Standards:
> Text Types and
> Purposes

Analyzing Narrative

As we noted in Chapter 9, when guiding students into reading and writing higher-level themes, it is often quite effective to introduce and develop understanding of literary structure and elements with picture books, often intended for younger readers. Elaine shared a number of such works with her class. Afterward, her students chose a picture book from the several titles that

FIGURE 10.12 Eighth-Grade Skillful Reader's Response to *Warriors Don't Cry*

"Be patient, our people's turn will come. You'll see. Your lifetime will be different from mine. I might not live to see the changes, but you will . . . Oh, yes, my child, you will." —Grandma India, page 10, Chapter 1

Within her words—
Grandma's voice,
Holds a hint of truth,
A pinch of promise,
And a glint of hope.
Her words bring me a dream,
That maybe what I am doing
Will change things,
And bring our people what they deserve.

In this quote Grandma India brings Melba a hope that in the years to come she will be treated differently. Grandma says this after reading a portion of the Bible, she is adding to God's words. Melba puts her trust in her, and believes that one day what she has done will change things for the better.

★★★

"Then there was one that stuck in my mind and made me tighten my jaw. 'Are you going back tomorrow?' I wasn't ready to think of another tomorrow at Central High." —Melba, page 104, Chapter 8

Today's Tomorrow—
Today's tomorrow
Seems so far from that of yesterday.
It seems forever ago,
That I could be free of worries.
Now I have seen the ugly truth,
And I realize that it is my duty,
As a warrior,
To change it.

Melba's world changes after her first day inside Central High School, and she realizes that one day has so much impact. She is unsure if she will be able to accomplish what she set out to do. The reporters ask her all sorts of questions, but most important is the one that involves her future as a Central High student.

★★★

"After three full days inside Central, I know that integration is a much bigger word than I thought." —Melba, page 113, Chapter 9

Integration—
Who would have thought,
That only eleven letters
Could stand for all their hate,
Their signs,
The hate in their eyes,
Their chants,
Our perseverance,
Our pain,
Our determination,
Our dreams,
Eventually becoming reality.

At this point in the story Melba recognizes the importance of what she is doing. She sees the struggle that lies before her, but in the future she sees the results. She is baffled by the hatred she receives every day, and although hurt, she must push through.

★★★

FIGURE 10.12 *(Continued)*

"Dignity is a state of mind, just like freedom. These are both precious gifts from God that no one can take away unless you allow them to." —Grandma India, page 164, Chapter 14

I am what I believe—
In my heart I know that I am no different.
I am just the same as all of the white children.
I am what I know I am inside.
And therefore,
I am what I believe.

In this quote Grandma India give Melba the idea that she will never have to live up to the white people because she already is her own person. Grandma understands that Melba might question whether she is equal to the white children, but tries to explain that there is no need to compare herself to them. This quote is very powerful to me because it holds true to everyone, and outlines the rights that everyone is entitled to.

Elaine provided and applied their developing understanding over the next couple of days in their own analytical writing. Figure 10.13 presents excerpts from seventh-grader Abbie's analytical essay, *Learn to Love*, based on Maurice Sendak's *Where the Wild Things Are* (1963/1980).

Abbie frames her analysis in narrative form, beginning with a question tapping familiar experiences to engage her reader. The evidence that she uses to support her analysis is based on common experiences and emotions she assumes most of her readers have had. She moves back and forth between sharing her *own* experiences and, indirectly acknowledging her audience, those that *they* have had—establishing a bond between writer and reader: "I'll bet that after you talked back . . ." / "I can remember many times where I have talked back . . . ." Abbie firmly grounds her shared experience with her readers before proceeding to her analysis of *Where the Wild Things Are*, but makes sure the reader will keep this foundation in mind: "Think about this throughout the rest of this paper."

After a brief synopsis of the book, Abbie explicitly signals her focus: "Now, we're going to go back to the beginning of the book and take a deeper look . . . ." As her analysis unfolds, she builds her case by continuing to reference the perspective of a young child, angry and trying to gain control over the situation as he battles his mother's authority: "If Max were to eat his mother, he would be taking her in, therefore controlling her." She signals her reader that she is going to move to the next point in establishing her argument: "Next, let's look a little bit further into the book and check out another time when Max is in the manipulative position." Her close reading of both text and illustration yields the insight that Max's wolf suit is a metaphor for his behavior. Her argument continues in this fashion, leading to her conclusion regarding Max's journey: an allegory for learning "how to control himself and his emotions," as well as for negotiating the complex dynamic of parent/child in the context of growing and learning boundaries. While Abbie concludes that *Where the Wild Things Are* is "a book full of lessons," she makes sure she signals this by wording her title as if it were a lesson: *Learn to Love*.

Analyzing and Constructing an Argument

Hillocks (2011) emphasizes that "the process of working through an argument is the process of inquiry" (p. xxii), and inquiry is at the core of critical thinking. We engage students in this process, walking them through their inquiry and demonstrating *how* to think critically at these higher levels. Rather than beginning with a thesis statement or question, when students are going to compose an argument, we show them how to begin by examining the evidence, much

FIGURE 10.13 Skillful Seventh-Grade Reader's Analysis of *Where the Wild Things Are* (Excerpt)

Have you ever talked back to your mother because your anger and/or frustration took over? I know I have. I bet you have too. Also, I'll bet that after you talked back you felt badly. This bad feeling was the growth of love for your mother. I can remember many times where I have talked back to my mother. Typically, I was sent to my room to "think about my behavior."

When I first got sent to my room, I would always be frustrated. After a while of being in there I would start to feel bad about what I did or said. Sometimes it was saying something like, "I hate you!" Or I was violent and kicked or punched. Of course, I don't really hate my mother. That's just what I say because I don't like what she is telling me.

So, while thinking in my room, I began to feel bad and regret my choices. This bad feeling was the growth of love for my mom. In the book *Where The Wild Things Are*, by Maurice Sendak, Max goes through these same changes. Think about this throughout the rest of this paper.

The book starts with Max acting and dressing as a wolf. He wears his wolf costume day and night. Max builds a fort in his mother's house. While building his fort, he breaks and damages some of her things. Next, Max chases his dog with a fork – he is still wearing his wolf costume. Max is having trouble controlling himself, he does not know how to act. His mother calls him "Wild Thing," he responds with "I'll eat you up." That night, he is sent to bed without his dinner ...

Now, we're going to go back to the beginning of the book and take a deeper look into Max's actions and choices.

When Max chases his dog with a fork, he is wearing a wolf suit. Wolves are untamed wild dogs. This means that Max is acting troublesome and "untamed." He is acting as the alpha, because he is unsure of how to "tame" himself. His mother calls him "Wild thing." Max shouts, "I'll eat you up." That night Max is sent to bed without his dinner. In this example, Max tries to be in charge of his mother by talking back. If Max were to eat his mother, he would be taking her in, therefore controlling her. His mother stops Max by sending him to bed with no dinner. This represents Max's mother taking control of her son. As you may have noticed, Max doesn't know how to show his love for his mother yet. He has not had enough time to reflect on his behavior, so, he hasn't learned his lesson yet. Clearly, in the beginning of the book, Max is out of control. He's acting as if he is the one with authority. Next, let's look a little bit further into the book and check out another time when Max is in the manipulative position.

Max's wolf suit is a metaphor. It relates his costume to his behavior. At the start of the book, Max wears a full wolf suit and acts poorly to his mother. By the end of the book, Max had taken the hood off of his wolf suit, and he is now able to show more love and respect to his mother ...

Where The Wild Things Are, in my mind, is not a silly children's book with tamed wild animals; it's a book full of lessons. As I see it, Max goes on a journey to the wild things to learn how to control himself and his emotions. Also, he learns to show his love for his mother.

---

like *CSI* investigators or scientists—actually, *any* role or situation in which we find ourselves. Hard data give rise to questions about that data, and when students re-examine the facts and try to answer those questions, the data that support their answer becomes the evidence they will use in their argument. This gives rise to a claim about the evidence, and we often refer to that claim as our **thesis statement**. We then need to demonstrate *how* the evidence supports our claim, or thesis, and how it counters competing claims (Hillocks, 2011; Toulmin, 1958).

Hillocks suggests a progression in teaching argument writing. This progression is based on moving from a very specific topic with concrete evidence, to topics with a broader scope and a larger database/potential evidence:

- Arguments based on *fact*
- Arguments based on *judgment*
- Arguments based on *policy*

FIGURE 10.14 Cartoon: Analyze for Constructing an Argument of Fact

Source: Hillocks (2011)

Many of the informational texts that students read at this level are good examples of *arguments*. They provide the type of organization, language, and vocabulary for writing effective arguments—for example, Sojourner Truth's *Ain't I a Woman?* (Daley, 2008); Winston Churchill's *Blood, Toil, Tears, and Sweat* (2004); and Franklin Delano Roosevelt's first "fireside chat" on "The Banking Crisis" to a nation mired in the Great Depression (Ahuja, 2008). However, it is important that we understand that our students will gain a deeper sense and understanding of *constructing* arguments if they begin their exploration with motivating issues and topics.

Hillocks (2011) begins instruction in argument writing based on *fact* with "crime scene" drawings such as the one in Figure 10.14. In discussing the woman's explanation that her husband stumbled on the stairs and fell, leading to his death, the teacher engages seventh-graders in discussing the data provided in the drawing: Do they believe it supports the woman's story or suggests she instead murdered her husband? As they consider this, the teacher guides them in understanding how to think about what "counts" as evidence.

- They discuss the position of the husband's body.
- If he tripped and fell, would he have landed facing up?
- The glass in his hand isn't broken—wouldn't it have broken in a fall? And wouldn't he have dropped it?
- Objects on the wall have not been disturbed—wouldn't he have tried to grab something if he was falling down the stairs?
- The carpet where he landed hasn't been disturbed—wouldn't it be rumpled if something heavy, like a body, landed on it?

This examination of evidence, in small groups, then with the whole class, with teacher as mediator/facilitator, helps students develop a more consistently *objective* stance. They understand how and why it's important to move beyond the preconceptions and assumptions in their own thinking—which can make effective analysis difficult. This process takes time, especially if we're not used to thinking this way. After students have, through discussion, identified relevant evidence, they will in small groups write a one-paragraph argument, based on fact, in support of their claims. When understanding this structure in paragraphs is clear, teachers can then move students to writing longer compositions.

Until now, the common practice in writing has often been to require students to write an argument *without* examining relevant underlying evidence. They write about what they already believe, choosing evidence that supports their point of view. There is a place for this type of writing—*persuasive* writing—but unless we also teach *argumentative* thinking and writing, students will have difficulty growing beyond their own preconceptions and biases—even if they write well.

Understanding and constructing *arguments of policy* begin by addressing problems students care about. Disturbed about rising violence in their community, for example, the middle school students in Danielle Taggart's class wanted to find ways *they* might address this challenge. Danielle knew they would be developing an argument based on *policy*: They brainstormed ideas, but then needed to address the practicality of these ideas. What, as students, is more in their direct control? The next steps involve researching the possibilities they brainstormed:

- What has already been done?
- How effective has it been? Why? Why not?
- What possible solutions will they find that they have not brainstormed?
- Based on these findings, what might they be able to try in *their* community?

As Danielle moves the students through this process, she is addressing the Common Core's emphasis on research: The class's final report, each section of which will be written by a different group of students, will be structured much like the research reports written by those in various disciplines (Hillocks, 2011):

I. Introduction: What is the problem you're investigating? What is your primary question? What are related questions?
II. Research Design and Methods: Explain *how* you conducted your investigation of the main question and the related questions.
III. Results: What did you find?
IV. Discuss Your Results: *Explain* your results, what they *mean*, and *why* they are valid.
V. Conclusions/Recommendations: Based on your findings, what might now be done?

Common Core Connection

Writing Standards: Research to Build and Present Knowledge

If this outline if familiar to you, the odds are it is probably because you have taken a course in research methodology in education. As demonstrated by Danielle's students, however, it's not necessary to wait until students are undergraduates or graduate students to learn about and use this format. The cognitive foundation for understanding this type of argument and writing is in place in the middle grades—we just need to start teaching to that foundation.

Remember, once students have been guided through this process of constructing an argument of policy, they are better prepared to understand, evaluate, and appreciate such arguments in their reading. Excerpts from the speeches represented in Figure 10.15, for example, are not "objective" in the usual sense: Winston Churchill wished to reassure and inspire the British people who, in May 1940, were standing alone against Nazi Germany; Cesar Chavez wished to encourage farm workers and others to push back against the power of pesticide producers to impose deadly chemicals on defenseless workers. Still, however, these examples illustrate the argument form. Students can evaluate each, then compare them together, to see how an effective argument may be built through language and the arrangement and presentation of evidence:

FIGURE 10.15 The Argument Form in Two Speeches: Winston Churchill and Cesar Chavez

Winston Churchill, after being appointed Prime Minister of England, addressed the House of Commons on May 13, 1940. Three days earlier, Nazi Germany had invaded the Netherlands, Belgium, Luxembourg, and France; Germany had already invaded Czechoslovakia, Austria, Poland, Norway, and Denmark.	Cesar Chavez, civil rights leader and leader of the United Farm Workers movement for decades, addressed the issue of pesticides and their deadly effects in a speech delivered in March, 1989. He began with the words, *"What is the worth of a man or a woman? What is the worth of a farm worker? How do you measure the value of a life?"*
. . . I have nothing to offer but blood, toil, tears, and sweat. We have before us an ordeal of the most grievous kind. We have before us many, many months of struggle and suffering. *. . .* *You ask, what is our policy? I say it is to wage war by land, sea, and air. War with all our might and with all the strength God has given us, and to wage war against a monstrous tyranny never surpassed in the dark and lamentable catalogue of human crime. That is our policy.* *. . .* *You ask, what is our aim? I can answer in one word. It is victory. Victory at all costs—Victory in spite of all terrors—Victory, however long and hard the road may be, for without victory there is no survival.* *. . .* *I take up my task in buoyancy and hope. I feel sure that our cause will not be suffered to fail among men. I feel entitled at this juncture, at this time, to claim the aid of all and to say, "Come then, let us go forward together with our united strength."*	*The misery that pesticides bring farm workers—and the dangers they pose to all consumers—will not be ended with more hearings or studies. The solution is not to be had from those in power because it is they who have allowed this deadly crisis to grow.* *. . .* *The times we face truly call for all of us to do more to stop this evil in our midst.* *. . .* *The answer lies with you and me. It is with all men and women who share the suffering and yearn with us for a better world.* *. . .* *Our cause goes on in hundreds of distant places. It multiplies among thousands and then millions of caring people who heed through a multitude of simple deeds the commandment set out in the book of the Prophet Micah, in the Old Testament: "What does the Lord require of you, but to do justice, to love kindness, and to walk humbly with your God."*

- *Identifying the immediate challenge (problem):* "ordeal" and "struggle and suffering" for Churchill; "misery" for Chavez
- *Nature of the challenge:* "monstrous tyranny" for Churchill; "evil" for Chavez
- *Nature of the response:* "our task" for Churchill; "our cause" for Chavez
- *Conclusion:* Both conclude with compelling quotations.

Churchill's complete speech is fairly brief, because he knew his audience understood the threat that faced them. Chavez's speech is longer, because many in his audience did *not* understand the facts—were not even aware of the magnitude of the threat. Consequently, Chavez documents the suffering of many families (children who have developed cancer or who were born with deformities, many of whom died before reaching the age of 10) and the research that clearly demonstrates the harm done by pesticides to both workers and the entire population that consumes fruits and vegetables. Two speeches, both using the argument form, separated by almost 50 years, one delivered by a child of privilege, son of an English lord and lady; the other delivered by a Latino migrant farm worker who left school after eighth grade to help support his family. Both Churchill and Chavez understood the power of well-constructed arguments.

Common Core Connection

Reading Standards for Informational Text: Craft and Structure

Chapter Summary

Skillful readers and writers have the foundation to adjust their reading to the demands of texts in different disciplines. When they read silently, skillful readers read between 150–250 words correctly per minute, and they are able to adjust their rate of reading more flexibly to the type of material they are reading and to their purpose for reading. They extend their potential to read deeply in different disciplines and types of texts, and this in turn extends their ability to think critically in these different contexts as well. As they exercise this thinking in their writing, the process of writing becomes one that also extends their thinking. The full reciprocity of reading different types of texts and writing different types of texts is developed.

Word knowledge at this level reflects the exploration of more advanced features of morphology—deeper investigation of Greek and Latin roots and their combination with affixes. This understanding supports *generative* vocabulary learning, and it also supports understanding of the close relationship between the spelling of words and their meaning.

Suggested Extension Activities

- Using a story from the literature that sixth-, seventh-, and eighth-grade students are expected to read this year, plan for conducting a Narrative Directed Reading Activity (Chapter 9) with a group of students. Where will you have them pause in their reading to check predictions? Select two or three questions from those provided in Figure 10.2 to ask after students finish the narrative.
- At the intermediate and the middle grades, you are likely to be challenged at one time or another about a particular title you have made available to your students. With a fellow student or colleague, visit the National Banned Book Week website (www.ala.org/advocacy/banned) and follow the link to the Top 100 Banned/Challenged Books in 2000–2009. For those titles with which you are familiar, discuss why you believe these books might be challenged. How might you justify using them?
- Share one of the examples of the etymology/history of words in this chapter with a group of middle grade students. Do they "get it"? Do they ask further questions?

Recommended Professional Resources

The journal *Voices from the Middle,* published by the National Council of Teachers of English, provides excellent information about reading and writing, and the social and political contexts of learning how to negotiate effective instruction and learning at this level. It is the best resource for middle school English/language arts educators interested in these topics.

Danner, H. G., & Noel, R. (1996). *Discover it! A better vocabulary the better way.* Occoquan, VA: Imprimis Books.

Templeton, S., Bear, D., Invernizzi, M., & Johnston, F. (2010). *Vocabulary their way: Word study with middle and secondary students.* Boston: Pearson/Allyn & Bacon.

Templeton, S., Johnston, F., Bear, D., & Invernizzi, M. (2009). *Words their way: Word sorts for derivational relations spellers* (2nd ed.). Boston: Pearson/Allyn & Bacon.

Silvey, A. (2006). *500 great books for teens.* Boston: Houghton Mifflin.

Wolf, S. A., Coats, K., Encisco, P., & Jenkins, C. A. (2011). *Handbook of research on children's and young adult literature.* New York: Routledge/Taylor & Francis.

Online Resources

Cooperative Children's Book Center

www.education.wisc.edu/ccbc/

This site, developed and continuously updated in the School of Education at the University of Wisconsin, Madison, has excellent reviews and links to suggested books for middle school students/young adults, including graphic novels and multicultural literature.

Young Adult Library Services Association

www.ala.org/yalsa/booklistsawards/booklists

A division of the American Library Association, the YALSA provides a comprehensive array of resources and booklists. Focusing on teens from ages 12 to 18, their links and lists include, for example, "Best Fiction for Young Adults," "Great Graphic Novels for Teens," "Outstanding Books for the College Bound," and "Quick Picks for Reluctant Young Readers."

Word Generation

http://wg.serpmedia.org/

A vocabulary resource that addresses middle school vocabulary instruction, words are taught through a number of activities and approaches that reflect the effective instruction described in this chapter. Instruction is embedded in a number of different contexts, including discussion focusing on contemporary issues. Math, science, and social studies disciplines are included.

11

Response to Instruction: Intervention and Acceleration for Readers Who Struggle

Chapter Outline

» **What Is Response to Instruction?**

» **Profiles of Students Experiencing Difficulty in Learning to Read**

» **Accommodating Students Experiencing Difficulty with Literacy**

» **Supporting the Development of *All* Students: Research-Based Best Practices**

11 Focus Questions

1. What is Response to Instruction/Response to Intervention? How is it similar to and different from the discrepancy model?

2. How can your comprehensive literacy assessment system help you plan instruction and intervention for readers who struggle?

3. Name and describe several common profiles of readers who struggle and describe the kind of instruction that can help accelerate these students' progress.

4. When is it appropriate to explore the possibility of a learning disability?

5. What are some research-based instructional strategies that can help all readers, especially those who experience difficulty?

It's mid-September and third-grade teacher Kevin Hayes schedules a meeting with his school's reading specialist, Abbey McGowan, to talk about his new student, Paul. Kevin is concerned about Paul's level of achievement and he isn't quite sure what to do about it. Abbey reassures Kevin that it can be overwhelming to have a student who is achieving below grade level and this is true for novice teachers and veterans alike. Abbey also acknowledges there are things they both can do to help accelerate Paul's achievement. She proceeds to ask Kevin a few questions:

- What are Paul's strengths?
- What can he do independently?
- What is he "using but confusing" or experimenting with?
- What can he do with support?

These questions catch Kevin by surprise and he quickly realizes that he's been so focused on Paul's deficits, he's not exactly sure how to answer Abbey's questions. All he really knows is that Paul is far behind his peers and he's not sure what to do about it. Abbey affirms that Kevin's response to these questions is not uncommon. She understands that it's often a teacher's first inclination to focus on what students *can't* do when they're not achieving grade-level standards, but

that's not a particularly helpful stance. Instead, she explains, it's more effective to focus on what students can do independently and what they are using but confusing, so we can identify students' "zones of proximal development" and build from their strengths. Teaching in a developmentally responsive way is something Kevin knows a great deal about, but he didn't immediately think of it when working with Paul. This is an important reminder for him.

With Abbey's help, Kevin looks over Paul's assessment data beginning with his Qualitative Spelling Inventory. They start with Paul's spelling inventory because word knowledge is the foundation of reading, and spelling is the best indicator of a student's knowledge about written words:

1. bed	11. spoil
2. ship	12. serving
3. when	13. chooed (chewed)
4. lump	14. carys (carries)
5. flote (float)	15. marched
6. trane (train)	16. shouer (shower)
7. plase (place)	17. botil (bottle)
8. driv (drive)	18. faver (favor)
9. bright	19. ripen
10. throte (throat)	20. seler (seller)

As they analyze the inventory, Abbey and Kevin see that Paul independently uses initial and final consonants as well as short vowels, as in the word *bed*. He also accurately uses digraphs (as in <u>*ship*</u>) *and* preconsonantal nasals (as in <u>*lump*</u>). As they continue to look down the list, they're looking for the first place where Paul "uses but confuses" a given spelling feature. Soon they notice Paul beginning to experiment with long vowel patterns, as in the words *flote/float, trane/train,* and *throte/throat*. These spelling attempts suggest that Paul is an early within word pattern speller—a stage many children enter at the end of first grade or the beginning of second grade, but it's not unusual for some students to remain in this stage throughout third grade and even into the beginning of fourth grade.

Next, Kevin and Abbey look at Paul's unedited writing samples and they notice that his spelling is relatively consistent with his spelling on the primary spelling inventory, though he's using a little more phonic or sound spelling than he was when writing words in isolation. For example, he spells *DIV* for dive, *FELS* for feels, and *BORD* for bored. They also notice Paul correctly spells many sight words (*the, and, is, like*) as well as most short vowel words. This suggests that he is indeed in the early within word pattern stage. Identifying the knowledge and strategies Paul's beginning to use and understand helps Kevin and Abbey know where to begin word study instruction.

Kevin then shares several records of oral reading. As he and Abbey look them over, they see that Paul can read level-12 texts independently with very few, if any, miscues and he can retell the stories, too. When they look at Kevin's running records for level 14 and level 16 texts, they see that Paul is reading at a very slow pace with some miscues on multisyllabic words such as *certainly/suddenly* as well as some confusions on words that are visually similar: *on/now, them/then, were/where,* and *quiet/quit*. These reading behaviors suggest that Paul is an early transitional reader—a finding consistent with his spelling achievement.

Kevin asks Abbey if she thinks Paul has a learning disability. Abbey explains that it's sometimes hard to tell if a student's difficulty is the result of a mismatch between instruction and the child's stage of development or if it's a sign of a learning difference. Since Paul is new to the school and has never had intervention services, the first thing Abbey recommends is providing Paul with developmentally responsive instruction in the classroom and a supplemental "second dose" of instruction provided by a reading specialist like herself. Since Paul's reading, writing, and spelling seem to be consistent with students in the early within word pattern stage, Abbey is inclined to believe that developmentally responsive instruction is going to make a significant difference for Paul. If Paul doesn't respond well to this regimen, it may suggest that he needs more explicit and/or intensive instruction, or it may indicate the presence of a learning disability. It's simply too soon to tell, but they'll closely monitor his progress and meet again to adjust their plan based on Paul's progress. ■

What Is Response to Instruction?

In this opening vignette, Kevin Hayes and Abbey McGowan engaged in a problem-solving process commonly called *Response to Instruction* or *Response to Intervention (RTI)*. The RTI process is used to identify and respond to students experiencing academic or behavioral challenges, including difficulties with reading, writing, and language. RTI is also used to identify and respond to students at risk for developing learning or behavioral challenges. In this way, RTI is intended to prevent these problems from developing by providing **early intervention**.

Response to Intervention is a relatively new approach that's frequently associated with the reauthorization of the Individuals with Disabilities Education Act of 2004 (IDEA) (PL 108-446). This act was first passed into law in 1990. Together with its predecessor, the Education for All

Handicapped Children Act (PL 94-142), it guarantees all children, regardless of intellectual or physical disability, a free appropriate public education (FAPE). Children eligible for special education services under this law receive **individualized education plans** (IEPs) and support services that are intended to prepare them for "further education, employment, and independent living" (NICHCY, 2010a). Approximately 14 percent of the total U.S. public school population is served under IDEA and about half of those students have a **specific learning disability** (NCES, 2007) (see Figure 11.1). Of these students, about 80 percent experience difficulty with reading (Lyon, 1995).

FIGURE 11.1 What Is a Specific Learning Disability?

A *specific learning disability (SLD)* is a neurological disorder that affects the way a person processes information or expresses knowledge. The effects from a SLD can range from mild to severe. Students with learning disabilities may have difficulty learning to read, spell, or express themselves in writing or when speaking. When you note a significant difference between a child's intellectual ability and her or his achievement, it may signal the presence of a learning disability. Children with learning disabilities may learn differently, but this doesn't mean they aren't intelligent. Children with specific learning disabilities are often very bright. For this reason and others, some people prefer to use the term *learning differences* rather than *learning disabilities*. The following information highlights some common disabilities that can affect students' performance in literacy.

Common Learning Disabilities that Affect Literacy Development

Dyslexia Dyslexia is a language-based learning disability in which the student's brain processes the sounds of language differently and less effectively than others. This often affects the child's ability to read, write, spell, and even express his or her thoughts clearly when speaking. Dyslexia, like so many learning disabilities, tends to run in families. Symptoms of dyslexia in young children include:

- Mispronouncing words that children of similar ages don't have difficulty saying, often changing the order of sounds in words (*packback* for *backpack*) or confusing words that sound similar (*bit* and *bet*)
- Trouble rhyming and learning the sequence of items (days of the week, letters, numerals)
- Difficulty matching letters and sounds when spelling or decoding words

Symptoms of dyslexia in older students include:

- Significant difficulty reading, writing, and spelling
- Poor reading and writing fluency
- Illegible handwriting
- Difficulty with word problems in math
- Difficulty comprehending texts and/or developing logical arguments based on reading.

Although students with dyslexia often reverse or invert letters when writing (*b* for *d*, *m* for *w*) and confuse visually similar words (*was* and *saw*), dyslexia is *not* a visual disability. These confusions are the result of an underlying issue with phonological processing and orthographic memory (Vellutino, 1987).

Dysgraphia Dysgraphia is a learning disability that affects how students process visual-spatial information. Students with dysgraphia can have difficulty organizing letters, numerals, words, and lines of text. Writing is difficult for these students, and this often results in poor handwriting, spelling, and overall written expression. Illegible handwriting in and of itself is not indicative

(*Continued*)

FIGURE 11.1 *(Continued)*

of dysgraphia, but several of the following symptoms may signal the presence of this learning disability:

- Difficulty drawing, forming letters or numerals, and inconsistent spacing between letters or words beyond the beginning stage of development
- Poor writing fluency and poor stamina for writing
- Difficulty expressing oneself in writing
- Saying words out loud while writing them
- Omitting words in sentences when writing
- Difficulty with syntax and grammar in writing
- A significant difference between the student's oral expression of ideas and written compositions

Nonverbal Learning Disabilities Students with nonverbal learning disabilities experience difficulty with visual-spatial tasks including handwriting and symbol recognition in mathematics. These students often have difficulty with organization, following directions, reading comprehension, and written expression. Students with nonverbal learning disabilities are sometimes characterized as being uncooperative, lazy, or lacking motivation because they don't respond as expected to verbal or written directions. This characterization is simply not fair or accurate. With appropriate accommodations, students with nonverbal learning disabilities, like all learning disabilities, can achieve as their typically developing peers.

For more information about these and other specific learning disabilities, visit the Learning Disabilities Association of America's website or LDonline's website.

The Individuals with Disabilities Education Act has been revised several times and the 2004 reauthorization was in response to a threefold increase in the number of students identified as having a specific learning disability over the past 30 years (NCES, 2007). One of the most significant changes in the new IDEA is how students become eligible for special education services (Shinn, 2007). Historically, students were found eligible for special education when there was a "severe" difference between their intellectual ability and academic achievement as measured by standardized tests. This *discrepancy model*, as it's often called, essentially required students to "fail" before they were eligible to receive special education services (Vaughn & Fuchs, 2003). This led to a disproportionately high rate of identification among specific populations of children at risk for learning difficulties, including minorities, English learners, and those experiencing poverty (Snow, Burns, & Griffin, 1998; Walmsley & Allington, 1995). As Vaughn and Fuchs (2003) observed, these students were, in effect, "waiting to fail" in order to receive intervention services. The reauthorization of IDEA responded to this very serious concern by allowing states, at their own discretion, to implement a process-oriented approach to identification with an emphasis on:

1) Universal screening to identify students experiencing learning difficulties, or those at risk for learning difficulties
2) The prevention of learning problems through responsive, research-based classroom instruction and early intervention
3) Intervention that increases in intensity for students who are experiencing ongoing learning challenges
4) Ongoing progress monitoring of all students, especially those receiving intervention

This new process has become known as *Response to Instruction* or *Response to Intervention*.

The Language of Your Instruction

Student-First Language

Over the years you've probably heard children with learning differences referred to as "struggling readers," "special needs kids," and even "disabled learners." All of these terms give priority and power to the label rather than the student. Student-first language shifts our focus to the student first and foremost. Instead of saying "struggling readers," you might say, "students with reading difficulties"; instead of "disabled kids," you could say "children with learning challenges" or "students with learning differences." Although this shift may appear subtle, its implications are quite profound: A disability does not define a student any more than his or her race, ethnicity, socioeconomic status, gender, or sexual orientation. By focusing on student-first language, we show our respect for the individual, and the student's disability becomes just one of many descriptors (Snow, 2012).

Tiered Instruction

In an RTI system, intervention is often categorized into three or four tiers or levels of instruction. Each tier increases not only in terms of how frequently the lessons occur but also the duration of these lessons as well as the explicitness of instruction (Fuchs & Fuchs, 2011; Gehsmann, 2008). When students do not respond to regular classroom instruction, what's known as Tier 1 instruction, they are moved along the continuum of tiers until their achievement begins to accelerate. When a student responds to lower-tiered interventions, it's assumed that the student does not have a learning disability (Mesmer & Mesmer, 2008). In order to achieve the best possible results in an RTI system, the person providing instruction should be the most highly qualified professional available—a certified teacher or reading specialist (Allington, 2009, 2012). It's generally not advisable for paraeducators to be the primary provider of intervention services for readers who struggle. (See the feature titled "Working and Collaborating" in Chapter 3 for more information about appropriate roles and responsibilities for paraeducators.)

Tier 1

Tier 1 instruction refers to instruction that is delivered in the regular classroom setting—instruction that is differentiated based on students' stages of development and instructional needs. Examples include your differentiated guided reading, guided writing, and word study lessons. Some students may also benefit from additional practice and instruction in specific areas such as decoding or fluency. Other students may need additional support comprehending text or organizing their writing pieces. It's important to remember that *all* students benefit from Tier 1 instruction.

Tier 2

Tier 2 intervention is instruction that is *in addition* to Tier 1 instruction. This instruction is usually provided by an interventionist—someone with specialized training in teaching students with reading difficulties: a reading specialist or special educator. To achieve the best results, your students' intervention services should be coordinated with the Tier 1 instruction they receive in your classroom. Tier 2 interventions are typically appropriate for students performing in the lowest 10 to 20 percent of a given grade level.

In many systems, Tier 2 interventions are provided at least three times per week for about 30 minutes each session. These interventions are intended to provide a temporary scaffold for students so they can successfully participate in the regular classroom program without the need for long-term supplemental services. However, it is possible that some students, including those with learning disabilities, will continue to need Tier 2 interventions for longer periods of time. Tier 2 interventions, like Tier 1 interventions, are based on students' ongoing needs and they're usually optimized when delivered in groups of one to three students (Hiebert & Taylor, 2000; Mathes et al., 2005; Vaughn, Gersten, & Chard, 2000).

Tiers 3 and 4

Most approaches to RTI include Tier 3 and sometimes Tier 4 interventions. Tiers 3 and 4 interventions are provided more regularly, sometimes every day, and for 30 or more minutes per day. These interventions are often delivered in a one-to-one setting. Tier 3 and Tier 4 interventions are usually reserved for students whose achievement is considerably behind their peers and a learning disability may be present or suspected. Importantly, these tiers of intervention are usually *in addition* to tier 1 instruction, although occasionally, in some cases, Tier 3 or 4 intervention may replace regular classroom instruction. Less than ten percent of a given population would typically be eligible for Tier 3 or Tier 4 intervention.

The Role of Assessment in Response to Instruction

As you learned in Chapter 3 and again in the opening vignette, assessment data are critical in determining your students' stages of development, as well as their strengths and instructional needs. In schools and districts that implement RTI, teachers use **universal screening** to identify students whose achievement warrants further diagnostic assessment and/or supplemental instruction. Screening assessments generally take place in the first weeks of the school year, and ongoing formative progress monitoring and interim/benchmark assessment are administered throughout the school year to monitor students' progress and identify students who are not progressing. Decisions about which students receive intervention services should be made based on teacher observation, trends in students' assessment data, and student work samples. It is not appropriate to identify students for intervention services based on a single test score (Afflerbach, 2004; Lipson & Wixson, 2010). It's also critical that your comprehensive literacy assessment system assess each of the essential elements of literacy to get a complete picture of students' strengths and needs: word structure, fluency, vocabulary, comprehension, writing, and motivation (Buly & Valencia, 2002; Gehsmann, 2008).

Accommodating English Learners

Determining the Presence of a Learning Disability in an English Learner

English learners are inherently at risk for reading difficulties because they often lack enough exposure to spoken English to acquire the phonological, syntactic, orthographic, and vocabulary knowledge needed to accurately read words and comprehend texts. For many English learners, early reading skills develop at about the same rate as their native speaking peers. But as texts become more complex around third or fourth grade, English learners can begin to struggle and this is usually related to a lack of vocabulary and background knowledge (Goldenberg, 2011). This phenomenon is sometimes referred to as the *fourth-grade slump* (Chall, 1983; Chall & Jacobs, 2003) and it occurs in populations of English learners and native speaking students, too. Some ELs' difficulties begin even earlier, and these early difficulties *may* signal the presence of a learning disability. In either scenario, when English learners experience significant difficulty with reading and writing, it's important to consider the role of their language proficiency, as well as the possibility of a learning disability.

Fortunately in most schools today, students at risk for or experiencing reading difficulties receive intervention services through RTI. However, it can still be helpful to pursue a more formal special education evaluation to better understand the root cause of an English learner's difficulty, particularly if the student is not responding to instruction and intervention. If you're wondering about the presence of a learning disability in one of your English learners, it may be helpful to consider these questions in advance of initiating a formal evaluation for special education services (Spear-Swerling, 2006):

- Assuming the child has received adequate exposure to his or her native language, is there evidence of a disability in the child's native language? Evidence may include any of the following:
  - A delay in speaking
  - Difficulty pronouncing words or difficulty speaking in syntactically correct sentences
  - Poor phonological awareness (particularly in languages with deep orthographies)
  - Difficulty acquiring literacy in the native language (assuming adequate instruction)
- Is there a family history of a language delay or disability in the native language?
- Is there a history of reading problems in parents, siblings, or other close relatives (assuming there's been adequate access to instruction for these people, too)?
- Is the student's progress significantly different than that of other English learners at the same level of proficiency who have had similar access to high-quality, research-based reading instruction?

If you answered yes to one or more of these questions, you might decide to pursue a formal special education evaluation. If you do, you'll want to provide your student with the most equitable assessments available. Consider using assessments in the child's native language, assuming it's the stronger of the two languages, or other appropriate accommodations to get the most valid results possible (Garcia, McKoon, & August, 2008; Gunderson & Siegel, 2001; Jimenez, 2004). See the feature "Accommodating English Learners" in Chapter 4 for more about assessing English learners.

English learners *with*, and even those *without*, learning disabilities typically respond well to many of the same accommodations used with native speaking students experiencing learning challenges. However, English learners differ in at least one important way: They will need considerably more support and instruction in general academic and domain-specific vocabulary. These students will also benefit from other language supports such as the use of visual aids (pictures, props, and gestures) and culturally responsive instruction. Refer to Chapter 5 and throughout each of the instructional chapters to find additional suggestions for teaching literacy to English learners.

Profiles of Students Experiencing Difficulty Learning to Read

A number of empirical studies have confirmed that readers with low achievement vary quite little from readers who are learning disabled (Fletcher et al., 1994; Stanovich & Siegel, 1994; Vellutino, Scanlon, & Lyon, 2000). The key to both groups' success is understanding their specific strengths and needs, and responding with appropriate instruction (Clay, 1987; Valencia & Buly, 2004; Wanzek, Wexler, Vaughn, & Ciullo, 2010).

Over the years, a number of researchers have worked to better understand the similarities and differences among readers who struggle (Buly & Valencia, 2002; Kamil, Borman, Dole, Kral, Salinger, & Torgesen, 2008; Leach, Scarborough, and Rescorda, 2003). In doing so, they've developed profiles that can help you better understand the characteristics of these readers, as well as plan instruction that can make a real difference in their achievement. In the sections that follow, we share several profiles from Valencia and Buly's study of a large sample of students who did not meet the fourth-grade reading standard in the state of Washington. We selected this age group as our focus because studies of fourth- and fifth-graders experiencing difficulty with reading are most instructive for teachers of students in grades 4 through 12 (Wanzek et al., 2010).

FIGURE 11.2 Research-Based Approaches to Early Intervention

Reading Recovery

Reading Recovery is an approach to early intervention that is intended to help the lowest-achieving first-grade students. These students meet with specially trained Reading Recovery teachers one-to-one for 30 minutes per day, five days a week, for 12 to 20 weeks of individualized early reading instruction.

The *What Works Clearinghouse* found that Reading Recovery has significant positive effects on general reading and other measures of early reading as well. Upward of 75 percent of program completers read at grade level (RRCNA, 2012). For more information, go to the *What Works Clearinghouse* (http://ies.ed.gov/ncee/wwc/AboutUs.aspx) or the Reading Recovery Council of North America's website (http://readingrecovery.org).

Book Buddies

Book Buddies is a research-based tutoring framework for students experiencing reading difficulties in kindergarten through third grade. These tutoring lessons are approximately 30 minutes long and are delivered one-to-one under the supervision of a trained reading specialist. In wide-scale implementations, Book Buddies has achieved impressive results, with 85 percent of students reaching grade level after 40 or more lessons (Johnston, Invernizzi, Juel, & Lewis-Wagner, 2009). For more information, including videos of Book Buddies lessons in action, see *Book Buddies, A Tutoring Framework for Struggling Readers* by Johnston and colleagues (2009).

Howard Street Tutoring Program

The Howard Street Tutoring Program is a supplemental after-school intervention program specifically designed for second- and third-grade readers who struggle. Students meet with their mentors one-to-one two days per week for about an hour. The tutoring includes reading an instructional-level text, word study instruction, writing, and easy reading practice. Students who participate in this program achieve significantly better results on various measures of reading and, in general, make more than one year's gain in reading achievement in as few as 50 hours of tutoring (Morris, Shaw, & Perney, 1990). For more information see *The Howard Street Tutoring Manual: Teaching At-Risk Readers in the Primary Grades* (Morris, 2005).

Understanding the developmental continuum and appropriate instruction in phonological awareness, phonemic awareness, oral language development, and word recognition are probably most helpful for understanding and planning instruction and intervention for readers who struggle before fourth grade (Scanlon, Vellutino, Small, Fanuele, & Sweeney, 2005; Scarborough, 2002; Walpole & McKenna, 2007 Wanzek et al., 2010). Figure 11.2 highlights some research-based approaches to early intervention in these grades.

Although profiles of readers who struggle can provide a useful lens for analyzing students' assessment data and planning your instruction, it's also important to realize that no two readers are exactly alike. Even students who share the same profile will vary from one another. When planning your instruction and intervention for readers who struggle, it's critical that you use all your assessment data, as well as student work samples, data from interviews and conferences, and information from other teachers and families to create a holistic plan that meets each student's unique needs.

Automatic Word Callers: Readers with Strong Word Recognition, Weak Vocabulary and Comprehension

Automatic word callers (Valencia & Buly, 2004) are students who read words accurately and quickly, but do not monitor their reading to be sure it makes sense. These students exhibit difficulty with language-based skills such as understanding and using general academic and domain-specific vocabulary, and comprehending texts at both the basic and inferential level. Written expression can also be challenging for them.

Automatic word callers benefit from coaching and instruction that helps them read with appropriate rate, phrasing, and expression, as well as explicit comprehension strategy instruction. By focusing on both reading for meaning and reading with appropriate fluency, automatic word callers can begin to better comprehend, enjoy, and learn from the texts they read independently. Teaching automatic word callers to monitor their comprehension is also important.

English learners and children experiencing poverty often fall into this category of readers who struggle, and this makes sense given their backgrounds. Both groups of students are often proficient in what's referred to as *surface-level* communication (Cummins, 1991). But it will likely take years of exposure to rich language and explicit instruction in vocabulary to help them understand the more nuanced meanings of written text and to develop their inferential thinking skills. Their vocabulary knowledge "sets the ceiling" (Biemiller, 1999) on their comprehension and so your ongoing vocabulary instruction *and* comprehension strategy instruction are critical. In one study, automatic word callers account for nearly one in five readers who struggle (Buly & Valencia, 2002).

EL Connection

Word Stumblers: Readers with Strong Vocabulary and Comprehension, Weaker Word Recognition and Fluency

Another common group of readers who struggle are *word stumblers;* these students account for almost a fifth of all readers who struggle (Buly & Valencia, 2002). Unlike automatic word callers, word stumblers tend to be native English speakers and they're often from middle-class or upper-middle-class backgrounds. They have strong vocabularies and background knowledge, and these strengths facilitate their comprehension, and to some degree, their word recognition. As you might expect, these students often overrely on context to help them read individual words, and when the meaning of the sentence doesn't help them readily identify words, they have great difficulty decoding the unknown word(s). Because their word recognition is so labored, their fluency suffers considerably. Given how difficult labored reading can be, you'd expect their reading comprehension would suffer, too, but their strong vocabulary and knowledge of the world in general help them when it comes to understanding the texts they read. As they progress through the upper grades, however, these supports become much less effective, and their lack of knowledge about word structure significantly impacts their reading.

Word stumblers benefit from explicit instruction in decoding and word recognition. By coordinating your word study instruction with your guided reading instruction, you'll help word stumblers begin to see the logic of letter–sound correspondences, as well as spelling patterns in words. Word stumblers sometimes benefit from repeated exposure to these patterns, so matching their word study instruction with guided reading texts, including some decodable text, can really help these readers progress. We've found that many, if not most, word stumblers are transitional readers in the within pattern stage of spelling. Targeted word study instruction with a simultaneous focus on building automaticity and fluency will help accelerate these students' growth.

Struggling Word Callers: Readers Experiencing Difficulty with Word Recognition and Comprehension

Another common profile is that of *struggling word callers* (Buly & Valencia, 2002). In Buly and Valencia's study (2002), this group of students accounted for about 15 percent of readers who struggle. Students with this profile sometimes perform better when reading words in isolation or spelling words in blind writing sorts, but their word recognition and spelling suffer in terms of accuracy and automaticity when reading or writing connected texts. Their comprehension is also quite limited.

Struggling word callers benefit from word study instruction that is coordinated with their guided reading, making explicit the predictable spelling patterns of words with a focus on reading them automatically in isolation *and* in context. In contrast to *word stumblers* who are able to compensate and better comprehend texts, *struggling word callers* need a concentrated focus on reading for meaning—this will also help these students use semantic knowledge to monitor their reading of individual words. Students who fall into this category of readers benefit from extended practice reading just-right texts with appropriate levels of support and feedback.

Slow and Steady Comprehenders: Readers with Strong Comprehension and Word Recognition and Weaker Fluency

This group of readers, *slow and steady comprehenders* (Buly & Valencia, 2002), are typically native English speakers with good oral language and strong background knowledge. These readers often appear stronger than they really are because their comprehension is solid; however, their reading rate is unusually labored and this will likely be uncovered through your comprehensive literacy assessment program. Unlike struggling word callers, slow and steady comprehenders have a number of strategies for decoding words—they just aren't efficient in using these strategies. This often results in a lot of rereading and self-correcting, which negatively affect fluency. In Buly and Valencia's study (2002), nearly one in four readers who struggle fit into this category.

Slow and steady comprehenders may nearly meet the standard on your assessments. Without intervention, however, students with this profile will likely become overwhelmed and fall further behind as the volume and expectations for reading increase throughout the late elementary and middle school years. This phenomenon is known as the *Matthew effect*—a reference to the biblical story where the rich get richer and the poor get poorer (Stanovich, 1986). Your well-coordinated word study and guided reading instruction will help address this phenomenon, particularly when you focus on building automaticity through recognizing spelling patterns, as well as reading in phrasal units. Repeated readings and other techniques such as Readers' Theater would be equally beneficial, as would extended reading practice in high-success texts (Allington, 2009; Morris & Gaffney, 2011).

Slow Word Callers: Readers with Strong Word Recognition and Weak Fluency and Comprehension

Slow word callers are quite similar to automatic word callers (Buly & Valencia, 2002). The difference, however, is that these students are able to decode and recognize words, but they do so quite slowly. Because they are so accurate, they rarely need to reread or self-correct. However, their slow processing of words negatively impacts their fluency, and this may contribute to their poor comprehension. For some students in this group, comprehension might be impeded by poor general and/or academic vocabulary knowledge as well. Only further diagnosis will help you determine the extent to which you need to supplement your fluency and comprehension instruction with intensive vocabulary instruction.

Students with Specific Learning Disabilities in Reading

Approximately ten percent of readers who struggle have a specific learning disability (Buly & Valencia, 2002). These students not only learn differently, they often experience difficulties in several aspects of reading including word recognition, fluency, *and* comprehension

Reading and Writing in Digital Contexts

Assistive Technology in the Literacy Classroom

Students experiencing difficulty with reading can often gain increased access to grade-appropriate learning through assistive technology. Computer software programs that read text aloud and speech-to-print software were only dreams just a generation ago. Today, they're nearly as common as textbooks and computers themselves, but these tools are just the tip of the iceberg. To explore the research on assistive technologies and the countless products available, visit http://techmatrix.org.

It's important to recognize that support for students learning to write is much more limited. So much of learning how to write depends on students' ability to organize and sequence thoughts and ideas. But speech-to-print technology doesn't help with that, because students must have a good idea what they want to express before this technology is helpful. On the other hand, if there's a particular word a student wants to use but is hesitant to because the spelling isn't known, this technology can be a helpful resource.

Most older students do not struggle with the physical requirements of writing; it's the overall structure, organization, and logic of compositions they need to learn. Their success with these will depend on your writing instruction, including your specific feedback and support. It's important to remember that supportive technology doesn't teach—it's you and your instruction that will make the most lasting impact on your students' learning.

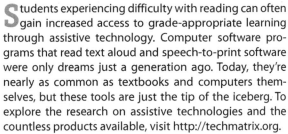

(Buly & Valencia, 2002; Morris, 2008; Wanzek et al., 2010). Older readers with specific learning disabilities typically achieve significantly below their peers—on average 3.4 years behind them (Melekoglu, 2011)—and one in five students with a learning disability reads at least five grade levels below their peers (NJCLD, 2008; Wagner et al., 2003). This does not have to be the case. With developmentally appropriate instruction and individualized accommodations, students with learning differences *can* and *should* achieve at the same level as their peers (Allington, 2012; Connor, Morrison, Fishman, Schatschneider, & Underwood, 2007; Klenk & Kibby, 2000). Your developmentally responsive instruction and student-centered accommodations, along with supplemental intervention services, will help ensure your students' optimal levels of achievement.

Accommodating Students Experiencing Difficulty with Literacy

Accommodations are defined as intentional and essential instructional modifications that are legally guaranteed to students who are identified as having a specific learning disability, as well as to English language learners. Accommodations make the regular curriculum accessible to these students. Appropriate accommodations are usually specified in students' IEPs and/or specially designed instruction. Typically, accommodations fall into the following five different categories: extended time, grouping and special settings, differentiated materials and assistive technology, instructional modifications, and student response (NICHCY, 2010b; NCLD, 2006). Examples of each type of accommodation follow:

Extended Time

- Providing students extra time to complete assignments and/or tests
- Breaking longer assignments or long-term projects into small parts or spreading the work across several days or class periods
- Allowing frequent breaks if needed

Grouping and Special Settings

- Providing students opportunities for small group instruction
- Working one-to-one with qualified teachers
- Working with peers or older reading buddies
- Providing quiet workspaces
- Using preferential seating

Differentiated Materials and Assistive Technology

- Providing access to grade-level appropriate content through technology-assisted reading material (books on tape or electronic readers)
- Using technology to record your class presentations and instruction for future reference
- Using word processors instead of writing assignments by hand, or using voice-activated transcription software
- Providing materials and directions in the child's native language
- Using texts at the student's independent and instructional levels in both reading class and in content area instruction

Instructional Modifications

- Reducing the length of assignments
- Providing graphic organizers or other scaffolds
- Supplementing oral directions with written directions and vice versa
- Offering bilingual education
- Adjusting the pace of instruction
- Providing opportunities for extended practice
- Simplifying the language of directions, using pictures, icons, or gestures

Student Response

- Allowing students to provide answers orally, providing a scribe, or using assistive technology so writing does not get in the way of the student demonstrating his or her knowledge
- Allowing students to answer test questions in their native language
- Providing an interpreter

Accommodations are intended to "level the playing field" for students with learning disabilities; they do not give these students an added or unfair advantage. If your students' accommodations do not seem to be helping them gain access to the regular curriculum, it's important to continue to monitor their progress and make additional modifications with input from the student, other teachers, parents, and other caregivers.

Supporting the Development of *All* Students: Research-Based Best Practices

Children with learning differences often benefit from the very same instruction typically developing students benefit from—they sometimes just need more practice, more time to move through the scope and sequence, or more explicit modeling and coaching. In short, research-based best practices for typically developing students are often the very same practices we recommend for students who struggle and for English learners (Allington, 2012; McCormick & Zutell, 2010). In this

Working and Collaborating

Helping Students with Learning Disabilities Be Successful with Homework

Homework can be a chore for students and families alike, but for students with learning disabilities it can present an extra challenge! Before addressing specifically how you can be supportive of your students' homework efforts, however, be sure to keep this observation in mind: When teaching any new strategy or understanding for the first time, do *not* assign homework on that new material to be completed that night. Homework should be assigned only *after* the initial instruction has been applied by the students under the teacher's watchful eye and discussed with other students. In other words, be sure to apply the "gradual release of responsibility" model to your assignment of homework as well. Once you have done so, you may help your students be successful with homework by following these five tips (adapted from Warger, 2001):

1) **Assign homework that's predictable, clear, and appropriate.** Make your expectations for homework explicit by providing directions for completing homework in writing. You'll also make homework more manageable if you:

   - Differentiate homework based on students' developmental stage.
   - Define the criteria by which the homework will be evaluated.
   - Support the completion of long-term assignments by periodically checking on students' progress or breaking the assignment into more manageable pieces.
   - Coordinate with other teachers to avoid homework overload.

2) **Provide students with appropriate accommodations for homework assignments**. Whatever accommodations are appropriate in the classroom are appropriate for homework, too. Common accommodations include fewer problems/examples; adjusting the length of an assignment; differentiating the materials, particularly reading materials; providing graphic organizers to support reading comprehension or to assist with the planning of a writing assignment; and allowing alternative response formats (instead of writing the answers to questions, the student may dictate and record the answers). Students should also have access to assistive technologies in their home settings if they're necessary or helpful for the completion of homework assignments.

3) **Teach study and organizational skills.** All students benefit from instruction in how to set up a home-work space that's free of distractions and appropriately stocked with learning materials such as pens and pencils, index cards, highlighters, Post-it notes, paper, and so on. Students also benefit from time management and project management tips including:

   - How to estimate the time it will take to complete an assignment
   - How to plan the use of time and prioritize tasks
   - How to take good notes
   - How to prepare for a test or exam
   - Knowing when (and how) to ask for help

4) **Teach students how to use a homework notebook.** Many students with learning disabilities have difficulty with organization and task completion. You'll support their development by teaching them how to use a homework notebook and calendar, as well as helping them develop systems for keeping their important papers and materials organized.

5) **Focus on regular home/school communication.** Parents, grandparents, and other adult caregivers are partners in all aspects of your students' educational experience, and particularly in the area of homework. Be sure to support them in this important role by following some of these tips:

   - Provide a list of things they might do to assist their student with homework—for example, setting up a daily homework routine or reading word problems aloud.
   - Provide helpful articles, website links, and your specific expectations for parental involvement with homework.
   - Share regular feedback with parents and care-givers about how their student is doing with homework.
   - Provide ways to reach you at school by phone and/or e-mail and make it clear how soon they can expect a response (for example, within 24 or 48 hours).

You can learn more about helping students with learning disabilities manage homework, develop study skills, and succeed in the general education program by visiting this website: www.ldonline.org. For more specific information about engaging the support of parents whose children have learning disabilities, visit www.ldonline.org/article/c668.

section we'll review a few suggestions for making your instruction more effective for *all* students, not just those experiencing difficulties. You'll find additional suggestions for research-based best practices in each of the developmental chapters (Chapters 6 through 10) as well as in Chapter 5.

Word Sorts: Varying the Complexity

Common Core Connection

Reading Standards:
Foundational Skills –
Phonological
Awareness; Phonics
and Word Recognition

Sorting is a basic staple of word study instruction and it's something you'll probably do with your students nearly every day. Sorts can be as simple or complex as you wish to make them: For students who *excel* in word study, you may wish to make your sorts more difficult, and you can do so by adding more categories or less obvious contrasts. The sounds of /m/ and /r/, for example, are obvious contrasts, /m/ and /n/ are less obvious and therefore quite difficult. To ensure your students' success, begin with the more obvious contrasts before introducing the more difficult, less obvious contrasts. You can also increase the difficulty of sorts by including more words, more difficult words or more oddballs. As always, when varying the complexity of your word sorts, be sure you continue to work at your students' instructional levels.

If some of your students find a sort too difficult, and this may be the case with many of your readers who struggle, you can do one of several things to accommodate their learning, including:

- Reduce the number of categories.
- Reduce the total number of words.

Children's Literature Connection

Great Books about Children and Adolescents with Learning Difficulties

Picture Books

Bunting, E. (1989). *The Wednesday surprise*. New York: Clarion.

Cheltenham Elementary School Kindergartners. (1991). *We are all alike . . . we are all different*. New York: Scholastic.

Fox, M. (1997). *Whoever you are*. New York: Harcourt Children's Books.

Polacco, P. (1998). *Thank you, Mr. Falker*. New York: Philomel.

Polacco, P. (2010). *The junkyard wonders*. New York: Philomel.

Stuve-Bodeen, S. (1998). *We'll paint the octopus red*. Bethesda, MD: Woodbine House.

Yashima, T. (1955). *Crow boy*. New York: Viking.

Books for the Upper Elementary Grades

Draper, S. M. (2002). *Double dutch*. New York: Atheneum Books for Young Readers.

Gavalda, A., & Rosner, G. (2003). *95 pounds of hope*. New York: Viking.

Lord, C. (2006). *Rules*. New York: Scholastic.

Martino, A. C. (2005). *Pinned*. New York: Harcourt Children's Books.

Petrillo, G. (2007). *Keep your ear on the ball*. Gardiner, ME: Tilbury House.

Philbrick, R. (1993). *Freak the mighty*. New York: Scholastic/Blue Sky.

Spinelli, J. (1999). *Maniac Magee*. New York: Little Brown Books for Young Readers.

Spinelli, J. (2000). *Stargirl*. New York: Knopf Books for Young Readers.

Winkler, H., & Oliver, L. (2003). *Niagara falls, or does it? #1*. New York: Grosset & Dunlap.

Books for Middle School Students

Abeel, S. (2001). *Reach for the moon*. New York: Orchard.

Abeel, S. (2005). *My thirteenth winter: A memoir*. New York: Scholastic.

Alexie, S. (2007). *Flight*. New York: Grove/Black Cat.

Baskin, N. R. (2009). *Anything but typical*. New York: Simon & Schuster Books for Young Readers.

Bloor, E. (1997). *Tangerine*. New York: Harcourt.

Flake, S. (2012). *Pinned*. Scholastic.

Trueman, T. (2001). *Stuck in neutral*. New York: Harper Teen.

- Use the categories from the previous week's list and add just one new category.
- Use the sort for more than one week of instruction.

These accommodations may be appropriate for some of your learners *every* week, particularly those who need additional time and/or repetition to learn new material, and students with decoding and spelling challenges.

Common Core Connection

Language Standards:
Conventions of
Standard English

Building Background Knowledge and Using Graphic Organizers

Many of your students, particularly English learners and students from high-poverty back-grounds, will need your assistance with building background knowledge for the subjects they're studying or a text they're reading. For example, middle school students listening to selected read-ings from a primary source such as the *Narrative of the Life of Frederick Douglass, an American Slave, Written by Himself* (Douglass,1845), usually need additional information about the histori-cal context surrounding the life of Frederick Douglass before they're able to listen (or read) with adequate comprehension. You can build this background knowledge through a number of ways, including video snippets, short stories, lectures and discussion, by examining artifacts from the time period, and by reading and discussing less complex texts on these topics.

Common Core Connection

Reading Standards
for Literature and
Informational Text:
Key Ideas and Details

As students acquire more background knowledge, it is helpful for them to arrange this information in a graphic organizer such as a **concept map** as seen in Figure 11.3. You'll introduce graphic organiz-ers like this as a means to keep track of new learning, but also as a tool to help students plan their

FIGURE 11.3 Concept Map of Frederick Douglass

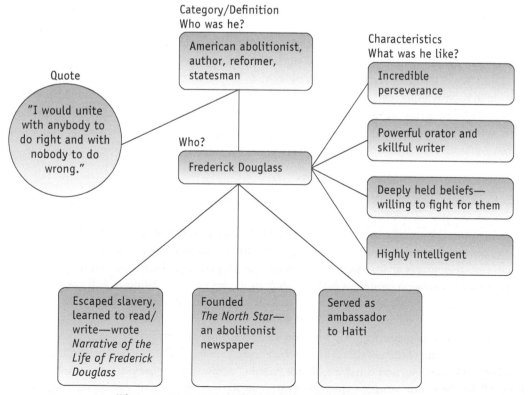

Source: Flanigan et al., 2011.

FIGURE 11.4 Sentence Frame to Support Reading Comprehension and to Teach Text Structure

Issue: Federalists vs. Anti-Federalists

Sentence Frame: One of the major issues that confronted the framers of the Constitution was _____. On one side were the_____. They believed _____. On the other side were the _____. They believed _____.

The eventual solution to this problem was _____. This solved the problem by _____.

Source: Flanigan et al., 2011.

Common Core Connection

Reading Standards for Literature and Informational Text: Craft and Structure

Common Core Connection

Writing Standards: Production and Distribution of Writing

writing. Over time, you'll expect your students to create their own graphic organizers before reading, and they'll add to them during and after reading. Graphic organizers can also be a great study tool.

Sentence Frames

Another common graphic organizer that can support students' developing understanding of text structure, particularly informational text, are sentence frames, as seen in Figure 11.4 (Flanigan et al., 2011). Here, we see how a teacher scaffolded a student's comparative essay on the Federalists and the Anti-Federalists. Sentence frames, like other graphic organizers, can help students identify the big ideas in their reading, but also provide a structure by which they can respond to writing prompts (Graff & Birkenstein, 2006; Zwiers, 2006). When using sentence frames, you'll intentionally help students identify the underlying structure of the text (in this example, a comparative essay) and related signal words and phrases—for instance, "One of the major issues...," "On one side...," and "On the other side...." Identifying and talking about the structure helps them begin to apply these structures and signal words to other writing experiences.

The goals of using sentence frames is twofold: to help students identify the important information in their reading, and also to learn how to effectively express this information by using appropriate text structure and signal words in their writing. Graphic organizers should always be seen as a temporary scaffold to achieve improved reading comprehension, deeper thinking, and/or more effective written expression. They are a *means* to an *end*.

Teach Comprehension Routines

Effective readers use comprehension strategies automatically and effortlessly when they read, and more intentionally when meaning breaks down (Duke & Pearson, 2002). While we want all students to use comprehension strategies flexibly and as needed, many readers who struggle do not reach this level of integration or intentionality (Gersten, Fuchs, Williams, & Baker, 2001). Reciprocal teaching is an instructional strategy that helps readers learn how to integrate and use key comprehension strategies *before*, *during*, and *after* reading (Palincsar & Brown, 1984). Reciprocal teaching has been found effective with readers who struggle, English learners, and typically developing students as well (NRP, 2000).

When modeling reciprocal teaching, you'll select a passage, paragraph, chapter, or text (usually something relatively short) and demonstrate four specific strategies: predicting, summarizing, questioning, and clarifying. *Before* reading, demonstrate how you predict what the text will be about; don't forget to provide a rationale for your prediction! *During* reading, you'll periodically stop to summarize what you read and ask questions about the text and the author's purpose, as well as attempt to clarify any confusing parts. Before you resume reading, you'll model another prediction. *After* reading you'll repeat the comprehension routine again.

After sufficient modeling, invite your students to lead the routine and become the "teacher"—this is how the teaching is "reciprocal." After some guided practice, your students will begin to internalize this comprehension routine, and with your encouragement and scaffolding, they will begin to use it as a discussion protocol for small group conversations, too (Oczkus, 2010). As you get to know your students, you'll become aware of the students who *really* need texts broken down into smaller, more manageable chunks. With these students, you may begin with a paragraph, then gradually work from there toward larger chunks of text—a page, several pages, a section, and later a chapter. For more information on reciprocal teaching, refer to Chapter 8.

Common Core Connection

Speaking and Listening: Comprehension and Collaboration

Increase "High-Success" Reading Practice

It stands to reason that the more you practice something, the better you get. Think about it: Musicians need to practice every day, professional athletes practice every day, and effective readers, well, they need to practice every day, too! Studies of time spent reading consistently show that the more you read, the better reader you become (Anderson, Wilson, & Fielding, 1988; Brozo, Shiel, & Topping, 2008; Cipielewski & Stanovich, 1992; Krashen, 2004). The same is true for readers who struggle. Studies of the most effective teachers affirm the importance of reading practice in the regular literacy classroom (Allington & Johnston, 2001; Pressley et al., 2001; Taylor, Pearson, Clark, & Walpole, 1999) as well as in intervention settings (Mathes et al., 2005; Pinnell, Lyons, DeFord, Bryk, & Seltzer, 1994; Scanlon, Vellutino, Small, Fanuele, & Sweeney, 2005). Unfortunately, all too often, readers who struggle get the least amount of reading practice because their instruction is so focused on skill and strategy development, and they're not particularly motivated to read on their own (McGill-Franzen & Allington, 1990; Rowan & Guthrie, 1989; Vaughn et al., 2003). Your classroom will be different.

Common Core Connection

Reading Standards for Literature and Informational Text: Range of Reading and Level of Text Complexity

Strategies for the Classroom

Tips for Teaching Comprehension Strategies

One of the single most powerful things you can do to help readers who struggle is teach them how to monitor their reading and use comprehension strategies effectively (Allington & McGill-Franzen, 2008; Duke & Pearson, 2002; Knapp, 1995). Keene (2002) and Pressley (2005) offer several tips for teaching comprehension strategies:

- Model the use of comprehension strategies using the "gradual release of responsibility model": demonstration, guided practice, and independent application (Pearson & Gallagher, 1983).
- Explicitly teach students one strategy at a time for a brief amount of time.
- Model how to apply these strategies in both fiction and informational texts.

- After teaching the strategies individually, move to comprehension routines such as reciprocal teaching. Be sure students understand that the goal of strategy instruction is to monitor and understand what they're reading.
- Encourage students to become more metacognitive so they intentionally use their comprehension strategies when meaning breaks down.
- Reinforce strategy instruction in small guided reading groups.
- Regularly confer with readers to ensure that they're attending to meaning when reading.

Readers not only need time to practice 30 or more minutes during each school day—they also need books they *want* to read and *can* read. Allington (2009) calls this "high-success" reading. In other words, students need interesting books they can read with high levels of accuracy; high levels of accuracy can foster successful practice with word recognition, fluency, and comprehension. Helping students select just-right books—books at their independent reading level—will help ensure productive reading practice each day.

Morphological Analysis: Helping Students "Unlock" the Meaning of Words

As you've learned, most words in English are created by combining free and bound roots with affixes. Readers who struggle are usually capable of becoming aware of and understanding the role of morphology (for example, see Katz & Carlisle, 2009; Wolter, Wood, & D'zatko, 2009). This knowledge will help older beginning and transitional readers, and intermediate-level readers as well. The value of this knowledge for older readers who are at the earlier developmental levels may lie in supporting their vocabulary development and word consciousness—an awareness that word structure is logical and follows certain rules. When students understand basic morphological processes, they realize that words and their structure are predictable, and printed words are not randomly arranged sequences of letters that frustrate them when they attempt to read them. This insight gives all students, particularly readers who struggle, the keys needed to unlock, understand, and remember the meanings of words, as well as assist them in their decoding and word recognition attempts. Perhaps most important, vocabulary knowledge is strongly related to reading comprehension.

Increasingly, published materials are incorporating the insights from the most effective and engaging ways to teach vocabulary, especially the morphological, *generative* aspect. Figure 11.5 presents the first part of a lesson from a vocabulary unit in a program developed specifically for adolescent readers who are experiencing difficulty with reading, and for English learners.

FIGURE 11.5 Example of Generative Activity in a Published Program

> **2. Related Words**
>
> **All in the Family** Remind students that a group of words that has the same root or base word is called a word family and that words belonging to the same word family have related meanings. Knowing about root or base words and their word families can help students to figure out the meanings of unfamiliar words encountered in their reading.
>
> Explain that the base word and word family for **concentrating** is *concentrate,* as in "We need to **concentrate** on our new words so we will learn them well." Have students brainstorm related words from the word family *concentrate.* (See the following list to aid in your class discussion.)

Source: Consortium on Reaching Excellence in Education, 2012.

FIGURE 11.6 Supplemental Programs: Technology as an Instructional Tool

Software and Programs

Interactive games can support the development and practice of literacy skills in your classroom. Software and websites such as Starfall (www.starfall.com), Earobics (www.earobics.com), and Earobics REACH (www.hmhinnovation.com/Earobics-Reach.php) provide students with supplemental practice and skills development. Many students find these experiences quite motivating. Other print-based supplemental programs such as *Word Study in Action* (Bear, Invernizzi, Templeton, & Johnston, 2012) have also been found to be effective with readers who struggle (Eddy, Ruitman, Hankel, Matelski, & Schmalstig 2011).

Study Aids

Many students also appreciate digital study aids, including graphic organizers, flash cards, and quiz and game generators as found on www.flashcard.com, www.eduplace.com/graphicorganizer/, and www.quizlet.com, to name just a few.

Evaluating the Effectiveness of Supplemental Programs

Although no supplemental program is perfect, you can get information about the effectiveness of different programs and resources by visiting the *What Works Clearinghouse* (http://ies.ed.gov/ncee/wwc/topic.aspx?sid=8) or *RTI4Success* (rti4success.org). Of course, monitoring your own students' motivation and skills development is the most important indicator of a program or tool's success.

Another program, Earobics REACH, provides generative vocabulary instruction in the form of an online, interactive intervention resource designed for intermediate and middle school readers who struggle (Brady, Morrison, Rasinski, Shanahan, & Templeton, 2006). In this program, students design avatars who walk through morphological processes explicitly and engagingly. For example, an avatar provides the student with a sense of how the root *–auto–* combines with other roots, and why. This kind of computer animation not only supports morphological development, but for some students, can provide exactly the type of motivation and engagement necessary to build their vocabulary and hook them on reading. (See Figure 11.6 for more on using technology as an instructional tool.) Importantly, you'll connect this kind of vocabulary instruction to authentic reading and writing tasks, as well as help students apply their understanding of morphology to strategically "unlock" the meaning of unknown words. These insights can also support students' decoding of multisyllabic words.

Common Core Connection

Language Standards:
Vocabulary
Acquisition and Use

Attend to Motivation and Engagement

All too often, students who experience reading challenges are characterized as being unmotivated. This is not the case in most instances, but it's sometimes true, and these students' lack of motivation might even be understandable. They often experience frustration with the task of reading—it isn't easy, it often doesn't make sense, and they see little value in it. This is especially true for students who have few opportunities to engage in real reading for real purposes. Again, this doesn't have to be the case for readers who struggle or any other student in your classroom.

Motivation and engagement include three dimensions: cognitively stimulating activities, socially interactive learning, and intrinsic motivation (Guthrie, 2004; Guthrie & Wigfield, 2000). Figure 11.7 highlights some ways these three factors will express themselves in your classroom.

Motivation is a powerful factor in learning to read. Researchers have found that engaged, purposeful reading is a *greater predictor* of reading success than students' gender, ethnicity, socioeconomic status, or parents' education level (Guthrie, 2004)! Engaged readers spend 500 percent more time reading than disengaged readers, and a student's ability to choose his or her reading materials seems to be a critical factor in developing and sustaining motivation and reading engagement. Researchers point out that teachers who provide students with easy access to interesting texts see an effect size of 1.6 for comprehension and 1.5 for motivation (Guthrie & Humenick, 2004). This may not seem like much, but an effect size of 1.0 would move a

FIGURE 11.7 Dimensions of Motivation and Engagement

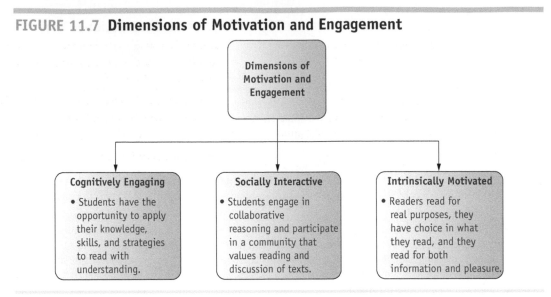

student's level of achievement from the 16th percentile (well below average) to a solidly average performance at the 50th percentile! Students who choose only some of their reading materials still see positive effects (1.2 for comprehension and 0.95 for motivation).

Providing all your students, including those with reading challenges, the opportunity to engage in sustained and meaningful reading experiences and conversations with their peers, as well as some choice in their reading materials, can have a powerful effect on their motivation, engagement, and reading achievement.

Chapter Summary

Readers who struggle vary little from students with learning disabilities, yet each one has her or his own unique set of circumstances and characteristics. Profiles of students who experience reading challenges can help teachers like you analyze assessment data and plan developmentally responsive instruction and intervention. By using the strategies outlined in this chapter and throughout this book, accelerating the achievement of *all* learners, including readers who struggle, is well within your reach.

Suggested Extension Activities

- Select one of the strategies for improving the achievement of all learners found at the end of this chapter and plan a content-area lesson that incorporates one—or more—of those strategies.
- Examine the assessment data of several readers experiencing difficulty. Use the questions in the opening vignette and the profiles of readers who struggle to plan classroom-based small group instruction that will help accelerate these students' growth in literacy.

- Meet with a cooperating teacher or look over your own class list and create an accommodations matrix that specifies each student's name, disability or area of difficulty, general accommodations, and specific accommodations for reading, writing, and word study. Keep this matrix handy when planning future lessons for these students.

Recommended Professional Resources

Allington, R. L. (2012). *What really matters for struggling readers* (3rd ed.). Upper Saddle River, NJ: Pearson.

Flanigan, K., Hayes, L., Templeton, S., Bear, D. R., Invernizzi, M., & Johnston, F. (2010). *Words their way with struggling readers: Word study for reading, vocabulary, and spelling instruction, grades 4–12.* Upper Saddle River, NJ: Pearson.

Johnston, F., Invernizzi, M., Juel, C., & Lewis-Wagner, D. (2009). *Book buddies: A tutoring framework for struggling readers* (2nd ed.). New York: Guilford.

McCormick, S., & Zutell, J. (2011). *Instructing students who have literacy problems.* Boston: Pearson Education.

Morris, D. (2005). *The Howard Street tutoring manual: Teaching at-risk readers in the primary grades* (2nd ed.). New York: Guilford.

Morris, D. (2008). *Diagnosis and correction of reading problems.* New York: Guilford.

Walpole, S., & McKenna, M. C. (2009). *How to plan differentiated reading instruction: Resources for grades K–3.* New York: Guilford.

Walpole, S., McKenna, M. C., & Philippakos, Z. A. (2011). *Differentiated reading instruction in grades 4 and 5: Strategies and resources.* New York: Guilford.

Online Resources

Information on Specific Learning Disabilities

Resources for understanding and teaching students with specific learning disabilities can be found at a number of reputable sites, including:

Learning Disabilities Online: *www.ldonline.org*
The International Dyslexia Association: *www.interdys.org*
Council for Exceptional Children: *www.cec.sped.org*
Learning Disabilities Association of America: *www.ldanatl.org*

Response to Intervention and Instruction

As your school and district begin to implement RTI, you might find some of these online resources valuable:

National Center for Response to Intervention: *www.rti4success.org*
RTI Action Network: *www.rtinetwork.org*
Wisconsin RTI Center: *www.wisconsinrticenter.org*

Glossary

academic language   Includes new and abstract or technical *vocabulary* and more complex *sentences*.

Adequate Yearly Progress (AYP)   A formula that measures a school's progress toward *all* students meeting or exceeding the standards in key content areas.

affix   Bound morphemes that attach to the beginning or the end of a root word or Greek/Latin root; the "umbrella" term for a prefix or suffix.

alliteration   The same beginning sound repeated to reinforce letter names and sounds; for example, *Sita and Sasha see the sack.*

alphabetic layer   The layer of the spelling system explored by beginning readers and writers; the sequential, left-to-right correspondence between letters and sounds within words.

alphabetic principle   The understanding that letters represent sounds and are matched in a left-to-right sequence within printed words.

analytic phonics or analogy phonics   Applying knowledge of a spelling pattern (rime, phonogram) in a known word to determine the pronunciation of an unfamiliar word.

analytic talk   Supports readers' focus in analyzing and responding to aspects of narrative or informational text.

argument   Measured and logical presentation of a point of view. Well-constructed and presented arguments are invaluable in both education and the workplace. The argument form is used to change points of view, move others to act in a certain way, or convince others of the reasonableness of your position.

assimilated prefix   A prefix in which the spelling and sound of the consonant have been changed so that it is easier to pronounce when added to a root word or bound root; for example, *ad- + count = account*; *com- + duct = conduct*.

basal readers   The traditional term for textbooks that are designed and used to teach reading to schoolchildren.

base   (see *base word*)

base word   A word to which prefixes and/or suffixes may be added; for example, *camp, wrestle* (synonymous with *base*).

beginning stage   Learners attend much more closely to print in the beginning stage of literacy. They learn to "read the spaces," developing a concept of word in text, and full phonemic awareness.

big books   Oversized children's books or texts usually measuring about 18" × 24" so they can be viewed by some distance; typically used in shared reading in the primary grades.

blended words   Blended words are sounds and/or syllables from different words that have been blended together to form a new word, such as *soundscape* (sound and landscape) and *ginormous* (gigantic and enormous).

blind writing sort   One partner calls out the words while the other writes the words in the appropriate spelling pattern category; for example, *faint* would be written in the column under the key word *train*, *gate* would be written in the column under the key word *game*.

book talks   Short and lively "infomercials" designed to encourage students to read specific books.

bound morpheme   A unit of meaning that cannot occur by itself but must be *bound* or connected to another morpheme (prefixes, suffixes, and many Greek and Latin roots are bound morphemes).

choral reading   When students read a piece of text aloud together in unison.

clipped words   Clipped words are those such as deli (delicatessen) and grad (graduate).

cognates   Words in different languages that are spelled the same or similarly and have the same or similar meanings; for example, English/Spanish *artistic/artistíco*, Spanish/French *inquisitivo/inquisiteur*.

cognition   Thought; the act of thinking.

cohesion   Connections among sentence-, paragraph-, and text-level relationships. A text with a *high* degree of cohesion reflects explicit connections among words and sentences, shows more concrete language, and repeats and/or summarizes important points along the way. Texts with *low* cohesion place more demands on readers, requiring them to infer more connections among the information.

compounding   The morphological process from which we derive compound words; for example, *rainbow* and *overkill*.

comprehensive core reading programs   Commercially available reading programs that typically include a teacher's manual, student books, and other supplemental materials including workbooks and technology used to teach reading at a given grade level.

concept of word in text   A child's ability to point to each word accurately as reading lines of a memorized text.

concepts about print   An understanding of the ways print works, including directionality, spacing, punctuation, letters, and words.

connotation   The associations that a word takes on—what the word suggests to us, how it makes us feel, and the personal associations we bring to it beyond the word's denotative meaning.

constructivist approach   An active, hands-on, learner-centered approach to instruction that encourages students to collaborate and co-construct understandings and knowledge through talk and shared experiences.

Content Directed Reading Activity (CDRA)   A strategy for approaching informational texts; teachers teach, facilitate, and move students toward independence in applying knowledge of how to use the features of informational texts as they *actively* preview, question/make predictions, read, and review the information presented in the text.

continuant sounds   Sounds that can be isolated and elongated without distorting the sound the letter represents; for example, *mmmm*an and *sssss*it).

conversational vocabulary   The most frequent, basic words in the language. They frequently label common things or actions and they seldom require direct instruction because they are used so often; for example, *chair, fun, happy,* and *ran*.

criterion-referenced assessments   Assessments that compare students' achievement to a criterion or standard; sometimes referred to as *standards-based assessments* and *outcomes-based assessments*.

critical literacy   A stance readers take that allows them to critically analyze, question, and understand an author's perspective as well as any underlying issues of power, inequality, or injustice within a text.

cultural diversity   Any perceived difference from the dominant culture; for example, differences in race, ethnicity, socioeconomic status, linguistic ability, or language use (Dee & Henkin, 2000).

culture   Reflects the language, beliefs, values, literature, art, and institutions of a group. A culture is a framework for making meaning, and the students in our classrooms see themselves in terms of the culture from which they come.

cumulative assessment   Assessment that comes at the end of a series of lessons or unit. Sometimes called *summative assessment* and *outcomes assessment*.

curriculum-based assessment measures   Assessments that are strategically distributed throughout the school year and used to monitor students' progress toward meeting the standards at a given grade level.

D

decodable texts   Short texts that are written to contain several examples of the phonic/spelling patterns children are learning in their word study and reading instruction.

decode   Translating printed letters into sound in order to identify words and their meanings.

deep orthography   A spelling system in which the relationship between sound and spelling is complex. Sounds are often spelled depending on where they occur within a word, as well as on other sounds that are around them. Meaning or *morphological* features are also represented in the system; although their pronunciation may vary depending on the word in which they occur, their spelling usually remains consistent; for example, *resign*/*resignation*. English is an example of a deep orthography.

denotation   The literal or dictionary meaning of a word.

derivational morphology   The processes by which hundreds of thousands of words in English are *derived* from root words and Greek and Latin roots through combinations with affixes and other roots.

derivational suffixes   The "workhorses" of derivational morphology, these suffixes usually change the syntactic role of a root, although the core meaning of the root is usually retained; for example, *predict* (verb), *predict + –able* (adjective), *predict + –ion* (noun).

differentiated instruction   Instruction that is responsive to students' developmental needs.

digital immigrants   People who are not as comfortable with technology and therefore have to work rather intentionally to integrate it into their lives and teaching.

digital natives   People who see and use technology as a natural part of their environment.

disciplinary literacy   Learning and communicating the specific information, ideas, and ways of thinking that characterize each discipline or subject-matter area: English/language arts, the sciences, mathematics, and the social sciences/history. Developing these more specialized strategies and skills will enable students to read and write more effectively in particular disciplines.

domain-specific vocabulary   Words that occur in specific content areas/disciplines such as mathematics *(numerator, rectilinear)*, science *(enzyme, magnetic field)*, the arts *(bass clef, impressionism)*, and history and social science *(ante bellum, preamble)*.

E

early intervention   Intervention designed for children at risk for developing reading difficulties. The goal of early intervention is the prevention of later reading problems.

echo read   When students read a section of text aloud after it has been read aloud to them.

emergent stage   The emergent stage of literacy ranges from the preschool years through kindergarten (though some first-graders will still be in this stage). Children begin to develop concepts about print in this stage of development.

environmental print   Signs, labels, and other print found in the classroom environment or the students' broader community.

expressive vocabulary   Words that an individual understands and is able to use in speech and/or writing.

F

figurative language　Words or phrases that are not used in their literal sense but instead to compare, emphasize, clarify, or open up a new way of looking at and thinking about our world; for example, simile/metaphor, hyperbole, and personification.

finger-point reading　When a child in the emergent or beginning stages of reading uses a finger to help maintain voice–print match.

fluency　The ability to identify words quickly and accurately and to read orally with expression.

formative assessment　Assessment that is ongoing and used to inform your teaching and evaluate its effectiveness.

free morpheme　A unit of meaning (word) that can occur by itself (*snitch, cattle*) and that cannot be broken down into smaller meaning units.

functional print　A form of informational text that is accessed to get practical information; for example, menus, directions, recipes, or schedules.

G

general academic vocabulary　Words that students encounter frequently in their reading and should be able to use in their writing. These words are also likely to occur in formal oral language contexts such as lectures. They occur across all content areas; for example, *coincidence, analyze, evaluate,* and *paradox.*

generalizations　Students' reflections about the "rules" of the English spelling system.

Gradual Release of Responsibility　A model of instruction that makes explicit what and why something is to be learned. Teachers use this model as a vehicle for (1) modeling, demonstrating, or sharing what is to be learned; (2) supporting and guiding students as they together attempt to apply what is being learned; then (3) ensuring that students will be able to successfully and independently apply and use what they have learned.

grand conversation　A term often used in literacy instruction to refer to students' reading in which they read deeply, discuss thoroughly, and experience a book in depth through collaborative conversations.

H

headers　Pictures, words, or objects that are used to identify the features or categories of a sort.

High stakes testing　A testing program used for accountability purposes.

high-frequency word　One of the approximately 300 words that occur most frequently in spoken and written English, and which children are expected to learn by the end of second grade. These words are sometimes called *sight words,* as students are expected to read them "on sight" and without hesitation.

high success reading or independent-level reading　Unsupported reading practice in which children will be reading text with a high rate of accuracy—95 percent or better.

homographs　Words that have the same spelling but different meanings, and quite often have different pronunciations as well; for example, *lead* a movement versus *lead* is removed from gas and paint.

homophones　Words that sound the same but are spelled differently and have different meanings; for example, *main/mane, sight/site/cite.* The meaning of a homophone determines its spelling.

I

idiomatic expressions/idioms　Groups of words whose meanings can't be understood by putting together the meanings of each of the words in the group; for example, *dead as a doornail, higher than a kite.*

individualized education plan (IEP)　Under the Education for All Handicapped Children Act and Individuals with Disabilities Education Act, children eligible for special education services receive individualized education plans that address appropriate accommodations in the following categories: extended time, grouping and special settings, differentiated materials and assistive technology, instructional modifications, and student response.

inflectional morphology　Adding suffixes that indicate verb tense and number; for example, crawl*ed*/crawl*ing*; desk*s*. These suffixes are most commonly referred to as *inflectional endings.*

informational patterns/text structures　These patterns are *signaled* by particular words and phrases, and are a critical part of *academic language;* for example, description, temporal/sequential, cause/effect, compare/contrast, and problem/solution.

informational text features　Transitional readers begin exploring these features in greater depth; for example, the role of *headings* to signal importance, *captions* to describe pictures or illustrations, *boldface print* to highlight important words that can also be found in the glossary.

interactive writing　Identical in purpose to the *language-experience approach,* interactive writing includes children's (and teachers') attempts to compose a story or message. Interactive writing is sometimes referred to as *sharing the pen, shared writing,* or *guided writing.*

intermediate stage　Students' developing understanding of texts supports their reading of more extensive texts, over longer periods of time. Reading interests may expand considerably. This is the stage during which students' acquisition of vocabulary from wide reading begins to increase dramatically.

interrater reliability　A measure of how consistently teachers score student work.

invented spelling　The type of spelling that characterizes emergent and early beginning learners' attempts with writing. These children will sound out and spell the most salient sounds they hear in words, usually leaving out less-obvious sounds. Also called *sound spelling* or *phonic spelling.*

I.R.E. cycle   A discourse pattern in which the teacher *Initiates* a question, the child *Responds* to the question, and then the teacher *Evaluates* the response. A common pattern in many literacy classrooms, it usually discourages active thinking, engagement, and the collaborative construction of meaning.

key pictures   Pictures that exemplify the sounds being studied in a given sort. Key pictures are often used as headers and are placed at the top of a column in sort.

keywords   Words that exemplify the features of a given sort. These words are usually placed at the top of a column in a word sort and can be used as headers.

language-experience approach (LEA)   Based on their discussion about a common experience, the teacher writes down verbatim the contributions from several children. These compositions or *dictations*, as they're often called, are an important source for developing children's concepts about print, the relationship between print and speech, and their beginning sight-word vocabularies.

lexical knowledge   The automatic engagement and integration of phonological knowledge, orthographic knowledge, and children's familiarity with words.

linguistic modification   To simplify one's language when speaking with or giving directions to students who are English learners.

liquid sounds   The sounds /r/ and /l/. They affect the sounds of vowels, as with *a* (*-ar*) and *i* (*-ill*). They tend to "roll around" in the mouth, which is why they have been termed liquid.

literary devices   Aspects of an author's craft that are used to develop a narrative; for example, *metaphor*, *simile*, *allusion*, *symbolism*, and *personification*.

M

meaning layer   The layer of the spelling system explored primarily by intermediate and skillful readers and writers; how morphology is *visually* represented by the spelling system; the consistent spelling of affixes, root words, and Greek and Latin word roots among words that are related in meaning; for example, *humane humanity*; *beneficial/ benefactor/benevolent*.

media literacy   Having the skills, knowledge, and dispositions to safely and effectively use, create, analyze, and interpret messages in both print and nonprint forms.

metacognition   The ability to think about one's thinking (for example, to realize that one is having difficulty comprehending during reading, and adjusting one's reading strategy use to attend to the difficulty).

metalinguistic skill   The ability to attend to *sound* apart from the meaning of a word or words. Such skills include

the components of *phonological awareness;* for example, detecting rhyme, clapping syllables in words, and attending to individual consonant and vowel sounds within a syllable.

miscue   When a reader misreads a word. Teachers attend to a student's miscues because they provide insight into what type(s) of information that reader may be relying on to decode words.

morpheme   The smallest unit of meaning in a language.

morphological knowledge   Understanding of the processes by which morphemes are combined into words and how that process determines the meaning of words (affixes plus root words; affixes plus Greek and Latin word roots).

morphology   The correspondence between meaningful word parts and their underlying meaning, and the processes by which those word parts combine to form words.

multiple-meaning words   Words that represent different meanings, depending on the context in which they occur; for example, *find* the missing toy versus an archaeological *find*.

Narrative Directed Reading Activity   A strategy for approaching the reading of narratives, fictional and literary; teachers guide students in combining their prior knowledge with information in the story they are reading to make predictions, and then confirm or revise those predictions. Students are also supported in applying their developing word analysis/decoding knowledge.

norm-referenced assessments   Formal assessments that compare students' achievement to that of other students of the same age, grade, or other demographic.

novel words   New and interesting words that are more often found in children's books than in spoken vocabularies. These words are often considered *Tier 2 words*, or *general academic vocabulary*.

O

onset-rime   The *onset* is the beginning element in a spoken syllable (usually a consonant); the *rime* is the rest of the syllable—the vowel and what follows; for example, in the word /lag/ the /l/ is the onset, /ag/ is the rime.

open sort   Students sort pictures, words, or objects into categories of their own choosing and provide a rationale for these categories.

orthographic knowledge   The learner's underlying knowledge of word structure that supports the ability to decode words in reading and encode words in writing.

outcomes assessment   Assesses students' learning at the end of a learning unit or the end of the school year. It is sometimes called *summative assessment* and *cumulative assessment*.

out-of-level test   Tests administered to students that are not at the students' grade level—they are either above or below students' current grade level.

P

pattern layer   The layer of the spelling system explored by transitional readers and writers; the regular sound/spelling correspondences *within* syllables and *between* syllables. *Within* a single syllable, a group or pattern of letters functions as a single unit that corresponds to sound. *Between* syllables, the pattern principle influences the spelling where syllables join—the number of consonants, for example, and whether consonants are doubled or letters dropped when prefixes and suffixes are added.

personal readers   A special folder customized for each child, containing a collection of texts, often memorized or familiar, that the children are encouraged to reread and interact with during free play, center time, and independent reading time.

phoneme   The smallest unit of speech in a language; for example, the word *snack* has four phonemes: /s/ /n/ /ă/ /k/.

phonemic awareness   The ability consciously to attend to every consonant and vowel sound within a syllable, including the substitution and manipulation of sounds within a word.

phonic spelling   The process children are attempting to use as they learn phonic correspondences and apply this knowledge in their writing; synonymous with *invented spelling*, but *phonic spelling* is the preferred term.

phonological awareness   Awareness of aspects of speech, apart from the meaning the speech conveys: syllables, onset/rime, phonemes. This awareness is essential in learning to read.

point of articulation   When pronouncing sounds, the placement of the tip of the tongue in conjunction with the lower lip or teeth.

popcorn reading   An outdated and ineffective form of small group reading instruction where the teacher randomly selects students to read aloud.

prefix   A bound morpheme at the beginning of a root word or word root.

print-rich environment   A learning environment where teachers intentionally display words and texts as a means to engage their learners in reading, writing, and oral language activities.

prosody   The natural, more rhythmic flow of speech, which is an important aspect of fluency or "reading with expression." This flow varies in terms of loudness, duration, pitch or intonation, and pausing. Speakers use these features to give particular emphasis to what they are saying.

R

Reader Response Theory   A reader's response to text follows a continuum from acquiring and taking away information (an *efferent* stance), through a response in which the reader attends to connotations, nuanced meaning, and more personal and affective connections (an *aesthetic* stance).

receptive vocabulary   Words that an individual understands when hearing them in context; the person may or may not be able to use the words in speech or writing depending on his or her stage of development. Students' receptive vocabularies are predictably larger than their expressive vocabularies.

reciprocal teaching   A comprehension routine that incorporates four key comprehension strategies—predicting, clarifying, questioning, and summarizing; can be used in whole class read-alouds, guided reading groups, and intervention lessons.

records of oral reading   Systematic notations of children's oral reading behaviors including their reading errors, self-corrections, and strategy use. Sometimes referred to as *running records*.

register   Different formats/types of language use; for example, one type of register is a more relaxed, *informal* use of language (talking with friends); another is a more *formal*, academic use of language (presenting a report to a class). Often the term *code switch* is used to refer to one's ability to change registers depending on the context and the audience.

root   The root word or Greek/Latin root to which affixes (prefixes and suffixes) are attached.

root word   A word to which prefixes and/or suffixes may be added; for example, *camp*, *wrestle* (synonymous with *base word*).

round robin reading   An outdated and ineffective form of small group reading instruction where students read aloud one by one, usually in sequential order.

rudimentary concept of word   Children have developed this concept when they can recite a piece of memorized text while maintaining fairly accurate finger-point reading.

running records   Systematic notations of children's oral reading behaviors including their reading errors, self-corrections, and strategy use. Sometimes referred to as *records of oral reading*.

S

schema theory   Provides an important perspective for much of our understanding about comprehension in reading. Our *schemas* (or *schemata*) for different types of experiences apply to all our social and cognitive activity. These understandings provide the foundation for new learning.

schwa   A vowel sound in English that usually occurs in an unstressed syllable, such as the /uh/ sound in the first syllable of *about*. It is represented by the symbol /ə/.

shallow orthography   A spelling system in which the relationship between sound and spelling is direct; letters stand for a sound consistently. Spanish is an example of a more shallow orthography.

sight vocabulary   Words that a reader recognizes immediately both in text and in isolation.

sight word   A word that a reader can identify immediately, in text or in isolation, when seeing it. Many sight words are also high-frequency words.

signal words   Words that "signal" certain text patterns/structures; for example, *most important* and *for instance* signal a "description" pattern, *after* and *when* signal a temporal/sequential pattern, *although* and *similarly* signal a compare/contrast pattern, *as a result* and *if . . . then* signal cause/effect and problem/solution patterns.

skillful stage   The ability to read deeply, thoughtfully, and critically may be applied to a wide range of genres in this stage of development. Morphology is explored in depth, including a wide range of Greek and Latin roots and affixes, as well as etymology.

sophisticated words   Words that are not generally part of a child's spoken vocabulary, but are often found in children's books and used by more mature language users. These words are often considered *Tier 2 words*, or *general academic vocabulary*.

specific learning disability (SLD)   A neurological disorder that affects the way a person processes information or expresses knowledge. The effects from an SLD can range from mild to severe. Students with learning disabilities may have difficulty learning to read, spell, or express themselves in writing or when speaking.

spelling–meaning connection   Words that are related in meaning are often related in spelling as well, despite changes in sound; for example, *punish/punitive, allege/allegation, condemn/condemnation*.

standardized tests   Assessments that are administered and scored in a consistent or "standardized" way.

stop sounds   Sounds made with a burst of air that cannot be continued without adding the schwa sound; for example, */b/* - "buh" and */t/* - "tuh."

story schema   The understanding of how narrative text works.

strategy group   Small groups of students who may be at different developmental stages but have a common need. Strategy groups tend to be very short in duration (5 to 10 minutes) and may meet only once or twice, or until the strategy is improved or mastered.

suffix   A bound morpheme at the end of a root word or word root.

summative assessment   Assesses students' learning at the end of a series of lessons or unit. It is sometimes called *outcomes assessment* and *cumulative assessment.*

syllable   A unit of speech that contains a vowel. A consonant or consonants may come before or after the vowel; for example, the word *vocabulary* has five syllables: vo·cab·u·lar·y and the word *stop* has one.

target vocabulary words   New vocabulary words that are selected for instruction over the course of a week and/or a unit. These words are heard in reading (usually a teacher read-aloud at the primary grades) and explored through a variety of different activities.

thesis statement   A claim about the evidence. The claim, or thesis statement, comes from careful examination of hard data and the questions that arise from that examination. When students try to answer those questions, the data that support their answers become the evidence they will use in their argument to support their claims.

Tiered Instruction   A system of instruction and intervention that contains three or four tiers that vary in intensity, duration, and frequency

trade books   Books that are commercially published and widely available in book stores and libraries.

transactional model   A reader brings her or his prior knowledge, purposes, and expectations for reading a particular text to the act of reading. As the reader interacts with the author's intended meaning, a "transaction" occurs—a new meaning that results from this transaction between reader and author.

transitional stage   Learners' increasing word knowledge and their growing familiarity with narrative and informational texts support their moving toward fluency in their reading and in their writing; learners' store of sight words increases dramatically in this stage of development.

universal access   A term that refers to providing equitable access to learning and assessment through eliminating bias or practices that limit accessibility. It is sometimes referred to as *universal design.*

universal screening   A systematic approach to assessing all students at the beginning of a school year to determine who is in need of further diagnostic assessment and/or intervention services.

vernacular   A dialect that differs from the standard dialect enough to present challenges for students who enter classrooms in which the standard dialect is spoken.

visual literacy   The ability to "read" or make meaning from a visual image.

vowel markers   Long vowel sounds are represented with more than one letter. A silent letter that is used to indicate the sound of the vowel "marks" the long sound; for example, vowel markers are the silent *e* in *grape*, the *i* in *plain*, and the *y* in *tray*.

W

whole language   An approach to teaching reading that focuses primarily on making meaning.

word banks   Children's collection of known words that are practiced each day to increase automatic word recognition.

word families   Words that share the same rimes or phonograms; for example, *bam, jam, Pam, ram, Sam* are all members of the same word family.

word families   Words that share the same rimes or phonograms; for example, *bam, jam, Pam, ram, Sam* are all members of the same word family.

word reading   As much as possible, children read a variety of texts and genres every day.

word root   A Greek or Latin root to which affixes and/or other roots are added. Many word roots are *bound* roots; they cannot stand alone as words; for example, -*fect*- (in*fect*) and -*pon*- (ex*pon*ent).

writing traits   The characteristics and the teaching of writing are addressed by "traits"; traditionally, the "Six Traits" model has been emphasized in the teaching of writing and are evident in the writing criteria of the Common Core State Standards. The traits in the Common Core are idea development, organization, sentence fluency, voice, word choice, and conventions.

References

Abbott, R. D., Berninger, V. W., & Fayol, M. (2010). Longitudinal relationships of levels of language in writing and between writing and reading in grades 1 to 7. *Journal of Educational Psychology, 102*(2), 281–298.

ACT, Inc. (2006). *Reading between the lines: What the ACT reveals about college readiness in reading.* Iowa City, IA: Author.

Adams, M. J. (1990). *Beginning to read: Thinking and learning about print.* Cambridge, MA: MIT Press.

Adams, M. J. (2010/2011, Winter). Advancing our students' language and literacy: The challenge of complex texts. *American Educator,* 3–11, 53.

Afflerbach, P. (2002). The road to folly and redemption: Perspectives on the legitimacy of high-stakes testing. *Reading Research Quarterly, 37,* 348–360.

Afflerbach, P. (2004). *High stakes testing and reading assessment.* Position paper of the National Reading Conference. www.literacyresearchassociation.org/publications/HighStakesTestingandReadingAssessment.pdf. Retrieved September 16, 2012.

Afflerbach, P. (2010). *Essential readings on assessment.* Newark, DE: International Reading Association.

Afflerbach, P., Pearson, P. D., & Paris, S. G. (2008). Clarifying differences between reading skills and reading strategies. *Reading Teacher, 61*(5), 364–373.

Akhavan, N. (2006). *Help! My kids don't all speak English.* Portsmouth, NH: Heinemann.

Alexander, P. A., & Jetton, T. L. (2000). Learning from text: A multidimensional and developmental perspective. In M. L. Kamil, P. B. Mosenthal, P. D. Pearson, & R. Barr (Eds.), *Handbook of reading research* (vol. 3, pp. 285–310). Mahwah, NJ: Erlbaum.

Alliance for Excellent Education. (2013). *About the crisis.* www.all4ed.org/about_the_crisis. Retrieved January 25, 2013.

Allington, R. (1977). If they don't get to read much, how they ever gonna get good? *Journal of Reading, 21,* 57–61.

Allington, R. (2002). *Big brother and the national reading curriculum: How ideology trumped evidence.* Portsmouth, NH: Heinemann.

Allington, R. (2009). *What really matters in response to intervention: Research-based designs.* Boston: Allyn & Bacon.

Allington, R. (2012). *What really matters for struggling readers: Designing research-based programs* (3rd ed.). Boston: Pearson/Allyn & Bacon.

Allington, R. L. (1983). The neglected reading goal. *Reading Teacher, 36,* 556–561.

Allington, R., & Johnston, P. (2001). Characteristics of exemplary fourth-grade instruction. In C. Roller (Ed.), *Research on effective teaching.* Newark, NJ: International Reading Association.

Allington, R., & Johnston, P. (2002). *Reading to learn: Lessons from exemplary fourth-grade classrooms.* New York: Guilford.

Allington, R., & McGill-Franzen, A. (2008). Comprehension difficulties of struggling readers. In S. Israel & G. G. Duffy (Eds.), *Handbook of comprehension research.* Mahwah, NJ: Erlbaum.

American Heritage children's dictionary, The. (2009). Boston: Houghton Mifflin Harcourt.

Amrein, A. L., & Berliner, D. (2002). High-stakes testing, uncertainty, and student learning. *Educational Policy Analysis Archives, 10*(18).

Anderson, C. (2000). *How's it going? A practical guide to conferring with student writers.* Portsmouth, NH: Heinemann.

Anderson, L. W., & Krathwohl, D. R. (Eds.). (2000). *A taxonomy for learning, teaching and assessing: A revision of Bloom's Taxonomy of Educational Objectives.* Boston: Allyn & Bacon.

Anderson, R. C., & Biddle, W. B. (1975). On asking people questions about what they are reading. In G. H. Bower (Ed.), *The psychology of learning and motivation* (vol. 9). New York: Academic Press.

Anderson, R. C., Chinn, C., Waggoner, M., & Nguyen, K. (1998). Intellectually stimulating story discussions. In J. Osborn & F. Lehr (Eds.), *Literacy for all* (pp. 170–196). New York: Guilford.

Anderson, R. C., Hiebert, E. F., Scott, J. A., & Wilkinson, I. A. G. (1985). *Becoming a nation of readers: The report of the Commission on Reading.* Washington, DC: The National Institute of Education.

Anderson, R. C., Nguyen-Jahiel, K., McNurlen, B., Archodidou, A., Kim, S., Reznitskaya, A., Tillmanns, M., & Gilbert, L. (2001). The snowball phenomenon: Spread of ways of talking and ways of thinking across groups of children. *Cognition and Instruction, 19* (1), 1–46.

Anderson, R. C., Spiro, R. J., & Montagu, W. E. (Eds.). (1977). *Schooling and the acquisition of knowledge.* Hillsdale, NJ: Erlbaum.

Anderson, R. C., Wilson, P. T., & Fielding, L. G. (1988). Growth in reading and how children spend their time outside of school. *Reading Research Quarterly, 23,* 285–303.

Anglin, J. M. (1993). *Vocabulary development: A morphological analysis.* Monographs of the Society for Research in Child Development (Serial No. 238), *58*(10).

Apol, L., & Certo, J. L. (2011). A burgeoning field or a sorry state: U.S. poetry for children, 1800–present. In S. A. Wolf, K. Coats, P. Enciso, & C. A. Jenkins (Eds.), *Handbook of research on children's and young adult literature* (pp. 275–287). New York: Routledge/Taylor & Francis.

Applebee, A. (1978). *The child's concept of story, ages two to seventeen.* Chicago: University of Chicago Press.

Applegate, M. D., Quinn, K. B., & Applegate, A. J. (2002). Levels of thinking required by comprehension questions in informal reading inventories. *Reading Teacher, 56,* 174–180.

Armbruster, B., Lehr, F., & Osborn, J. (2006). *Put reading first: The research building blocks for teaching children to read.* Washington, DC: National Institute for Literacy.

Asimov, I. (1960). *Words from the myths.* Boston: Houghton Mifflin.

Atwell, N. (1998). *In the middle: New understandings about reading, writing and learning* (2nd ed.). Portsmouth, NH: Heinemann.

Au, K. (2005). *Literacy instruction in multicultural settings.* Fort Worth, TX: Holt, Rinehart and Winston.

Au, K. (2005). *Multicultural issues and literacy achievement.* Mahwah, NJ: Erlbaum.

August, D., & Shanahan, T. (Eds.). (2006). *Developing literacy in second-language learners: Report of the National Literacy Panel on Language-Minority Children and Youth.* Mahwah, NJ: Erlbaum.

Ayers, D. M. (1986). *English words from Latin and Greek elements* (2nd ed., rev. by Thomas Worthen). Tucson: The University of Arizona Press.

Ayto, J. (2009). *Oxford school dictionary of word origins: The curious twists and turns of the cool and weird words we use.* Oxford: Oxford University Press

Ayto, J. (1991). *Dictionary of word origins.* New York: Arcade.

Baca, J. (2010a). *Adolescents on the edge: Stories and lessons to transform learning.* Portsmouth, NH: Heinemann.

Bahr, R. H., Silliman, E. R., & Berninger, V. W. (2009). What spelling errors have to tell about vocabulary learning. In C. Wood & V. Connelly (Eds.), *Reading and spelling: Contemporary perspectives* (pp. 109–129). New York: Routledge.

Baker, L. (2000). Metacognition in comprehension instruction. In C. Collins Block & M. Pressley (Eds.), *Comprehension instruction: Research-based best practices* (pp. 77–95). New York: Guilford.

Bang-Jensen, V. (2010). Insights into book selection, social relationships, and reader identity. *Language Arts, 87*(3), 169–175.

Barone, D. (1989). *Young children's written responses to literature: Exploring the relationship between written response and orthographic knowledge.* Unpublished doctoral dissertation, University of Nevada, Reno.

Barton, P. E. (2000). *What jobs require: Literacy, education and training, 1940–2006.* Washington, DC: Educational Testing Service.

Barton, P. E. (2005). *One-third of a nation.* Princeton, NJ: Educational Testing Service.

Bauer, S. W. (2006). *The story of the world: Volume 1 (Ancient times).* Charles City, VA: Peace Hill Press.

Baumann, J. F., Blachowicz, C. L. Z., Graves, M., Olejnik, S., & Manyak, P. (2009). *Multifaceted comprehensive vocabulary improvement project.* Washington, DC: Institute of Education Sciences.

Bauman, J. F., Chard, D. J., Cooks, J., Cooper, J. D., Gersten, R., Lipson, M., Morrow, L. M., Pikulski, J. J., Rivera, H. H., Rivera, M., Templeton, S., Valencia, S. W., Valentino, C., & Vogt, M. (2012). *Journeys—Grade 1 teacher's edition* (p. T290). Boston: Houghton Mifflin Harcourt.

Baumann, J. F., Ware, D., & Edwards, E. C. (2007). "Bumping into spicy, tasty words that catch your tongue": A formative experiment on vocabulary instruction. *Reading Teacher, 61*(2), 108–122.

Bear, D. R. (1992). The prosody of oral reading and stage of word knowledge. In S. Templeton & D. Bear (Eds.), *Development of orthographic knowledge and the foundations of literacy: A memorial Festschrift for Edmund H. Henderson* (pp. 137–189). Hillsdale, NJ: Erlbaum.

Bear, D. R., & Barone, D. (1997). *Developing literacy: An integrated approach to assessment and instruction.* Boston: Houghton Mifflin.

Bear, D. R., Casserta-Henry, C., & Venner, D. (2004). *Personal readers and literacy instruction with emergent and beginning readers.* Berkeley, CA: Teaching Resource Center.

Bear, D. R., Invernizzi, M., Johnston, F., & Templeton, S. (2010). *Words their way: Letter and picture sorts for emergent spellers* (2nd ed.). Boston: Allyn & Bacon.

Bear, D. R., Invernizzi, M., Templeton, S., & Johnston, F. (2012). *Words their way: Word study for phonics, vocabulary, and spelling instruction* (5th ed.). Boston: Pearson/Allyn & Bacon.

Bear, D. R., & Smith, R. E. (2009). The literacy development of English learners: What do we know about each student's literacy development? In L. Helman (Ed.), *Literacy development with English learners: Research-based instruction in grades K–6* (pp. 87–116). New York: Guilford.

Bear, D. R., & Templeton, S. (1998). Explorations in developmental spelling: Foundations for learning and teaching phonics, spelling, and vocabulary. *Reading Teacher, 52,* 222–242.

Bear, D. R., Templeton, S., Helman, L., & Baren, T. (2003). Orthographic development and learning to read in different languages. In G. C. Garcia (Ed.), *English learners: Reaching the highest level of English literacy* (pp. 71–95). Newark, DE: International Reading Association.

Beaver, J. M. (2006). *Developmental reading assessment: Teacher guide (DRA2 K-3).* Parsippany, NJ: Celebration Press, Pearson Learning Group.

Beaver, J. M., & Carter, M. A. (2003). *Teacher guide: Developmental reading assessment grades 4–8* (2nd ed.). Parsippany, NJ: Pearson.

Beaver, J. M., & Carter, M. A. (2006). *Developmental reading assessment* (2nd ed.). Parsippany, NJ: Celebration Press, Pearson Learning Group.

Beck, I. L., & McKeown, M. G. (1991). Conditions of vocabulary acquisition. In R. Barr, M. Kamil, P. Mosenthal, & P. D. Pearson (Eds.), *Handbook of reading research* (vol. 2, pp. 789–814). New York: Longman.

Beck, I. L., & McKeown, M. G. (2001). Text talk: Capturing the benefits of read aloud experiences for young children. *The Reading Teacher, 55,* 10–20.

Beck, I. L., & McKeown, M. G. (2006). *Improving comprehension with questioning the author: A fresh and expanded view of a powerful approach.* New York: Scholastic.

Beck, I. L., McKeown, M. G., Hamilton, R. L., & Kucan, L. (1997). *Questioning the author: An approach for enhancing student engagement with text.* Newark, DE: International Reading Association.

Beck, I. L., McKeown, M. G., & Kucan, L. (2002). *Bringing words to life: Robust vocabulary instruction.* New York: Guilford.

Beck, I. L., McKeown, M. G., & Kucan, L. (2008). *Creating robust vocabulary: Frequently asked questions and extended examples.* New York: Guilford.

Benjamin, R. G., & Schwanenflugel, P. J. (2010). Text complexity and oral reading prosody in young readers. *Reading Research Quarterly, 45*(4), 388–404.

Berninger, V. W., Abbott, R. D., Nagy, W., & Carlisle, J. (2009). Growth in phonological, orthographic, and morphological awareness in grades 1 to 6. *Journal of Psycholinguistic Research—Online First.* www.springerlink.com. innopac.library.unr.edu/content/gpu4572318l52242/. Retrieved October 16, 2009.

Biancarosa, G., & Snow, C. E. (2006). *Reading next: A vision for action and research in middle and high school literacy*. Washington, DC: Alliance for Excellent Education.

Biemiller, A. (1999). *Language and reading success* (vol. 5). Cambridge, MA: Brookline.

Biemiller, A. (2005). Size and sequence in vocabulary development: Implications for choosing words for primary grade vocabulary instruction. In E. H. Hiebert & M. L. Kamil (Eds.), *Teaching and learning vocabulary: Bringing research to practice* (pp. 223–242). Mahwah, NJ: Erlbaum.

Biemiller, A. (2010). *Words worth teaching: Closing the vocabulary gap*. Columbus, OH: McGraw-Hill.

Biemiller, A., & Slonim, N. (2001). Estimating root word vocabulary growth in normative and advantaged populations: Evidence for common sequence of vocabulary acquisition. *Journal of Educational Psychology, 98,* 44–62.

Bilingual Education Office of the California Department of Education. (2012). *Student Oral Language Observation Matrix*. www.cal.org/twi/EvalToolkit/appendix/solom.pdf. Retrieved August 11, 2012.

Birch, B. (2002). *English L2 reading: Getting to the bottom*. Mahwah, NJ: Erlbaum.

Blachowicz, C., & Fisher, P. J. (2010). *Teaching vocabulary in all classrooms* (4th ed.). Boston: Allyn & Bacon/Pearson.

Black, P., & Wiliam, D. (1998). Assessment and classroom learning. *Assessment in Education: Principles, Policy and Practice, 5*(1).

Black, P. & Wiliam, D. (2010). Inside the black box: Raising standards through classroom assessment. *Kappan, 92*(1), 81–90.

Blackburn, M. V., & Clark, C. T. (2011). Becoming readers of literature with LGBT themes. In S. A. Wolf, K. Coats, P. Enciso, & C. A. Jenkins (Eds.), *Handbook of research on children's and young adult literature* (pp. 148–163). New York: Routledge/Taylor & Francis.

Blair, C., Protzko, J., & Ursache, A. (2011). Self-regulation and early literacy. In S. B. Neuman & D. K. Dickinson (Eds.), *Handbook of early literacy research* (vol. 3). New York: Guilford.

Block, C. C., & Pressley, M. (2007). Best practices in teaching comprehension. In L. B. Gambrell, L. M. Morrow, & M. Pressley (Eds.), *Best practices in literacy education* (3rd ed.). New York: Guilford.

Bloom, B. S. (1956). *Taxonomy of educational objectives: The classification of educational goals*. Harlow, Essex, England: Longman Group.

Bomer, R., & Bomer, K. (2001). *For a better world: Reading and writing for social action*. Portsmouth, NH: Heinemann.

Books, S. (2004). *Poverty and schooling in the U.S.: Contexts and consequences*. Mahwah, NJ: Erlbaum.

Boscolo, P., & Gelati, C. (2007). Best practices in promoting motivation for writing. In S. Graham, C. A. MacArthur, & J. Fitzgerald (Eds.), *Best practices in writing instruction* (pp. 202–221). New York: Guilford.

Boushey, G., & Moser, J. (2006). *The daily 5: Fostering literacy independence in the elementary grades*. Portland, ME: Stenhouse.

Bracey, G. (2000). *High stakes testing*. Milwaukee, WI: Center for Education Research, Analysis, and Innovation.

Brady, B., Morrison, A., Rasinski, T., Shanahan, T., & Templeton, S. (2006). Earobics REACH. Boston: Houghton Mifflin Harcourt.

Bravo, M. A., Hiebert, E. H., & Pearson, P. D. (2005). Tapping the linguistic resources of Spanish/English bilinguals: The role of cognates in science. In R. K. Wagner, A. E. Muse, & K. R. Tannenbaum (Eds.), *Vocabulary acquisition: Implications for reading comprehension* (pp. 140–156). New York: Guilford.

Brock, C., Lapp, D., Salas, R. G., & Townsend, D. (2009). *Academic literacy for English learners: High quality instruction across content areas*. New York: Teachers College Press.

Brophy, J. (2004). *Motivating students to learn* (2nd ed.). Mahwah, NJ: Erlbaum.

Brozo, W., & Afflerbach, P. (2011). *Adolescent literacy inventory, grades 6–12*. Boston: Pearson/Allyn & Bacon.

Brozo, W., Shiel, G., & Topping, K. (2008). Engagement in reading: Lessons learned from three PISA countries. *Journal of Adolescent and Adult Literacy, 51*(4), 304–315.

Bruner, J. S. (1973). *Beyond the information given: Studies in the psychology of knowing*. Oxford, England: W. W. Norton.

Bruner, J. S. (1991). *Actual minds, possible worlds*. Cambridge, MA: Harvard University Press.

Bruner, J. S. (1996). *The culture of education*. Cambridge, MA: Harvard University Press.

Buly, M. R., & Valencia, S. W. (2002). Below the bar: Profiles of students who fail state reading assessments. *Educational Evaluation and Policy Analysis 24*(3), 219–239.

Busching, B., & Slesinger, B. A. (2002). *"It's our world too": Socially responsive learners in middle school language arts*. Urbana, IL: National Council of Teachers of English.

Bussis, A., Chittenden, E., Amarel, M., & Klausner, E. (1985). *Inquiry into meaning: An investigation of learning to read*. Hillsdale, NJ: Erlbaum.

Calderón, M., Slavin, R., & Sánchez, M. (2011). Effective instruction for English learners. *The Future of Children, 21*(1), 103–127.

Caldwell, K., & Gaine, T. (2000). *"The phantom tollbooth" and how the independent reading of good books improves students' reading performance*. San Raphael, CA: Reading and Communication Skills Clearinghouse. (ERIC Document Reproduction Service No. ED449462.)

California Invasive Plant Council. (2010). *Invasive plant inventory*. http://www.cal-ipc.org/ip/inventory/index.php.

Calkins, L. (1983). *Lessons from a child*. Exeter, NH: Heinemann.

Calkins, L. (1994). *The art of teaching writing* (2nd ed.) Portsmouth, NH: Heinemann.

Calkins, L. (2000). *The art of teaching reading*. Boston: Allyn & Bacon.

Calkins, L., & Hartman, A. (2003). *Authors as mentors*. Portsmouth, NH: Firsthand.

Calkins, L., Ehrenworth, M., & Lehman, C. (2012). *Pathways to the common core: Accelerating achievement*. Portsmouth, NH: Heinemann.

Calkins, L., & Oxenhorn, A. (2003). *Small moments: Personal narrative writing*. Portsmouth, NH: Firsthand.

Capps, R., Fix, M., Murray, J., Ost, J., Passel, J., & Herwantoro, S. (2005). *The new demography of America's schools: Immigration and the No Child Left Behind Act*. Washington, DC: The Urban Institute. www.urban.org. Retrieved August 11, 2012.

Carey, S. (1978). The child as a word learner. In M. Haller, J. Bresnan, & G. A. Miller (Eds.), *Linguistic theory and psychological reality*. Cambridge, MA: MIT Press.

Carlisle, J. F. (2000). Awareness of the structure and meaning of morphologically complex words: Impact on reading. *Reading and Writing, 12,* 169–190.

Carnevale, A. P. (2001). *Help wanted . . . college required*. Washington, DC: Educational Testing Service, Office for Public Leadership.

Carnine, D., Silbert, J., Kame'enui, E. J., & Tarver, S. G. (2009). *Direct instruction reading* (5th ed.). Upper Saddle River, NJ: Prentice Hall.

Carpenter, K. (2010). The relationships among concept sorts, storybook reading, language-based print awareness, and language proficiency in the vocabulary learning of kindergarten children. Unpublished doctoral dissertation, University of Nevada, Reno.

Carr, S. (2011). *The shallows: What the Internet is doing to our brains.* New York: W. W. Norton.

Causton-Theoharis, J. N., Giangreco, M. F., Doyle, M. B., & Vadasy, P. F. (2007). Paraprofessionals: The "sous chefs" of literacy instruction. *Teaching Exceptional Children, 40*(1), 56–62.

Cazden, C. (1988). *Classroom discourse: The language of teaching and learning.* Portsmouth, NH: Heinemann

Chall, J. S. (1983). *Stages of reading development.* New York: McGraw-Hill.

Chall, J. S. & Dale, E. (1995). *Readability revisited—The new Dale-Chall readability formula.* Cambridge, MA: Brookline Books.

Chall, J. S. (1996). *Stages of reading development* (2nd ed.). Fort Worth, TX: Harcourt-Brace.

Chall, J. S., Bissex, G. L., Conrad, S. S., & Harris-Sharples, S. (1996). *Qualitative assessment of text difficulty: A practical guide for teachers and writers.* Cambridge, MA: Brookline Books.

Chall, J. S., & Jacobs, V. A. (2003). Poor children's fourth-grade slump. *American Educator, 2*(1), 14–15.

Chall, J. S., Jacobs, V. A., & Baldwin, L. E. (1991). *The reading crisis: Why poor children fall behind.* Cambridge, MA: Harvard University Press.

Chomsky, N. (1959). A review of B. F. Skinner's "Verbal Behavior." *Language, 35*(1), 25–58.

Cipielewski, J., & Stanovich, K. E. (1992). Predicting growth in reading ability from children's exposure to print. *Journal of Experimental Child Psychology, 54,* 74–89.

Clark, E. V. (2003). *First language acquisition.* Cambridge: Cambridge University Press.

Clay, M. (1975). *What did I write?* Exeter, NH: Heinemann.

Clay, M. (1991). *Becoming literate: The construction of inner control.* Portsmouth, NH: Heinemann.

Clay, M. (1991). Introducing a new storybook to young readers. *Reading Teacher, 45,* 264–273.

Clay, M. (2000). *Concepts about print: What have children learned about the way we print language?* Portsmouth, NH: Heinemann.

Clay, M. (2001). *Change over time in children's literacy development.* Portsmouth, NH: Heinemann.

Clay, M. (2002). *An observation survey of early literacy achievement* (2nd ed.). Portsmouth: Heinemann.

Clay, M. M. (1979). *Reading: The patterning of complex behavior* (2nd ed.). Aukland, New Zealand: Heinemann.

Clay, M. M. (1982). *Observing young readers—Selected papers.* Portsmouth, NH: Heinemann.

Clay, M. M. (1985). *The early detection of reading difficulties* (3rd ed.). Auckland, New Zealand: Heinemann.

Clay, M. M. (1987). Learning to be learning disabled. *New Zealand Journal of Educational Studies, 22*(2), 155–173.

Clay, M. M. (2000a). *Running records for classroom teachers.* Portsmouth, NH: Heinemann.

Clay, M. M. (2000b). *Concepts about print: What have children learned about the way we print language?* Portsmouth, NH: Heinemann.

Cleland, J. V. (1999). We can charts: Building blocks for student-led conferences. *Reading Teacher, 54-4 2*(6), 588–595.

Cobb, C. (2003). Effective instruction begins with purposeful assessments. *Reading Teacher, 57*(4), 386–388.

Cobin, P., Templeton, S., & Burner, K. (2011). Worry or wait: The dilemma to refer English Learners to special education. *AccELLerate! The Quarterly Review of the National Clearing House for English Language Acquisition, 3*(3), 12–13.

Common Core Curriculum Maps. (2012). http://commoncore.org/maps/.

Common Core State Standards (CCSS). (2010). *Common Core State Standards.* www.corestandards.org. Retrieved on March 12, 2010.

Common Core State Standards Initiative. (2010). National Governors Association Center for Best Practices and the Council of Chief State School Officers. www.corestandards.org.

Connor, C., Morrison, F., Fishman, B., Giuliani, S., Luck, M., Underwood, P., Bayraktar, A., Crowe, E., & Schatschneider, C. (2011). Testing the impact of characteristics x instruction interactions on third graders' reading comprehension by differentiating literacy instruction. *Reading Research Quarterly,* 46, 189–221.

Connor, C. M., Morrison, F. J., Fishman, B. J., Schatschneider, C., & Underwood, P. (2007, January). Algorithm-guided individualized reading instruction. *Science, 315,* 464–465.

Consortium on Reaching Excellence in Education. (2012). *Word intelligence: Developing academic and content vocabulary.* Berkeley, CA: Author.

Cooper, J. D. (2001). *Soar to success: The intermediate intervention program.* Boston: Houghton Mifflin.

Cooper, J. D., & Pikulski, J. J. (1996). *Early success: An intervention program.* Boston: Houghton Mifflin.

Council of Chief State School Officers & National Governors Association. (2013). *Supplemental information of Appendix A of the Common Core State Standards for English language arts and literacy: New research on text complexity.* www.corestandards.org/assets/ E0813_Appendix_A_New_Research_ on_Text_Complexity.pdf.

Courtney, A. M., & Abodeeb, T. L. (1999). Diagnostic-reflective portfolios. *Reading Teacher, 52*(7), 708–714.

Cross, D. R., & Paris, S. G. (1988). Developmental and instructional analyses of children's metacognition and reading comprehension. *Journal of Educational Psychology, 80*(2), 131–142.

Crumpler, T. P., & Wednick, L. (2011). Readers, texts, and contexts in the middle: Re-imagining literature education for young adolescents. In S. A. Wolf, K. Coats, P. Enciso, & C. A. Jenkins (Eds.), *Handbook of research on children's and young adult literature* (pp. 63–75). New York: Routledge/ Taylor & Francis.

Cummins, J. (1991). Language development and academic learning. In L. Malave & G. Duquette (Eds.), *Language, culture and cognition.* Clevedon, UK: Multilingual Matters.

Cummins, J. (Ed.). (1991). *Heritage languages.* Special issue of the *Canadian Modern Language Review, 47*(4).

Cunningham, A. E., Nathan, R. G., & Schmidt Rather, K. (2011). Orthographic processing in models of word recognition. In M. Kamil, P. D. Pearson, E. Birr Moje, & P. P. Afflerbach (Eds.), *The handbook of reading research* (vol. 4, pp. 259–285). New York: Routledge.

Cunningham, A. E., Perry, K. E., & Stanovich, K. E. (2001). Converging evidence for the concept of orthographic processing. *Reading and Writing, 14,* 549–568.

Cunningham, A. E., & Stanovich, K. E. (1992). Tracking the unique effects of print exposure: Associations with vocabulary, general knowledge, and spelling. *Journal of Educational Psychology, 83*(2), 264–274.

Cunningham, P. (2005). *Phonics they use: Words for reading and writing.* Boston: Allyn & Bacon.

Cunningham, P. (2008). *Phonics they use* (5th ed.). Boston: Allyn & Bacon.

Cunningham, P. (2009). *What really matters in vocabulary: Research-based practices across the curriculum.* Boston: Pearson/Allyn & Bacon.

Cunningham, P., & Allington, R. (1999). *Classrooms that work: They can all read and write* (2nd ed). Boston: Allyn & Bacon.

Díaz, J. (2012). *By the book.* www .nytimes.com/2012/09/02/books/ review/junot-diaz-by-the-book. html?pagewanted=all.

Daane, M. C., Campbell, J. R., Grigg, W. S., Goodman, M. J., & Oranje, A. (2005). *Fourth-grade students reading aloud: NAEP 2002 Special Study of Oral Reading.* Washington, DC: U.S. Department of Education, Institute of Education Sciences.

Daniels, H. (1994). *Literature circles: Voice and choice in the student-centered classroom.* Portland, ME: Stenhouse.

Daniels, H. (2002). *Literature circles: Voice and choice in book clubs and reading groups.* Portland, ME: Stenhouse.

Danner, H. G., & Noel, R. (1996). *Discover it! A better vocabulary the better way.* Occoquan, VA: Imprimis Books.

Darling-Hammond, L. (1999). *Teacher quality and student achievement: A review of state policy evidence.* Seattle: University of Washington, Center for the Study of Teaching and Policy.

Dee, J. R. & Henkin, A. B. (2002). Assessing dispositions toward cultural diversity among preservice teachers. *Urban Education, 37*(1), 22–40.

Delpit, L. (1995/2006). *Other people's children: Cultural conflict in the classroom.* New York: New Press.

Denton, P., & Kriete, R. (2000). *The first six weeks of school.* Greenfield, MA: Northeast Foundation for Children.

Dickinson, D. McCabe, A., & Sprague, K. (2003). Teacher rating of oral language and literacy (TROLL): Individualizing early literacy instruction with a standards-based rating tool. *Reading Teacher, 56*(6), 554–564.

Dickinson, D., & Tabors, P. (Eds.). (2001). *Beginning literacy with language: Young children learning at home and school.* Baltimore: Brookes.

Dickinson, D., McCabe, A., & Essex, M. J. (2006). A window of opportunity we must open to all: The case for preschool with high-quality support for language and literacy. In D. K. Dickinson & S. B. Neuman (Eds.), *Handbook of early literacy research* (vol. 2). Baltimore: Brookes.

Dickson, D., & Smith, M. W. (1994). Long-term effect of preschool teachers' book readings on low-income children's vocabulary and story comprehension. *Reading Research Quarterly, 29,* 104–122.

Diederich, P. (1974). *Measuring growth in English.* Urbana, IL: NCTE.

Diller, D. (2008). *Spaces and places: Designing classrooms for literacy.* Portland, ME: Stenhouse.

Djikic, M., Oatley, K., Zoeterman, S., & Peterson, J. (2009). On being moved by art: How reading fiction transforms the self. *Creativity Research Journal, 21,* 24–29.

Donahue, P. L., Finnegan, R. J., Lutkus, A. D., Allen, N. L., & Campbell, J. R. (2001). The Nation's Report Card: Fourth Grade Reading, 2000: Executive Summary. http://nces.ed.gov/nation-sreportcard/pubs/main2000/2001499. asp. Retrieved June 12, 2012.

Dornheim, R. (Director). (2001). *Anne Frank: The whole story* [Television movie]. New York: ABC.

Duke, N. K. (2000). 3.6 minutes per day: The scarcity of informational text in first grade. *Reading Research Quarterly, 35,* 202–224.

Duke, N. K., Bennett-Armistead, V. S., & Roberts, E. M. (2003). Bridging the gap between learning to read and reading to learn. In D. M. Barone & L. M. Morrow (Eds.), *Literacy and young children: Research-based practices* (pp. 226–242). New York: Guilford.

Duke, N. K., & Carlisle, J. (2011). The development of comprehension. In M. L. Kamil, P. D. Pearson, E. B. Moje, & P. P. Afflerbach (Eds.), *Handbook of reading research* (vol. IV, pp. 199–228). New York: Routledge.

Duke, N. K., & Pearson, P. D. (2002). Effective practices for developing reading comprehension. In A. E. Farstrup & S. J. Samuels (Eds.), *What research has to say about reading instruction* (3rd ed., pp. 205–242). Newark, DE: International Reading Association.

Dunn, L. M., & Dunn, D. M. (2007). *Peabody Picture Vocabulary Test* (3rd ed.) Circle Pines, MN: American Guidance Service.

Echevarria, J., Vogt, M., & Short, D. (2012). *Making content comprehensible for English learners: The SIOP model* (4th ed.). Boston: Pearson/Allyn & Bacon.

Eddy, C. (2010). A morphological approach for English language learners. www.vocabulogic.com. Retrieved September 21, 2012.

Eddy, R. M., Ruitman, T., Hankel, N., Matelski, M. H., & Schmalstig, M. (2011). *Pearson Words Their Way: word study in action intervention efficacy study, final report.* La Verne, CA: Cobblestone Applied Research & Evaluation.

Editors (2006). *Longman Study Dictionary of American English.* Harlow, England: Pearson Longman.

Editors (2007). *The American Heritage Children's Dictionary.* Boston: Houghton Mifflin.

Editors (2009). *The American Heritage Children's Dictionary.* Boston: Houghton Mifflin Harcourt.

Edwards, C., Gandini, L, & Forman, G. (1998). *The hundred languages of children: The Reggio Emilia approach* (2nd ed.). Burlington, MA: Elsevier.

Ehri, L. C. (1997). Learning to read and learning to spell are one and the same, almost. In C. A. Perfetti, L. Rieben, & M. Fayol (Eds.), *Learning to spell: Research, theory, and practice across languages* (pp. 237–269). Mawah, NJ: Erlbaum.

Ehri, L. C. (2000). Learning to read and learning to spell: Two sides of a coin. *Topics in Language Disorders, 20*(3), 19–36.

Ehri, L. C. (2005). Learning to read words: Theory, findings, and issues. *Scientific Studies of Reading, 9*(2), 167–188.

Ehri, L. C., Dreyer, L. G., Flugman, B., & Gross, A. (2007). Reading rescue: An effective tutoring intervention model for language-minority students who are struggling readers in first grade. *American Educational Research Journal, 44*(2), 414–448.

Ehri, L. C., & McCormick, S. (1998). Phases of word learning: Implications for instruction with delayed and disabled readers. *Reading and Writing Quarterly: Overcoming Learning Disabilities, 14,* 134–164.

Ehri, L. C. & Roberts, T. (2006). The roots of learning to read and write: Acquisition of letters and phonemic awareness. In D. K. Dickinson & S. B. Neuman (Eds.), *Handbook of early literacy research* (vol. 2). New York: Guilford.

Ehri, L. C., & Wilce, L. S. (1980). Do beginning readers learn to read function words better in sentences or lists? *Reading Research Quarterly, 15,* 675–685.

Elbow, P. (1999). *Writing with power* (2nd ed.). New York: Oxford University Press.

Eldredge, J. L. (2004). *Teach decoding: Why and how* (2nd ed.). Upper Saddle River, NJ: Pearson/Merrill/Prentice Hall.

Elkonin, D. (1973). Reading in the USSR. In J. Downing (Ed.), *Comparative reading* (pp. 551–579). New York: Macmillan.

Ellis, N., & Cataldo, S. (1992). Spelling is integral to learning to read. In C. M. Sterling & & C. Robson (Eds.), *Psychology, spelling, and education* (pp. 122–142). Clevedon, UK: Multilingual Matters.

Elmore, R. (2002a). *Unwarranted intrusion.* http://educationnext.org/ unwarranted-intrusion. Retrieved March 31, 2003.

Evertson, C. M., & Weinstein, C. S. (2006). Classroom management as a field of inquiry. In C. M. Evertson & C. S. Weinstein (Eds.), *Handbook of classroom management: Research, practice, and contemporary issues* (pp. 3–16). Mahwah, NJ: Erlbaum.

Fan, M. (2000). How big is the gap and how to narrow it? An investigation into the active and passive vocabulary knowledge of low learners. *RELC Journal, 31,* 105–119.

Farr, R. (1992). Putting it all together: Solving the reading assessment puzzle. *Reading Teacher, 46,* 26–37.

Ferreiro, E., & Teberosky, A. (1982). *Literacy before schooling.* Exeter, NH: Heinemann.

Fielding, L. G., Anderson, R. C., & Pearson, P. D. (1990). *How discussion questions influence children's story understanding* (Technical Report No. 490). Urbana: Center for the Study of Reading, University of Illinois.

Fischer, W. R. (1989). Clarifying the narrative paradigm. *Communication Monographs, 56,* 55–58.

Fisher, D., & Frey, N. (2012). *Common Core English language arts in a PLC at work, grades 3–5.* Bloomington, IN: Solution Tree.

Fisher, D., Frey, N., & Lapp, D. (2012). *Text complexity: Raising rigor in reading.* Newark, DE: International Reading Association.

Fisher, D., Frey, N., & Rothenberg, C. (2011). *Implementing RTI with English learners.* Bloomington, IN: Solution Tree.

Flanigan, K. (2007). A concept of word in text: A pivotal event in early reading acquisition. *Journal of Literacy Research, 39*(1), 37–40.

Flanigan, K., Hayes, L., Templeton, S., Bear, D. R., Invernizzi, M., & Johnston, F. (2011). *Words their way with struggling readers: Word study for reading, vocabulary and spelling instruction, grades 4–12.* Boston: Pearson/Allyn & Bacon.

Flanigan, K., Hayes, T., Helman, L., Bear, D. R., & Templeton, S. (2013). *Vocabulary their way with American History: Vocabulary and concept development* (vols. 1 and 2). Boston: Pearson/Allyn & Bacon.

Flanigan, K., Templeton, S., & Hayes, L. (2012). What's in a word? Using content vocabulary to *generate* growth in general academic vocabulary knowledge. *Journal of Adolescent and Adult Literacy, 56*(2), 140–148.

Flesch, R. (1956). *Why Johnny can't read (and what you can do about it).* New York: Harper & Brothers.

Fletcher, J. M., Shaywitz, S. F., Shankweiler, D. P., Katz, L., Liberman, I. Y., Stuebing, K. K., Francis, D. J., Fowler, A. E., & Shaywitz, B. A. (1994). Cognitive profiles of reading disability: Comparisons of discrepancy and low achievement definitions. *Journal of Educational Psychology, 86,* 6–23.

Fletcher, R. (1996). *A writer's notebook.* New York: HarperCollins.

Fletcher, R., & Portalupi, J. (2007). *Craft lessons: Teaching writing K–8.* Portsmouth, NH: Heinemann.

Florio-Ruane, S. (2001). *Teacher education and the cultural imagination: Autobiography, conversation, and narrative.* Mahwah, NJ: Erlbaum.

Foorman, B., Francis, D., Shaywicz, S., Shaywicz, B., & Fletcher, J. (1997). The case for early reading intervention. In B. Blachman (Ed.), *Foundations of reading acquisition and dyslexia: Implications for early intervention* (pp. 243–264). Mahwah, NJ: Erlbaum.

Ford, K., & Invernizzi, M. (in press). *PALS Español.* Charlottesville: University of Virginia Press.

Fountas, I. C., & Pinnell, G. S. (1996). *Guided reading: Good first teaching for all children.* Portsmouth, NH: Heinemann.

Fountas, I. C., & Pinnell, G. S. (1999). *Benchmark assessment system.* Portsmouth, NH: Heinemann.

Fountas, I. C., & Pinnell, G. S. (2001). *Guiding readers and writers (grades 3–6): Teaching, comprehension, genre, and content literacy.* Portsmouth, NH: Heinemann.

Fountas, I. C., & Pinnell, G. S. (2005). *Leveled books, K–8: Matching texts to readers for effective teaching.* Portsmouth, NH: Heinemann.

Fountas, I. C., & Pinnell, G. S. (2010). *Benchmark assessment system 1: Grades K–2.* Portsmouth, NH: Heinemann.

Fountas, I. C., & Pinnell, G. S. (2010). *Benchmark assessment system 2: Grades 3–8.* Portsmouth, NH: Heinemann.

Freebody, P., & Anderson, R. C. (1983). Effects of vocabulary difficulty, text cohesion and schema availability on reading comprehension. *Reading Research Quarterly, 18,* 277–293.

Freeman, D., & Freeman, Y. (2003). *Essential linguistics: What you need to know to teach reading, ESL, spelling, phonics, and grammar.* Portsmouth, NH: Heinemann.

Freeman, D., & Freeman, Y. (2007). *English language learners: The essential guide.* New York: Scholastic.

Freire, P. (1970). *Pedagogy of the oppressed.* New York: Continuum.

Frey, N., Fisher, D., & Berkin, A. (2009). *Good habits, great readers.* Upper Saddle River, NJ: Celebration Press, Pearson.

Frith, U. (1985). Beneath the surface of developmental dyslexia. In K. Patterson, J. Marshall, & M. Coltheart (Eds.), *Surface dyslexia: Neuropsychological and cognitive studies of phonological reading* (pp. 301–330). London: Erlbaum.

Fry, E. (1968). A readability formula that saves time. *Journal of Reading, 11*(7), 265–271.

Fry, E. B., & Kress, J. E. (2006). *The reading teacher's book of lists: Grades K–12* (5th ed.). San Francisco: Jossey-Bass.

Fry, E. B., Kress, J. E., & Fountoukidis, D. L. (2000). *The reading teacher's book of lists* (4th ed., p. 41). Paramus, NJ: Prentice Hall.

Fuchs, D., & Fuchs, L. S. (2006). Introduction to response to intervention: What, why, and how valid is it? *Reading Research Quarterly, 41*(1), 92–99.

Funk, W. (1950/1998). *Word origins: An exploration and history of words and language.* New York: Wings Books.

Gambrell, L., Koskinen, P., & Kapinus, B. (1991). Retelling and the reading comprehension of proficient and less-proficient readers. *Journal of Educational Research, 84,* 356–362.

Garcia, G. E., McKoon, G., & August, D. (2008). Language and literacy assessment. In D. August & T. Shanahan (Eds.), *Developing reading and writing in second-language learners: Lessons from the Report of the National Literacy Panel on Language-Minority Children and Youth* (pp. 251–274). Newark, DE: Routledge, the Center for Applied Linguistics, and the International Reading Association.

Gee, J. P. (2007). *What video games have to teach us about learning and literacy* (2nd ed.). New York: Palgrave Macmillan.

Gehsmann, K. (2008). Response to Intervention: What is it and how do schools and districts plan for it? *Michigan Reading Journal, 40*(3), 22–30.

Gehsmann, K., & Templeton, S. (2011/2012). Of stages and standards in literacy: Teaching developmentally in the age of accountability. *Journal of Education, 192*(1), 5–16.

Gehsmann, K., & Templeton, S. (2013). Foundational skills. In L. M. Morrow, T. Shanahan, & K. K. Wixson (Eds.), *Teaching with the Common Core Standards for English Language Arts: PreK–2* (pp. 67–84). New York: Guilford.

Gehsmann, K., & Woodside-Jiron, H. (2005). Becoming more effective in the age of accountability: A high-poverty school narrows the literacy achievement gap. In B. Maloch, J. V. Hoffman, D. L. Schallert, C. M. Fairbanks, & J. Worthy (Eds.), *54th Yearbook of the National Reading Conference* (pp. 182–197). Oak Creek, WI: National Reading Conference.

Gerber, S. B., Finn, J. D., Achilles, C. M., & Boyd-Zaharis, J. (2001). Teacher aides and students' academic achievement. *Educational Evaluation and Policy Analysis, 23*(2), 123–143.

Gewertz, C. (2011). Educators need training to understand common standards, experts warn. *Education Week.* Published online June 30, 2011.

Giangreco, M. F. (2003). Working with paraprofessionals. *Educational Leadership, 61*(2), 50–53.

Goldenberg, C. (2011). Reading instruction for English language learners. In M. L. Kamil, P. D. Pearson, E. Birr Moje, & P. P. Afflerbach (Eds.), *Handbook of reading research* (vol. 4, pp. 684–710). New York: Routledge.

Goldman, S. R., & Rakestraw, J. A. (2000). Structural aspects of constructing meaning from text. In M. L. Kamil, P. B. Mosenthal, P. D. Pearson, & R. Barr (Eds.), *Handbook of reading research* (vol. 3, pp. 311–336). Mahwah, NJ: Erlbaum.

Gonzales, N., Moll, L. C., & Amanti, C. (2005). *Theorizing education practice: Funds of knowledge in households.* Mahwah, NJ: Erlbaum.

Good, T., & Brophy, J. (2003). *Looking into classrooms* (9th ed.) Boston: Allyn & Bacon.

Goodman, K. (1986). *What's whole in whole language?* Portsmouth, NH: Heinemann.

Goodman, K. (1993). *Phonics phacts.* Portsmouth, NH: Heinemann.

Goodman, Y., & Owacki, G. (2002). *Kidwatching: Documenting children's literacy development.* Portsmouth, NH: Heinemann.

Goswami, U. (2001). Early phonological development and the acquisition of literacy. In D. K. Dickenson & S. B. Neuman (Eds.), *Handbook of early literacy research* (vol. 2). New York: Guilford.

Graesser, A. C., McNamara, D. S., & Louwerse, M. M. (2011). Methods of automated text analysis. In M. L. Kamil, P. D. Pearson, E. B. Moje, & P. P. Afflerbach (Eds.), *Handbook of reading research* (vol. IV, pp. 34–35). New York: Routledge.

Graff, G., & Birkenstein, C. (2006). *"They Say/I Say": The moves that matter in academic writing.* New York: W. W. Norton.

Graff, H. (2010). *Literacy myths, legacies, and lessons: New studies on literacy.* Piscataway, NJ: Transaction Publishers.

Graham, S., & Harris, K. (2007). Best practices in teaching planning. In S. Graham, C. A. MacArthur, & J. Fitzgerald (Eds.), *Best practices in writing instruction* (pp. 119–140). New York: Guilford.

Graham, S., Harris, K., & Fink, B. (2000). Is handwriting causally related to learning how to write? Treatment of handwriting problems in beginning readers. *Journal of Educational Psychology, 92*(4), 620–633.

Graves, D. (1983). *Writing: Teachers and children at work.* Portsmouth, NH: Heinemann.

Graves, M. F. (2006). *The vocabulary book: Learning and instruction.* New York: Teachers College Press.

Gray, C., McCloy, S., Dunbar, C., Mitchell, D., & Ferguson, J. (2007). Added value or familiar face? The impact of learning support assistants on young readers. *Early Childhood Research 5*(3), 285–300.

Green, L. J. (2002). *African American English: A linguistic introduction.* Cambridge: Cambridge University Press.

Greenwood, S.C., & Flanigan, K. (2007, November). Overlapping vocabulary and comprehension: Context clues complement semantic gradients. *The Reading Teacher, 61*(3), 249–254.

Grossman, P., & Thompson, C. (2004). *Curriculum materials: Scaffolds for new teacher learning?* (Research Report R-04-1). Seattle: Center for the Study of Teaching and Policy, University of Washington.

Gunderson, L., & Siegel, L. S. (2001). The evils of the use of IQ tests to define learning disabilities in first- and second- language learners. *Reading Teacher, 55*(1), 48–55.

Guthrie, J. T. (2002). Engagement and motivation in reading instruction. In M. L. Kamil, J. B. Manning, & H. J. Walberg (Eds.), *Successful reading instruction* (pp. 137–154). Greenwich, CT: Information Age.

Guthrie, J. T. (2004). Teaching for literacy engagement. *Journal of Literacy Research, 36*(1), 1–28.

Guthrie, J. T., & Humenick, N. M. (2004). Motivating students to read: Evidence for classroom practices that increase motivation and achievement. In P. McCardle & V. Chhabra (Eds.), *The voice of evidence in reading research* (pp. 329–354). Baltimore: Brookes.

Guthrie, J. T., McGough, K., & Wigfield, A. (1994). *Measuring reading activity: An inventory* (Instructional Resource No. 4). Athens: National Reading Research Center, University of Georgia and University of Maryland.

Guthrie, J. T., & Wigfield, A. (2000). Engagement and motivation in reading. In M. L. Kamil, P. B. Mosenthal, P. D. Pearson, & R. Barr (Eds.), *Handbook of reading research* (vol. 3, pp. 403–422). Mahwah, NJ: Erlbaum.

Guthrie, J. T., Wigfield, A., & Perencevich, K. C. (2004). *Motivating reading comprehension: Concept-oriented reading instruction.* Mahwah, NJ: Erlbaum.

Halladay, J. L. (2012). Revisiting key assumptions of the reading level framework. *Reading Teacher, 66*(1), 53–62.

Halliday, M. A. K. (1993/2003). Towards a language-based theory of learning. In M. A. K. Halliday (Ed.), *The language of early childhood* (pp. 327–352). London: Continuum.

Halliday, M. A. K. (1999/2003). Grammar and the construction of educational knowledge. In M. A. K. Halliday (Ed.), *The language of early childhood* (pp. 353–372). London: Continuum.

Halliday, M. A. K., & Hasan, R. (1976). *Cohesion in English*. London: Longman.

Halliday, M. A. K., & Martin, J. R. (1993). *Writing science: Literacy and discursive power*. Pittsburgh, PA: University of Pittsburgh Press.

Hammond, W. D., & Nessel, D. D. (2011). *The comprehension experience: Engaging readers through effective inquiry and discussion*. Portsmouth, NH: Heinemann.

Hancin-Bhatt, B., & Nagy, W. (1994). Lexical transfer and second language morphological development. *Applied Psycholinguistics, 15*(3), 289–310.

Hansen, J. (2001). *When writers read* (2nd ed.). Portsmouth, NH: Heinemann.

Hansen, J., & Pearson, P. D. (1984). An instructional study: Improving inferential comprehension of fourth grade good and poor readers. *Journal of Educational Psychology, 75*, 821–829.

Harre, R. (1984). *Personal being: A theory for individual psychology*. Cambridge, MA: Harvard University Press.

Harris, J., Golinkoff, R. M., & Hirsch-Pasek, K. (2011). Lessons from the crib for the classroom: How children really learn vocabulary. In S. B. Neuman & D. K. Dickinson (Eds.), *Handbook of early literacy research* (vol. 3). New York: Guilford.

Harris, K., & Graham, S. (1996). *Making the writing process work: Strategies for composition and self-regulation* (2nd ed.). Cambridge, MA: Brookline Books.

Hart, B., & Risley, T. (1995). *Meaningful differences in the everyday experiences of young American children*. Baltimore: Brookes.

Hasbrouk, J. E., & Tindal, G. (2006). Oral reading fluency norms: A valuable assessment tool for reading teachers. *Reading Teacher, 59*, 636–644.

Hattie, J. (2009). *Visible learning: A synthesis of over 800 meta-analyses relating to achievement*. New York: Routledge.

Havelock, E. (1983). *The literate revolution in Greece and its cultural consequences*. Cambridge, MA: Harvard University Press.

Havelock, E. (1988). *The muse learns to write: Reflections on orality and literacy from antiquity to the present*. New Haven, CT: Yale University Press.

Heibert, E., & Mesmer, H. (2006). Perspectives on text difficulty of beginning reading texts. In D. K. Dickinson & S. B. Neuman (Eds.), *Handbook of early literacy research* (vol. 2). New York: Guilford.

Helman, L. (Ed.). (2009). *Literacy development with English learners: Research-based instruction in grades K–6*. New York: Guilford.

Helman, L., & Bear, D. R., Templeton, S., Invernizzi, M., & Johnston, F. (2012). *Words their way with English learners: Word study for phonics, vocabulary, and spelling* (2nd ed.). Boston: Pearson/Allyn & Bacon.

Helman, L., & Burns, M. K. (2008). What does oral language have to do with it? Helping young English-language learners acquire a sight word vocabulary. *Reading Teacher, 62*(1), pp. 14–19.

Helsel, L., & Greenberg, D. (2007). Helping struggling writers succeed: Self-regulated strategy instruction program. *The Reading Teacher, 60*(8), 752–760.

Henderson, E. H. (1981). *Learning to read and spell: The child's knowledge of words*. DeKalb: Northern Illinois Press.

Henderson, E. H. (1985). *Teaching spelling*. Boston: Houghton Mifflin.

Henderson, S., Petrosino, A., Guckenburg, S., & Hamilton, S. (2008). *A second follow-up year for "Measuring how benchmark assessments affect student achievement"* (REL Technical Brief No. 002). Washington, DC: National Center for Educational Evaluation and Regional Assistance, Institute of Education Sciences, U.S. Department of Education.

Henk, W. A., & Melnick, S. A. (1995). Reader Self-Perception Scale (RSPS): A new tool for measuring how children feel about themselves as readers. *The Reading Teacher, 48*, 470–482.

Hersch, J., & Andrews, S. (2012). Lexical quality and reading skill: Bottom-up and top-down contributions to sentence processing. *Scientific Studies of Reading, 16*(3), 240–262.

Hess, K. (2011). *Local assessment toolkit*. khess@nciea.org.

Hess, K. (2011). *Learning progressions frameworks designed for use with the Common Core State Standards in English Language Arts & Literacy K–12*. National Center for the Improvement of Educational Assessment.

Hiebert, E. (2005). State reform policies and the reading task for first graders. *Elementary School Journal, 105*, 245–266.

Hiebert, E. (2011, December/2012, January). The Common Core's staircase of text complexity: Getting the size of the first step right. *Reading Today*. Newark, DE: International Reading Association.

Hiebert, E. H. (2005). State reform policies and the reading task for first graders. *Elementary School Journal, 105*, 245–266.

Hiebert, E. H., & Lubliner, S. (2008). The nature, learning, and instruction of general academic vocabulary. In A. Farstrup & S. J. Samuels (Eds.), *What research has to say about vocabulary instruction* (pp. 106–129). Newark, DE: International Reading Association.

Hiebert, E. H., & Raphael, T. E. (1998). *Early literacy instruction*. Orlando, FL: Harcourt Brace.

Hiebert, E. H., & Sailors, M. (2008). *Finding the right texts: What works for beginning and struggling readers*. New York: Guilford.

Hiebert, E. H., & Taylor, B. M. (2000). Beginning reading instruction: Research on early interventions. In M. Kamil, P. Mosenthal, R. Barr, & P. D. Pearson (Eds.), *Handbook of Reading Research* (vol. 3, pp. 455–482). Mahwah, NJ: Erlbaum.

Hiebert, E. H., & Taylor, B. M. (2011). Beginning reading instruction: Research on early interventions. In M. L. Kamil, P. Mosenthal, P. D. Pearson, & R. Barr (Eds.), Handbook of reading research (vol. 3, pp. 455–482). Mahwah, NJ: Erlbaum.

Hillocks, G., Jr. (2011). *Teaching argument writing, grades 6–12*. Portsmouth, NH: Heinemann.

Hoffman, J. (2000). The de-democratization of schools and literacy in America. *Reading Teacher, 53*, 616–623.

Hoffman, J., Sailors, M., Duffy, G. G., & Beretvas, N. (2004). The effective elementary classroom literacy environment: Examining the validity of the TEX-IN3 observation system. *Journal of Literacy Research, 36*, 289–320.

Holdaway, D. (1979). *The foundations of literacy*. Sydney: Ashton Scholastic.

Horsford, P. L. (1978). The silent curriculum: Its impact on teaching the basics. *Educational Leadership, 36*(3), 211–215.

Howard, G. (2006). *We can't teach what we don't know: White teachers, multiracial schools* (2nd ed.). New York: Teachers College Press.

Huffman, L. E. (1998). Spotlighting specifics by combining focus question with K-W-L. *Journal of Adolescent and Adult Literacy, 41,* 470–472.

Hughes, M., & Searle, D. (1997). *The violent e and other tricky sounds: Learning to spell from kindergarten through grade 6.* York, ME: Stenhouse.

Ikpeze, C. H, & Boyd, F. B. (2007). Web-based inquiry learning: Facilitating thoughtful literacy with WebQuests. *The Reading Teacher, 60*(7), 644–654.

Invernizzi, M., Abouzeid, M., & Gill, T. (1994). Using students' invented spellings as a guide for spelling instruction that emphasizes word study. *The Elementary School Journal, 95*(2), 155–167.

Invernizzi, M., & Hayes, L. (2004). Developmental-spelling research: A systematic imperative. *Reading Research Quarterly, 39,* 216–228.

Invernizzi, M., Johnston, F., Bear, D. R., & Templeton, S. (2009). *Words their way: Word sorts for within word pattern spellers* (2nd ed.) Boston: Pearson/Allyn & Bacon.

Invernizzi, M., Juel, C., Swank, L., & Meier, J. (2009). *Phonological Awareness Literacy Screening, Kindergarten (PALS-K).* Charlottesville: University of Virginia Press.

Invernizzi, M., Landrum, T. J., Howell, J. L., & Warley, H. P. (2005). Toward the peaceful coexistence of test developers, policymakers, and teachers in an era of accountability. *Reading Teacher, 57*(7), 610–618.

Invernizzi, M., Meier, J., & Juel, C. (2006). *Phonological Awareness Literacy Screening, Grades 1–3 (PALS 1–3).* Charlottesville: University of Virginia Press.

Invernizzi, M., Sullivan, A., Meier, J., & Swank, L. (2004). *Phonological Awareness Literacy Screening, Preschool (PALS-PreK).* Charlottesville: University of Virginia Press.

Irwin, J. (2006). *Teaching reading comprehension processes* (3rd ed.). Boston: Allyn & Bacon.

Israel, S. E. D., & Duffy, G. G. (Eds.). (2009). *Handbook of research on reading comprehension.* New York: Taylor & Francis.

James, W. (1958). *Talks to teachers on psychology and to students on some of life's ideals.* New York: W. W. Norton. (Original work published 1899.)

Jensen, E. (2005). *Teaching with the brain in* mind (2nd ed.). Alexandria, VA: Association for Supervision & Curriculum Development.

Jimenez, R. T. (2004). More equitable literacy assessment for Latino students. *Reading Teacher, 57,* 576–578.

Johns, J. J. (1980). First graders' concepts about print. *Reading Research Quarterly, 15*(4), 529–549.

Johns, J. J. (2012). *Basic reading inventory: Pre-primer through Grade Twelve and Early Literacy Assessments* (11th ed.). Dubuque, IA: Kendall/Hunt.

Johnson, D. W., & Johnson, R. T. (1998). *Learning together and along: Cooperative, competitive, and individualistic learning.* Boston: Allyn & Bacon.

Johnson, M. H., Munakata, Y., & Gilmore, R. O. (Eds.). (2008). *Brain development and cognition: A reader* (2nd ed.). New York: Wiley and Sons.

Johnston, F. (1998). The readers, the text, and the task: Learning words in first grade. *The Reading Teacher, 51,* 666–675.

Johnston, F. (2000). Word learning in predictable text. *Journal of Educational Psychology, 92,* 258–255.

Johnston, F., Bear, D. R., Invernizzi, M., & Templeton, S. (2009). *Words their way: Word sorts for letter name-alphabetic spellers* (2nd ed.). Boston: Pearson/Allyn & Bacon.

Johnston, F., Invernizzi, M., Bear, D. R., & Templeton, S. (2009). *words their way: word sorts for syllables and affixes spellers.* Boston: Pearson/Allyn & Bacon.

Johnston, F., Invernizzi, M., Bear, D. R., Templeton, S., & Helman, L. (in press). *Words their way for preK–K.* Boston: Pearson/Allyn & Bacon.

Johnston, F., Invernizzi, M., Juel, C., & Lewis-Wagner, D. (2009). *Book buddies: A tutoring framework for struggling readers* (2nd ed.). New York: Guilford.

Johnston, P. (2004). *Choice words: How our language affects children's learning.* Portland, ME: Stenhouse.

Johnston, P. (2012). *Opening minds: Using language to change lives.* Portland, ME: Stenhouse.

Johnston, P., & Costello, P. (2005). Principles for literacy assessment. *Reading Research Quarterly, 40* (2), 256–267.

Juel, C. (1988). Learning to read and write: A longitudinal student of 54 children from first through fourth grades. *Journal of Educational Psychology, 80,* 437–447.

Juel, C. (1991). Beginning reading. In R. Barr, M. Kamil, P. Mosenthal, & P. D. Pearson (Eds.), *Handbook of reading research* (vol. II, pp. 759–788). New York: Longman.

Juel, C., Biancarosa, G., Coker, D., & Deffes, R. (2003). Walking with Rosie: A cautionary tale of literacy instruction. *Educational Leadership, 60*(7), 12–18.

Juel, C., & Minden-Cupp, C. (2000). Learning to read words: Linguistic units and instructional strategies. *Reading Research Quarterly, 35,* 458–492.

Justice, L., Invernizzi, M., & Meier, J. (2002). Designing and implementing an early literacy screening protocol: Suggestions for the speech-language pathologist. *Speech and Hearing Services in Schools, 33,* 84–101.

Justice, L. M., Pence, K., Bowles, R., & Wiggins, A. (2006). An investigation of four hypotheses concerning the order by which 4-year-old children learn the alphabet letters. *Early Childhood Research Quarterly, 21*(3), 374–389.

Justice, L. M., & Piasta, S. (2011). Developing children's print knowledge though adult-child storybook reading interactions: Print referencing as an instructional practice. In S. B. Neuman & D. K. Dickinson (Eds.), *Handbook of early literacy research* (vol. 3). New York: Guilford.

Kalyuga, M., & Kalyuga, S. (2008). Metaphor awareness in teaching vocabulary. *Language Learning Journal, 36*(2), 249–257.

Kamil, M. L. (2003). *Adolescents and literacy: Reading for the 21st century.* Washington, DC: Alliance for Excellent Education.

Kamil, M. L., Borman, G. D., Dole, J., Kral, C. C., Salinger, T., & Torgesen, J. (2008). *Improving adolescent literacy: Effective classroom and intervention practices: A practice guide* (NCEE#2008-4027). Washington, DC: National Center for Education Evaluation and Regional Assistance, Institute of Education Sciences, U.S. Department of Education.

Kansas Department of Education. (2011). Kansas College and Career Ready Standards. Retrieved October 17, 2012. http://www.ksde.org/Default.aspx?tabid=5280. Retrieved Ocrober 17, 2012.

Karmilov, K., & Karmilov-Smith, A. (2001). *Pathways to language: From fetus to adolescent.* Cambridge, MA: Harvard University Press.

Katz, L. A., & Carlisle, J. F. (2009). Teaching students with reading difficulties to be close readers: A feasibility study. *Language, Speech, and Hearing Services in Schools, 40,* 325–340.

Kaufman, G. F., & Libby, L. K. (2012). Changing beliefs and behavior through experience-taking. *Journal of Personality and Social Psychology, 103*(1), 1–19.

Keene, E. O. (2002). From good to memorable: Characteristics of highly effective comprehension teaching. In C. C. Block, L. Gambell, & M. Pressley (Eds.), *Improving comprehension instruction: Rethinking research, theory, and classroom practice* (pp. 80–105). San Francisco: Jossey-Bass.

Kermode, F. (Ed.). (1975). *Selected prose of T. S. Eliot.* Boston: Houghton Mifflin.

Kieffer, M. (2012). Before and after third grade: Longitudinal evidence for the shifting role of socioeconomic status in reading growth. *Reading & Writing, 25*(7), 1725–1746. doi: 10.1007/s11145-011-9339-2

Klenk, L., & Kibby, M. W. (2000). Re-mediating reading difficulties: Appraising the past, reconciling the present, constructing the future. In M. L. Kamil, M. Mosenthal, P. D. Pearson, & R. Barr (Eds.), *Handbook of reading research* (vol. III, pp. 667–690). New York: Longman.

Kletzien, S. B. (2009). Paraphrasing: An effective comprehension strategy. *Reading Teacher, 63*(1).

Knapp, M. S. (1995). *Teaching for meaning in high poverty classrooms.* New York: Teachers College Press.

Kohlberg, L. (1987). *Child psychology and childhood education: A cognitive-developmental view.* New York: Longman.

Kohn, A. (1999). *Punished by rewards: The trouble with gold stars, incentive plans, A's, praise, and other bribes.* New York: Houghton Mifflin.

Kozlow, M., & Bellamy, P. (2004). *Experimental study on the impact of the 6+1 writing model on student achievement in writing.* Portland, OR: Northwest Regional Educational Laboratory.

Krashen, S. (2004). *The power of reading: Insights from the research* (2nd ed). Portsmouth, NH: Heineman.

Krashen, S. D. (1987). *Principles and practice in second language acquisition.* New York: Prentice-Hall International.

Krashen, S. D. (2003). *Explorations in language acquisition and use: The Taipei lectures.* Portsmouth, NH: Heinemann.

Krech, B. (2000). *Fresh and fun: Teaching with kids' names.* New York: Scholastic.

Kretovics, J. R. (1985). Critical literacy: Challenging the assumptions of mainstream educational theory. *Journal of Education, 167*(2): 50–62.

Kuhn, D., Shaw, V., & Felton, M. (1997). Effects of dyadic interaction on argumentative reasoning. *Cognition and Instruction, 15*(3), 287–315.

Kuhn, M. R. & Stahl, S. A. (2004). Fluency: A review of developmental and remedial practices. In R. B. Ruddell & N. J. Unrau (Eds.), *Theoretical models and processes of reading* (5th ed., pp. 412–451). Newark, NJ: International Reading Association.

Kuhn, M. R., Schwanenflugel, P. J., & Meisinger, E. B. (2010). Review of research: Aligning theory and assessment of reading fluency: Automaticity, prosody, and definitions of fluency. *Reading Research Quarterly, 45*(2), 230–251.

Kuhn, M., & Stahl, S. (2003). Fluency: A review of developmental and remedial strategies. *Journal of Educational Psychology, 95*(1), 3–21.

Kuhn, M., Schwanenflugel, P., Morris, R., Morrow, L, Woo, D., Meisinger, E., Sevcik, R., Bradley, B., & Stahl, S. (2006). Teaching children to become fluent and automatic readers., *Journal of Literacy Research, 38*, 357–387.

LaBerge, D., & Samuels, S. J. (1974). Toward a theory of automatic processing in reading. *Cognitive Psychology, 6*, 293–323.

Labov, W. (1972). *Language in the inner city: Studies in the Black English vernacular.* Philadelphia: University of Pennsylvania Press.

Labov, W. (2001). *Principles of linguistic change, II: Social factors.* Oxford: Blackwell.

Ladson-Billings, G. J. (1998). Just what is critical race theory and what's it doing in a nice field like education? *International Journal of Qualitative Studies in Education, 11*(1).

Ladson-Billings, G. J. (1999). Preparing teachers for diverse student populations: A critical race theory perspective. *Review of Research in Education, 24*, 211–247.

Landauer, T. K., & Dumais, S. T. (1997). A solution to Plato's problem: The latent semantic analysis theory of acquisition, induction, and representation of knowledge. *Psychological Review, 104*, 211–240.

Lane, H. B., & Wright, T. L. (2007). Maximizing the effectiveness of reading aloud. *Reading Teacher, 60*(7), 668–675.

Lanehart, S. (Ed.). (2001). *Sociocultural and historical contexts of African American English.* Amsterdam: John Benjamins.

Lanehart, S. L. (Ed.). (2009). *African American women's language: Discourse, education and identity.* Newcastle upon Tyne, UK: Cambridge Scholars Publishing.

Langer, J. (2001). Beating the odds: Teaching middle and high school students to read and write well. *American Educational Research Journal, 38*, 837–880.

Lawrence, J., & Snow, C. (2011). Oral discourse and reading. In M. Kamil, P. D. Pearson, E. Birr Moje, & P. P. Afflerbach (Eds.), *The handbook of reading research* (vol. IV). New York: Routledge.

Leach, J. M., Scarborough, H., & Rescorda, L. (2003). Late-emerging reading disabilities. *Journal of Educational Research, 52*(4), 557–578.

Lefstein, A. (2009). Rhetorical grammar and the grammar of schooling: Teaching "powerful verbs" in the English National Literacy Strategy. *Linguistics and Education, 20*, 378–400.

Lefstein, A., & Snell, J. (2011). Promises and problems of teaching with popular culture: A linguistic ethnographic analysis of discourse genre mixing in a literacy lesson. *Reading Research Quarterly, 46*(1), 40–69.

Lehmann, N. (1997, November). The reading wars. *The Atlantic Monthly, 280*(5), 128–134. www.theatlantic.com/past/docs/issues/97nov/read.htm.

Lenneberg, E. (1967). *The biological foundations of language.* New York: Wiley & Sons.

Lenski, S., Ehlers-Zavala, F., Daniel, M., & Sun-Irminger, X. (2006). Assessing English language learners in mainstream classrooms. *Reading Teacher 60*(1), 24–34.

Lesaux, N. (2010, May). George Graham Memorial Lecture, University of Virginia.

Lesaux, N. K., Koda, K., Siegel, L. S., & Shanahan, T. (2008). Development of literacy. In D. August & T. Shanahan (Eds.), *Developing literacy in second-language learners: Report of the National Literacy Panel on language-minority children and youth* (pp. 75–122). Mahwah, NJ: Erlbaum.

Leslie, L., & Caldwell, J. (2011). *Qualitative Reading Inventory–5.* Boston: Allyn & Bacon.

Leslie, L., & Calhoon, A. (1995). Factors affecting children's reading of rimes, reading ability, word frequency, and rime-neighborhood size. *Journal of Educational Psychology, 87*, 576–586.

Lexile Framework for Reading. (2013). www.lexile.co.

Lipson, M. J., Mosenthal, J., & Mekkelson, J. (1999). The nature of comprehension among grade two children: Variability in retellings as a function of development, text, and task. In T. Shanahan & F. V. Rodriguez-Brown (Eds.), *Forty-eighth yearbook of the National Reading Conference* (pp. 104–119). Chicago: National Reading Conference.

Lipson, M. Y., & Wixson, K. K. (2009). *Assessment and instruction of reading and writing differences* (4th ed.). Boston: Pearson/Allyn & Bacon.

Lipson, M. Y., & Wixson, K. K. (Eds.). (2010). *Successful approaches to RTI: Collaborative practices for improving K–12 literacy.* Newark, DE: International Reading Association.

Lonigan, C. J., Burgess, S. R., & Anthony, J. L. (2004). Development of emergent literacy and early reading skills in preschool children: Evidence from a latent variable longitudinal study. *Developmental Psychology, 36,* 596–613.

Longman study dictionary of American English. (2006). Harlow, England: Pearson Longman.

Lyon, G. R. (1995). Research initiatives in learning disabilities: Contributions from scientists supported by the National Institute of Child Health and Development. *Journal of Child Neurology, 10* (suppl. S120-S126).

Lyons, C. (2001). The role of emotion in memory and comprehension. In G. S. Pinnell & P. L. Scharer (Eds.), *Extending our reach: Teaching for comprehension in reading grades K–2.* Columbus: Literacy Collaborative at the Ohio State University.

MacArthur, C., Schwartz, S., Graham, S., Molloy, D., & Harris, K. R. (1996). Integration of strategy instruction into a whole language classroom: A case study. *Learning Disability Research and Practice, 11,* 168–176.

MacGinitie, W. H., MacGinitie, R. K., Maris, K., & Dreyer, L. (2000). *The Gates-MacGinitie reading tests* (4th ed). Itasca, IL: Riverside.

Macon, J. M., Bewel, D., & Vogt, M. (1991). *Responses to literature.* Newark, NJ: International Reading Association.

Madaus, G., & Russell, M. (2010/2011). Paradoxes of high-stakes testing. *Journal of Education, 190*(1/2), 21–30.

Madura, S. (1995). The line and texture of aesthetic response: Primary children study authors and illustrators. *Reading Teacher, 49*(2), 110–118.

Madura, S. (1998). *Transitional readers and writers respond to literature through discussion, writing, and art.* Unpublished doctoral dissertation, University of Nevada, Reno.

Madura, S. (1998). An artistic element: Four transitional readers and writers respond to the picture books of Patricia Polacco and Gerald McDermott. *National Reading Conference Yearbook, 47,* 366–376.

Marciano, J. (1997). *Civic illiteracy and education.* New York: Peter Lang.

Martinez, M. (1993). Motivating story reenactments. *Reading Teacher, (46)*8, 682–688.

Martinez, M., Roser, N., & Stecker, S. (1999). "I never thought I could be a star": A readers' theatre ticket to reading fluency. *Reading Teacher, 52,* 326–334.

Marx, S., & Pennington, J. (2003). Pedagogies of critical race theory: Experimentations with white preservice teachers. *International Journal of Qualitative Studies in Education, 16*(1), 91–110. doi:10.1080/0951839022000036381

Marzano, R. J., Pickering, R. J., & Pollock, J. E. (2004). *Classroom instruction that works: Research-based strategies for increasing student achievement.* Englewood Cliffs, NJ: Prentice Hall.

Mashburn, A. J., Justice, L. M., Downer, J. T., & Pianta, R. C. (2009). Peer effects on children's language achievement during pre-kindergarten. *Child Development, 80*(3), 686–702.

Mathes, P. G., Denton, C. A., Fletcher, J. M., Anthony, J. L., Francis, D. J., & Schatschneider, C. (2005). The effects of theoretically different instruction and student characteristics on the skills of struggling readers. *Reading Research Quarterly*, 40(2), 148–182.

McBride-Chang, C., Shu, H. Y. W., Ng, J., Meng, X., & Penney, T. (2007). Morphological structure awareness, vocabulary, and reading. In R. K. Wagner, A. E. Muse, & K. R. Tannebaum (Eds.), *Vocabulary acquisition: Implications for reading acquisition* (pp. 104–122). New York: Guilford.

McCarrier, A., Pinnell, G. S., & Fountas, I. (1999). *Interactive writing: How language and literacy come together, K–2.* Portsmouth, NH: Heinemann.

McConachie, S. M., & Petrosky, A. R. (2010). *Content matters: A disciplinary literacy approach to improving student learning.* San Francisco, CA: Jossey-Bass.

McCormick, S., & Zutell, J. (2010). *Instructing students who have literacy problems* (6th ed.). Boston: Pearson/Allyn & Bacon.

McGee, L., & Richgels, D. (1990). *Literacy's beginnings: Supporting young readers and writers.* Boston: Pearson.

McGee, L., & Schickedanz, J. (2007). Repeated interactive read-alouds in preschool and kindergarten. *Reading Teacher, 60,* 742–752.

McGill-Franzen, A. (2000). Policy and instruction: What is the relationship? In M. L. Kamil, P. Mosenthal, P. D. Pearson, & R. Barr (Eds.), *Handbook of reading research* (vol. 3, pp. 889–908). Mahwah, NJ: Erlbaum.

McGill-Franzen, A. M., & Allington, R. L. (1990). Comprehension and coherence: Neglected elements of literacy instruction in remedial and resource room services. *Journal of Reading, Writing, and Learning Disabilities, 6*(2), 149–182.

McIntyre, E., Rightmyer, E., Powell, R., Powers, S., & Petrosko, J. (2006). How much should young children read? A study of the relationship between development and instruction. *Literacy Teaching and Learning, 11*(1), 51–72.

McKenna, M. (2001). Development of reading attitudes. In L. Verhoeven & C. Snow (Eds.), *Literacy and motivation: Reading engagement in individuals and groups* (pp. 135–158). Mahwah, NJ: Erlbaum.

McKenna, M., Labbo, L., Conradi, K., & Baxter, J. (2010). Effective use of technology in literacy instruction. In L. Morrow & L. B. Gambrell (Eds.), *Best practices in literacy instruction* (4th ed.). New York: Guilford.

McKenna, M. C., & Kear, D. J. (1990). Measuring attitude toward reading: A new tool for teachers. *Reading Teacher, 43*(9), 626–639.

McKenna, M. C., & Stahl, S. A. (2003). *Assessment for reading instruction.* New York: Guilford.

McKeough, A., Palmer, J., Jarvey, M., & Bird, S. (2007). Best narrative writing practices when teaching from a developmental perspective. In S. Graham, C. A. MacArthur, & J. Fitzgerald (Eds.), *Best practices in writing instruction* (pp. 50–73) New York: Guilford.

McLaughlin, M. (2009). *Guided comprehension in grades 3–8* (2nd ed.). Newark, DE: International Reading Association.

McLaughlin M., & DeVoogd, G. (2011). Critical literacy as comprehension: Understanding at deeper levels. In D. Lapp & D. Fisher (Eds.), *Handbook of research on teaching the English*

Language Arts (pp. 272–282). New York: Taylor & Francis.

McMahon, S. I., Raphael, T. E., Goatley, V. J., & Pardo, L. S. (1997). *The book club connection: Literacy learning and classroom talk.* New York: Teachers College Press.

McMaster, K. L., Fuchs, D., & Fuchs, L. S. (2006). Research on peer-assisted learning strategies: The promise and limitations of peer-mediated instruction. *Reading & Writing Quarterly, 22*(1), 5–25.

McVee, M. B., Dunsmore, K., & Gavelek, J. R. (2005). Schema theory revisited. *Review of Educational Research, 75,* 531–566.

McWhorter, J. (2000). *Spreading the word: Language and dialect in America.* Portsmouth, NH: Heinemann.

McWhorter, J. (2001). *Word on the street: Debunking the myth of "pure" Standard English.* New York: Basic Books.

Meier, D., & Wood, G. (Eds.). (2004). *Many children left behind: How the No Child Left Behind Act is damaging our children and our schools.* Boston: Beacon.

Melekoglu, M. C. (2011). Impact of motivation to read on reading gains for struggling readers with and without learning disabilities. *Learning Disability Quarterly, 34*(4), 248–261.

Merriam-Webster new book of word histories. (1991). Springfield, MA: Merriam-Webster.

Mesmer, E. M., & Mesmer, H. A. E. (2008). Response to intervention (RTI): What teachers of reading need to know. *The Reading Teacher, 62*(4), 280–290.

Mesmer, H. A. (2006). Beginning reading materials: A national survey of primary teachers' reported uses and beliefs. *Journal of Literacy Research, 38,* 389–425.

Metcalfe, J., & Shimamura, A. P. (1994). *Metacognition: Knowing about knowing.* Cambridge, MA: MIT Press.

Metsala, J. (2011). Lexical reorganization and the emergence of phonological awareness. In S. B. Neuman & D. K. Dickinson (Eds.), *Handbook of early literacy research* (vol. 3). New York: Guilford.

Meyer, B. J. F., & Rice, G. E. (1984). The structure of text. In P. D. Pearson, R. Barr, M. D. Kamil, & P. Mosenthal (Eds.), *Handbook of reading research* (vol. 1, pp. 319–351). White Plains, NY: Longman.

Michaels, S., O'Connor, C., & Resnick, L. B. (2008) Deliberative discourse idealized and realized: Accountable talk in the classroom and in civic life. *Studies in Philosophy and Education, 27*(4), 283–297.

Miller, D. (2002). *Reading with meaning: Teaching comprehension in the primary grades.* Portland, ME: Stenhouse.

Miller, G. A. (1999). On knowing a word. *Annual Review of Psychology, 50,* 1–19.

Mills, K. A. (2010). A review of the "digital turn" in the New Literacy studies. *Review of Educational Research, 80*(2), 246–271.

Milner, H. R. (2003). Teacher reflection and race in cultural contexts: History, meanings, and methods in teaching. *Theory into Practice, 42*(3), 173–180.

Moll, L. (2005). Reflections and possibilities. In N. González, L. Moll, & C. Amanti (Eds.), *Funds of knowledge: Theorizing practices in households, communities, and classrooms* (pp. 275–288). Mahwah, NJ: Erlbaum.

Moll, L. C., & Gonzalez, N. (1994). Critical issues: Lessons from research with language-minority children. *Journal of Reading Behavior, 26*(4), 439–457.

Moore, B., & Moore, M. (1997). *NTC's dictionary of Latin and Greek origins: A comprehensive guide to the classical origins of English words.* Chicago: NTC Publishing Group.

Morris D. (2005). *The Howard Street tutoring manual: Teaching at-risk readers in the primary grades* (2nd ed.). New York: Guilford.

Morris, D. (2008). *Diagnosis and correction of reading problems.* New York: Guilford.

Morris, D., Bloodgood, J. W., Lomax, R. G., & Perney, J. (2003). Developmental steps in learning to read: A logitudinal study in kindergarten and first grade. *Reading Research Quarterly, 38*(3), 302–328.

Morris, D., & Gaffney, M. (2011). Building reading fluency in a learning-disabled middle school reader. *Journal of Adolescent & Adult Literacy, 54*(5), 331–341.

Morris, D., & Perney, J. (1984). Developmental spelling as a predictor of first grade achievement. *Elementary School Journal, 84*(4), 441–457.

Morris, D., & Slavin, R. (Eds.). (2003). *Every child reading.* Boston: Allyn & Bacon.

Morris, D., Blanton, L., Blanton, W. E., Nowacek, J., & Perney, J. (1995). Teaching low-achieving spellers at their "instructional level" *Elementary School Journal, 96*(2), 163–178.

Morris, D., Shaw, B., & Perney, J. (1990). Helping low readers in grades 2 and 3: An after-school volunteer tutoring program. *The Elementary School Journal, 91*(2), 133–150.

Morris, D., Woodrow, T., Lomax, G. G., Perney, J., Kucan, L., Frye, E. M., Bloodgood, J. W., Ward, D., & Schlagal, R. (2010). Modeling aspects of print-processing skills: Implications for reading assessment. *Reading and Writing, 25*(1), 189–215.

Morrow, L. M. (1985). Retelling stories: A strategy for improving children's comprehension, concept of story structure and oral language complexity. *Elementary School Journal, 85*(5), 647–661.

Morrow, L. M. (1986). Effects of structural guidance in story retelling on children's dictation of original stories. *Journal of Reading Behavior,18,* 135–152.

Morrow, L. M. (1996). Story retelling: A discussion strategy to develop and assess comprehension. In L. B. Gambrell & J. F. Almasi (Eds.), *Lively discussions, Fostering engaged reading* (pp. 265–285). Newark, DE: International Reading Association.

Morrow, L. M., Reutzel, D. R., & Casey, H. (2006). Organization and management of language arts teaching: Classroom environments, groping practices, and exemplary instruction. In C. Evertson (Ed.), *Handbook of classroom management* (pp. 559–582). Mahwah, NJ: Erlbaum.

Morrow, L. M., & Schickedanz, J. A. (2006). The relationships between sociodramatic play and literacy development. In D. K. Dickinson & S. B. Neuman (Eds.), *Handbook of early literacy research* (vol. 2). New York: Guilford.

Morrow, L. M., & Smith, J. K. (1990). The effect of group setting on interactive storybook reading. *Reading Research Quarterly, 25,* 213–231.

Morrow, L. M., & Tracey, D. (1997). Instructional environments for language and learning: Considerations for young children. In J. Flood, S. B. Heath, & D. Lapp (Eds.), *Handbook of literacy educators: Research on teaching the communicative and visual arts* (pp. 475–485.) New York: Macmillan.

Morrow, L. M., & Weinstein, C. S. (1986). Encouraging voluntary reading: The impact of a literature program on children's use of library centers. *Reading Research Quarterly, 21,* 330–346.

Mosenthal, J., Lipson, M., Torncello, S., Russ, B., & Mekkelsen, J. (2004). Contexts and practices of six schools successful in obtaining reading achievement. *Elementary School Journal, 104* (5), 343–367.

Mountain, L. (2005). ROOTing out meaning: More morphemic analysis for primary pupils. *The Reading Teacher, 58*(8), 742–749.

Murray, D. M. (1982). Teaching the other self: The writer's first reader. *College Composition and Communication, 33*(2), 140–147.

Muter, V., Hulme, C., Snowling, M. J., & Stevenson, J. (2004). Phonemes, rimes, vocabulary, and grammatical skills as foundations of early reading development: Evidence from a longitudinal study. *Developmental Psychology, 40*(5), 665–681.

Nagy, W. (2007). Metalinguistic awareness and the vocabulary-comprehension connection. In R. K. Wagner, A. Muse, & K. Tannenbaum (Eds.), *Vocabulary acquisition: Implications for reading comprehension* (pp. 52–77). New York: Guilford.

Nagy, W., & Anderson, R. C. (1984). How many words are there in printed school English? *Reading Research Quarterly, 19*, 304–330.

Nagy, W., Berninger, V. W., & Abbott, R. D. (2006). Contributions of morphology beyond phonology to literacy outcomes of upper elementary and middle-school students. *Journal of Educational Psychology, 98*(1), 134–147.

Nagy, W., & Scott, J. (2000). Vocabulary processes. In M. L. Kamil, P. Mosenthal, P. D. Pearson, & R. Barr (Eds.), *Handbook of reading research* (vol. 3, pp. 269–284). Mahwah, NJ: Erlbaum.

Nagy, W., & Townsend, D. (2012). Words as tools: Learning academic vocabulary as language acquisition. *Reading Research Quarterly, 47*(1), 91–108.

Nagy, W., García, G., Durgunogiu, A., & Hancin-Bhatt, B. (1993). English–Spanish bilingual students' use of cognates in English reading. *Journal of Reading Behavior, 25*(3), 241–259.

National Center for Education Statistics. (2007). *The condition of education 2007.* http://nces.ed.gov/programs/coe/2007/pdf/07_2007.pdf. Retrieved March 17, 2008.

National Center for Educational Statistics. (2012), *The condition of education: Elementary and secondary education.* www.http://nces.ed.gov/pubsearch/pubsinfo.asp?pubid=2012045.

National Center for Learning Disabilities (NCLD). (2006). *Accommodations for students with LD.* www.ldonline.org/article/Accommodations_for_Students_with_LD.* Retrieved November 23, 2012.

National Commission on Excellence in Education. (1983). *A nation at risk.* Washington, DC: National Commission on Excellence in Education.

National Dissemination Center for Children with Disabilities (NICHDY). (2010a). *Subpart A: General provisions.* http://nichcy.org/laws/idea/partb/subparta#300.1. Retrieved November 23, 2012.

National Dissemination Center for Children with Disabilities (NICHDY). (2010b). *Supports, modifications, and accommodations for students.* http://nichcy.org/schoolage/accommodations#part2. Retrieved November 23, 2012.

National Institute of Child Health and Human Development (NICHHD). (2000). *Report of the National Institute of Child Health and Human Development. Teaching children to read: An evidence-based assessment of the scientific research literature on reading and its implications for reading instruction* (NIH Publication No. 00-4769). Washington, DC: U.S. Government Printing Office.

National Institute of Child Health and Human Development. (2000). *Report of the National Reading Panel. Teaching children to read: An evidence-based assessment of the scientific research literature on reading and its implications for reading instruction: Reports of the subgroups* (NIH Publication No. 00-4754). Washington, DC: U.S. Government Printing Office.

National Joint Committee on Learning Disabilities (NJCLD). (2008). Adolescent literacy and older students with learning disabilities. *Learning Disability Quarterly, 31*(2), 1–218.

National Reading Panel (NRP). (2000). *Teaching children to read: An evidence-based assessment of the scientific research literature on reading and its implications for reading instruction.* Washington, DC: National Institute of Child Health and Human Development.

Negrete, S. (2010). *Oral reading rate and accuracy and within word pattern spelling.* Unpublished doctoral dissertation, University of Nevada, Reno.

Nelson, K. (1981). Social cognition in a script framework. In J. H. Flavell & I. Ross (Eds.), *Social cognitive development: Frontiers and possible futures* (pp. 97–118). Cambridge: Cambridge University Press.

Nelson, K. (1996). *Language in cognitive development: The emergence of the mediated mind.* New York: Cambridge University Press.

Neuman, S. (2006). The knowledge gap: Implications of leveling the playing field for low-income and middle-income children. *Reading Research Quarterly, 41,* 176–201.

Neuman, S. B. (1999). Books make a difference: A study of access to literacy. *Reading Research Quarterly, 34*(3), 2–31.

Neuman, S. B., & Dickinson, D. K. (2011). *Handbook of early literacy research* (vol. 3). New York: Guilford.

Neuman, S. B., & Roskos, K. (1992). Literacy objects as cultural tools: Effects on children's literacy behavior in play. *Reading Research Quarterly, 27*(3), 203–225.

Newell, G. E., Beach, R., Smith, J., VanDerHeide, J., Kuhn, D., & Andriessen, J. (2011). Teaching and learning argumentative reading and writing: A review of research. *Reading Research Quarterly, 46*(3), 273–304.

Newman, D., Griffin, P., & Cole, M. (1989). *The construction zone: Working for cognitive change in school.* Cambridge: Cambridge University Press.

Nguyen, A., Shin, F., & Krashen, S. (2001). Development of the first language is not a barrier to second-language acquisition: Evidence from Vietnamese immigrants to the United States. *International Journal of Bilingual Education and Bilingualism, 4*(3), 159–164.

Nichols, S. L., & Berliner, D. (2007). *Collateral damage: How high-stakes testing corrupts America's schools.* Cambridge, MA: Harvard Education Press.

Nieto, S. (2009). *The light in their eyes: Creating multicultural learning communities* (2nd ed.). New York: Teachers College Press.

Nippold, M. A. (2007). *Later language development.* Austin, TX: Pro-Ed.

Notarnicola, A., Angelelli, P., Judica, A., & Zoccolotti, P. (2012). Development of spelling skills in a shallow orthography: The case of Italian language. *Reading & Writing: An Interdisciplinary Journal, 25*(5), 1171–1194.

Oatley, K. (1999). Why fiction may be twice as true as fact: Fiction as cognitive and emotional simulation. *Review of General Psychology, 3*(2), 101–117.

Oczkus, L. (2003). *Reciprocal teaching at work: Strategies for improving* reading comprehension. Newark, DE: International Reading Association.

Office of the Inspector General (2006, September). The Reading First Program's grant application: Final inspection report (ED-OIG/I13-F0017). Washington, DC: U.S Department of Education, Office of Inspector General. www.ed.gov/about/offices/list/oig/aireports/i13f0017.pdf. Retrieved September 19, 2012.

Ogle, D. (1986). K-W-L: A teaching model that develops active reading of expository texts. Reading Teacher, 39, 564–570.

Olson, D. (1996). The world on paper: The conceptual and cognitive implications of writing and reading. New York: Cambridge University Press.

Ong, W. (2002). Orality and literacy. London: Routledge.

Optiz, M. F., & Raskinski, T. (2008). Good-bye round robin reading: 25 effective oral reading strategies. Portsmouth, NH: Heinemann.

Ouellette, G. P., & Sénéchal, M. (2008). A window into early literacy: Exploring the cognitive and linguistic underpinnings of invented spelling. Scientific Studies of Reading, 12(2), 195–219.

Palincsar, A. S., & Brown, A. (1984). Reciprocal teaching of comprehension-fostering and comprehension-monitoring activities. Cognition and Instruction, 1(2), 117–175.

Palincsar, A. M., & Brown, A. L. (1986). Interactive teaching to promote independent learning from text. Reading Teacher, 39, 771–777.

Paris, S., & Carpenter, R. D. (2003). FAQs about IRIs. Reading Teacher, 12, 32–50.

Paris, S. G., Wasik, B. A., & Turner, J. C. (1991). The development of strategic readers. In R. Barr, M. L. Kamil, P. Mosenthal, & P. D. Pearson (Eds.), Handbook of reading research (pp. 609–640). White Plains, NY: Longman.

Patterson, F. R. A. (2000). The politics of phonics. Journal of Curriculum and Supervision, 15, 179–211.

Patterson, F. R. A. (2002). The politics of phonics. In R. L. Allington (Ed.), Big brother and the national reading curriculum: How ideology trumped evidence (pp. 157–194). Portsmouth, NH: Heineman

Paul, A. M. (2012). Your brain on fiction. www.nytimes.com/2012/03/18/opinion/sunday/the-neuroscience-of-your-brain-on-fiction.html?_r=1&pagewanted=all. Retrieved March 17, 2012.

Pearson, P. D. (2012, August). The Common Core Standards for English Language Arts: Launching pad for innovation or a rerun of No Child Left Behind. Presentation at The Vermont Reads Institute, Stowe, VT.

Pearson, P. D., & Gallagher, M. (1983). The instruction of reading comprehension. Contemporary Educational Psychology, 8, 317–344.

Pennington, J. L. (2007). Silence in the classroom/whispers in the halls: Autoethnography as pedagogy in white pre-service teacher education. Race, Ethnicity and Education, 10(1), 93–113.

Pennington, J. L., Brock, C. H., & Ndura, E. (2012). Unraveling the threads of white teachers' conceptions of caring: Repositioning white privilege. Urban Education, 47(4), 743–775. doi: 10.1177/0042085912441186

Pennington, J. L., & Sallas, R. G. (2009). Examining teacher dispositions toward linguistically and culturally diverse students. In L. Helman (Ed.), Literacy development with English learners: Research-based instruction in grades K–6 (pp. 213–233). New York: Guilford.

Perfetti, C. (1985). Reading ability. New York: Oxford University Press.

Perfetti, C. (2007). Reading ability: Lexical quality to comprehension. Scientific Studies of Reading, 11, 357–383.

Perfetti, C. A., Landi, N., & Oakhill, J. (2005). The acquisition of reading comprehension skill. In M. J. Snowling & C. Hulme (Eds.), The science of reading: A handbook (pp. 227–247). Oxford, England: Blackwell.

Peterson, R., & Eeds, M. A. (2007). Grand conversations: Literature groups in action. New York: Scholastic.

Phenix, J., & Cole, K. (2003). The spelling teacher's book of lists: Words to illustrate spelling patterns—And tips for teaching them (2nd ed.). Portland, ME: Stenhouse.

Piaget, J., & Inhelder, B. (1969). The psychology of the child. New York: Basic Books.

Pikulski, J. J., & Chard, D. J. (2005). Fluency: Bridge between decoding and reading comprehension. The Reading Teacher, 58, 510–519.

Pinnell, G. S., Lyons, G. A., DeFord, D. E., Bryk, A. S., & Seltzer, M. (1994). Comparing instructional models for the literacy education of high-risk first graders. Reading Research Quarterly, 29(1), 8.

Prensky, M. (2001). Digital natives, digital immigrants. On the Horizon, 9(5), 1–6.

Pressley, M. (2005). Reading instruction that works: The case for balanced teaching (3rd ed.). New York: Guilford.

Pressley, M., Allington, R., Wharton-McDonald, R., Collins Block, K., & Morrow, L. (2001). Learning to read: Lessons from exemplary first-grade classrooms. New York: Guilford.

Pritchard, R. J., & Honeycutt, R. L. (2006). The process approach to teaching writing: Examining its effectiveness. In C. A. MacArthur, S. Graham, & J. Fitzgerald (Eds.), Handbook of writing research (pp. 275–290). New York: Guilford.

Puranik, C. S., & Lonigan, C. J. (2011). From scribbles to scrabble: Preschool children's developing knowledge of written language. Reading and Writing, 24, 567–589.

Quint, J. C., Sepanik, S., & Smith, J. K. (2008). Using student data to improve teaching and learning: Findings from an evaluation of the Formative Assessments of Student Thinking in Reading (FAST-R) program in Boston elementary schools. New York: MDRC.

RAND Reading Study Group. (2002). Reading for understanding: Toward an R&D program in reading comprehension. Santa Monica, CA: RAND Corporation.

Raphael, T. E., & Au, K. (2005). QAR: Enhancing comprehension and test taking across grades and content areas. The Reading Teacher, 59(3), 206–221.

Raphael, T. E., Highfield, K., & Au, K. (2006). QAR Now: A powerful and practical framework that develops comprehension and higher-level thinking in all students. New York: Scholastic.

Raphael, T., & Pearson, P. D. (1985). Increasing students' awareness of sources of information for questioning answers. American Educational Research Journal, 22, 217–236.

Rapp, B., & Lipka, K. (2011). The literate brain: The relationship between spelling and reading. Journal of Cognitive Neuroscience, 23(5), 1180–1197.

Rasinksi, T. (2011). Teaching reading fluency. In T. Rasinski (Ed.), Rebuilding the foundation: Effective reading instruction for the 21st century (pp. 180–198). Bloomington, IN: Solution Tree.

Rasinski, T., Reutzel, D. R., Chard, D., & Linan-Thompson, S. (2011). Reading fluency. In M. L. Kamil, P. D. Pearson, E. B. Moje, & P. P. Afflerbach (Eds.), Handbook of reading research (vol. IV, pp. 286–319). New York: Routledge.

Rasinski, T., Rikli, A., & Johnston, S. (2009). Reading fluency: More than automaticity? More than a concern for the primary grades? *Literacy Research and Instruction, 48,* 350–361.

Ravitch, D. (2011). *The death and life of the great American school system.* New York: Basic Books.

Rayner, K., Foorman, B., Perfetti, C., Pesetsky, D., & Seidenber, M. (2001). How psychological science informs the teaching of reading. *Psychological Science in the Public Interest, 2,* 31–74.

Read, C. (1971). Pre-school children's knowledge of English phonology. *Harvard Educational Review, 41*(1), 1–34.

Reading Recovery Council of North America. (2012). *I'm a reflection of you.* readingrecoveryworks.org. Retrieved November 23, 2012.

Reutzel, D., Jones, C. D., Fawson, P. C., & Smith, J. A. (2008). Scaffolded silent reading: A complement to guided repeated oral reading that works! *Reading Teacher, 62*(3), 194–207.

Reutzel, R., Morrow, L. M., & Casey, H. (2009). Organization and management of the language arts program with children from diverse backgrounds. In L. Morrow, D. Lapp, & R. Rueda (Eds.), *Handbook of research on literacy instruction: Issues of diversity, policy, and equity.* New York: Guilford.

Reznitskaya, A., & Anderson, R. C. (2002). The argument schema and learning to reason. In C. Collins Block & M. Pressley (Eds.), *Comprehension instruction: Research-based best practices* (pp. 314–334). New York: Guilford.

Roberts, T. A., Christo, C., & Shefelbine, J. A. (2011). Word recognition. In M. L. Kamil, P. D. Pearson, E. B. Moje, & P. P. Afflerbach (Eds.), *Handbook of reading research* (vol. IV, pp. 229–258). New York: Routledge.

Rodriguez, R. (1981/2004). *Hunger of memory: The education of Richard Rodriguez.* New York: Dial.

Rosenblatt, L. (1978). *The reader, the text, the poem: The transactional theory of the literacy work.* Carbondale: Southern Illinois University Press.

Rosenshine, B., & Meister, C. (1994). Reciprocal teaching: A review of the research. *Review of Educational Research, 64,* 479–530.

Roskos, K. A., Tabors, P. O., & Lenhart, L. A. (2004). *Oral language and early literacy in preschool: Talking, reading, and writing.* Newark, DE: International Reading Association.

Roth, F. P., Speece, D. L., & Cooper, D. H. (2002). A longitudinal analysis of the connection between oral language and reading. *Journal of Educational Research, 95,* 259–272.

Rothenberg, C., & Fisher, D. (2006). *Teaching English language learners: A differentiated approach.* Boston: Pearson.

Routman, R. (2005). *Writing essentials: Raising expectations and results while simplifying teaching.* Portsmouth, NH: Heinemann.

Rowan, B., & Guthrie, L. F. (1989). The quality of Chapter 1 instruction: Results from a study of twenty-four schools. In R. E. Slavin, N. Karweit, & N. Madden (Eds.), *Effective programs for students at risk* (pp. 195–219). Boston: Allyn & Bacon.

Samuels, S. J. (1979). The method of repeated reading. *Reading Teacher, 32,* 403–408.

Samuels, S. J., & Farstrup, A. (2006). *What the research has to say about fluency instruction.* Newark, DE: International Reading Association.

Santa, C. M., Havens, L. T., & Valdes, B. J. (2004). *Project CRISS: Creating independence through student-owned strategies* (3rd ed.). Dubuque, IA: Kendall/Hunt.

Saunders, W., & Goldenberg, C. (1999). Effects of instructional conversations and literature logs on limited- and fluent-English-proficient students' story comprehension and thematic understanding. *Elementary School Journal, 99,* 277–301.

Saunders, W., & Goldenberg, C. (2010). Research to guide English language development instruction. In *Improving education for English learners: Research-based approaches.* Sacramento: California Department of Education.

Scanlon, D. M., Vellutino, F. R., Small, S. G., Fanuele, D. P., & Sweeney, J. M. (2005). Severe reading difficulties: Can they be prevented? A comparison of prevention and intervention approaches. *Exceptionality, 13*(4), 209–227.

Scarborough, H. (2002). Connecting early language and literacy to later reading (dis)abilities: Evidence, theory, and practice. In S. B. Neuman & D. K. Dickinson (Eds.), *Handbook of early literacy research* (vol. 1). New York: Guilford.

Scardamalia, M. (1981). How children cope with the cognitive demands of writing. In C. Frederiksen & J. Dominic (Eds.), *Writing: The nature, development, and teaching of written communication.* Hillsdale, NJ: Erlbaum.

Schickedanz, J. (1986). *More than ABCs: The early stages of writing.* Washington, DC: National Association for the Education of Young Children.

Schlagal, B. (2007). Best practices in spelling and handwriting. In S. Graham & C. MacArthur (Eds.), *Best practices in writing* (pp. 179–201). New York: Guilford.

Schleppegrell, M. (2004). *The language of schooling: A functional linguistics perspective.* New York: Routledge.

Schreiber, P. A. (1987). Prosody and structure in children's syntactic processing. In R. Horowitz & S. J. Samuels (Eds.), *Comprehending oral and written language* (pp. 243–270). New York: Academic Press.

Schreiber, P. A. (1991). Understanding prosody's role in reading acquisition. *Theory into Practice, 30,* 158–164.

Schreiber, P. A., & Read, C. (1980). Children's use of phonetic cues in spelling, parsing and maybe reading. *Bulletin of the Orton Society, 20,* 209–224.

Schwanenflugel, P. J., Meisinger, E., Wisenbaker, J. M., Kuhn, M. R., Strauss, G. P., & Morris, R. D. (2006). Becoming a fluent reader and automatic reader in the early elementary school years. *Reading Research Quarterly, 41*(4), 496–522.

Scott, J. A., Skobel, B. J., & Wells, J. (2008). *The word-conscious classroom: Building the vocabulary readers and writers need.* New York: Scholastic.

Sekeres, D. C. (2009). The market child and branded fiction: A synergism of children's literature, consumer culture, and new literacies. *Reading Research Quarterly, 44*(4), 399–414.

Shanahan, T., & Shanahan, C. (2008). Teaching disciplinary literacy to adolescents: Rethinking content-area literacy. *Harvard Educational Review, 78*(1), 40–59.

Shannon, P. (1998). *Reading poverty.* Portssmouth, NH: Heinemann.

Shefelbine, J. A. (1990). A syllabic-unit approach to teaching decoding of polysyllabic words to fourth- and sixth-grade disabled readers. In J. Zutell & S. McCormick (Eds.), *Literacy theory and research: Analyses from multiple paradigms* (pp. 223–229). Chicago: National Reading Conference.

Sheridan, M., & Rowell, J. (2010). *Design literacies: Learning and innovation in a digital age.* London: Routledge.

Shinn, M. R. (2007). Identifying students at risk, monitoring performance and determining eligibility within Response to Intervention: Research on educational need and benefit from academic intervention. *School Psychology Review, 36*(4), 601–617.

Silverman, R., & DiBara-Crandell, J. (2010). Vocabulary practices in prekindergarten and kindergarten classrooms. *Reading Research Quarterly, 45*(3), 318–340.

Silvey, A. (2006). *500 great books for teens.* Boston: Houghton Mifflin.

Sinatra, G. M., Brown, K. J., & Reynolds, R. E. (2002). Implications of cognitive resources for comprehension strategies instruction. In C. C. Block & M. Pressley (Eds.), *Comprehension instruction: Research-based practices* (pp. 62–76). New York: Guilford.

Skillings, M. J., & Ferrell, R. (2000). Student-generated rubrics: Bringing students into the assessment process. *Reading Teacher, 53*(6), 452–455.

Smith, F. (2004). *Understanding reading* (6th ed.). Mahwah, NJ: Erlbaum.

Smith, M. C. (2000). The real-world reading practices of adults. *Journal of Literacy Research, 32,* 25–32.

Smith, N. B. (1965/2002). *American reading instruction.* Newark, DE: International Reading Association.

Smith, R. E. (2012). *Developmental gradations of kindergartners' concept of word in text: An examination of the relationship between fingerpoint reading skills and other early literacy measures.* Unpublished doctoral dissertation, University of Nevada, Reno.

Smitherman, G. (1985). *Talkin and testifyin: The language of Black America.* Detroit: Wayne State University Press.

Smolkin, L. B., & Donovan, C. A. (2001). The contexts of comprehension: The information book read aloud, comprehension acquisition, and comprehension instruction in a first-grade classroom. *Elementary School Journal, 102*(2), 97–122.

Smolkin, L. B., Yaden, D. B., Jr., Brown, L., & Hofius, B. (1992).The effects of genre, visual design choices, and discourse structure on preschoolers' responses to picture books during parent-child read-alouds. In C. K. Kinzer & D. J. Leu (Eds.), *Literacy research, theory, and practice: Views from many perspectives* (41st yearbook of the National Reading Conference, pp. 291–301). Chicago: National Reading Conference.

Snow, C. E., Burns, M. S., & Griffin, P. (Eds.). (1998). *Preventing reading difficulties in young children.* Washington, DC: National Academy Press.

Snow, K. (2012). *People first language.* www.disabilityisnatural.com/images/PDF/pfl09.pdf. Retrieved October 16, 2012.

Sousa, D. (2011). *How the brain learns* (4th ed.). Thousand Oaks, CA: Corwin.

Spandel, V. (2008). *Creating writers through 6-trait writing assessment and instruction* (5th ed.). Boston: Pearson/Allyn & Bacon.

Sparks, R., Patton, J., Ganschow, L., & Humbach, N. (2012). Relationships among L1 print exposure and early L1 literacy skills, L2 aptitude, and L2 proficiency. *Reading & Writing, 25*(7), 1599–1634.

Spear-Swerling, L. (2006). Learning disabilities in English learners. www.ldonline.org/spearswerling/Learning_Disabilities_in_English_Language_Learners. Retrieved November 20, 2012.

Spear-Swerling, L., & Sternberg, R. J. (Contributor). (1997). *Off track: When poor readers become "learning disabled."* Boulder, CO: Westview.

Spector, K., & Jones, S. (2007). Constructing Anne Frank: Critical literacy and the Holocaust in eighth-grade English. *Journal of Adolescent and Adult Literacy, 10*(1), 36–48.

Speece, D., Mills, C., Ritchey, K., & Hillman, E. (2003). Initial evidence that evidence that letter fluency tasks are valid indicators of early reading skill. *Journal of Special Education, 36,* 223–233.

Spiro, R. J. (1980). Constructive processes in prose comprehension and recall. In R. J. Spiro, B. C. Bruce, & W. F. Brewer (Eds.), *Theoretical issues in reading comprehension* (pp. 245–278). Hillsdale, NJ: Erlbaum.

Stage, S., Sheppard, J., Davidson, M. M., & Browning, M. M. (2001). Prediction of first graders' growth in oral reading fluency using kindergarten letter fluency. *Journal of School Psychology, 29*(3), 225–237.

Stahl, S. A., Heubach, K. M., & Holcomb, A. (2005). Fluency-oriented reading instruction. *Journal of Literacy Research, 37*(1), 25–60.

Stahl, S. A., & Nagy, W. (2006). *Teaching word meanings.* Mahwah, NJ: Erlbaum.

Stanovich, K. E. (1980). Toward an interactive-compensatory model of individual differences in the development of reading fluency. *Reading Research Quarterly,* 16, 32–71.

Stanovich, K. E. (1986). Matthew effects in reading: Some consequences of individual differences in the acquisition of literacy. *Reading Research Quarterly, 21,* 360–407.

Stanovich, K. E. (1992). Are we overselling literacy? In C. Temple & P. Collins (Eds.), *Stories and readers: New perspectives on literature in the elementary classroom* (pp. 209–231). Norwood, MA: Christopher-Gordon.

Stanovich, K. E. (2000). *Progress in understanding reading: Scientific foundations and new frontiers.* New York: Guilford.

Stanovich, K. E., & Siegel, L. S. (1994). Phenotype profiles of children with reading disabilities: A regression based test of the phonological-core variable-difference model. *Journal of Educational Psychology, 86,* 24–53.

State Educational Technology Directors Association (SETDA). (2012). *Out of print: Reimagining the K–12 textbook in a digital age.* http://setda.org/web/guest/outofprint. Retrieved October 10, 2012.

Stauffer, R. (1969). *Directing reading maturity as a cognitive process.* New York: Harper & Row.

Stauffer, R. (1970). *The language-experience approach to the teaching of reading.* New York: Harper & Row.

Stauffer, R. (1980). *The language experience approach to the teaching of reading* (2nd ed.). New York: Harper & Row.

Stenner, A. J., Smith, D. R., Horiban, I., & Smith, M. (1987). *Fit of the Lexile Theory to sequenced units from eleven basal series.* Durham, NC: MetaMetrics.

Sterbinsky, A. (2007). *Words Their Way Spelling Inventories: Reliability and validity analyses.* Memphis, TN: Center for Research in Educational Policy, University of Memphis.

Sticht, T. G., & James, J. H. (1984). Listening and reading. In P. D. Pearson, R. Barr, M. L. Kamil, & P. Mosenthal (Eds.), *Handbook of reading research* (pp. 293–317). New York: Longman.

Storch, S. A., & Whitehurst, G. J. (2002). *Preparing our teachers: Opportunities for better reading instruction.* Washington, DC: Joseph Henry Press.

Storch, S. A., & Whitehurst, G. J. (2002). Oral language and code-related precursors to reading: Evidence from a longitudinal structural model. *Developmental Psychology, 38,* 934–947.

Strecker, S., Roser, N., & Martinez, M. (1998). Toward understanding and oral reading fluency. *National Reading Conference Yearbook, 47,* 295–310.

Strickland, D., & Snow, C. (2002). *Preparing our teachers: Opportunities for better reading instruction.* Washington, DC: Joseph Henry Press.

Student Oral Proficiency Assessment. (2000). Washington, DC: Center for Applied Linguistics.

Suárez-Orozco, C., Suárez-Orozco, M. M., & Todorova, I. (2008). *Learning a new land: Immigrant students in American society.* Cambridge, MA: Harvard University Press.

Sulzby, E. (1985). Children's emergent reading of favorite storybooks. *Reading Research Quarterly, 20,* 458–481.

Taylor, B. M., Pearson, P. D., Clark, K., & Walpole, S. (1999). *Beating the odds in teaching all children to read* (No. 2-006). Ann Arbor, MI: CIERA.

Taylor, B., Pearson, P. D., Clark, K., & Walpole, S. (2000). Effective schools and accomplished teachers: Lessons about primary-grade reading instruction in low-income schools. *Elementary School Journal 101*(2), 121–165.

Taylor, B. M., Pearson, P. D., Peterson, D., & Rodriguez, M. C. (2003). Looking inside classrooms: Reflecting on the "how" as well as the "what" in effective reading instruction. *Reading Teacher, 56*(3), 270–279.

Taylor, I., & Taylor, M. M. (1983). *The psychology of reading.* New York: Academic.

Teachers of English to Speakers of Other Languages (TESOL). (2006). *PreK–12 English language proficiency standards.* Alexandria, VA: TESOL. www.tesol.org. Retrieved August 10, 2012.

Teale, W. (2003). Reading aloud to young children as a classroom instructional activity: Insight from research and practice. In A. van Kleeck, S. A. Stahl, & E. B. Bauer (Eds.), *On reading books to children: Parents and teachers* (pp. 114–139). Mahwah, NJ: Erlbaum.

Telgemeier, R. (2002). *Beginnings.* http://goraina.com/webcomics/beginnings.html

Templeton, S. (1983). Using the spelling/meaning connection to develop word knowledge in older students. *Journal of Reading, 27*(1), 8–14.

Templeton, S. (1986). Metalinguistic awareness: A synthesis and beyond. In D. B. Yaden, Jr., & S. Templeton (Eds.), *Metalinguistic awareness and beginning literacy: Conceptualizing what it means to learn to read and write.* Portsmouth, NH: Heinemann.

Templeton, S. (1996). *Children's literacy: Contexts for meaningful learning.* Boston: Houghton Mifflin.

Templeton, S. (1997). *Teaching the integrated language arts* (2nd ed.). Boston: Houghton Mifflin.

Templeton, S. (2004). The vocabulary-spelling connection: Orthographic development and morphological knowledge at the intermediate grades and beyond. In J. F. Baumann & E. J. Kame'enui (Eds.), *Vocabulary instruction: Research to practice* (pp. 118–138). New York: Guilford.

Templeton, S. (2010). Spelling-meaning relationships among languages: Exploring cognates and their possibilities. In L. Helman (Ed.), *Literacy development with English learners: Research-based instruction in grades K–6* (pp. 196–212). New York: Guilford.

Templeton, S. (2012). *Word study guide: Grade 1.* Boston: Houghton Mifflin Harcourt.

Templeton, S. (2012). *Word study teacher's guide.* Boston: Houghton Mifflin Harcourt.

Templeton, S. (2012). The vocabulary-spelling connection and generative instruction: Orthographic development and morphological knowledge at the intermediate grades and beyond. In J. F. Baumann & E. J. Kame'enui (Eds.), *Vocabulary instruction: Research to practice* (2nd ed., pp. 116–138). New York: Guilford.

Templeton, S., & Bear, D. R. (Eds.). (1992). *Development of orthographic knowledge and the foundations of literacy: A Memorial Festschrift for Edmund Henderson.* Hillsdale, NJ: Erlbaum.

Templeton, S., & Bear, D. R. (2011). Phonemic awareness, word recognition, and spelling. In T. Rasinski (Ed.), *Developing reading instruction that works* (pp. 153–178). Bloomington, IN: Solution Tree.

Templeton, S., Bear, D. R., Invernizzi, M., & Johnston, F. (2010). *Vocabulary their way: Word study with middle and secondary students.* Boston: Pearson/Allyn & Bacon.

Templeton, S., Johnston, F., Bear, D. R., & Invernizzi, M. (2009). *Words Their Way: Word sorts for derivational relations spellers* (2nd ed.). Boston: Pearson/Allyn & Bacon.

Thomas, W. P., & Collier, V. P. (2002). A national study of school effectiveness for language minority students' long-term academic achievement. Santa Cruz, CA: Center for Research on Education, Diversity & Excellence. www.Thomasandcollier.com. Retrieved August 1, 2012.

Tierney, R. J., Carter, M. A., & Desai, L. E. (1991). *Portfolio assessment in the reading-writing classroom.* Norwood, MA: Christopher-Gordon.

Tierney, R. J., & Readence, J. E. (2005). *Reading strategies and practices: A compendium* (6th ed.). Boston: Pearson/Allyn & Bacon.

Tolchinsky, L. (2003). *The cradle of culture and what children know about writing and numbers before being taught.* Mahwah, NJ: Erlbaum.

Tomasello, M. (2008). *Origins of human communication.* Cambridge, MA: MIT Press.

Torgesen, J. K., Wagner, R. K., Rashotte, C. A., Burgess, S., & Hecht, S. (1997). Contributions of phonological awareness and rapid naming ability to growth of word-reading skills in second and fifth grade. *Scientific Studies of Reading, 12,* 161–185.

Touchstone Applied Science Associates. (2013). *The degrees of reading power.* Brewster, NY: Touchstone Applied Science Associates.

Toulmin, S. E. (1958). *The uses of argument.* Cambridge: Cambridge University Press.

Townsend, D. (2011). If you want them to learn academic English—Teach it to them. In D. Lapp & B. Moss (Eds.), *Teaching with rigor: Supporting multiple ways of learning.* New York: Guilford.

Townsend, D., & Collins, P. (2008). English or Spanish? Assessing Latino/a children in the home and school languages for risk of reading disabilities. *Topics in Language Disorders, 28*(1), 61–73.

Townsend, D., Lee, E., & Chiappe, P. (2006). *English or Spanish? The efficacy of assessing Latino/a children in Spanish for risk of reading disabilities.* Paper presented at the meeting of the Society for the Scientific Study of Reading, Vancouver, BC, Canada.

Townsend, D., & Templeton, S. (2012, May). *What makes academic language academic?* Presentation at the 57th annual convention of the International Reading Association, Chicago.

Treiman, R., Goswami, U., & Bruck, M. (1990). Not all nonwords are alike: Implications for reading development and theory. *Memory & Cognition, 18,* 559–567.

Treiman, R., Tincoff, R., Rodriguez, K., Mousake, A., & Francis, D. (1998). The foundations of literacy: Learning the sounds of letters. *Child Development, 69*(6), 1524–1540.

Turkle, S. (2012, April 22). www.nytimes.com/2012/04/22/opinion/sunday/

the-flight-from-dconversation.html?_r=1&hp. Retrieved April 22, 2012.

Tyack, D., & Cuban, L. (1995). *Tinkering toward Utopia.* Cambridge, MA: Harvard University Press.

U.S. Department of Education, Institute of Education Sciences, National Center for Educational Statistics, National Assessment of Educational Progress (NAEP). (2002). *Oral reading study.* http://nces.ed.gov/nationsreportcard/studies/ors/scale.asp. Retrieved September 6, 2012.

Usher, A. (2012, May). *AYP results for 2010–2012 update.* Washington, DC: Center for Education Policy. www.cep-dc.org/displayDocument.cfm?DocumentID-402.

Valencia, S. W. (2011). Using assessment to improve teaching and learning. In S. J. Samuels & A. E. Farstrup (Eds.), *What the research has to say about reading instruction* (4th ed.). Newark, DE: International Reading Association.

Valencia, S. W., & Buly, M. R. (2004). Behind test scores: What struggling readers really need. *Reading Teacher, 57,* 520–531.

Valencia, S. W., & Place, N. A. (1994). Literacy portfolios for teaching, learning, and accountability: The Bellevue literacy assessment project. In S. W. Valencia, E. H. Hiebert, & P. P. Afflerbach (Eds.), *Authentic reading assessment: Practices and possibilities* (pp. 134–166). Newark, DE: International Reading Association.

Valencia, S. W., & Wixson, K. K. (2000). Policy-oriented research on literacy standards and assessment. In M. L. Kamil, P. Mosenthal, P. D. Pearson, & R. Barr (Eds.), *Handbook of reading research* (vol. 3, pp. 909–936). Mahwah, NJ: Erlbaum.

Valencia, S. W., Wixson, K. K., & Pearson, P. D. (2011). *Issues in developing reading comprehension assessments aligned with the Common Core State Standards.* Paper presented at the 61st Annual Conference of the Literacy Research Association, Jacksonville, FL.

Van Deusen-Scholl, N. (2003). Toward a definition of heritage language: Sociopolitical and pedagogical considerations. *Journal of Language, Identity, and Education, 2,* 211–230.

Vasilyeva, M., & Waterfall, H. (2011). Variability in language development: Relation to socioeconomic status and environmental input. In S. B. Neuman & D. K. Dickinson (Eds.), *Handbook of early literacy research* (vol. 3). New York: Guilford.

Vaughn, S., & Fuchs, L. S. (2003). Redefining learning disabilities as inadequate response to instruction: The promise and potential problems. *Learning Disabilities Research & Practice, 18*(3), 137–146.

Vaughn, S., Gersten, R., & Chard, D. J. (2000). The underlying message in LD intervention research: Findings from research syntheses. *Exceptional Children, 67*(1), 99–114.

Vaughn, S., Linan-Thompson, S., Kouzekanani, K., Bryant, D. P., Dickinson, S., & Blozis, S. A. (2003). Reading instruction grouping for students with reading difficulties. *Remedial and Special Education, 24*(5), 301–315.

Vega, S., Crawford, H. G., & Van Pelt, J. (2012). Safe schools for LGBTQI students: How do teachers view their role in promoting safe schools? *Equity & Excellence in Education, 45*(2), 250–260.

Vellutino, F. R. (1987). Dyslexia. *Scientific American, 256*(3), 34–41. doi: 10.1038/scientificamerican0387-34

Vellutino, F. R., Scanlon, D., & Lyon, G. R. (2000). Differentiating between difficult-to-remediate and readily remediated poor readers. More evidence against IQ-achievement discrepancy of reading disability. *Journal of Learning Disabilities, 33,* 223–238.

Vellutino, F. R., Scanlon, D. M., Sipay, E. R., Small, S. G., Pratt, A., Chen, R., et al. (1996). Cognitive profiles of difficult to remediate and readily remediated poor readers: Early interventions as a vehicle for distinguishing between cognitive and experiential deficits as basic causes of specific reading disability. *Journal of Educational Psychology, 88,* 601–638.

Venezky, R. L. (1999). *The American way of spelling: The structure and origins of American English orthography.* New York: Guilford.

Vidoni, K. L., & Maddux, C. D. (2002). WebQuests: Can they be used to improve critical thinking skills in students? *Computers in the Schools, 19,* 101–117.

Villanueva, V. (1993). *Bootstraps: From an American academic of color.* Urbana/Champaign IL: National Council of Teachers of English.

Vygotsky, L. (1962). *Language and thought.* Cambridge, MA: MIT Press.

Vygotsky, L. (1978). *Mind in society: The development of higher psychological processes.* Cambridge, MA: Harvard University Press.

Wadsworth, B. J. (2003). *Piaget's theory of cognitive and affective development: Foundations of constructivism* (5th ed.). Boston: Allyn & Bacon.

Waggoner, M., Chinn, C., Yi, H., & Anderson, R. C. (1995). Collaborate reasoning about stories. *Language Arts, 72,* 582–588.

Wagner, M., Marder, C., Blackorby, J., Cameto, R., Newman, L., Levine, P., . . . Bavies-Mercer, E. (2003). *The achievement of youth with disabilities during secondary school. A report from the National Longitudinal Transition Study – 2 (NLTS2).* Menlo Park, CA: SRI International. www.nlts2.org/reports/2003_11/nlts2_report_2003_11_complte.pdf. Retrieved on March 9, 2013.

Wagner, R. K., Torgeson, J. K., & Rashotte, C. A. (1994). Development of reading-related phonological processing abilities: New evidence of bidirectional causality from a latent variable longitudinal study. *Developmental Psychology, 30*(1), 73–87.

Wagner, T. (2010). *The global achievement gap.* New York: Basic Books.

Walmsley, S. A., & Allington, R. L. (1995). Redefining and reforming instructional support programs for at-risk students. In R. L. Allington & S. A. Walmsley (Eds.), *No quick fix: Rethinking literacy programs in America's elementary schools* (pp. 19–41). New York: Teachers College Press.

Walpole, S. & McKenna, M. (2009). *Differentiating reading instruction: Strategies for the primary grades.* New York: Guilford.

Walpole, S., McKenna, M., & Philippakos, Z. A. (2011). *Differentiated reading instruction in grades 4 & 5: Strategies and resources.* New York: Guilford.

Wanzek, J., Wexler, J., Vaughn, S., & Ciullo, S. (2010). Reading interventions for struggling readers in the upper elementary grades: A synthesis of 20 years of readers. *Reading and Writing, 23,* 889–912.

Warger, L. (2001). *Five homework strategies for teaching students with learning disabilities.* www.ldonline.org/article/Five_Homework_Strategies_for_Teaching_Students_With_Learning_Disabilities?theme=print. Retrieved November 21, 2012.

Weismann, K. E. (1996). Using paragraph frames to complete a K-W-L. *The Reading Teacher, 50,* 271–272.

Wells, G. (1986). *The meaning makers: Children learning language and using language to learn*. Portsmouth, NH: Heinemann.

Wells, G., & Chang-Wells, G. L. (1992). *Constructing knowledge together: Classrooms as centers of inquiry and literacy*. Portsmouth, NH: Heinemann.

White, T. G., Stowell, J., & Yanagihara, A. (1989). Teaching elementary students to use word practices. *The Reading Teacher, 42*, 302–308.

Whitehurst, G. J., Arnold, D. S., Epstein, J. N., & Angell, A. L. (1984). A picture book reading intervention in day care and home for children from low income families. *Developmental Psychology, 30,* 679–689.

Whitehurst, G. J., & Lonigan, A. (2002). Emergent literacy: Development of prereaders to readers. In D. K. Dickinson & S. B. Neuman (Eds.), *Handbook of early literacy research* (vol. 2). New York: Guilford.

Whitehurst, G. J., Zevenbergen, A. A., Crone, D. A., Schultz, M. D., Velting, O. N., & Fischel, J. E. (1999). Outcomes of an emergent literacy intervention from Head Start through second grade. *Journal of Educational Psychology, 91*, 261–272.

WIDA Consortium. (2011). *The English language development standards* (draft). www.wida.us. Retrieved August 10, 2012.

Wiggins, G. (1998). *Educative assessment: Designing assessments to inform and improve student performance*. San Francisco: Jossey-Bass.

Wiggins, G., & McTighe, J. (2005). *Understanding by design* (2nd ed.). Boston: Pearson.

Wilcox, J. (2006, February). Less teaching, more assessing: Teacher feedback is key. *Education Update* (ASCD), *48*(2).

Williams, G. (2005). Grammatics in schools. In R. Hasan, C. M. I. M. Matthiessen, & J. Webster (Eds.), *Continuing discourse on language* (pp. 281–310). London: Equinox.

Williams, J. P. (1993). Comprehension of students with and without learning disabilities: Identification of narrative themes and idiosyncratic text representations. *Journal of Educational Psychology, 85*, 631–641.

Williams, K. T. (2006). *Expressive Vocabulary Test–2*. Bloomington, MN: American Guidance Service/Pearson.

Willows, D. (2002, January). The balanced literacy diet: Using a food pyramid concept to cut through the great debate over phonics vs. whole language. *The School Administrator*.

Wilson, J. K. (2008). *Activity-system analysis of a highly effective first-grade teacher and her students*. Unpublished doctoral dissertation, University of Nevada, Reno.

Wilson, P. T., & Anderson, R. C. (1986). What they don't know will hurt them: The role of prior knowledge in comprehension. In J. Oransano (Ed.), *Reading comprehension from research to practice* (pp. 31–48). Hillsdale, NJ: Erlbaum.

Wineburg, S. (1991). On the reading of historical texts: Notes on the breach between school and academy. *American Educational Research Journal, 28*(3), 495–519.

Wineburg, S. (2001). *Historical thinking and other unnatural acts: Charting the future of teaching the past*. Philadelphia: Temple University Press.

Wolf, M. (2007). *Proust and the squid: The story and science of the reading brain*. New York: Harper/Perennial Press.

Wolf, S. A., Coats, K., Enciso, P., & Jenkins, C. A. (2011). *Handbook of research on children's and young adult literature*. New York: Routledge/Taylor & Francis.

Wolter, J. A., Wood, A., & D'Zatko, K. W. (2009). The influence of morphological awareness on the literacy development of first-grade children. *Language, Speech & Hearing Services in Schools, 40*(3), 286–298.

Wong, H. K., & Wong, R. T. (2009). *The first days of school: How to be an effective teacher* (4th ed.). Mountain View, CA: Harry K. Wong Publications.

Wong-Fillmore, L., & Fillmore, C. J. (2012). What does text complexity mean for English learners and language minority students? *Understanding Language*. Stanford, CA: Stanford University School of Education.

Woodcock, R. W. (1998). *Woodcock Reading Mastery Test–Revised*. Circle Pines, MN: American Guidance Service.

Woodside-Jiron, H., & Gehsmann, K. (2009). Peeling back the layers of policy and school reform: Revealing the structural and social complexities within. *International Journal of Disability, Development, and Education, 56*(1), 49–72.

Wulffson, D. (2000). *Toys! Amazing stories behind some great inventions*. New York: Henry Holt.

Yolen, J. (2012). *Where do I get my ideas?* http://janeyolen.com/for-kids/. Downloaded February 14, 2012.

Yopp, R. E. (1988). Questioning and active comprehension. *Questioning Exchange, 2*, 231–238.

Young, K. (2007). Developmental stage theory of spelling: Analysis of consistency across four spelling-related activities. *Australian Journal of Language and Literacy, 30*(3), 203–220.

Zambo, D., & Brozo, W. (2009). *Bright beginnings for boys: Engaging young boys in active literacy*. Newark, DE: International Reading Association.

Zehler, A. M., Fleischman, H. L., Hopstock, P. J., Stephenson, T. G., Pendzick, M., & Sapru, S. (2003, September). *Descriptive study of services to LEP students and LEP students with disabilities*: Volume I: Research Report (Contract No. EO-00-CO-0089). Office of English Language Acquisition, Language Enhancement, and Academic Achievement of Limited English Proficient Students (OELA).

Zwiers, J. (2008). *Building academic language: Essential practices for content classrooms*. San Francisco: Jossey-Bass.

Ziegler, J. C., & Goswami, U. (2005). Reading acquisition, developmental dyslexia, and skilled reading across languages: A psycholinguistic grain size theory. *Psychological Bulletin, 13*(1), 3–29.

References for Children's and Young Adult Literature

Aardema, V. (1975). *Why mosquitoes buzz in people's ears: A West African tale.* New York: Dial.

Abbott, T. (2006). *Firegirl.* New York: Little, Brown.

Abeel, S. (2001). *Reach for the moon.* New York: Orchard.

Abeel, S. (2005). *My thirteenth winter: A memoir.* New York: Scholastic.

Abercrombie, B. (1990). *Charlie Anderson.* New York: M. K. McElderry.

Ahuja, B. N. (Ed.). (2008). *The world's great speeches.* New York: Goodwill.

Alborough, J. (1992). *Where's my Teddy?* Cambridge, MA: Candlewick.

Alexandros, S. (2008). *Curious George and the nwspapers.* Boston: Houghton Mifflin.

Alexie, S. (2007). *Flight.* New York: Grove/Black Cat.

Aliki. (1992). *My hands!* New York: Crowell.

Alvarado, A. (2009). *Dad's garden.* Boston: Houghton Mifflin.

Amery, H. (2009). *Greek myths for children.* London: Usborne Books.

Anderson, L. H. (2008). *Chains.* New York: Simon & Schuster.

Andrews, J. (1991). *Explorer books: Jungles & rain forests.* New York: Trumpet Club.

Asimov, I. (1961). *Words from the myths.* Boston: Houghton Mifflin.

Auch, M. (2009). *The plot chickens.* New York: Holiday House.

Babbitt, N. (1975). *Tuck everlasting.* New York: Farrar, Straus, Giroux.

Baca, J. (2010). *Stories from the edge.* Portsmouth, NH: Heinemann.

Baer, E. (1990). *This is the way we go to school: A book about children around the world.* New York: Scholastic.

Barton, B. (1987). *Airport.* New York: HarperCollins.

Base, G. (1987). *Animalia.* New York: Harry N. Abrams.

Baskin, N. R. (2009). *Anything but typical.* New York: Simon & Schuster Books for Young Readers.

Bass, H. (2009). *The secret life of Walter Anderson.* Cambridge, MA: Candlewick.

Bauer, S. W. (2006). *The story of the world: Volume 1—Ancient times* (2nd ed.) Charles City, VA: Peace Hill Press.

Baumann, J. F., Chard, D. J., Cooks, J., Cooper, J. D., Gersten, R., Lipson, M., Morrow, L. M., Pikulski, J. J., Templeton, S., Valencia, S., Valentino, C., & Vogt, M. (2002/2012). *Journeys.* Boston: Houghton Mifflin Harcourt.

Baumgartner, B., & Hall, A. (1998). *Good as gold.* New York: DK Publishing.

Beals, M. P. (1994). *Warriors don't cry: A searing memoir of the battle to integrate Little Rock's Central High.* New York: Washington Square Press.

Bemelmans, L. (1963). *Madeline.* New York: Viking.

Bliss, H. (2003). *The diary of a worm.* New York: Joanna Cutler.

Bloom, V. (2000). *Time.* From *The world is sweet.* New York: Bloomsbury Children's Books

Bloor, E. (1997). *Tangerine.* New York: Harcourt.

Blume, J. (1971). *Freckle juice.* New York: Simon & Schuster.

Brett, J. (1994). *Town mouse, country mouse.* New York: Putnam.

Briggs, R. (1978). *The snowman.* New York: Random House.

Brinkhole, J. (1986). *Fireflies.* New York: Aladdin.

Brown, M. T. (1996). *Arthur writes a story.* Boston: Little, Brown.

Brown, M. W. (1947). *Goodnight moon.* New York: Harper.

Brown, M. W., & Weisgard, M. (1949). *The important book.* New York: Harper.

Browne, A. (1998). *Voices in the park.* New York: DK Publishers.

Bryant, M. E. (2009). *Mythlopedia: Oh my gods! A look-it-up guide to the gods of mythology.* New York: F. Watts/Scholastic.

Bryant, M. E. (2009). *Mythlopedia: She's all that! A look-it-up guide to the goddesses of mythology.* New York: F. Watts/Scholastic.

Bryant, M. E. (2010). *Mythlopedia: All in the family: A look-it-up guide to in-laws, outlaws, and offspring of mythology.* New York: Scholastic.

Bulla, C. R. (1994). *What makes a shadow?* New York: HarperCollins.

Bunting, E. (1989). *The Wednesday surprise.* New York: Clarion Books.

Bunting, E. (1990). *The wall.* New York: Clarion Books.

Bunting, E. (1991). *Fly away home.* New York: Clarion Books.

Bunting, E. (1994). *A day's work.* New York: Clarion Books.

Bunting, E. (1994). *Smoky night.* New York: Harcourt Children's Books.

Burnett, F. H. (1962). *The secret garden.* Philadelphia: Lippincott.

Caduto, M. J. (1988). *Keepers of the earth: Native American stories and environmental activities for children.* Golden, CO: Fulcrum.

Cameron, A. (1981). *The stories Julian tells.* New York: Pantheon.

Cameron, A. (1995). *The stories Huey tells.* New York: Knopf.

Cameron, P. (2003). *"I can't" said the ant.* New York: Scholastic.

Campbell Pearson, T. (2002). *Where does Joe go?* New York: Farrar Straus Giroux.

Cannon, J. (2004). *Pinduli.* New York: Harcourt Children's Books.

Carle, E. (1970). *The tiny seed.* Natick, MA: Picture Book Studio, Alphabet Press.

Carle, E. (1978). *The very hungry caterpillar.* New York: Collins.

Carpenter, E. (1996). *Young Thurgood Marshall: A fighter for equality.* New York: Scholastic.

Carroll, L. (1963). *Alice's adventures in Wonderland* and *Through the looking glass.* New York: Macmillan.

Carter, D. (1991). *In a dark, dark wood.* New York: Simon & Schuster Books for Young Readers.

Cassino, M. (2009). *The story of snow: The science of winter's wonder.* San Francisco: Chronicle Books.

Chauffe, E., & Chauffe, E. (2009). *Kids show kids how to make balloon animals.* Austin, TX: Casey Shay.

Cheltenham Elementary School Kindergartners. (1991). *We are all alike . . . We are all different.* New York: Scholastic.

Cherry, L. (1990). *The great kapok tree: A tale from the Amazon Rain Forest.* San Diego, CA: Harcourt Brace Jovanovich.

Child, L. (2004). *I am absolutely too small for school.* Somerville, MA: Candlewick.

Choi, Y. (2003). *The name jar.* New York: Dragonfly Books.

Choldenko, G. (2004). *Al Capone does my shirts.* New York: Penguin.

Choldenko, G. (2009). *Al Capone shines my shoes.* New York: Dial Books for Young Readers.

Churchill, Winston. (1940/2004). "Blood, Toil, Tears and Sweat: Address to Parliament on May 13th, 1940." *Lend Me Your Ears: Great Speeches in History* (3rd ed.). Edited by William Safire. New York: W. W. Norton, 2004.

Cisneros, S. (1991). *The house on Mango Street.* New York: Vintage Books.

Cisneros, S. (2008). *Woman hollering creek and other stories.* New York: Random House.

Clements, A. (1996). *Frindle.* New York: Atheneum Books for Young Readers.

Clements, A. (2007). *No talking.* New York: Aladdin/Simon & Schuster.

Cole, J. (1989). *Anna Banana: 101 jump rope rhymes.* New York: Morrow Junior Books.

Cole, J., & Calmenson, S. (1990). *Miss Mary Mack and other children's street rhymes.* New York: Morrow Junior Books.

Cole, R. (2010). *The story of Ruby Bridges.* New York: Scholastic.

Collins, S. (2008). *The hunger games.* New York: Scholastic.

Cooper, S., & Cober, A. E. (1973). *The dark is rising.* New York: Atheneum.

Cooper, S., & Gill, M. (1966). *Over sea, under stone.* New York: Harcourt, Brace & World.

Craighead, G. J. (2000). *How to talk to your dog.* New York: HarperCollins.

Creech, S. (2001). *A fine, fine school.* New York: HarperCollins.

Crews, D. (1992). *Shortcut.* New York: Greenwillow.

Crews, D. (1993). *Freight train.* New York: Greenwillow.

Crews, D. (1998). *Bigmama's.* New York: Greenwillow.

Cronin, D. (2000). *Click, clack, moo: Cows that type.* New York: Simon & Schuster.

Curtis, C. P. (1995/2000). *The Watsons go to Birmingham—1963.* New York: Delacorte.

Dahl, R. (1980). *The Twits.* New York: Knopf.

Daley, J. (2006). *Great speeches by African Americans: Frederick Douglass, Sojourner Truth, Dr. Martin Luther King, Jr., Barack Obama, Jr., and others.* Mineola, NY: Dover.

Daley, J. (Ed.). (2008). *Great speeches by American women.* New York: HarperCollins.

Daniel, C. (1996). *Sparky's bone.* Parsippany, NJ: Modern Curriculum Press.

Davies, N. (2001). *One tiny turtle.* Cambridge, MA: Candlewick.

Day, A. (1985). *Good dog Carl.* La Jolla, CA: Green Tiger.

Day, T. (2006). *Guide to savage earth.* New York: DK Publishing.

DeGross, M. (1994). *Donavan's word jar.* New York: HarperCollins.

Delmar, G. (1983). *Children's counting out rhymes, fingerplays, jump-rope and bounce-ball chants and other rhymes. A comprehensive English-language reference.* Jefferson, NC: McFarland.

dePaola, T. (1973). *Charlie needs a cloak.* New York: Aladdin.

dePaola, T. (1975). *Strega Nona: An old tale.* Englewood Cliffs, NJ: Prentice-Hall.

dePaola, T. (1975). *The cloud book.* New York: Holiday House.

dePaola, T. (1978). *Pancakes for breakfast.* New York: Harcourt Brace Jovanovich.

dePaola, T. (1985). *Tomie dePaola's Mother Goose.* New York: Putnam.

dePaola, T. (1988). *Cookie's week.* New York: Putnam.

DiCamillo, K. (2000). *Because of Winn-Dixie.* Cambridge, MA: Candlewick.

Douglass, F. (1845/2005). *Narrative of the life of Frederick Douglass: An American slave.* New York: Sterling.

Douglass, F. (2013). *A narrative in the life of Frederick Douglass.* New York: CreateSpace.

Dowd, N. (1996). *A rainbow somewhere.* Parsippany, NJ: Modern Curriculum Press.

Draper, S. (2002). *Double dutch.* New York: Atheneum Books for Young Readers.

Draper, S. (2010). *Out of my mind.* New York: Atheneum Books for Young Readers.

Duke, K. (1992). *Aunt Isabel tells a good one.* New York: Dutton Children's Books.

Edwards, K. (2003). *Invaders.* New York: Newbridge.

Ehlert, L. (1984). *Eating the alphabet: Fruits and vegetables from A to Z.* New York: Harcourt Brace Jovanovich.

Elfman, E., & Pruitt, G. (1994). *Almanac of the gross, disgusting, and totally repulsive.* New York: Random House.

Ellis, D. (2001). *The breadwinner.* Toronto: Groundwood Books.

Evslin, B., & Hofmann, W. (1967). *Heroes, gods and monsters of the Greek myths.* New York: Four Winds.

Falwell, C. (2001). *David's drawings.* New York: Lee & Low Books.

Feelings, M. (1992). *Jambo means hello: Swahili alphabet book.* New York: Puffin.

Fine, E. H., & Doner, K. (2004). *Cryptomania: Teleporting into Greek and Latin with the CryptoKids.* Berkeley, CA: Tricycle.

Flake, S. (2012). *Pinned.* New York: Scholastic.

Fleischman, P. (1988). *Joyful noises: Poems for two voices.* New York: Harper & Row.

Fleischman, P. (1999). *Weslandia.* New York: Scholastic.

Fleischman, P. (2000). *Big talk: Poems for four voices.* Cambridge, MA: Candlewick.

Fletcher, R. J. (2005). *A writing kind of day: Poems for young poets.* Honesdale, PA: Wordsong/Boyds Mills Press.

Fox, M. (1988). *Koala Lou.* San Diego: Harcourt Brace Jovanovich.

Fox, M. (1997). *Whoever you are.* New York: Harcourt Children's Books.

Franco, B. (Ed.). (2001). *Things I have to tell you: Poems and writing by teenage girls.* Cambridge, MA: Candlewick.

Franco, B. (Ed.). (2001). *You hear me? Poems and writing by teenage boys.* Cambridge, MA: Candlewick.

Frank, A. (1991/2001). *The diary of a young girl: The definitive edition.* (O. H. Frank, M. Pressler, & S. Massotty, Eds. & Trans.). New York: Bantam Books and Doubleday.

Fraser, D. (2000). *Miss Alaineus.* Orlando, FL: Harcourt.

Frazee, M. (2003). *Roller coaster.* San Diego, CA: Harcourt Brace Jovanovich.

Freeman, D. (1968). *Corduroy.* New York: Viking.

Galdone, P. (1973). *The little red hen.* New York: Seabury Press.

Galdone, P. (1984). *Henny Penny.* San Anselmo, CA: Sandpiper.

Garland, S. (1993). *The lotus seed.* San Diego, CA: Harcourt Brace Jovanovich.

Gavalda, A., & Rosner, G. (2003). *95 pounds of hope.* New York: Viking.

Gephart, D. (2010). *How to survive middle school.* New York: Yearling/Random House.

Gibbons, G. (1984). *The seasons of Arnold's apple tree.* San Diego: Harcourt Brace Jovanovich.

Gibbons, G. (1990). *How a house is built.* New York: Holiday House.

Gibbons, G. (1991). *From seed to plant*. New York: Holiday House.

Gibbons, G. (1997). *The honey makers*. New York: Morrow Junior Books.

Gibson, R. (1999). *I can draw people*. London: Usbourne.

Giles, J. (2000). *Max rides his bike*. Crystal Lake, IL: Rigby.

Goodrich, F., & Hackett, A. (1956). *The diary of Anne Frank: A play*. New York: Random House.

Graves, D. (1996). *Baseball, snakes, and summer squash: Poems about growing up*. Honesdale, PA: Wordsong/Boyds Mills Press.

Greenburg, J. (2002). *Action Jackson*. Brookfield, CT: Roaring Brook Press.

Greenfield, E. (1978). *Honey, I love, and other love poems*. New York: Crowell.

Grimm, J., & Grimm, W. (1980). *The fisherman and his wife: A tale from the Brothers Grimm*. New York: Farrar, Straus, Giroux.

Grindley, S. (1997). *Why is the sky blue?* New York: Simon & Schuster Books for Young Readers.

Gustafson, S. (2007). *Favorite nursery rhymes from Mother Goose*. Seymour, CT: Greenwich Workshop.

Haarsma, P. J. (2006). *The softwire: Virus on Orbis 1*. Cambridge, MA: Candlewick.

Hakim, J. (1993). *The new nation* (Vol. 4 in *A history of U.S.*). New York: Oxford University Press.

Hakim, J. (1999). *Making thirteen colonies*. New York: Oxford.

Havill, J. (1989). *Jamaica tag-along*. Boston: Houghton Mifflin.

Hazen, B. S. (1979). *Tight times*. New York: Viking.

Heard, G. (2002). *The place I know: Poems of comfort*. Cambridge, MA: Candlewick.

Hearne, B. G. (2000). *Who's in the hall? A mystery in four chapters*. New York: Greenwillow.

Heller, R. (1983). *The reason for a flower*. New York: Grosset and Dunlap.

Henkes, K. (1990). *Julius, the baby of the world*. New York: Greenwillow.

Henkes, K. (1991). *Chrysanthemum*. New York: Greenwillow.

Henkes, K. (1996). *Lilly's purple plastic purse*. New York: Scholastic.

Henkes, K. (2000). *Wemberly worried*. New York: Greenwillow.

Herrera, J. F. (2000). *The upside down boy/El niño de cabeza*. New York: Children's Books Press / Lee & Low Books.

Hesse, K. (1997). *Out of the dust*. New York: Scholastic.

Hesse, K. (1999). *Come on rain*. New York: Scholastic.

Hest, A., & Sawaya, L. D. (1995). *How to get famous in Brooklyn*. New York: Simon and Schuster Books for Young Readers.

Hill, K. (2000). *The year of Ms. Agnes*. New York: M. K. McElderry.

Hoban, T. (1985). *Is it larger? Is it smaller?* New York: Greenwillow.

Hoffman, M. (1991). *Amazing Grace*. New York: Dial.

Holm, J., & Castaldi, E. (2007). *Middle school is worse than meatloaf: A year told through stuff*. New York: Atheneum Books for Young Readers

Holub, J. (2001). *The pizza we made*. New York: Viking.

Hoose, P. (1998). *Hey, little ant*. Berkeley, CA: Tricycle.

Hoose, P. M. (1993). *It's our world, too! Stories of young people who are making a difference*. Boston: Joy Street Books.

Hughes, L. (1991). *Thank you, ma'am*. Mankato, MN: Creative Education.

Hurd, T. (1997). *Art dog*. New York: HarperCollins.

Isadora, R., & Grimm, J. (2008). *Rapunzel*. New York: G. P. Putnam's Sons.

James, S. (1991). *Dear Mr. Blueberry*. New York: M. K. McElderry.

Janeczko, P. B. (2005). *A poke in the I: Collection of concrete poems*. London: Walker Books.

Katz, A. (2001). *Take me out of the bathtub*. New York: Scholastic.

Kaufman, O. K. (2004). *I wanna iguana*. New York: Putnam.

Keats, E. J. (1962). *The snowy day*. New York: Viking.

Keats, E. J. (1964). *Whistle for Willy*. New York: Viking.

Keats, E. J. (1971). *Over in the meadow*. New York: Four Winds.

Keats, E. J. (1998). *A letter to Amy*. New York: Viking.

Keats, E. J. (1998). *Peter's chair*. New York: Puffin.

Kellogg, S. (1971). *Can I keep him?* New York: Dial.

Kellogg, S. (1998). *Oh, a-hunting we will go*. New York: HarperCollins.

Kijak, A. (1996). *Humpback whales*. Parsippany, NJ: Modern Curriculum Press.

Krause, A., & Rosenthal, T. (2009). *Duck! Rabbit!* San Francisco: Chronicle Books.

Krauss, R. (1973). *The carrot seed*. New York: HarperCollins.

L'Engle, M. (1962). *A wrinkle in time*. New York: Farrar, Straus, Giroux.

Langstaff, J., & Parker, N. W. (1974). *Oh, a-hunting we will go*. New York: Antheneum.

Lanning, R., & Grimm, J. (1983). *Rumplestiltskin*. London: Abelard.

Layne, S. (2003). *My brother Dan's delicious*. Gretna, LA: Pelican.

Lester, H. (1997). *Author: A true story*. Boston: Houghton Mifflin.

Lewis, C. S. (1950/1994). *The lion, the witch, and the wardrobe*. New York: HarperCollins.

Lewis, C. S. (1950/2013). *The chronicles of Narnia*. London: HarperCollins.

Lewis, R. (2009). *Coyote and rabbit—A tale from the Southwest*. Boston: Houghton Mifflin.

Lin, G. (2002). *Kite flying*. New York: Knopf.

Lisson, A. (1996). *My cat*. Parsippany, NJ: Modern Curriculum Press.

Lobel, A. (1979). *Frog and toad are friends*. New York: HarperCollins.

Lobel, A. (1983). *Fables*. New York: Harper & Row.

Lobel, A. (1997). *The Arnold Lobel book of Mother Goose: A treasury of more than 300 classic nursery rhymes*. New York: Knopf.

Lord, C. (2006). *Rules*. New York: Scholastic.

Louis, S. (2009). *My dog*. Boston: Houghton Mifflin.

Lowry, L. (1993). *The giver*. Boston: Houghton Mifflin.

Lowry, N. J. (1988). *If you were a writer*. New York: Four Winds.

Macauley, D. (1973). *Cathedral: The story of its construction*. Boston: Houghton Mifflin.

MacCuish, I. (2001). *100 best-loved nursery rhymes*. Great Bardfield, England: Miles Kelly.

MacLachlan, P. (1985). *Sarah, plain and tall*. London: MacRae.

Maloney, B., Morehouse, M., & Chauhan, S. (Eds.). (2011, October). *National Geographic Explorer: Spiders*. Washington, DC: National Geographic Learning.

Martin, B. (1992). *Brown bear, brown bear, what do you see?* New York: Henry Holt.

Martin, R. (1992). *The rough-face girl*. New York: G. P. Putnam's Sons.

Martino, A. C. (2005). *Pinned*. New York: Harcourt Children's Books.

Mathis, S. (1971). *Sidewalk story*. New York: Penguin.

Mayer, M. (1990). *There's a nightmare in my closet*. New York: Dial Book for Young Readers.

McCloskey, R. (1941). *Make way for ducklings*. New York: Viking.

McCloskey, R. (1948). *Blueberries for Sal*. New York: Viking.

McCully, E. A. (1992). *Mirette on the high wire*. New York: Puffin.

McDermott, G. (1972). *Anansi the spider*. New York: Holt, Rinehart and Winston.

McGovern, A. (1986). *Stone soup*. New York: Scholastic.

McManus, D. (2009). *Bear's tail*. Boston: Houghton Mifflin.

Messner, K. (2010). *Sugar and ice*. New York: Walker Children's.

Mikaelsen, B. (2002). *Touching spirit bear*. New York: HarperCollins.

Milton, J. (1985). *Dinosaur days*. New York: Random House.

Miranda, A. (1996). *The city cat and the country cat*. Parsippany, NJ: Modern Curriculum Press.

Mitten, The. (2007). (Adapted by Katalina Page). Learning from A-Z (Downloaded from www.readinga-z.com).

Morris, A. (1989). *Bread, bread, bread (Foods of the world)*. New York: Lothrop, Lee, and Shepard.

Morris, A. (1997). *Houses and homes*. New York: Viking.

Moss, M. (2006). *Amelia's notebook*. New York: Simon & Schuster.

Munoz, P. R. (2000). *Esperanza rising*. New York: Scholastic.

Murphy, C. R. (2006). *Children of Alcatraz: Growing up on the rock*. New York: Walker.

Napoli, D. J. (1992). *The prince of the pond*. Toronto: Penguin.

Nelson, R. (2003). *From wax to crayon*. Minneapolis, MN: Lerner.

O'Dell, S. (2010). *Island of the blue dolphins*. San Anselmo, CA: Sandpiper. [Originally published by Houghton Mifflin, 1960.]

O'Neill, A. (2002). *The recess queen*. New York: Scholastic.

Orozoco, J. (2002). *Diez deditos and other play rhymes and action songs from South America*. New York: Puffin.

Palacio, R. J. (2012). *Wonder*. New York: Knopf.

Parish, P. (1971). *Come back, Amelia Bedelia*. New York: HarperCollins.

Park, F., & Parker, G. (2000). *The royal bee*. Honesdale, PA: Boyds Mill Press.

Park, L. S. (2010). *A long walk to water*. New York: Clarion Books.

Paterson, K. (1977/2004). *Bridge to Terabithia*. New York: Harper Teen. [Originally published by HarperCollins]

Paulsen, G. (1987). *Hatchet*. New York: Bradbury.

Paulsen, G. (1991). *The river*. New York: Delacorte.

Peek, M. (1981). *Roll over! A counting song*. New York: Houghton Mifflin.

Peek, M. (1993). *Mary wore her red dress, Henry wore his green sneakers*. New York: Clarion Books.

Penn, A. (1993). *The kissing hand*. Washington, DC: Child Welfare League of America.

Peterson, P. (1996). *Eyes are everywhere*. Parsippany, NJ: Modern Curriculum Press.

Petrillo, G. (2007). *Keep your ear on the ball*. Gardiner, ME: Tilbury House.

Pfister, M. (1992). *Rainbow fish*. New York: North-South Books.

Philbrick, R. (1993). *Freak the mighty*. New York: Scholastic/Blue Sky.

Pilkey, D. (1999) *Paperboy*. New York: Scholastic.

Pinkney, J. (1999). *The ugly duckling*. New York: Morrow Junior Books.

Pinkney, J. (2000). *Aesop's fables*. New York: SeaStar Books.

Piper, W. (1930). *The little engine that could*. New York: Platt & Munk.

Polacco, P. (1998). *My rotten redheaded older brother*. New York: Aladdin.

Polacco, P. (1998). *Thank you, Mr. Falker*. New York: Philomel.

Polacco, P. (2010). *The junkyard wonders*. New York: Philomel.

Prelutsky, J. (1984). *New kid on the block*. New York: Greenwillow.

Prelutsky, J. (1986). *Read aloud rhymes for the very young*. New York: Knopf.

Prelutsky, J. (2005). *It's raining pigs and noodles*. New York: Greenwillow.

Prelutsky, J., & Dorman, B. (2008). *Be glad your nose is on your face and other poems: Some of the best of Jack Prelutsky*. New York: Greenwillow.

Rappaport, D. (2001). *Martin's big words: The life of Dr. Martin Luther King Jr.* New York: Hyperion Books for Children.

Rappaport, D. (2008). *Lady Liberty: A biography*. Cambridge, MA: Candlewick.

Raschka, C. (1993). *Yo! Yes?* New York: Orchard Books.

Reed, J. (2009). *Hide and seek*. New York: Weldon Own Education (published by Scholastic).

Reed, J. (2009). *No snacks, Jack!* New York: Weldon Own Education (published by Scholastic).

Riordan, R. (2006). *The sea of monsters: Percy Jackson & the Olympians, Book Two*. New York: Scholastic.

Rockwell, A. (1989). *Apples and pumpkins*. New York: Scholastic.

Rockwell, A. (2005). *Honey in a hive*. New York: HarperCollins.

Roessel, D., & Rampersad, A. (Eds.). (2006). *Poetry for young people: Langston Hughes*. New York: Sterling.

Rosen, D. (2009). *Louise Arner Boyd and glaciers*. Boston: Houghton Mifflin.

Roth, V. (2011). *Divergent*. New York: Katherine Tegen/HarperCollins.

Rumford, J. (2008). *Silent music: A story of Baghdad*. New York: Roaring Brook Press.

Rylant, C. (1985). *Every little thing*. New York: Bradbury.

Rylant, C. (1986). *Night in the country*. New York: Bradbury.

Rylant, C. (1990). *Checkouts*. From *A couple of kooks and other stories about love*. New York: Orchard.

Rylant, C. (1996). *An angel for Solomon Singer*. New York: Orchard Books.

Rylant, C. (1997). *Poppleton*. New York: Blue Sky Press.

Schotter, R. (1999). *Nothing ever happens on 90th Street*. New York: Orchard Books.

Schwartz, J. (2002). *Gold*. Washington, DC: National Geographic Society.

Scieszka, J. (2008). *Knucklehead: Tall tales & mostly true stories about growing up*. New York: Viking.

Seely, J., & Kitchen, D. (1990). *Priscilla and the wimps: Stories and poems*. New York: Pearson Longman.

Selznick, B. (2007). *The invention of Hugo Cabret*. New York: Scholastic.

Sendak, M. (1963/1988). *Where the wild things are*. New York: HarperCollins.

Sharmat, M. (1994). *Nate the great and the stolen base*. New York: Yearling.

Shaw, N. (1986). *Sheep in a Jeep*. Boston: Houghton Mifflin.

Shepherd, M. (2007). *Tian Tian, a giant panda*. Learning A-Z. (Downloaded from www.learninga-z.com on May 5, 2012.)

Showers, P. (1994). *Where does the garbage go?* New York: HarperCollins.

Shulman, L. (2002). *Old MacDonald had a workshop*. New York: Putnam.

Shusterman, N. (2001). *The downsiders*. New York: Simon Pulse.

Shusterman, N. (2006). *The Schwa was here*. New York: Puffin.

Silverstein, S. (1964). *A giraffe and a half*. New York: Harper & Row.

Silverstein, S. (1974). *Where the sidewalk ends: The poems & drawings of Shel Silverstein*. New York: Harper & Row.

Simon, S. (1997). *Lightning*. New York: Morrow Junior Books.

Simon, S. (2002). *Planets around the Sun*. New York: Seastar Books.

Slate, J. (2003). *Miss Bindergarten takes a field trip with kindergarten*. New York: Dutton Children's Books.

Solomon, F. (2009). *A snowy day*. Boston: Houghton Mifflin.

Soto, G. (1990). *Baseball in April and other stories*. San Diego: Harcourt Brace Jovanovich.

Speigelman, A. (1986) *Maus: A survivor's tale (Volume 1: My father bleeds history)*. New York: Pantheon.

Speigelman, A. (1993). *Maus: A survivor's tale (Volume 2: And here my troubles began)*. New York: Pantheon.

Spinelli, E. (2008). *The best story*. New York: Dial Books for Young Readers.

Spinelli, J. (1990). *Maniac Magee*. Boston: Little, Brown.

Spinelli, J. (2000). *Stargirl*. New York: Knopf Books for Young Readers.

Steig, W. (1971). *Amos & Boris*. New York: Farrar, Straus, Giroux.

Steptoe, J. (1987). *Mufaro's beautiful daughters*. New York: Lothrop, Lee & Shepard.

Stevens, J. (1984). *The tortoise and the hare: An Aesop fable*. New York: Holiday House.

Stone, T. L. (2008). *Elizabeth leads the way: Elizabeth Cady Stanton and the right to vote*. New York: Henry Holt.

Stone, T. L. (2008). *Sandy's circus: A story about Alexander Calder*. New York: Viking.

Stone, T. L. (2009). *Almost astronauts: 13 women who dared to dream*. Somerville, MA: Candlewick.

Stone, T. L. (2010). *The good, the bad, and the Barbie: A doll's history and her impact on us*. New York: Viking.

Stuve-Bodeen, S. (1998). *We'll paint the octopus red*. Bethesda, MD: Woodbine House.

Taback, S. (1997). *There was an old lady who swallowed a fly*. New York: Viking.

Taback, S. (1999*). Joseph had a little overcoat*. New York: Viking.

Tatham, B. (2002*). Penguin chick*. New York: HarperCollins.

Trueman, T. (2001). *Stuck in neutral*. New York: Harper Teen.

Truss, L., & Timmons, B. (2007). *The girl's like spaghetti: Why you can't manage without apostrophes!* New York: Putnam.

Van Allsburg, C. (1986). *The stranger*. Boston: Houghton Mifflin.

Van Allsburg, C. (1990). *Just a dream*. Boston: Houghton Mifflin.

Viorst, J. (1972). *Alexander and the terrible, horrible, no good, very bad day*. New York: Atheneum.

Viorst, J. (1990). *Earrings*. New York: Atheneum.

Waber, B. (1965). *Lyle, Lyle crocodile*. Boston: Houghton Mifflin.

Waddel, M. (1992). *Owl babies*. Cambridge, MA: Candlewick.

Watt, M. (2006). *Scaredy Squirrel makes a friend*. Toronto: Kids Can Press.

Westcott, N. B. (1988). *The lady with the alligator purse*. Boston: Joy Street Books.

Westcott, N. B. (1996). *I've been working on the railroad*. New York: Hyperion Books for Children.

White, E. B. (1952). *Charlotte's web*. New York: Harper & Row.

White, M. M., Moore, E., Deregniers, B. S., & Carr, J. (Eds.). (1988). *Sing a song of popcorn: Every child's book of poems*. New York: Scholastic.

White, N. (1993). *Seeds get around*. New York: Newbridge Communications.

Wiesner, D. (1991). *Tuesday*. New York: Clarion Books.

Wildsmith, B. (1982). *Cat on the Mat*. New York: Oxford University Press.

Wiles, D. (2001). *Freedom summer*. New York: Atheneum Books for Young Readers.

Wiles, D. (2005). *Each little little bird that sings*. New York: Harcourt.

Willems, M. (2004). *Knuffle Bunny: A cautionary tale*. New York: Hyperion Books for Children.

Williams, J., & Clark-Ford, L. (2000). *Fat cat*. Parsippany, NJ: Modern Curriculum Press.

Williams, J., & Clark-Ford, L. (2000). *The wet pet*. Parsippany, NJ: Modern Curriculum Press.

Williams, M. (2005). *Brothers in hope: The story of the lost boys of Sudan*. New York: Lee & Low Books.

Williams, M. (2011). *Greek myths*. Somerville, MA: Candlewick.

Williams, S. (1989). *I went walking*. San Diego: Harcourt Brace Jovanovich.

Williams, V. B. (1982). *A chair for my mother*. New York: Greenwillow.

Williams, V. B. (1984). *Music, music for everyone*. New York: Greenwillow.

Williams, V. B. (1994). *Un sillón para mi mama*. New York: Greenwillow.

Wilson, E. G. (Ed.). (2007). *Poetry for young people: Maya Angelou*. New York: Sterling.

Wilson, K. (2002) *Bear snores on*. New York: M. K. McElderry.

Winkler, H., & Oliver, L. (2003). *Niagara falls, or does it? #1*. New York: Grosset & Dunlap.

Wood, A. (1994). *Silly Sally went to town*. Orlando, FL: Harcourt Brace.

Wormell, C. (2005). *Mice, morals, and monkey business: Lively lessons from Aesop's fables*. Philadelphia: Running Press Kids.

Yashima, T. (1955). *Crow boy*. New York: Viking.

Yeats, W. B. (1956). *The collected poems of W. B. Yeats*. New York: Macmillan.

Yolen, J. (1987). *Owl moon*. New York: Philomel.

Yolen, J. (1990). *The devil's arithmetic*. New York: Puffin.

Yolen, J., & Degen, B. (1990). *Dinosaur dances*. New York: Putnam.

Young, C. (1996). *The little red hen: A play*. Bothell, WA: Wright Group.

Young, E. (1982). *Yeh-Shen: A Cinderella story from China*. New York: Philomel.

Young, E. (2002). *Seven blind mice*. New York: Philomel.

Zelinsky, P. (1990). *The wheels on the bus*. New York: Dutton Children's Books.

Zolotow, C. (1972). *William's doll*. New York: HarperCollins.

Index

A

ABC center, 181
–*able* suffix, 392
ab– prefix, 393
absorbed prefixes, 67
academic language
    defined, 9, 46
    general academic vocabulary, 15, 239
    informational text patterns, 319–320
    skillful literacy, 368, 381–384
    systematic instruction, 346–349
accommodations
    Response to Instruction, 425–426
    universal access, 126
accountable talk, 322
accuracy, of informational text, 186
active involvement, 86
activities, 346
adding/comparing words, 383
addition, phoneme, 210
adequate yearly progress (AYP), 113
ad– prefix, 391, 394
advanced English proficiency, 164
Aesop's fables, 302
aesthetic stance, 287
affixes, 43
    morphology with, 336, 339–340
    spelling, 63
African American Vernacular English
    (AAVE), 162–163
Al Capone Does My Shirts (Choldenko), 9,
    12, 36, 45
    "best guess" meaning of a word,
      checking, 345–346
    book club example, 316–317
    collaborative reasoning, 291–292
    contextual analysis, 344
    figurative language, 36
    historical fiction, 12
    idiomatic expressions, 170
    narrative, 373
    oral language development, 64
    persuasive stance, 372
    problems and plot, 45–46
    themes, 371–372
    vocabulary words, 15
"All-About Texts," 264
alliteration, 203, 325
alphabet books, 204
alphabetic layer, 41–42
alphabet knowledge
    assessment, 144

beginning conventional reading and
    writing, 20, 222–223
ambiguous vowels, 277–279, 331, 334–335
analogy phonics, 232
analytic phonics, 232
analytic talk, 184
analyzing, 39
    higher-order questions, 256
    text, 85
ana– prefix, 394
anchored vocabulary instruction, 196
Annenberg Learner, 111, 314
annotated vocabulary instruction, 197
an– prefix, 393
antonym, 344
apostrophes, 355
applying
    as characteristic of thought, 39
    higher-order questions, 256
a– prefix, 393
Arabic, 170
argument
    analyzing and constructing, 407–411
    in Common Core State Standards, 13
art center, 181
articulation, point of, 235
assessment
    adequate yearly progress (AYP), 113
    Common Core State Standards,
      118–120
    comprehensive literacy assessment
      program, 127–144
    conferring, 144–145
    criterion-referenced assessment,
      122–123
    emergent and beginning readers,
      143–144
    English learners, 127
    "essentials," 129
    fluency, 139–141
    formative assessment, 123–124
    foundational skills, 132–133
    high-stakes testing, 113–115
    history of, 115–118
    informal reading inventories, 136–139
    instructional transparency, 126
    interest inventories and motivation
      surveys, 143
    mistakes and unintended conse-
      quences, 118
    norm-referenced tests, 121–122
    planning, 125
    portfolios, 150

    reading comprehension, 133–136
    reliability, 125–126
    rubrics, 145–146
    student self-assessment and ongoing
      feedback, 146–150
    summative assessment, 123
    validity, 126
    vocabulary and morphological knowl-
      edge, 141–142
    word structure, 129–132
    word study, 108, 239
assimilated prefixes, 391, 392, 394
assistive technology, 425, 426
audience, 361
author's craft lessons, 360, 404–405
automaticity, word study, 238–239
automatic word callers, 422–423

B

background knowledge, 346
basal readers. *See* comprehensive core
    reading programs
base/base word, 44. *See also* root word.
Basic Interpersonal Communication Skills
    (BICS), 159
beginning conventional reading and writing
    alphabet knowledge, 222–223
    characteristics, 221–222, 267–268
    comprehension development, 254–260
    concept of word in text, 224–225 in
      developmental model of literacy,
      58–60
    English learners, 166
    five-day shared reading lesson plan,
      226–228
    five-day word study lesson plan,
      238–239
    fluency instruction, 252–253
    guided reading, 242–247
    independent word knowledge, 247–252
    letter name-alphabetic spellers,
      233–237
    narrative writing, 263
    phonics, 232–233
    phonological and phonemic aware-
      ness, 224
    sight word vocabulary, 228–232
    small group reading instruction,
      241–252
    vocabulary development, 237,
      239–241

word knowledge, 222–232
word study, 232–241
writing process, 264–266
writing to inform, 264
writing workshop, 261–263
beginning English proficiency, 164
beginning sound sorts, 205–206
beginning stage
    developmental approach to literacy,
        20–21
    reading assessment, 143–144
bell curve, 122
–bene– root, 393
big books, 79, 182, 191
bilingual instruction/programs, 161
Black English. See African American
    Vernacular English
blended words, 379–381
blending, phoneme, 210
blind sorts, 103
blocks center, 181
blogging, 294
Book Buddies, 422
book clubs, 87–90, 167, 305, 316, 325,
    327–329
    strategies in the classroom, 327–329
    sample, 316–317
books
    about learning difficulties, 428
    critical thinking, interactive read-
        alouds for, 290
    evaluating cultural authenticity, 167
    fables, 302
    fingerplays, chants, and rhymes, 189
    folktales, 302
    high-quality informational text, 186
    historical fiction — Al Capone Does
        My Shirts, 12
    lesbian, gay, bisexual, transgender,
        questioning, or intersex (LGBTQI)
        students, 379
    middle school students at intermedi-
        ate stage, 330
    mythology, 369–370
    myths, 302
    nursery rhymes, 189
    perseverance and overcoming
        obstacles, 136
    poetry, 189
    questions, texts that stimulates chil-
        dren to ask, 257
    read-aloud books, resources for
        selecting, 192
    reading for boys and young adult
        males, 49
    selection for guided reading, 242–243
    songs, 189
    start of school year, 84
    supporting children's conversations
        about, 289–291
book talks, 79
bound morphemes, 36

boys, reading for, 49
brainstorming, 104
buddy/partner sorts, 103

C

categorization, phoneme, 210
cause/effect, 46, 319
CCSS. See Common Core State Standards
    (CCSS)
–ced–/–ceed–/–cess– root, 393
The Center for Media Literacy, 78
Center for Universal Design in Education,
    126
centers, literacy-rich, 181
chants, 189
chaos, 369
characterization, 326
children's literature connection
    about learning difficulties, 428
    critical thinking, interactive read-
        alouds for, 290
    evaluating cultural authenticity, 167
    fables, 302
    fingerplays, chants, and rhymes, 189
    folktales, 302
    high-quality informational text, 186
    historical fiction — Al Capone Does
        My Shirts, 12
    myths, 302
    nursery rhymes, 189
    perseverance and overcoming
        obstacles, 136
    poetry, 189
    questions, texts that stimulate
        children to ask, 257
    read-aloud books, resources for
        selecting, 192
    reading for boys, 49
    songs, 189
    start of school year, 84
Chinese, 158
    characters, 163
    spelling, 170
choral read, 352
choral reading, 224
classroom environment
    emergent literacy, 176–181
    teachers, 74–77
classroom library, 78–81
classroom strategies
    accountable talk, 322
    anchored vocabulary instruction, 197
    author's craft lessons, 360, 404–405
    "best method" for teaching reading, 5
    book clubs, 327–329
    building a tower of talk, 179
    comprehension strategies, teaching,
        431
    hearing and representing sounds, 225
    literacy-rich centers, 181
    "modeling" academic language, 171

morphology, 339–340, 342–343
planning assessment before instruc-
    tion, 125
prefix "un–", 284–285
shared reading, print referencing, and
    rhyme, 209
skillful readers with "spelling issues," 395
speech discrimination, 57
text-leveling system, 80–81
word study, sample five-day lesson
    plan, 238–239
written response and note taking, 319
clipped words, 379–381
closed sorts, 100–101
close reading, 382
–clud–/–clus– root, 393
coaching beginning readers, 245
code switching, 37
cognates
    English learners (EL), 351
    intermediate readers, 317–318
cognition
    intermediate statge, 22
    thought, characteristics of, 38
Cognitive Academic Language Proficiency
    (CALP), 159
cohesion, 47
cohesive words and phrases, 383
collaborative reasoning, 291–292
Colorín Colorado, 172
commas, 355
Common Core Curriculum Mapping
    Project, 363
Common Core State Standards (CCSS),
    118–120
    argument in, 13
    assessment, 119–120
    closer, deeper reading of texts, 325
    influence on teaching, 18
    interpretive strategies, 287–288
    Narrative Directed Reading Activities,
        325
    research and technology, 78
    third-grade response to text, sample,
        288
    writing traits, 356, 357
Common Sense Media, 203
compare/contrast, 46, 319
compare/contrast table, 349
complexity
    text, teacher decision-making and, 119
    text level of written language, 46–48
compounding, 43
compound words, 285–286
com– prefix, 391, 394
comprehension
    assessment, 133–136
    beginning conventional reading and
        writing, 254–260
    described, 7–12
    intermediate reading and writing,
        318–330

comprehension *(continued)*
    reading to children, 191–198
    routines, teaching, 430–431
    schema theory, 8
    skillful literacy, 371–384
    skills vs. strategies, 11–12
    strategies, 9–11
    teaching strategies, 431
    transitional reading and writing,
        303–305
comprehensive core reading programs, 16,
    108–110
concept books, 189
concept map, 347, 429–430
concept of word in text, 20
Concepts about Print (CAP), 19, 143–144
concept sorts
    skillful literacy level, 401
    vocabulary terms, 347
    word study instruction, 102
conceptual knowledge, 196–198
conceptually related words, 195
concrete operations, 299
conferring
    assessment, 144–145
    reading workshop, 83
    small group instruction, 96
    with transitional readers and writers,
        305–306
connotative meaning of word, 35
con– prefix, 394
consonant blend, 41
consonant digraph, 41
consonants
    beginning assessment, 223
    confusion for English learners, 207
    defined, 41
    different sounds, 16
    single-syllable words, 279–280
    sounds, 204–205
    standard American English, 35
    that influence vowel sounds, 236
constructivist approach, 75
Content Directed Reading Activity,
    320–322
content learning, technological literacy
    and, 360–361
content-specific academic vocabulary, 15,
    239–240
context/meaning clues, 246
contexts, meaningful
    emergent literacy, 180
    modeling contextual analysis, 344
    text talk, 193
continuant sounds, 204–205
contracts, individual learning, 108, 109
contra– prefix, 392
conventions, 295
conversation
    authentic and sustained, 178–180
    conversational vocabulary, 15
    emergent literacy, 178–180

Cooperative Children's Book Center
    (CCBC), 363, 413
co– prefix, 394
cor– prefix, 394
–corp– root, 393
counter– prefix, 392
–crat/–cracy suffix, 392
–cred– root, 393
criterion-referenced assessment, 122–123
critical literacy
    in action on Web, 386–387
    development, 368
    highly effective teachers, 73
critical reading comprehension, 7
critical thinking, interactive read-alouds,
    290
cultural authenticity, children's literature,
    167
cultural diversity, 156
cultural responsive and culturally inclu-
    sive teaching
    defined, 157
    English learners (EL), 159–164
culture, 25
cumulative learning, assessing, 123
curriculum-based assessment measures
    (C-BAM), 128

D

DARE strategy, 311
decodable texts, 20
    for beginners, 251–252
decode, 17
decoding, word stumblers and, 423
deep orthography, 280
deep thinkers, building community of, 74
Degrees of Reading Power (DRP), 135
deletion, phoneme, 210
demographics, English learners (EL),
    158–159
denotations, 35
density of talk, 177
derivational morphology, 43
derivational relationships, developmental
    spelling, 384–385, 388–394
derivational suffixes, 43
description, 46, 319
details, 383
developmental appropriateness, informa-
    tional text, 186
developmental model of literacy, 18–23.
    See also beginning conventional reading
    and writing; emergent literacy; transi-
    tional reading and writing
    developmental continuum, 49
    English learners, 166
    intermediate reading and writing,
        62–64
    skillful reading and writing, 65–67
    stages, tables of, 50–54
developmental spelling, 384–385, 388–394

developmental word knowledge,
    330–349
diagnostic assessment, 128
dialects, 162–163
dialogic read-alouds, 191–193
dia– prefix, 393
dictionary use, 345–346
–dict– root, 343
differentiated materials, for struggling
    readers, 426
differentiating instruction
    literacy, 27
    sight vocabulary for English learners,
        230
digital contexts
    assistive technology, 425
    blogging in response to text, 294
    content learning, connecting to tech-
        nological literacy, 360–361
    critical literacy in action on Web,
        386–387
    electronic data management systems,
        133–135
    learning applications, resources for
        evaluating, 203
    as study topic, 78
    technology as learning tool, 78
    technology-assisted repeated read-
        ings, 253
digital immigrants, 78
digital literacy, 4–5
digital natives, 78
diphthong, 41, 277–278
disciplinary literacy, 367
discrepancy model, 418
dis– prefix, 339
domain-specific vocabulary, 15, 239–240,
    346–349
Double versus Don't Double patterns, 333
drafting
    beginning conventional writing, 265
    intermediate writing stage, 354–355
dramatic play center, 181
dramatic reenactment center, 181
draw and label, 104
Drop Everything and Read (DEAR), 90–91
–duc–/–duct– root, 393
dysgraphia, 417–418
dyslexia, 417
dystopian novels, 368

E

early intermediate English proficiency,
    164
early intervention, 416
early receptive language, 164
Earobics REACH, 433
ebonics. *See* African American Vernacular
    English
echo reading, 224

editing
    beginning conventional writing,
        265–266
    intermediate writing stage, 355
Education, U.S. Department of, 268–269
The Education Alliance at Brown University, 70
efferent stance, 287
8th grade
    books to start school year, 84
    developmental stages, 54
    intermediate reading and writing,
        62–64
    skillful reading and writing, 65–67
electronic data management systems,
    133–135
Elementary and Secondary Education Act
    of 1965 (ESEA), 115
elementary school students. See grades
    listed by year
Elementary Spelling Inventory (ESI),
    130–132
emergent literacy
    authentic and sustained conversation,
        178–180
    big books, 191
    classroom environment, enriching,
        176–181
    concept books, 189
    density of talk, 177
    English learners, 166
    environmental and functional print,
        188–189
    fingerplays, 188
    independent reading practice, 200–202
    informational text, 185–187
    introduction, 174–176
    meaningful contexts, 180
    nursery rhymes, 188
    oral language development, 176
    phonemic awareness, 202–206
    poetry, 188
    predictable pattern books, 190
    quality of talk, 177
    reading to children (listening compre-
        hension and vocabulary), 191–198
    reading-writing-language connection,
        214–217
    shared reading, 198–200
    songs, 188
    storybook reading, 182–184
    syntax, 178
    units of print and language, 206–212
    wordless picture books, 190
    writing, 213–214
    written texts, 182–187
emergent reading and writing
    as developmental stage, 19–20
    as part of developmental model of
        literacy, 55–58
    reading assessment, 143–144
engagement, Response to Instruction,
    433–434

English learners (EL)
    cognates, 317–318, 351
    cultural responsive and culturally
        inclusive teaching, 159–164
    demographics, 158–159
    equitable literacy assessment, 127
    home languages and literacy experi-
        ences, 161–164
    instructional practices, 160–161
    learning disabilities, finding, 420–421
    levels of English proficiency, 164–165
    literacy instruction similarities and
        differences, 155–156
    predictable consonant confusions, 207
    sight vocabulary, 230
    special instruction, 165–171
    teachers' dispositions and identities,
        156–158
    variant/vernacular dialects, 162–163
    vowel sounds, teaching, 280
en- prefix, 392
entrance/exit cards, 124
environment, print in, 190
environmental and functional print, 182,
    188–189
epi- prefix, 393
episodes, 45
e- prefix, 392
equitable literacy assessment, 127
The Equity Alliance at Arizona State
    University, 172
error detection, in mathematics, 382
"essentials," comprehensive literacy
    assessment program, 129
evaluating, 39, 63
    higher-order questions, 256
events, 45
everyday experiences, books about, 263
exclamation marks, 355
explanatory dialogue, 180
ex- prefix, 392
expressive reading, 303–304
expressive vocabulary, 55
Expressive Vocabulary Test (EVT), 142
Extended Scale Score (ESS), 121
extensions, 101, 206

F

fables, 302
-fac- root, 393
families. See working and collaborating
-fec- root, 393
feedback, ongoing, 146–150
-fer- root, 393
-fic- root, 393
5th grade
    books to start school year, 84
    developmental stages, 53
    intermediate reading and writing,
        62–64
figurative language, 36

fingerplays
    children's literature connection, 189
    emergent literacy, 188
fingerpoint reading, 59, 200
1st grade
    beginning conventional reading and
        writing, 58–60
    books to start school year, 84
    CCSS, 18
    developmental stages, 50–51, 55–58
    transitional reading and writing,
        60–62
fist to five assessment strategy, 124
five-day shared reading lesson plan,
    beginning conventional reading and
    writing, 226–228
five-day word study lesson plan, begin-
    ning conventional reading and writing,
    238–239
fluency
    assessment, 139–141
    beginning conventional reading and
        writing, 252–253
    intermediate reading and writing,
        349–352
    literacy, 17
    transitional reading and writing,
        303–305
    wide reading, 303
Fluency-Oriented Reading Instruction
    (FORI), 253
folktales, 302
follow-up queries, 322
fore- prefix, 392
format, 361
formative assessment, 114, 123–124
formative progress monitoring, 128
foundational skills assessment, 132–133
4-square diagram, 348, 350
    in math, 401
fourth-grade slump, 420
4th grade
    books to start school year, 84
    developmental stages, 53
    intermediate reading and writing,
        62–64
    transitional reading and writing, 60–62
frames, sentence, 322, 430
free appropriate public education (FAPE),
    417
free morphemes, 36
free verse, 381
French, 159
Fry's Instant Word List, 228
functional print, 182, 188–189
-fy- root, 393

G

games
    instructional supplements, 433
    word study, 104–105, 239

Gates-MacGinitie Reading Assessment, 135–136
generalizations, 98
generative activity, 432
generative vocabulary, 13, 67, 403
German, 159
goals of informational text, 186
Grade Equivalent (GE), 121
Gradual Release of Responsibility model, 27, 306
Graduate Record Exam (GRE), 114
grammar
    scaffolding syntax, 178
    variant dialects, accommodating, 162–163
grammar check, 355
grand conversation, 293
grapheme, 41
graphic novels, 378
graphic organizers, 124, 346
    narrative text, prewriting and planning, 307
    Response to Instruction, 429–431
graphics, in informational texts, 383
Gratiae, 370
Greek roots. *See also* roots.
    assimilation of prefixes, 391, 392
    morphology with, 336, 338, 340–341, 342–343
    orthographic knowledge, 67
    skillful literacy stage, 23
    sorting words by, 396–398
green, yellow, red assessment strategy, 124
grouping, for struggling readers, 426
Guess My Category sort, 101–102
guided reading
    beginning conventional reading and writing, 242–247
    small group reading instruction, 87–88, 95–96

H

handwriting instruction, 204
headers, 100
hearing sounds, 225
Heritage language, 161
heuristic function of language, 38
high-frequency words, 228
high-quality informational text, 186
high-stakes testing, 113–115
    helping students succeed, 117
    online resources, 152
    talking with parents and families about, 120
high success reading, 297, 431–432
high utility words, 195
historical fiction, 12
history, of words, 23
history texts, 383
Hmong/Miao, 159

home languages, 161–164
home links. *See* working and collaborating
homework, students with learning disabilities, 427
homographs, 43
homophones, 42
Howard Street Tutoring Program, 422
"How-To" text, 264
hyperbole, 36

I

–ian suffix, 389
–ible suffix, 392
idea completions, 194
IDEA (Individuals with Disabilities Education Act) of 2004, 416–418
identification, phoneme, 210
idiomatic expressions, 170
illustrations, 167
il– prefix, 392
imaginative function of language, 38
im– prefix, 392
independent level text, 297
independent reading
    reading workshop, 83
    skillful literacy, 378–381
independent reading practice
    books for, 297–302
    emergent literacy, 200–202
independent reading time, 90–93
independent word knowledge, 247–252
independent writing practice, 95
individualized education plans (IEPs), 417
individual learning contracts, 108, 109
Individuals with Disabilities Education Act of 2004 (IDEA), 416–418
infer, teaching children to, 10, 299–300
inferential reading comprehension, 7
inflectional morphology, 43
inform, writing to, 264
informal reading inventories
    assessment, 136–139
    list of common, 137
information, identifying important, 10–11
informational text
    comprehension and understanding, 319–320
    constructed response, example of, 359
    described, 9
    emergent literacy, 185–187
    features, 301
    interactive read-alouds, transitional stage, 290
    language, racial, ethnic and culturally diverse learners, 167
    late transitional readers, 300–301

predicting, 254
    skillful literacy, 381–384
    structure, 46
    third-grade common core standards, 288
    types of, 45
informative writing, 353
–ing suffix, 331–333
initiating queries, 322
in– prefix, 392
instructional focus, 89
instructional-level texts, 87
instructional modifications, 426
instructional transparency, 126
instructions, special
    accommodations, 126
    English learners (EL), 165–171
    for struggling readers, 426
interactional function of language, 38
interactive read-alouds
    Reading Workshop, 83–84
    transitional reading and writing, 286–293
interactive writing, 214
interest
    assessment, 143
    in informational text, 186
interim/benchmark assessment, 128
intermediate English proficiency, 164
intermediate reading and writing
    characteristics of learners, 362
    comprehension and understanding of texts, 318–330
    decoding and learning longer words in reading, 341–346
    as developmental stage, 22
    developmental word knowledge, 330–349
    English learners, 167
    fluency, 349–352
    overview, 317–318
    as part of developmental model of literacy, 62–64
    spelling, 330–336
    systematic instruction in general academic and domain-specific vocabulary, 346–349
    vocabulary development, 336–341
    writing, 352–361
International Reading Association, 269
inter-rater reliability, 126
invented spelling, 214
inventories
    informal reading, 136–139
    spelling, 130–132
–ion suffix, 340, 388–389
I.R.E. cycle, 290–291
ir– prefix, 392
irregular verbs, 56
–ism suffix, 392
isolation, phoneme, 210
–ist suffix, 392

J

–ject– root, 393
Jeopardy assessment strategy, 124
–jud– root, 393
junctures, 330–331, 334
just-right books, 91

K

key pictures, 98
keywords, 98
kindergarten
    beginning conventional reading and
        writing, 58–60
    books to start school year, 84
    CCSS, 18
    developmental stages, 50, 55–58
The Knowledge Loom, 314
Korean, 158–159
    spelling, 170

L

label and draw, 104
language
    conventionality and clarity, 48
    phonological awareness and, 211–212
    of stories, 182–184
    and thought, characteristics of, 38–39
    used at home by English learners
        (EL), 161–164
language-experience approach, 214
Language-minority students, 161
language of instruction
    building community of thoughtful com-
        municators and deep thinkers, 74
    collaborative reasoning in action,
        291–292
    complexity, emphasis on, 47
    conferring with transitional readers
        and writers, 305–306
    environment, print in, 190
    high-stakes assessment, helping
        students succeed with, 117
    idiomatic expressions, 170
    infer, teaching children to, 299–300
    persuasive stance, provoking, 372
    prompting readers to be strategic, 246
    schema theory and comprehension, 8
    spelling features at intermediate
        stage, 331
    standards, influence of, 18
    student-first language, 419
    writing traits, 356
Latin roots See also root
    assimilation of prefixes, 391, 392
    and Greek, 392. (See also Greek roots;
        root words)
    morphology with, 336, 338, 340–341,
        342–343

numbers and dates, 399
orthographic knowledge, 67
revising, 355
skillful literacy stage, 23
sorting words by, 396–398
learning applications, digital, 203
learning difficulties. See also Response to
    Instruction
        children's literature about, 428
        in English learners (EL), 420–421
        homework, 427
–leg– root, 393
lesbian, gay, bisexual, transgender, questioning, or intersex (LGBTQI) students,
young adult literature, 379
lesson plan
    five-day shared reading for beginning
        conventional reading and writing,
        226–228
    five-day shared reading lesson plan,
        beginning conventional reading
        and writing, 226–228
    five-day word study lesson plan, be-
        ginning conventional reading and
        writing, 238–239
    word study instruction, 107
letter name-alphabetic spellers, 233–237
levels of English proficiency, 164–165
lexical knowledge, 230
library, classroom, 78–81, 181
Limited English proficient, 161
linguistic modification, 127
liquid sounds, 236
listening, as common core standard, 288
literacy. See also developmental model of
    literacy; skillful literacy
        beginning stage, 20–21
        centers rich in, 181
        comprehension, 7–12
        defined, 3–4
        differentiating instruction, 27
        emergent stage, 19–20
        English learners (EL), similarities and
            differences, 155–156
        experiences for English learners (EL),
            161–164
        fluency, 17
        intermediate stage, 22
        motivation, 17
        presentations of, 5–6
        print and digital, importance of, 4–5
        reciprocal processes of reading and
            writing, 6
        sociocultural contexts, 24–25
        standards, 18
        support, levels of, 26–27
        transitional stage, 21–22
        vocabulary, 13–16
        word structure, 16–17
        writing, 12–13
literal reading comprehension, 7
literary devices, 94
literary nonfiction, 46

literature
    interactive read-alouds, transitional
        stage, 290
    skillful literacy, 371–377
    third-grade common core standards,
        288
    types of, 45
literature circles, 88–89, 327–329
    sample, 316–317
literature connection, children's
    about learning difficulties, 428
    critical thinking, interactive read-
        alouds for, 290
    evaluating cultural authenticity, 167
    fables, 302
    fingerplays, chants, and rhymes, 189
    folktales, 302
    high-quality informational text, 186
    historical fiction, 12
    myths, 302
    nursery rhymes, 189
    perseverance and overcoming
        obstacles, 136
    poetry, 189
    questions, texts that stimulate chil-
        dren to ask, 257
    read-aloud books, resources for
        selecting, 192
    reading for boys, 49
    songs, 189
    start of school year, 84
literature connection, young adult's
    lesbian, gay, bisexual, transgender,
        questioning, or intersex (LGBTQI)
        students, 379
    middle school students at intermedi-
        ate stage, 330
    mythology, 369–370
    reading for young adult males, 49
logos, recognizing, 57
–logy/–logist suffix, 392

M

mal– prefix, 393
–man– root, 393
"markup" feature, 354
mathematics
    four-square diagram, 401–402
    texts, 382
Matthew effect, 424
meaning
    correspondences at level of (See
        morphology)
    levels of, 48
    word knowledge, 42–43
meaningful contexts, 180
media literacy, 78
mental dictionary, 229
mentor texts
    Writing Workshop, 94
metacognition, 38

metalinguistic skill, 224
metaphor, 36, 325
meta– prefix, 393
micro– prefix, 342
middle school students. *See also* grades
    listed by year
        literature for, 330
mini-lesson
    Reading Workshop, 83, 84–87
    Writing Workshop, 95
miscues, 229
–*mis*– root, 393
mistakes
    assessment, 118
    error detection in mathematics, 382
–*mit*– root, 393
model/demonstrate, 86
modeling, 86
    academic language, 171
    contextual analysis, 344
modifications, instructional, 426
monitoring, 11
    strategic reading, 246
morpheme, 36
morphological analysis
    beginning conventional reading and
        writing, 240–241
    Response to Instruction, 432–433
morphological knowledge
    assessment, 141–142
    word correspondences, 43–44
morphology
    defined, 36
    with Greek and Latin roots, 342–343
    with root words and affixes, 339–340
    vocabulary development, 336
    word correspondences, 43–44
motivation
    of informational text, 186
    literacy, 17
    Response to Instruction, 433–434
    surveys, 143
multiple-meaning words, 43
mythology
    children's literature connection, 302
    young adult's literature, 369–370

N
NAEP (National Assessment of Educational
    Progress), 119, 123
NAEP (National Assessment of Educational
    Progress) Fluency Rubric, 141
NAEYC (National Association for the
    Education of Young Children), 70
narrative
    analyzing, 405–407
    beginning, middle- to late-intermedi-
        ate level, 359
    described, 9
    engagements with, 373–376
    exemplar questions, 326

literature connection, 167
    prewriting and planning, 307, 309
    retelling, 258–259
    structure, 44–46
Narrative Directed Reading Activities, 325
narrative writing, 353
    beginning conventional reading and
        writing, 263
nasals, preconsonantal, 235–236
National Assessment of Educational
    Progress (NAEP), 119, 123
National Assessment of Educational
    Progress (NAEP) Fluency Rubric, 141
National Association for the Education of
    Young Children (NAEYC), 70
National Center on Response to
    Intervention, 132
National Council of Teachers of English,
    269
National Literacy Panel on Language-
    Minority Children and Youth, 155
National Reading Panel Report, 116, 139
National Writing Project, 314
A Nation at Risk, 115
nature, things found in, 197
NCLB (No Child Left Behind) Act of 2001,
    114, 116–118
Newcomer programs, 161
No Child Left Behind (NCLB) Act of 2001,
    114, 116–118
nonverbal learning disabilities, 418
normal curve, 122
normal distribution, 122
norm-referenced tests, 121–122
Northern Nevada Writing Project, 111, 363
notebooks
    vocabulary, 347
    word study, 106
note taking, 319
novel words, 177, 195
nursery rhymes
    children's literature connection, 189
    emergent literacy, 188

O
obstacles, books about overcoming, 136
onset, 56
onset-rime, awareness of, 208–209
open sort, 98
opinion/persuasive writing, 353, 358
oral language
    characteristics, table of, 68
    emergent literacy, 176
    emergent reading and writing, 55
    phonological knowledge, 34–35
    pragmatic knowledge, 37–38
    semantic knowledge, 35–37
    syntactic knowledge, 37
oral reading accuracy, 137–138
orthographic knowledge, 40. *See also* word
    knowledge

outcomes (outcomes-based) assessment,
    114, 122, 128
out-of-level test, 136
overgeneralize, 56

P
paired reading, 247
paragraph
    academic language, 382
    relationship among, 447
    understanding, 44
    unpacking, 384
paraprofessionals, 81–82
parents. *See* working and collaborating
Parents' Choice, 203
partner read, 352
Partnership for Assessment of Reading
    for College and Career (PARCC), 119,
    123
pattern layer word knowledge, 41–42
pattern sorts, word study instruction, 103
Peabody Picture Vocabulary Test (PPVT),
    142
Percentile Rank (PR), 121
periods, 355
per– prefix, 393
perseverance stories in children's litera-
    ture, 136
personal essay rubric, 149
personal function of language, 38
personal readers, 200
personification, 325
persuasive "argument" texts, 264
persuasive stance, 372
persuasive writing, 353
-*phobia/phobic* suffix, 392
phonemes
    awareness of, 20, 209–211
    defined, 34
    major, table of, 35
phonemic awareness
    beginning conventional reading and
        writing, 224
    emergent literacy, 202–206
phonics, 211
    beginning conventional reading and
        writing, 232–233
    strategic reading, 246
    word study instruction vs., 97–98
phonic spelling, 214
phonograms, 232
phonological awareness, 56
    beginning conventional reading and
        writing, 224
    language and, 211–212
Phonological Awareness Literacy Screen-
    ing (PALS), 128, 132–133, 268
phonological knowledge
    English learners, accommodating,
        162
    oral language, 34–35

Phonological Literacy Awareness Screening (PALS), 132–135
    Concepts about Print (CAP), 143–144
phonological sensitivity, 207–208
phon– prefix, 342
photo– prefix, 342
pictionaries, 345
picture books
    interactive read-alouds, transitional stage, 290
    as mentor texts, 94
    wordless, 190
picture sorts, 103
planning
    assessment, 125
    beginning conventional writing, 264–265
plot, 45, 326
poetry
    children's literature connection, 189
    emergent literacy, 188
    independent reading, 378–379
    interactive read-alouds, transitional stage, 290
point of articulation, 235
point of view, 326
popcorn reading, 87
portfolios, 150
–pos–/–pon– root, 393
power relationships, 367
practice reading for beginning readers, 245
pragmatic knowledge, 37–38
Praxis exam, 114
preconsonantal nasals, 235–236
predictable consonant confusions, English learners (EL), 207
predictable pattern books, 190
predictions
    Content Directed Reading Activity, 321
    teaching children, 10
prefixes, 14, 284, 337
    assimilated, 391, 392, 394
    classroom strategies, 339
    Greek/Roman, 392
preK
    books to start school year, 84
    developmental stages, 50, 55–58
preview, 321
prewriting
    beginning conventional writing, 264–265
    intermediate stage, 354
Primary Spelling Inventory (PSI), 130, 276
print
    concepts about, 19
    environmental and functional, 188–189
    functions, 198
    independent reading practice, 200–202
    literacy, 4–5
    shared reading, 198–200
print referencing, 199–200, 209

print-rich environment, 75–76
problem/solution, 46, 319
procedural lessons, 85
prompting readers to be strategic, 246
pro– prefix, 392
prosody, 34
publishing
    beginning conventional writing, 265–266
    intermediate writing stage, 355
punctuation, 355
purpose, text reading, 8, 324–325
purposeful reading, 433–434
purposeful writing, 169–170

Q

qualitative text measures, 47–48
    spelling inventory, scoring, 130–132
quantitative text measures, 47–48
Quartile, 121
Question-Answer Relationships (QARs), 257, 323
Questioning the Author, 322
question marks, 355
questions
    asking during reading, 10
    as formative assessment strategy, 124
    text that stimulate children to ask, 257
    vocabulary words, 347
Quick Checks, 132–133
quotation marks, 355

R

RAFT papers (Role, Audience, Format, and Topic), 358, 361
Raw Score (RS), 121
read-alouds
    dialogic, 191–193
    interactive, 84, 286–293
Reader Response Theory, 287
Readers' Theater, 272, 304, 424
reading
    beginning reading stage, 267
    "best method" for teaching, 5
    with child at home, 201
    comprehension, 133–136
    developmental model of literacy, 65–67
    difficulties, profiles of students with, 421–425
    emergent literacy stages, 216
    high success, 297
    intermediate stage, 362
    rate, assessing, 139–141
    storybook, 182–184
    transitional reading stage, 313
    wide, 169–170
    writing and, 6

Reading, Writing, Word Study Workshop, 81
reading conferences, 89–90
Reading Excellence Act of 1998 (REA), 116
Reading First of 2002, 116
Reading Recovery, 422
Reading Rockets, 268–269
reading to children
    anchored vocabulary instruction, 196
    conceptual knowledge, developing, 196–198
    dialogic read-alouds, 191–193
    listening comprehension and vocabulary, 191–198
    text talk, 193–195
    words to teach, 195–196
Reading Workshop
    components, table of, 83
    English learners, 166–167
    independent reading time, 90–93
    interactive read-aloud, 84
    mini-lessons, 84–87
    reading, shared, 82–83
    share time, 93
    small group reading instruction, 87–90, 92–93
    time management, 82
reading-writing-language connection, emergent literacy, 214–217
reasoning
    collaborative, 291–292
    levels of understanding, 39
receptive vocabulary, 55
reciprocal teaching, 299, 303
records of oral reading, 138
reflection, 99, 101
register, 37
regulatory function of language, 38
reliability of assessments, 125–126
remembering, 39
    higher-order questions, 256
representational function of language, 38
representations, of words, 195
research
    best practices, 426, 428–434
    reading conferences, 89
Response to Instruction
    accommodations, 425–426
    graphic organizers, 429–431
    "high-success" reading practice, 431–432
    morphological analysis, 432–433
    motivation and engagement, 433–434
    profiles of students with difficulty learning to read, 421–425
    research-based best practices, 426, 428–434
    Response to Intervention, 416–421
    word sorts, 428–429

Response to Intervention (RTI), 27–28, 416–421
retelling
    informational text, 260
    narrative text, 258–259
retro– prefix, 393
revising
    beginning conventional writing, 265–266
    intermediate writing stage, 355
rhymes
    children's literature connection, 189
    classroom strategies, 208, 209
rime, 56
R-influenced vowel patterns, 276–277
role, 361
Role, Audience, Format, and Topic (RAFT) papers, 358, 361
Roman times. *See* Latin
root, 14, 28, 34, 35, 36, 43, 44, 64, 67, 68, 69, 97, 102, 104, 142, 167, 169, 240–241, 284, 318, 330, 331, 332, 333, 336–338, 339, 340–347, 355, 362, 365–366, 379, 384, 385, 386–387, 391–392, 396–400, 404, 412, 432–433. *See also* Individual root words; Greek roots; Latin roots.
root words and affixes, 43–44, 339–340
round robin reading, 87
RTI (Response to Intervention), 27–28, 416–421
rubrics, 145–146
rudimentary concept of word, 212
running records, 138
    interpreting, 145
Russian, 159

S

Scale Score (SS), 121
schema, story, 184
schema theory, 8
Scholastic Achievement Test (SAT), 114
school year start, 84
schwa sound, 205, 331
    spelling, secret to, 390
science center, 181
science texts, 383
screening, 128
2nd grade
    beginning conventional reading and writing, 58–60
    books to start school year, 84
    developmental stages, 50–52
    transitional reading and writing, 60–62
segmentation, phoneme, 210
self-assessment, 146–150
self-correction, 246
semantically related words, 195
semantic knowledge, 35–37
semantic maps, 402
semicolons, 355

sentences
    academic language, 382
    frames, 322, 430
    relationships among, 47
sequence, 46
series books, 299–300, 369, 404–405
setting, 326
7th grade
    books to start school year, 84
    developmental stages, 54
    intermediate reading and writing, 62–64
    skillful reading and writing, 65–67
sexuality, 368
shallow orthographies, 280
shared reading, 209
    components, 82–83
    emergent literacy, 198–200
share time, 83, 93
sharing
    Think-Pair-Share assessment strategy, 124
    Writing Working, 97
Sheltered English, 161
sight vocabulary, 41
    beginning stage, 20
    English learners (EL), 230
sight words, 41, 228–232
signal words, 320
"silent curriculum," 156–157
simile, 36, 325–326
6th grade
    books to start school year, 84
    developmental stages, 53
    intermediate reading and writing, 62–64
    skillful reading and writing, 65–67
Six Trait Model, 356
Sketch-to-Stretch assessment strategy, 124
skillful literacy
    argument, analyzing and constructing, 407–411
    comprehension and understanding, developing, 371–384
    developmental spelling, derivational relationships and, 384–385, 388–394
    English learners, 167
    independent reading, 378–381
    informational texts and academic language, 381–384
    as literacy stage, 23
    literature, 371–377
    narrative, analyzing, 405–407
    overview, 367
    texts, characteristics of, 367–371
    vocabulary development, 394–404
    writing, 405–411
skillful readers with "spelling issues," 395
SLD (specific learning disability), 417–418, 424–425
slow and steady comprehenders, 424

slow word callers, 424
small groups
    reading, books for, 297–302
    reading instruction, 83, 87–90, 92–93, 241–252
    writing instruction and conferring, 95–97
Smarter Balanced Assessment Consortium (SBAC), 119, 123
social injustice, 368
social studies center, 181
sociocultural contexts, 24–25
SOLOM (Student Oral Language Observation Matrix), 165, 169
Somebody-Wanted-But-So graphic organizer, 259–260
songs
    children's literature connection, 189
    emergent literacy, 188
sophisticated words, 177, 195
sorting
    sample five-day lesson plan, 238
    syllables, 334
    word study instruction, 98–99, 101
sounds
    hearing and representing, 225
    sorts, beginning, 205–206
Spanish, 158, 159
    spelling, 170
speaking, in third-grade common core standards, 288
special instructions
    accommodations, 126
    English learners (EL), 165–171
    for struggling readers, 426
specific learning disability (SLD), 417–418, 424–425
speech discrimination, 57
speed sorts, 103
spell check, 355
spelling
    assessment, 130–132
    developmental model of literacy, 64
    features at intermediate stage, 331
    intermediate reading and writing, 330–336
    intermediate stage, 362
    letter name-alphabetic, 233–237
    meaning, connection to, 16–17
    phonic or invented spelling, 214
    skillful readers with spelling issues, 395
    vocabulary and, 390–391
    vowels, 234–235
    word study instruction vs., 97–98
spoken language
    characteristics, table of, 68
    emergent literacy, 176
    emergent reading and writing, 55
    phonological knowledge, 34–35
    pragmatic knowledge, 37–38
    semantic knowledge, 35–37
    syntactic knowledge, 37

spoken reading accuracy, 137–138
standardized tests, 121–122
standards, influence of, 18
Stanine (ST), 121
start of school year, 84
–sta–/–stit– root, 393
State Educational Technology Directors
    Association (SETDA), 4
Stop and Jot
    assessment strategy, 124
    text responses, 293
Stop and Think, 305
stop sounds, 205
storybook
    reading in emergent literacy,
        182–184
    transitional writing, 307
story schema, 184
strategy lessons, 85
    small group reading instruction, 88,
        96
    test-taking, 117
strategy use, 246
"strikeout" feature, 355
structure
    language, 178
    text, 48
struggling word callers, 423–424
student-first language, 419
Student Oral Language Observation
    Matrix (SOLOM), 165, 169
student response, 426
student self-assessment and ongoing
    feedback, 146–150
student talk and reflection, 99
study topic, digital contexts as, 78
style, narrative, 326
sub– prefix, 391
substitution, phoneme, 210
suffixes, 14, 337
    classroom strategies, 340
suffragettes, 386–387
suffragist, 386
summarizing, 11, 383
summative assessment, 114, 123
super– prefix, 392
support, levels of, 26–27
surface-level communication, 423
Sustained Silent Reading (SSR), 90–91
syllables
    awareness of, 208
    defined, 34, 41
    junctures, 330–331, 334
    open and closed, 331
    pattern layer, 42
    spelling, 63
syl– prefix, 394
sym– prefix, 394
synonyms
    contextual analysis, 344
    Synonym and Antonym Lines activity,
        283

syn– prefix, 394
syntax
    emergent literacy, 178
    oral language knowledge, 37
    strategic reading, 246
synthesizing, 39, 63
    higher-order questions, 256

T

talk
    accountable, 322
    building a tower of, 179
    density of, 177
    emergent literacy, 177
    quality of, 177
    speaking well to writing well, 293–297
    talking with, not just to, your students,
        26
teacher-directed closed sorts, 100–101
teachers
    classroom environment, 74–77
    classroom library, 78–81
    dispositions and identities, English
        learners (EL) and, 156–158
    highly effective, characteristics of,
        73–74
    observation of beginning readers, 245
teachers' aides. See paraprofessionals
Teachers of English to Speakers of Other
    Languages (TESOL), 164
teaching point, 86
    beginning reading, 245–246
technology
    as learning tool, 78
    repeated reading, 304
    repeated readings, 253
tele– prefix, 342
temporal/sequential, 319
Test of Morphological Structure (Carlisle),
    142
text
    blogging in response to, 294
    complexity and teacher decision-
        making, 19
    concept of word in, 20
    relationships within, 47
    skillful literacy, 367–371
textbooks, 46, 320
text feature notebooks, 301
text-leveling system, 80–81
text level of written language
    complexity, 46–48
    narrative structure, 44–46
    paragraph-level understanding, 44
TextProject, 70
text talk, 193–195
text type, informational text, 186
textual analysis, 86
themes
    narrative, 326
    skillful literacy, 371–372

thesis statement, 408
Think-Pair-Share assessment strategy, 124
3rd grade
    books to start school year, 84
    developmental stages, 52
    intermediate reading and writing,
        62–64
    transitional reading and writing,
        60–62
thought, characteristics of
    language and, 38–39
    metacognition, 38
thoughtful communicators, building com-
    munity of, 74
3-2-1 assessment strategy, 124
tiered instruction, 27
time, extended to accommodate chal-
    lenged students, 425
time management, 82
topic, 361, 383
Tower of Talk, 179, 327
trade books, 79, 182
traits, of writing, 356–357
transactional model of reading, 287
transitional reading and writing
    books for independent and small
        group reading practice, 297–302
    conferring with, 305–306
    connections to writing well, 306–312
    as developmental stage, 21–22
    English learners, 166
    fluency and comprehension, 303–305
    interactive read-alouds, 286–293
    overview, 272–273
    as part of developmental, 60–62
    from talking well to writing well,
        293–297
    vocabulary development, 282–286
    within word pattern spellers,
        273–280
Two or Three Column Notes assessment
    strategy, 124

U

understanding, 39
    constructed response scoring rubric,
        295
    higher-order questions, 256
    paragraph-level, 44
    skillful literacy, 371–384
unintended consequences, 118
universal access, 126
universal design, 152
universal screening, 420
unpacking paragraphs, 384
unvoiced sounds, 205
un– prefix, 284–285
Upper Level Spelling Inventory, 385, 388
Upper Spelling Inventory (USI), 130
U.S. Department of Education, 268–269

V

validity, assessment, 126
variant/vernacular dialects
    English learners (EL), 162–163
    instructional practices, 160
Venn diagrams, 347, 349
–ven–/–vent– root, 393
verbs, irregular, 56
Vernacular English, 161
–vers–/–vert– root, 393
–vid– root, 343
Vietnamese, 158
    spelling, 170
–vis– root, 343, 355
visual literacy, 77
Vocab-o-gram, 402–403
vocabulary
    academic, 381–384
    anchored vocabulary instruction, 196
    annotated vocabulary instruction, 197
    assessment, 141–142
    classical myths and legends, 369–370
    general academic and domain-
        specific, systematic instruction in,
        346–349
    high-stakes assessments, 117
    informational text, 9
    intermediate stage, 64
    layers of instruction, 14
    literacy, 13–16
    notebooks, 347, 403–404
    reading to children, 191–198
    spelling and, 390–391
    three major types, 14–15
    word study instruction vs., 97–98
vocabulary development
    beginning conventional reading and
        writing, 237, 239–241
    intermediate reading and writing,
        336–341
    skillful literacy, 394–404
    transitional reading and writing,
        282–286
voiced sounds, 205
voice-print match, 246
vowel markers, 276
vowels
    ambiguous, 277–279, 331, 334–335
    consonants that influence sounds, 236
    defined, 41
    pattern layer, 42
    related words, sorting across, 390
    sounds, English learners (EL), 280
    spelling, 234–235
    standard American English, 35

W

Web
    critical literacy in action, 386–387
    publishing, 355
WebQuests, 360–361
webs, word, 348, 350
What Works Clearinghouse, 422
whisper read, 352
whole-language approach, 116
wide reading, 303
Wikipedia, 386
within word pattern speller, 132
word associations, 194
word banks, 229, 231
word families, 232
Word Generation, 413
word hunt, 99, 104
word knowledge
    alphabetic layer, 41–42
    beginning conventional reading and
        writing, 222–232
    correspondences at meaning level
        (morphology), 43–44
    meaning, 42–43
    pattern layer, 41–42
    underlying role and importance,
        40–41
wordless picture books, 190
word pattern spellers, 273–280
word recognition, 423
words
    awareness of, 207–208
    compound, 285–286
    concept of, 212
    longer, decoding and learning,
        341–346
    maps, 347
    novel, 177, 195
    recognition in isolation, 137
    sophisticated, 177, 195
    to teach, reading to children,
        195–196
    in text, beginning conventional
        reading and writing, 224–225
    in text, concept of, 20, 144
    unknown, discussing, 325
Words Correct Per Minute (WCPM), 139,
    141, 317
word sorts, 428–429
word structure, 14
    assessment, 129–132
    literacy, 16–17
word study
    beginning conventional reading and
        writing, 232–241
    beginning reading stage, 267
    emergent literacy stages, 216
    Reading, Writing, Word Study
        Workshop, 81
    transitional reading stage, 313
word study instruction, 97–98
    assessment, 108
    blind sorts, 103
    blind writing sorts, 103
    brainstorming, 104
    buddy/partner sorts, 103
    concept sorts, 102
draw and label, 104
English learners, 166–167
games and other activities, 104–105
guess my category sort, 101–102
individual learning contracts, 108,
    109
lesson plan sequence, 107
pattern sorts, 103
picture sorts, 103
preparing sorts, 102–103
sample schedule, 107
sorting, 98–99
speed sorts, 103
student talk and reflection, 99
talking with families about, 281–282
teacher-directed closed sorts,
    100–101
vs. other forms of phonics, spelling,
    and vocabulary instruction, 97–98
word hunts, 104
word study notebooks, 106
writing sorts, 103
word stumblers, 423
word walls, 232
working and collaborating
    high-stakes assessment, talking with
        parents and families about, 120
    home-school communication, 159
    paired reading, 247
    paraprofessionals, 81–82
    reading with child, 201
    reading with child at home, 201
    students with learning disabilities,
        homework and, 427
    word study instruction, talking with
        families about, 281–282
World-class Instructional Design and
    Assessment (WIDA), 164
writing
    beginning reading stage, 267
    beginning stage, 20–21
    center, 181
    constructed response scoring rubric,
        295
    developmental model of literacy,
        65–67
    emergent literacy, 58, 213–214
    emergent literacy stages, 216
    to inform, 264
    intermediate reading and writing,
        352–361
    intermediate stage, 362
    literacy, 12–13
    process, beginning conventional
        reading and writing, 264–266
    purposeful, 170
    Reading, Writing, Word Study
        Workshop, 81
    reading and, 6
    skillful literacy, 405–411
    third-grade common core standards,
        288
    traits, language of instruction, 356

transitional stage, 21, 313
well from talking well, 293–297
writing sorts, 103
Writing Workshop
beginning conventional reading and
writing, 261–263
independent writing practice, 95
mentor texts, 94
sharing, 97
small group writing instruction and
conferring, 95–97

written language
characteristics, table of, 69
text level, 44–48
word level, 40–44
written response classroom strategy, 319
written texts, emergent literacy, 182–187

Young Adult Library Services
Association, 413

young adult's literature connection
lesbian, gay, bisexual, transgender,
questioning, or intersex (LGBTQI)
students, 379
middle school students at
intermediate stage, 330
mythology, 369–370
reading for young adult males,
49
young adult males, books
for, 49

Credits

Photo Credits

DESIGN IMAGES: Strategies for the Classroom icon, Jasmin Merdan/Fotolia; Reading and Writing in Digital Contexts icon, Scanrail/Fotolia; Working and Collaborating icon, Screenshot from Pearson videos created for *Words Their Way: Word Study for Phonics, Vocabulary, and Spelling Instruction*, 5th Edition, Copyright © 2012. Director: Mark Gandolfo, University of Nevada, Reno. Videographers: Theresa Danna-Douglas, Maryan Tooker. Editor and Production Sound Mixer: Shawn Sariti. Producer: Donald Bear; The Language of Your Instruction icon, Annie Fuller/Pearson Education; Accommodating English Learners icon, Alexander Kaludov/Fotolia; Children's Literature Connection icon (open book), Romvo/Fotolia; Children's Literature Connection icon (eBook), "Children's Literature Connection" eBook—eLearning concept, Claudio Bravo/Fotolia; Children's Literature Connection icon (stack of books), Trotzolga/Fotolia; TEXT IMAGES: p. vi, left, Shane Templeton; p. vi, right, Kristin M. Gehsmann; p. 1, Karen Struthers/Fotolia; p. 12, *Al Capone Does My Shirts* by Gennifer Choldenko. Used by permission of Penguin Group (USA) Inc. All rights reserved; p. 32, Steve Gorton/DK Images; p. 65, Copyright © 2002 by Raina Telgemeier; p. 71, Monkey Business/Fotolia; p. 112, ZouZou/Shutterstock; p. 153, Monkey Business Images/Shutterstock; p. 173, WaveBreakMedia/Shutterstock; p. 219, Fotolia; p. 249, From *Ready Readers, Stage 0/1, Book 27, The Wet Pet* by Jacklyn Williams and Linda Clark-Ford, illustrated by Kristina Stephenson. Copyright © 2000 Pearson Education, Inc., or its affiliates. Used by permission. All rights reserved; p. 250, bottom, from *Ready Readers, Stage 2, Book 46, Eyes are Everywhere* by Polly Peterson, illustrated by Yoshi Miyake. Copyright © 1996 Pearson Education, Inc., or its affiliates. Used by permission. All rights reserved; p. 250, top, From *Ready Readers, Stage 2, Book 18, The City Cat and the Country Cat* by Anne Miranda, illustrated by Deborah Melmon. Copyright © 1996 Pearson Education, Inc., or its affiliates. Used by permission. All rights reserved; p. 251, From *Ready Readers, Stage 3, Book 7, Sparky's Bone* by Claire Daniel, illustrated by Eldon Doty. Copyright © 1996 Pearson Education, Inc., or its affiliates. Used by permission. All rights reserved; p. 270, WaveBreakMedia/Shutterstock; p. 298, From *Ready Readers, Stage 3, Book 19, Grandpa, Grandma, and the Tractor* by Deb Eaton, illustrated by Joe Boddy. Copyright © 1996 Pearson Education, Inc., or its affiliates. Used by permission. All rights reserved; p. 301, top, Excerpt from *Gold* by Jaime Schwartz. Copyright © 2013 National Geographic Learning. Reprinted by Permission of National Geographic Learning/Cengage Learning. All rights reserved. Photos: (left) Kenneth Garrett/National Geographic Stock, (right) James L. Stanfield/National Geographic Stock; p. 301, bottom, Used with permission from Brian MacDonald (photo) and Janet Bellavance (chart); p. 315, Wow/Shutterstock; p. 364, Screenshot from Pearson videos created for *Words Their Way: Word Study for Phonics, Vocabulary, and Spelling Instruction*, 5th Edition, Copyright © 2012. Director: Mark Gandolfo, University of Nevada, Reno. Videographers: Theresa Danna-Douglas, Maryan Tooker. Editor and Production Sound Mixer: Shawn Sariti. Producer: Donald Bear; p. 386, Courtesy of George Eastman House, International Museum of Photography and Film; p. 409, Cartoon from "Crime and Puzzlement 2: More Solve-Them-Yourself Picture Mysteries" by Lawrence Treat, illustrations by Kathleen Borowick. Copyright © 1982 by Kathleen Borowick. Reprinted by permission of David R. Godine, Publisher, Inc.; p. 414, ZouZou/Shutterstock.

Text Credits

Inside Back Cover, Based on Common Core State Standards; Inside Front Cover, Based on Common Core State Standards; Figure 1.4, p. 22, Templeton (1997). *Teaching the Integrated Language Arts* (2nd Ed.) (p. 433). Boston: Cengage Learning; Figure 1.5, p. 23, Courtesy of Kristin Gehsmann; Figure 2.2, p. 39, Adapted from Bloom, 1956; Anderson & Krathwohl, 2000; Figure 2.6, p. 60, Reprinted with permission; Figure 2.7, p. 61, Courtesy of Mandy Grotting; Table 2.1, pp. 51–54: "We can run." from Louis, S. (2009). *My dog.* Boston: Houghton Mifflin; "The cat sat on the mat." from Wildsmith, B. *Cat on the Mat.* New York: Oxford University Press; The Mitten: "The bear was cold. The bear got into the warm mitten." The Mitten (adapted by Katalina Page); "Dad had a sandwich. Len and Kate had popcorn Jack wanted snacks, too," from Reed, J. (2009). *No snacks, Jack!* New York: Weldon Own Education (published by Scholastic); "George rode his bike down the street. He gave the newspapers to all the people." from Alexandros, S. (2008). *Curious George and the nwspapers.* Boston: Houghton Mifflin; "Snow is made from water in the sky. In winter, the water freezes and becomes snow." from Solomon, F. (2009). *A snowy day.* Boston: Houghton Mifflin; "Bear liked to talk. Beart alked about the sky and the snow. He talked about the lake and the trees. But most of all, Bear loved to talk about his long, brown tail." from McManus, D. (2009). *Bear's tail.* Boston: Houghton Mifflin; "This is Tian Tian. He is a giant Panda. Most giant pandas have black and white fur like Tian Tian." from Shepherd, M. (2007). *Tian Tian, a giant panda.* Learning A–Z. (Downloaded from www.learninga-z.com on May 5, 2012.); "Charlie was a shepherd. He had a cozy house, a big hat, a crook, and a flock of fat sheep." from DePaola, T. (1973). *Charlie needs a cloak.* New York: Aladdin; "I, Nate the Great, am a detective. Sometimes I'm a baseball player. This morning I was a detective and a baseball player." from Sharmat, M. (1994). *Nate the great and the stolen base.* New York: Yearling; "'Good morning,' said Amelia Bedelia. 'I will have some cereal with my coffee this morning, said Mrs. Rogers. All right,' said Amelia Bedelia. 'Mrs Rogers went into the dining room. . . .'" from Parish, P. (1971). *Come back, Amelia Bedelia.* New York: HarperCollins; "Coyote was very excited about